The SAGE Handbook of
E-learning Research

The SAGE Handbook of
E-learning Research

Edited by
Richard Andrews
and Caroline Haythornthwaite

SAGE Publications
Los Angeles • London • New Delhi • Singapore

 SAGE Publications Ltd
1 Oliver's Yard
55 City Road
London EC1Y 1SP

SAGE Publications Inc.
2455 Teller Road
Thousand Oaks, California 91320

Sage Publications India Pvt Ltd
B1/I1 Mohan Cooperative Industrial Area
Mathura Road
New Delhi 110 044

SAGE Publications Asia-Pacific Pte Ltd
33 Pekin Street #02-01
Far East Square
Singapore 048763

Library of Congress Control Number: 2006937732

British Library Cataloguing in Publication data

A catalogue record for this book is available from British Library

ISBN 978-1-4129-1938-8

Typeset by Pantek Arts Ltd, Maidstone, Kent
Printed in Great Britain by Cromwell Press Ltd, Trowbridge, Wiltshire
Printed on paper from sustainable resources

Contents

List of Contributors

Richard Andrews is Professor in English at the Institute of Education, University of London and Visiting Professor at New York University's Steinhardt School of Education, Culture and Human Development. He has edited *Narrative and Argument* (1991), *Learning to Argue in Higher Education* with Sally Mitchell (2000) and *The Impact of ICT on Literacy Education* (2004), as well as bestselling editions of *Hamlet* (with Rex Gibson) and *The Comedy of Errors* for the Cambridge School Shakespeare. His work in e-learning has included co-directing a series of systematic research reviews on the impact of ICT on literacy learning for the EPPI-Centre (Evidence for Policy and Practice Information and Co-ordinating Centre), part of the UK government's drive to develop the research evidence base for education. He is a member of the expert group for the OECD-CERI project 'New Millennium Learners' which first met in Florence at INDIRE in 2007.

Sasha Barab is an Associate Professor in Learning Sciences, Instructional Systems Technology and Cognitive Science at Indiana University. He holds the Barbara Jacobs Chair of Education and Technology, and is Director of the Center for Research on Learning and Technology. His research has resulted in dozens of peer-reviewed articles, chapters in edited books, and he is editor of the book *Designing for Virtual Communities in the Service of Learning* (2004). His current work involves the design of rich learning environments, frequently with the aid of technology, that are designed to assist children in developing their sense of purpose as individuals, as members of their communities, and as knowledgeable citizens of the world.

Janina Brutt-Griffler is Associate Professor of Foreign and Second Language Acquisition and Director of Polish Studies at the State University of New York, Buffalo. Prior to taking up her current position, she taught on the graduate faculty at the University of York, England. She has published widely in the area of bilingualism, sociolinguistics, and second language learning. Her current research programme examines the extent to which language curricula address the development of advanced levels of foreign/second language competence and how technology aids it. She is the author of *World English: A Study of its Development* (2002), winner of the Modern Language Association's 2004 Kenneth W. Mildenberger Prize. Her other recent publications include *English and Ethnicity* (2002) and *Bilingualism and Language Pedagogy* (2004).

Andrew Burn is Reader in Education and New Media in the School of Culture, Language and Communication and the London Knowledge Lab at the Institute of Education, University of London, and Associate Director of the Centre for the Study of Children, Youth and Media. He has published work on many aspects of the media, including the use of horror films in schools, young people's production work with digital equipment, the semiotics of computer games, and the multimodal nature of media texts. He is especially interested in the use of digital video: he has pioneered work in schools with non-linear editing software and computer animation, and continues to be involved in the development of innovation in this area. He has previously taught English, drama and media studies in comprehensive schools for over twenty years. He has been a Head of English and was Assistant Principal at his last school, Parkside Community College in Cambridge, the first specialist Media Arts College in the country.

Carol A. Chapelle, Professor of TESL/applied linguistics, is Vice-president of the American Association of Applied Linguistics. Her research explores issues at the intersection of computer technology and applied linguistics. Recent books are *Computer Applications in Second Language Acquisition: Foundations for Teaching, Testing, and Research* (2001) and *English Language Learning and Technology: Lectures on Applied Linguistics in the Age of Information and Communication Technology* (2003). Recent books focus on language assessment and research methods: *Assessing Language through Technology* (with Dan Douglas, 2006), *Inference and Generalizability in Applied Linguistics* (with Micheline Chalhoub-Deville and Patricia Duff, editors, 2006), *ESOL Tests and Testing: A Resource for Teachers and Administrators* (with Stephen Stoynoff, 2005). She is former editor of *TESOL Quarterly* (1999–2004), and her papers have appeared in journals such as *TESOL Quarterly, Language Learning, Language Testing,* and *Language Learning and Technology.* She teaches courses in applied linguistics at Iowa State University and has taught in Arizona, Hawaii, Michigan, Spain, and Canada. She has lectured at conferences in Chile, Denmark, England, France, Japan, Morocco, Scotland, Singapore, South Korea, Spain, and Taiwan.

Gráinne Conole is Professor of E-learning in the Institute of Educational Technology at the Open University. Previously she was Professor of Educational Innovation in Post-compulsory Education at the University of Southampton. She has research interests in the use, integration and evaluation of information and communication technologies and e-learning and their impact on organizational change. She serves on and chairs a number of national and international advisory boards, steering groups, committees and international conference programmes. She has research, development and project management experience across the educational and technical domains; funding sources have included HEFCE, ESRC, EU and commercial sponsors. She has published and presented over 200 conference proceedings, workshops and articles, including over fifty journal publications on a range of topics, including the use and evaluation of learning technologies, and is editor of the Association of Learning Technologies journal, *ALT-J*.

Susan J. Doubler is co-leader of the Center for Science Teaching and Learning at TERC (an educational research and development center for K-12 mathematics and science learning) and Associate Professor of Science Education at Lesley University in Cambridge, Massachusetts. She is Co-Principal Investigator of the Fulcrum Leadership Institute, a Math and Science Partnership with Tufts University funded by the US National Science Foundation. She led the development and implementation of a fully online master's programme in science education for K-8 teachers. Her work focuses on the interface of science education, teacher professional development and technology with the aim of improving inquiry-based science learning. Before going to TERC and Lesley University she was an instructional specialist and teacher in the Winchester, Massachusetts Schools.

Leigh S. Estabrook is Professor of Library and Information Science and of Sociology at the University of Illinois, Urbana–Champaign. She also directs the Library Research Center. Her research on educational policy began in the 1970s with a study of the impact of school desegregation on parents' attitudes toward schools. Her experience with educational policy, particularly as it applies to e-learning, included fifteen years as dean of the Graduate School of Library and Information Science (1986-2001). She is a past president of the Association for Library and Information Science Education and the recipient of the American Library Association Beta Phi Mu Award.

Linda Harasim is a Professor in the School of Communication, Simon Fraser University, and has been Network Leader and CEO of Canada's TeleLearning Network of Centres of Excellence. She also leads the Virtual-U research activities and has been involved in designing, implementing and researching Online Collaborative Learning (OCL) since 1983. Linda's focus has been on OCL pedagogical design, and on system design to support Online Collaborative Learning. She has also been active in developing a theory of online learning and a research methodology to study and assess effective collaborative learning. Pedagogical and technological designs to assist researchers and instructors in assessing and advancing collaborative learning and knowledge building are key aspects of her research and practice.

Wynne Harlen has held several high-ranking positions, including Sidney Jones Professor of Science Education and Head of the Education Department at the University of Liverpool and Director of the Scottish Council for Research in Education. She is now semi-retired, has an honorary position as Visiting Professor at the University of Bristol and undertakes some consultancies. She was an Osher Fellow at the Exploratorium, San Francisco, in 1995 and a consultant and co-director of a research project, funded by the NSF, at TERC, Cambridge, Massachusetts, from 1999 to 2002. She was awarded the OBE by the Queen for services to education in 1991. She serves on the editorial board of three international journals. Her publications include twenty-five research reports, over 150 journal articles, twenty-six books of which she is sole or joint author and contributions to thirty-five books. She graduated from Oxford University with an honours degree in physics and obtained her Ph.D. through research in educational evaluation at the University of Bristol.

Gail E. Hawisher is Professor of English and founding Director of the Center for Writing Studies at the University of Illinois, Urbana–Champaign. Her work probes the many connections between literate activity and new information technologies as reflected in her most recent book with Cynthia Selfe, *Literate Lives in the Information Age* (2004). In 2004 she received the Lynn Martin Award for Distinguished Women Faculty and the Campus Award for Excellence in Undergraduate Teaching. In 2005 she was also honoured as a University Distinguished Teacher/Scholar.

Caroline Haythornthwaite is Associate Professor in the Graduate School of Library and Information Science at the University of Illinois, Urbana–Champaign. Her research focuses on the way computer-mediated interaction supports and affects interaction for learning, community, information exchange, and the construction of knowledge. She is co-editor of *Learning, Culture and Community in Online Education: Research and Practice*, with Michelle M. Kazmer (2004) and *The Internet in Everyday Life* with Barry Wellman (2002). She has published widely, including papers in *The Information Society, Journal of Computer-Mediated Communication, New Media and Society, Information Communication and Society, Annual Review of Information Science and Technology*, and in Steve Jones's Doing *Internet Research* and Jayne Gackenbach's *Psychology and the Internet*.

Starr Roxanne Hiltz is Distinguished Professor, College of Computing Sciences, New Jersey Institute of Technology. Her research interests include group support systems (virtual teams and online communities), asynchronous learning networks, and pervasive computing. In particular, with major funding from the Corporation for Public Broadcasting and the Alfred P. Sloan Foundation, she has created and experimented with a Virtual Classroom™ for delivery of college-level courses. This is a teaching and learning environment that is constructed, not of bricks and boards, but of software structures within a computer-mediated communication system. One of her earliest books was the award-winning *The Network Nation: Human Communication via Computer*, co-authored with Murray Turoff (1978, revised edition 1993). Her most recent book, co-edited with Ricki Goldman, is *Learning together Online: Research on Asynchronous Learning Networks* (2005).

Chris Hoadley is an Associate Professor of Education and of Information Sciences and Technology at Penn State University (split appointment). He designs, builds, and studies ways for computers to enhance collaboration and learning. Chris Hoadley has degrees in cognitive science, computer science, and education from MIT and the University of California at Berkeley. He is Director of dolcelab, the Laboratory for Design of Learning, Collaboration and Experience. He is affiliated with the Penn State Center for Human–Computer Interaction and the American Center for the Study of Distance Education. He has chaired the American Educational Research Association's Special Interest Group for Education in Science and Technology, and served as the first president of the International Society for the Learning Sciences. Hoadley was the Director of the Center for Innovative Learning Technologies Knowledge Network. He founded and leads the Design-based Research Collective, funded by the Spencer Foundation.

Michelle M. Kazmer is an Assistant Professor at the College of Information, Florida State University. Her research focuses on social processes in online social worlds, especially online worlds that are designed to be temporary. Her research has examined the social world disengaging processes of distance learners and academic researchers, as well as community-embedded online learning. She is especially interested in how knowledge is shared among people who have left a social world, and in how individuals' local environment shapes their online experiences. She works with an interdisciplinary research team that uses a hermeneutics approach for studying virtual communities. She has worked with online learners as a teacher and researcher since 1997, in the LEEP programme at the University of Illinois, Urbana–Champaign, and at Florida State. Her research has been published in journals such as *Library Quarterly, Library and Information Science Research*, and *New Media and Society*.

Terry Locke is Associate Professor of English Language Education and Chairperson of the Arts and Language Education Department in the School of Education, University of Waikato, New Zealand. His research interests, besides e-learning, include the literacy/technology nexus, constructions of English as a subject, teacher professionalism, curriculum and assessment reform and pedagogies of literature. His most recent book is *Critical Discourse Analysis* (2004).

He is co-ordinating editor of the international online journal *English Teaching: Practice and Critique* and is on the board of a number of journals, including *L1: Educational Studies in Language and Literature* and *English in Australia.*

Jane Lund is the Online Teaching and Learning Manager in the Department of Social Policy and Social Work at the University of York, England, responsible for online pedagogy in its broadest sense. A background in teaching IT brought her into contact with technologies around the time when the expectation was that CDs would revolutionize the way we teach and learn. E-learning has come a long way since then and Jane has had the privilege of working as a practitioner, developer and collaborator in the use of learning technologies with adults ever since. Her research interests include how groups develop into an online learning community (or not) and the role of the e-tutor.

Angela McFarlane is Professor in Education in the Graduate School of Education at the University of Bristol, where she is head of department. She is also a Visiting Professor at the University of Oslo. She was a founder of the TEEM project on evaluation of digital content in the classroom, and is on the board of the UK government-funded blue-sky Futurelab project. A former science teacher, she ran a software R&D unit at Homerton College, Cambridge, for over ten years and has experience of educational software development from concept to market. During this time she worked closely on computer-based assessment with the University of Cambridge Local Examination Syndicate, to which she remains an adviser. In addition, Angela has designed and directed national UK research and evaluation projects on ICT and Learning, and was part of the team that designed the longitudinal study of the impact of networked technologies on home and school learning – Impact2. She has also evaluated the £350 million Curriculum Online investment, and NCSL online, the first online learning community for school leaders. She continues to work with Learning2Go, Europe's largest hand-held learning project, in Wolverhampton, and WebPlay, the UK and US-based blended drama program for elementary schools. She was a member of the OECD expert group on quality in educational software and the first Evidence and Practice Director at Becta, the UK government agency for ICT. Current research interests include the role of e-learning in professional development, personal and mobile computing, computer games in learning and in particular the creative online learning communities they spawn. Professor McFarlane is a member of the board of the government-funded Teachers' TV and the Becta Board Education Committee. She has given keynote presentations at a range of international conferences in a number of countries, including the United Kingdom, the United States, Chile, Malaysia, Spain and Norway, and writes regularly for the UK *Times Educational Supplement.*

Naomi Miyake is Professor in the School of Information Technology and Science, Chukyo University, and holds a Ph.D. in Psychology from the University of California, San Diego, and an M.Ed. from the Graduate School of the University of Tokyo. She is interested in collaborative cognition in general, in understanding both of its socio-cultural aspects like socially constrained, sustainable motivation, and its cognitive processes such as how each individual maintains her own intrinsic intellectual enthusiasm to go beyond the cultural boundaries while being constrained socio-culturally. She has been Principal Investigator for an eight-year learning science project to establish effective curriculum using collaborative activities as scaffolds for undergraduate cognitive science. Collaboration support applications developed through the project include ReCoNote (relational concept mapping tool for collaborative reflection), comment-sharing tools for lecture video clips and lecture notes and some assessment/observation tools using tablet PCs for mobility.

Rae-Anne Montague is Assistant Dean of Student Affairs in the Graduate School of Library and Information Science at the University of Illinois, Urbana–Champaign. Her research interests include multimodal education, learning technologies, and diversity. Rae-Anne has written several articles and given many presentations on innovative and effective practice for online and distance education. She holds a Ph.D. and an M.S. in Library and Information science – the M.S. was completed through the UIUC GSLIS online option, LEEP – as well as an M.Ed. in Curriculum and Instruction from St Mary's University in Halifax, Nova Scotia.

Konrad Morgan is Professor of Human Computer Interaction and Director of the InterMedia research centre on Digital Learning and New Media at the University of Bergen. His research interests focus on understanding the human and social impact of information and communications technology. His scientific work includes a number of original contributions: the first empirical evaluations and explanations of why direct manipulation and graphical user interfaces are superior in usability terms; some of the first explanations of gender differences and attitudes in ICT use; revealing the role of personality types in computer-based behaviour; and finally, the influence of early parental encouragement in later technology competence and attitudes.

Madeleine Morgan has a background in both law and information science. She co-ordinated the intellectual property division of a leading blue-chip technology multinational before forming her own highly successful new media organization MadBagus. Now living in her apartment overlooking the picturesque Mount Fløyen in Bergen, Norway she works on her current research interests, including the impact of ICT on gender, personality and cross-cultural issues. She has been involved with national and European-funded research projects, including the IDEELS and MASSIVE EU projects. Author of numerous peer-reviewed scientific articles, and an invited contributor to numerous edited books, her work is both well respected and known internationally.

Ellen Roberts is programme director of a number of online postgraduate programmes in public policy and management, delivered by the Department of Social Policy and Social Work at the University of York. Ellen is seconded to York from the civil service, where she has worked in a range of policy and management roles. Posts have included Ministerial Private Office, the Cabinet Office and the development of career progression policies in the former Department of Social Security. Her interests are in enabling practitioners to connect theory and practice, and in the role of e-learning in fostering international learning communities in public policy and management.

Cynthia L. Selfe is Humanities Distinguished Professor of Humanities at Ohio State University, Columbus. In 1996 Selfe was recognized as an EDUCOM Medal award winner for innovative computer use in higher education—the first woman and the first English teacher ever to receive this award. Among her numerous publications about computer use in educational settings are *Literacy and Technology in the Twenty-first Century: The Perils of not Paying Attention* (1999) and the co-authored *Writing New Media* (2004). With Gail Hawisher, Selfe continues to edit *Computers and Composition: an International Journal.*

Mike Sharples is Professor of Learning Sciences and Director of the Learning Sciences Research Institute at the University of Nottingham. He has over twenty-five years' experience in human-centred design of new technologies for learning, knowledge working and social interaction. He is the author of seven books, thirty journal articles and over 150 other publications in the areas of interactive systems design, artificial intelligence and educational technology. Through a series of projects funded by the UK research councils, the European Commission and industry he has developed a systematic approach to the design, deployment and evaluation of socio-technical systems (people and their interaction with technology).

Ilana Snyder is an associate professor in the Faculty of Education, Monash University. Her research focuses on changes in literacy, pedagogical and cultural practices associated with the use of new media in local and global contexts. Her books that explore these changes include *Page to Screen* (1998), *Teachers and Technoliteracy*, co-authored with Colin Lankshear (2000) and *Silicon Literacies* (2002). Intrinsic to her work is the understanding that there are increasingly urgent social and economic imperatives to investigate the complex ways in which new technologies allow an expanded network of communication and intellectual exchange, but a network that is not equally available to all. She is working on a project investigating the digital literacy practices of Australian young people in home, school and community that will be contrasted with parallel studies in Brazil, Greece and South Africa. She is also writing a book, *The Literacy Wars*, to be published in 2008.

Bronwyn Stuckey has been a classroom teacher, researcher, community facilitator, lecturer, educational technologist, instructional designer, trainer and teacher educator. She has worked in teacher education and professional development over ten years as a trainer, lecturer, researcher, and community and project developer, for education departments, universities, distance education organizations and vocational education providers in Australia and the US. She is a foundation member of CPsquare and coaches in the Etienne Wenger CPsquare Foundations of Communities of Practice Workshop. She has over the past four years designed for, facilitated and consulted to online community groups and communities of practice. She is collaborating as a researcher in the Learning, Cognition and Instruction/Learning Sciences at Indiana University with Sasha Barab in research issues surrounding a three-dimensional multi-user game environment, Quest Atlantis, in which students around the world learn together.

Josie Taylor is Professor of Learning Technology at the Open University, and Co-director of the UserLab in the Institute of Educational Technology, a group of researchers investigating pedagogy and learning in technology-enhanced environments. Major projects include the European Commission-funded projects MOBIlearn and GUARDIANS, both looking at pedagogically sound tools to support learning. She has advised on strategies for e-learning and effective pedagogy nationally and internationally, and on evaluation methodology. She was funded by EPSRC to conduct a UK-wide consultation process to establish priorities for research in e-learning in the UK to inform funding policy, and is leading the CRC/BCS Grand Challenge in Computing on 'Learning for Life'.

Melody M. Thompson is Assistant Professor of Education and Co-ordinator of Doctoral Programs in Penn State's adult education programme. In that role she teaches and advises Masters and doctoral students, with much of her teaching being done online through the Penn State World Campus. She is also the Faculty Satisfaction editor for the Sloan Consortium's Effective Practices database. Her primary research interests are faculty satisfaction and the institutional policy environment for online learning, as well as diversity issues in adult education. Dr Thompson received her bachelor's degree in English from Bryn Mawr College and both her M.Ed. and her D.Ed. from Penn State. Her past positions include Director of Planning and Research for the World Campus and Director of the American Center for the Study of Distance Education (ACSDE). Dr Thompson is the author of numerous articles and book chapters, as well as co-author of the *McGraw-Hill Handbook of Distance Learning*.

Murray Turoff is a Distinguished Professor in the Information Systems Department at the New Jersey Institute of Technology. He has been engaged in research and development of Computer-Mediated Communication systems since the late 1960s. He was the designer of EMISARI (Emergency Management Information

System And Reference Index) which was the first group communication-oriented crisis management system and which was used for the 1971 wage price freeze and assorted federal crisis events in the US until the mid-1980s. He is co-author of the award-winning book *The Network Nation: Human Communication via Computer* that predicted all the current Web-based communication systems in 1978. He is a co-founder of ISCRAM (Information Systems for Crisis Response And Management) and he was programme chair of their third international meeting in 2006. He has published a number of papers on the design of information systems for all aspects of crisis planning and emergency management.

Virgil E. Varvel is a finishing graduate student in the Department of Curriculum and Instruction at the University of Illinois, Urbana–Champaign, who has an M.S. in biomolecular chemistry and an Ed.M. in science teaching. He is also a Computer-Assisted Instruction specialist for University Outreach and Public Service for the University of Illinois, working with online education, throughout the state of Illinois, and is a certified grades 6-12 instructor in Illinois. He researched the use of wireless networks in education, evaluated online programs, and researches various issues related to online education including policy, understanding instructor–student relations, and online research methods. He was part of the Illinois Online Network program to receive the award for Excellence in ALN Faculty Development from the Sloan Consortium in 2002. In 2005 he won a WebCT Exemplary Course Award, the first one awarded for a faculty development course.

Giasemi Vavoula is a lecturer at the University of Birmingham, and a research fellow at the Institute of Educational Technology, the Open University. She has worked as a research fellow on the EU project MOBIlearn, and the EU Kaleidoscope NoE JEIRP Mobile Learning in Informal Science Settings, conducting literature reviews and diary studies of informal and mobile learning practices. She has co-authored a literature review in mobile technologies for learning for NESTA Futurelab.

Andrew Whitworth is Programme Director for the Masters in ICT in Education at the University of Manchester, England. After some years working in the ICT industry he completed a degree then a Ph.D. in politics at the University of Leeds, studying critical theory as applied to the study of micropolitical interactions in organizations. His ICT background and the newly emerging World Wide Web kept pulling at him, however, and he subsequently taught Web design and the politics of ICT at Leeds until moving to Manchester in 2005. His research and teaching now stand at the intersection of technology, education and the organization of higher education.

Zhao Yuan is a Ph.D. student in the department of Educational Studies at the University of York. Her study focuses on the impact of computer technology on teaching and learning English listening and speaking as a second language in UK higher education. The fundamental theoretical basis of Yuan's research is the interaction among students, teachers and computers, and the primary aim of the research is to investigate the impact of computer technology on learning in the context of language classrooms. Specifically, Yuan has extended her research to how computer technology expands the opportunities of learning, how computer technology increases the communication across various contexts, and how different types of information and communication technology stimulate and improve learning.

Introduction to E-learning Research

Richard Andrews and Caroline
Haythornthwaite

The publication of the *SAGE Handbook of E-learning Research* marks a significant point in studies in e-learning. Although there has been considerable
development in teaching and learning, as well as in learning design, there is as
yet no coherent view of what constitutes research in the field nor of how best to
undertake it. The present volume takes stock of progress in e-learning research,
addressing a range of issues from student experience to policy and provides a
foundation for further research and development.

By e-learning research, we mean primarily research *into*, *on*, or *about* the use
of electronic technologies for teaching and learning. This encompasses learning
for degrees, work requirements and personal fulfilment, institutional and non-
institutionally accredited programmes, in formal and informal settings. It
includes anywhere, anytime learning, as well as campus-based extensions to
face-to-face classes. E-learning includes all levels of education from pre-school
to secondary/high school, higher education and beyond. The potential for this
area is broad. For this handbook, the focus is primarily on e-learning in the
formal setting of degree-granting institutes of higher education. However, with
many kinds of e-learning and computer-assisted teaching entering all arenas of
education, from schools to workplaces, examples from other arenas of education
enter into and carry important information for the discussion.

As a working definition of e-learning, the following from the Higher
Education Funding Council for England (HEFCE) can serve as a starting point:

The use of technologies in learning opportunities, encompassing flexible learning as well as distance learning; and the use of information and communication technology as a communications and delivery tool, between individuals and groups, to support students and improve the management of learning.

(HEFCE, 2005: 12)

However, this definition is not an end point, and at points in the Introduction and throughout the *Handbook* we will take issue with some aspects of this initial definition. In particular we take issue with the way the HEFCE definition appears to portray technology as simply a delivery mechanism, and fails to address the co-evolutionary nature of technology and its use. The *Handbook* chapters together help provide a more nuanced and elaborated definition and appreciation of e-learning.

Since the mid-1980s or so we have seen the rapid evolution of Computer-Assisted Learning (CAL) and Computer-Assisted Instruction (CAI) into Course Management Systems (CMS) and Virtual Learning Environments (VLEs). From early forays into the use of computers to assist, or indeed provide the entire basis for learning with particular topics to more recent activities involving VLEs and other custom-designed interfaces, the computer has held a fascination for teachers, lecturers, learning designers and learners alike. At times claims have been hyped: it has been variously claimed that computers would revolutionize learning, bring about the end of the book, put an end to institutionalized learning and/or improve the quality of learning. Rarely have these claims been properly tested. At other times its impact has been overly downplayed, as in the many studies that find 'no significant difference' between face-to-face learning and online learning outcomes. Rarely do these studies look at the more transformative effects of e-learning, such as creating a distributed community, and learning new genres of communication and collaborative work practice. We now appear to be at a stage of development where we can gauge the impact of the computer on learning in a more measured, critical way, as well as taking a more comprehensive view of changes accompanying e-learning. It is in the spirit of such critique, realism, and expanded view that the present volume has been conceived.

This introduction begins the discussion of e-learning research which is continued in subsequent chapters. The introduction addresses definitional issues, taking time to explore the 'e' and 'learning' in e-learning, then theoretical and methodological issues, before presenting a model of co-evolutionary processes of technology and learning.

In choosing to use the term 'e-learning' we have turned away from other names that might equally have been useful, such as computer-assisted learning, technology-enhanced learning, instructional technologies or online learning. To us, these terms fall into the trap that many previous studies of the relationship between technology and learning/education have fallen into, of assuming that learning exists independently of technologies and that in various ways technologies enhance it. The causal assumptions behind terms such as 'technology-enhanced learning' are ones we critique in this introduction.

'E-learning' as a term is a hybrid. Like many compounds, the two elements have worked together to create a new hybrid. Nevertheless, it is made up of two parts: e + learning. The 'e' of e-learning has a longer history than many will assume, including long-term efforts to capture voice and images, and to store and then transmit those recordings. With each capture – from records to CDs, film to DVD, conversation to text chat – there are trade-offs in quality, interactivity, and transferability: trade-offs that mark both the pros and cons of technology mediation. The following section takes us through some of this journey, giving historical and theoretical perspectives on electronic media.

But first we give an example based on the use of one technology – electronic whiteboards, implemented primarily in secondary/high school settings – that shows the kind of work that needs to be done to bring experience with technologies together into a research framework.

AN EXAMPLE OF RESEARCH ISSUES: ELECTRONIC WHITEBOARDS

Symptomatic of the problems facing researchers in e-learning is the case of electronic interactive whiteboards – touch-sensitive screens that work in conjunction with a computer and projector – and their efficacy in learning. The issue is that there is little substantial research on the topic (though see Smith *et al.*, 2005), and yet many schools have installed them in place of blackboards or other forms of large-scale projection in a classroom. Reports are anecdotal, based on perceptions of pro-technology innovators and even of the technology vendors, with reviews of their use describing and justifying, *post hoc*, the use of whiteboards in the classroom. Whiteboards are examined in isolation, without considering their place in the social and technological context of the classroom, or of the evolution of technology and practice over time.

Most of the studies of whiteboards have been small-scale and descriptive, the most in-depth and evaluative being those by Glover and Miller (2001) and Goodison (2002; see also Gerard and Widener, 1999; Levy, 2002). Glover and Miller (2001) report on the views of both students and staff on the impact of interactive whiteboards in a secondary/high school. They discuss and describe the use, teaching and learning implications, problems and potential of whiteboards. They find that the attitudes of teachers towards the use of interactive whiteboards are particularly critical: where teachers adapt their pedagogy, the use of whiteboards has more impact; where they are used as a surrogate blackboard, the impact is less significant. Whiteboards are described as increasing efficiency, enabling teachers to draw on a range of ICT resources fluently and with pace; as extending learning and creating new learning styles stimulated by interaction with the whiteboard (BECTA, 2003b). Because of the role of the teacher, Glover and Miller conclude that training in the use of whiteboards is key to the transformation of classrooms and of the learning experience for young people. Goodison (2002) used interviews to collect data on the views of primary/elementary school children on the use of interactive whiteboards. Goodison found that whiteboards played a significant role in facilitating classroom instruction, social learning and student engagement with technology. However, it was not clear from this work what effect or impact the electronic whiteboard had on learning. As with many such articles, the results are presented as a positive finding about whiteboards.

In the UK, the British Educational Communication and Technology Agency (BECTA, 2003a) has been appropriately cautious about the research on electronic whiteboards. It acknowledges that they were a relatively recent technology with little research literature relating to them in refereed academic journals. BECTA (2003b) concludes that much of the evidence about the impact of whiteboards on learning is anecdotal, conducted by schools or school boards and local authorities, and carried out on a small scale. That the research is largely qualitative is not a problem, in that such a study could provide key insights into the way an electronic whiteboard is used. But as most of the studies are of the *perceptions* of use (elicited via questionnaires and interviews, anecdotes and personal testimony), and as most of those reporting their perceptions are excited – like pioneers – by the new technology, it is probably too early to say that there is much reliable or substantial research evidence to hand. In a more recent review (BECTA, 2006) the indication is that the installation and use of interactive whiteboards in the UK have spread rapidly, with 93 per cent of primary schools and 97–8 per cent of secondary schools reporting that they had installed such technology (some under political pressure from bodies like the Office for Standards in Education). This review also notes that there has been a pilot evaluation of the use of interactive/electronic whiteboards in mathematics and literacy lessons in primary schools (Higgins *et al.*, 2005), with a more large-scale evaluation of the Department of Education and Skills Schools Whiteboard Expansion program due in 2006/07. The most recent presentation on the latter evaluation at time of writing was by Somekh and Haldane (2006), who report on behalf of a larger project team that they used multi-level modelling of attainment of individual children, based on gains in national test scores, questionnaire surveys, observations of interactive whiteboard training, and digital video classroom observation from ten case study primary schools. They suggest that the interactive whiteboard can act as a mediating tool between teacher and pupils; that its size can excite and motivate children; that it has potential for special needs use; that it can speed up learning as well as provide an archived record of use. Questions are also raised about the nature of interactivity. It could be that this particular Department for Education Skills (DfES) evaluation, when completed, will provide a foundation or benchmark for further study and research on the topic; or, as BECTA (2006) puts it, a 'robust assessment of the impact of interactive display technologies which we currently lack' (p. 11).

Other information on whiteboard use comes from the vendors themselves. In a 'review of classroom case studies and research literature' from the US, the UK and Australia, SMART Technologies (2004) – the self-described 'industry leader in interactive whiteboard technology' (online) – conclude that interactive whiteboards affect learning in several ways:

> They serve to raise the level of student engagement in a classroom, motivate students and promote enthusiasm for learning. In at least one case, the addition of an interactive whiteboard positively influenced student attendance. Interactive whiteboards support many different learning styles and have been successfully employed in hearing and visually impaired learning environments. Research also indicates higher levels of student retention, and notes taken on an interactive whiteboard can play a key role in the student review process. In addition to student learning, observations also indicate that designing lessons around interactive whiteboards can help educators streamline their preparation and be more efficient in their ICT integration.

(2004: 3)

The problem with such a review is, of course, that it is not independent. And, again, it is the positive results that are highlighted. Thus, it is unclear what educators may take from such a review in order to make informed decisions about the adoption of such tools. But it is also clear that the technology itself, as well as its use, develops over time. Somekh and Haldane (2006) suggest that teachers were largely confident in the use of the tool because of their daily use of it, which cannot be said of practice even five years earlier in a range of ICTs.

This example shows the potential and the need for various kinds of examinations of e-learning and its technologies. There is room for systematic and independent research reviews on e-learning topics, ones that balance a pro-innovation view with the realities of large-scale implementation. Chapters in this *Handbook* serve as reviews for a number of topics relating to e-learning. There is also substantial room for small and large-scale primary research studies using techniques such as direct observation, control and experimental groups, and longitudinal dimensions. As in the example above, the focus is too often on the new computing technology as a single entity, introduced and used in one way at one time. This ignores implementation and adoption effects, the use of other complementary technologies, and the reciprocal, co-evolutionary nature of the relationship between technologies and learning. These are the kinds of issues addressed when research steps in to make sense of e-learning as a system- and societal-wide change in teaching and learning.

We turn now to beginning the task of addressing e-learning and e-learning research. We start by providing context for the current wave of e-learning technologies, reviewing important trends in recording and dissemination of materials that form the historical background for the 'e' in e-learning, before joining it up again with 'learning'.

THE 'E' IN E-LEARNING

What is the 'e' in e-learning, and what does it mean for learning? The 'e' in e-learning joins many common hybrids such as e-mail and e-commerce in signifying enactment through electronic means, typically interpreted as computer-based. Essential components of all 'e' enterprises are the computer hardware and software, but also the networking infrastructures that make it possible to collect and distribute data, information and knowledge to people at different times and locations. Devices that permit access to these data streams now no longer need to be the fixed desktop computer. The mobility and multimedia capabilities afforded by laptops, palmtops (also known as Personal Digital Assistants, PDAs), mobile phones, and media players (e.g. MP3 players), shatter our notions of where and by what means 'e' activities can take place. Thus, in considering e-learning, we include a range of electronically networked Information and Communication Technology (ICT) via which learning can take place.

While we often find e-learning reified as a particular course management system, its flexibility lies in the way new technologies are quickly appropriated into the e-learning toolkit. This is possible because of continuing efforts to cross hardware platforms. At its basis, e-learning technology, like all other e-enterprises, depends on *hardware* to process digital or analogue *signals*; *software* that can encode and decode, collect, store and forward, and present communications in visual, textual and/or audio *modes*; applications and *systems* that bring together tools to support data storage and retrieval, course management, computer-mediated communication, and collaborative virtual environments. As we will discuss below, equally important in this technological mix are the people who use the systems – teachers, instructors, administrators, students – each bringing to the e-learning enterprise their ideas of how teaching, learning, and communication should be enacted.

Educators have long been appropriating technologies into the classroom, from radio and television, records and record players, video reels and projectors, to today's computers, CDs, DVDs, podcasts, and more. What the digital revolution has done is free the information and its carriers from the classroom, making the information available in ever increasingly mobile ways. What is often forgotten is how each of these technologies performs a slightly different way of coding and decoding data and information, at times enhancing one mode of communication over another, but each changing where and when we receive information and communication. The following presents a brief historical background to emphasize that computing technologies represent the current culmination of many years of electronic encoding protocols and devices, each with its own limits and affordances. Later, we pick up again the notion of affordances to discuss contemporary computing technologies.

Coding and decoding signals

The historical shift from analogue to digital technology has revolutionalized the resources for learning by making material available that is high-fidelity, and which can be repurposed, easily reproduced (within copyright constraints), and reviewed in a number of different modes via a number of different types of hardware. E-learning, as we define it in this volume, could hardly be imagined without the digital shift. The vast majority of electronic information, in the broad, technical sense of the word, is now transferred in digital form. In the UK and US, for example, there are plans to switch the entire broadcasting of television to digital format (by 2010 in the UK and 2009 in the US).

The translation of a message via digital coding generally makes for less interference and thus better quality of the communication. Indeed, since such recordings can be made without even travelling through the vibrating air, e.g. from a digital piano direct to the recording device, they represent more 'purely' the origin of the sound. However, such 'purity' can come across as clinical, without the attendant sounds that accompany live music, such as the performer's breathing or the audience reaction. The analogy for e-learning is that an instructor's words, flawlessly typed into text for distribution to students, can fail to convey the enthusiasm they express verbally, the pacing they use to present the text, and the gaze they use while speaking. However, an advantage of digital coding is that the original message can be reproduced on an infinite number of occasions, without the deterioration that takes place in the course of translation through repeated use of the kinds of materials that tend to be used with analogue recording, like vinyl or tape. Similarly, the instructor's words remain available, distributable and reproducible long after the lecture presentation has taken place. Thus, at the recording and transmission level, there are differences in the kind of message and translation of communication that occurs, and that are likely to have an impact on e-learning.

Digital recording is now not only easy to do, but easy to disseminate. Neither tapes nor CDs need to be distributed to remote sites; nor is specialized equipment (beyond the computer) needed to decode the recording. There are a few caveats. First that non-specialized and widely available recording and playback equipment provides a generic representation without the fidelity available in dedicated, high-end technologies such as those for audio, photography, or film. However, one might argue that this has always been the case, since high-fidelity recordings have for a long time been played back on simpler, less expensive, stereo equipment. In the Computer Age, this issue may be more important because of more widespread, low-fidelity, data recording devices that combine with wide dissemination, e.g. cameras in cell phones, audio recording in laptops, and movie capability in digital cameras. Media production is changing from high fidelity/low number to low fidelity/high number. Dissemination is changing from specialized and controlled to widespread and grass-roots.

Second, newer translations from full-screen to smaller handheld or mobile phone interface truncate and reinterpret text and visual representations (both in sending messages, e.g. by Short Messaging Service (SMS), and in receiving them, e.g. in receiving Web pages on very small screens). Whereas dedicated technologies formerly ensured that decoding was approximately the same for all receivers (within the range, say, of the size of a television screen, or quality of record-playing audio equipment), current message receivers may be using markedly different decoding schemes. This is an issue not just for formerly analogue messages. Information produced and published on the Web may appear differently depending on the colour palette of the computer screen, the Web browser in use, the size of the window and the operating system of the computer. What *you* see on retrieving from the Web is not necessarily what we see from the Web.

Third, the ubiquity of computer access and the expectation that 'everyone, everywhere' can have equal access to digital signals must be questioned: we are not yet at the stage where broadband capabilities are equally available. Service arrives late to low-population areas; wireless may be taken for granted in some cities and on some campuses, but this is by no means a universal service; and cell/mobile phone signals can be limited by geography and terrain. As well as technical obstacles, cost can be a significant barrier in the acquisition of computers as well as of Internet services. The digital divide remains a real issue within societies and particularly internationally (see Gorard and Taylor, 2005; Haythornthwaite, this volume).

Modes of communication

Communication signals can carry sound, text, and images. These major forms of communication are often called, metaphorically, 'languages'. The aural and visual modes translate directly into sounds and moving and still images; the textual mode is, interestingly, based on an aural code (speech) but given visual form (text, letters). 'Text' is thus an abstracted, second-level symbolic system, a highly powerful medium or mode of communication that is itself hybrid. It can be conveyed visually and/or through sound and has, through history, manifested itself in various languages, each using different symbolic representation systems (e.g. Latin, Greek, Sumerian, Mandarin). The term 'text' can also be used to refer to multimodal texts as well as to linguistic texts.

Text is of particular importance for e-learning because not only is education heavily weighted toward the use and production of texts, but e-learning increases the textual load with conversations and interactions occurring largely through the texts of chat rooms, blogs, e-mail, bulletin boards, etc. Notions of Asynchronous Learning Networks (ALN), prevalent since the mid-1990s, stress near-exclusive use of text-based postings. It is only recently that proponents of ALN have begun to see this as a supplement or extender to face-to-face interaction, in ideas of *blended learning* (see below). This despite the fact that programmes which have long been including synchronous and oral/aural components have found the interactivity and ability to hear others as the main attractions of real-time meetings on e-learning (e.g. Haythornthwaite and Kazmer, 2004). In e-learning in general, text has led the way, partly for technical considerations (e.g. slow Internet connections lead to video and even audio delays that make real-time interaction unworkable) and partly because the educational emphasis on text tends to place audio and video modalities second in importance and relevance.

As Stuckey and Barab suggest in this volume, to move away from single, text-mode communication for e-learning requires both social and technical planning. Multimodality occurs naturally in face-to-face settings, transparently combining visual, oral, aural and other physical cues with immediacy of communication.[1] Not so online. E-multimodality or multimedia must be planned, making choices between presentation via text, audio and/or video connection, as well as working out the social logistics of synchronicity, turn taking, and cross-modal interaction (e.g. live audio with text chat for questions, recorded video with audio questions and asynchronous text response). However, as multimedia options expand online, e-learning can move away from the notion that to learn something must be to abstract it, classify it, and simplify it. Instead, learning could be conceived as a framed activity, that entails bringing to the frame an open mind, willingness to learn, and a degree of concentration necessary to learn. In addition, learning would be expressible or (more likely) recastable in a different medium or media; and thus assessable, if necessary. Whole experiences may be captured and disseminated in multimodal formats, including moving image, sound, and text. However, the ability to include everything, from everywhere leads quickly to information overload. Like the writer Borges's mnemonist, we would need whole days to evaluate others' experiences of whole days. Thus, issues of selectivity come more to the fore, particularly in choosing what real-time capture to spend time viewing.

Information and communication technologies

In considering the 'e' side of e-learning, we need to address the products that have been made to store, access, and use information and which support the information and communication activities of e-learning. Computer use in e-learning is, at the most immediate level, experienced via software. Computers run on operating systems, like Windows, Linux or MacOS which provide the basic architecture. Specific software packages for particular purposes, like word processing, games, and spreadsheets created by commercial enterprises or collaborative efforts in open source computing, run on the foundation provided by the operating system. Collections of applications are then brought together into single environments – virtual learning environments, Collaborative Virtual Environments (CVEs), course management systems – with a common look and feel that signifies entry into a particular set of norms, practices and participants.

Computer interfaces provide the *entré* into online environments. At their best for information access they are easy to use, follow known conventions, are consistent, and support both the novice and advanced user; at their best, for communication, they allow seamless interaction with others through computers rather than with the computer. This is not the place to recapitulate the extensive work in human computer interaction (HCI; see, for example, Nielsen, 1994; Carroll, 2002), but it is the place to point out the importance of the interface in the user's experience of the e-learning environment. Upcoming research issues include not just what the best computer interface is for particular learning environments, but also how these will scale to handheld devices, provide interoperability between devices, and convergence of technologies on single devices (e.g. laptops, palmtops and third-generation (3G) mobile phones).

Before computing, our electronic communication devices included the phone (dating from the 1870s), radio (1890s), and television (1920s). The advent of the computer (1940s) and its desktop (early 1980s), laptop (late 1980s), palmtop (1990s), and PDA/3G phone (2000s) versions have brought increased and extended mediated access to information as well as, more recently, convergence with communication devices. In particular, the palmtop computer (or PDA) and third-generation (3G) mobile phones are converging, not only using advanced digital technology to access and use all three modes of communication described earlier (text, sound, image), but also to function as radios and televisions. Of course, none of this mobility would be possible without the rise of network infrastructures, including phone networks, computer cable networks, and wireless networks, as well as the accepted standards for communicating along these networks and rendering data on devices. Again, the history is too vast to discuss here (for further reading, see, for example, Abbate, 1999).

These multimodal devices suggest the future for ICT and e-learning. However, at present, they are little used. When we refer to e-learning and ICT, it is still, at this early point of the twenty-first century, the (increasingly wireless) desktop or laptop computer that is central to our concerns. While the small display features of palmtops and mobile phones may not be the major platform for e-learners, their existence suggests trends in how, when, and where we access information and communicate with others. These general trends cannot help but affect the habits of e-learners and thus also of e-learning instructors and administrators. (For more on mobile learning, see Sharples, Taylor and Vavoula, this volume.)

As well as the technology advances noted above, ICT for e-learning also includes many new and emerging technologies specifically designed to support learning activities. These include in-class tools such as the electronic whiteboards noted above; large tablet displays that accept and project writing on top of pre-formatted data so notes can be added during presentations; and clickers used by students to vote for their answers to questions. Added to these are the new online games used as media for learning and communication (see McFarlane, this volume), immersive technologies for virtual world and whole-body interaction, and blogs and wikis as media for class writing and collaborative writing. We note these few here to highlight the rapidly expanding technological base that is evolving in conjunction with learning both in and outside the traditional classroom.

Features and affordances

Technologies are useful to the extent that they allow users – instructors, students, administrators – to achieve their goals. Sometimes technology facilitates application in education, sometimes it inhibits it. In discussing the use of technology, many analysts turn to Gaver's (1996) use of the term *affordances* (following Gibson, 1979; see also Norman, 1988) to make the distinction between the explicit features of technology and what these allow or facilitate for users. Explicit features of ICTs include such things as whether multiple modes are supported; whether design is for single or group use; whether interaction is effected through the keyboard, mouse, joystick or glove; whether data storage and retrieval occur to and from the Internet or on the local desktop. What a technology affords are ways of communicating and connecting with others, being visible in the online context, viewing and using data and information, creating and displaying content, and linking with others and with resources.

Affordances signify the possibilities for users, but, for these to become reality, systems must actually be used. Yet, in keeping with much that has been written about the adoption of technologies (Rogers, 1995), users may resist new uses, may not know how to use new features, or may avoid them as too complicated or incompatible with previous practice. Some of the affordances listed above are *social affordances* that provide possibilities for awareness and co-ordinated action with others (Bradner *et al.*, 1999). These affordances may be particularly difficult to enact because users need to work together to create collective uses that are of benefit to the group as a whole. In these cases, some users may need to lead use by seeding a shared database, starting discussion and activity on a listserv, or modelling communication behaviours until a critical mass of users and behaviours is established (Connolly and Thorn, 1990; Haythornthwaite, 2002a, b, 2005; Markus, 1990). Social affordances are of particular relevance for e-learning since instructors strive to be aware of students and their contributions, and collaborative learning advocates promote the advantages of peer-to-peer awareness, exchange, and engagement (e.g. Bruffee, 1993; Koschmann, 1996; Koschmann *et al.*, 2002; Miyake, this volume). Thus, rather than looking only at the features of a medium, it is important to examine what these features mean for users of the environment.

As an example of this issue, we take the key feature of asynchronicity and see what this affords for communication and e-learning.

Asynchronous technology and its affordances for e-learning

Perhaps one of the most talked about characteristics of computer-mediated communication and, one might argue, the most transformative is the ability to carry on conversations asynchronously. To be completely correct, asynchronous communication is in fact an affordance based on systems designed to store and retrieve messages. Computer technologies such as e-mail, listservs, bulletin boards, blogs, and wikis store messages for retrieval, review and response at times of the user's making. For the user, these each afford anytime communication. Depending on the availability of computing and networks, they can also afford anywhere communication. The applications differ in their affordances for routing messages specifically to others. For e-mail, unique identifiers for senders and receivers route messages to just the specified audience. In listservs and bulletin boards, posters are identified, but receivers may gain access more generally by entering passwords to view all posted information. The same is true of postings on blogs and wikis, although their use is more prevalent without password protection and thus anyone with computer and Web access can view the posted information in the same way as other kinds of Web pages.

These differences across these media may appear subtle, but each system affords different visibilities of messages, senders, and audience, which in turn afford different kinds of uses. E-mail affords privacy and control of readership (notwithstanding legal precedence for access to e-mail archives), which in turn may encourage discussion of more sensitive, personal information. Bulletin boards provide threading, grouping topics as they are discussed, affording easier review of message history. Blogs afford easy posting to the Web and a stage on which to perform for a broad, unspecified audience. Identifiers for senders and receivers may range from a set of anonymous-looking numbers to user-selected 'handles' that afford self-expression about identity or character. They may be easily traceable to the actual individual or provide protection from actual identification. Individuals may use one or many identifiers to present themselves to others, deliberately or by accumulation maintaining multiple identities within one type of medium (e.g. as we keep multiple e-mail addresses on various e-mail servers). Groups of receivers may be indicated by single names, e.g. when sending to a listserv address, obscuring whether the message is being sent to a few or many others. Thus identifiers can afford anonymity, role playing, and disguise, and can equally afford open identification.

Contemporary computing has made it possible to use many kinds of devices to interact with servers where messages are stored. This affords *mobility*. A poster no longer needs to be hardwired from their desktop to the institution's servers, but instead can access systems on and via the Web, through wireless communication initiated on their laptop, palmtop, or mobile phone. Mobility of individuals also means *distribution* of participants. Online engagement of this kind does not specify how many learners can be in the engagement at any one time, nor where they are embedded at the time they are members of the learning community. They could be accessing the engagement for different periods of time each, from different machines (desktop, laptop, palmtop, phone), in different situations (café, home, hilltop, bus, etc.) and in different locations around the world. This affords the opportunity to bring in experiences from these different locations and suggests the ability to apprentice locally at the same time as obtaining education remotely. Thus the notion of 'situated learning' (Lave and Wenger, 1991) is not abandoned, but instead is given new identity through e-learning. It now operates at two levels: the local embedding, potentially leveraging an apprenticeship (see Kazmer, this volume) and the online embedding, creating an apprenticeship in the ways and means of online interaction and in the online practices of a future professional or interest-based community. Thus the 'situation' provides a dual education – in the subject and the online environment (Haythornthwaite *et al.*, 2000) – and the potential for a dual apprenticeship in the local and online communities. Such contextualizing will come into play again later in this chapter, when we address theoretical issues.

ICTs also afford a new rhythm of interaction, one that differs from face-to-face and classroom dynamics. Many find the new rhythm liberating, but others decry the loss of immediacy. What underpins much of the discussion of the pros and cons of asynchronous, distributed education is the degree of *interactivity* provided by these various modes and means of communication. Interactivity can best be characterized by depicting a spectrum of degrees relating to both what the technology affords for the granularity of interactivity and interactivity among participants in online communities.

Interactivity with ICT devices ranges from low-degree – as occurs in interactive television or touch-screen panels, where operations are limited to a few functional buttons – to a high degree of interactivity, as might be found for situations in which virtual reality headsets and hand controls provide fine-grained manipulations. Typical practice in the use of a computer interface would be somewhere between these two extremes, but such interaction is often taken for granted. It is usually mediated via a conventional typewriter-derived keyboard (though there are other kinds, like concept keyboards). The user's input, whether via a keyboard or via a point-and-click mouse, is a significant limitation on the degree of interactivity possible. A mouse, for example, can point only to operations that have already been programmed into the computer; whereas a keyboard allows the textual possibilities of language to be exploited. However, a keyboard can be a barrier to communication for those who find its operation cumbersome (e.g. those with physical disabilities). In such cases, speech recognition technologies might yet prove to play a major part in interactivity. However, although available for some time, such technologies have yet to attain a sufficient degree of sensitivity to the varieties of the voice to become easy-to-use and reliable interface devices, and they have not yet become standard with a computer purchase.

This approach to interactivity describes the affordances of the technology, but interactivity also has a social, communicative dimension, one that may or may not be achieved in practice. Interactivity can depend on the immediacy of question and response. This is inherently delayed in asynchronous settings compared to synchronous settings. Yet social norms about response times and social practices to respond in a timely manner go a long way to increasing the perceived interactivity of online communication. Rafaeli and Sudweeks (1997) use the term 'interactivity' to address responsive behaviour in communication, viewing this as a likely process that explains cohesion in online groups. As they state,

> Interactivity is not a characteristic of the medium. It is a process-related construct about communication. It is the extent to which messages in a sequence relate to each other, and especially the extent to which later messages recount the relatedness of earlier messages ... Interactivity describes and prescribes the manner in which conversational interaction as an iterative process leads to jointly produced meaning. Interactivity merges speaking with listening.

(online, n.p.)

Thus key issues to bear in mind regarding interactivity are not only what the technology affords for iterative and respondent processes but also the extent to which responsiveness is actually achieved using the medium.

Overall, posting messages for storage through contemporary networked computing affords the presentation of self online, sometimes anonymously and always pseudonymously (at least to the extent an e-mail address is a pseudonym), usually abiding by group communication conventions, and originating from any computer device, located anywhere with Internet access, at any time of the day or night. These are the essential elements bound up in the terms 'asynchronous communication' and 'asynchronous learning'; it is the reason the area is called *asynchronous learning networks*, signifying the computer network, but perhaps more importantly the social network that sustains learning efforts (Harasim *et al.*, 1995; Hiltz, Turoff and Harasim, this volume). Thus, more than anytime, anywhere input, it is anytime, anywhere access to a community where conventions and common interests reside and where individuals pull together to define the way their community will work. We will return to the notion of the community of enquiry below, when we consider the 'learning' side of the e-learning equation, and when discussing theoretical models.

Beyond asynchronous

Text-based asynchronous communication is not the only option for e-learning. As outlined above many new technologies make it possible to include audio, still and moving images into e-learning offerings, both from the instructor side, with formally produced audio or video, and from the student side, with informally produced pictures, audio, and video. Also as noted, including multimodal communication in e-learning requires planning. It also requires an understanding of the affordances that make such planning worthwhile. This is an area of research that deserves more attention from a learning perspective and that can inform the introduction of new media into e-learning offerings.

Synchronous communication is found in many e-learning environments, including text, audio and video transmissions. Audio-conferencing has been with us for a while; new meeting software systems and better networking infra-structures now make video-conferencing a reality for multiple participants at multiple sites (e.g. Internet2 in the US, http://www.internet2.edu/). Synchronous text-based interaction is most prevalent and most available at present. Internet chat, instant messaging and more recently the short message text (SMS) available on mobile phones are examples. Text chat is used in e-learning for live class sessions that permit all participants to type and enter comments simultaneously. This kind of interaction underpins popular multi-player games (Multi-User Dungeons or Dimension, MUDs) and is increasingly used for online conferences. Extensions add graphical interfaces to create virtual worlds for gaming (Massively Multiplayer Online Roleplaying Games, MMORPG; and Virtual Reality, VR), which are also being adopted and adapted for education.

Not only new technologies, but also new venues are opening up for e-learning. Where e-learning inherits from distance learning (see Thompson, this volume) it is taken to be synonymous with online interaction only, happening away from educational settings such as classrooms. However, the continued pen-etration of Internet use into everyday life, combined in some instances with increased familiarity with online education, has led to a reverse trend of incor-porating online features into on-campus classrooms. This trend in *blended learning* is developing strongly as students entering higher education are increasingly computer-savvy and highly conversant with online communication.

What is emerging is a *spectrum of different combinations of e-learning with conventional learning*. The term 'blended learning' has appeared to indicate prac-tices that sit in the middle of the spectrum between online, distributed approaches at one end and traditional, face-to-face teaching at the other. At the distributed end, a course or programme can be entirely delivered and engaged with electroni-cally. Every stage of the process of learning, from enquiry about the course to registration, from access to the materials to their use, from the submission of assignments to their marking, and so on to the final award of the degree or other qualification, could be handled electronically, via a computer interface. Such engagement could include synchronous communication or it could be handled without any synchronicity. In theory, as well as in practice, a course or programme could replicate the notion of the correspondence course in which the learner acted individually and had very little contact with teachers, lecturers or fellow students.

Moving along the spectrum, many online programmes build some face-to-face interaction (i.e., including physical proximity as well as synchronous engagement) into their schedule of largely electronic contact. For example, a programme might begin with a short residential course in which the learning community (lecturers, students, administrators) get to know each other, engage in joint learning and set up contacts and allegiances which they will develop electronically while taking the degree. They might meet again for a week after one year and again for a week towards the end of the programme. Such a pattern is a type of blended learning. However, nothing is actually blended in such a model. Rather, there is a combination of types of learning situations.

A mid-point on the spectrum would be a course or programme that was divided fifty–fifty between e-learning and conventional learning, in whatever forms those types of learning took.

Towards the other end of the spectrum, e-learning can be used as a support for more conventional types of learning. An example would be a conventional undergraduate programme that provided reading material, a chat room, feedback facilities and e-mail contact with the lecturer or tutor in support of the programme. The Internet is there as a resource for electronic searching; some programmes provide guides or portals to enable students to access relevant databases, Web sites and other resources.

Finally, at the far end of the spectrum is conventional learning, by which we mean non-electronically mediated learning, fully offline, requiring no Internet access, online communication or online resource delivery. Even as we write we cannot imagine such a situation for higher education. Only retreats beyond the reach of Internet access and without the power to recharge portable devices could now fit this bill. As for fully online learning, we imagine the benefits of including use of ICTs in learning will be best achieved when attention is paid to the affordances of the technologies. Again, there is much research yet to be done on looking at these affordances for learning.

We end this section on e-learning by emphasizing again the need to consider the way technologies have modified – for better or for worse – the way information is recorded, stored, disseminated, and reviewed. E-learning as a whole is no more or less of a transformation than the one that takes place when knowledge is packaged for conventional learning and disseminated in a physical classroom; it is, however, a different transformation, and that is what we are all in the throes of living through and researching.

We turn now to address the 'learning' side of the e-learning enterprise.

THE 'LEARNING' IN E-LEARNING

The second element in the 'e-learning' equation is *learning* itself. While this is not the place for a consideration of the various theories of learning *per se*, it is necessary to say briefly what we mean by learning. We recognize that there is already much material on learning theory relevant to e-learning (e.g. work on collaborative learning, Bruffee, 1993, and computer-supported collaborative learning, Koschmann, 1996), and discussion of this and the nature of (e)learning will take place in the chapters of the *Handbook*, particularly those on modes and models of learning, and communities of learning. Here we highlight four general aspects of learning.

First, learning is a personal and social/political *transformative* act in which new knowledge is gained by the learner. The degree of transformation is critical to the kinds of learning that will take place. For example, the learning of a new fact by rote may in itself constitute a fairly minor transformative function, and thus be seen as learning to a small degree (accretive, gradual, a step forward). However, at some point such a small step might afford a more extensive vista. The analogy is the poet Alexander Pope's: that learning is like climbing a mountain, often in the mist. Steps are small, uphill, and hard work; but every now and again larger vistas open up, each one more extensive than the last. When such an expansive vista opens to the learner, the transformation can be said to be greater. The nature of the transformation can be purely intellectual, and/or it can be (a combination of) emotional, spiritual, physical.

Second, although learning is experienced by the individual, it is essentially an *effect of community*: not only is knowledge generated and preserved by a community throughout history, it is also learnt as an effect of being part of a community (Bourdieu, 1986; Crook, 2002; Haythornthwaite, 2006 Rogoff, 1990; Vygotsky, 1986). Some of the knowledge will be tacit, some will be explicit. The kinds of communities in which knowledge is made and transferred are varied: some are relatively informal, like families and peer groups; others are institutionalized and formal like schools or universities. Knowledge is packaged differently in these different communities, and also gained and tested differently. It is one of the main preoccupations of the present *Handbook* to define and explore the electronic communities in which e-learning takes place, considering them in relation to non-electronically mediated communities but also moving beyond a polarized distinction between online and offline communities to chart the new territory of e-learning. Indeed, this latter topic is a major area for research in e-learning, both theoretically and empirically.

Third, in order to distinguish it from experience, the transformative aspect of learning takes place in relation to *bodies of knowledge*. This does not mean to say that all knowledge is outside the learner because learning may take the form of enhanced self-knowledge; but it does mean that the learning is given definition by the way it transforms the learner in relation to knowledge of some kind. Hence learning and knowledge are inextricably related. To be able to say 'I now know that …' is to acknowledge that learning stands in relation to what was known before by the individual learner and also in relation to what is known and recognized as knowledge by a wider community.

Fourth, in keeping with the transformative and community aspects of learning, we add that knowledge is not simply delivered to a learner. The transformative act creates *new knowledge* that is the product of a learner's (or learners') research and exploration in territory previously unrecognized or uncharted. But this journey is not taken alone. New knowledge is tested against the world – the physical world, the social world, or the mental world of others' ideas – and so modified through practice, discussion, use, and interaction (Cook and Brown, 1999; Engeström,

1999a, b). In this interaction we find the community action on learning as a whole and knowledge development for all members of the community.

Of the four aspects of learning, it is probably the second – the nature and effect of the community of learners – that is the most distinctive in an e-learning environment. It is here that notions of distance learning come to the fore (as they had already in extension classes in the late nineteenth century; and via correspondence courses, for example those of the UK's Open University from the 1970s). E-learning allows the learners that make up a community to be far-flung in terms of physical distance, but also, as discussed earlier in this introduction, to operate asynchronously as well as synchronously. The fact of physical distance between learners and a lecturer/teacher, mediated by chat rooms, Web logs, e-mail, and other forms of group communication, means that: interaction can be recorded for future reference; learners operate largely from their computers or mobile devices; that physicality is largely absent; text, image, and sound provide the major modes through which communication happens; co-learners in the community may never meet face-to-face; the learning experienced is not situated in the physical, contextual ways we have come to expect; and contexts outside the classroom probably play a larger part in the learning experience than might be the case in a traditional programme or course conducted on the premise of regular, co-located, face-to-face meetings.

FROM 'E' + 'LEARNING' TO E-LEARNING

We have discussed the 'e' and 'learning' in e-learning, but this separation to discuss the technical, computer-based means of delivery and social perspectives on learning must now be recombined to consider the social and technological construct that is e-learning.

E-learning

E-learning is not a computer system. You cannot buy it off the shelf and plug it in. You cannot hand it to network administrators and be done with the job. To have an e-learning system means having *people* talking, writing, teaching, and learning with each other online, via computer-based systems. While e-learning is usually found implemented via a suite of software tools, such implementation is only the surface of the e-learning environment. E-learning encompasses any and all means of communication available to participants, from dedicated course management systems to late-night phone calls and e-mail in the early hours of the morning, from instructor-prepared lectures to collaborative products generated through discussion boards, blogs and wikis. E-learning is a leaky system; it spreads to take advantage of any and all opportunities for communicating, learning, and seeking resources, and, like an invasive species, turns up in many places not traditionally associated with formal instruction – the kitchen table, coffee shop, workplace, hotel room on corner of the bedroom. Through instructor and student push-and-pull, e-learning colonizes new technologies and new spaces, with each new generation of technologies providing, but also creating demand for, new kinds of delivery (e.g. gaming environments, podcasting based on MP3 players, video streaming and mobility inherent in cell and mobile phones, PDAs, and laptops).

The question then remains – what does define and distinguish e-learning? The HEFCE definition cited at the start of this chapter is a good starting place, but some modification is needed. E-learning *needs to be more than* the 'use of technologies' and it *is more than a* 'communications and delivery tool ... to support students and improve the management of learning'. At its best, e-learning is a reconceptualization of learning that makes use of not only instructor-led pedagogy but all the flexibility that asynchronous, multi-party contribution can bring. At its worst, e-learning is a substitution of one delivery mechanism for another; but even such implementations will be overwhelmed by the demands and expectations of users (both instructors and learners) and will change through social contracts, disuse, and idiosyncratic use. E-learning is *continuously emergent*, emanating from the possibilities of ICT in the hands of administrators, instructors, and learners, and created and recreated by use.[2] The forms and shapes of technology, learning, and technology-in-use for learning co-evolve, one pushing, pulling, and modifying the other.

This co-evolutionary view emphasizes the social and emergent nature of e-learning, i.e., the way people, operating with and through ICT, in communication and interaction with others, form what e-learning means. This is the core of our definition of e-learning. As such, it puts stand-alone learning programmes at the periphery; although successful learning can result from computer-based learning systems, such as self-paced tutorials, these are not centrally what e-learning is about. Similarly, use of ICT for resource delivery is not e-learning even though it is part of the e-learning phenomenon, just as delivery of books is not teaching although library collections are part of the learning activity. Teaching and teaching presence are essential parts of e-learning (Garrison and Anderson, 2003) and thus e-learning is more than delivery alone. Finally, e-learning is not (just) computer-mediated communication, in the same way that learning is not (just) conversation, although both are important in e-learning as a whole. The directed, purposeful pursuit of understanding, with resultant changes in knowledge, skill and/or practice, are inherent in learning and thus also in e-learning.

E–learning is a complex, multi-faceted phenomenon. Its scope includes the entirety of the social and technical system, from administrative decisions to systems developers, curriculum designers, and learners at the kitchen table. A range of educational systems and practices falls within e-learning. Children and adolescents are addressed in K-12/pre-school to senior high school/sixth-form online teaching and learning, as in virtual high schools (e.g. Zucker *et al.*, 2003); young and not-so-young adults are addressed through full- and part-time education in community colleges, training colleges, post-secondary undergraduate and graduate pro-grammes. E-learning includes formally structured, degree-based programmes, as well as non-degree, continuing education programmes in museums, art galleries and other locations; and in proprietary in-house corporate training systems.

E-learning may be implemented to take advantage of as many technologies as possible, or only a few. Thus we include in e-learning single application addi-tions to traditional teaching, such as electronic voting systems that add interactivity to large face-to-face lectures, online discussion added to on-campus courses, and myriad other blended learning configurations. E-learning may involve students and faculty geographically located on or off-campus, at a dis-tance from each other and campus, or distributed with no corresponding physical campus. Distance may be as close as the local dormitory room, or as remote as thousands of miles away, from sites accessing the latest in Internet connectivity to those with less than perfect networking capabilities. Indeed, defining the campus may be a challenge, not only for locating the physical home of an online university, but also where rapidly emerging, multi-institutional pro-grammes include students enrolled from many different campuses.

Social processes and technology

Researchers have been examining the interplay of social processes and ICTs for many years, building on a foundation of study of social processes and workplace interventions that include the 'time and motion' studies by Taylor (1911), the wiring room group behaviour studies by Roethlisberger and Dickson (1939) and the longwall miners studies by Trist and Bamford (1951) and the Tavistock group. These studies laid a foundation for identifying the importance of context in the presentation of technology in use and the recognition that similar tech-nologies will take dissimilar forms depending on the social, political, and institutional contexts in which they are implemented. This has become known as a 'socio-technical systems' approach. It is popular in management for jointly optimizing the social and technical systems in the workplace.

With the advent of computing, the socio-technical perspective became an important approach for understanding changes in work practices brought about by the implementation of computer systems (see Whitworth's chapter in this volume). As researchers looked at early computing systems they noted a number of issues that still factor into contemporary uses and presentations of ICT. These are reviewed briefly here because the history of the progression of computer systems provides background to the kinds of processes seen in current systems and helps tease out where effects of ICT on learning may be found.

Early computing systems were designed with the primary purpose of automating office processes, reproducing paper-based systems for the mainte-nance of records and automating the production of statistical reports. Terms like 'electronic data processing' captured the essence of these computing applications. However, as Zuboff (1988) observed, these systems began to *informate* as they automated. With the rise of computing also came a rise in the observability of processes; and then of systems to process these observations, including statistical analyses and benchmarking of human performance. Zuboff eloquently demonstrated the impact of this computerization on individuals at work. Clerical workers who had worked in social groups now found themselves isolated at computer terminals, entering data on their own. Their productivity could now be assessed in terms of keystrokes. The *social impact* of this instance of computerization was both the isolation of data entry personnel and increased monitoring of the minutiae of performance.

Technological determinists see such changes as the inevitable outcome of technology, with human activity shaped by the technologies that are imposed on them. Others see technology use as more malleable and affected by strategies of individual or joint human action: strategies such as non-use, or more complicated appropriations of the technology to local contexts (Danziger *et al.*, 1982; Rice and Rogers, 1980; Rogers, 1995; Rogers *et al.*, 1977). These two sides are often portrayed against each other – technology determining social behaviour, or social behaviour determining technology – with neither technology nor social behaviour changing. This approach to computing followed earlier work in management trying to find the best *task–technology fit*, where the technology was the kind of organizational structure and process most appropriate for the manufacturing task at hand (e.g. Thompson, 1967), taking into consideration the nature of the incoming raw materials and the needed transformation process to create outputs (Perrow, 1970) and the context in which the work took place (e.g. contingency theory, Lawrence and Lorsch, 1967).

This idea of looking for fit was transferred directly to examination of computing implementations because the data management capabilities of information technologies (IT) reconfigured organizational structures and processes. For a while there was an effort to explore computer system–organization fit, including communication–technology fit (Daft and Lengel, 1986; Trevino *et al.*, 1990). Studies of fit in the computing arena are best summed up in notions of *organizational validity* and *invalidity*, used to refer to how well the computing system corresponded to existing organizational structures and what could or should be done about it (Markus and Robey, 1983; Noble and Newman, 1993). Noble and Newman (1993) in particular noted that where fit was not made, the system could change, the people could change, or both could change. The socio-technical systems approach to computing emerges from this kind of observation: aligning social practices and technological support in the service of work outcomes is the essence of socio-technical systems evaluation, an approach that begins to make headway in thinking about systems design and implementation.

But, it is not enough to view the problem as one of accommodation, of making technology 'fit' the social or vice versa, or even of simultaneous adjustment, in part because this assumes a knowing observer, and relatively stable and identifiable social/technical conditions. However, the rapid development of computing technology, at first the personal computer revolution and now the mobile technology revolution, have pushed change ahead of planned fit, making developers out of users. Grass-roots movements such as Usenet, the Web and open-source software show that systems and use have a general, societal-level implementation that is under the control of no one organization or entity. New practices are emerging at a societal level that influence what can be done, and what is expected, within any organization or institution.

A number of systems design approaches emerged during the 1980s and early 1990s that have strongly influenced approaches to computerization. These include workplace studies that articulate everyday workplace processes, using this as input to systems design that better reflects actual practice (e.g. Luff *et al.*, 2000; Suchman, 1987), participatory design that brings the user into the design process rather than leaving the process to systems specialists alone (also known as user-centred design, e.g. see the work by Pelle Ehn, Morton Kyng) and shared cognition, with its emphasis on joint processes of learning and collaboration (e.g. Engeström and Middleton, 1996; Resnick *et al.*, 1991 and Whitworth in this volume, who suggests that the social shaping of technology can be a contested process). Systems development has changed from *a priori* definition of all operations in a sequence of systems analysis, design and implementation to more responsive and flexible design techniques such as rapid prototyping and scenario-based design. Whole sectors of computer science have emerged to engage with human–computer issues, such as Human–Computer Interaction (HCI, or CHI) which centres on interface design (e.g. Nielsen, 1994; Carroll, 2002), and Computer Supported Co operative Work (CSCW) with its attention to systems for working jointly with others in and through online applications (e.g. Baecker, 1993; Bannon and Schmidt, 1991; Crabtree *et al.*, 2005; Schmidt and Bannon, 1992; see also the proceedings of the CSCW and ECSCW (European) conferences). Research in Computer-Mediated Communication (CMC), which examines behaviour in and through computer media (for a review, see Herring, 2002), owes much of its heritage to the initiators of the CSCW field with their focus on understanding social processes and collaborative work on the way to designing support systems.

Examination of computing systems has also inherited from historical and sociological studies of technology, particularly in areas known as Social Studies of Technology (SST), Social Studies of Science (SSS) and Social Construction of Technology (SCOT). Work in this area is not limited to computers; some classic work has looked at how the particular design of bicycles we know today came about (Bijker, 1995). These areas look more broadly at how science and technology are constructed in society, and how this works with, and affects, society. Reviewing this area is beyond the scope of this chapter, but the attention these researchers give to the shaping of technology is an important construct for considering the place and presentation of e-learning technologies, and should prove a useful resource for researchers interested in this perspective. (For further reading, see, for example, Bijker *et al.*, 1987; MacKenzie and Wajcman, 1985; Pinch and Bijker, 1984; Williams and Edge, 1996).

Collectively, these approaches have provided a more holistic view of systems development: one that sees the social and technical sides of computerization not as two immutables in tension, but as two forces each shaping the other. As a whole, these new approaches to development and analysis of the unfolding of systems, plus the co-evolution of social and technical practices, are being gathered under the name *social informatics*.

Social informatics is one of two theoretical perspectives we find particularly relevant for e-learning. The other is rhetorical theory, which focuses on the relation between speaker, audience, and subject matter. Both of these are discussed at length in the next section as we turn now to look at theories that inform an e-learning research agenda.

THEORETICAL BACKGROUND

As noted at the outset of this introduction, our aim here and in the following chapters is to address the transformative effects of e-learning with a focus on research problems and challenges. In defining and building a research agenda for e-learning, it is necessary to find the theoretical base that informs evolving processes in a rapidly advancing technological environment, yet also addresses the kind of transformative activity that is entailed in e-learning and e-learning communities. Some key questions can be asked. What theories are useful for examining and understanding e-learning? Where does e-learning research fit in terms of theory? What are the parameters of the field? What are or will be our theories of e-learning? Is research conducted *about* the technology or *via* the technology – or both? These questions are essential for the conduct of research programmes, whether at masters and doctoral level or in terms of larger-scale joint research projects.

We make a start here on describing theoretical frameworks for e-learning. We do not attempt in this *Handbook* a 'grand theory' of e-learning, as we feel that the field is not in a sufficiently mature state for such theorizing; however, at the end of the section we present a number of questions that will help research move toward an overarching theory (or theories) in the field. Other chapters in the *Handbook* continue this theoretical framing. There are yet more theories that may prove useful for understanding the e-learning phenomenon coming from the fields and sub-fields of education, information science, communication, computer science, management, psychology, and sociology, to name a few. While we begin the process here, we expect more and new theories to be brought to bear on e-learning in the future.

As far as the electronic dimension of the field goes, communications theory and social informatics provide important perspectives. Communications theory is not a coherent field with a competing and/or convergent set of theories underpinning it. Rather, it draws on contemporary rhetorical theory and other sources to map out the nature and functions of the communicative acts that take place. Thus we begin with outlining the basics of rhetorical theory.

Rhetorical theory

Late twentieth-century thinking in the field of rhetoric sees it as an overarching theory that has a long tradition (Corbett, 1965), is grounded in historical and political change (Eagleton, 1983), has a pragmatic, Aristotelian pedigree rather than an idealist, Platonic one (Vickers, 1988), is centrally concerned with the arts of discourse (Andrews, 1992) and, through ICT, is intimately connected with democracy (Lanham, 1992) and argumentation. Contemporary rhetoric is concerned with the relationship among three key elements: the speaker/writer, the audience, and the subject matter. This communicative triangle (Kinneavy, 1971) enables exploration and definition of the purpose of the communicative act, as well as the possibility of investigation of the means by which the communication takes place. A key term in contemporary rhetoric is *dialogue*, deriving from the Greek for *through speech/logic* rather than from any notion of two people speaking.

Rhetoric can be used to analyse communication once it has taken place and also to predict (in ancient and medieval times, to *prescribe*) the patterns and means of communication that might be necessary in a particular situation. Behind such an understanding of the nature and purposes of communication is the philosophy of Habermas (1984), with his theory of communicative action and the function of argumentation (a subsection of rhetoric) in a society to bring about consensus before action.

Why is rhetoric a useful foundation for considering what happens in e-learning? All e-learning is contextualized, as suggested earlier in this introduction with reference to the work of Lave and Wenger (1991). It takes place in particular situations. Describing the contingencies and particularities of those situations is important because not all e-learning *acts* are the same. E-learning varies the relationship among the elements of speaker/writer, audience, and the 'thing to be communicated'. For example, a single teacher, lecturer, or course e-tutor may at one time address a whole class of e-learners; at other times, the communication may be one-to-one; and at yet other times, a single e-learner may send a message to the class as a whole on a bulletin board or as part of an ongoing dialogue. While these patterns of communication are no different in some respects from their face-to-face versions, the asynchrony available to e-learners potentially makes for a more reflective dynamic. Critically, from the audience's point of view in rhetorical theory, the reader/student/e-learner is more in control of the rhetorical process. Readers can choose when and whether they will respond to others or to the communication.

Rhetorical theory has already been used as a platform for understanding online communication. Studies have applied rhetorical concepts such as genres and discourse communities (Bakhtin, [1953] 1986; Frye, [1957] 1969; Miller, 1984, 1994; Swales, 1990) to online communication (Bregman and Haythornthwaite, 2003; Cherny, 1999; Orlikowski and Yates, 1994; Yates and Orlikowski, 1992). Concepts such as speech–act theory (Austin, 1962; Searle 1969) have been applied to the formalization of communicative action and design of communication systems (Flores *et al.*, 1988; Malone *et al.*, 1989; Winograd and Flores, 1986). However, this application has not been without controversy because of its overdetermination of actions (see Suchman, 1994; Winograd, 1994). Genre, rhetorical, and linguistic approaches also underpin the new rhetoric of *persistent conversation* (Erickson, 1999), which situates online communication somewhere between speech and writing.

Thus, rhetorical theory, with its basis in purposive communication and its recent application to communication via ICTs, is an important starting point for applying theory to e-learning. In what follows, we draw on Kinneavy's communication triangle as a basis for exploring e-learning. The discussion shows how the simple triangle of interaction between speaker, audience, and communication, when considered in relation to evolutionary processes of language, technology and purpose, shows a dynamic system, modified and modifiable by communicators' actions. The ideas echo those of others who point to the emergent nature of communication and technology use in group settings (e.g. Poole and DeSanctis's (1990) ideas of adaptive structuration which builds on Giddens's (1984) structuration theory; see also Monge and Contractor, 1997; Orlikowski, 1992).

To explore the emergent nature of communication in e-learning, we start with Kinneavy's (1971) basic notion of the communicative triangle, which is depicted in Figure 1.1: An adaptation of Kinneavy's model for e-learning (Figure 1.2) adds elements associating the writer/speaker with the teacher, the audience with the learners, and the body of knowledge with the 'substance of communication' or the 'thing to be communicated'.

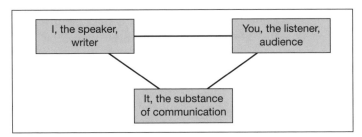

Figure 1.1 Kinneavy's (1971) model of communication

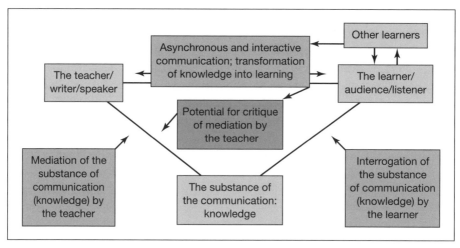

Figure 1.2   Adaptation of Kinneavy's (1971) model

In this adapted model, learning is conceived as a dialogic and dialectical exchange, not only between the learner and the teacher, but also between the learner and the body of knowledge that is being explored. Whereas, in Kinneavy's original model, the 'audience' was relatively passive; in this model the learner as audience is in a more powerful, active position in relation to the social dynamics of learning. He/she can even critique the teacher's mediation of existing knowledge, as indicated by the box in the middle of the communicative triangle. Furthermore, he/she is part of a community of enquiry with other learners.

This model not only retains the communicative element in e-learning, but provides a way of understanding how the individual learner positions him/herself in relation to a community of learners, a teacher/lecturer, and a body of knowledge. The *communicative* dimension of e-learning is an essential foundation to studies in the field. Moreover, although the model might just as well apply to learning, the asynchronous possibilities of exchange between learner and teacher, and between learner and co-learners, enables reflection to become an integrated part of the actual dialogic interaction between the participants *while in the process of learning*. Such reflection is possible in a conventional, face-to-face classroom, but the immediacy of the classroom environment and its many contextual cues – lecturer at the head of the class, students in desks, black/whiteboards and projectors, the presence of other students – and our natural reluctance to tolerate silence in face-to-face settings weigh against reflection during class sessions. But asynchronous communication as well as synchronous computer-mediated communication provides and tolerates a much longer lag between question and response, an expectation of silence, and a lack of visual scrutiny while thinking, all of which affords reflection in the learning process.

Another aspect of communication theory that might be helpful in understanding the use of language in e-learning is that made by Austin (1962) in *How to*

Do Things with Words, where he makes the distinction between locutionary speech acts – 'sayings' – and illocutionary acts (and their perlocutionary effects) in which language performs an 'action' or 'does something'. Although the distinction itself was critiqued by Searle (1969), it remains a potentially useful one in that it enables distinctions to be drawn between different types of language use in e-learning. For example, there is a distinct difference between online synchronous 'chat' on the one hand, which has a social as well as communicative function, and asynchronous dialogic exchange on the other, where there is less emphasis on the social and there may be less attention on the building of a co-constructed understanding of a particular phenomenon. There is considerable potential for studies in speech-act theory and e-learning in that the 'map' of communication exchanges in e-learning is yet to be fully charted.

Furthermore, Kinneavy's adapted model or other theoretical attempts to chart communication in relation to e-learning can be further adapted in order to better describe, explain, and analyse the rhetorical dimensions of e-learning. There are many research projects to be undertaken here and there is much exciting work to be done.

Social informatics

Social informatics refers to the interdisciplinary study of the design, uses, and consequences of ICTs that takes into account their interaction with institutional and cultural contexts.

(Kling *et al.*, 2005: 6)

Social informatics provides another theoretical foundation for addressing e-learning, deriving not so much from rhetoric and communication theory as from the sociology of contemporary culture, particularly where it intersects with computing use by groups, organizations, communities, and societies. A few studies of e-learning using this perspective are just beginning to appear (e.g. Dutton *et al.*, 2004; see also Haythornthwaite and Kazmer, 2004).

Many fields contribute to the social informatics perspective. Sociology has provided background pertinent to the study of information systems and e-learning in studies and theories about diffusion and adoption of innovations (Rogers, 1995), social construction and social shaping of technology (e.g. MacKenzie and Wajcman, 1985; Williams and Edge, 1996), activity theory (Engeström and Middleton, 1996), social networks (Wellman and Berkowitz, 1997) and actor networks (Latour, 1987). Perhaps not as well integrated into social informatics, but of particular importance to e-learning is work on literacy, particularly online literacy (Andrews, 2004; Hawisher and Selfe, 1999), language (Clark, 1996; Crystal, 2001), linguistics (e.g. Cherny, 1999; Herring, 2002) and genre (Bregman and Haythornthwaite, 2003; Orlikowski and Yates, 1994). Also important are many different approaches to community from social network definitions (Wellman, 1979,

1999) to discourse communities (Miller, 1994; Warschauer, 2000), knowledge communities (e.g. Collins, 1998; Knorr-Cetina, 1999) and communities of practice (Wenger, 1998). Studies in sociology, linguistics and communication have contributed to our understandings of community and its manifestation online (Baym, 2000; Cherny, 1999; Haythornthwaite *et al.*, 2000; Kendall, 2002; Warschauer, 2003; Wellman, 1997; Wellman *et al*, 1996), as well as how offline communities are affected by online interaction (in studies of community networking initiatives and an area of research now often referred to as *community informatics*, e.g. Bishop, 2000; Cohill and Kavanaugh, 2000; Keeble and Loader, 2001 see also the studies in Wellman and Haythornthwaite, 2002).

New systems of social relationships

These many studies and theories share a common focus on the way new technologies change social interaction: with new language, meeting places, means of meeting, and meaning of associations. Castells (2001), for example, argues that 'a new system of social relationships centred on the individual' (p. 128) is emerging, in which the individual creates his or her own individualized communities in a society which creates emphasis on the individual through the relationship between capital and labour, between workers and the work process, and 'the crisis of patriarchism, and the subsequent disintegration of the nuclear family' (p. 129). Although individual networks have existed for a long time, supported through letters, travel by car and plane, and the telephone (Wellman, 1979, 1999), the Internet in particular has been cited as supporting (and creating) such individualized sociability (Wellman, 2002; Wellman *et al.*, 1996; Wellman *et al.*, 2003), with consequent positive or negative effects (e.g. Kraut, *et al.*, 1998; Kraut, Kiesler *et al.*, 2002; for a review, see Haythornthwaite and Wellman, 2002). The Internet is effective in maintaining weak ties and perhaps also instrumental in creating the space or the opportunities in which strong ties can be made stronger (Haythornthwaite, 2005). Online communities, suggests Castells (2001), 'are better understood as networks of sociability, with variable geometry and changing composition, according to the evolving interests of social actors and to the shape of the network itself' (p. 130). (For a review of social networks and online community, see Haythornthwaite, forthcoming-b.)

Although Castells (2001) does not address issues of e-learning *per se* in his book, the implications for networked communities of learners are clear: e-learning communities are social communities of a different kind from conventional learning communities, which may allow the individual to assert him- or herself more at the centre of a range of networks. Although the individual and his or her learning are defined by those networks, it is also the case that he or she defines the networks. A number of e-learning researchers have begun to examine networked aspects of ties built in association with e-learning (e.g. Aviv *et al.*, 2003; Cho *et al.*, 2002; Haythornthwaite, 2002a, b; Hrastinski, 2006; Saltz *et al.*, 2004). These studies hold promise as a theoretical platform on which to build e-learning research.

Exploring the nature of e-learning communities, Haythornthwaite and Kazmer (2002), in presenting findings about on- and offline relations for e-learning, discuss the claims and counter-claims that the Internet both 'reduces involvement with those whom we share strong, local, interpersonal ties, taking us away from face-to-face involvement and potentially decreasing our well-being' and also 'is seen as providing the means for increased contact with others' (p. 434), for example with those with whom we share an interest, such as co-learners in a distance learning programme. They argue that often each side of the argument has been simplified, the truth of the matter being in elaborately textured networks of strong and weak ties that change in time (weak ones faster than strong ones). The Internet is seen, not so much as a social world, 'but as a medium through which we have the opportunity to maintain our multiple social worlds' (p. 442).

Scott and Page (2001) see learning communities as 'social spaces, physical and/or virtual, within which users are invited or enabled to engage in a shared learning process, while respecting the diversity of their knowledge base' (2001: 152). If, as Scott and Page suggest, learners in such an environment 'are encouraged to set their own learning goals' (2001: 152) and if such networks encourage and support individualism, then there are interesting questions to be asked about the nature of the common experience of e-learners: in particular, can it be said that an e-learning programme can set such goals itself, or should it err on the side of the individuals setting their own goals? As ever, some kind of balance has to be struck; it may be important to determine exactly what the possibilities of balance are in any e-learning context. Loader (1997) provides further discussion of the governance of cyberspace. One of the many interesting aspects of that discussion pertains to notions of information polity or informationality, with clear connections to the nature and accessibility of knowledge, its location (on- or offline) and its use. Mere accessing of information may not, in itself, be akin to learning; some transformation of the material into new knowledge for the individual must, we think, take place if such activities are to be called 'e-learning'. Thus the term 'e-learning' becomes something greater than the sum of its parts, inviting research and examination in terms of an independent phenomenon rather than a re-purposed version of offline learning.

From social informatics to educational informatics

Extending the principles of social informatics into the learning sphere leads logically to the adoption of the term *educational informatics*, as Levy *et al.* (2003) have done. They define the domain of educational informatics as: 'the study of the application of digital technologies and techniques to the use and communication of information in learning and education' (p. 299) and the main concerns as twofold:

> First, research in educational informatics seeks to understand the effects on people of using digital information (re)sources, services, systems, environments and communications media for learning and education. It examines the issues and problems that arise from their

practice and how these relate to factors such as educational and professional context, communication and information practices, psychological and cognitive variables, and ICT design and use. Second, it seeks to contribute to the development of practical knowledge that is relevant to diverse forms of ICT-supported learning.

(Levy *et al.*, 2003: 299)

In reviewing how computer systems have been received, there are many parallels in the receipt of learning technologies. For instance, unquestioned technological or social deterministic views hold back an effective transformation to e-learning. Teachers may avoid online teaching because they feel constrained by the technology (a technological determinist view, resisted through non-use), or they may come online expecting to transfer existing teaching practices wholesale to the online enterprise (a social determinist view, expecting no change in their pedagogy). But neither approach serves the long-term interests of educators and neither approach can be maintained for long. In the former case, student use and demand for technology plus campus initiatives to 'keep up' with the technology use of other campuses will remove the option of non-use for teachers; and in the latter case, as has been shown from many studies, simple transfer from offline to online does not make good pedagogy – teachers interested in good pedagogy learn to modify their practices in accordance with the online environment.

There are parallels in the way computerization automates and informates e-learning in the same way it has done for other operations. Formerly transient and ephemeral processes are now routinely recorded as part of the delivery process. Conversations, discussions and lectures that remain in digital records facilitate asynchronous participation, but their persistence also allows interrogation and review. They create a source of information about the course progress and conduct. As Berge (1997: 15) notes, an 'interesting line of research involves the fact that computer conferencing programs can produce complete transcripts of all interactions they have mediated. These transcripts are a rich data source.' Beyond research, however, they are also an interesting source of data for monitoring, accountability and benchmarking.

Paralleling the concerns described by Zuboff of workers cut off from human contact (see also Kraut *et al.*, 1998, for similar concerns about Internet use), many conceive of e-learning as an individual working alone at their computer. What is different now is that the isolated student is just as likely to be carrying on conversations with many others via class discussion boards, e-mail and whispering, moulding and forming the communication dialogue they prefer. Invisible to the outside observer is the communication that goes on between students, and between students and instructors, as the student sits 'alone' at their terminal, as well as the actions they take to initiate and sustain that interaction. Perhaps now we should say that computers automate, informate, and 'communicate' (in the sense that computers facilitate communication). The turn from HCI to CSCW marks a turn from humans interacting with computers to interacting with others *through* computers, an observation made early in relation to education in a collection of papers concerned with computer-supported collaborative learning (CSCL; O'Malley, 1989). In that volume, Bannon connects ideas from CSCW with CSCL, describing the computer's role 'as a medium through which individuals and groups can collaborate with others' (Bannon, 1989: 271; see also Crook, 1989; Kaye, 1991, 1995). These interests in collaboration have led to the development of more all-embracing systems developments for supporting knowledge work, such as collaboratories (also known as collaborative virtual environments, Finholt, 2002) which lead naturally to the idea of collaborative learning and collaborative learning environments (Lunsford and Bruce, 2001).

Bringing together rhetorical and social/educational informatics perspectives

If rhetorical theory and social/educational informatics provide some theoretical basis to the field, what are the field's parameters? How do we know what is included and what is excluded from research in e-learning? Our answer comes from one aspect of discourse theory that itself derives from sociological theory: the notion of framing. Put simply, any research study needs to be framed in some way: it needs to define its boundaries, state what area it intends to cover and provide a 'map' (literature review) of the field.

Tannen (1993), in *Framing in Discourse*, traces the concept of framing back to Bateson's 'A theory of play and fantasy' ([1954] 1972). Bateson, she suggests, 'demonstrated that no communicative move, verbal or nonverbal, could be understood without reference to a metacommunicative message, or metamessage, about what is going on – that is, what frame of interpretation applies to the move' (p. 3). The notion of framing – itself deriving metaphorically from the framing of paintings in the visual arts or other forms of art, like theatre and its framed spaces – has been taken up by researchers in communication and psychology, anthropology, and most notably in sociology in Goffman's *Frame Analysis* (1974). As far as rhetoric and the arts of discourse go, it is a central organizing principle of communication. (See also Engeström and Middleton, 1996, on activity theory and complex systems theory.) Frames are systemic (political assumptions, ideologies, historical tendencies), concrete (a school, other institutions), genre-based (socially habitual forms of communication, like debates, conversations) as well as 'inside the head' – a kind of cultural programming. Frames can be transgressed as well as observed. They can also be imposed by others. Such imposition can be made directly or through technologies and/or organizational structures which make it literally impossible to do things in certain ways.

In terms of the field of e-learning research, what frames are brought to bear in its interpretation? We could posit these as technical, sociological and pedagogical. *Technically*, there now appears to be no limit to what is possible in terms of connectivity. Wireless connection, access grid technology, and broadband Internet connection allow multimodal communication between two or more people. There is the possibility of synchronous and asynchronous communication, albeit without physicality and with the constraints of access to equipment, networks and the technical skill required to make such connection reliably. *Sociologically*, the dispersed, sometimes international nature of communities of enquiry makes for distributed learning, often more informally than has been the case in the past. *Pedagogically*, the teacher comes and goes in the class – a presence which co-ordinates, directs, supports, and challenges the learners. It could be said that the relation between teacher and learner has the potential to be equalized in e-learning, with authoritative, canonical positions adopted by teachers less likely to be accepted by learners; on the other hand, anecdotal evidence suggests that a teacherly presence and/or leadership is important for sustaining the group. Whatever the precise and specific dynamic of an e-learning community, the nature and power (and extent) of networks becomes more telling and more influential in the nature of the actual learning that takes place. Rogoff (1990) has suggested that 'learning is an effect of community'; that is, what we learn is a read-off or affordance of being part of a community, whether that community is a school, family, street corner, club, society or looser group of friends. Essentially, without a community of some sort, the learning that arises from involvement in it cannot take hold. Community, therefore, is a *sine qua non* of learning. To adapt Rogoff's (1990) phrase for the twenty-first century and in particular for e-learning, learning becomes an effect of computer *networked communities* rather than an effect of local, geographical community.

It is exactly at the point where questions are asked about networked communities of practice that current theory in e-learning begins to break down. Questions that suggest themselves for future work include: What do we mean by a community of enquiry? How do e-communities relate to situated, real-world communities? (see Kazmer, this volume) What kinds of community experience are best suited to high-quality learning? Where and what are the boundaries between being, and acting in the world, and learning? What could an ecology of learning mean, and, once defined, how would e-learning fit into it?

A central theme emerging from such questions is the relationship between the social control of learning and individual agency in learning. From the identification of such a theme – one that is not confined to e-learning, but which applies to learning more generally – further questions arise. When engaged in e-learning, what are you learning? Whose model of learning and whose selection of knowledge are you adopting? What are the unexpected consequences of the drive for e-learning initiatives, such as the continued exclusion of non-ICT users? What is the digital divide (see Haythornthwaite, this volume) in terms of access to and use of ICT in learning?

This is a short list of questions, and there is much scope for examination. As said above, this is an exciting time to be exploring this phenomenon. To help in that exploration, we turn now from theoretical considerations to issues of methodology and method.

METHODOLOGICAL CHALLENGES FOR E-LEARNING RESEARCH

Methodologically, e-learning research requires inventive approaches. The complexity of e-learning situations cannot always be easily described, let alone investigated and analysed. In this section, we explore some of the difficulties of finding the right methodology (overall approach) and methods (techniques) for researching e-learning; we also propose some possible solutions. In particular, we are concerned to point out that conventional approaches to research in education may not be adequate to the task in hand; and that finding appropriate methodologies may be more important than discovering new methods. More specifically, we think that one-way models of research (the simple causal model in which an intervention has an effect on an existing state of affairs) and two-way models ('there is a symbiotic relationship between technologies and learning') need to give way to reciprocal co-evolutionary models of the relationship between the 'e-' and 'learning' in e-learning research. In order to demonstrate an emerging model, we will use the specific case of research into the relationship between ICT and literacy education, scaling up the model to apply to research into e-learning.

One of the problems with research in education – and it no doubt applies to other fields of enquiry too, and to research in particular disciplines – is that the object of research is often framed too simply. To put it more precisely, the object of research is conceived of as a single entity that is affected or influenced by one or more factors or variables. Such a single entity is often the focus of whatever method or methods is/are used to understand it and to shed light on it.

Whichever approach we take, the problem of a single entity on which we are focusing remains. It is, perhaps, a vestige of what is assumed to be a 'scientific' approach to the investigation of a single entity – something we try to isolate, by controlling variables, in order to understand it. However, conceiving of e-learning situations in terms of their singularity will not help us progress far in research terms, because the very nature of e-learning is enmeshed within social and informational contexts of the kind we have described in the theoretical section of this introduction.

To explain our emerging sense of what is needed in e-learning research, we start with the example of studies of the relationship between ICTs and literacy development. We suggest that the lessons learnt from trying to interrogate this relationship at the level of literacy development can be scaled up to apply to learning in general and thus provide a more powerful methodological model for the future of e-learning research.

The remainder of the introduction articulates a model for examining e-learning that incorporates elements of rhetorical, communication, and social informatics theories. This model has been developed by Andrews, and was first presented at conferences in 2005 (Andrews, 2005a, b).

Modelling e-learning processes

If we are interested in the effectiveness of a particular intervention – say the computer interface – on some educational outcome – say learning development for 5–16 year olds, or for undergraduate students – we could set up a controlled experiment in which we try to isolate and measure the impact of the intervention from effects from all other variables. Or we could study the case of a single pupil, or a group of pupils, or the equivalent at undergraduate level and undertake a holistic study in which we embraced all the variables or factors that were at play in order to get a better understanding of what was going on with our particular case. In the former approach, the methodology is exclusive; in the latter, it is inclusive.

What most researchers and reviewers of research have been asking to date in the field of ICT and literacy education in schools is 'What is the *impact* of ICT on literacy development?' When it has been hard to pin down exactly what is meant by 'impact', researchers have narrowed the aperture to ask a more precise question: 'What is the *effect* (or effectiveness) of ICT on literacy development?' and thus narrowed the attention to controlled trials, and randomized controlled trials where they can be found (see Andrews, 2004; Andrews *et al.*, 2002; Andrews *et al.*, 2005; Burn and Leach, 2004; Locke and Andrews, 2004; Low and Beverton, 2004: Torgerson and Zhu, 2003). Rather than discuss this and other research, we will depict the progress from the one-way model of research methodology – which we now find too limited for our purposes – to a dialectic and longitudinal model that is appropriate for the study of e-learning in higher education and other contexts. The progress from conventional approaches to cause–effect study through to a new model is depicted through stages.

In the stage depicted in Figure 1.3 the relationship between an intervention (x) and the phenomenon which it affects or has impact on (y) is basically causal; x is assumed to be unchanging, but its arrival on the scene, its presence, its actions make a difference to y. Most studies in the field of ICT and literacy education have used this model in the 1980s and 1990s and indeed into the first part of the twenty-first century. In fact, most short-term evaluations are of this nature (of which there have been many in the field of ICT's impact on literacy and other aspects of education since 1980 or so; see Tweddle, 1997). The most reliable and highly controlled experiments of this kind are randomized controlled trials, which, by controlling for wayward variables and randomizing participants to experimen-

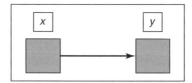

Figure 1.3   One-way model of causality. This model assumes the impact or effect on *x* and *y*. It assumes that, although *y* is affected by *x*, *x* remains unchanged

tal and control groups, can claim to say something about the causal relationship between x and y. Discussions of the nature and complexity of causality are often put aside in such research projects, as they would interfere with what looks like a relatively simple model. We all know this model: it is one of a number of default models in educational research, often removing considerations of context from a study in order to identify an internal and single causal relationship.

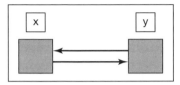

Figure 1.4   Two-way model. This model assumes there is some kind of *dialogic* **relationship between** *x* **and** *y***. In other words, although** *x* **may affect** *y***, it may also be the case that** *y* **affects** *x* **– perhaps to the same degree, or perhaps to a lesser extent (or even, possibly, to a greater extent). In studies in literacy development the relationship has been described as 'symbiotic' by Haas (1996)**

While the one-way model provides a starting point, neither life nor learning stops after one interaction. Thus, we build on to the one-way model a reaction or simultaneous action of y on x. Figure 1.4 shows that the relationship between x and y is complicated by the fact that the reaction of y may have a bearing upon x. This relationship can be described as symbiotic, in that the two parties or entities affect each other, with each adapting to the other's characteristics. It is a two-way process; indeed, each party comes to depend on the other. For example, the advent of word-processing software may have affected writing practices, but writing practices in turn have affected word-processing programmes. Word-processing software has evolved from its earlier simplicity to include features permitting tracking changes, adding editorial comments, and reformatting documents. But such features do not entirely arise from the technology; they were practised by scribes in the medieval period and are part of writing process practice that re-emerged in the work of Graves (1983) and others (e.g. Andrews and Noble 1982) in the early 1980s. In this case, writing practices have had a backwash or informing effect on software design, thus enabling the inclusion of tracking and other editorial devices in the word-processing packages.

Co-evolutionary model

The model depicted in Figure 1.4 is closest to what Haas (1996) calls the *symbiotic* relationship between ICT and development. This acceptance of a two-way process in the interaction between ICT and learning, in our model, can be scaled up to a two-way process in understanding the relationship between any two phenomena, as long as there is some degree of mutability in both phenomena.

However, symbiosis is not the appropriate term to characterize the relationship between ICT and learning development, nor any scaled-up dialectical relationship between mutable phenomena. The problem is that *symbiosis* is essentially conservative, i.e., a symbiotic relationship is one where the two parties try to preserve and conserve the equilibrium that they have reached. Such conservatism clearly isn't the case with the relationship between ICT and learning, nor in most dialectical, developmental situations. So, in order to reflect more accurately what goes on between the two phenomena, it is necessary to move towards a model that biologists call 'reciprocal co-evolution'.

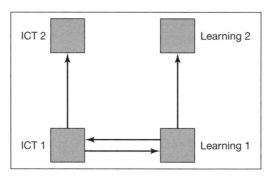

Figure 1.5   Co-evolutionary model, stage 1. Both ICT and learning change in time. What counts for ICT in 1990 is different by the year 2000, and again different in 2010. Similarly, what counts as being a learner also changes.

For the moment, let us concentrate on the internal dynamics of the relationship, though it is obvious that there are external factors at play in bringing about change in ICT and in learning. Figure 1.5 introduces a temporal dimension into the relationship. In research terms, it would be characterized as longitudinal. In the fast-changing world of information and communication technology, what counts as standard one year is not the same as what is standard a year or two later. If we compared 1980 with 1990, and then with 2000 and 2010, for example, we would register considerable change in the ICT field, not only in terms of what is available, but also in the degree of accessibility to that technology. Similarly, what counts as learning also changes (though more slowly) and educational changes – in curricula, classroom design, social practices within schooling, etc. – tend to follow even more slowly. Rather than complicate the model at this point, the educational contexts and the individual growth of the learner are left out, though they clearly have a bearing on the learning that takes place and they also change over time.

Thus, methodologically, any study of the relationship between ICT and learning needs a dialectical as well as a temporal dimension if it is to give a full account of the relationship. Figure 1.6 depicts the fact that a new state of affairs has come about – which we have called ICT 2 and Learning 2. There is not only a new 'two-way' or quasi-symbiotic relationship between the two phenomena, but there are also backwash or delayed influences, indicated by the diagonal arrows. For example, the use of Microsoft's PowerPoint as a presentational tool was extensive in the first part of the first decade of the twenty-first century, even though other presentation software or approaches were available (e.g. through the creation of a Web site with hot spots to reveal information, using hypertextual principles). As individuals 'discovered' PowerPoint and added it to their repertoire they operated at different levels: plain slide presentations using given templates; the creation of individual and/or corporate templates; the introduction of images; the introduction of moving images and/or sound; the creation of hot spots to automate links to Web sites. Presenters often back up their electronic presentations with acetate slides for an overhead projector. 'New' technologies and practices, like presentation through a Web site or PowerPoint, thus backwash on to older technologies and practices.

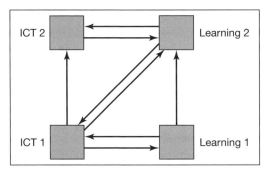

Figure 1.6 Co-evolutionary model, stage 2. Both ICT and learning change in time, but so do the learners as they grow up and develop. A new 'symbiosis' is established at ICT 2 and Learning 2; but there are also residual influences

Such residuality, backwash, and consolidation are important both for ICT development and for learning development. As suggested earlier in this introduction, residual technologies take their place in relation to new forms of learning rather than being replaced by them, creating a new economy in communicative and educational practices. To put it another way: old technologies and practices don't necessarily disappear as new technologies come along. They are absorbed, added to, or find their place, rather than being replaced. Their place is determined by the economies of use: the key rhetorical principle of what is or are the best medium/media of communication in any particular situation and set of circumstances. So, as indicated in Figure 1.6, ICT 1 may have effects and impacts on Learning 2 and (perhaps to a lesser extent) vice versa. The emergent complexity of the model is shown in Figure 1.7.

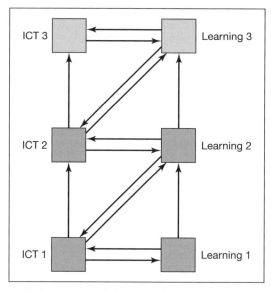

Figure 1.7   Co-evolutionary model, stage 3

The diagonal effects can also be from an advanced state of ICT development in relation to less advanced states of learning development, as shown in Figure 1.8. Here we have the almost fully-fledged model describing the complex of relationships between two entities that are both developing in time. The figure also

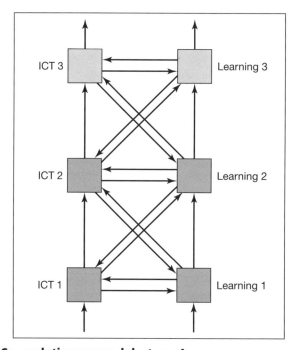

Figure 1.8   Co-evolutionary model, stage 4

suggests that each of the entities brings a history with it and that both are likely to continue changing into the future. To put it another way: every new form of ICT runs through old ways of use until new forms – many of them hybrid – are found.

The value of the co-evolutionary model is that it can provide a framework for studies in ICT and development of learning practices. While research studies may concentrate on only one aspect of the model – for example, the effect of ICT 1 on Learning 1 – such limited study needs to be placed within a bigger picture, without making claims that would apply to the whole of the relationship between the two entities.

In broad methodological terms, the co-evolutionary model posited here goes beyond simplistic notions of causality and introduces a temporal dimension. In research methods terms, the model suggests the need for an approach that is more able to describe and analyse such a dialectical relationship. Although it is not possible to explore all possibilities in detail in this introduction, one approach that looks useful is cross-lagged panel analysis (or cross-lagged panel design; Oud, 2002). This approach was first mooted by Lazarsfeld (Lazarsfeld, 1940; Lazarsfeld and Fiske, 1938). It has been used more recently to study the reciprocal relationship between parenting and adolescent problem-solving behaviour (Rueter and Conger, 1998). There is room for further exploration of the applicability and worth of cross-lagged panel designs in educational research, in particular in paying attention to the problem of how continuous (and sometimes erratic) development can be adequately mapped in staged analyses of reciprocity. This standard approach to dynamic phenomena in natural science could be used to explore the relationship between ICT and learning with the use of qualitative as well as quantitative data.

Before we leave this model, however, there is one further consideration to take into account: that these phenomena – ICT development and use – do not take place in a vacuum and are in themselves phenomena affected by and affecting context.

Adding societal context

To complete the model, we need to take into account something that has arisen already in systematic reviews of the relationship between ICT and literacy/learning development, i.e. neither ICT nor literacy/learning is a simple entity in itself (see, for example, Cope and Kalantzis, 2000, on multiliteracies). Similarly, learning is not a self-contained entity, but instead is heavily influenced by local, regional, national, and international contexts. To take ICT: the term itself covers a multitude of different technologies and modes of communication. When researchers take 'ICT' as one of their points of reference, they take much for granted. Are they talking about desktop computer interfaces and their use, or are they talking about the same software interfaces being used on a laptop, palmtop or via mobile phone? Are moving images, as experienced in the cinema, at home, or in the classroom, included or excluded from the definition of ICT?

Such considerations suggest the need for another dimension of classification – what biologists refer to as a *phylogeny* of the field. A phylogeny of e-learning would track the historical/longitudinal and taxonomic progress of ICT and learning (separately) and then show at what points they converge. The nearest analogy outside Biology is probably the 'family tree' model. We have not space in this introduction to create such a phylogeny, but invite future researchers to do so. Such a phylogeny would have the advantage of defining exactly the social and political provenance of a particular aspect of e-learning, distinguishing it from other related activities that might otherwise be confused with it.

Similarly, contexts of family, educational and social policy, economic funding and international competition affect the learning context; and technology advances, networking infrastructures and ICT developments constitute and affect the e-learning context. In the light of these considerations, the co-evolutionary model depicted above needs to be extended to accommodate wider contexts. Figure 1.9 presents a version of a co-evolutionary contextual model that can act as a starting point for theoretical models of research in e-learning in general. The new model shows how factors external to the internal dynamics of the model need to be taken into account when investigating phenomena like ICT and learning. These include factors that determine the changing nature of ICT, like economic, design and scientific factors; the changing nature of electronic communities; and the determinants of longitudinal growth.

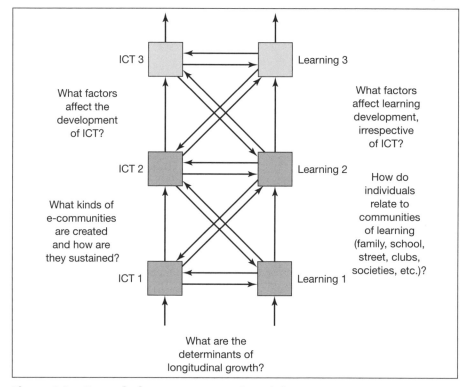

Figure 1.9   Co-evolutionary contextual model

Clearly a conclusion at this point in time would be inappropriate for a developing, exploratory model. Better approaches for the time being are: to critique the proposed model itself; to look for ways of testing the efficacy of the model's power to explain; and to ask questions of its scalability.

In the sense that the model itself is predicated on a dialectical principle, there is probably scope for its use. Not only horizontal and diagonal effects are equally or unevenly reciprocated, but vertical ones might also exist which describe the advances made from one state to another for a particular phenomenon. These vestigial or residual elements might be investigated in themselves. They are developmental and diachronic, as opposed to synchronic. The opportunity for dialectical interaction between states/snapshots of development is full of potential.

To sum up: the vertical axes represent change in time. We can research these by identifying points in time at which measures will be taken of the state of technological development or the state of learning (whether the latter is a particular age group growing over a number of years, or a cohort changing over a short period of time) and by modelling the changes alongside each other. The horizontal axes represent the causal and symbiotic relationships between the two entities. The diagonal axes represent residual and predicted changes as a result of interaction between the two entities.

Research studies in the field of e-learning may not explore every axis, nor each particular link in the structure, but by referring to a larger picture of reciprocal co-evolution between ICT and learning, may be able to position themselves more clearly and accurately in a complex and intra-related field of enquiry.

A FRAMEWORK FOR EXAMINING EMERGENT PROCESSES IN E-LEARNING

The model of emergent processes described above, and the social informatics research perspective, both draw our attention to the way e-learning is itself an emergent process. While some view it as a new delivery mechanism for education, and others view it as a new pedagogical challenge, what that delivery looks like and what frames the pedagogical challenge emerges from the interplay between new educational strategies, new teaching approaches, new technologies, and new participants in this endeavour. A key need for e-learning research is, then, to consider how this phenomenon unfolds in educational settings. Emergent, socio-technical change is not random. Knowing what is likely to influence the changing face of e-learning lets us predict, and, indeed, shape its future form – though these forms are going to be adapted on the 'shop floor' and in individual contexts. As a final presentation in this introduction, the following framework and its examples are offered as a beginning to exploration of the co-evolutionary developments in e-learning.

In grappling with the complexity of the area, four primary areas of action stand out for examining change processes in e-learning. These are actions taken by or emanating from *administration, pedagogy, technology*, and *community*.

Change in any of these areas not only drives further change within the area itself, but also drives and is driven by change in each other area. *Administration* encompasses the decisions made about e-learning initiatives in education, and the decision makers who direct this agenda. *Pedagogy* entails the knowledge accumulated about teaching and learning, as well as the teachers and instructors who build and deliver courses. *Technology* in this instance is narrowly defined as the delivery mechanisms for e-learning, i.e., primarily computer-based technology, including course management systems, e-mail, the Internet, and newly emergent information and communication technologies. *Community* refers here to potential and actual elearners and the communities they live in, both physical and virtual, on-campus and off.

As decisions and implementations are made in each area, they have direct and indirect effects on other areas. Table 1.1 presents a first run at sorting out and describing the complex interactions of the four prime areas. It is offered as a beginning of such explanation. Future research will be able to refine and verify impacts, as well as considering other areas and streams of influence (e.g. economic factors). In Table 1.1, the direct and indirect effects are classified as *driver, passenger, emergent* and *second-order effects*. *Driver effects* are evident when an action stemming from one of the four identified areas has an impact on other aspects of e-learning, e.g. when administrative decisions about technology drive what options are available for giving online classes and for maintaining an online community. *Passenger effects* are evident in the way practices are transformed by the driving forces, e.g. in the way pedagogy can or must now proceed because of an administrative choice about technology. All driver effects have an impact on a passenger, but to save redundancy the passenger side impact is not given in the table. Instead, identification of a passenger effect is limited to instances where the effect is less immediately expected. Readers may, however, prefer to see them all as driver effects, since even the unexpected passenger effect then becomes a driver for further change.

Outcomes that arise from action within the same area are identified as *emergent effects*; these appear primarily along the diagonal in Table 1.1. Such influences may come from action within the local institution or programme, but also from outside, e.g. as institutions look to and emulate peers, as colleagues share pedagogical techniques at conferences, and as new technologies appear. (See Scott, 1992, for more on the many kinds of ways organizations pay attention to their environments, for example, following the actions of peer institutions, regional competitors, etc.).

Finally, outcomes that emerge because of new practices are indicated in the table as *second-order effects*. These do not arise immediately but emerge later in time as a set of less expected outcomes; sometimes these become further driver, passenger, or emergent effects.

The effects described in Table 1.1 begin the work of identifying the major push-and-pull between developments in each of these areas. The ideas presented in the table are not intended to be exhaustive, but instead illustrative of the kind of iterative action and reaction that is of importance to e-learning. It is hoped that it will be taken up, expanded and tested by future e-learning research.

Table 1.1: E-learning driver, passenger, emergent, and second-order effects

	Administration drives …	Pedagogy drives …	Technology drives …	Community drives …
Administration	External A drives A: decisions about the adoption of new practices that are made at peer institutions drive decisions and practices made for the local institution	P drives A: early adopters of technology experiment with new technologies in their classes, driving class transformation, outreach programmes and distributed learning, even before wider administration choices are made New P drives A: the need to meet new technology-based pedagogy drives administration to implement support mechanisms for non-early adopters to learn to teach online	T drives A: availability of learning technology systems determines development versus off-the-shelf purchase options for administrative choices T drives A: local adoption of technologies increases need for hardware and software purchase, management and training and system upgrading	C drives A: community use of technology drives administrative response to keep up with incoming student expectations and employers' expectations about training
Pedagogy	A drives P: administrative decisions and directives drive how education will be delivered and thus the priorities for pedagogy	External P drives P: changes in pedagogical practice are discovered and exchanged through professional organizations, research and publication affecting local practice New P drives P: norms of use are built, creating a comparison set for e-learning practices as well as a set to learn from and copy	T drives P: technology choices drive how teaching can be delivered and who can receive it P and T co-evolve: limitations of technology drive changes in pedagogy, but pedagogical requirements drive technology design and improvement	C drives P: changing community work and knowledge needs drive need for lifelong learning, distributed and mobile learning
Technology	A drives T: administration makes decisions about institution-wide technology adoption and support A drives T: administrative decisions push use of technology and can limit choice of technology (e.g. campus-wide selection of a learning platform limits instructor options to use different systems and approaches)	P drives T: teachers adopt and then experiment with technology in their classes, determining their technology preferences, and sit on working committees determining technology adoptions New P drives A and T: e-learning solutions are adopted and implemented in response to opportunities for outreach, new pedagogy, etc.	External T drives T: technology trends are matched in e-learning, e.g. enterprise-wide systems with course management systems; computer-mediated communication with e-mail accounts and support for students; Internet with online course reserves, electronic publication licences; distributed computing with distributed learning; mobile computing with mobile learning New T drives T: e-learning systems offer a standard range of options, driving conformity but also narrowing e-learning options	C drives T: community expectations about what technology makes an institution and its programme progressive drive attention to technology within the institution

Table 1.1: continued

	Administration drives …	Pedagogy drives …	Technology drives …	Community drives …
Community	☞ A drives C: expectations of technology use in classes in higher education drive the need for the community to prepare students appropriately	�j ☞ P drives C: pedagogical requirements for use of online resources have the unexpected consequence of distributing responsibility to public access points, e.g. public and university libraries at locations local to the students; such institutions then act as nests for the distributed learning 'cuckoos' (Searing, personal communication)* �j ☞ P drives External A: use of local university libraries by non-enrolled students leads to new inter-organizational administrative practices	☞ T drives C: technology presence drives community efforts to promote information and computer literacy, thus affecting how well students are able to take advantage of technologies and e-learning �j ☞ T drives C: distribution possible because of technology now places teachers and learners in the community, at work, at home while at school	✤ C drives C: community technology use, and support for use, bootstraps community readiness to use technology and to take part in e-learning �j ☞ C drives C: embedded learners enact new relationships with embedding context �j ☞ C drives C: increased use of online interactions for education drives norms for how to communicate and do work, changing the skill set available to employers

A administration, C community, P pedagogy, T technology
☞ Driver effects ☞ Passenger effects ✤ Emergent effects �j Second-order effects
*Personal communication, Sue Searing, Library and Information Science Librarian, University of Illinois at Urbana-Champaign

STRUCTURE AND LIMITATIONS OF THE *HANDBOOK*

We have taken the opportunity in this introduction to begin work on building a framework for e-learning research, emphasizing the key elements involved in the e-learning enterprise – learners, teachers, information and communication technology, local and societal level knowledge, and embedding contexts – leading to a focus on two theoretical perspectives – rhetorical theory and social informatics – and an emergent, co-evolutionary process of development. Ours is just a beginning, and invites testing and debate. It is now time to turn to the work of others in this *Handbook* who can illuminate other areas of research and exploration for e-learning.

The *Handbook* is organized in five parts. The first chapters set the *context for research in e-learning*, providing histories of important predecessors to e-learning, including reviews of the now long-standing fields of asynchronous learning networks (Hiltz, Turoff and Harasim) and computers and writing (Hawisher and Selfe); the state of the digital divide (Haythornthwaite); the online experience of gamers (McFarlane); and of the learning sciences that design and study learning environments (Hoadley). The chapters in Part II address *theory*, including a plea to maintain the understanding of 'distance' in our new e-learning contexts (Thompson), explorations of the rhetoric of new spaces and cultures of e-learning (Locke), the ways in which e-learning research, development and implementation can be (and actually are) organized (Whitworth), a theoretical approach to learning in a mobile age (Sharples, Taylor and Vavoula) and computer-supported collaborative learning (Miyake). From there, in Part III, we turn to *policy*, including issues of copyright and ownership in relation to e-learning intellectual property (Varvel, Montague and Estabrook), an examination of international policy (Conole), e-learning in the community (Kazmer), and what we know about individual differences and the effectiveness of digital learning systems (Morgan and Morgan). In Part IV issues of *language and literacy* are addressed, beginning with two chapters addressing multilingual issues: one on bilingualism (Brutt-Griffler), and one reviewing second language learning online (Chapelle); and one applying literacy, learning and technology research to e-learning (Snyder). A further chapter examines the practicalities of researching e-learning (Zhao). Part V examines *design issues*, starting with how to design technically and socially for community (Stuckey and Barab), and continuing with chapters on programme design for professional development (Harlen and Doubler) and graduate education (Roberts and Rostron); and a final chapter looking at current and future possibilities in digital video production and literacy in schools (Burn).

Inevitably, in such a large and expanding field of enquiry, there are limitations to the *Handbook*. While we have concentrated on the social dimensions of e-learning, the nature of e-learning itself, communities of e-learning, theoretical and methodological issues, and modelling e-learning processes, we acknowledge that we have hardly touched on technical or technological issues, pedagogical issues, the visual dimension of e-learning, forms of argumentation within e-learning, e-learning in the global south (see Leach *et al.*, 2005), or

computer modelling of learning. These are all important and fascinating sub-
fields, worthy of handbooks to themselves. Nevertheless, we hope to have
provided at least an initial map for further research in the field.

NOTES

1 For more on modalities, see Halliday (1985) for detailed discussion of the distinctions between field,
   tenor and mode in systematic functional linguistics, and Kress (2001, 2003, 2005) for a development
   of the Hallidayan model into the semiotics and multimodalities of communication in education.
2 The continuously emergent nature of social interaction is inherent in Giddens' (1984) structuration
   theory. This has been taken up in relation to ICT use by Poole and DeSanctis (1990), Orlikowski
   (1992) and Galegher and Kraut (1990). For more on emergent communication processes see Monge
   and Contractor (1997, 2003).

REFERENCES

Abbate, J. (1999) *Inventing the Internet*. Cambridge, MA: MIT Press.
Andrews, R. (ed.) (1992) *Rebirth of Rhetoric: Essays in Language, Culture and Education*. Abingdon:
   Routledge.
Andrews, R. (ed.) (2004) *The Impact of ICT on Literacy Education*. Abingdon: RoutledgeFalmer.
Andrews, R. (2005a) 'A dialogic model for research in education', ESRC Research seminar on Dialogue
   and Development, King's College London, June.
Andrews, R. (2005b) 'Problems in e-learning research – and a possible solution', Association of Internet
   Researchers conference, Chicago, October.
Andrews, R. and Noble, J. (1982) *From Rough to Best*. London: Ward Lock.
Andrews, R., Burn, A., Leach, J., Locke, T., Low, G. and Torgerson, C. (2002) 'A systematic review of the
   impact of networked ICT on 5–16 year olds' literacy in English', EPPI-Centre Review, in *Research
   Evidence in Education Library*. London: EPPI Centre, Social Science Research Unit, Institute of
   Education. Retrieved 20 May 2006 from: http://eppi.ioe.ac.uk/reel.
Andrews, R., Freeman, A., Hou, D., McGuinn, N., Robinson, A. and Zhu, J. (2005) 'The effectiveness of
   different ICTs in the teaching and learning of English (written composition), 5–16', in *Research
   Evidence in Education Library*. London: EPPI-Centre, Social Science Research Unit, Institute of
   Education. Retrieved 20 May 2006 from: http://eppi.ioe.ac.uk/reel.
Austin, J. L. (1962) *How to do Things with Words*. Cambridge, MA: Harvard University Press.
Aviv, R., Erlich, Z., Ravid, G. and Geva, A. (2003) 'Network analysis of knowledge construction in asyn-
   chronous learning networks', *Journal of Asynchronous Learning Networks*, 7 (3): 1–23.
Baecker, R. (ed.) (1993) *Readings in Groupware and Computer-Supported Cooperative Work*. San
   Mateo, CA: Morgan Kaufmann.
Bakhtin, M. M. ([1953] 1986) 'The problem of speech genres', in C. Emerson and M. Holquist (eds),
   M. M. Bakhtin Speech Genres and other Late Essays, (Trans. V. W. McGee, C. Emerson and M.
   Holquist). Austin, TX: University of Texas Press. pp. 60–102.
Bannon, L. (1989) 'Issues in computer supported collaborative learning', in C. O'Malley (ed.), *Computer
   Supported Collaborative Learning*. Berlin: Springer-Verlag. pp. 267–82.
Bannon, L. and Schmidt, K. (1991) 'CSCW: four characters in search of a context', in J. M. Bowers and
   S. D. Benford (eds), *Studies in Computer Supported Cooperative Work: Theory, Practice, and Design*.
   Amsterdam: Elsevier. pp. 3–16.
Bateson, G. ([1954] 1972) 'A theory of play and fantasy', in *Steps to an Ecology of Mind*. New York:
   Ballantine. pp. 117–93.
Baym, N. K. (2000) *Tune in, Log on: Soaps, Fandom and Online Community*. Thousand Oaks, CA: Sage.
BECTA (2003a) *Educational Research on Interactive Whiteboards: a Selection of Abstracts and Further
   Sources*. Coventry: British Educational Communication and Technology Agency.
BECTA (2003b) *What the Research Says about Interactive Whiteboards*. Coventry: British Educational
   Communication and Technology Agency.

BECTA (2006) T*he BECTA Review: Evidence on the Progress of ICT in Education*. Coventry: British Educational Communication and Technology Agency.

Berge, Z. L. (1997) 'Computer conferencing and the online classroom', *International Journal of Educational Telecommunications*, 3 (1): 3–21.

Bijker, W., (1995) *Of Bicycles, Bakelite, and Bulbs: Toward a Theory of Sociotechnical Change*. Cambridge, MA: MIT Press.

Bijker, W., Hughes, T. P. and Pinch, T. (eds) (1987) *The Social Construction of Technological Systems: New Directions in the Sociology and History of Technology*. Cambridge, MA: MIT Press.

Bishop, A. P. (2000) 'Communities for the new century', *Journal of Adolescent and Adult Literacy*, 43 (5): 472–8.

Bourdieu, P. (1986) 'The forms of capital', in J. G. Richardson (ed.), *Handbook of Theory and Research for the Sociology of Education*. Westport, CT: Greenwood Press. pp. 241–58.

Bradner, E., Kellogg, W. and Erickson, T. (1999) 'The adoption and use of "Babble": a field study of chat in the workplace', in *Proceedings of the VI European Conference on Computer Supported Cooperative Work*. Copenhagen. pp. 139–58.

Bregman, A. and Haythornthwaite, C. (2003) 'Radicals of presentation: visibility, relation, and co-presence in persistent conversation', *New Media and Society*, 5 (1): 117–40.

Bruffee, Kenneth A. (1993) *Collaborative Learning: Higher Education, Interdependence, and the Authority of Knowledge*. Baltimore, MD: Johns Hopkins University Press.

Burn, A. and Leach, J. (2004) 'A systematic review of the impact of ICT on the learning of literacies associated with moving image texts in English, 5–16', in *Research Evidence in Education Library*. EPPI-Centre, Social Science Research Unit, Institute of Education, London. Retrieved 20 May 2006 from: http://eppi.ioe.ac.uk/reel.

Carroll, J. M. (2002) *Human–Computer Interaction in the New Millennium*. Reading, MA: Addison-Wesley.

Castells, M. (2001) *The Internet Galaxy: Reflections on the Internet, Business and Society*. New York: Oxford University Press.

Cherny, L. (1999) *Conversation and Community: Chat in a Virtual World*. Stanford, CA: CSLI Publications.

Cho, H. Stefanone, M. and Gay, G. (2002) *Social Network Analysis of Information Sharing Networks in a CSCL Community*. Proceedings of the Computer-Supported Collaborative Learning conferences, Boulder, CO.

Clark, H. H. (1996) *Using Language*. Cambridge: Cambridge University Press.

Cohill, A. M. and Kavanaugh, A. L. (2000) *Community Networks: Lessons from Blacksburg, Virginia* (2nd edn). Boston, MA: Artech House.

Collins, R. (1998) *The Sociology of Philosophies: A Global Theory of Intellectual Change*. Cambridge, MA: Belknap Press of Harvard University Press.

Connolly, T. and Thorn, B. K. (1990) 'Discretionary data bases: theory, data and implications', in J. Fulk and C. W. Steinfield (eds), *Organizations and Communication Technology*. Newbury Park, CA: Sage. pp. 219–34.

Cook, S. D. N, and Brown, J. S. (1999) 'Bridging epistemologies: the generative dance between organizational knowledge and organizational knowing', *Organization Science*, 10 (4): 381–400.

Cope, B. and Kalantzis, M. (ed.) (2000) *Multiliteracies*. Abingdon: Routledge.

Corbett, E. (1965) *Classical Rhetoric for the Modern Student*. New York: Oxford University Press.

Crabtree, A., Rodden, T. and Benford, S. (2005) 'Moving with the times: IT research and the boundaries of CSCW', *Computer Supported Cooperative Work*, 14 (3): 217–51.

Crook, C. (1989) 'Educational practice within two local computer networks', in C. O'Malley (ed.), *Computer Supported Collaborative Learning*, Berlin: Springer-Verlag. pp. 165–82.

Crook, C. (2002) 'Learning as cultural practice', in M. R. Lea and K. Nicoll (eds) *Distributed Learning: Social and Cultural Approaches to Practice*. New York: RoutledgeFalmer. pp. 152–69.

Crystal, D. (2001) *Language and the Internet*. Cambridge. Cambridge University Press.

Daft, R. L. and Lengel, R. H. (1986) 'Organizational information requirements, media richness and structural design', *Management Science*, 32 (5): 554–71.

Danziger, J. N., Dutton, W. H., Kling, R. and Kraemer, K. L. (1982) *Computers and Politics*. New York: Columbia University Press.

Dutton, W. H., Cheong, P. H. and Park, N. (2004) 'An ecology of constraints on e-learning in higher education: the case of a virtual learning environment', *Prometheus*, 22 (2): 131–49.

Eagleton, T. (1983) *Literary Theory: An Introduction.* Oxford: Blackwell.

Engeström, Y. and Middleton, D. (1996) *Cognition and Communication at Work.* Cambridge: Cambridge University Press.

Engeström, Y. (1999a) 'Innovative learning in work teams: analyzing cycles of knowledge creation in practice', in Y. Engeström, R. Miettinen and R. Punamäki (eds), *Perspectives on Activity Theory,* Cambridge: Cambridge University Press. pp. 377–404.

Engeström, Y. (1999b) 'Learning by expanding: ten years after', trans. F. Seege. *Lernen durch Expansion.* Marburg: BdWi-Verlag, Retrieved 1 August, 2006 from: http://lchc.ucsd.edu/MCA/Paper/Engestrom/expanding/intro.htm.

Erickson, T. (1999) 'Persistent conversation: an introduction', *Journal of Computer-Mediated Communcation,* 4 (4). Available online at: http://www. ascusc. org/jcmc/vol4/issue4/ericksonintro.html

Finholt, T. (2002) 'Collaboratories', *Annual Review of Information Science and Technology,* 36: 73–107.

Flores, F., Graves, M., Hartfield, B. and Winograd, T. (1988) 'Computer systems and the design of organizational interaction', *ACM Transactions on Office Information Systems,* 6 (2): 153–72.

Frye, N. ([1957] 1969) *Anatomy of Criticism: Four Essays.* New York: Athenaeum Press.

Galegher, J. and Kraut, R. E. (1990) 'Technology for intellectual teamwork: perspectives on research and design', in J. Galegher, R. E. Kraut and C. Egido (eds), *Intellectual Teamwork: Social and Technological Foundations of Cooperative Work.* Hillsdale, NJ: Erlbaum. pp. 1–20.

Garrison, D. R. and Anderson, T. (2003) *E-learning in the Twenty-first Century.* Abingdon: RoutledgeFalmer.

Gaver, W. (1996) 'Situating action' II: 'Affordances for interaction: the social is material for design', *Ecological Psychology,* 8: 111–29.

Gerard, F. and Widener, J. (1999) 'A SMARTer Way to Teach Foreign Languages: the SMART Board™ Interactive Whiteboard as a Language Learning Tool'. Retrieved 2 August, 2006, from: http://education.smarttech.com/NR/rdonlyres/3CABE650-1C29-4E3A-BC21-45BB97F08B0D/0/SBforeignlanguageclass.pdf.

Gibson, J. J. (1979) *The Ecological Approach to Visual Perception.* Boston, MA: Houghton Mifflin.

Giddens, A. (1984) *The Constitution of Society: Outline of a Theory of Structuration.* Berkeley, CA: University of California Press.

Glover, D. and Miller, D. (2001) 'Running with technology: the pedagogic impact of the large-scale introduction of interactive whiteboards in one secondary school', *Journal of Information Technology for Teacher Education,* 10 (3): 257–76.

Goffman, E. (1974) *Frame Analysis.* New York: Harper and Row.

Goodison, T. A. M. (2002) 'Learning with ICT at primary level: pupils' perceptions', *Journal of Computer Assisted Learning,* 18: 282–95.

Gorard, S. and Taylor, C. (2005) *Adult Learning in the Digital Age.* London: Continuum.

Graves, D. (1983) *Writing: Teachers and Children at Work.* Portsmouth, NH: Heinemann.

Haas, C. (1996) *Studies in the Materiality of Literacy.* Hillsdale, NJ: Erlbaum.

Habermas, J. (1984) *The Theory of Communicative Action I, Reason and the Rationalization of Society.* London: Heinemann.

Halliday, M.A.K. (1985) *An Introduction to Functional Grammar.* London: Edward Arnold.

Harasim, L., Hiltz, S. R., Teles, L. and Turoff, M. (1995) *Learning Networks: A Field Guide to Teaching and Learning Online.* Cambridge, MA: MIT Press.

Hawisher, G. and Selfe, C. L. (eds) (1999) *Passions, Pedagogies, and twenty-first Century Technologies.* Logan, UT: Utah State University Press; Urbana, IL: NCTE.

Haythornthwaite, C. (2002a) 'Strong, weak and latent ties and the impact of new media', *Information Society,* 18 (5): 385–401.

Haythornthwaite, C. (2002b) 'Building social networks via computer networks: creating and sustaining distributed learning communities', in K. A. Renninger and W. Shumar (eds), *Building Virtual Communities: Learning and Change in Cyberspace.* Cambridge: Cambridge University Press. pp. 159–90.

Haythornthwaite, C. (2005) 'Social networks and Internet connectivity effects', *Information, Communication and Society,* 8 (2): 125–47.

Haythornthwaite, C. (forthcoming-a) 'Articulating divides in distributed knowledge practice', *Information, Communication and Society.*

Haythornthwaite, C. (forthcoming-b) 'Social networks and online community', in A. Joinson, K. McKenna, U. Reips and T. Postmes (eds), *Oxford Handbook of Internet Psychology.* Oxford: Oxford University Press.

Haythornthwaite, C. and Kazmer, M. M. (2002). 'Bringing the Internet home: adult distance learners and their Internet, home and work worlds', in B. Wellman and C. Haythornthwaite (eds), *The Internet in Everyday Life*. Oxford: Blackwell. pp. 431–63.

Haythornthwaite, C. and Kazmer, M. M. (eds) (2004) *Learning, Culture and Community in Online Education: Research and Practice*. New York: Peter Lang.

Haythornthwaite, C., Kazmer, M. M., Robins, J. and Shoemaker, S. (2000) 'Community development among distance learners: temporal and technological dimensions', *Journal of Computer-Mediated Communication*, 6 (1). Available online at: http://www.ascusc.org/jcmc/vol6/issue1/haythornthwaite.html.

Haythornthwaite, C. and Wellman, B. (2002). 'Introduction: Internet in everyday life', in B. Wellman and C. Haythornthwaite (eds), *The Internet in Everyday Life*. Oxford: Blackwell. pp. 3–44.

Herring, S. C. (2002) 'Computer-mediated communication on the Internet', *Annual Review of Information Science and Technology*, 36: 109–68.

Higgins, S., Falzon, C., Hall, I., Moseley, D., Smith, H. and Wall, K. (2005) *Embedding ICT in the Literacy and Numeracy Strategies*. Newcastle upon Tyne: University of Newcastle upon Tyne. Available online at: http://www.becta.org.uk/page_documents/research/univ_newcastle_evaluation_whiteboards.pdf.

Higher Education Funding Council for England (2005) *HEFCE Strategy for e-learning*. Bristol: HEFCE.

Hrastinski, S. (2006) 'Introducing an informal synchronous medium in a distance learning course: how is participation affected?' *Internet and Higher Education* (in press).

Kaye, A. R. (1995) 'Computer supported collaborative learning', in N. Heap, R. Thomas, G. Einon, R. Mason and H. MacKay (eds), *Information Technology and Society*, London: Sage. pp. 192–210.

Kaye, A. R. (ed.) (1991) *Collaborative Learning through Computer Conferencing: The Najaden Papers*. Berlin: Springer-Verlag.

Keeble, L. and Loader, B. (eds) (2001) *Community Informatics: Shaping Computer-Mediated Social Relations*. Abingdon: Routledge.

Kendall, Lori (2002) *Hanging out in the Virtual Pub: Masculinities and Relationships Online*. Berkeley, CA and Los Angeles: University of California Press.

Kinneavy, J. (1971) *A Theory of Discourse*. Englewood Cliffs, NJ: Prentice-Hall.

Kling, R., Rosenbaum, H. and Sawyer, S. (2005) *Understanding and Communicating Social Informatics*. Medford, NJ: Information Today.

Knorr-Cetina, Karin (1999) *Epistemic Cultures: How the Sciences make Knowledge*. Cambridge, MA: Harvard University Press.

Koschmann, T. (ed.) (1996) *CSCL: Theory and Practice of an Emerging Paradigm*. Mahwah, NJ: Erlbaum.

Koschmann, T., Hall, R. and Miyake, N. (eds) (2002) *CSCL 2: Carrying Forward the Conversation*. Mahwah, NJ: Erlbaum.

Kraut, R., Kiesler, S., Boneva, B., Cummings, J., Helgeson, V. and Crawford, A. (2002) 'Internet paradox revisited', *Journal of Social Issues*, 58 (1): 49–74.

Kraut, R., Patterson, V. L., Kiesler, S., Mukhopadhyay, T. and Scherilis, W. (1998) 'Internet paradox: a social technology that reduces social involvement and psychological well-being?', *American Psychologist*, 53 (9): 1017–31.

Kress, G. (2001) *Multimodal Teaching and Learning: the Rhetorics of the Science Classroom*. London: Continuum.

Kress, G. (2003) *Literacy in the New Media Age*. Abingdon: Routledge.

Kress, G. (2005) *English in Urban Classrooms: Multimodal Perspectives in Teaching and Learning*. Abingdon: RoutledgeFalmer.

Lanham, R. (1992) *The Electronic Word*. Chicago, IL: University of Chicago Press.

Latour, B. (1987) *Science in Action: How to follow Scientists and Engineers through Society*. Philadelphia, PA: Open University Press.

Lave, J. and Wenger, E. (1991) *Situated Learning: Legitimate Peripheral Participation*. Cambridge: Cambridge University Press.

Lawrence, P. R. and Lorsch, J. W. (1967) 'Differentiation and integration in complex organizations', *ASQ*, 12: 1–47.

Lazarsfeld, P. (1940) '"Panel" studies', *Public Opinion Quarterly*, 4: 122–8.

Lazarsfeld, P. F. and Fiske, M. (1938) 'The panel as a new tool for measuring opinion', *Public Opinion Quarterly*, 2: 596–612.

Leach, J., Ahmed, A., Makalima, S. and Power, T. (2005) *Deep Impact: an Investigation of the Use of Information and Communication Technologies for Teacher Education in the Global South*. London: Department for International Development

Levy, P. (2002) *Interactive Whiteboards in Learning and Teaching in Two Sheffield Schools: a Developmental Study*. Sheffield: Department of Information Studies, University of Sheffield.

Levy, P., Ford, N., Foster, J., Madden, A., Miller, D., Nunes, M. B., McPherson, M. and Webber, S. (2003) 'Educational informatics: an emerging research agenda', *Journal of Information Science*, 29 (4): 298–310.

Loader, B. (1997) *The Governance of Cyberspace: Politics, Technology and Global Restructuring*. Abingdon: Routledge.

Locke, T. and Andrews, R. (2004) 'A systematic review of the impact of ICT on literature-related literacies in English, 5–16', in *Research Evidence in Education Library*. EPPI-Centre, Social Science Research Unit, Institute of Education, London. Retrieved 20 May 2006 from: http://eppi.ioe.ac.uk/reel.

Low, G. and Beverton, S. (2004) 'A systematic review of the impact of ICT on literacy learning in English of learners between 5 and 16, for whom English is a second or additional language', in *Research Evidence in Education Library*. EPPI Centre, Social Science Research Unit, Institute of Education, London. Retrieved 20 May 2006 from: http://eppi.ioe.ac.uk/reel.

Luff, P., Hindmarsh, J. and Heath, C. (2000) *Workplace Studies: Recovering Work Practice and Informing System Design*. Cambridge: Cambridge University Press.

Lunsford, K. J. and Bruce, B. C. (2001) 'Collaboratories: working together on the web', *Journal of Adolescent and Adult Literacy*, 45 (1): 52–8.

MacKenzie, D. and Wajcman, J. (1999). *The Social Shaping of Technology*. Buckingham: Open University Press.

Malone, T. W., Grant, K. R., Lai, K. Y., Rao, R. and Rosenblitt, D. A. (1989) 'The information lens: an intelligent system for information sharing and coordination', in M. H. Olson (ed.), *Technological Support for Work Group Collaboration*. Hillsdale, NJ: Erlbaum. pp. 143–72.

Markus, M. L. (1990) 'Toward a 'critical mass' theory of interactive media', in J. Fulk and C. W. Steinfield (eds), *Organizations and Communication Technology*. Newbury Park, CA: Sage. pp. 194–218.

Markus, M. L. and Robey, D. (1983) 'The organizational validity of management information systems', *Human Relations*, 36 (3): 203–26.

Miller, C. (1984) 'Genre as social action', *Quarterly Journal of Speech*, 70 (2): 151–67.

Miller, C. (1994) 'Rhetorical community: the cultural basis of genre', in A. Freedman and P. Medway (eds), *Genre and the New Rhetoric*. Abingdon: Taylor and Francis. pp. 67–78.

Monge, P. R. and Contractor, N. S. (1997) 'Emergence of communication networks', in F. M. Jablin and L. L. Putnam (eds), *Handbook of Organizational Communication* (2nd edn). Thousand Oaks, CA: Sage. pp. 440–502.

Monge, P. R. and Contractor, N. S. (2003) *Theories of Communication Networks*. Oxford: Oxford University Press.

Nielsen, J. (1994) *Usability Engineering*. San Francisco, CA: Morgan Kaufmann.

Noble, F. and Newman, M. (1993) 'Integrated system, autonomous departments: organizations, invalidity and system change in a university', *Journal of Management Studies*, 30 (2): 195–219.

Norman, D. (1988) *The Design of Everyday Things*. New York: Basic Books.

O'Malley, C. (ed.) (1989) *Computer Supported Collaborative Learning*. Berlin: Springer-Verlag.

Orlikowski, W. J. (1992) 'The duality of technology: rethinking the concept of technology in organizations', *Organization Science*, 3 (3): 398–427.

Orlikowski, W. J. and Yates, J. (1994) 'Genre repertoire: the structuring of communicative practices in organizations', *Administrative Science Quarterly*, 39: 541–74.

Oud, J. H. L. (2002) 'Continuous time modelling of the cross-lagged panel design', *Kwantitatieve Methoden*, 69: 1–26.

Perrow, C. (1970) *Organizational Analysis: A Sociological View*. Monterey, CA: Wadsworth.

Pinch, T. J. and Bijker, W. E. (1984) 'The social construction of facts and artefacts: or how the sociology of science and the sociology of technology might benefit each other', *Social Studies of Science*, 14: 399–441.

Poole, M. S. and DeSanctis, G. (1990) 'Understanding the use of group decision support systems: The theory of adaptive structuration', in J. Fulk and C. W. Steinfield (eds), *Organizations and Communication Technology*. Newbury Park, CA: Sage. pp. 173–93.

Rafaeli, S. and Sudweeks, F. (1997) 'Networked interactivity', *Journal of Computer-Mediated Communication*, 2 (4). Available online at: http://www.ascusc.org/jcmc/vol2/issue4/rafaeli.sud-weeks.html.

Resnick, L. B. Levine, J. M. and Teasdale, S. D. (eds) (1991) *Perspectives on Socially Shared Cognition.* Washington, DC: American Psychological Association.

Rice, R. E. and Rogers, E. M. (1980) 'Reinvention in the innovation process', *Knowledge*, 1 (4): 499–514.

Roethlisberger, F. and Dickson, W. (1939) *Management and the Worker: An Account of a Research Programme conducted by the Western Electric Company, Chicago.* Cambridge, MA: Harvard University Press.

Rogers, E. M (1995) *Diffusion of Innovations.* (4th edn). New York: The Free Press.

Rogers, E. M., Eveland, J. D. and Klepper, C. (1977) *The Innovation Process in Organizations.* Ann Arbor, MI: Michigan: Department of Journalism, University of Michigan. NSF Grant RDA 75–17952.

Rogoff, B. (1990) *Apprenticeship in Thinking.* New York: Oxford University Press.

Rueter, M. A. and Conger, R. D. (1998) 'Reciprocal influences between parenting and adolescent problem-solving behaviour', *Developmental Psychology*, 34: 1470–82.

Saltz, J. S., Hiltz, S. R., and Turoff, M. (2004). 'Student Social Graphs: Visualizing a Student's Online Social Network'. Proceedings of the CSCW '04 conference, Chicago.

Schmidt, K. and Bannon, L. (1992) 'Taking CSCW seriously: supporting articulation work', *Computer Supported Cooperative Work*, 1: 7–41.

Scott, A. and Page, M. (2001) 'Change agency and women's learning: new practices in community informatics', in L. Keeble and B. Loader (eds), *Community Informatics: Shaping Computer-Mediated Social Relations.* Abingdon: Routledge. pp. 49–174.

Scott, W. R. (1992). *Organizations: Rational, Natural, and Open Systems.* Toronto: Prentice-Hall.

Searle, J. R. (1969) *Speech Acts: an Essay in the Philosophy of Language.* Cambridge, MA: Cambridge University Press.

SMART Technologies (2004) *Interactive Whiteboards and Learning: A Review of Classroom Case Studies and Research Literature.* Retrieved 2 August, 2006, from: http://education.smarttech.com/NR/rdon-lyres/30258C60-24D0-43D5-A1D2-BDE1A93B6F93/0/InteractiveWhiteboardsAndLearning.pdf.

Smith, H. J., Higgins, S., Wall, K. and Miller, J. (2005) 'Interactive whiteboards: boon or bandwagon? A critical review of the literature', *Journal of Computer Assisted Learning*, 21 (2): 90–101.

Somekh, B. and Haldane, M. (2006) 'How can Interactive Whiteboards contribute to Pedagogic Change? Learning from Case Studies in English Primary Schools'. Paper given at FIP WG 3.1/3.3/3.5 conference, Ålesund, June.

Suchman, L. (1987) *Plans and Situated Actions: The Problem of Human–Machine Communication.* Cambridge: Cambridge University Press.

Suchman, L. (1994) 'Do categories have politics? The language/action perspective reconsidered', *Computer Supported Cooperative Work*, 2: 177–90.

Swales, J. M. (1990) *Genre Analysis: English in Academic and Research Settings. Cambridge*: Cambridge University Press.

Tannen, D. (ed.) (1993) *Framing in Discourse.* New York: Oxford University Press.

Taylor, F. W. (1911) *The Principles of Scientific Management.* New York: Harper.

Thompson, J. D. (1967) *Organizations in Action.* New York: McGraw-Hill.

Torgerson, C. and Zhu, D. (2003) 'A systematic review and meta-analysis of the effectiveness of ICT on literacy learning in English, 5–16', in *Research Evidence in Education Library.* EPPI-Centre, Social Science Research Unit, Institute of Education, London. Retrieved 20 May 2006 from: http://eppi.ioe.ac.uk/reel.

Trevino, L. K., Daft, R. L. and Lengel, R. H. (1990) 'Understanding managers' media choice: a symbolic interactionist perspective', in J. Fulk and C. W. Steinfield (eds), *Organizations and Communication Technology.* Newbury Park, CA: Sage. pp. 71–94.

Trist, E. L. and Bamford, K. W. (1951) 'Some social and psychological consequences of the longwall method of coal-getting', *Human Relations*, 4 (1): 6–24, 37–8.

Tweddle (1997) 'A retrospective: fifteen years of computers in English', *English in Education*, 31 (2): 5–13.

Vickers, B. (1988) *In Defence of Rhetoric.* Oxford: Clarendon Press.

Vygotsky, L. (1986) *Language and Thought*. Cambridge, MA: Harvard University Press.

Warschauer, M. (2000) 'Language, identity, and the Internet', in B. E. Kolko, L. Nakamura and G. B. Rodman (eds) *Race in Cyberspace*, New York: Routledge. pp. 151–70.

Warschauer, M. (2003) *Technology and Social Inclusion*. Cambridge, MA: MIT Press.

Wellman, B. (1979) 'The community question', *American Journal of Sociology*, 84: 1201–31.

Wellman, B. (1997) 'An electronic group is a social network', in S. Kiesler (ed.), *Cultures of the Internet*. Mahwah, NJ: Erlbaum. pp. 179–205.

Wellman, B. (2002) 'Little boxes, glocalization, and networked individualism?' in M. Tanabe, P. van den Besselaar and T. Ishida (eds), *Digital Cities II, Computational and Sociological Approaches*, Berlin: Springer-Verlag. pp. 10–25

Wellman, B. (ed.) (1999) *Networks in the Global Village*. Boulder, CO: Westview Press.

Wellman, B. and Berkowitz, S. D. (eds) (1997) *Social Structures: A Network Approach* (updated edn). Greenwich, CT: JAI Press.

Wellman, B. and Haythornthwaite, C. (eds) (2002) *The Internet in Everyday Life*. Oxford: Blackwell.

Wellman, B., Salaff, J., Dimitrova, D., Garton, L., Gulia, M. and Haythornthwaite, C. (1996) 'Computer networks as social networks: collaborative work, telework, and virtual community', *Annual Review of Sociology*, 22: 213–38.

Wellman, B., Quan-Haase, A., Boase, J., Chen, W., Hampton, K., de Diaz, I. I. and Miyata, K. (2003) 'The social affordances of the Internet for networked individualism', *Journal of Computer-Mediated Communication*, 8 (3). Available online at: http://jcmc.indiana.edu/vol8/issue3/wellman.html.

Wenger, E. (1998) *Communities of Practice: Learning, Meaning, and Identity*. Cambridge: Cambridge University Press.

Whitworth, A. (2006) 'Dynamic but prosaic: a methodology for studying e-learning environments', *International Journal of Research and Method in Education*, 29: 2, 149–61.

Williams, R. and Edge, R. (1996) 'The social shaping of technology', *Research Policy*, 25: 856–99.

Winograd, T. (1994) 'Categories, disciplines, and social coordination', *Computer Supported Cooperative Work*, 2: 191–7.

Winograd, T. and Flores, F. (1986) *Understanding Computers and Cognition: A New Foundation for Design*. Norwood, NJ: Ablex.

Yates, J. and Orlikowski, W. J. (1992) 'Genres of organizational communication: a structurational approach to studying communication and media', *Academy of Management Journal*, 17 (2): 299–326.

Zuboff, S. (1988) *In the Age of the Smart Machine: The Future of Work and Power*. New York: Basic Books, Inc.

Zucker, A., Kozma, R. and Dede, C. (2003) *The Virtual High School: Teaching Generation V*. New York: Teachers College Press.

ACKNOWLEDGEMENTS

The authors wish to thank the Worldwide Universities Network (WUN) and the UK's Economic and Social Research Council (ESRC) for support of a series of seminars on e-learning organized on behalf of the Universities of Bristol, Leeds, Manchester, Sheffield, Southampton and York by Richard Andrews, held in 2004–6. Richard Andrews thanks colleagues for feedback and discussion on the model described in the introduction, especially Professor Angela Douglas of the Biology Department at the University of York. Caroline Haythornthwaite thanks the University of Illinois at Urbana–Champaign Research Board for travel funds to attend the UK seminars, and WUN for support of a workshop she organized on e-learning held at the Association of Internet Researchers conference, in Chicago in 2005. We thank David Pilsbury and WUN for the opportunity to participate in e-learning meetings held in 2005 and 2006, and for WUN's series of video-conferences on e-learning topics, organized by Andrew Whitworth, who has also commented helpfully on an earlier version of the introduction. We also wish to thank all contributors to the *Handbook* for their efforts and scholarship in creating this collection.

PART I

Contexts for
Researching E-learning

2

Development and Philosophy of the Field of Asynchronous Learning Networks

Starr Roxanne Hiltz, Murray Turoff
and Linda Harasim

This chapter reviews the history and pedagogical philosophy of the field of Asynchronous Learning Networks (ALN), a major type of e-learning. 'Asynchronous' refers to computer-mediated communication (CMC) systems that allow 'anytime' communication via the Internet, systems such as computerized conferencing or bulletin boards that support threaded discussions. 'Learning Networks' refer to the social network or community of learners that emerges when students and faculty communicate and work together to build and share knowledge. ALN thus integrates social and technical aspects; it depends upon technologies such as the Internet to link together teachers and learners, but it is an effective means of learning only when collaborative social/pedagogical processes emerge from the communication that is supported by the technology.

The objective of ALN is not just to be 'as good as' traditional classroom-based learning, but to use CMC to encourage and support new forms of collaboration and learning together online. This has led to changes in the roles of both students and faculty. Research on how ALNs change student and faculty roles, and on the nature and effectiveness of collaborative learning within ALNs, is reviewed. The chapter ends with a discussion of issues facing higher education as a result of the transformative nature of ALN and other forms of e-learning.

WHAT IS ALN AND WHY IS IT IMPORTANT? (A CONCEPTUAL HISTORY)

Asynchronous learning networks have been defined in several ways (Bourne *et al.*, 2006). First, the asynchronous part of the acronym is intended to convey the idea that people can learn at different times, and the network term connotes both support through a computer network such as the Internet, so that people can learn 'anytime, anywhere', and a social network of people who are learning together through this technology. The most widely used definition of ALNs is the definition that appears on the ALN Web (http://www.aln.org):

> ALNs are people networks for anytime–anywhere learning. ALN combines self-study with substantial, rapid, asynchronous interactivity with others. The major point in this definition is that ALN is a 'people network'; that is, ALN permits improved interaction between people.

> (Bourne *et al.*, online)

What distinguishes ALN courses from Online Distance Education (ODE), synchronous learning networks, Computer Supported Collaborative Learning (CSCL) or other forms of e-learning such as Online Computer-Based Training (OCBT)? While these terms are related, we argue that ALN is distinct because of its focus on collaborative learning, and how online attributes such as asynchronicity, anyplace and text-based communication enable new and more powerful forms of collaboration and knowledge work.

Note that the etymology of the term 'asynchronous' focuses solely on time, and not place. The 'anywhere' aspect is included explicitly by the Sloan Consortium and often included implicitly by others who use the term, but we recognize that it is a separate and distinct attribute. By the above definition, online courses that primarily rely on a synchronous audio or video presentation or chat are not ALN because these require learners and instructors to be available to communicate at the same time. A video-taped course or mail-based correspondence course or computer-based training is not ALN because these do not include substantial and rapid interactivity with others, even though the learner might mail in a paper or test and receive a reply many days later. 'Distance learning' might employ any or all of these modes, and refers to anything that does not require the teacher and learners to be gathered in the same place. 'E-learning' is also a very broad term, and applies to any form of online course, including those that may not be asynchronous, and those that may not include any interaction among the members of a class. 'Computer-supported collaborative learning' is most similar in concept, but it applies to same-place or same-time use of computers to support learners working together, as well as to anytime, anyplace use of computers to support such processes.

Why did the name ALN, which is admittedly a mouthful, stick? A major reason is that it was institutionalized by funding and sponsorship by the Alfred P.

Sloan Foundation: Sloan helped to support an annual international conference, summer research workshops, a journal (*JALN* or *Journal of Asynchronous Learning Networks*), as well as the funding of dozens of educational programmes using ALN at US universities. Second, the term does precisely describe the nature of the communication and collaboration supported by this approach. We will define ALN more systematically by decomposing it into its parts: the A, the L and the N.

Asynchronous means anytime (anywhere)

A fundamental characteristic of ALN is that each person can work at his or her own pace and preferred times. Each participant sends and receives communications at the pace and time that is most convenient to them (within the course syllabus parameters, such as within a specific week), and the software system being used stores and orders these communications so that the other participants can read and respond to them whenever they wish. Asynchronicity enables every participant to contribute at the time, place, and pace that is most convenient for him or her and appropriate to the activity. Asynchronous communication and interaction can accommodate different schedules and learning readiness. For example, the fact that one of the group members can take part only after dinner hours, for instance, or that some members of the class (such as those for whom English is not the native language) take two to three times longer than others to be able to read and respond to material, does not negatively impact their ability to participate equitably, nor does it affect the ability of others to work at the time and pace that best suit them (Harasim *et al.*, 1995; Hiltz, 1994; Hiltz and Goldman, 2005).

Asynchronous communication, as contrasted to real-time chat or face-to-face meetings, has both advantages and disadvantages. Among the advantages are that each person can think about, consult references, compose and revise their contributions at their own optimal speed, before posting them. Because more time is spent on reflection and on refining contributions to a discussion before sharing them, online discussions are generally found to be 'deeper' and more considered than synchronous classroom discussions. Linked with asynchronicity is the availability of a verbatim transcript of the discussion. Participants can thus read, reread and reflect on previous messages to thereby ensure a more appropriate and thoughtful response. Another advantage is that the time and place of participation can accommodate the schedules of busy people who have jobs and/or family responsibilities in addition to coursework.

Among the disadvantages of ALN is the decreased 'immediacy' of response – it may be hours or even days until a reply is received to a posting, and this can be frustrating. Moreover the delayed response can contribute to communication anxiety, in which the sender may experience concern as to whether the message was sent to the correct destination, or whether it was received but deemed unworthy of a reply.

Learning networks and communities

Any use of e-mail or computer conferencing can be an example of asynchronous computer-mediated communication. What distinguishes ALN is that it is focused not only on education, but on a particular form and philosophy of education: using collaborative discussion, team work and other activities to co-labour to share and build knowledge about a particular subject area. The main pedagogical quality of ALN is its amenability to the design and use of asynchronous CMC to support educational advances such as progressive discourse and Online Collaborative Learning (OCL: the term used by Harasim in many of her prior publications, rather than ALN). Thus another key characteristic of ALN is that it involves students 'learning together' in a co-operative or collaborative manner that ideally leads to the development of a learning community or 'learning network' (Harasim *et al.*, 1995). The 'network' term refers not only to the technology that is used to support this activity – the computer networks – but also to the social network of co-learners that emerges and forms a 'class', a social group with an identity and a shared purpose and social ties. Building a learning community, a social and mutually supportive network of learners, is perhaps the greatest challenge and the greatest opportunity for the faculty member who teaches a class using ALN (Hiltz and Goldman, 2005).

ALN'S BEGINNINGS AND GROWTH

Educational adoption of computer networking began in the mid-1970s, following closely upon the invention of packet-switched networks in 1969 and of e-mail and computer conferencing in 1971 (Hafner and Lyon,1996; Hiltz and Turoff, 1978). Many of the researchers involved in early networking experiments were also academics. As these faculties introduced e-mail and computer conferencing into their academic curricula, they discovered expanded opportunities for student communication, interaction, and collaboration (Harasim, 2006).

Table 2.1 very briefly reviews the emergence of ALN. Figuring prominently is EIES, the Electronic Information Exchange System, developed and operated with National Science Foundation funding at New Jersey Institute of Technology. As Harasim (2006: 30–1) relates:

> Murray Turoff, credited as the father of computer conferencing, designed the first computer conferencing system in 1971 as a Delphi System (EMISARI). By 1974 he was at New Jersey Institute of Technology, following his 'dream of developing and evaluating Computer Mediated Communication technology to facilitate group decisions so that groups might act with their collective intelligence instead of the lowest common denominator' (Turoff, 1999, p. 39). There he created EIES, the Electronic Information Exchange System, for scientific research communities … .

EIES computer conferencing was primarily designed to support 'invisible colleges' of scientists building knowledge together and applying 'collective intelligence' to decision making and problem solving, and included its own tailoring language to create special communication structures for specific types of tasks or objectives. However, it also served as the host for online educational programmes developed by the Western Behavioural Sciences Institute (WBSI), which provided graduate-level education for executives, and Connect-Ed, which offered a graduate degree in communications media. A later version of EIES, called the Virtual Classroom®, was specifically tailored to support ALN, an activity financed by the Annenberg/CPB project. This project supported the initial development and delivery of ALN courses to undergraduates at the New Jersey Institute of Technology.

Table 2.1 Brief history of asynchronous learning networks

Year	Event	Example
Mid 1970s	University courses are supplemented by e-mail and conferencing	NJIT and several others
1981	First totally online courses (Nonformal, adult education)	The source EIES
1982	First online programme (executive education)	WBSI executive education (EIES)
1986	First totally online undergraduate 'Classroom'	Virtual classroom (NJIT)
1985	First totally online graduate courses	Connect-Ed (New School of Social Research) OISE (University of Toronto)
1986	First online degree programmes	Connect-ED (1986) 1989 University of Phoenix
1989	*Internet launched*	
1989	First large-scale online courses	Open University (UK)
1992	*World Wide Web is invented*	*CERN (Switzerland)*
1993	First national educational networks	1993 SchoolNet (Canada)
1999	First large-scale online education field trials	Virtual-U research project

Source: Adapted from Harasim, 2006.

The pedagogy of ALN: collaborative learning

From its beginnings in the 1980s the use of what came to be called ALN focused on collaborative learning as a pedagogy, and the tailoring of CMC virtual spaces to support specific kinds of collaborative activities in a course. The principle of collaborative learning is probably the single most important factor for the effectiveness of online networked learning, since it is this principle which provides the strong socio-affective and cognitive power of learning.

The pedagogical assumption that students learn by constructing knowledge through group interaction is the theoretical foundation of ALN (Harasim *et al.*, 1995). Collaborative learning is based upon a model that treats the student as an active participant in group activities. The learner becomes actively involved in constructing knowledge by applying concepts to problems, and/or formulating ideas into words, and these ideas are built upon through reactions and responses of others (Alavi, 1994; Bouton and Garth, 1983). In other words, learning is not only active but also interactive. Active involvement can take place through communication with the instructor, or with peers. Collaborative learning refers to instructional methods that encourage students to work together on academic tasks. It involves interpersonal processes as a small group of students work together to complete an academic problem-solving task that promotes learning.

The online asynchronous environment of the Web both enables and requires collaborative learning: collaboration provides the motivation and social glue of a community that engages learners and encourages them to participate and contribute to common goals; and the asynchronous nature of interaction facilitates much more extensive involvement in group projects and discussion activities over time, since one does not have to co-ordinate the time schedules of the participants. Instructional models where faculty 'present' or publish information on the Web are less engaging and have resulted in higher drop-out rates.

As Linda Harasim (2006: 38) relates in her account of the development and delivery of the first totally online graduate courses, at OISE in Toronto:

> The online courses that I first designed and implemented in 1985, until today, use a variety of activities based on collaborative learning. For example, a totally online course may start and end with a set of plenary activities, to build the sense of group identity and community. Seminars, small group discussions, and small group assignments might comprise the core curriculum, each lasting for one online week or for a set number of online weeks. Courses designed and offered in the mid to late 1980s at the Ontario Institute for Studies in Education (OISE) illustrate this approach (Harasim, 1993). The courses were graduate level credit courses, with a limit of about 25 students to a course (although some were considerably smaller and a few significantly larger). The first activities were plenary group discussions. Topics included a conference for 'Self-introductions', a conference for setting personal and class 'Learning Objectives', and a conference for engaging in a 'Great Debate'. And there was also the very important 'Café' for socializing and a conference entitled 'Mutual Assist' for peer technical help. The graduate courses employed the following types of group learning activities: Seminars (plenary and small group); Dyads; and Project Teams. The twelve-week course was organized into four weeks of seminar activity, followed by two weeks of a dyad assignment; four weeks of project work and class presentations and concluded with two weeks of debates structured around dyad interaction.

Only a small number of educators and educational researchers were seriously involved with creating, and teaching, ALN courses by the beginning of the 1990s, and the number of online students totalled only in the thousands. Access was difficult; it required dialling into a central server over telephone lines (with few if any instructions or support services), on connections that were low-speed, frequently unreliable, difficult to access, and expensive.

The Internet and the World Wide Web and the subsequent advent of high-speed connections to homes have made a remarkable difference. A decade later millions of students are online, not only in the US, but around the world. Overall online enrolment increased from 1.98 million in 2003 to 2.35 million in 2004 (Allen and Seaman, 2005); of this number, of course, it is not possible to tell how many are enrolled in truly ALN courses and how many are taking other forms of Web-based courses. Online learning is not just a North American phenomenon, though it began there. The UK Open University has experimented for some time with the use of ALN in its courses, first under the leadership of Tony Kaye and then his colleague, Robin Mason (1989, 1998). The largest field trials of online post-secondary education in the twentieth century occurred in Canada, through the Tele-learning Networks of Centers of Excellence and the Virtual-U project headed by Linda Harasim, which studied over 500 e-learning courses, taught by 250 instructors, and reached 1,500 students (Harasim, 2006: 48–9). Among the many other nations in which studies of ALN have been conducted are Ireland, Australia (Klobas and Haddow, 2000), Finland (Marttunen, 1998), Germany (Stahl *et al.*, 2003), and Taiwan (Jehng, 1997).

Besides offerings by individual, traditional colleges and universities, there are also for-profit online programmes, of which the largest is the University of Phoenix Online, with over 37,000 students as of 2002. There are many statewide systems to organize and integrate online offerings throughout many different institutions, such as the SUNY Learning Network, part of the State University of New York. In its first academic year in 1995–96, the SUNY Learning Network (SLN) enrolled 119 students in eight courses on two campuses. By 2005, SLN's online enrolments had increased to over 100,000 students from around the world, in 4,300 courses, with 100 online degree programmes and courses offered through 56 different SUNY campuses, and over 2000 SUNY faculty members teaching online (http://www.sln.suny.edu/index.html). Another major online education provider is the Illinois Virtual University (2005), which reported offering over 6,500 online class sections that generated 105,207 student enrolments during the fall 2005 term.

HOW ALN CHANGES STUDENT AND FACULTY ROLES

At the core of asynchronous learning networks is the concept of the student as an active – and socially interactive – learner. The many empirical studies of ALN (e.g., see www.ALNResearch.org) demonstrate evidence of a tendency for ALN courses to elicit more active participation from students than do typical face-to-face (Face-to-face) courses.

ALN courses have been shown to be more learner-centred than traditional courses, meaning that the learner takes a more active part in class activities (Hiltz and Shea, 2005). At Syracuse University, Heckman and Annabi (2003) similarly documented this phenomenon. In a field experiment with four groups of students, each of whom completed two case study discussions, one Face-to-face and one via ALN, they found significant differences in teacher and student roles in the two modes of learning. The presence of the teacher was much more pervasive in Face-to-face (141 utterances) versus ALN (eleven utterances) discussions; most strikingly, the ratio of student to teacher utterances was 5:1 in ALN, compared to 1:1 in the Face-to-face discussions. Moreover, student utterances were longer in ALN (100 words versus thirty words), while teacher utterances were shorter in ALN (fifty words versus eighty words). These results are confirmed with a different type of evidence at SUNY: students report more active participation in online courses relative to similar Face-to-face courses. Student respondents ($n = 935$) were approximately twice as likely to report more active participation in online class discussion when compared to their participation levels in similar Face-to-face courses they had taken (Shea *et al.*, 2002).

We know from over thirty empirical studies comparing the effectiveness of ALN and Face-to-face courses that, overall, ALN courses are, on the average, as effective or more effective than FtF ones, whether this is measured by objective or subjective methods of measuring learning. However, there is much more variability within modes than between them (Fjermestad *et al.*, 2005; Hiltz, 1994). Though there are many, many variables that contribute to and help explain the effectiveness of courses taught using the ALN paradigm, the most important is the pedagogy and the presence that the instructor brings to the course. Anderson *et al.* (2001) split the 'multifaceted components of teaching and learning in a text based environment' into three elements: cognitive presence, social presence and teaching presence. They further propose that the 'teaching presence' construct consists of three roles, namely the role of design and administration, the role of facilitating discourse and the role of direct instruction.

The instructor's success can be greatly aided, however, by a software platform that supports collaborative learning and allows forms of interaction that would be difficult to achieve in a traditional classroom, thus capitalizing on the power of computer-mediated communication. And of course, what occurs online is also affected by what the students bring to the course, especially their motivation in regard to the course.

Demographic characteristics such as age or gender are weak predictors of success of students in ALNs; much stronger predictors include student characteristics having to do with motivation, general academic ability (e.g., grade point average), and being able to make regular times for online interaction (Hiltz and Shea, 2005). Not surprisingly, students who are motivated, self-directed and confident about having the computer skills necessary to use the technology are those who are most likely to thrive in the ALN environment. In the 1990s, these were often students who were older than traditional on-campus undergraduates. Currently, the 'new millenials' – those late teens and twenty-somethings who 'grew up online' – also have a proclivity to thrive in the online learning environment, though they are much more critical than previous students of software that is not 'state of the art'. Females seem on the average to be somewhat more comfortable in ALN courses than males, perhaps because of their generally higher verbal skills and their greater tendency to like collaborative learning styles (Hiltz and Shea, 2005).

Examinations of student characteristics explain a little of the variance in terms of succeeding in online learning environments, and raise the important issues of how we can help most or all students seeking online education to succeed. Motivated, self-directed, self-disciplined students are likely to succeed in any learning environment, but we need to know more about how to support weaker students – online environments pose additional challenges and opportunities in this regard.

Frederickson *et al.* (2000) report that pedagogical elements are more important than demographic characteristics in predicting learning outcomes. Interaction with the teacher was found to be the most significant contributor to perceived learning in a large-scale survey of SUNY Online students. Among the findings for which this and many other empirical studies provide support is the applicability of Chickering and Gamson's (1987) general principles of effective learning to the ALN environment as well as the traditional classroom. The greater the student–faculty contact online, and the higher the student collaboration, course expectations, time on task, and the more prompt the feedback given for student postings the higher the student learning and satisfaction (Arbaugh and Hornik, 2002; Shea *et al.,* 2001, 2002). In order to be effective, this feedback should be timely, and should incorporate what has been termed 'instructor immediacy behaviours', which refers to communication behaviours that reduce social and psychological distance between people (Mehrabian, 1971). Immediacy behaviours include both non-verbal and verbal behaviours in the traditional classroom, but since most non-verbal behaviour is excluded from online communication, it is especially important that the instructor's verbal style incorporate immediacy behaviours.

Using the fourteen items from Gorham's (1988) verbal immediacy scale, Arbaugh and Hornik (2002) surveyed twenty five Web-based class sections at the University of Wisconsin, Oshkosh. Two factors emerged from the analysis: 'classroom demeanour' and 'name recognition'. Classroom demeanor is the extent of an instructor's use of personal examples, humour, and openness toward and encouragement of student ideas and discussion. Name recognition refers to the extent to which the instructor was addressed by name by students, and vice versa. Both of these immediacy factors were significant predictors of student learning, and were also positively associated with course satisfaction.

Although the 'principles of good teaching' remain the same in ALN as for Face-to-face, there are several fundamental shifts in the nature of faculty roles. Discussion facilitation rather than presentation skills becomes most important for online faculty in an ALN. The most frequently reported change in studies of ALN faculty is more and higher-quality interaction with students. This is especially important in the beginning of a course, when the students need to gain trust in one another and in the responsiveness of the instructor and the environment (Coppola *et al.*, 2004).

Coppola *et al.* (2002) used semi-structured interviews of faculty, coded with pattern analysis software, to capture the perceived role changes enacted by instructors in ALN settings, in terms of cognitive roles, affective roles, and managerial roles. The cognitive role, which relates to mental processes of learning, information storage, and thinking, shifts to one of deeper cognitive complexity in terms of the depth of discussion obtained. The affective role, which relates to influencing the relationships among students, the instructor, and the classroom atmosphere, requires faculty to find new tools to express emotion in a text environment, yet the instructors found the relationship with students more intimate. The managerial role, which deals with class and course management, requires greater attention to detail, more structure, and additional student monitoring. Overall, faculty reported a change in their teaching persona, towards more precision in their presentation of materials and instructions, but also towards becoming a 'digital socrates', who shifts from conveying information to raising questions and engaging in dialogues guided by the instructor.

Engaging in dialogue and facilitating the collaboration of students in an ALN is a continuous job; it takes seven-days-a-week attention. Instructors tend to report that teaching online takes significantly more time than teaching a course in a traditional classroom, which is 'over' when the set time for the class ends. However, there are indications that once the course has been developed, then the teaching time required is not very different in terms of total time; but it is spread out over the whole week, rather than being concentrated in one or two days, so it 'feels' like it takes more time. At least, this is what was found by Hislop (2001), who paid Drexel instructors to record detailed time logs for matched Face-to-face and online sections of courses. Although they perceived teaching online as taking substantially more time, in fact the differences were small and not consistent. Differences in the type, amount, and distribution of efforts throughout the week and the course are a topic that needs much further research. In addition, we need to know more about the motivators and demotivators that lead faculty to choose initially to teach a course online, and then to continue to choose to teach online or to reject this mode of instruction.

COLLABORATIVE LEARNING AS A KEY CHARACTERISTIC OF EFFECTIVE ALNs

As summarized by Swan (2006) in her introduction to a special issue of the *Journal of Asynchronous Learning Networks*, a wide range of theoretical and empirical analyses emphasizes the importance of both active participation and collaboration among students in promoting the effectiveness of online learning. The two phenomena are closely related, because collaboration allows students to interact socially and develop a feeling of community in online courses, and thus motivates them to actively and regularly participate. As Garrison (2006: 27) emphasizes, 'the ultimate goal is to create a community of inquiry where learners are fully engaged and responsible learners'. Besides its motivational aspects, collaborative learning also helps students to actively construct knowledge and enhances their understanding of course materials (Scardamalia and Bereiter, 1996).

Haythornthwaite (2006) reviews the kinds of teaching interventions that facilitate successful collaboration in online environments. These are dependent upon the overall goal of the collaboration and the forms it can take, 'from division of labor to joint construction, from application of knowledge to creation of shared, co-constructed knowledge' (2006: 12). Among the most basic facilitation skills for collaborative learning is the ability to structure discussions to create meaningful discourse. Gilbert and Dabbagh (2005) define meaningful discourse as the ability of learners to demonstrate critical thinking skills by (1) relating course content to prior knowledge and experience, (2) interpreting content through the analysis, synthesis, and evaluation of others' understanding, and (3) making inferences. Structuredness is defined in their study as the instructional design elements that guide asynchronous online discussions. These include facilitator guidelines, posting protocols (e.g. number of postings required, length of posting, pacing of postings), evaluation criteria, grade weight, nature of topic discussed, number of participants, length of discussion, and degree of instructor or facilitator participation, among others. Gilbert and Dabbagh's (2005) research design was a multiple case study of the use of minimal, low, medium, and high structure in a course over four different semesters, with content analysis of samples of the transcripts. They found that:

- Facilitator guidelines increase the number and type of student facilitator postings in the online discussion forums.
- Postings protocols, specifically, limiting the length of a posting and mandating reading citations, had a negative impact on meaningful discourse.
- Evaluation rubrics, specifically the requirement of even distribution of postings over the semester and increased grade weight, had a positive impact on online discourse.

Evaluation rubrics are part of a second key aspect of the pedagogy for guiding collaborative learning online, the use of assessment techniques that directly reward and involve collaborative behaviour among students rather than grading only individual work (Swan *et al.*, 2006). Among the most basic principles is that participation must be a significant part of the grading for a course if it is to be rewarded. Discussion should be graded or rewarded not just by counting posts, but by assessing their relevance, depth, and responsiveness to others. This is one of the most time-consuming tasks for the ALN instructor, but there are semi-automated means emerging that can assist. For example, Saltz (2005) developed, and tested in a field experiment, a Web-based tool, iPET (integrated

Participation Evaluation Tool). It aims to enable facilitators (i.e., instructors) to more quickly and accurately understand and, where appropriate, grade participation within an ALN. In brief, the results of the study demonstrate that when instructors have access to iPET, they have an increased confidence in their understanding of student participation without increasing their work load. In addition, when students had access to iPET reports, they felt that instructors provided more feedback and that they had an increased motivation for online discussion. Taken together, iPET established an environment of increased focus on participation, without increasing instructor work load.

There have been few empirical studies that measure the effectiveness of collaborative learning strategies for online learning as compared to individually oriented activities and grading. However, surveys tend to show correlations between collaborative learning and student perceptions of learning. For example, Fredericksen *et al.* (2000) report the results of an online survey of 1,406 SLN students, which represented a response rate of 42 per cent of the enrollees in spring 1999. Interaction with the teacher was the most significant contributor to perceived learning in these courses. However, levels of participation compared to traditional classrooms, interaction with classmates and motivation are all important factors that affected student perceived learning at a highly significant level ($p=<0.00$).

In a quasi-experimental field study, Benbunan-Fich and Hiltz (1999) compared groups and individuals solving an ethical case scenario, Face-to-face or with an ALN, to determine the separate and joint effects of communication medium and teamwork. Dependent variables included quality and length of the reports, and subjective perceptions of learning and satisfaction. ALN-supported participants had significantly better solution quality than their manual counterparts. Group reports were significantly longer than individual reports and students in online conditions submitted longer reports. As for perceived learning, there was a significant interaction effect between teamwork and technology: collaborative groups online reported better perceived learning than all the other conditions. Thus there is some experimental evidence for a causal link between collaborative learning and outcomes. However, there is need for more research on this issue, which disentangles mode of communication and collaborative versus individual work, examines a range of different kinds of collaborative assignments in different disciplines, and measures objective as well as subjective perceptions of learning.

CHALLENGES AND OPPORTUNITIES

Although ALN began at the university level, it has since the early 1980s been increasingly incorporated into the curriculum of primary and secondary education and in recent years in the provision of virtual schooling and parent–teacher networks. More recently, the use of ALN for formal and non-formal educational applications in workplace and executive education has begun to flourish (i.e., NACTEL, EPCE, CAEL, etc.).

Thus it is important to consider how to make ALNs most effective, given the growing number of learners and educators becoming involved. Moreover, the nature of the leading providers – large-scale inter-institutional consortia and for-profit operations – shows that the importance of ALN goes well beyond the numbers involved, and challenges the traditional structure of educational institutions, as well as the traditional role of faculty members.

Besides offering individual courses, online or 'virtual' universities increasingly offer a full range of services and activities for their students, such as online registration, advising, and grade reporting. Innovations abound; this is an exciting and also perilous time in higher education, with online programming raising many issues about the future of the university. The position of the authors is not that virtual universities or e-learning programmes should replace or displace the traditional classroom, but that there is a huge pent-up need to increase university access beyond current time and space boundaries. Innovations such as asynchronous group communication technologies enable an unprecedented set of opportunities to advance the quality and accessibility of education, worldwide. Collaborative learning and knowledge building are increasingly possible. We have the technology. We need the vision, the designs, and the research to develop evidence-based models and programmes.

ALN, as we argue in this chapter, brings powerful new inventions to innovate the university curricula, and to reinvent the pedagogy from one that is based on a view of learning as passing on a body of foundational knowledge (memorizing a set of ideas and information) to that of collaborative learning based on learning and applying the analytical terms and processes of a field. While these two perspectives continue to struggle, there are other aspects of a university that arguably need to be supported or transformed in a virtual university. The traditional university is a powerful paradigm and model of not only academic discourse but also of the social, political, and other aspects that university life provides. Thus far, most online or virtual university offerings have focused on the academic programming. Yet, as the trend to increased adoption of ALN continues, there is a powerful argument to be made for including other aspects of university life and experience. For example, facilities can be added to support student unions, special interest groups, politics and governance; faculty unions, associations, etc., enriching the political, social, cultural, and personal experience of all participants. Virtual football may be an important portent.

EDUCATIONAL TRANSFORMATION: ALTERNATIVE FUTURES

In at least one respect, the use of computer-mediated communication to support 'ALN' types of course delivery can be seen as coming full circle during the approximately thirty years of its history thus far. The initial applications in higher education were to augment the traditional classroom with online communication and group activities between class meetings, variously termed 'blended', 'mixed mode' or 'hybrid' courses. Blended courses are once again in vogue, and are the fastest-growing form of online learning. In 2002 online learning programme directors projected that not only will totally online courses continue growing at a fast pace, but many courses that are now offered entirely face-to-face, on-campus, will become 'blended' courses that combine on-campus meetings with continued online interaction. The survey was conducted in 2002 by Allen and Seaman (2003). It gathered responses from over fifty US online learning programme directors who belonged to a foundation-supported (not-for-profit) consortium of colleges and universities that offer fully online university degree programmes (Allen and Seaman, 2003). The survey also projected the number of students enrolled in blended courses as tripling in three years, from about 7 per cent to about 21 per cent. Generally, these blended courses meet face-to-face for many fewer hours of instructor contact than on-campus classes, e.g. every other week, or for half the conventional classroom time.

This kind of spread of e-learning – both from on-campus to off-campus, and from on-campus only to blended forms – is a major trend in transforming the nature of traditional institutions of higher education. At the same time, there are other forces at work that push changes in the direction of commercialization and a shift of pedagogical roles towards the division of labour and a factory system (Turoff, 1997). In the UK one such force is the rise in the cost of higher education in which the teaching (delivery) is done by the highly trained and well paid professoriate, who are responsible for the production of knowledge (research) as well as its 'delivery'. The rise in tuition for public education has been fuelled by the drive for tax cutting in government, with a resultant steep decrease in the level of state support for public universities. As a result, many would-be university students are priced out of the traditional market, or graduate with financially crippling loans that they may be paying off for decades.

One change that seems inevitable is that there will emerge several very large, international 'mega-universities' that educate hundreds of thousands of students online. Some of these will be for-profit organizations that do not see themselves as having the kinds of multiple roles that traditional residential universities play for their students and their communities, but rather, simply deliver education in a cost-effective way that satisfies their customers. Many will adopt the 'factory' model in which the Ph.D.-bearing professoriate become the 'producers' of the content of knowledge modules, which are packaged in multimedia formats by educational technology specialists, and delivered by less skilled and less expensive teachers employed part time or in non-tenure track positions. In fact, the 'teachers' may become software 'agents' in many cases. As related by Britt (2005), a University of Florida professor, Amy Baylor, is experimenting with 'pedagogical agents'. The software will adapt to a student's skill level in a given subject and provide feedback, both cognitive and emotional:

'Up until now, the personal computer's potential to be a valuable teaching and learning tool has been stymied by its "soulless" nature … We're using computers to simulate human beings in a controlled manner so we can investigate how they affect and persuade people.' … Baylor's work is focusing on friendly facial expressions, soothing hand gestures, and a 'coolly intelligent voice' to create characters that are 'both disarmingly lifelike and surprisingly persuasive' … 'Unlike a human mentor, we can control all aspects of a pedagogical agent – its gender, age, ethnicity, personality, message, and interaction style – to represent the ideal persona for facilitating learning,' Baylor says.

(Britt, 2005)

In a special issue of *Communications of the ACM* on 'The Digital Society' Hiltz and Turoff (2005: 60) state:

We argue that the current evolutionary changes in educational technology and pedagogy will be seen, 50 years from now, as revolutionary changes in the nature of higher education as a process and as an institution. We are in the process of moving:

From: face-to-face courses using objectivist, teacher-centered pedagogy and offered by tens of thousands of local, regional, and national universities;

To: online and hybrid courses using digital technologies to support constructivist, collaborative, student-centered pedagogy, offered by a few hundred 'mega-universities' that operate on a global scale.

The university as we know it must change to compete in the international market for tuition dollars.

Too many educators live with the illusion that they have a choice about whether or not these changes will occur … whether we like it or not, the restructuring that corporations underwent as they moved from an industrial to a postindustrial or information economy is now occurring in higher education.

(Mark Taylor, in *Educause Review*, 2000)

Will the next forms of computer-mediated communication preserve the role of the instructor as mentor and facilitator? Can software agents act to facilitate collaborative learning, on their own or as automated teaching assistants? How will the shift towards digital audio that can be listened to on iPods or similar mobile devices affect collaborative learning? These are among the issues that undoubtedly will be the subject of research in the next decade.

REFERENCES

Alavi, M. (1994) 'Computer-mediated collaborative learning: an empirical evaluation', *MIS Quarterly*, 18 (2): 150–74.

Allen, I. E. and Seaman, J. (2003) *Sizing the Opportunity: The Quality and Extent of Online Education in the United States, 2002 and 2003*. Needham, MA: SCALE.

Allen, I. E. and Seaman, J. (2005) *Growing by Degrees: Online Education in the United States, 2005*. Needham, MA: SCALE.

Anderson, T., Rourke, L., Garrison, R. and Archer, W. (2001) 'Assessing teaching presence in a computer conferencing context', *Journal of Asynchronous Learning Networks*, 5 (2): np. Available online at: http://www.sloan-c.org/publications/jaln/ v5n2/v5n2_anderson.asp.

Arbaugh, J. B. (2001) 'How instructor immediacy behaviours affect student satisfaction and learning in Web-based courses', *Business Communication Quarterly*, 64 (4): 42–54.

Arbaugh, J. B. and Hornik, S. C. (2002) 'Predictors of Perceived Learning and Satisfaction in Web-based MBA Courses: A Test and Extension of Chickering and Gamson's (1987) Seven Principles of Good Practice in Education'. Paper presented at the XXXIII annual meeting of the Decision Sciences Institute, San Diego, CA.

Benbunan-Fich, R. and Hiltz, S. R. (1999) 'Impacts of asynchronous learning networks on individual and group problem solving: a field experiment', *Group Decision and Negotiation*, 8: 409–26.

Bourne, J. R., Mayadas, A. F. and Campbell, J. O. (2006) *Asynchronous learning networks: an information-technology-based infrastructure for engineering education*. Retrieved 8 May 2006 from: http://www.sloan-c.org/consulting/docu/sc/36/40.doc.

Bouton, C. and Garth, R. Y. (1983) *Learning in Groups*, San Francisco, CA: Jossey-Bass.

Britt, R. R. (2005) 'Attractive virtual professors draw student attention', *LiveScience*, 16 November. Retrieved from: http://www.livescience.com/technology/ 051116virtual_teachers.html.

Chickering, A. W. and Gamson, Z. (1987) 'Seven principles of good practice in undergraduate education', *AAHE Bulletin*, 39: 3–7.

Coppola, N. W., Hiltz, S. R. and Rotter, N. (2002) 'Becoming a virtual professor: pedagogical roles and asynchronous learning networks', *Journal of Management Information Systems*, 18 (4): 169–90.

Coppola, N. W., Hiltz, S. R. and Rotter, N. (2004) 'Building trust in virtual teams', *IEEE Transactions on Professional Communication*, 47 (2): 95–104.

Fjermestad, J., Hiltz, S. R. and Zhang, Y. (2005) 'Effectiveness for students: comparisons of "in-seat" and ALN courses', in S. R. Hiltz and R. Goldman (eds), *Learning Together Online: Research on Asynchronous Learning Networks*. Mahwah, NJ: Erlbaum. pp. 39–80.

Frederickson, E., Pickett, A., Shea, P., Pelz, W. and Swan, K. (2000) 'Student satisfaction and perceived learning with online courses: principles and examples from the SUNY Learning Network', *Journal of Asynchronous Learning Networks*, 4 (2): np. Available online at: http://www.sloan-c.org/ publications/jaln/v4n2/v4n2_fredericksen.asp.

Garrison, D. R. (2006) 'Online collaboration principles: facilitating collaboration in online learning', *Journal of Asynchronous Learning Networks*, 10 (1): 25–34. Available online at: http://www.sloan-c.org/publications/jaln/v10n1/v10n1_3garrison.asp.

Gilbert, P. K., Dabbagh, N. (2005) 'How to structure online discussions for meaningful discourse: a case study', *British Journal of Educational Technology*, 36 (1): 5–18.

Gorham, J. (1988) 'The relationship between verbal teacher immediacy behaviours and student learning', *Communication Education*, 37 (1): 40–53.

Hafner, K. and Lyon, M. (1996) *Where Wizards stay up Late: The Origins of the Internet*. New York: Simon & Schuster.

Harasim, L. (2006) 'A history of e-learning: shift happened', in J. Weiss, J. Nolan and P. Trifonas (eds), *International Handbook of Virtual Learning Environments*. Dordrecht: Kluwer. pp. 25–60.

Harasim, L., Hiltz, S. R., Teles, L. and Turoff, M. (1995) *Learning Networks: A Field Guide to Teaching and Learning Online*. Cambridge, MA: MIT Press.

Haythornthwaite, C. (2006) 'Facilitating collaboration in online learning', *Journal of Asynchronous Learning Networks*, 10 (1): 7–24. Available online at: http://www.sloan-c.org/publications/ jaln/v10n1/v10n1_2haythornthwaite.asp.

Heckman, R. and Annabi, H. (2003) 'A content analytic comparison of face to face and ALN case-study discussion', in *Proceedings of 36th Hawaii International Conference on Systems Science*. Washington, DC: IEEE Press.

Hiltz, S. R. (1994) *The Virtual Classroom: Learning without Limits via Computer Networks*. Norwood, NJ: Ablex.

Hiltz, S. R. and Goldman, R. (eds) (2005) *Learning Together Online: Research on Asynchronous Learning Networks*. Mahwah, NJ: Erlbaum.

Hiltz, S. R. and Shea, P. (2005) 'The student in the online classroom', in S. R. Hiltz and R. Goldman (eds), *Learning Together Online: Research on Asynchronous Learning Networks*. Mahwah, NJ: Erlbaum. pp. 145–68.

Hiltz, S.R. and Turoff, M. (1978) *The Network Nation: Human Communication via Computer*. Reading, MA: Addison-Wesley.

Hiltz, S. R. and Turoff, M. (2005) 'Education goes digital: the evolution of online learning and the revolution in higher education', *Communications of the ACM*, 48 (10): 59–64.

Hislop, G. W. (2001) 'Does teaching online take more time?' in *Proceedings, 31st ASEE/IEEE Frontiers in Education Conference*, Oct 10–12, Reno, NV (CD-rom edn). Washington, DC: IEEE Computer Society.

Illinois Virtual Campus (2005) *Distance Education Enrollments at Illinois Colleges and Universities*. Retrieved 9 May 2006 from: http://www.ivc.illinois.edu/pubs/enrollment/Fall05.pdf.

Jehng, J. C. (1997) 'The psycho-social processes and cognitive effects of peer-based collaborative interaction with computers', *Journal of Educational Computing Research*, 17 (1): 19–46.

Klobas, J. and Haddow, G. (2000) 'International computer-supported collaborative teamwork in business education: a case study and evaluation', *International Journal of Education Technology*, 2 (1): np. Retrieved 19 July 2004 from: http://smi.curtin.edu.au/ijet/v2n1/klobas/index.html.

Marttunen, M. (1998) 'Electronic mail as a forum for argumentative interaction in higher education studies', *Journal of Educational Computing Research*, 18 (4): 387–405.

Mason, R. (1989) 'An evaluation of CoSy on an Open University course', in R. Mason and A. Kaye (eds), *Mindweave: Communication, Computers and Distance Education*. Oxford: Pergamon Press. pp. 115–45.

Mason, R. (1998) *Globalising Education: Trends and Applications*. Abingdon: Routledge.

Mehrabian, A. (1971) *Silent Messages*. Belmont, CA: Wadsworth.

Saltz, J. (2005) 'Dynamic Measuring Tools for Online Discourse'. Unpublished doctoral dissertation, New Jersey Institute of Technology.

Scardamalia, M. and Bereiter, C (1996) 'Computer support for knowledge-building communities', in T. Koschmann (ed.), *CSCL: Theory and Practice of an Emerging Paradigm*. Mahwah, NJ: Erlbaum. pp. 249–68.

Shea, P., Swan, K., Fredericksen, E. and Pickett, A. (2002) 'Student satisfaction and reported learning in the SUNY Learning Network', in J. Bourne and J. C. Moore (eds), *Quality Online Education* III. Needham, MA: Sloan Center for Online Education. pp. 145-55.

Shea, P., Fredericksen, E., Pickett, A., Pelz, W. and Swan, K. (2001) 'Measures of learning effectiveness in the SUNY Learning Network', in *Online Education: Learning Effectiveness, Faculty Satisfaction, and Cost Effectiveness*. Needham, MA: Sloan Center for Online Education.

Stahl, G. and The_BSCW_Development_Group (2003) 'Knowledge negotiation in asynchronous learning networks', in *Proceedings of the 36th Hawaii International Conference on System Sciences*. Washington, DC: IEEE Computer Society Press.

Swan, K. (2006) 'Online collaboration: introduction to the special issue', *Journal of Asynchronous Learning Networks*, 10 (1): 3-5. Available online at: http://www.sloan-c.org/publications/jaln/v10n1/v10n1_1swan.asp.

Swan, K., Shen, J. and Hiltz, S. R. (2006) 'Assessment and collaboration in online learning', *Journal of Asynchronous Learning Networks*, 10 (1): 45–62. Available online at: http://www.sloan-c.org/publications/jaln/v10n1/v10n1_5swan.asp.

Taylor, M. C. (2000) 'Useful devils', *Educause Review* (July–August), 38-46. Available online at: http://www.educause.edu/apps/er/erm00/articles004/taylor.pdf.

Turoff, M. (1997) 'Alternative futures for distance learning: the force and the dark side', keynote presentation at the UNESCO/Open University international colloquium, *Virtual Learning Environments and the Role of the Teacher*, Open University, Milton Keynes, 27–29 April. Retrieved 29 July 2006 from: http://web.njit.edu/~turoff/Papers/darkaln.html.

ACKNOWLEDGEMENTS

Portions of this chapter were adapted from previous works by the authors: from Harasim, 'A history of e-learning: shift happened', in Weiss, Nolan and Trifonas (eds), *The Handbook of Virtual Learning Environments* (2006); and from Hiltz and Goldman, *Learning Together Online* (2005). The NJIT-related research reported in this chapter was partially supported by the Alfred P. Sloan Foundation.

3

On Computers and Writing

Gail E. Hawisher and Cynthia L. Selfe

The intense interest in research methods and research design continues to create a kairos of significance and of caring for our collective work in computers and writing.

(Hugh Burns, 2004: 8)

The field of computers and writing – also called computers and composition studies and recently known for its study of what are now termed digital literacies in the US – has a rich, if relatively short, history dating back to 1977 with the mass production of the first fully assembled microcomputer. At that time, personal computers began making their way into university writing programs and a decade later were well on their way to establishing themselves as integral to postsecondary writing contexts. But this beginning ties a history of computers and writing, and e-learning more generally, too closely to the technologies that enable online writing without taking fully into account those who have participated in its history: the writers, students, instructors, and writing program administrators who have all shaped the field and its current use of information technologies to abet learning. A more accurate starting date, if such a date does indeed exist, might begin with arguably the first dissertation appearing in 1979. Entitled 'Stimulating Rhetorical Invention in English Composition through Computer-Assisted Instruction' and written by Hugh Burns (1979), the study represents the first of many attempts to assess the possible impact of computing software on learning and to devise a research methodology that recognizes the complexities related to new technologies, new theoretical understandings, and composing. As Burns notes in the epigraph at the start of our chapter, research has marked the field from its outset and continues to evolve as the contexts for enquiry expand out from the classroom into our professional lives. In this chapter, then, we attempt to bring together the research in computers and writing of the past decades while at the same time focusing on the many individuals who have shaped current practices and the constellation of factors that continue to contribute to e-learning.

In this project, we are influenced by Brian Street (1995), James Gee (1996), Harvey Graff (1987), and Deborah Brandt (2001), who remind us that we can understand literacies – and, we would argue, digital literacies and e-learning – as social practices and values *only* when we properly situate them within the context of a particular historical period, a particular cultural milieu, and a specific cluster of material conditions. Thus we hope that by focusing on the relationships between computers and writing, people, and the cultural ecologies within which people practise and learn digital literacies, this chapter will provide individuals, scholars, and researchers with guidance in thinking about the critical research issues that e-learning foregrounds. In the twenty-first century, as Sullivan and Porter (1997) have pointed out, 'Technology and writing research focuses at various times on the various relationships among places, writers, readers, texts, and institutions. Often it proceeds from the assumption that all of these relationships occur inside a framework that accepts technology as an inevitable part of writing (for good or ill)' (p. 171). This tendency to view computers and literacy practices as inextricable from one another (C. Selfe, 1999; Hawisher and Selfe, 2000) has become increasingly accepted regardless of whether we consider free-standing word-processing programmes or multimodal composing environments, which provide authors access to text, image, audio, and video as digital design resources.

We organize the discussion that follows along broad chronological lines – a cautionary note, however, is in order. Although we begin by presenting research in computer-assisted instruction and word processing and then move on to studies of electronic networks, hypertext, and multimodal composing, we do not want to suggest that the field has been characterized by a tidy sequence of investigations that proceeds along a coherently organized timeline. Technologies for composing and digital communication environments may emerge as distinct historical innovations, but the community of computers and writing scholars – as a diverse disciplinary group – actually take up and examine these technologies *unevenly, recursively* and in many different forms. The use and study of communication technologies occur as social formations, time, institutional infrastructure, economic factors, educational policies, and many other elements establish a fit between any specific invention and a broad range of cultural conditions (Deibert, 1997).

Thus scholars in the community of computers and writing did not discover word processing, electronic networks, hypertext, and then multimodal composing in a strict temporal order. In many places, for example, electronic networks of mainframe computers exerted a significant influence on communications long before word-processing packages became available on personal computers.

Similarly, many teachers of composition were using texts that combined the modalities of visual and alphabetic information long before word processing became popular. Reducing history to monodimensional chronologies tends to ignore the perspective that individuals within the field are always changing methodological directions, revisiting research perspectives, discovering new reasons and ways to investigate every new technology – some engaging now in research that others began experimenting with twenty years ago. Our broad chronological organization, then, provides only one view of the field's research and is not meant to deny its general complexity.

We also hope to resist a deterministic understanding of technology uptake. This perspective, too, we believe, reduces the study of computers and writing to overly simplistic terms. Hence the discussion that follows – while recognizing that the field has often responded with pedagogical enthusiasm to new technological innovations soon after they have been released – also tries to describe how subsequent research projects typically help temper such initial excitement, shifting educators' focus from the technology itself to the ways in which such technologies shape and are shaped by students and teachers, rhetorical and pedagogical contexts, composing products and composing processes.

HISTORICAL OVERVIEW OF THREE METHODOLOGICAL TRENDS IN COMPUTERS AND WRITING

Readers of this chapter will note that the studies and investigations range widely in terms of their methodology. To mirror some of the complexity that characterizes computers and composition research, we have included references to quantitative as well as qualitative work; projects that rely on inferential statistics as well as those that employ various kinds of descriptive statistics; investigations that focus on case studies, survey data, and ethnographic observation. Despite this diversity and despite the fact that a range of methodological perspectives have always characterized the work in computers and composition and are likely to continue to do so, some broad historical patterns of methodological approach seem worth mentioning, even though these trends are, inevitably, shot through with contradiction, variation, and exception.

In many instances, the trends we note here were influenced by related trends in rhetoric and composition studies, one of the fields out of which computers and writing has grown. In the late 1970s and early 1980s, for example, composition studies were a relatively young discipline intent on establishing a tradition of authoritative and scientifically informed research that would set it apart from literary studies. One solution to this dilemma, for compositionists, was to study the cognitive processes of experienced writers and then teach the processes systematically to less experienced student writers. During this period, researchers in computers and writing – like many compositionists (e.g. Elbow, 1981; Flower,

1981; Flower and Hayes, 1980; Murray, 1980) – turned to cognitive science for methodologies that would allow them to trace processes. A number of these scholars, for instance, borrowed the tool of speak-aloud protocols (Collier, 1983; Nichols, 1986; C. Selfe, 1985; Woodruff *et al.*, 1986) to trace and analyse the invention, composing, and revision processes of computer-using students. Their goal was to tease out the effects of word-processing environments on specific areas of students' writing practices. By the latter half of the 1980s, however, some scholars in composition studies had become disenchanted with the methodological approaches of cognitive scientists (Cooper and Holzman, 1983; Petrosky, 1983; Stewart, 1992), which, they claimed could not fully represent the many tacit decisions that writers made as they composed. In a related move, scholars were also posing questions about experimental methodologies and the kinds of pedagogical guidance with which they could actually provide classroom teachers (e.g. Connors, 1983; Cooper, 1997; Dudley-Marling and Rhodes, 1989; Voss, 1983).

Converging with these methodological trends in composition studies was the development of new networking technologies in the 1980s and the World Wide Web in the early 1990s. To computers and writing researchers these new composing environments suggested complicated new questions about the social dynamics of computer use, among just a few of these: How were teachers and students communicating in online contexts? How did computer users exercise discursive power in digital composing environments? Was online communication gendered and racialized in the same ways as face-to-face communications? Were new forms of digital composition instantiating postmodern theories of language? Answers to these types of complex, 'wicked' questions (Selber *et al.*, 1997) did not seem likely to emerge from narrowly controlled investigations based on experimental research designs.

Recognizing this context, some computers and composition researchers – like their counterparts in the larger field of rhetoric and composition studies – traded the generalizable claims of experimental investigations for the explanatory power of social theory (e.g. critical theory, feminism, Marxism, among others), and more qualitative methodologies. This trend was fuelled by the fact that computers, increasingly, were becoming ubiquitous in the public sphere and the workplace, as well as in the academy. As a result, fewer scholars felt the need to prove that computer use or word processing was of value to writers, or to quantify the nature of the value added by computers in writing instruction (e.g. Cohen, 1986).

This situation meant that scholars in computers and writing conducted increasing numbers of qualitative investigations in the later 1980s and into the twenty-first century. Among these investigations were ethnographic case studies of individuals (Bridwell Bowles *et al.*, 1987; Daiute, 1985, 1986; Flinn, 1987; C. Selfe, 1985), surveys of computer-using teachers and students (C. Selfe and Wahlstrom, 1986; R. Selfe, 2005), online observations or discursive analyses of electronic discussions (Faigley, 1992; Herring, 2001; Romano, 1993; Sproull and Kiesler, 1991), and ethnographic studies of classrooms (Herrmann, 1987;

Klem and Moran, 1992). These qualitative methodologies were better suited, some felt, to identifying the multiple and complex ways in which specific computer-supported communication environments shaped, and were shaped by, local and global social relationships.

BEGINNINGS: STUDENTS, TEACHERS, AND COMPUTER-ASSISTED INSTRUCTION IN WRITING (CAI)

The grand debate in English composition circles these days concerns the problem of whether or not we teachers of composition should be more concerned with the processes of composition or the products of composition – whether we should be helping the students understand how they can create a piece of sustained thought or whether we should teach the students how to evaluate their own written work. … Enter rhetorical invention. Enter creativity theory. Enter the computer.

(Hugh Burns, 1981: 31)

Research in the early years of computers and writing primarily concerned itself with determining the role computers might play in the learning of writing through CAI, often examining and testing tutorials that individual faculty members and emerging software companies were developing for use in college settings. As Burns notes in the epigraph above, computers entered the field almost simultaneously with the field's turn to writing as a process – that is, the theoretical recognition that activities such as planning, drafting, evaluating, revising and editing grounded writers' work and should be introduced to students. In these years, then, research such as Burns' study (1984) often went hand in hand with a focus on a particular activity within the writing process, such as planning or invention, and the attempt to measure the effects of the software on students' thinking and writing. As mentioned, quantitative studies were very much at the forefront of research in composition or writing studies at the time, and Burns' study was no exception. Although Burns (1984) admits readily that it is difficult to 'quantify' any changes in students' writing as a result of his 'first-generation prewriting programmes' (p. 31), experimental research was integral to these first attempts to look at the connections between writing and computer-assisted instruction. These views of learning and writing, and the research accompanying them, were meant to contribute to an understanding of what it means to engage in literacy learning and of how computers can help students in this process. They also reflect the ways in which views of instruction, software, and research have changed as the field has moved away from looking at computers as delivery systems for instruction to viewing the user/learner as a more active and engaged participant.

In trying to understand the trajectory of research of the past decades, we find it instructive to turn to Bizzell's (1986) words. In a review of research on composing, she notes that when a particular theoretical perspective prevails in a discipline, research results are interpreted in light of the assumptions that the particular view embraces. At this time she was arguing that writing research was persistently interpreted with expressive – what she called 'personal-style'– ped-agogical assumptions or with an emphasis on what goes on within the writer's head, cognitive assumptions. In arguing that this sort of interpretation is unavoidable, she writes: 'Scholars writing up their research, like students strug-gling with their first essay assignments, must work within the language-using practices of a particular community, which are in turn shaped by its social, cul-tural, and political circumstances' (p. 68). Thus research in computers and writing at this time often focused on the cognitively based composing processes in computer environments – mirroring the interest that composition studies had in cognitive composing processes more generally. The research continued in this vein through the next barrage of studies that responded to the increasingly ubiq-uitous use of word processing in college settings. Such investigations were important, in part, because they established a habit – within the arena of com-puters and writing research – of questioning and testing technological solutions systematically against the goals of effective writing instruction.

COLLEGE WRITERS AND WORD PROCESSING

Despite the problems inherent in the new technology, word-processing is not going to go away. It will become the norm at colleges and universities, as it is now the norm for profes-sional writers. It will, and should, become part of the writing classroom.

(Charles Moran, 1983: 115)

As Moran suggests in the above quotation, word processing did not go away. It remains an essential part of the writing classroom and has received all sorts of attention over the years as to whether or not college students' writing improves as a result of its use. By far the most prolific area of research in computers and writing, studies in word processing continue to abound in the research literature. And, although word processing today appears very matter-of-fact, a huge shift occurred when researchers moved from examining CAI contexts in which com-puters are programmed as instructional delivery systems to writing contexts in which computers are programmed as spaces for writing. Unfortunately, however, questions driving the research were often framed too simplistically as some ver-sion of 'What is the effect of computers on writing quality?' which attribute far too much power to computers rather than to how writers or writing instructors might use computers. Today the quality question seems somewhat naive and beside the point; word processing occupies centre stage as the writing technol-ogy of choice in university and workplace settings. And, just as English professionals stopped asking a long time ago whether tools such as typewriters improve students' writing, many regard the quality question in relation to word processing as wrongheaded as well (e.g. Cohen, 1986). As word processing has become indispensable for student and professional writers alike, other research questions need to be formulated. Little research, for example, has looked at the reciprocal relationships between electronic class discussions and the face-to-face contexts in which instructors and students meet together; little research has looked at how today's writers move out from word processing to the Web or presentation and photo-editing software programmes; and few have examined how word-processing programmes have changed to include a wide variety of capabilities within the programmes themselves. Yet a review of a meta-analysis (e.g. Goldberg *et al.*, 2003) reveals that researchers still ask whether the use of word processing will enhance writing abilities.

Other research questions have included how word processing in combination with process-oriented teaching influences writers' processes – planning, drafting, revising, editing – and products – quality, syntax, length, and number of mechanical errors. Researchers have also been interested in whether students tend to enjoy writing at computers and whether the technology is more appropriate for one group of writers than another. Results of the research with post-secondary students are many and varied. Students report positive attitudes toward writing and word processing after working with computers; student writers often exhibit finished products that have fewer mechanical errors than those written with traditional tools; and many writers produce longer texts with word processing than with traditional methods (Hawisher, 1989). Over the years, however, conflicting results have emerged around the variables of revision and writing quality. Although many studies have found an increase in revision, only a few studies have claimed that writing quality improves. In fact, regardless of which group of writers has been the focus of the research and regardless of whether the research was college-based or otherwise, investigations of writing quality continue to yield conflicting results. (For another meta-analysis of word processing in writing instruction, see Bangert-Drowns, 1993.)

The qualitative research – case studies and ethnographic research – asked somewhat different questions from the early quantitative studies. Questions focused on how writers adapt their strategies to computer writing, on whether their composing habits change with the technology, and on how the introduction of computers influences the cultural context into which they are introduced. A general theme drawn from these studies was similar to one from the comparative or experimental studies; that is, a writer's particular habits and strategies for composing take precedence over the influence of computers. Writers bring their routines and patterns of writing with them. Thus, if students were not extensive revisers before word processing, they probably will not become extensive revisers with computers even when revision strategies are part of the instruction (Bridwell *et al.*, 1985). It is interesting to speculate on how this may have changed with the current generation of university students who are likely to have learned most of their writing processes on computers. The ethnographic studies that have been conducted tend also to contribute new knowledge that the comparative studies cannot reveal. They suggest that while students often do their paper-and-pencil writing silently and privately, the move to writing online in conjunction with word processing and the Internet often transforms the process from a private to a public activity. In seeking to elucidate the subtle influences of computers in social interactions among students and teachers, the qualitative research, like studies of online discussions, suggests the probable importance of the cultural context in shaping writers' work and learning with word processing (Blair and Monske, 2004).

One of the earliest qualitative studies, Collier's research (1983) of four nursing students, set the stage for the kinds of questions that would drive subsequent inquiries. Collier asked how the use of a computer application (in this case, a mainframe text editor) would influence the student nurses' writing processes (in this case, revision) as well as the quality of the texts they produced. And although he saw no improvement in quality, he found that the writers he studied revised more and produced longer texts with word processing than with conventional tools. Since Collier's study, researchers have continued to probe the relationship among writers and various kinds of computer applications, aiming much of the research at university-based writing and often with an eye toward examining how the teaching of writing might benefit from the use of the new technologies. In recent years, moreover, researchers have extended their study to the newer technologies of electronic communication networks and hypertextual and multimodal contexts. Yet, despite the considerable attention research in computers and composition studies has received over the years, there have been few studies that look in detail at how the use of computers affects students' interactions with the cultural context or learning environment in which students participate. In other words, little systematic attention has been paid to the kinds of research that have the potential to inform fundamental changes in teaching writing – changes which must be realistically played out within current social, political, economic, educational, and ideological contexts.

ELECTRONIC NETWORKS

The use of conferencing software in the classroom has been accompanied by a pedagogical shift toward student-based, active learning. Instead of listening to a lecture about a subject, students are actively engaged in exploring a topic. Electronic conferencing empowers students in several ways that have been impractical or impossible without computers – most notably by increasing the level of participation, by improving individual facility with language, and by promoting an understanding of discourse communities.

(Paul Taylor, 1992: 139)

A major difference between research aimed at word processing and the early research on electronic networked discourse or computer-mediated communication (CMC) is its cross-disciplinary emphasis. Unlike word processing, which was largely studied in English composition classes, studies on electronic networks range across the disciplines including but not limiting themselves to the writing classes that Taylor references in the epigraph above. Studies in distance education, communication research, linguistics, social psychology, and library and information science, to mention a few of the fields in which scholars actively study CMC (e.g. Haythornthwaite, 2001; Jones, 1998; Kiesler, 1997) have also contributed to work in computers and writing.

Since the research is cross-disciplinary, it is somewhat surprising that studies have converged on similar issues, asking similar research questions. The questions focus first on identifying the characteristics of electronic discourse, examining how participants contribute and respond to the discourse, and, then, for those working in educational settings, exploring its potential for teaching and learning. Gender considerations also come into play regardless of whether the research is within the realm of distance learning (e.g. Hawisher and Selfe, 2003; Kramarae, 2001), classroom contexts (e.g. George, 1990), or in professional exchanges on the Internet (Hawisher and Sullivan, 1998; Selfe and Meyer, 1991). Many initial findings were more in the spirit of observations gleaned from experience in working with the medium, not unlike early exploratory studies in word processing. But regardless of whether the research was conducted within or outside educational settings, common questions, findings, and observations emerged.

Researchers seem to agree that networked discourse often employs a language that is somewhere on a continuum between spoken and written language. Indeed, researchers often refer to online communication as 'talk' or 'dialogue' while acknowledging that this 'talk' takes place in a totally written context (Taylor, 1992). Erickson (1999) also notes that it enables 'persistent conversation' and that 'its persistence means that it may be far more structured, or far more amorphous, than an oral exchange, and that it may have the formality of published text or the informality of chat' (n.p.). Some participants write profusely on the networks; others seem terse, almost 'telegraphic'. Instant messaging or 'IMing', adopted as the synchronous medium of choice first among teenagers, seems indeed to employ a language of its own as students go about using IM to communicate with friends wherever they find it available. Conventions of language and style are still evolving and will change as asynchronous (e.g. blogs, text messaging) and synchronous (e.g. IMing) capabilities continue to change and proliferate. A number of researchers have noted that a writer's relation to a screen and electronic communication seems different from a writer's relation to a written letter or memorandum. In writing to a screen, writers may at times lose the sense of an audience and, with that, the constraints and inhibitions that the imagined audience provides (Eldred, 1989). At its most dramatic, this difference produces what has been termed 'flaming', or emotionally laden language sometimes inappropriate to classroom settings (Mann and Stewart, 2000; Rouzie, 2005). Some researchers contend that in classrooms the more focused the task the less likely flaming is to occur. In those studies where the electronic activity was goal-directed, and the roles of participants were clearly defined, no flaming was reported (Hartman *et al.*, 1991).

Research in various fields, moreover, has suggested that the lack of paralinguistic cues such as one's appearance, tone of voice, and facial expression also invites participation on networks from those who normally refrain from speaking frequently in face-to-face contexts. Sensitivity to the position of individuals within organizations, corporate or academic, tends to silence those who perceive themselves as having lower status. Dubrovsky and his colleagues (1991) looked specifically at electronic discussion in four-person groups with first-year college students and MBA graduate students; the researchers confirmed what they call 'the equalization phenomenon', that is, those with 'lower status', the first-year college students, asserted themselves more and had greater influence on the group than the first-year college students in the face-to-face groups. Such studies can have important implications for writing instructors who hope to encourage all students regardless of their class, race, or gender to participate, but the social science research needs to be scrutinized carefully before being imported directly into literacy classes (Eldred and Hawisher, 1995).

Basing their claims on similar research in the social sciences, those in computers and writing often argue that electronic discussion has the potential to encourage students who are sometimes silenced because of their status to 'speak up', to participate electronically in ways that they avoid in traditional class settings (e.g. Cooper and Selfe, 1990). As of yet, however, little empirical research in educational settings has supported or contradicted such claims. Blair and Monske (2004) sum up early CMC research in computers and writing with the following statement:

> Ultimately, research reported in *College English, College Composition and Communication, Written Communication* (Cooper and Selfe, 1990; Eldred and Hawisher, 1995; Hawisher and Moran, 1993; and Selfe and Meyer, 1991), and in edited collections (e.g. Hawisher and LeBlanc, 1992 and Hawisher and Selfe, 1991) were consistent in their postmodern conclusions that almost any networked activity will be a means to decenter the traditional classroom space and to disrupt the position of teacher as the figure of master; authority is moved away from the teacher in electronic space, allowing students from all backgrounds to be heard (Eldred, 1989; Selfe, 1990; Sommers, 1992). . . . Inevitably, the use of networks in the classroom was frequently presented as a win/win proposition – although students could resist teacher authority, this resistance benefited the entire class because it shifted focus from teacher-centered to student-centered learning.

> (p. 444)

Thus networked classrooms were often thought capable of transforming teaching practices for the better, a conclusion that must – like other emerging claims – continue to be carefully examined. As research on CMC in computers and writing turns to twenty-first century contexts, its reach extends beyond class-room practices, taking into consideration how audio and moving images become part of the larger digital communicative context (e.g. Shankar, 2005).

HYPERTEXT AND THE MOVE TO THE WORLD WIDE WEB

As a global hypertext system, the Web has provided the most convincing evidence of the computer's potential to refashion the practice of writing. For better or worse, the Web is hypertext for us today; all the earlier applications of stand-alone hypertext seem experimental or provisional by comparison.

(Jay David Bolter, 2001: xi)

Researchers began to explore the implications of hypertext for writing and writing instruction in the late 1980s, but, as Bolter suggests in the quotation above, the studies have less currency and value than they might as a result of the exponential development of the World Wide Web. Even before the Web's 1993 nascent entry, however, one of the problems researchers encountered is that hypertext, like networked discourse, exists only online and takes many different forms, ranging from hyperfiction (e.g. Joyce, 1987), to CD-rom guides, to museums (Snyder and Bulfin, in press), to online textbooks (e.g. Porter *et al.*, 2004), to online, collaboratively generated repositories of information like Wikipedia. Indeed, new genres, such as the early appearance of personal home pages, seem to emerge on a daily basis. Hypermedia programmes, whether stand-alone or on the Web, can be assembled so as to mimic old CAI programmes with their workbook-like structure and exercises, or they can take on an interactive form, such as video games, where individuals choose their own paths through online text with print, graphics, sound, and video as part of the text. With the extraordinary growth of the Web since 2000, the number and complexity of different kinds of Web genres are probably fast approaching those of print.

For educational settings, the early research on hypertextual environments existed primarily outside the field of computers and writing and often examined readers' and writers' navigational capabilities; that is, researchers looked at how users moved through large, complex, non-linear bodies of information without losing their sense of connection. Other questions driving the research focused on the design of hypertext systems and asked how material can be presented in such a way as to optimize learning (Spiro *et al.,* 1990).

An early approach to using hypertextual environments within the field encouraged students to author their own hypertexts and then asked them to describe their experiences in working with the new medium. One exploratory study in a first-year writing class found that students responded generally favourably to reading and writing hypertexts (Kaplan and Moulthrop, 1991).

While they sometimes wondered how they would know when they finished a reading assignment (there are no pages or specific paths to follow), they devoted large amounts of time and energy to reading and writing their own interactive fictions. In these kinds of hypertext environments it is difficult to know where reading stops and writing begins, since both occur in the same space often at the same time (Bolter, 2001). When the Web, the hypertextual component of the Internet, is used in such a way as to allow readers and writers to make their own connections, with a speed, incidentally, that is unknown in print contexts, and then to create new knowledge based on these connections, researchers enter a world that we have only begun to imagine, much less study in all its complexity.

EMERGING RESEARCH CONTEXTS

Technology is the medium of daily life in modern societies. Every major technical change reverberates at many levels, economic, political, religious, cultural. Insofar as we continue to see the technical and the social as separate domains, important aspects of these dimensions of our existence will remain beyond our reach as a democratic society.

(Andrew Feenberg, 1999: vii)

Each of the technologies discussed so far – computer-assisted instruction, word processing, electronic networks, hypertext and hypermedia, and their convergence in the World Wide Web – offer new challenges for research. Recent years, for example, have appropriately seen cultural issues surrounding the use of new technologies within computers and writing incorporated into the research. The work by cultural critics such as Feenberg (1999, 2002) quoted above, along with Castells (1996, 1997, 1998), Giddens (1979), and Norris (2001) remind us, for example, that computers fundamentally shape – and are shaped by – cultural values. Hence these machines magnify and reproduce the complex social conditions connected with those values. Computers, then, far from encouraging productive change, can also serve to support the *status quo* within the existing educational and cultural systems. And, unfortunately, there has been insufficient research on writing classes and technology that traces how these cultural processes unfold or that identifies the locations of gaps in the web of cultural, political, economic, and ideological relations.

Studies of the use of electronic discourse within local classrooms (e.g. Faigley, 1992; Regan, 1993; Romano, 1993) began to show us the complexities that attend its instructional use and the difficulties of bringing about reform even in classrooms led by critical pedagogues. Faigley (1992), Romano (1993), and Regan (1993) in separate studies, for example, suggest that issues of gender, multiculturalism, and sexual orientation cannot be addressed so easily. Even when teachers are able to encourage students to be more sensitive to the problems of the marginalized – which Faigley, Romano, and Regan as instructors weren't always able to do – translating this new awareness into venues for productive action remains a pressing challenge in computers and writing. How to incorporate these concerns into a research agenda is also not so easy. Below are a few attempts the two authors have made or observed over the years.

One study conducted by Selfe and Meyer (1991) looked at networked discourse on Megabyte University, a listserv aimed at English professionals who taught with computers. The two researchers tried to assess the power relationships within the online conference and used descriptive statistical data from their analysis of the postings along with an analysis of the patterns of individual participation in the conference. Although this research wasn't aimed at writing classes *per se*, the study revealed that men and those who are perceived as having higher status in the field often get more air time than women on the net. Hawisher and Selfe (1991) subsequently applied some of the same research perspectives to a study conducted within their university classes at separate universities. And although the study did not document similar gender inequities in online classroom discourse, interesting conversational patterns emerged regarding the role of instructors in online discussions. The electronic spaces had been set aside as discussion areas for students, and the instructors had purposely refrained from participating, hoping that the students would claim ownership of the discussion group. Hawisher and Selfe, however, dominated the conversation every bit as much as they might have in offline class discussions in that they were hailed and referred to more than any other participants on the list. Rather than being spaces uninhabited by instructors – even when the instructors don't contribute to the discussion – the pattern of participation in some electronic conferences may demonstrate just how central instructors are in undergraduate writing classes, even as decentred writing classes continue to be prized (Blair and Monske, 2004).

In the late 1990s Hawisher and Sullivan (1998) conducted a study of the online lives of academic women in writing studies. Questions driving the research concerned how thirty women academics perceived power as circulating in electronic contexts and how they negotiated authority within these spaces. The research took place entirely online and focused on two sources of data: e-mail interviews and transcripts from a listserv named 'women@waytoofast'–an electronic discussion group that the women themselves constructed in connection with the study. While the online interviews began to shed light on how these women in rhetoric and writing studies – graduate students and faculty – understood their participation in electronic discussion groups, the listserv transcripts reflected the ways in which the women carved out online identities for themselves. In looking at a particular group of women, whom the 'equalization phenomenon' is said to benefit, and in tying the research to a study of online gender roles the enquiry illustrated another approach to research open to computers and writing researchers. The tentative conclusion from the study is that online environments are neither egalitarian spaces for women nor spaces devoid of power–some women prevail on the nets despite what feminists have sometimes regarded as rather hostile environments for women (e.g. Spender, 1995). When this thinking is used to inform studies of other groups of women – adolescent women, for example – we might well find different patterns of participation.

In an attempt to consider generational differences in the acquisition of digital literacies, Selfe and Hawisher (2004) in a book-length study, *Literate Lives in the Information Age*, feature twenty case studies of people aged from 13 to 62. Culled from a larger corpus of over 350 interviews conducted over several years, the interviews reveal that such literacies – like all literacies we would argue – are situated in the cultural ecology of the time. That is, the life-history accounts reveal that people's acquisition of digital literacies is influenced by political, social, and educational factors that tend also to be influenced by the experiences of the individuals themselves. In addition to documenting several gateways – schools, homes, workplaces, and communities – through which those in the US came to know computers during these years, the study probes the contested nature of the literacy landscape during the late twentieth century and early twenty-first century, when technological change has been extremely rapid, and when various forms of digital literacy have been competing with various forms of print literacy for ascendancy. In the early 1990s, for example, as studies in computers and writing reveal, although young people were working in electronic environments, most of their online literacy practices in academic settings were still primarily alphabetic. At that time, while desktop publishing, e-mail, and photo manipulation software were gaining considerable currency, the Web and graphical browsers were just emerging. Only a decade later, however, young people were commonly using visual presentation software, downloading Web documents, designing sites for the Web, rendering three-dimensional land-scapes, animating human figures, manipulating photographs, and inserting both audio and video clips into their online communications. Their online communi-cations, at this point in time, could no longer be considered primarily alphabetic; they had taken a 'turn to the visual' (Kress, 1999: 66) and to the multimodal.

Clearly there was a close fit between these students' newly acquired digital literacies and the existing cultural ecology. Their new literacies could not have flourished, for instance, without the invention of the World Wide Web, Web browsers, and Web search engines. Neither could they have existed without new kinds of hardware and software that supported multimedia design and communi-cation, nor would they have experienced such exponential growth without the accompanying explosion of online communities that used chat rooms, designed and played video games, experimented with digital photography, and designed Web sites – communities made up of people who shared the interests of the young people in the case studies we have mentioned. Their interests were sup-ported as well by parents and friends convinced of the value of digital literacies, the growing enthusiasm of educators who saw the potential of multimedia tech-nology, the technologizing of the US workplace, the establishment of federal and state programmes for technological literacy, the increasing global invest-ment in information services, the influence and growth of globalization and transnational finances, to mention only a few influences. All of these factors and many more have contributed to a cultural ecology in which digital literacy prac-tices have been, and continue to be, valued.

But Selfe and Hawisher (2004) also learned through the study that the cul-tural ecology young people inhabit has not been at all uniform in its predisposition to digital and non-alphabetic literacies. Analyses of the inter-views revealed that conventional print literacy remains central to schooling, although this tendency is also likely to be generational. While the culture of print literacy continues to shape the expectations of parents and the historically defined literacy ideals of the larger society in which educational institutions exist and are expected to thrive, those who have been brought up almost exclu-sively with digital media have begun to develop different literacy experiences. Similar findings from other recent studies can help those of us working in com-puters and writing respond to emerging generations of students (e.g. Johnson-Eilola, 2005; Rouzie, 2005; Snyder and Beavis, 2004).

Another book-length study that takes on issues of how members of the upcom-ing generation in the US are negotiating literacy practices in digital contexts is Jonathan Alexander's *Digital Youth* (2006). In looking at how today's youth – in this case a sub-set of first-year writing students – use the Internet to write and communicate, Alexander (2006) examines the kinds of literate practices in which 'e-savvy youth' (p. 16) participate on the World Wide Web. For Alexander, this group consists of 'college youth who bring with them, often into the classroom, interest in, knowledge of, and frequently great facility with composing in Web-based venues and for Web publication' (p. 16). Instead of conducting extensive interviews, Alexander initially selected several sites, constructing rich case stud-ies, and then used a few selected interviews to support his analyses. In describing his methodology, Alexander states that each of the chapters in his book 'surveys a few sites that seem representative of the rhetorical issues of Web genres at which [he was] looking, and [that he then provides] an in-depth case study ...' (2006: 16) Like Selfe and Hawisher (2004), he does not regard his sample as representative, but he does see his ethnographic method as multi-sited and drawing upon various elements from online and offline contexts. Although Alexander also acknowledges throughout his research that the youth with whom he worked may well be the exception, they produced routinely 'electronically enabled communications' (p. 383) that featured multimedia formats and regular use of visuals, video, and sound. At the same time, however, he observed his participants bringing tradi-tional literacies to their work with digital media whenever it suited their needs Thus while Alexander (2006), along with Selfe and Hawisher (2004), identify changing literacy practices, their research also recognizes the vital role that print contexts continue to play in literate activities among the young.

RESEARCH INTO MULTIMODAL COMPOSING

Multimedia composition is the craft of inventing, shaping, producing, and delivering text, audio, video, and images purposefully. As a craft (or art), it is a set of skilled practices for integrating content that may appear in various forms – words, sound, moving and still images, even physical objects – all in the interest of communicating, entertaining, or persuading.

(David Blakesley and Karl Stolley, 2004)

In this final section on research in computers and writing, we return to multimodal composing or multimedia composition as David Blakesley and Karl Stolley (2004) refer to it in the above quotation. Although by the mid-1990s, as we have noted, networked computers and the World Wide Web exerted an increasingly strong influence on education, culture, and communication in the US, the composing of multimodal texts and their connection to literate activity and writing classes only recently has attracted widespread attention (Hawisher and Selfe, 2004; Selfe *et al.*, 2002; Shipka, 2005). Hence, fewer studies have been conducted at this point than one might expect.

As readers well know, however, the availability of communication technologies has continued to grow and the Internet has continued to change dramatically. Recognizing the importance of Web communications, for example, in the 1990s the US White House, the United Nations, and the Vatican came online; RealAudio provided computer users with access to near-real time audio; Radio HK was developed in the Hajjar/Kaufman New Media Lab and became the first commercial twenty-four-hour Internet-only radio station; and the visual browser Mosaic, followed by Netscape, changed the ways that people sought and represented information (Zakon, 2005).

Converging with the rapid pace of change on the Internet was a global educational movement that stressed the multimodal nature of twenty-first century communications. In 1996 the New London Group published a groundbreaking article in the *Harvard Educational Review* explicitly naming this approach and connecting it to literacy instruction. Variously termed 'multimedia composition' (Blakesley and Stoll, 2004), 'multiliteracies' (Cope and Kalantzis, 2000), and 'multimodal literacy' (Jewitt and Kress, 2003), its theoretical base attempts to accommodate the rapidly changing social, economic, linguistic, and technological demands of complex and globalized communication environments. This theory acknowledges that contemporary authors, faced with complex rhetorical situations, need the ability to draw on an increasingly rich set of design resources and representational modalities to make meaning and create texts – among them, still photography, video, audio, alphabetic, animation, graphical drawings, colour. The New London Group (1996) maintains that any single mode – including the alphabetic – is capable of representing only a portion of the meaning that authors might want to convey. The theory of multiliteracies draws, at least in part, on the research of Kress (1999), who continues to document the increasing importance of visual information as a semiotic channel in twenty-first century communications.

With its strong emphasis on rhetorical understanding and innovative pedagogies for literacy instruction, the work of the New London Group (1996) and Kress and van Leeuwen (1996) resonated with related research and scholarship in the arena of computers and composition. As George (2002) points out, visual modes of representation have a long history of being used in US composition courses as support for writing assignments and instruction, but they have generally been considered the handmaiden of alphabetic texts – a less sophisticated, less precise mode of conveying semiotic content than written language. As a result, George (2002) notes, the visual has been given short shrift as a composing resource that students could draw on to create their own compositions.

Supporting this convergence of interests in multimodality are the proliferation of sophisticated computers in schools and English composition programmes – machines that include not only word-processing programmes but photo manipulation packages, digital video production and editing environments, drawing and animation software, and audio editing and production capabilities. Increasingly, everyday computers provide students with access to environments within which they can draw on multiple semiotic channels to produce effective multimodal texts, if teachers of composition can avoid, in the words of Wysocki and Johnson-Eilola, being 'blinded by the letter' (1999: 349), allowing their ideological relationship with alphabetic literacy to constrain their understanding of new multimodal texts created in electronic environments.

Research on visual modalities of representation became, throughout the late 1990s and early years of the new century, a rich area of composition research. Hawisher and Sullivan (1999), for example, explored the visual representations on women's Web pages in the light of arguments by feminist Susan Bordo (1993), examining how the self of Web pages can challenge, or reinforce, stereotypical representations of gender. Hawisher and Sullivan (1999) connected their explorations to the cyborg studies of Haraway (1991) and Star (1989) and sought connections 'that might extend or refashion pre-existing categories' (Hawisher and Sullivan 1999: 273) of body images on the Web. Handa also contributed to the research in visual rhetoric, editing two special issues of *Computers and Composition* (2001) and publishing the first critical sourcebook on the subject, *Visual Rhetoric in a Digital World* (2004), both projects aimed at studying the intersection of rhetorical theory, visual representation, and digital environments for composing.

Importantly, research on multimodality and visual rhetoric in computers and composition studies connects closely to pedagogical issues through the concepts of production and agency. This approach to composition pedagogy requires writing instructors not only to incorporate new kinds of texts into their classrooms but new kinds of multimodal compositional processes that ask students to envision and create something that may not yet exist. Hocks (2003), for example, argues that student writers need not only be sophisticated readers of visual rhetoric, but also sophisticated authors of such texts: as students identify useful written, visual, and aural resources in digital environments, rearrange, manipulate, and reconfigure them, they become producers of knowledge, and not just critics of existing knowledge.

The increased attention to digital and multimodal literacy not only began to generate new research projects, but also spawned academic journals devoted to representing research in new ways using photography, visual elements, text, video, sound, animation, hypertext, and multimedia. In 1996, for example, *Kairos*, a journal focusing on rhetoric, technology, and pedagogy edited by Eyman and Inman came online with its first coverweb, that is, writings tailored exclusively to take advantage of the affordances of the Web. The new submission policy for the journal noted:

> *Kairos* publishes 'webtexts,' which means projects developed with specific attention to the World Wide Web as publishing medium. ... [W]e invite each author or collaborative writing team to think carefully about what unique opportunities the web offers. Some projects may best be presented in hypertextual form, others more linear, and in some instances multimedia and graphical architecture may be critical, while other projects may be less suited to such approaches.
>
> (*Kairos*, 1996)

Such invitations attracted a wide range of academic texts from those such as Alexander's 'Ravers on the Web: resistance, multidimensionality, and writing (about) youth culture' (2002) that used a hypertextual organization of alphabetic writing to those such as Wysocki's 'Bookling Monument' (2003) that explored visual possibilities of representation.

Other journals, too, took up the challenge of representing new forms of scholarly research. Following close on the heels of *Kairos*, for example, was *Enculturation: An Electric Journal for Cultural Studies, Rhetorics, and Theories*, edited by Hawke *et al.* which published its first online issue in 1997. And, by 2005, *Computers and Composition Online*, a companion journal to *Computers and Composition* under the editorship of Kristine Blair, featured the following policy:

> Submissions for *Computers and Composition Online* need to be Web-aware, meaning that they not only use the World Wide Web as a medium, they also take advantage of the benefits of this kind of publishing. Rhizomatic structures that disrupt traditional linear forms are welcome. Artful use of graphical interfaces and hypertext are [sic] also encouraged. Multimedia use, including digital video and audio, is also welcome.

Computers and Composition has sent out calls for papers to appear in special issues of the journal devoted exclusively to scholarship and research on multimodal composition. Thus work on multimodal literacies continues in traditional print forms even as researchers experiment in online venues. Allen (2002), for instance, edited *Working with Words and Images: New Steps in an Old Dance*, and Wysocki *et al.* (2004) authored *Writing New Media: Theory and Applications for Expanding the Teaching of Composition* – both books attempt to apply research in visual rhetoric and multimodality to the teaching of composition.

IN CONCLUSION, BUT ONLY FOR THE MOMENT ...

Although a great number of research studies have been conducted at the intersections of literacy and technology, too few have been successful in mapping a nuanced understanding of digital environments in writing classrooms and programmes onto the medial- and macro-level cartographic landscapes of global cultures. While we have learned that the new information technologies have radically altered activities related to writing and its teaching – to the extent that the definition of writing has expanded out from the alphabetic to the multimodal – more thoughtful research must be undertaken if we are to understand the relationships among technology, existing cultural formations, literacy practices and values, educational institutions, economic and material conditions, and the literate lives of instructors, writers, and students. Although it is not possible to predict the degree or magnitude of the changes that will continue to occur on the technological front, we need to make sure that the claims made for the use of digital media are intimately related to the conditions under which those of us in the twenty-first century live out our professional and personal lives.

REFERENCES

Alexander, J. (2002) 'Ravers on the Web: resistance, multidimensionality, and writing (about) youth cultures', *Kairos* 7 (3). Available online at: http://english.ttu.edu/kairos/7.3/binder2.html?cover web.html#de.

Alexander, J. (2006) *Digital Youth: Emerging Literacies on the World Wide Web*. Cresskill, NJ: Hampton Press

Allen, N. (2002) *Working with Words and Images: New Steps in an Old Dance*. Cresskill, NJ: Greenwood Press.

Bangert-Drowns, R. L. (1993) 'The word processor as an instructional tool: a meta-analysis of word processing in writing instruction', *Review of Educational Research*, 63: 69–93.

Bizzell, P. (1986) 'Composing processes: an overview', in A. Petrosky and D. Bartholomae (eds), *The Teaching of Writing*. Chicago, IL: University of Chicago Press. pp. 49–70.

Blair, K. (2005) *Submissions*. Computers and Composition Online. Retrieved 26 December 2005 from: http://www.bgsu.edu/cconline/sub.htm.

Blair, K. and Monske, E. (2004) '*Cui bono?* Revisiting the promises and perils of online learning', *Computers and Composition*, 20 (2): 441–54.

Blakesley, D. and Stolley, K. (2004) *Kairosnews*. Retrieved 2 January 2006 from: http://kairosnews.org/node/4066.

Bolter, J. D. (2001) *Writing Space: Computers, Hypertext, and the Remediation of Print*. Mahwah, NJ: Erlbaum.

Bordo, S. (1993) *Unbearable Weight: Feminism, Western Culture, and the Body*. Berkeley, CA: University of California Press.

Brandt, D. (2001) *Literacy in American Lives*. Cambridge: Cambridge University Press.

Bridwell, L. S., Sirc, G. and Brooke, R. (1985) 'Revising and computing: case studies of student writers', in S. Freedman (ed.), *The Acquisition of Written Language: Revision and Response*. Norwood, NJ: Ablex. pp. 172–94.

Bridwell-Bowles, L. S., Johnson, P. and Brehe, S. (1987) 'Composing and computers: case studies of experienced writers', in A. Matsuhashi (ed.), *Writing in Real Time: Modeling Production Processes*. Norwood, NJ: Ablex. pp. 81–107.

Burns, H. (1979) 'Stimulating Rhetorical Invention in English Composition through Computer-Assisted Instruction'. Unpublished doctoral dissertation. University of Texas. ERIC Document Reproduction Service ED 188 245.

Burns, H. (1981) 'Stimulating thinking with computer technology', *Proceedings of the Task Force on the Implications of Educational Technology*. Denver, CO: Colorado Commission on Higher Education.

Burns, H. (1984) 'Recollections of first-generation computer-assisted prewriting', in W. Wresch (ed.), *The Computer in Composition Instruction*. Urbana, IL: NCTE. pp. 34–46.

Burns, H. (2004) 'Four dimensions of significance: tradition, method, theory, and originality', *Computers and Composition*, 21 (1): 5–14.

Castells, M. (1996) *The Rise of the Network Society*. Malden, MA: Blackwell.

Castells, M. (1997) *The Power of Identity*. Malden, MA: Blackwell.

Castells, M. (1998) *End of the Millennium*. Malden, MA: Blackwell.

Cohen, M. (1986) 'In search of the Writon', in L. Gerrard (ed.), *Writing at Century's End*. New York: Random House.

Collier, R. (1983) 'The word processor and revision strategies', *College Composition and Communication*, 35: 49–55.

Computers and Composition Online. 'Submissions'. Retrieved 2 January 2006 from: http://www.bgsu.edu/cconline/sub.htm.

Connors, R. J. (1983) 'Composition studies and science', *College English*, 45: 1–20.

Cooper, M. M. (1997) 'Distinguishing critical and post-positivist research', *College Composition and Communication*, 48: 556–61.

Cooper, M. and Holtzman, M. (1983) 'Talking about protocols', *College Composition and Communication*, 34 (3): 284–93.

Cooper, M. M. and Selfe, C.L. (1990) 'Computer conferences and learning: authority, resistance, and internally persuasive discourse', *College English*, 52 (8): 847–69.

Cope, B. and Kalantzis, M. (2000) *Multiliteracies: Literacy Learning and the Design of Social Futures*. Abingdon: Routledge.

Daiute, C. (1985) 'Do writers talk to themselves?', in S. Freedman (ed.), *The Acquisition of Written Language: Revision and Response*. Norwood, NJ: Ablex. pp. 133–59.

Daiute, C. (1986) 'Physical and cognitive factors in revising: insights from studies with computers', *Research in the Teaching of English*, 20: 141–59.

Deibert, R. (1997) *Parchment, Printing, and Hypermedia: Communications in World Order Transformation*. New York: Columbia University Press.

Dubrovsky, V. J., Kiesler, S. and Sethna, B. N. (1991) 'The equalization phenomenon: status effects in computer-mediated and face-to-face decision-making groups', *Human–Computer Interaction*, 6: 119–46.

Dudley-Marling, C. and Rhodes, L. K. (1989) 'Reflecting on a close encounter with experimental research', *Canadian Journal of English Language Arts*, 12: 24–8.

Elbow, P. (1981) *Writing with Power: Techniques for Mastering the Writing Process*. New York: Oxford University Press.

Eldred, J. C. (1989) 'Computers, composition pedagogy, and social view', in G. E. Hawisher and C. Selfe (eds), *Critical Perspectives on Computers and Composition Instruction*. New York: Teachers College Press. pp. 201–18

Eldred, J. C. and Hawisher, G. E. (1995) 'Researching electronic networks', *Written Communication*, 12: 330–59.

Erickson, T. (1999) 'Persistent conversation: an introduction', *Journal of Computer-Mediated Communication*. Retrieved 3 June 2006 from: http://jcmc.indiana.edu/vol4/issue4/ericksonintro.html.

Faigley, L. (1992) *Fragments of Rationality: Postmodernity and the Subject of Composition*. Pittsburgh, PA: University of Pittsburgh Press.

Feenberg, A. (1999) *Questioning Technology*. New York: Routledge.

Feenberg, A. (2002) *Transforming Technology*. Oxford: Oxford University Press.

Flinn, J. Z. (1987) 'Case studies of revision aided by keystroke recording and replaying software', *Computers and Composition*, 5 (1): 31–44.

Flower, L. S. (1981) *Problem-Solving Strategies for Writing*. New York: Harcourt Brace.

Flower, L. S. and Hayes, J. R. (1980) 'The cognition of discovery: defining a rhetorical problem', *College Composition and Communication*, 31: 21–32.

Gee, J. P. (1996) *Social Linguistics and Literacies: Ideology in Discourses*, 2nd edn. London: Taylor and Francis.

George, D. (2002) 'From analysis to design: visual communication in the teaching of writing', *College Composition and Communication*, 54 (1): 11–39.

George, E. L. (1990) 'Taking women professors seriously: female authority in the computerized classroom', *Computers and Composition*, 7: 45–52.

Giddens, A. (1979) *Central Problems in Social Theory: Action, Structure, and Contradiction in Social Analysis*. Berkeley, CA: University of California Press.

Goldberg, A, Russell, M. and Cook, A. (2003) 'The effect of computers on student writing: a meta-analysis of studies from 1992–2002', *Journal of Technology, Learning, and Assessment*, 2 (1): 3–52.

Graff, H. J. (1987) *The Legacies of Literacy: Continuities and Contradictions in Western Culture and Society*. Bloomington, IN: Indiana University Press.

Handa, C. (ed.) (2001) 'Digital rhetoric, digital literacy, computers, and composition', *Computers and Composition*, 18 (1–2), whole issues.

Handa, C. (ed.) (2004) *Visual Rhetoric in a Digital World: A Critical Sourcebook*. New York: Bedford St. Martin's.

Haraway, D. J. (1991) *Simians, Cyborgs, and Women: The Reinvention of Nature*. New York: Routledge.

Hartman, K., Neuwirth, C., Kiesler, S., Sproull, L., Cochran, C., Palmquist, M. and Zubrow, D. (1991) 'Patterns of social interaction and learning to write: some effects of network technologies', *Written Communication*, 8 (1): 79–113.

Hawisher, G. E. (1989) 'Research and recommendations for computers and composition', in G. E. Hawisher and C. L. Selfe (eds), *Critical Perspectives on Computers and Composition Instruction*. New York: Teachers College Press. pp. 44–69.

Hawisher, G. E. and LeBlanc, P. (1992) *Re-imagining Computers and Composition*. Portsmouth, NH: Boynton/Cook.

Hawisher, G. E. and Moran, C. (1993) 'The electronic classroom and the writing instructor', *College English*, 55: 627–43.

Hawisher, G. E. and Selfe, C. L. (eds) (1991) *Evolving Perspectives on Computers and Composition Studies: Questions for the 1990s*. Urbana, IL: National Council of Teachers of English.

Hawisher, G. E. and Selfe, C. L. (eds) (2000) *Global Literacies and the World Wide Web*. Abingdon: Routledge.

Hawisher, G. E. and Selfe, C.L. (2003) 'Teaching writing at a distance? What's gender got to do with it?', in P. Takayoshi and B. Huot (eds), *Teaching Writing with Computers*. Boston, MA: Houghton Mifflin. pp. 128–49.

Hawisher, G. E. and Sullivan, P. (1998) 'Women on the networks: searching for e-spaces of their own', in S. Jarratt and L. Worsham (eds), *Feminism and Composition Studies*. New York: Modern Language Association. pp. 172–97.

Hawisher, G. E. and Sullivan, P. (1999) 'Fleeting images: women visually writing the web', in G.E. Hawisher and C.L. Selfe (eds), *Passions, Pedagogies, and 21st Century Technologies*. Logan, UT: Utah State University Press. pp. 268–91.

Hawisher, G. E., Selfe, C.L., Moraski, B. and Pearson, M. (2004) 'Becoming literate in the information age: cultural ecologies and the literacies of technology', *College Composition and Communication*, 55 (4): 642–92.

Hawk, B., Brooke, C. G. and Rickert, T. (eds) *Enculturation: Rhetoric and Composition*. Retrieved 5 June 2006 from: http://enculturation.gmu.edu/index.html.

Haythornthwaite, C. (2001) 'Exploring multiplexity: social network structures in a computer-supported distance learning class', *Information Society*, 17 (3): 211–26.

Herring, S. C. (2001) 'Computer-mediated discourse', in D. Schiffrin, D. Tannen and H. Hamilton (eds), *The Handbook of Discourse Analysis*. Oxford: Blackwell. pp. 612–34.

Herrmann, A. W. (1987) 'An ethnographic study of a high school writing class using computers: marginal, technically proficient, and productive learners', in L. Gerrard (ed.), *Writing at Century's End: Essays on Computer-Assisted Composition*. New York: Random House. pp. 79–91.

Hocks, M. E. (2003) 'Understanding visual rhetoric in digital writing environments', *College Composition and Communication*, 54 (4): 629–56.

Hocks, M. E. and Kendrick, M. R. (2003) 'Eloquent images', in M.E. Hocks and M.R. Kendrick (eds), *Eloquent Images: Word and Image in the Age of New Media*. Cambridge, MA: MIT Press. pp. 1–18.

Jewitt, C. and Kress, G. (2003) *Multimodal Literacy*. New York: Peter Lang.

Johnson-Eilola, J. (2005) *Datacloud: Toward a New Theory of Online Work*. Cresskill, NJ: Hampton Press.

Jones, S. (ed.) (1998) *Doing Internet Research: Critical Issues and Methods for Examining the Net*. Thousand Oaks, CA: Sage.

Joyce, M. (1987) *Afternoon, a Story*. Boston, MA: Eastgate.

Kairos (1996) *Guide for Prospective Authors*. Retrieved 26 December 2005 from: http://english.ttu.edu/kairos/guides/author/index.htm.

Kaplan, N. and Moulthrop, S. (1991) 'Something to imagine: literature, composition, and interactive fiction', *Computers and Composition*, 9: 7–23.

Kiesler, S. (1997) *Culture of the Internet*. Mahwah, NJ: Erlbaum.

King, B., Birnbaum, J. and Wageman, J. (1984) 'Word processing and the basic college writer', in T. Martinez (ed.), *The Written Word and the Word Processor*. Philadelphia, PA: Delaware Valley Writing Council.

Klem, E. and Moran, C. (1992) 'Teachers in a strange LANd: learning to teach in a networked writing classroom', *Computers and Composition*, 9(3): 5–22.

Kramarae, C. (2001) *The Third Shift: Women Learning Online*. Washington, DC: American Association of University Women.

Kress, G. (1999) 'English at the crossroads', in G. E. Hawisher and C. L. Selfe (eds), *Passions, Pedagogies, and 21st Century Technologies*. Logan, UT: Utah State University Press. pp. 66–88.

Kress, G. R. and van Leeuwen, T. (1996) *Reading Images:The Grammar of Visual Design*. New York: Routledge.

Mann, C. and Stewart, F. (2000) *Internet Communication and Qualitative Research: A Handbook for Searching Online*. Thousand Oaks, CA: Sage.

Moran, C. (1983) 'Word processing and the teaching of writing', *English Journal*, 72: 113–15.

Murray, D. (1980) 'Writing as process: how writing finds its own meaning', in T. R. Donovan and B. W. McClelland (eds), *Eight Approaches toTeaching Composition*. Urbana, IL: NCTE. pp. 3–20.

New London Group (1996) 'A pedagogy of mulitliteracies: designing social futures', *Harvard Educational Review*, 66 (1): 60–92.

Nichols, R. (1986) 'Word processing and basic writers', *Journal of Basic Writing*, 5: 81–97.

Norris, P. (2001) *Digital Divide: Civic Engagement, Information Poverty, and the Internet Worldwide*. New York: Cambridge University Press.

Petrosky, A. (1983) Review of *Problem-Solving Strategies for Writing* by Linda Flower, *College Composition and Communication*, 34: 233–5.

Proter, J., Sullivan, P. and Johnson-Eilola, J. (2004) *Professional Writing Online, Version 2.0*. New York: Pearson Longman.

Regan, A. (1993) '"Type normal like the rest of us": writing, power, and homophobia in the networked composition classroom', *Computers and Composition*, 10: 11–26.

Romano, S. (1993) 'The egalitarianism yardstick', *Computers and Composition*, 10 (3): 5–28.

Rouzie, A. (2005) *At Play in the Fields of Writing: A Serio-Ludic Rhetoric*. Cresskill, NJ: Hampton Press.

Selber, S., Johnson-Eilola, J. and Mehlenbacher, B. (1997) 'Online support systems, turtorials, documentation, and design', in *CRC Handbook of Computer Science and Engineering*. Boca Raton, FL: CRC Press, pp. 1619–43.

Selfe, C. L. (1985) 'The electronic pen: Computers and the composing process', in J. Collins and E. Sommers (eds), *Writing Online: Using Computers in the Teaching of Writing*. Upper Montclair, NJ: Boynton/Cook, pp. 55–66.

Selfe, C. L. (1999) *Technology and Literacy in the Twenty-first Century: The Perils of Not Paying Attention*. Carbondale, IL: Southern Illinois University Press.

Selfe, C. L. and Meyer, P. R. (1991) 'Gender and electronic conferences', *Written Communication*, 8 (2): 163–92.

Selfe, C. L. and Hawisher, G. E. (2004) *Literate Lives in the Information Age: Narratives of Literacy from the United States*. Mahwah, NJ: Erlbaum.

Selfe, C. L. and Wahlstrom, B. J. (1985) 'Fighting the computer revolution: a field report from the walking wounded', *Computers and Composition*, 2: 63–8.

Selfe, C. L., Hawisher, G. E., and Ericsson, P. (2002) 'Stasis and change: the role of independent composition programs and the dynamic nature of literacy', in P. O'Neill, A. Crow and L. Burton (eds), *Field of Dreams: Independent Writing Programs*. Logan, UT: Utah University Press. pp. 268–77.

Selfe, R. (2005) *Sustainable Computer Environments: Cultures of Support in English Studies and Language Arts*. Cresskill, NJ: Hampton Press.

Shankar, T. R. (2005) 'Speaking on the Record'. Unpublished doctoral dissertation, Massachusetts Institute of Technology, Cambridge, MA.

Shipka, J. (2005) 'A multimodal task-based framework for composing', *College Composition and Communication*, 57 (2): 277–306.

Snyder, I. and Beavis, Catherine (eds) (2004) *Doing Literacy Online: Teaching, Learning and Playing in an Electronic World*. Cresskill, NJ: Hampton.

Snyder, I. and Bulfin, S. (in press) 'Electronic reading and writing: what it means for arts education', in L. Bresler and P. Webster (eds), *International Handbook of Research in Arts Education*. Amsterdam: Kluwer.

Sommers, E. (1992) 'Political impediments to virtual reality', in G. E. Hawisher and P. LeBlanc (eds), *Re-imagining Computers and Composition: Teaching and Research in the Virtual Age*. Portsmouth, NH: Heinemann/Boynton Cook. pp. 43–57.

Spender, D. (1995) *Nattering on the Net: Women, Power and Cyberspace*. Aurora, Ontario: Garamond Press.

Spiro, R., and Jehng, J. (1990) 'Cognitive flexibility theory and hypertext: theory and technology for the nonlinear and multidimensional traversal of complex subject matter', in D. Nix and R. Spiro (eds), *Cognition, Education, and Multimedia: Exploring Ideas in High Technology*, Hillsdale, NJ: Erlbaum. pp. 163–205.

Sproull, L. and Kiesler, S. (1991) *Connections: New Ways of Working in the Networked Organization*. Cambridge, MA: MIT Press.

Star, S. L. (1989) 'The structure of ill-structured solutions: boundary objects and heterogeneous distributed problem solving', in M. Hahns and L. Gasser (eds), *Distributed Artificial Intelligence* II. Menlo Park, NY: Morgan Kauffman. pp. 37–54.

Stewart, D. C. (1992) 'Psychologists, social constructionists, and three nineteenth-century advocates of an authentic voice', *JAC* 12 (2). Available online at: http://jac.gsu.edu/jac/12.2/Articles/2.htm.

Street, B. V. (1995) *Social Literacies: Critical Approaches to Literacy in Development, Ethnography, and Education*. Harlow: Longman.

Sullivan, P. and Porter, J. E. (1997) *Opening Spaces: Writing Technologies and Critical Research Practices*. Greenwich, CT: Ablex.

Taylor, P. (1992) 'Social epistemic rhetoric and chaotic discourse', in G. E. Hawisher and P. LeBlanc (eds), *Re-imagining Computers and Composition*. Portsmouth, NH: Heinemann. pp.131–48.

Voss, R. F. (1983) 'Composition and the empirical imperative', *JAC* 4. Available online at: http://jac.gsu.edu/jac/4/Articles/1.htm.

Woodruff, E., Lindsay, P., Bryson, M. and Joram, E. (1986) 'Some Cognitive Effects of Word Processors on Enriched and Average 8th Grade Writers'. Paper presented at the annual meeting of the American Educational Research Association, San Francisco, CA.

Wresch, W. (ed.) (1984) *A Writer's Tool: The Computer in Composition Instruction*. Urbana, IL: NCTE.

Wysocki, A. (2002) 'A bookling monument', *Kairos* 7 (3). Retrieved 26 December 2005 from: http://english.ttu.edu/kairos/7.3/coverweb.html.

Wysocki, A. F. and Johnson-Eilola, J. (1999) 'Blinded by the letter: why are we using literacy as a metaphor for everything else?' in G. E. Hawisher and C. L. Selfe (eds), *Passions, Pedagogies, and 21st Century Technologies*. Logan, UT: Utah State University Press. pp. 349–68.

Wysocki, A. F., Johnson-Eilola, J., Selfe, C. L., and Sirc, G. (2004) *Writing New Media: Theory and Applications for Expanding the Teaching of Composition*. Logan, UT: Utah State University Press.

Zakon, R. H. (2005) *Hobbes' Internet Timeline*, version 8.1. Retrieved 23 December 2005 from: http://info.isoc.org/Internet/history/.

4

Digital Divide and E-learning

Caroline Haythornthwaite

E-learning presupposes access to the Internet for delivery and receipt of instruction, contact with instructors, and communication with fellow students. But such access also presupposes connection via telecommunications technologies, ownership or borrowed access to computer hardware and software, and the skills to use them all. Too often this kind of access is assumed, particularly in developed countries, with rhetoric about e-learning suggesting it is a way to provide equitable access to education. But is this so? Who can take advantage of e-learning, and who is excluded? What makes an e-learning-ready participant? And how does the digital divide play into the accessibility of e-learning? What does it mean for e-learning if we continue to assume it is accessible for all learners?

This chapter examines how the digital divide matters for e-learning. This has both a contemporary and a historical aspect. Contemporary issues involve who is online now and who is not, their access to computers and the Internet, their competence and confidence in computer use, and their current information literacy (e.g., how well they can use the Internet to find resources). Their history of use also matters. As Rice (2002) points out, delayed use is impoverished use, in keeping with 'the argument held by Castells and others that such differential timing in access to power and information – even if the later adopters catch up after several years – [the delay] is itself a significant source of social inequality and unequal participation' (Rice and Haythornthwaite, 2006: 94; see also Rice, 2002). Long-standing lack of access carries into the picture of use in higher education (Ching *et al.*, 2005). Thus the digital divide is more than just whether someone now passes the abstract line between being online or not, but includes how their experience with being online affects their contemporary skill and confidence levels. Access, use, confidence, and experience all play into the likelihood that someone will choose e-learning as an option, and as such it is important to know who is being reached when there is increased use and dependence on e-learning strategies for distributed learners as well as supplements to on-campus courses.

The following provides a review of current thinking on the digital divide with an emphasis on how it affects e-learning. The review includes statistics on who is and is not online, differences between users and non-users, bandwidth connectivity issues, and the role of computers and the Internet in schools. Throughout this chapter statistics are presented that address the current (mid-2006) state of Internet access. Undoubtedly the statistics reported here will be out of date soon. However, while the numbers change, access differences persist and remain relevant into the future. The aim of this chapter is to highlight the issue of continuing differences in access and use of computers and the Internet that will, in turn, have a continuing impact on e-learning. (For more complete treatments of the digital divide, see the original reports noted below, and DiMaggio *et al.*, 2001; Katz and Rice, 2002; Rice, 2002; Rice and Haythornthwaite, 2006; Strover, 2003; Wellman and Haythornthwaite, 2002).

FROM A DIGITAL DIVIDE TO A DIGITAL SPECTRUM

The *digital divide* refers to the division between those with and without access to computers and the Internet, and their resultant inclusion and exclusion from full participation in the Information Age.[1] Although the term likely has earlier origins, it became most popular after the publication by the US National Telecommunications and Information Administration (NTIA) of the report entitled *Falling Through the Net: Defining the Digital Divide* (NTIA, 2000). However, many researchers now feel the term *divide*, while highly useful in early analyses, fails to capture the full measure of digital inclusion and exclusion. Many question the measure of access as the primary indicator of 'electronic equity' (Patterson and Wilson, 2000: 80) since differences continue to be present across demographics in time spent online, activities engaged in online, bandwidth used, and perceived usefulness of Internet technology (CEC, 2005; Horrigan, 2005; Howard and Jones, 2003; Katz and Rice, 2002). Persistent differences in interest between users and non-users suggest that current divides are not passing phenomena, but instead represent different ways of approaching and participating for information needs (CEC, 2005; Lenhart *et al.*, 2003).

A report by the Commission of the European Communities (CEC, 2005) sees the disappearance of the digital divide as unlikely. The report identifies three patterns of Internet uptake, and describes how these are evident in traditional categories of the digital divide. The first pattern suggests the digital divide may be a *temporary issue*, with groups catching up to forerunners in the medium term. At present this looks like the case for the gender divide, and for older populations, particularly as the latter increasingly include digitally-aware age cohorts. The second pattern suggests the digital divide is an issue of *ever evolving delays*, with groups catching up in the very long term, but lagging behind with every new innovation. The CEC report finds this likely to be the case for low-income and less educated groups, and possibly the case for some countries newly entering the EU, and for rural areas and users. (The methodological model presented in Chapter 1 of this volume would be able to accommodate such a pattern.) The third pattern suggests the digital divide is a continuing issue of *delay and exclusion*, with considerable delay between social groups, and some groups never catching up. At present, this is possibly the case for low-income, less educated groups, and looks like it is the case for some countries, and for rural areas and users.

These kinds of results have led many researchers to reject the rhetoric of the divide, with its implications of a 'bipolar division between the haves and the have-nots' (Warschauer, 2003b: 297), in favour of a *spectrum of access* (see CEC, 2005; Kling, 1999; Lenhart and Horrigan, 2003; Lenhart *et al.* 2003; Livingstone and Bober, 2005; Patterson and Wilson, 2000; Pinkett, 2000; van Dijk and Hacker, 2000; Warschauer, 2002, 2003a; Wellman and Haythornthwaite, 2002). This rhetorical move also acknowledges that the divide is not a single entity to be closed by providing everyone with a computer and an Internet connection, but instead that some regions and some people will always lag behind in their access to, and ability to make use of the latest in technology as measured by use in developed countries and by advanced users (e.g., CEC, 2005; Lenhart *et al.,* 2003).

The character of digital inclusion, or *e-inclusion* (a term popular in European discussions of the digital divide[2]), as shown in access, use, skills, and competence, is a critical issue for e-learning. Where universal access and use of the latest, most recently produced, technology are assumed, there is a danger of distributing learning only to the elite, leaving behind the very people who were supposed to benefit from anywhere, anytime access to the people and resources that are part of the e-learning enterprise. It is necessary for e-learning enterprises to understand the incoming skills and persistent differences among their potential students. This may become of even greater importance as e-learning reaches across borders; providing education from one country to another also means bridging across different hardware, software, and telecommunications infrastructures, as well as general preparedness for learning online.

THE SPECTRUM OF DIGITAL ACCESS

Much of the research about differences in access and use has considered who is (and is not) online by gender, race, age, socio-economic status, and region. Tables 4.1–4.4 give a sample of such statistics about Internet use and users and will be discussed further below.

Table 4.1 Demographics of US Internet users: percentage of members of each category who are Internet users,[a] 2003, 2006

Category	US census (2003)	Pew (2006)
Adults 18+		
All US	59.5[b]	73[c]
Men	59.1	74
Women	59.8	71
Age		
15–24	47.1	
18–29		88
25–34	60.4	
30–49		84
35–44	65.3	
45–54	65.1	
50–64		71
55–64	56.6	
65+	29.4	32
Race/ethnicity		
Asian	66.7	
Black	36.0	61
Hispanic	36.0	76
White	57.0	73
Household income per year		
Less than $25,000	30.7	
Less than $30,000		53
$25,000–$30,000 to $49,999	57.3	80
$50,000 to $74,999	77.9	86
$75,000 to $99,999	85.8	
$75,000 or more		91
$100,000 or more	92.2	

Education

Less than high school	20.2	40
High school	43.1	64
Some college	62.2	84
College and beyond		91
Bachelor's degree	76.8	
Advanced degree	81.1	

Children aged 6–17 in household

No	50.2
Yes	67.0

Type of community

Rural	63
Suburban	73
Urban	75

Notes

a US census: 'use of a computer at home, school or work, and the Internet at any location'. Pew: 'use the Internet'.

b Of US population.

c Of representative sample of 4,001.

Sources

US Census Bureau. Data from the Internet Use supplement to the October 2003 Current Population Survey; civilian non-institutionalized population living in the United States; report, *Computer and Internet Use in the United States,* 2003 (retrieved 9 July 2006 from http://www.census.gov/prod/2005pubs/p23-208.pdf). *Pew Internet and American Life Project,* February–April 2006, Tracking Survey, *n* = 4,001 adults eighteen and older. (Retrieved 10 July 2006 from the Latest Trends, Who's Online, update for 26 April 2006, site at http://www.pewinternet.org/trends/User_Demo_4.26.06.htm.) *Note* This table is continuously updated with more recent figures; access the latest version via http://www.pewinternet.org/trends.asp.

Table 4.2 Internet use in the UK, April 2002 (%)

Adults

All UK	Women	Men
55	54	57

Age

16–24	25–44	45–54	55–64	65+
89	74	60	40	12

Source National Statistics Omnibus Survey, (*National Statistics,* 2002:5) retrieved 10 July 2006 from http://www.statistics.gov.uk/pdfdir/intacc0702.pdf. Crown copyright material is reproduced with the permission of the Comptroller of the Stationery Office.

Table 4.3 Internet use by world regions (%)

Region	Latest data (% of population)	Growth 2000–05
Africa	2.6	423.9
Asia	9.9	218.7
South Korea	67.0	78.0
Japan	67.2	83.3
China	8.5	393.3
Europe	36.1	177.5
EU	49.8	147.3
EU candidate countries	17.3	450.7
Rest of Europe	18.0	397.5
Middle East	9.6	454.2
North America	68.6	110.3
US	68.6	115.3
Canada	67.9	72.4
Latin America/Caribbean	14.4	342.5
Oceania/Australia	52.6	134.6
Australia	68.4	115.0
World total	15.7	183.4

Source Internet World Statistics, which aggregates data from a number of surveys; statistics updated on 31 March 2006. Retrieved 10 July 2006 from http://www.Internetworldstats.com/stats4.htm.

Table 4.4 Percentage of US households with a computer and Internet access 1984–2003

	1984	1989	1993	1997	1998	2000	2001	2003
Computer	8.2	15.0	22.8	36.6	42.1	51.0	56.3	61.8
Internet access	–	–	–	18.0	26.2	41.5	50.4	54.7

Source US Census Bureau. Numbers taken from Figure 1 on p. 1 of US Census Bureau (October 2005), 'Computers and Internet use in the United States', 2003, retrieved 9 July 2006 from http://www.census.gov/prod/2005pubs/p23-208.pdf.

Many sources of statistics exist and this review cannot be comprehensive. Discussion highlights only some reports, largely from the US, but also from the UK and Europe. Sources that can be consulted for more details include reports from government and foundation studies. Some commercial sites exist that aggregate data from multiple sources, providing easy cross-country comparison, although sampling frames may differ across countries (e.g., Internet World

Statistics, http://www.internetworldstats.com). In the US, the Bureau of the Census gathers information on computers and Internet use from a representative sample of the US population (http://www.census.gov/population/www/socdemo/computer.html); the National Telecommunications and Information Administration (NTIA) issues regular reports (http://www. ntia.doc.gov); and the Pew Internet and American Life projects conduct frequent surveys on many aspects of Internet use, although on a smaller scale than the census data (http://www.pewInternet.org/; Howard and Jones, 2003). In the UK, National Statistics releases reports regularly and has reports on Internet Use and connectivity (http://www.statistics.gov.uk/). In the EU, the European Commission and Eurostat, the statistical office of the European Commission, carry out surveys and issue reports, including ones related to Internet use (CEC, 2005; Demunter, 2005), and e-learning (http://www.e-learningeuropa.info/).

A number of researchers also conduct important survey studies that address Internet use. Some examples are: the Digital Living project for Europe and the UK (Anderson and Tracy, 2002); Livingstone and Bober's (2005) study of UK children's Internet use; Robinson, Neustadtl and Kestnbaum's Web Use project in the US (http://webuse.umd.edu/; Neustadtl *et al.*, 2002; Robinson *et al.*, 2003); Nie and Erbring's US studies at the Stanford Institute for the Quantitative Study of Society (http://www.stanford.edu/group/siqss/home/home.htm; Nie and Erbring, 2000; Nie, 2001; Nie *et al.*, 2002); Katz, Rice and Aspden's Syntopia project (Katz and Rice, 2002); and Cole and colleagues' Digital Future projects, and World Internet Report (http://www.digitalcenter.org/; Cole *et al.,* 2000). See also the Internet studies reported in Wellman and Haythornthwaite (2002).

DIFFERENCES IN ACCESS AND USE

Results from the earliest of studies of computers and Internet use revealed a population of young, white, affluent males, living in developed countries. It was these findings that promoted concerns about the digital divide. In education settings there was concern that students without access to computers would fail to gain the skills needed for future work and higher education. As the site for equitable access, schools carried the responsibility of making sure such skills were acquired. Thus, in the 1980s, schools grappled with how to afford computers and train teachers to include their use in the curriculum. Computer labs became an important addition to schools, and computer skills became an important new area of the curriculum from junior to senior grade levels.

With the advent of the Internet in the 1990s, connection to the Web becomes important, as do skills in searching the Web. In all such additions, schools with students on the affluent side of the digital divide have been ahead of others. For example, in the US in 1998, the ratio of students to Internet-connected computers in schools was 16.8 students per computer in schools with the poorest students (75 per cent or more students eligible for free or reduced school lunch), but 10.6 in schools with the lowest concentration of poor students (35 per cent or less eligible for the lunch programme; Parsad and Jones, 2005). These numbers have improved dramatically since 1998 due to concerted efforts by government and school initiatives; in 2003 the ratio was 5.1 students per computer for the highest poverty category and 4.2 for the lowest. However, across the years, note that those with more students in the poorest category have always lagged behind others (see Table 4.5). This also holds in relation to the percent of minority students in schools, a measure that is related to poverty. In 1998, the ratio of students per computer for schools with 50 per cent or more minority students was 17.2 versus 10.1 for schools with less than 6 per cent minority students; in 2003 the ratios were 5.1 and 4.1. Thus, while there is overall improvement in access for schools, there has been greater and faster improvement in schools with more affluent students. Different growth rates lead to the 'ever evolving delays' noted by the CEC report.

Table 4.5 Ratio of students to computers in US schools, by poverty level, 1998–2003

Poverty level (%)[a] 1998	1999	2000	2001	2002	2003
<35	10.6	7.6	6.0	4.9	4.6	4.2
35–49	10.9	9.0	6.3	5.2	4.5	4.4
50–74	15.8	10.0	7.2	5.6	4.7	4.4
75 +	16.8	16.8	9.1	6.8	5.5	5.1
All	12.1	9.1	6.6	5.4	4.8	4.4

Notes [a] Percentage of students eligible for free or reduced-price lunch. Poverty level is based on percent of students in the school eligible for free or reduced-price lunch because of low household income.
Source US Department of Education, National Center for Education Statistics report (Parsad and Jones, 2005).

This trend of inclusion and exclusion continues with e-learning. In the US, well funded school districts have been able to offer online courses. These offerings allow students to gain early access to university courses, and acquire what is known as 'advanced placement' (AP) credits that let them take higher-level courses once at university. A 2001 report found that over 60 per cent of virtual high schools reported funding as a barrier to success (e.g., start-up funding for staff and technology; course creation costs), with other barriers being outdated technology infrastructure, finding qualified staff, coalition building, and public relations.

Thus, even with school access, students coming into higher education, and into e-learning, from affluent homes and school districts, and most likely from urban rather than rural settings, will have more years of experience online, which will in turn make them more confident with the technology. This may in turn make them more confident to take on AP courses online, once again allowing them to take advantage of this elite offering. It is ironic that these particular virtual courses are being offered online as a means of creating equitable access to these AP courses. (Small schools, and schools with few takers, cannot offer the courses.) Although such provision may include more remote users, it will be interesting to see exactly who, in terms of demographics, is actually being reached by these courses.

Access versus use

Heading into the 2000s, many felt the digital divide might be overcome. Evidence shows gaps across age, race, and socio-economic status diminishing, and the gender gap all but disappeared. However, as the numbers in Tables 4.1–4.4 show, these gaps have not completely closed. In the US, young, urban and suburban, Asian and white users, with higher education and household income levels, are much more likely to be online than blacks and Hispanics, rural residents, and those with a lower education attainment and income level. Across the globe, differences are great, making some countries information-rich and others information-poor.

Moreover, while gaps in the gross measure of 'access' appeared to be closing, new studies began to show that what people were doing once they had access was quite different across groups, and in particular by men versus women. Time online mirrored the earlier differences across the divide. Howard *et al.* (2002), for example, found that on any given day, among those with access, more of the men, whites, higher income earners, more educated and more experienced users were likely to be online. Among UK children, Livingstone and Bober (2005) found boys spend more time online than girls, have been online longer, have more online skills, and higher levels of self-efficacy; Hargittai and Shafer (2006) found that women judge their online skills lower than do men, which may affect what they choose to do online.

Online activities differ by gender, race, income, occupation, and experience online. Men use the Internet more than women for news, product, financial, sports, and hobby information, online trading, banking, and gaming (Howard *et al.* 2002; Cole *et al.* 2000; NTIA, 2002). Women and older users go online more for health information (NTIA, 2002), and women lead men in the proportion who say they use e-mail for relationship building and connecting with family (Boneva and Kraut, 2002; Haythornthwaite and Kazmer, 2002; Rainie *et al.*, 2000). Whites, those with higher income levels, and users below 55 years of age are online longer each day, and engage in more activities online, particularly spending more time on information than entertainment activities (Lenhart *et al.* 2003; NTIA, 2002).

DIFFERENCES BY LIFE STAGE

Age, or perhaps more appropriately, life stage (Anderson and Tracey, 2002), greatly influences online activity, in part due to requirements for school and work as well as the access these provide. Having a child in the household is a major reason for acquiring a computer and access to the Internet (Cole *et al.* 2000; Demunter, 2005; NSBF, 2000; Statistics Canada, 2000). In 1999, Statistics Canada (2000) found that 59 per cent of Canadian single-family households with unmarried children under 18 were connected to the Internet in 1999, compared to 39 per cent for other single-family households; and a US National School Board Federation study (NSBF, 2000) found 36 per cent of parents report children's education as a primary reason for computer purchase (27 per cent buy it for business reasons), and 39 per cent as the reason for Internet access at home.

School drives use by children and young adults, with differences present by income and race. The major online activities of this age group are school work, e-mail, playing games, listening to radio/watching movies, and use of chat rooms. Younger users in high-income households use the Internet in much higher proportions than those in low-income households: 87.5 per cent of US children (10–17 years) in the highest income level use the Internet, 82.5 per cent at home, while in the lowest income level 45.7 per cent use the Internet, with only 21.4 per cent using it at home. Being at school promotes use by 18–24 year olds: 85 per cent of those in school or college use the Internet, compared to 51.5 per cent of those not in school (NTIA, 2002; see also Livingstone and Bober, 2005). Race plays out in school access. The US National School Board Foundation (NSBF, 2000) found that low-income and African-American children were overwhelmingly more likely to use the Internet from school than home (46 per cent versus 86 per cent of use from home for households with incomes less than $40,000 versus over $75,000; 73 per cent versus 35 per cent of use from home for white versus African-American children; see Table 4.6).

Table 4.6 School and home use of the Internet (%)

% of use	Income (US$)			Race	
	<40,000 (US)	*40,000-74,999*	*75,000+*	*White*	*African-American*
School or pre-school	68	48	57	56	71
Home	46	78	86	73	35

Note Percentage of use at school and at home by income, and by race, according to responses from parents of children age two to seventeen.
Source National Center for Education Statistics, 2000

Livingstone and Bober (2005) point to schools as an important location for increasing all students' knowledge about computing and the Internet and raising their information literacy skills. However, they found children lacking in formal instruction about the Internet and in critical skills for evaluating Internet content. Combining concerns about computer and information literacy with the findings about access by income and race suggests an even greater need for such school-based learning as a means to address digital divide issues. Again, the issue for e-learning is the differential preparedness and confidence in computer and Internet use that will determine who is likely to look to e-learning as an option, and be ready to participate in it once enrolled.

Although Livingstone and Bober note that the issue is now one of 'quality of use (as assessed by time use, skills and range of online activities)' rather than of technology access (p. 12). Household lack of means or interest can bring the site of access into play in forging quality of use. School access serves an important role in children's confidence with use, as well as use in the household.

Livingstone and Bober (2005) report from their UK study of children's use of the Internet that:

> Children usually consider themselves more expert than their parents, gaining in social status within the family as a result. Among daily or weekly Internet users, 19 per cent of parents describe themselves as beginners compared with only 7 per cent of children, and only 16 per cent of parents consider themselves advanced compared with 32 per cent of children.

(p.14)

These children are also an important conduit for computer skills to enter the home. This can increase use among members of the household, either because the skills are entering the house, or because skills need to be acquired to help children learn. For example, the UCLA Center for Communication Policy study (Cole *et al.* 2000) found women's access to the Internet, but not men's, is markedly higher when there are children in the household (70 per cent versus 57 per cent) suggesting a learning/computing relationship between women and children.

In a similar way, work affects access and activities for those who are employed, and also for those at home. Computer use at work significantly enhances the likelihood of computer use at home and thus in the household for children and other household members (Lenhart *et al.* 2003; NTIA, 2002). The type of job determines how much computer and Internet use is part of daily activity (see Table 4.7), contributing to experience with and access to computers for e-learning, access to others who know how to use computers, and access for those at home to someone who knows how to use computers and the Internet. An NTIA (2002) report states that in 2001, 77 per cent of households in which someone used a computer or the Internet at work owned a computer or used the Internet from home, compared to 35 per cent for other households; this holds across other demographic factors (income, education, race, age of adults). As the NTIA report states for the US:

> Approximately 24 million of the 65 million employed adults who use a computer at work also do work on a computer at home. This underscores a critical connection between the workplace and home: exposure to a computer and the Internet in the workplace makes it substantially more likely for a computer and the Internet to be used at home.
>
> Undoubtedly, there are cases where enthusiastic home users introduce computers and the Internet to a workplace. [M]ore likely, however, use at work lends to use at home. Use at work not only acquaints someone with the utility of the technology, it also provides an opportunity to climb a sometimes frustrating learning curve in an environment with technical support. This acquired knowledge can then be taken home and shared with other members of a household.

(NTIA, 2002: 62–3)

Table 4.7 Internet use, by occupation

US Census		NTIA	
Management, business, and financial	71.1	Managerial and professional specialty	20.4
Professional	64.6	Technical, sales, and administrative support	21.5
Service	16.5	Precision production, craft, and repair	8.2
Sales	44.6	Farming, forestry, and fishing	10.0
Office and administrative support	52.0	Service	6.2
Farming, fishing, and forestry	6.2	Operators, fabricators, and labourers	3.6
Construction and extraction	12.5		
Installation, maintenance, and repair	25.8		
Production	16.3		
Transportation and material moving	11.4		

Sources US census: use of the Internet at work, as percentage of those employed in the job, eighteen years and older (data from 2001 survey); http://www.census.gov/population/www/socdemo/computer/2003.hmtl. NTIA: Internet/e-mail use at work by occupation, as a percentage of employed persons age twenty-five and over, 2001, from NTIA (2002: 62).

DIFFERENCES BY EXPERIENCE

Computers at home, school, or work combine to determine when individuals come online and how long they remain online. Research shows a difference in facility and range of use with somewhere between two and four years of experience. Experienced users spend considerably more time online (Cole *et al.*, 2000; Nie, 2001; Nie and Erbring, 2000), engage in more kinds of activities online (Howard *et al.*, 2002), and have higher confidence levels in their own skills (Eastin and LaRose, 2000; LaRose *et al.* 2001; Livingstone and Bober, 2005). Through use at work and more years online, these *Netizens*, as Howard *et al.*, (2002) call them, have acquired fluency with online life that too often is assumed for all users. They incorporate the Internet into all aspects of their lives, with greater comfort spending and managing their money online, and communicating online to support social relationships. They make less of a separation between being online and not being online, easily 'toggling' between on-and offline life (Fallows, 2005). However, not all users are so fluent. Howard *et al.* also find that, along with the approximately 16 per cent of adult Internet users who are Netizens (as of 2000), there are: *Utilitarians* (28 per cent) who approach the Internet as a tool; *Experimenters* (26 per cent), people who are moving beyond fun activities to information-related activities; and *Newcomers* (30 per cent) who have arrived online recently, using it primarily for entertainment activities, and generally from one place (e.g., work or home).

These data suggest that those most likely to choose e-learning, and most able to integrate it seamlessly into their daily life, will be those Netizens who easily toggle between on- and offline life. These, in turn, are most likely to be drawn from those who have had long-standing access to the Internet, with at least two years of working, communicating, searching and retrieving information, and conducting many kinds of activities online. Others who look like they might choose e-learning are the Utilitarians and the Experimenters. The former may not take to the Internet as a way of life, but can expect to use it as needed, and we might speculate that their style will be one that resists learning multiple new ways of getting that work done. Again, we might expect experimenters, by contrast, to be quite willing to play with new technologies. In an online class, each of these groups is likely to react differently, requiring different kinds of support. Newcomers have further to go in becoming fluent. Where they retain the interest in entertainment, they are far less likely to turn up in e-learning classes because they have yet to adopt the Internet as a tool for work and education. We do not have data on where in the online adoption sequence an individual might fit e-learning. This will be an interesting area for research, with implications for different kinds of support activities.

Regional differences

Even with means, skills, and sufficient engagement with online activity to consider e-learning, individuals may be prohibited from doing so by lack of a usable telecommunications infrastructure. Disparities across geography carry with them variation in local infrastructural support such as electricity, broadband, and wireless capabilities, typically privileging urban over rural users, and developed over developing countries (CEC, 2005; Davidson *et al.*, 2002; Nicholas, 2003; Warschauer, 2003b). It is often taken for granted that access via broadband or other high-speed connection is available, and thus applications can be written that require such transfer. For example, a study in the US by National Center for Academic Transformation (NCAT, 2005) examining the use of technologies for education of underserved students (in higher education) found that awareness of bandwidth for students was the second most important issue after access. For example, a quiz feature at one university did not work for dial-up users; and another university had to make a special endeavour to optimize 400 graphic, audio, and video files used in a particular course. However, the effort proved worthwhile. Results from the fifteen institutions examined showed the added online components to the courses (three fully online programmes, twelve blended with off- and online components) greatly helped the underserved students. Extra access to help for review of materials, and the added flexibility, helped working adult learners because of choices about when and where they could learn.

While geographical constraints are often cited as the reason broadband is not widely used, other factors such as Internet use and government policy play a large role. (See Wilhelm, 2003 for a discussion of US policy; for a discussion of

EU issues re broadband, see Europa, 2006.) Use of broadband is another indicator of the divide between users: broadband adopters are much more intense users than those continuing to use dial-up systems. A 2005 Pew survey (Horrigan, 2005) found that the 53 per cent of Americans who go online from home using broadband (33 per cent of the American adult population) engaged in 2.8 activities per day compared to 1.7 per day for dial-up users (indicating broadband users are 65 per cent more active than dial-up users); similarly, the 54 per cent of Canadians who use broadband are more intense users, spending 55 per cent more time online than dial-up users, and viewing twice as many Web pages (comScore Media Metrix survey 2003, cited by Nua, 2003)[3]. Those not using broadband show a disinclination toward adopting this technology. While intense US Internet users are adopting broadband and want broadband when they don't have it, 58 per cent of dial-up users report they do not want broadband (February 2004 data, Horrigan, 2005). This puts into question their ability to access e-learning and Internet content engineered to be broadcast and received via high-speed access, and assumed to be easily accessible to online users as a general category. The EU in particular is concerned about expanding broadband access, particularly outside urban areas, citing reports that indicate economic advantage to areas with such access (Europa, 2006). Figures for the EU for January 2006 show broadband reaches approximately 60 million subscribers, and 25 per cent of households.

Disabilities

Users with disabilities are proportionally underrepresented among those using the Internet and with computers in the household. In 2002, a Pew study found 38 per cent of Americans with disabilities were online compared to 58 per cent of all Americans (Lenhart *et al.*, 2003), and in 2003, 40 per cent lived in households with computers versus 63 per cent of Americans with no disability (US Census data, reported in Dobransky and Hargittai, 2006). Of the non-users, 28 per cent reported their disability made it 'difficult or impossible for them to go online' (Lenhart *et al.* 2003). Disabilities also affect children's use of the Internet. Livingstone and Bober (2005) found children and young adults with disabilities to be more highly represented among those using the Internet occasionally or not at all (14 per cent of this category included individuals with disabilities) compared to those using the Internet monthly or weekly (9 per cent disabled). These statistics are worrying for e-learning as, again, they show who is likely to be excluded from online education.

ACKNOWLEDGING NON-USE

In general, the digital divide has been considered a gap that will close with the right attention to providing computers, training, and connectivity. However, studies now suggest the rapid growth phase of computer ownership and Internet use has plateaued, and that there will remain a proportion of the population uninterested in Internet use. Research by Katz, Rice and Aspden that has explored differences in users and non-users finds no difference in demographics between who is and is not an Internet user, once the analysis had controlled for awareness of the Internet. However, that does not mean there are no differences. Attitudes differ considerably between users, potential users, and an emerging set of continuing non-users who have no interest, inclination, or support for Internet use.

A 2002 Pew study (Lenhart *et al.* 2003) examining who was not using the Internet and reasons for non-use found more nuance in use and non-use than suggested by an on/off-line dichotomy. Non-users were found to fit several categories: *Net Evaders* (20 per cent of non-users), *Net Dropouts* (17 per cent), and *Truly Unconnected* (69 per cent of non-users; 24 per cent of the US adult population). Net Evaders do not use the Internet. Although they may have access through others living in the household, they themselves do not go online, with some who 'proudly avoid the Internet on principled grounds' (p. 19).

Net Dropouts and their counterpart among users, *Intermittent Users* (estimated as 24–44 per cent of current users), represent turnover in Internet access. Net Dropouts were once online but have stopped; Intermittent Users dropped out but are back on. As noted in Rice and Haythornthwaite (2006):

> Often forgotten in considerations of connectivity are issues of dropouts. The UCLA (2000) study ... notes that in mid 2000, 10.3 per cent of non-users are actually Internet dropouts (formerly used the Internet at least once a month, but no longer); ... Katz and Rice (2002a) report that this 10 per cent figure is fairly consistent in surveys they conducted in 1995, 1996, 1997 and 2000. So, full connection rates should not be treated as a line that, once crossed, no longer needs to be addressed, but instead as a mark to constantly work towards.
>
> (Rice and Haythornthwaite, 2006: 94)

These partial users suffer from being behind in access to resources online, as well as gaining experience more slowly and more sporadically. This may make it even harder to acquire skills, as the types of hardware, software, and telecommunications connection may be constantly changing, preventing users from getting past the beginning of the learning curve.

Beyond those with intermittent or second-hand access to the Internet are the 24 per cent of US adult users who are *Truly Unconnected*. These individuals have no direct or indirect experience with the Internet, have never used the Internet, do not live with Internet users, and do not know many users. They do not see benefit in using the Internet, and have a more negative appraisal of the Internet than others:

> As a group, the Truly Unconnected have low incomes – 43 per cent live in households that earn under $30,000 yearly, and 29 per cent earn under $20,000. They also tend to be even older than other non-users, with 62 per cent over the age of 50. Seventy-four per cent have a high school education or less. Three-quarters are white, 15 per cent black, and 9 per cent are Hispanic.
>
> (Lenhart *et al.*, 2003)

Other studies describe a similar profile of non-users. A report on the expansion of Internet use in the EU by the Commission of the European Communities (CEC, 2005) finds 'Internet penetration among housepersons, especially women, older citizens, retired people and in rural areas is clearly lagging behind' (p. 8). And a study by the Consumer Federation of America (Cooper, 2000, cited in Rice and Haythornthwaite, 2006) comparing life style attributes across fully connected, partially connected, and disconnected users, found the disconnected were both 'disadvantaged and disenfranchised':

> The disconnected earn less than half the income of the fully connected ($25,500 versus $45,200), are much less likely to have a college degree (13 versus 46 per cent), and are more likely to be black (12 versus 7 per cent), older (53 versus 44 years) and have smaller house-holds (2.1 versus 2.8)

> (Rice and Haythornthwaite, 2006: 94).

Regional differences also go hand in hand with advantage and disadvantage. In its hopes for e-Inclusion, the CEC is most pessimistic about regional differences, including countries newly entering the EU, and rural–urban differences within countries. It concludes that, 'In general terms, it appears that those regions that are already more advanced are also better positioned to gain any additional advantage associated with the advent of the Information Society. More backward regions are slower in taking up ICTs, perpetuating their relative disadvantage' (CEC, 2005: 22). This commission's report, and indeed much of what has been reviewed above, concurs with conclusions drawn by Nie (2001) that connectivity goes to the already connected: the rich get richer, and, in the Internet Age, the elite get access to elite resources. The same may be true of e-learning.

IMPLICATIONS FOR E-LEARNING

These data set the scene for who can be reached with e-learning, and who is most likely to look to e-learning for their educational needs Where e-learning is billed as a means to provide education anywhere, anytime, it does not mean everyone. E-Learning – in its distributed, 'owner-operated' form (i.e., the learner is respon-sible for the equipment) – is yet another means for the elite to reap further benefit from being part of the elite (in this case in the form of education). As Demunter (2005) reports for the EU, 'Younger and highly educated persons and households in economically more prosperous regions are thus far consolidating their leading position in the information society' (p. 6). E-learning is poised to be another notch in their belt. The gap in Internet use between advantaged and disadvan-taged groups is not closing; Demunter's report actually shows the gap widening because, while more of each group are coming online, the rate of growth is slower for disadvantaged than for advantaged users. Another study also finds this kind of difference. According to van Dijk and Hacker (2000), data for the US and the Netherlands show increasing *relative differences* across demographics. Those in households with higher incomes, a head of household with a higher education, lower age of head of household, and of white ethnicity (US data only) show greater possession of computers, with the gap widening in percentage terms from 1984 to the late 1990s (1998 or 2000, depending on the studies available).

Moreover, the forms of e-learning being established now are being driven and operated by elite use and users, i.e., those with access to high-speed Internet, high-end computers, new software, and mobile access, living in regions where such services are available and affordable. It is not that high-end applications should not be developed; indeed, learning and using the latest technology are part of the benefit of e-learning (Haythornthwaite *et al.*, 2000). E-Learning should not give in to a high-technology and low-technology streaming as might be the unwitting result of choices made in some institutions. For example, a survey of US institutions that offer career and technical education (CTE; Johnson *et al.*, 2004) found that in 2000–01, 73 per cent offered CTE courses online, and that they rely on low-bandwidth technologies for course delivery (course management systems, e-mail, text chat, and asynchronous discussion). The authors speculate that one reason low bandwidth is used is to accommodate the range of end users:

> High-bandwidth technologies demand a fast connection speed for the end user as well as a computer that has a fast processor and lots of memory and file storage space. Incorporating high-bandwidth technologies into CTE courses may prevent students from participating because they do not have access to the computers or Internet connections needed to support these more advanced technologies. Since the colleges are using distance learning to attract nontraditional students, their decision to design their distance learning courses around the lowest common denominator is probably an appropriate choice.

However, as they also note,

> What is lacking in these technologies is the ability to incorporate multimedia and real-time exchange of information among individuals or groups within a course.

> (Johnson *et al.*, 2004: online)

Thus, accommodating the low-end users may work against some of the key benefits of e-learning, i.e., interactivity with peers, real-time exchanges, as well as training in the more technically sophisticated areas.

Nonetheless, it is important to maintain awareness of the implications of who can participate, and who is likely to be ready to participate, and balance this with technology choices and support. Every upgrade in equipment and telecommunications requirements, every change in technology, is an added barrier to economically disadvantaged e-learners. Those online longer are not only more able to afford new equipment, but also have greater confidence in their ability to learn to use it. They are more experienced with many kinds of online activity and particularly information-related activities. Who, then, do we really expect to choose and manage well with e-learning? Should our e-learning expectations assume this kind of incoming student or should it be planned for a less experienced, newer user? And, more so, should it be planned for a user who cannot afford and/or cannot get access to the latest hardware and telecommunication connection?

For many, access is achieved through schools and work. For example, in the EU, 85 per cent of students use the Internet versus 47 per cent of the whole population; 60 per cent of those employed versus 40 per cent of unemployed, and 13 per cent of retired persons (Demunter, 2005). Thus, when they leave school or work, they are also leaving their Internet Service Provider (ISP), and often their computers. Continuing education via the Internet then becomes a challenge for those without means.

Even with means and skills, individuals can be disadvantaged by the lack of availability of high-speed Internet access in their region. Distance, geographical features, and low population density weigh against creating and marketing broadband service to remote areas. Lack of infrastructure weighs against e-learning reaching people in these areas and in countries that lack affordable ISPs even in more reachable areas. Even in developed countries, high-speed home access costs money. Added to phone, cell phone, television cable costs or licences, broadband is another cost to carry. Again, this may seem light to an affluent user, but low-income earners choose between food and phone bills (Schement, 1996).[4] How will ISP and broadband costs fare in this hierarchy? How will the necessary upgrading of computers be achieved, as new hardware and software are needed to be compatible with contemporary technologies and e-learning strategies?

Although the focus in this book is on e-learning in higher education, informal learning is often wrapped into the general notion of e-learning. Where the Internet is used as a means to promote general learning, receipt of information disseminated in this way is seriously constrained by the ability of individuals and households to receive that information. For example, retired persons, 65+, are online far less than other groups. Where government and health information transfers to online delivery, EU figures show at present such information can be expected to reach directly only 11 per cent of those 65–74 years of age, 27 per cent of those 55–64, and 43 per cent of those 45–54. Although many will access this information through those in their close social network (see Boase *et al.* 2004; Lenhart *et al.*, 2003), individuals whose family, friends and acquaintances are also non-users will be isolated from information disseminated via the Internet. (See also Hagar and Haythornthwaite, 2005, who discuss how the UK government disseminated information about the 2001 foot-and-mouth disease crisis via the Internet when only 25 per cent of the area farmers had access to a computer and travel restrictions prevented access to public computing sites.)

In general, it is assumed that e-learning is an optional form of education, and hence that there is an alternative which does not require expensive equipment and infrastructure. However, place-based higher education now often includes and expects online connectivity. Universities and colleges act as service providers for the Internet, and make computers available across campus, but (barring some experiments) not personal computers for home and/or mobile use. Individuals are left to bear the cost of such devices (albeit with student discounts common), and telecommunication costs to connect to campus. Again, the digital divide statistics suggest that it will be the affluent, young users who have the means and skills to acquire such devices, and then have more continuous access to the Internet. Older, returning students and those from low-income households may lack these means and skills, disadvantaging them now even within the on-campus context.

SUMMARY

The digital divide statistics show us that income, education, occupation, age, race (in the US), association with schools, life stage, region, and ability/disability make a significant difference in who is online, and hence who is likely to look at e-learning as a viable means of pursuing a higher education degree or continuing education. It also suggests where success in e-learning will be most easily achieved – in postgraduate education, and among those at work or schooled in computer-using environments. The challenge will be extending the reach of e-learning to programmes for those most distanced from computing. The digital divide statistics suggest this challenge means reaching low-income, low-education, middle-aged and older users, those in non-computer-using industries, the unemployed, and those living in rural and other disadvantaged areas.

NOTES

1 The focus on Internet access followed on many years of looking at adoption of computing, notably measured by home ownership of computers. For example, the US Census Bureau began asking about computer ownership and use in 1984, with questions about Internet use beginning in 1997 (see Kominski and Newburger, 1999).
2 For example, see the European Commission's site on e-inclusion at http://europa.eu.int/information _society/eeurope/2005/all_about/einclusion/index_en.htm.
3 Broadband use is comparable in the UK, but research could not be found that explored the association with online activity as for the US and Canada. Statistics from March 2006 show 69.2 per cent of Internet subscriptions are broadband, and 30.8 per cent are dial-up. This is a major reversal of figures for March 2003, when only 15.3 per cent of subscriptions were for broadband, and 84.7 per cent for dial-up (National Statistics, 2006).
4 For more on cell phone ownership and use, see Rainie (April 2006), and Ling (2004).

REFERENCES

Anderson, B. and Tracey, K. (2002) 'Digital living: the impact (or otherwise) of the Internet in everyday British life', in B. Wellman and C. Haythornthwaite (eds), *The Internet In Everyday Life*. Oxford: Blackwell, pp. 139–63.

Boase, J., Horrigan, J. B., Wellman, B. and Rainie, L. (2006) *The Strength of Internet Ties: Pew Internet and American Life Project*. Retrieved 28 May 2006 from: www.pewInternet.org/pdfs/PIP_Internet _ties.pdf.

Boneva, B. and Robert K. (2002) 'E-mail, gender and personal relationships', in B. Wellman and C. Haythornthwaite (eds), *The Internet In Everyday Life*. Oxford: Blackwell, pp. 372–403.

Ching, C. C., Basham, J. D. and Jang, E. (2005) 'The legacy of the digital divide: gender, socioeconomic status, and early exposure as predictors of full-spectrum technology use among young adults', *Urban Education*, 40: 394–411.

CEC (Commission of the European Communities) (2005) *eInclusion Revisited: The Local Dimension of the Information Society*. Retrieved December 2005 from: http://europa.eu.int/comm/employment_ social/news/2005/feb/eincllocal_en.pdf.

Cole, M., Suman, M., Schramm, P., van Bel, D., Lunn, B., Maguie, P., Hanson, K., Singh, R. and Aquino, J-S. (2000) *The UCLA Internet Report: Surveying the Digital Future*. UCLA Center for Communication Policy. Retrieved 18 July, 2006 from: http://www.digitalcenter.org/pdf/InternetReportYearOne.pdf.

Cooper, M. (2000) *Disconnected, Disadvantaged, and Disenfranchised: Explorations in the Digital Divide*. New York: Consumer Federation of America.

Davidson, T., Sooryamoorthy, R. and Shrum, W. (2002) 'Kerala connections: will the Internet affect science in developing areas?', in B. Wellman and C. Haythornthwaite (eds), *The Internet in Everyday Life*. Oxford: Blackwell. pp. 496–519.

Demunter, C. (2005) 'The digital divide in Europe', *Statistics in Focus*, 38. Eurostat, European Communities. Retrieved 17 July 2006 from: http://epp.eurostat.ec.europa.eu/cache/ITY_OFFPUB/KS-NP-05-038/EN/KS-NP-05-038-EN.PDF.

DiMaggio, P., Hargittai, E., Neuman, W. R. and Robinson, J. P. (2001) 'Social implications of the Internet', *Annual Review of Sociology*, 27: 307–36.

Dobransky, K. and Hargittai, E. (2006) 'The disability divide in Internet access and use', *Information, Communication and Society*, 9 (3): 313–34.

Eastin, M. S. and LaRose, R. (2000) 'Internet self-efficacy and the psychology of the digital divide', *Journal of Computer-Mediated Communication*, 6 (1). Available online at: http://jcmc. indiana.edu/vol6/issue1/eastin.html.

Europa (2006) *The Commission's 'Broadband for all' Policy to Foster Growth and Jobs in Europe: Frequently Asked Questions*. Retrieved 17 July 2006 from: http://europa.eu.int/rapid/pressReleases Action.do?reference=MEMO/06/132.

Fallows, D. (2005) *How Women and Men use the Internet*. Retrieved 29 December 2005 from http://www.pewInternet.org/pdfs/PIP_Women_and_Men_online.pdf.

Hagar, C. and Haythornthwaite, C. (2005) 'Crisis, farming and community', *Journal of Community Informatics*, 1 (3). Available online at: http://ci-journal.net/viewarticle.php?id=89andlayout=html.

Hargittai, E. and Shafer, S. (2006). 'Differences in actual and perceived online skills: the role of gender', *Social Science Quarterly*, 87 (2): 432–48.

Haythornthwaite, C. and Kazmer, M. M. (2002) 'Bringing the Internet home: adult distance learners and their Internet, home and work worlds', in B. Wellman and C. Haythornthwaite (eds), *The Internet in Everyday Life*. Oxford: Blackwell. pp. 431–63.

Haythornthwaite, C., Kazmer, M. M., Robins, J. and Shoemaker, S. (2000) 'Community development among distance learners: temporal and technological dimensions', *Journal of Computer-Mediated Communication*, 6 (1). Available online at: http://www.ascusc.org/jcmc/vol6/issue1/haythornthwaite. html.

Horrigan, J. (2005) 'Broadband Adoption at Home in the United States: Growing but Slowing'. Paper presented to the XXXIII Annual Telecommunications Policy Research Conference. Retrieved 22 December 2005 from: http://www.pewInternet.org/pdfs/PIP_Broadband.TPRC_Sept05.pdf.

Howard, P. N. and Jones, S. (2003) (eds) *Society Online: The Internet in Context*. Thousand Oaks, CA: Sage.

Howard, P. N., Rainie, L. and Jones, S. (2002) 'Days and nights on the Internet', in B. Wellman and C. Haythornthwaite (eds), *The Internet In Everyday Life*. Oxford: Blackwell. pp. 45–73.

Johnson, S. D., Benson, A. D., Duncan, J. R., Shinkareva, O., Taylor, G. D. and Treat, T. (2004) 'Internet-based learning in postsecondary career and technical education', *Journal of Vocational Education Research*, 29 (2): 101–19. Available online at: http://scholar.lib.vt.edu/ejournals/JVER/v29n2/johnson.html.

Katz, J. E. and Rice, R. E. (2002) *Social Consequences of Internet Use: Access, Involvement and Expression*. Cambridge, MA: MIT Press.

Kling, R. (1999) 'Can the "next-generation" Internet effectively support "ordinary citizens"?', *Information Society*, 15 (1): 57–64.

Kominski, R. and Newburger, E. (1999) 'Access Denied: Changes in Computer Ownership and Use, 1984–1997'. Paper presented at the annual meeting of the American Sociological Association, Chicago. Retrieved 17 July from: http://www.census.gov/population/socdemo/computer/confpap99.pdf.

LaRose, R., Eastin, M. S. and Gregg, J. (2001) 'Reformulating the Internet paradox: social cognitive explanations of Internet use and depression', *Journal of Online Behavior*, 1 (2). Available online at: http://www.behaviour.net/JOB/v1n2/paradox.hmtl.

Lenhart, A. and Horrigan, J. B. (2003) 'Re-visualizing the digital divide as a digital spectrum', *IT & Society*, 1 (5): 23–39. Available online at: http://www.stanford.edu/group/siqss/itandsociety/v01i05/v01i05a02.pdf

Lenhart, A., Horrigan, J., Rainie, L., Allen, K., Boyce, A., Madden, M. and O'Grady, E. (2003) *The Ever-Shifting Internet Population: A New Look at Internet Access and the Digital Divide*. Retrieved 23 December 2005 from: http://www.pewInternet.org/pdfs/PIP_Shifting_Net_Pop_Report.pdf.

Ling, R. (2004) *The Mobile Connection: The Cell Phone's Impact on Society*. San Francisco, CA: Morgan Kaufmann.

Livingstone, S. and Bober, M. (2005) *UK Children go Online: Final Report of Key Project Findings*. Economic and Social Research Council, UK. Retrieved 16 January 2006 from: http://news.bbc.co.uk/1/shared/bsp/hi/pdfs/28_04_05_childrenonline.pdf.

NCAT (National Center for Academic Transformation) (2005) *Information Technology: A Problem or Solution for Underserved Students*. Retrieved 22 December 2005 from: www.thencat.org/Newsletters/Oct05.htm#1.

NSBF (National School Board Federation) (2000) *Safe & Smart: Research and Guidelines for Children's Use of the Internet* (28 March). Retrieved 14 January 2006 from: http://www.nsbf.org/safe-smart/full-report.htm.

National Statistics (2002) *Internet access: Households and Individuals*, retreived 10 July 2006, from http://www.statistics.gov.uk/pdfdir/intacc0702.pdf.

National Statistics (2006) *Internet Connectivity: March 2006 First Release*. Retrieved 17 July 2006 from: http://www.statistics.gov.uk/pdfdir/icfr0506.pdf.

Neustadtl, A., Robinson, J. and Kestnbaum, M. (2002) 'Doing social science research online', in B. Wellman and C. Haythornthwaite (eds), *The Internet in Everyday Life*. Oxford: Blackwell. pp. 186–211.

Nicholas, K. (2003) 'Geo-policy barriers and rural Internet access: the regulatory role in constructing the digital divide', *The Information Society* 19 (4): 287–95.

Nie, N. H. (2001) 'Sociability, interpersonal relations, and the Internet: reconciling conflicting findings', *American Behavioral Scientist*, 45 (3): 420–35.

Nie, N. H. and Erbring, L. (2000) 'Internet and society: a preliminary report', *IT & Society*, 1 (1): 275–83. Available online at: http://www.stanford.edu/group/siqss/itandsociety/v01i01/v01i01a18.pdf.

Nie, N. H., Hillygus, S. and Erbring, L. (2002) 'Internet use, interpersonal relations and sociability: a time diary study', in B. Wellman and C. Haythornthwaite (eds), *The Internet in Everyday Life*. Oxford: Blackwell. pp. 215–43.

NTIA (2000) *Falling through the Net: Toward Digital Inclusion*. Washington, DC: US Department of Commerce. Available online at: http://www.ntia.doc.gov/ntiahome/digitaldivide/.

NTIA (2002) *A Nation Online: How Americans are Expanding their Use of the Internet*. Washington, DC: US Department of Commerce. Retrieved 11 July 2006 from: http://www.ntia.doc.gov/ntiahome/dn/anationonline2.pdf.

NTIA (2004) *A Nation Online: Entering the Broadband Age*. Washington, DC: US Department of Commerce. Retrieved 11 July 2006 from: http://www.ntia.doc.gov/reports/anol/NationOnline Broadband04.pdf.

Nua (2003) *Canada Trumps US in Broadband Use*. http://www.nua.com/surveys/?f=VSart_ id=905358758rel=true.

Parsad, B. and Jones, J. (2005) *Internet Access in US Public Schools and Classrooms, 1994–2003* (NCES 2005–015). US Department of Education. Washington, DC: National Center for Education Statistics. Retrieved 17 July 2006 from: http://165.224.221.98/pubs2005/2005015.pdf.

Patterson, Rubin and Wilson, Ernest J. III (2000) 'New IT and social inequity: resetting the research and policy agenda', *The Information Society*, 16: 77–86.

Pew Internet and American Life Project (2005) *Internet and Cell Phone Facts*. (26 July). Retrieved 22 December 2005 from: http://www.pewInternet.org/pipcomments.asp?m=7y=2005.

Pinkett, R. (2000) 'Bridging the Digital Divide: Sociocultural Constructionism and an Asset-based Approach to Community Technology and Community Building'. Paper presented at the LXXXI Annual Meeting of the American Educational Research Association (AERA), New Orleans, LA, 24–28 April. Retrieved, 28 December 2005 from: http://llk.media.mit.edu/papers/archive/aera2000.pdf.

Rainie, L. (2006) *Cell Phone Use* (April). Pew Internet and American Life Project. Retrieved 5 August 2006 from: http://www.pewInternet.org/pdfs/PIP_Cell_phone_study.pdf.

Rainie, L., Fox, S., Horrigan, J., Lenhart, A. and Spooner, T. (2000) *Tracking Online Life: How Women use the Internet to Cultivate Relationships with Family and Friends* (10 May). Retrieved 6 March, 2006 from: http://www.pewInternet.org/pdfs/Report1.pdf.

Rice, R. E. (2002). 'Primary issues in Internet use: access, civic and community involvement, and social interaction and expression', in L. Lievrouw and S. Livingstone (eds), *Handbook of New Media*. London: Sage. pp. 105–29.

Rice, R. and Haythornthwaite, C. (2006) 'Perspectives on Internet use: access, involvement, and interaction', in L. Lievrouw and S. Livingstone (eds), *Handbook of New Media* (student edn). London: Sage. pp. 92–113.

Robinson, J. P., Dimaggio, P. and Hargittai, E. (2003) 'New social survey perspectives on the digital divide', *IT & Society*, 1 (5): 1–22. Available online at: http://www.stanford.edu/group/siqss/ itandsociety/v01i05/v01i05a01.pdf.

Schement, J. R. (1996) 'Beyond universal service: characteristics of Americans without telephones, 1980–1993', *Telecommunications Policy*, 16 (3): 477–85.

Statistics Canada (2000) 'Plugging in: household Internet use', *The Daily*, Monday 4 December 2000. Available online at: http://www.statcan.ca/Daily/English/001204/d001204a.htm.

Strover, S. (2003) 'Remapping the digital divide: exploring equity and politics', special issue, *The Information Society*, 19 (4): whole issue.

Cole, M., Suman, M., Schramm, P., van Bel, D., Lunn, B., Maguie, P., Hanson, K., Singh, R. and Aquino, J-S. (2000) *The UCLA Internet Report: Surveying the Digital Future*. UCLA Center for Communication Policy. Retrieved 18 July 2006 from: http://www.digitalcenter.org/pdf/InternetReportYearOne.pdf.

van Dijk, J. and Hacker, K. (2003) 'The digital divide as a complex and dynamic phenomenon', *The Information Society*, 19 (4): 315–26.

Wellman, B. and Haythornthwaite, C. (eds) (2002) *The Internet in Everyday Life*. Oxford: Blackwell.

Warschauer, M. (2002) 'Reconceptionalizing the digital divide', *First Monday*, 7 (7): 1–15. Available online at: http://firstmonday.org/issues/issue7_7/warschauer/index.hmtl.

Warschauer, M. (2003a) *Technology and Social Inclusion*. Cambridge, MA: MIT Press.

Warschauer, M. (2003b) 'Dissecting the "digital divide": a case study in Egypt', *The Information Society*, 19: 297–304.

Wilhelm, A. G. (2003) 'Leveraging sunken investments in communications infrastructure: a policy perspective from the United States', *The Information Society*, 19 (4): 279–86.

5

Learning and Lessons from the World of Games and Play

Angela McFarlane

A key element of e-learning has been the use of electronic communication to facilitate some form of co-learning among students on a course. The rationale for this approach lies in a model of learning as socially constructed, where exchange of views and information between students can lead to an enhanced outcome for all. Such meaningful exchange cannot, however, be taken for granted; the best known strategy for management of such exchanges is that of Salmon's five-step model for e-moderating where some form of social exchange is an essential precursor to meaningful learning exchanges (Salmon, 2000). Nevertheless examples of less than successful attempts to encourage learners to use online discussion to support their learning are common. Of the papers that made up a special issue of the *Journal of Computer Aided Learning* in late 2004 (Pilkington, 2004), none of the documents tells an entirely happy tale of deep engagement or spontaneous contribution, and these examples are far from isolated (McFarlane *et al.*, 2003). One recurring problem is that of non-contribution: even where this is a compulsory element of a credit-bearing course, it can be impossible to get students to post their own comments or respond to others.

Such non-participation is in stark contrast to the situation found in online communities associated with informal activities, such as digital game[1] play and fanfiction, where individuals voluntarily spend hours contributing their own input or offering feedback to others. The volume of output, and time taken to read content, would be the envy of anyone who has attempted to encourage online interaction as a vehicle of formal learning. In this chapter I will examine the nature of some of these communities of informal learning, and review what research there is into this relatively new and little known phenomenon; at least, that is, little known beyond the hundreds of thousands of individuals who constitute such communities. In order to offer some structure to an investigation of this area I will look at three types of participants in online communities: those forming to play a digital game online, those growing up as a result of a shared interest in a digital game, and those whose primary aim is to offer an outlet for creative work inspired by a work or works of fiction that may or may not be a digital game.

The way in which digital game players have embraced the opportunities afforded by online technologies to support communities should come as no surprise. Such virtual exchanges can be viewed as a natural extension of play in that most digital game play has a social element; the stereotypical lone desocialized digital gamer is not the norm. Although some researchers (e.g. Anderson and Dill, 2000) have treated digital game playing as an isolated psychological phenomenon and ignored the broader social contexts of such play, others such as Tobin (1998), McFarlane *et al.* (2002) and Squire (2004) have noted that playing digital games is a far from isolated, solitary activity. In an early study, Greenfield (1984) pointed out that half the young people who spent time in video games arcades were not actually playing games at all – rather they were using the arcade as a social gathering space. Tobin (1998) found that boys' digital game play was not simply a process of 'playing the game' but was embedded in social interactions. He stressed that boys were drawing on existing knowledge of such games from wide friendship groups, and were in fact increasing these friendship groups both physically and on the Internet, in order to become 'expert' players (see also Williamson and Facer, 2004). Digital games are often a focus or facilitator of social activities among peers (Kirriemuir and McFarlane, 2004), as indeed are non-digital games. Gee (2003) has noted that digital games players purposely gather into informal 'affinity groups' with shared interests in games, in which knowledge and expertise are shaped, enriched and expanded through the connections between all members of the group. In Becta's report on digital games use 'The Sims' is cited as an example where game-related

> discussion focused not just on how to use the software but on issues of science, government and citizenship. Specific issues such as alternative types of energy, pollution, planning of facilities and dealing with traffic congestion were raised for debate. Such group collaboration can help individuals to develop self-confidence coupled with respect for others. The games, as one teacher puts it, acted as 'platforms for social interaction'.
>
> (BECTA, 2001)

Thus digital game playing is more than simply a human–machine interaction; such play is embedded in social and cultural interactions. In some cases, Squire (2004) argues, discussion and collaboration emerging through game play and various kinds of reflection activities are as important as the game itself. Indeed, digital games could be regarded as 'mediating artefacts' that promote various kinds of social practices and activities. These practices are perhaps at their most advanced, and certainly nowhere more visible to outside observers, than when they are enacted online in virtual communities that leave at least a partial record of their interactions.

GAMES AND LEARNING

Before looking at learning within game-related communities, I want first to make some observations about the relationship between games and learning. The playing of digital games is now an established cultural practice for millions of individuals of all ages (Entertainment Software Association, 2005). The average age of game players has risen steadily, so this is clearly an adult as well as a children's pastime. The range of games available is large and varied, from online poker to simple puzzle games, from arcade-style shooting galleries to virtual worlds where hundreds of thousands of people interact in real time in a fantasy context. It is very difficult to make any meaningful general comments about this activity. However, a common feature of the majority of digital games is that, unlike most traditional games where the rules are explicit and known to all before play commences, the means to succeed are revealed through the actions and interactions of the players as they play. Thus the game environment must be designed to support such learning at a pace and in a style that ensures enough players will persist and succeed to make the game commercially viable. As Kücklich (2003) points out, it is not that the players necessarily elicit the rules of the game in this process, but they learn how to react in order to survive in the game.

In his book on the relationship between learning and digital games Gee (2003) sets out thirty-six models of learning that can be found in games. Becker (2006) offers an analysis of learning within games in terms of nine well established models of learning and learning style, from Gagné to Gardner, and makes a convincing case that, whatever the preferred guru or pedagogy, there is a digital game to suit every approach. What remains contentious is the degree to which such learning is relevant and transferable to contexts beyond gaming. Authors such as Gee and Jenkins (e.g. 1992) make strong cases for the relevance of such game literacy to wider competence in a multimodal connected world. In formal education, however, there remain concerns as to the applicability of such learning, in terms of content as well as context. The debate on the precise nature of the relationship between game play and education, especially in institutions such as schools and universities, remains active (Kirriemuir and McFarlane, 2004). It is beyond the scope of this chapter to rehearse these arguments here, and what follows offers no position for or against the incorporation of commercial games into the curriculum, or for the design of games to support the curriculum. Rather this chapter provides a view of the learning experiences offered in a range of online activities widely enjoyed beyond the experience of formal education, and offers some comments on what the implications of these experiences might be for those attempting to teach, learn and/or research within traditional settings. The communities that form in and around such activities are of particular interest, as their negotiated practice is relevant to many of the social and cultural issues raised in research and practice with computer-mediated communication in e-learning.[2]

IN-GAME COMMUNITIES

Research into Massively Multiplayer Online Games (MMOGs), which includes Massively Multiplayer Online Role Play Games (MMORPGs), is rather thin on the ground. This is almost certainly related to the fact that to research such a game requires the researcher to play for long periods over a sustained time frame. Such games are large and complex, and to gain insight into the game and the nature of the player community takes hours of dedication over a period of months if not years. Steinkuehler (2005) as part of her research for her doctoral thesis spent over two years playing Lineage to the level of a guild leader, which represents hundreds of hours of intense game play. This kind of research is akin to a participant observer ethnographic study, in which the researcher is observing her own and others' behaviour. There are many difficulties apart from the time involved in this kind of work, not least how one portrays oneself, and how others portray themselves. For example, if you declare yourself as a researcher on first contact with other player characters the impact is likely to be very marked, and subsequent interactions with them are likely to be atypical. Yet to record their interactions and behaviours without such declaration raises serious ethical issues. Further, it is not usual in such game environments to enquire about the identity of the player behind the character, yet without such information the inferences that can be made from data are limited. And yet, even if the researcher makes such enquiries, it is hard to verify the reliability of the responses. In an online environment sources of triangulating data, such as a school or college, are missing.

MMOGs are subscription-based games played online in a 2D, or more commonly 3D, world. Each player can see their own character or avatar, and those of any other players that are in their field of view, as well as the game environment. They can interact with player characters using on-screen chat facilities, and with computer-generated, non-player characters in the game. They can also interact with the environment and objects within it. The usual aim of play within an MMOG is to 'grow' your character through in-game experience and resource collection. In-game resources can take many forms, such as currency, magical powers, strength, health, weapons or pets. They can be accrued through various endeavours, purchased or won from in-game characters or other players. In order to work out how to do this, each player must discover the rules of the game, largely through exploration and experimentation. The suppliers of these gaming environments do not usually supply manuals, and in-game help is limited. Perhaps this is why fans create their own Web sites to record and exchange tips and techniques to aid play. These sites are the subject of the next section of this chapter.

What sets these games apart from the complex role-play games available offline, to be played on consoles or personal computers, is that as well as each player having their own character that they control, albeit within some limits set by the game rules, the majority of the characters encountered in the game are similarly controlled by other players. Thus the range of potential outcomes of any player–player interaction goes far beyond anything that is currently available in games, where the range of responses is the result purely of coding within the game, or interacting with the small number of players who can be active at one time – for example, using the ability of consoles to support up to four controllers at one time. In game design terms MMOGs are n-sum games as opposed to zero-sum games (Kampmann Walther, 2003), the former being characterized by a variety of outcomes and no clear winner, and the latter by a finite end with a winner and a loser .

The game environments are complex and dangerous, large enough that a player can walk through the wilderness for hours in real time before finding a town or settlement, and filled with dangerous creatures and other hazards, including in some cases other players who may kill them. This can make game play frustrating for new players, who may find it hard to get anywhere without being eaten, robbed or murdered by another player. In order to seek protection and help, players form into clans or guilds whose members help and support each other, form alliances, make and carry out joint plans and develop mutual strategies. The induction of new players into such groups is in the interest of experienced players, since the games require collaborative action to triumph, for example in a siege or battle, plus a turnover of players keeps the population vibrant and viable. It is also in the interest of the designers to encourage new players, and their subscriptions, thus the game is likely to contain some features that support such players. These can include areas of the game where no in-game hazards are found, such as towns where no monsters roam. The clans or guilds are very important, however, and it can be hard to survive without one. To strengthen the bonds within such groups they frequently engage in practices that go beyond the bounds of the game such as forming clan Web sites and e-mailing each other outside the game space. They also adopt shared in-game behaviours such as sporting symbols of membership, names or clothing, for example.

It is important to note that not all players are helpful to one another. The purpose of the game is to gain as much experience and as many resources for your avatar as possible. One way to do this is to trade with, or steal from, other players. And since the characters are all real people, communicating via written language, it is possible to cheat or abuse another player, as recorded by Kelly (2004). Such behaviour is, however, frequently moderated through clans, as recorded by Steinkuehler (2005), since aberrant behaviour by a clan member can bring adverse consequences for all clan members. Holland Oliver (2002) writes on the environment of the MMOG as a public space and offers insights into the behaviours of players in and around games in comparison to related behaviours in real space. Such moderation of individuals by a group is a typical example.

Such in-game communities are interesting in themselves, since they represent true communities of practice, at least within a clan or guild, where groups work together to achieve common goals through information sharing, negotiated action and partnership. Moreover that action may be beyond the rules or intention of the original game designers. An example of this is found when groups of players work together on carefully choreographed dance routines. At an agreed time and date, many hundreds of players send their avatar to an agreed space in the game, and perform complex, synchronized dance sequences together, to music. The whole sequence can also be recorded, which is the only way that anyone who has not actually performed in one of these mass actions is likely to observe one. This all takes place in real time, and the complex body movements and gestures of the avatars are all controlled through a conventional keyboard (for the most part) in an amazing display of speed and dexterity. Considering that this can take place in a game space primarily designed to support mass battle engagements, it shows how far players can subvert the original intention of designers and how creative they are in doing so.

A very different form of game subversion arises from the fact that in-game resources can also be purchased for cash through sites such as e-bay. This certainly goes against the general spirit of gaming, and may be explicitly excluded in the terms of the subscriber's licence and yet the real-world economy of some games is estimated to be larger than that of some countries (Castronova, 2001). Not only resources but entire characters can be bought in this way. This can be so lucrative in games with hundreds of thousands of players such as Lineage that playing in order to accrue in-game currency to then sell in the real world has become something of an organized industry. Adena is the Lineage currency, and playing in order simply to gain this to sell for cash is known as adena farming. The resultant imbalance in supply and demand, and the ruthless in-game behaviour of the farmers as they pursue adena, make them unpopular with mainstream gamers. Steinkuehler (2005) gives an account of this phenomenon as one example of the unanticipated outcomes that the interaction of games design and player behaviours can produce in the 'mangle' of play (Pickering, 1995). Dwarves, a normally useful and non-threatening class of player character, are now viewed with hostility and often killed in organized campaigns against them as likely adena farmers. Clans have been known to suspend normal game play to run campaigns against farmers. Indeed, the game is described as seriously broken by some players because of the effects of adena farming and the actions of and reactions to adena farmers. This is another reminder that the actions that arise within game communities may not be either sociable or benevolent. The identification of adena farmers as primarily Chinese has also led to some disturbing racial stereotyping, exacerbated when players do not share a common language and have problems communicating.

In her paper on learning in MMOGs Steinkuehler (2004) references the learning models of Lave and Wenger (1991), since clearly the process of joining and learning how to play an MMOG is indeed one of legitimate peripheral participation. A new player joins an established community of practice and, through observation and with support from experienced members, learns how to survive in the game. Through immersion in the culture of the game the shared discourse of the game can be learned (Gee, 1999). The learning built into Lineage is construed 'not as designed object but rather as a social practice … mastered not by overt instruction but rather through apprenticeship' (Steinkuehler, 2004: 5, referencing Gee, 1999, Lave and Wenger, 1991, and Tharp and Gallimore, 1998). Indeed, Tharp and Gallimore's model of teaching as assisted performance is manifest throughout the world of MMOGs as experienced players help the less experienced through demonstration and support.

When considering the richness and complexity of such online worlds it is interesting to compare it with the kind of game experience offered in formal learning contexts. Here the micro-worlds are more like those in offline games, e.g. in the military training games which are among the most sophisticated and have the largest development budgets, but still have limited player-to-player interaction and lack the level of social realism of MMOGs. Attempts to build MMOGs specifically to support formalized learning are in their infancy. The Quest Atlantis (QA) project is looking at this phenomenon; whether it is truly massive may be questionable, but it has had 3,000 users registered and active in the online game space, which is remarkable for a game aimed at the school curriculum (Barab *et al.,* 2005). QA does not, however, limit itself to the online space, but offers a 'distributed, transmedia narrative … spread across various media that come together and are given meaning as the user participates in the game …' (p. 87). The importance of intertextuality is a subject I will return to in the section on fanfiction.

The outcomes of QA are interesting. In terms of engagement with factual content it is not at all clear that the in-game experience is more effective than Web page or paper-based forms of presentation. Indeed, having to navigate a 3D space to find and interrogate the right characters in order to locate factual information is unlikely to be efficient as a search process. The question, then, is whether it is more compelling and more meaningful as a process than the alternatives. Results so far suggest that the learning from the game experience has been successful, with improvements related to curriculum objectives reported (although not as yet with data from a controlled trial). Perhaps more significant, however, is the project's success in achieving another of its goals, which is an advance in social commitment, including sense of purpose and of agency as individuals and citizens.

The Croquet project at University of Wisconsin, Madison, is building a form of MMOG environment to simulate the experiences of being on a real-world campus with all the social and cultural interactions one would find there (Lombardi, 2005). So far the outcomes are unclear, but it will be interesting to see if participation in such an immersive online world will prove more attractive than current online courses offered as alternatives to face-to-face higher education experiences, or even if they will compete with the real thing.

GAME-RELATED COMMUNITIES

Perhaps more closely related to formal e-learning formats in game communities are those that have grown up around a popular game and form 'self-organizing communities for knowledge production' (Squire and Giovanetto, 2005: 10). These offer players a chance to exchange information on all aspects of game play, with the aim of improving and developing each user's skills in the game. Researching such communities is slightly less challenging than researching MMOG communities in that many of the community interactions are conducted and recorded through a dedicated Web site. Once enrolled into such a community it is possible for a researcher to analyse the discussions and other products posted on the site, and even to contact individual contributors and seek their co-operation through online interviews, within or outside the community communication tools, or even face-to-face. Again there is a serious ethical question as to the point at which the researcher declares their role, and how widely. Clearly this is essential when approaching individual contributors, but should a researcher declare their interest to the whole community at the point they enrol and begin to observe the Web site?

The most well known of these fan-generated learning communities, thanks to the work of Kurt Squire (2004), is the Apolyton Civilization Site (ACS). Started in 1998 from the merger of two existing fan sites, ACS is the key Web site for players of what is widely (but not uniquely) described as the most successful computer game to date. The number of registered members surpassed 70,000 in 2005. The site's strap line states that 'ACS is a site created by Civilization fans, in an effort to provide information on the entire Civilization genre of computer gaming' (see www.Apolyton.net).

A fascinating development within the site is the Apolyton University (AU), described as 'a school of strategy, where students sharpen their Civ3 skills and share their experiences in a series of thematic games'. The underlying learning model is stated clearly on the site thus: 'When playing an Apolyton University game, gaining and sharing knowledge is more important than getting a high score, a fast finish, or even winning the game. Participants are encouraged to share their strategy after the game, and even to try several attempts.' Implicit in this is a model of supported trial-and-error learning that is both reflective and reflexive as well as collaborative. In each course – and there are over twenty – the 'student' plays the associated game while creating a During Action Report (DAR) that records in-game thinking to both aid reflection at the time, and be posted on the site for comment from other players. This process of the recording of a learner's process of thinking, ideas and strategies, which are then analysed and critiqued by other community members with different levels of expertise, is a holy grail of computer-mediated communication users in e-learning. It is actively and freely engaged in by AU community members in a way that is rare in formal education, so it is worth examining the features of AU that contribute to this practice.

Apolyton University is based on a series of specially modified – 'modded' in gaming terms – versions of the game itself, specifically designed to take a player through a progressively more difficult set of experiences, each of which emphasizes the effects and consequence of particular aspects of game play. The decisions presented to the player become more complex and more strategic with each iteration. Also the consequences of choices are made more context-sensitive, whilst not necessarily appearing obvious to the player in advance. The purpose of these mods is to offer balance and improved artifical intelligence when compared to the game as played 'out of the box', thus supporting the player as he or she gets to grips with the key elements of successful game play.

The variants of the main game are developed in discussion with the Apolyton University community before being implemented. Suggestions for new mods, or improvements to the main game, are sent to the Apolyton University Mod Panel, then discussed with the wider community via discussion fora if deemed sufficiently important. Ultimately a proposal may emerge, which is voted on by the panel after the wider community has had a chance to comment for or against. If a majority of the panel opt for the proposed change it will be accepted.

The membership and terms of reference of the panel are given on the site:

1   Listen to input from the Apolyton University community in order to identify possible changes to the standard game that fit into the AU mod philosophy, or problems with modifications already present in the AU mod. This includes reading this thread, as well as AARs (after action reports) and DARs for AU courses, as many scenarios are used as tests for the AU mod.

2   Formulate official proposals for any change to the AU mod. In the case of new modifications, present a proposal to the community for discussion through a new thread (which is to be linked from the mod's description found in this thread). In the case of changes to the existing AU mod modifications, bump the relevant discussion thread by formulating the new proposal.

3   Vote on the resolution of each official proposal. Modifications may be incorporated on a trial basis, in case real-game testing is required to further evaluate the change. Panelists cannot abstain.

4   Implement any accepted proposal in the editor, create and upkeep the official documentation for the AU mod, and ensure that both the mod and the documentation are readily accessible to the community.

The panel currently consists of these members (in alphabetical order):
alexman, lockstep, nbarclay, Nor Me, pvzh, Theseus, ZargonX.

The mixture of formalized language and roles and the use of game-related jargon and player identity names used in this process gives an insight into the flavour of this community. The reader is at once in a rule-based system, as formalized in its ways of working as any university validation process, and operating in a culture that embraces its own technical use of language and rather non-standard signifiers of identity.

It would be a mistake to think of such a site and its activities as either trivial or lacking in rigour in its activities or the way the community conducts its business. Playing games like Civilization is hard, complex and highly challenging. To gain any level of mastery requires hundreds of hours of dedicated play. As a result it is not surprising that offerings such as the Apolyton University courses find a ready audience. As Squire and Giovanetto (2005: 10) point out, Apolyton University is 'open' and 'emergent'. Anyone with sufficient interest can join, all they need is online access, and although you have to register there is no fee, and it has arisen from, and continues to respond to, the needs of its users.

It is perhaps easier for those less than enthusiastic about games and game culture to accept a game like Civilization, and the pursuit of its mastery, as genuine and valuable intellectual endeavour. After all, Civilization deals with the history of human culture within a simulation so powerful that it is used by teachers of history and historiography up to university level as a platform for teaching and learning. And it is perhaps the power of this simulation that is the key to the success of AU. The model of learning used here involves high levels of learner engagement with a system that can be understood through the process of 'playing' within it. Through such interaction it is possible to learn how the system works, and how the variables represented within the system can and do relate to one another. It is the power of process that is important here. As Friedman has observed, 'games are about process, and you can interact with a process and learn about it' (1995). This makes it possible for theories such as peripheral participation to be observed as action, as the process of play is explicit even to those who merely observe. The game experiences offer a 'sandbox' within which players can learn through discovery within a safe, bounded space (Gee, 2003). Moreover, anyone reading a DAR has a clear view of the space within which the writer has been operating and the possible actions and outcomes likely even though these are not entirely closed and combinations new to the community are possible. This is perhaps akin to viewing critiques or interpretations based on a well known work of literature, historical figure or scientific process, although these are less likely to reveal the process of the author's thinking in the same way as an auto-analysis of a decision-making process recorded in action as with a DAR.

For an example of an open site offering a support service in a more formal learning context, we can examine the Asynchronous Learning Network (ALN) Research site set up by New Jersey Institute of Technology with funding from the Arthur P. Sloan Foundation (see http://www.alnresearch.org/index.jsp).

This is a community Web site to support those engaged in research into asynchronous learning networks, particularly early career researchers and graduate students. All users must register, and then they can view the work submitted to the site, send articles for comment and review, and submit final drafts to the archive. Given the research interest of the intended audience for this site, it is reasonable to assume they might be more willing than most to take part in such an experimental exercise. Nevertheless, the potential audience for such a site is tiny when compared to Apolyton, yet a significant number of articles have been posted and some have hit counts in the several hundreds, so they are being viewed. However, comments on articles are hard to find, and when they have been posted they are often written to a wider audience, not the author(s), offering critique that may or may not be constructive in nature. Neither the number nor the nature of these comments suggests a spirit of excited engagement with the topic, or enthusiasm to produce new knowledge collectively that characterizes the posts to Apolyton. Perhaps researching ALN is just not as exciting as learning to play Civilization but, more important, such public collaborative negotiations of meaning are not common practice in the academic community and we are not therefore well equipped, nor do we have appropriate incentives, to utilize communications technologies to facilitate this process (Jacobs and McFarlane, 2005).

FAN COMMUNITIES

Fanfiction refers to original works of fiction based on forms of media such as television shows, movies, books, music, and video games. The work produced must relate in some way to the original source of inspiration but the nature and degree of the link, and the form in which it is made explicit, are negotiated within the community (Jenkins, 1992). The bond that unites members is a common passion for the inspiring fiction genres, an interest they are keen to display, share and develop. Fanfiction is not a new phenomenon but the appearance of the Internet has afforded an explosion in the visibility of this cultural practice. Many hundreds of fanfiction Web sites can readily be found on the Internet, carrying work based on a range of popular media. Although there is a trend for fan production to turn to multimodal output, language-based texts still form a large proportion of what is published.

There is no systematic research into the extent of fanfiction, or the level of participation in a given population. We have no clear idea, for example, how likely a person of any given age, stage, ethnicity or culture is to engage in this practice, or which forms of media inspire most fan activity. What we can see is the nature of the practice through examination of the sites, and a very small number of researchers have begun to do this. The challenges in researching these online communities are common to those facing researchers interested in game-related communities, set out in the last section.

In her research on Cardcaptor.com, an online fanfiction-based community, Black (2006) found over 20,000 Final Fantasy digital game-related fictions and approximately 107,000 Harry Potter-based texts within this single community. Final Fantasy belongs to the interactive story category, a kind of digital game that shares the most narrative elements with traditional forms of texts. Thus it could be assumed that players of these computer games already have an interest in narrative and are therefore more likely to create fanfiction based on the texts of the game. However, on the fanfiction.net site there are over 1,000 postings inspired by Halo, an action adventure as opposed to a narrative-based game, so this is clearly not the whole story (personal observation).

The fanfiction phenomenon is not restricted to English-language users. Chen and McFarlane (2006) report on the fanfiction inspired by a series of Chinese computer games known as Chinese Paladin (PAL), or Chinese Love Story, and published on a site known as PAL Union which is one of many fan sites devoted to this topic. PAL Union carries a great deal of fanfiction, but also has a play-related function with tips and techniques sections. The PAL games series is inspired by Chinese Wuxia literature. The word 'Wuxia' is composed of two characters, the first of which, Wu, can be translated into 'martial arts' and the second, Xia, into 'knight-errant' that gives a sense of the context and culture of the games. The games share a high degree of intertextuality with the original literature, incorporating, for example, traditional Wuxia-style poetry into the game. The resulting fanfiction shows clear mixtures of inspiration from the game and the originating literature in style, content and form. PAL fanfiction is very popular; PAL Union had over 44,000 registered users in late 2005, and members commonly posted large collections of work inspired by the PAL games. Whole novels, published chapter by chapter, are common.

The intertextuality of fanfiction is recognized as important by Robison (2004) and Chen and McFarlane (2006). Intertextuality refers to 'the potentially complex ways in which meanings (such as linguistic meanings) are formed through relationships to other texts (real or imaginary), text types (discourses or genres), narratives, and other modes of meaning' (New London Group, 1996: 80 ff.). Obviously the connection between the original media source and fanfiction itself is one kind of intertextuality. However, the intertextual connections extend far beyond the original media source. For example, it is perfectly acceptable to create fictions based on one computer game while borrowing characters or plots from other popular books or movies or inventing your own. The act of composition becomes easier when there is a framework to follow (Robison, 2004). Indeed, computer games themselves are increasingly placed within an intertextual world of related products such as books, comics, magazines and films (Marsh and Millard, 2000; Ito, in press). Thus there is a range of sources that authors can turn to, and a range of media they can use to construct their own work. The intertextual connections play a crucial role in the creative and discursive practices of design in online fanfiction communities.

Fanfiction is a clear example of the Rip, Mix and Burn phenomenon, terms that came to public notice in adverts for Apple computers in the 1990s, 'to "rip" it – meaning to copy it, to "mix" it meaning to reform it however the user wants, and finally, and most important, "burn" it, – to publish it in a way that others can see and hear' (Lessig, 2001). As Ito records (2006), emergent digital cultures are marked by the explosion in visible cultural production as opposed to consumption. She contrasts the passive television-viewing audience with those engaged in active production, in her case through the remixing of Animé film in yet another genre of fanfiction.

The growing importance of the phenomena of personal creativity and sharing in the context of digital media was recognised in the UK in 2005 when the BBC, Open University, British Film Institute and Channel 4 jointly launched the Creative Archive licence. This has much in common with the earlier Creative Commons Licence, and is an attempt to overcome some issues relating to intellectual property and copyright issues in electronic media. Under these licences, originators make content available for third-party use without charge provided that the exploitation of the material is not commercial, that anything made using the assets is also made available under the same terms, that the original source is acknowledged and that use of the original material implies no endorsement from the originator, and it applies to the UK only, which may be hard to enforce (see http://creativearchive.bbc.co.uk/). That such major content owners as the BBC and Open University have developed this agreement is a recognition of the growing importance of derivative personal production and publication in digital media. Fanfiction is one example of this phenomenon, and its Web sites support and reveal the social and cultural form of this activity.

There can be no doubt that the access to an audience is an important element of the success of fanfiction Web sites. There is substantial evidence to prove that students' sense of audience has a positive influence on their attitudes towards writing tasks and on the quality of writing they produce (Davison and Dowson, 1998). However, it is not passive readership that engages community members on fanfiction sites so much as interaction with and feedback from the audience. The tie between writers and audience is strengthened and develops in a positive and friendly way, encouraged through a common desire to read and write engaging fiction on topics that interest both author and reader.

Fanfiction sites facilitate a range of user practices that are used to develop and support community practices. As with MMOGs, communities' actual practices result from a combination of what the environment affords and negotiated behaviours of the community members. The fanfiction Web sites offer authors the opportunity to post a personal page with some information about themselves and their interests. They can also post comments within their fictions, explaining for example that they are inexperienced and requesting tolerance and understanding of this from the reader. Black (2006) has examined fanfiction from the perspective of English-language learning (ELL); she records the common practices that community members have adopted and which combine to create a supportive environment for ELL writers, especially those less confident in their writing. Comments are generally supportive in that they both express appreciation of the work and offer constructive feedback on content and structure as well as grammar and spelling. They are addressed to the author, not a wider audience, and intended to be helpful in the development of the story. A clear motive in many postings is a strong desire to read the rest of the narrative, with frequent urging to write more 'chappies' (chapters). Clues are taken from the author on the extent and nature of help sought, so for example where a lack of confidence in English is expressed, there is likely to be tolerance of a lack of technical competence and more emphasis on structural features such as content and plot (Robison, 2004).

Purely hostile and negative feedback is strongly discouraged within fanfiction communities through self-regulation. Negative postings usually elicit a set of positive responses from other community members. The overall effect, on Cardcaptor.com and PAL Union at least, is to produce a model socio-cultural learning community where members support one another in their development of their skills as storytellers and emergent writers (Black, 2006; Chen and McFarlane, 2006). It is also accepted practice that reading and commenting on the work of those who offer comments to you are reciprocated. This is not required by the site, but it is afforded. For example, the software displays 'favourites' on an author's own page, and allows them to link to other authors. Thus each contributor can promote and display the other authors whose work they interact with and review regularly. It is also acceptable, and possible, to offer comment even if you do not yourself post work, especially for newcomers or those less confident in their writing.

At the same time as fanfiction has proliferated, many educators, policy makers and researchers have acknowledged difficulties in the development of school-based literacy skills. The UK National Primary Strategy (see Department for Education and Skills, 2005) and the US No Child Left Behind policy (see Department for Education, 2002) both attempt to address this problem. This is not restricted to the anglophone world. In China, Han (2005) reports that first language literacy learning is not attractive to many learners. Most, if not all, pupils found writing tasks were not motivating enough. Many viewed such tasks as completely meaningless and boring, and were quite hostile towards them. Students' lack of motivation for writing tasks in school settings may be attributed to the artificial conditions under which writing takes place, where writing tasks are usually not set within larger social and communication frames. If students are given limited opportunities to use their personal experiences as well as their dreams and fantasies as a stimulus for writing tasks, then writing can lack authenticity for them. Yet writing becomes enjoyable when there is interest in the topic and things the author wants to write about (Bruning and Horn, 2000). The creativity such authentic engagement can evoke is readily evidenced by browsing any fanfiction site.

THE ESSENCE OF SELF-ORGANIZING LEARNING COMMUNITIES

All online communities described here are, without doubt, learning communities, even if they would not necessarily welcome or even recognize this description of themselves. Through engagement with virtual activities, individuals and groups develop skills and knowledge they did not previously possess. This happens in all cases through the enactment of a process, playing a game or creating a work of fiction, and it is visible and explicit to anyone involved as actor or observer. Communication within the virtual setting, through chat, bulletin board posts or review comments supports the negotiation of meaning and participation in the relevant Discourse. This is the now well known term used by Gee to describe the 'ways of behaving, interacting, valuing, thinking, believing, speaking and often reading and writing that are accepted as instantiations of particular roles (or 'types of people') by specific groups of people' (Gee, 1996: viii).

The relationship between expert and novice in these communities is clearly an apprenticeship model, where the inexperienced work beside the expert, developing shared practices and becoming more proficient over time. The parallels with the learning models of such theorists as Lave and Wenger, Vygotsky and Wertsch are clear. What is also apparent is that these communities afford the opportunity to engage in the development of an epistemic frame as described by Shaffer (2005) as 'ways of knowing, of deciding what is worth knowing, and of adding to the collective body of knowledge and understanding of a community of practice'. Each community of practice has its own epistemic frame, and Shaffer's group has explored this concept in a variety of contexts, including scientific journalism, urban planning and engineering (Svarovsky and Shaffer, in press). The games they have developed are a blended experience that uses digital tools in face-to-face contexts, not virtual communities. Shaffer and Gee (2005) make a strong argument that epistemic games could offer a solution to the failure of education in countries such as the US to prepare students adequately for life in an economy where innovation and innovative thinking will be critical to success. Similar arguments on the importance of children's games communities are made by Williamson and Facer (2004). They point out that those young people who are already exposed to the learning experiences in game and game-related communities of practice have a head start in such contexts, but that those who do not are at risk of being left behind.

It is clear that one uniting feature of all three forms of online community described so far is that the members participate voluntarily, motivated by intense interest in a given topic or form of activity and a strong desire to be part of a community that shares their passion. This is unlikely immediately to make most teachers think of their student body unless it is by way of contrast. And yet consider the populations who fill our universities. These individuals have worked hard, for many years, to achieve the credits they need to gain entry. They have committed years of their lives to pursuing a course with an institution they have chosen from the thousands of available combinations, and have successfully competed against many others to gain a place. So surely we could expect to find similar levels of commitment and engagement with their peers in online contexts as we see in a fanfiction site, or in a game site? Indeed, there may be some examples where this is so. In my own department, for example, our doctoral students maintain their own virtual learning environment site where they communicate with and support one another. This is valued especially by those who are not full-time in the university. What exactly they do on this site I cannot say, since staff are not members. It is their own site, maintained by them and for them, and it is likely that similar sites are maintained by countless groups of students in innumerable contexts throughout the world. Such private communities are by definition hard to research, and not widely documented. What is better known, however, are the attempts to seed socioculturally based learning communities online to support or replace those that form face to face. And these are not universally successful.

It seems the approach to learning in formal contexts differs from that in the online communities of informal learning in some key respects. There is a question of the degree of personal agency afforded the learner, especially in statutory education but perhaps also in higher education. To what extent are students in universities treated as autonomous learners? Clearly they are expected to take responsibility for their learning, but the persistence of the face-to-face lecture, and the demand for this format from students, reveals a continuing belief in an instructional model of teaching and learning. The model of professional learning as one of induction into a Discourse is not unknown in higher education, but examples of using an online community to achieve this are in their infancy. The virtual learning environments used commonly in schools and universities allow for a very formalized set of CMC options that are much less rich than those offered in online gaming worlds. There is little chance to act out the experience of being an engineer, art historian, physicist or Italian scholar in such a place.

There is evidence of reluctance by learners as well as teachers to move to online interactions as an alternative to face-to-face. The reasons for this are not fully understood but the importance of social presence is recognized. It is very hard to know how, if at all, raised levels of familiarity with online communications such as Internet Relay Chat (IRC) will affect notions of social presence in virtual spaces (Livingstone and Bober, 2005). Research in the 1990s showed clearly that at that time a sense of social presence had to be cultivated in virtual contexts, and that it was important for learning in virtual environments (see for example Lombard and Ditton, 1997, for a review of the topic of presence, and the importance of social engagement in Salmon's work (2000)). However, at that time online communications technology was in its infancy, the interfaces were awkward, and the cultural practices were not well established. For a generation that has grown up with technologies such as SMS messaging and chat, the semiotics of these media are second nature.

So the medium may not be the problem for the learners. But what of the shared model of education? It is striking that all of the community models described offer examples of successful implementations of learning as social constructivism. There is certainly a bias in the research here, since those few researchers who publish in this area start from a socio-cultural, constructivist perspective. It could be argued therefore that they find what they look for, but it is difficult to deny that in these communities there is collaborative action that leads towards the development of socially constructed knowledge as individuals work together in collaborative acts of knowledge building. The record of each series of actions is left in the community for all to see and learn from, or analyse in the case of the researcher. An analysis using Tharp and Gallimore's (1998) model of assisted performance would reveal clear evidence of scaffolding, modelling, questioning and so on as more and less experienced community members exchange information and comment to build a shared understanding or improved creative output (Ab-Jalil *et al.*, 2004).

It is perhaps here that the essence of the power of the online game-related communities lies. The model of learning is authentic in that it has high personal relevance, and the value of contribution from all community members is recognized. I suggest that this is in contrast with the model of learning underpinning much of formal education, where authenticity is low, and the value of comment from fellow learners is also low, since the 'teacher' is seen as the authority figure and arbiter of value. Such a model is endemic in an education system that is driven by evaluation through high stakes testing, as in the UK and US school systems. In test-based systems of this kind there is a privileged body of knowledge upon which tests are based, familiarity with which earns the student credit. Moreover the assessment model used almost universally in formal education militates against collaboration and group working. The unit of assessment is ultimately the individual, and her performance alone and only rarely within a group is what counts. To some extent there is also an element of competition since final results are usually fitted to a normal distribution, thus not all can gain the top classifications no matter how well they perform.

Such systems ill prepare students to participate in self-organizing responsive learning communities, and their informal learning activities might prepare them more readily. Indeed individuals with rich learning community experience may reject formal learning contexts or underperform in those they are obliged to join. There is little research into this phenomenon, but studies into the learning of computer-literate school pupils have shown that they can underperform on conventional tests by as much as a grade (e.g. Russell and Haney, 2000), while in contrast the extensive Impact 2 study showed a correlation between levels of ICT use at home and improvements in school performance (Harrison *et al.*, 2002). Clearly there is much left to unravel here, but the need to understand the implications of the rich and varied virtual community-based learning experiences for those who wish to attract and retain students in formal education is a pressing one. After all why would a 12 year old, given the choice of writing on a topic that excites her, for an audience of interested and encouraging fans throughout the world, choose instead to write on a topic with little personal relevance, just for her teacher?

NOTES

1 In the discourse relating to games, terminology is contested territory. Indeed, the term 'game' has no one unique definition. Many authors distinguish between computer and video games, the latter being available on games consoles or in arcades, the former on personal computers. Here I avoid this distinction, as it is not germane to any of the arguments that follow, using instead the term 'digital games' to mean any game played on a digital device.

2 The term 'community' here refers to a group of individuals who are drawn together by a common interest, share a set of cultural practices such as the use of specialist signs and symbols, including language, and use an online 'space' to enact these practices. There is a wide and diverse literature on both communities and communities of practice, where these terms are contested and developed. The term is used here primarily because it is commonly used by those involved to describe themselves.

REFERENCES

Ab-Jalil, H., McFarlane, A., Md. Yunus, M. and Mohd. Saufi, M. (2004) 'Assistance in Electronic Discussions'. Proceeding of the V International Conference on Information Communication Technologies in Education, Samos, Greece, 1–3 July.

Anderson, C. A. and Dill, K. E. (2000) 'Video games and aggressive thoughts, feelings and behaviour in the laboratory and in life', *Journal of Personality and Social Psychology*, 78: 772–90.

Barab, S., Thomas, M., Dodge, T., Carteaux, R. and Tuzun, H. (2005) 'Making learning fun: Quest Atlantis, a game without guns', *Educational Technology Research and Development*, (53) 1: 86–107.

Becker, K. (2006) 'Pedagogy in commercial video games', in D. Gibson, (ed.), *Games and Simulations in Online Learning: Research and Development Frameworks*, in press at Idea Group, http://www.idea-group.com/.

BECTA (2001) 'Computer Games in Education: Findings', report retrieved online at: http://www.becta.org.uk/research/research.cfm?section=1andid=2826, 15 September 2005.

Black, R. W. (2006). 'Convergence and divergence: online fanfiction communites and literacy pedagogy', to appear in Z. Bekerman, N. Burbules, H. Giroux, Silberman-Keller (eds), *Mirror Images: Popular Culture and Education*. Lanham, MD: Rowman and Littlefield.

Bruning, R. and Horn, C. (2000) 'Developing motivation to write', *Educational Psychologist*, 35 (1): 25–37.

Castronova, E. (2001) 'Virtual Worlds: A First-hand Account of Market and Society on the Cyberian Frontier', Centre for Economic Studies and Institute for Economic Research (CESifo) Working Paper Series 618. Retrieved from: http://papers.ssrn.com/sol3/papers.cfm?abstract_id=294828.

Chen, C. and McFarlane, A. E. (2006) 'Gaming culture and digital literacy: inspiration and audience', *Nordic Journal of Digital Literacy* 2 (1).

Davison, J. and Dowson, J. (1998) *Learning to Teach English in the Secondary School: A Companion to School Experience*. Abingdon: Routledge.

Department for Education and Skills (2005) UK National Primary Strategy Web site, at: http://www.standards.dfes.gov.uk/primary/.

Department for Education (US) (2002) *No Child Left Behind* policy, at: http://www.ed.gov/nclb/landing.jhtml?src=pb.

Entertainment Software Association (2005) 'Sales, Demographics and Usage Data: Essential Facts about the Computer and Video Games Market', retrieved online at http://www.theesa.com/files/2005EssentialFacts.pdf.

Friedman, T. (1995) 'Making sense of software', in S. Jones (ed.), *CyberSociety: Computer Mediated Communication and Community*. London: Sage.

Gee, J. P. (2003) *What Video Games Have to Teach us about Learning and Literacy*. New York: Palgrave Macmillan.

Gee, J. P. (1999) *An Introduction to Discourse Analysis: Theory and Method*, New York: Routledge.

Gee, J. P. (1996) *Social Linguistics and Literacies: Ideology in discourse*, (2nd edn). Abingdon: Falmer.

Greenfield, P. M. (1984) *Mind and Media: The Effects of Television, Computers and Video Games*. Cambridge, MA: Harvard University Press.

Han, J. (2005) 'What we have lost in Chinese Education?' Retrieved online at: http://www.njenet.net.cn/news/showjrtj.asp?id=982.

Harrison, C., Comber, C., Fisher, T., Haw, K., Lewin, C., Lunzer, E., McFarlane, A. E., Mavers, D., Scrimshaw, P., Somekh, B. and Watling, R. (2002) *Impact 2 – The Impact of Information and Communications Technology on Pupil Learning and Attainment*, Coventry: British Educational Communications and Technology Agency.

Holland Oliver, J. (2002) 'The Similar Eye: Proxy Life and Public Space in the MMORPG', in F. Myra, (ed.), *Proceedings of Computer Games and Digital Cultures Conference*, Tampere, Finland: Tampere University Press.

Ito, M. (2006) 'Technologies of the childhood imagination: Yugioh, media mixes and everyday cultural production', in J. Karaganis, and N. Jeremijenko (eds), *Structures of Participation in Digital Cultures*, Durham, NC: Duke University Press.

Jacobs, N. and McFarlane, A. E., (2005), 'Conferences as learning communities: some early lessons in using "back-channel" technologies at an academic conference – distributed intelligence or divided attention?', *Journal of Computer Assisted Learning*, 21 (5): 317–29.

Jenkins, H. (1992) *Textual Poachers: Television, Fans and Participatory Cultures*, New York: Routledge.

Kampmann Walther, B. (2003) 'Playing and gaming reflections and classifications', *Game Studies* 3 (1).

Kelly 2 [*sic*], R. V. (2004) *Massively Multiplayer Online Role-playing Games: The People, the Addiction and the Playing Experience*, Jefferson, North Carolina: McFarland.

Kirriemuir, J. and McFarlane, A. E. (2004) 'A Literature Review on Computer Games and Learning', Report 7, Nesta Futurelab Bristol, retrieved from: www.nestafuturelab.org.

Kücklich, J. (2003) 'Perspectives of computer game philology', *Games Studies* (3) 1, http://www.gamestudies.org/.

Lave, J. and Wenger, E. (1991) *Situated Learning: Legitimate Peripheral Participation*, Cambridge: Cambridge University Press.

Lessig, L. (2001) *The Future of Ideas*, New York: Random House.

Livingstone, S. and Bober, M. (2005) 'UK Children Go Online: Final report of Key Findings', retrieved from: http://www.children-go-online.net/.

Lombard, M. and Ditton, T. (1997) 'At the heart of it all: the concept of presence', *Journal of Computer Mediated Communication*, 3 (2).

Lombardi, M. M. (2005) 'Standing on the Plateau Looking Forward: The Croquet Project', Educause Resource Center, retrieved from: http://www.educause.edu.

Marsh, J. and Millard, E. (2000) *Literacy and Popular Culture: Using Children's Culture in the Classroom*, London: Paul Chapman Publishing.

McFarlane, A. E., Bradburn, A. and McMahon, A. (2003) 'E-learning for Leadership: Emerging indicators of Effective Practice', Nottingham: National College for School Leadership.

McFarlane, A. E., Sparrowhawk, A. and Heald, Y. (2002) 'The Role of Games in Education: a Research Report to the Department for Education and Skills', retrieved from: http://www.teem.org.uk.

New London Group (1996) 'A pedagogy of multiliteracies: designing social futures', *Harvard Educational Review*, 66: 60–92.

Pickering, A. (1995) *The Mangle of Practice: Time, Agency and Science*, Chicago, IL: University of Chicago Press.

Pilkington, R. (2004) 'Developing discussion for learning', *Journal of Computer Assisted Learning*, 20 (3): 161.

Robison, A. J. (2004) 'Video game designers as multiliteracy pedagogues: a discourse analysis of the designing process'. Presentation to CAL 05, Bristol.

Russell, M. and Haney, W. (2000) 'Bridging the gap between testing and technology in schools', *Education Policy Analysis Archives*, 8 (19).

Salmon, G. (2000) *E-moderating: The Key to Teaching and Learning Online*, London: Kogan Page.

Shaffer, D. W. (2005) 'Multisubculturalism: computers and the end of progressive education', under review by *Teachers College Record*. Retrieved from: http://coweb.wcer.wisc.edu/cv/papers/multisub-culturalism-draft1.pdf.

Shaffer, D. W. and Gee, J. P. (2005) 'Before every child is left behind: how epistemic games can solve the coming crisis in education', under review by *Educational Researcher*. Retrieved from: http://coweb.wcer.wisc.edu/cv/papers/learning_crisis.pdf.

Squire, K. D. (2004) 'Replaying History: Learning World History through Playing Civilization III', Ph.D. thesis, Bloomington, IN: Indiana University. Retrieved online at: http://Web site.education.wisc.edu/kdsquire/dissertation.html.

Squire, K. and Giovannetto, L. (2005) 'Self-organizing communities for knowledge production', *Interact*, 31, University of Bristol. Retrieved from: http://www.ltss.bris.ac.uk/interact/.

Steinkuehler, C. A. (2004) 'Learning in massively multiplayer online games', in Y. B. Kafai, W. A. Sandoval, N. Enyedy, A. S. Nixon and F. Herrera, (eds), Proceedings of the Sixth International Conference of the Learning Sciences. (pp. 521–8). Mahwah, NJ: Erlbaum.

Steinkuehler, C. A. (2005) 'Cognition and Learning in Massively Multiplayer Online Games: A Critical Approach', Ph.D. dissertation, Madison, WI: University of Wisconsin. Retrieved from: http://Web site.education.wisc.edu/steinkuehler/thesis.html.

Svarovsky, G. N., and Shaffer, D. W. (in press) 'SodaConstructing knowledge through exploratoids', *Journal of Research in Science Teaching*, retrieved from: http://coweb.wcer.wisc.edu/cv/papers/exploratoids.pdf.

Tharp, R. G. and Gallimore, R. (1998) *Rousing Minds to Life*. Cambridge: Cambridge University Press.

Tobin, J. (1998) 'An American "otaku"', in J. Sefton-Green, (ed.) *Digital Diversions: Youth Culture in the Age of Multi-media*, London: UCL Press.

Williamson, B. and Facer, K. (2004) 'More than "just a game": the implications for schools of children's computer games communities', *Education, Communication and Information*, 4 (2–3): 255–70.

6

Learning Sciences Theories and Methods for E-learning Researchers

Christopher Hoadley

The field of e-learning has been informed by a number of both theoretical and methodological traditions, ranging from education, psychology, and communications to computer science, media design, and informatics. Here, we explore the relationship between learning theories and in particular the theories and methods of the Learning Sciences (LS) and e-learning. We focus primarily on the relationship between research in the learning sciences and in e-learning (as opposed to practical design and development strategies). The learning sciences are, as will be discussed later, an interdisciplinary field concerned with the design of learning environments and studying them in context. In what follows, we examine three broad issues. First, what are the goals of e-learning research? Secondly, what are the learning sciences and what theories and methods do they draw upon? Third, how may these theories and methods be useful in e-learning research?

GOALS OF E-LEARNING RESEARCH

What are the goals of e-learning research? The goals of e-learning practice are relatively clear: producing and evaluating interventions using technology that lead to student learning outcomes in particular applications. E-learning research on the other hand has four more general goals: producing theories that explain phenomena with e-learning, producing tools or software for e-learning; producing activities, materials, curricula, and other non-technical elements of the e-learning environment that may be reused; and finally, producing design models that permit construction of improved e-learning interventions.

Theories

E-Learning theories overlap with many other categories of theory. For instance, a theory of the psychology of how people learn generally, a theory explaining how interfaces change individuals' behaviours in online course spaces, or a theory of information structuring for retrieval by computer systems might all be properly called e-learning theories because they relate to or have application in the domain of e-learning. However, it is important to note how these theories link to different disciplines outside e-learning (educational psychology, human–computer interaction, or information science, respectively, in these examples). One goal of e-learning research is to produce and test theories of these sorts.

Tools

E-learning practice uses tools to produce learning outcomes in students. E-learning research helps produce general tools such as server software, metadata specifications, interface designs, or authoring systems that can be applied in many practical applications. In the earliest days of e-learning, tools were often produced as 'one-off' applications for a particular set of learning goals. These days, one need not be (or hire) a programmer to create e-learning software from scratch; rather, the practical e-learning designer can make use of a wide variety of general tools. Thus, one area of e-learning research involves the creation and testing of tools that represent generalized solutions to commonly encountered problems in e-learning.

Activities, curricula, and other designs

Analogous to the issue of tools in e-learning, a third goal in e-learning research is to identify non-technical designs such as particular task structures, curricula, or other intangibles that can be used and reused in e-learning practice (for instance, the task structure of the WebQuest,[1] or grading rubrics for participation in online forums). Again, e-learning practitioners often apply these and other intangible design elements in their own practice, but it is a goal of e-learning research to create and test activities, curricula, or other intangibles that represent a more generalized platform on which specific e-learning applications may be built. An example of this is the e-LEN project of the European Union,[2] which is identifying design patterns in post-secondary e-learning through a consortium of university researchers and e-learning designers (Avgeriou et al., 2003).

Design models

Design models (Driscoll, 1984; Reigeluth, 1999) are an important final outcome of e-learning research. While some generalized tools, activities, curricula, or other design elements may be figured out 'once and for all' or for some generalized field of application, other elements of e-learning design may be contingent on the particular application. The e-learning designer may uncover these elements through experience or trial and error, or may uncover these elements through principled design processes. The creation and testing of such processes is a legitimate part of e-learning research. Design models represent a way to systematically transform generalized knowledge and solutions into specific solutions for particular circumstances.

Thus, we see four products of e-learning research: theories, tools, activities or other intangible design products, and design models. The following sections explore research methods and learning theory in the learning sciences and how these contribute to these four products of e-learning research.

THE LEARNING SCIENCES

The learning sciences are an interdisciplinary field that designs and studies learning environments, often technology-supported learning environments. As noted elsewhere (Hoadley, 2004a) a field may be characterized by its scope and goals, by its history, by its theoretical commitments, or by its epistemology and methods. To give context, I begin by describing the history, scope, and goals of the learning sciences. I then turn to a more detailed description of the theoretical commitments and methods of the learning sciences.

History, scope, and goals

Like cognitive science, the learning sciences arose from a number of disciplines that study similar phenomena, ranging from computer science to cognitive psychology, educational psychology, sociology, anthropology, and instructional design. As with cognitive science in its early days, there is some controversy over who is or isn't a learning scientist, and definitions are often conflicting or contested (see for example the discussion in the special issue of *Educational Technology* on this topic: 'Learning Sciences and Instructional Systems: Beginning the Dialogue', 2004).

Briefly, the moniker 'learning sciences' arose initially with the Institute for the Learning Sciences at Northwestern (connected tightly with cognitive and computer scientists there), and the first International Conference of the Learning Sciences in 1991; this conference was a relabelling and eventual spin-off of the existing AI-Ed (Artificial Intelligence in Education) conference. The

Journal of the Learning Sciences was founded in the same year with an aim of identifying 'what kinds of educational environments are effective in what kinds of situations' (Kolodner, 1991), with a heavy focus on how technology might play a role in such educational environments.

More recently, though, the learning sciences have evolved away from such a heavy connection to computer science or technology; in the first ten years of the *Journal of the Learning Sciences*, approximately half of the articles had a specific technology focus while half did not. Simultaneously, and with special relevance to the e-learning community, a community arose around the Computer-Supported Collaborative Learning conferences. These two communities had significant overlap in North America, although not necessarily elsewhere (Hoadley, 2005b). Eventually a professional organization, the International Society of the Learning Sciences, was founded and currently governs both conferences, *JLS*, and a new *International Journal of Computer-Supported Collaborative Learning*. The learning sciences community has been visible and successful; for instance, the *Journal of the Learning Sciences* was rated as the educational research journal with the highest impact factor by the Social Science Citation Index for 2004, and the *Handbook of the Learning Sciences* (Sawyer, 2006) showcases achievements in the field.

Notably, the learning sciences have not historically had a relationship with the instructional design or distance education fields (Kirby *et al.*, 2005), two fields frequently associated with e-learning, although this is changing (Hoadley, 2004a; Hung *et al.*, 2005).

Generally, the scope and goals of the learning sciences are to understand what makes learning environments work, and to design better ones. Obviously, this is a tremendously large scope and one that overlaps with the scope of many other disciplines, and for this reason the scope and goals of Learning Sciences are not perhaps the most distinctive characteristic of the field. In the sections that follow, I describe some of the major learning theories and research methods in which the learning sciences are grounded. For historical context, and also to highlight similarities and differences with other fields, this discussion is not limited to the theories espoused by Learning Sciences but also includes some of the important precursors to those theories.

Theories of learning

The twentieth century marks an explosion in the academic study of learning and teaching. The founding of psychology as a discipline (Freud published his first work on hysteria in 1895) helped pave the way for an increasingly empirical basis for making educational decisions. However, what assumptions underlie investigation of teaching and learning were (and continue to be) hotly debated. Some of the major theories of learning from the twentieth century onward are discussed below. Interestingly these theories were produced by a number of different intellectual paradigms, including philosophy, computer science, anthropology, and psychology, although psychology plays the largest role in this discussion.

Early twentieth century

Although Freud's psychoanalysis and the Gestaltists formed part of the early heritage of psychology, three major perspectives helped shape the early twentieth century's learning theories. Behaviorism, most closely identified with B. F. Skinner, was a reaction to the introspective methods of psychoanalysis. Mistrusting of self-reports, behaviorism tried to reduce learning to simple conditioning by only examining stimuli and responses of organisms. In the case of education, this led to teaching strategies in which learners are conditioned to perform correctly by using feedback and conditioning (Skinner, 1968). Edward Thorndike is closely identified with this approach in education, not only having studied animal and human behaviour and intelligence but also having advocated for the positivist, behaviorist paradigm as the way to conduct the scientific study of education (Lagemann, 2000). It should be noted that behaviorism is often linked with, but not identical to, the most commonly held folk theory of learning, that of instructivism. Instructivism holds that people learn things through simple transmission of messages ('I told them, so they must know'); this theory is implicitly evident in the use of language such as 'she gave a lesson' or 'he covered the concepts'. By contrast, behaviorism claims that people learn by being conditioned to respond to certain stimuli. Indeed, there is a deep contradiction between simple instructivism and radical behaviorism in that radical behaviorists reject the notion of mental states, at least as something accessible to science (Skinner, 1974). The behaviorist studies stimuli and responses (behaviors), and does not try to identify mental events such as thoughts, feelings, concepts, etc. This stance was in part a reaction to the Freudian methodology of studying human psychology through introspection, free association, etc. Instead, behaviorism treats the mind like a 'black box' where the inner workings must be revealed through careful experimentation and are presumed to be reducible to conditioned responses to stimuli.

In stark contrast to the behaviorism of Skinner and Thorndike, John Dewey developed a theory of progressive education based on a more practice-based, transactional view of learning. From Dewey's *My Pedagogic Creed* (1897):

> I believe that all education proceeds by the participation of the individual in the social consciousness of the race. This process begins unconsciously almost at birth, and is continually shaping the individual's powers, saturating his consciousness, forming his habits, training his ideas, and arousing his feelings and emotions. Through this unconscious education the individual gradually comes to share in the intellectual and moral resources which humanity has succeeded in getting together. He becomes an inheritor of the funded capital of civilization. The most formal and technical education in the world cannot safely depart from this general process. It can only organize it or differentiate it in some particular direction.
>
> (Dewey, 1929)

Dewey's philosophy is variously labelled progressivism, pragmatism, or functionalism. Rather than emphasizing the boundary between the learner and the environment and trying not to open the 'black box' of what might occur inside the learner, Dewey emphasized the tight connections between learner, social context, and resources. Dewey's pedagogy eventually came to be called progressive education, and emphasizes learning by doing and the relationship between authentic experiences and learning. Importantly, Dewey, although also an advocate of the empirical study of education, was not in agreement with Thorndike about what constituted appropriate methodology for educational research. Dewey was, perhaps primarily, a philosopher, but also helped found a famous laboratory school at the University of Chicago. Instead of conducting tightly controlled experiments of the sort Thorndike might have endorsed, Dewey was in many ways an advocate of doing research 'in the field' through collaboration with experienced teaching practitioners (at that time, generally women, while researchers or professors were generally men) (Lagemann, 2000).

A third early theory was developmentalism. The Swiss biologist, Jean Piaget, noted the similarities between his children's mental growth and the biological development of organisms more generally. Just as a flower's genetic program engendered a set of stages, from seed, to sprout, to plant, and finally to bloom, a child's mental development might be seen as progressing towards greater ability to think abstractly. And just as a flower might not bloom in exactly the same way as others (or even bloom at all) depending on environmental conditions, children's development could be enhanced or hindered by their experiences. This theory of development is highly influential in early childhood education and special education. Pedagogy is specifically targeted to be developmentally appropriate, that is, taking into account the limitations of what the learner can do at the current stage while trying to help them progress to the next. Piaget himself noted that while his early writings suggested a relatively rigid idea of development (i.e. that thinking abilities were strictly constrained by genes, and that everyone must progress through the exact same set of stages to reach more or less the same outcome) he became a cognitivist (explained below) later in life (Piaget, 1970).

Piaget's most famous educational contribution, however, was the notion of constructivism. Constructivism proposes that learning is the result of an individual's mental labour; the learner must create ideas and ways of thinking based on his or her experiences. He suggested that learning occurs through two processes, assimilation and accommodation – in assimilation, the learner incorporates ideas unproblematically into their current way of thinking, while in accommodation, learners must 'stretch their minds' to understand something. In either case, the learner's mental construction is the cause of learning (as opposed to the conditioning that took place). 'Constructivism' is probably one of the most overloaded terms in education, and means a great many different things to different groups of people. Most important, one must distinguish constructivism as a learning theory (learning is the result of mental work) from constructivism as a teaching philosophy. If one believes that students actively construct understandings, one may reasonably jump to a teaching strategy in which learners are autonomous, and discover ideas with minimal guidance, in the style of Jean-Jacques Rousseau (Ulich, 1954). However, this type of teaching strategy is not required by constructivist learning theory; the core idea of constructivism as learning theory is that successful learners do mental work to construct under-standings – even if their activities are rigidly structured. For instance, even in a brutally structured indoctrination camp, a constructivist would look to the learner's mental efforts to explain how learning could take place, and would hence be able to explain how some people might come to be brainwashed while others might develop sophisticated ways of resisting indoctrination.

Later twentieth century

The 1970s and 1980s saw a huge shift away from behaviorism, then the domi-nant paradigm in psychology and a hugely influential one in education. While the 'black box' of behaviorism was attractively objective, conditioned responses were not the most economical way to describe mental states – behaviorism did not extinguish the use of the words 'concept', 'thinking', 'imagining', and so on, and important aspects of learning were not well explained by behaviorism. The cognitive revolution was spurred by a number of developments in linguistics, neurology, anthropology, education, and the nascent computer science (Gardner, 1985). Rather quickly, cognitivism replaced behaviorism as the dominant para-digm in experimental psychology; clever experiments allowed researchers to begin to understand the mental machinery that allowed humans to process infor-mation, and the metaphor of mind-as-computer became a powerful influence on learning theory (Newell, 1990). In an information-processing view of learning, the human mind learns by essentially encoding information as symbols and pro-cedures, just as a computer encodes data and programmes using memory and CPUs. Cognitivism harkens back to instructivism, in that a learner reading a book might be viewed as learning through a process of decoding the squiggles on the page, encoding them as having semantic meaning, storing them into long-term memory, and so forth – teaching as telling, with the twist of active processing of messages coming in and going out. But cognitivists also embraced constructivism, the mental cogitation being the construction activity that Piaget identified. Cognitivism was begun in part by education researchers such as Jerome Bruner (Bruner, 1968). As mentioned earlier, Piaget later saw much of developmentalism as being compatible with cognitivism and began to view some developmental stages as being the product of biological processes, but others as being the product of cognitive ones.

Cognitivism gave rise to both a field and a meta-field. The field of Cognitive Psychology assimilated cognitive perspectives into the experimental methods of laboratory-based psychology. But cognitivism also led to the creation of the cog-nitive sciences, a loose affiliation of researchers from many disciplines, including philosophy, linguistics, neurology, computer science, psychology, sociology, anthropology, and education. In general, each component discipline retained its disciplinary methods, community, and theories, but cognitive science became a crossroads by which these disciplines informed or constrained each other on explanations of the same phenomena. In some cases, through collaboration or cross-training, multiple paradigms are blended to advance understanding of cognition. The process has clear parallels in Learning Sciences, in which a key characteristic of the field is its multidisciplinarity.

A final theory deserves mention. In the early twentieth century Lev Vygotsky, a Russian psychologist, developed theories of learning that were connected to social situations. Vygotsky was not well known in North America until his work was translated and interpreted in the 1970s and 1980s (Vygotsky, 1974; Wertsch, 1985). Vygotsky noted that what a child could accomplish with an adult helper was more expert than what the child could do alone; he defined the *zone of proximal development* to be the difference between these proficiencies. While this could be given a biological development interpretation, it today forms the basis of a large school of socially situated learning. Situated learning theory (Lave and Wenger, 1991) argues that learning is more of a social process than a mental one, that through processes of enculturation, individuals pick up the habits and practices of the cultures in which they are immersed, and that this is just as true of school-based learning as it is of ancient traditional apprenticeships. Hence a situated learning theorist might think less about how learners absorb the content of mathematics, and more about how learners 'become mathematicians', with all the social and cultural entailments, including the performance of mathematical practices.

Theoretical commitments within the learning sciences

Generally, learning scientists tend to draw most heavily on cognitive or situated learning theories in their work. Indeed, many of the most interesting theories within Learning Sciences today come from attempts to reconcile cognitive and situated perspectives, such as (to name just three of many such examples): models of distributed cognition (Hutchins, 1995) which analyse social and cultural phenomenon from the point of view of people and their tools as a distributed information processing systems; the model of cognitive apprenticeship (Collins *et al.*, 1989) in which learners are viewed as being supported or coached through cognitive processes by social actors and technologies; or the work of Geoffrey Saxe (Saxe, 1999) in which 'a core thesis is that a wide range of cognitive developments take form in and depend upon cultural practices and that new developments in culture [culture change] involve the cognitive constructions of individuals' (1999: 19).

Another theoretical commitment within Learning Sciences is towards constructivist theories of learning and pedagogies. In general, the learning sciences have not focused on more didactic information transmission teaching strategies, or on conditioning strategies, but rather the ways learners can be supported to construct understanding. Although some in the community adopt forms of constructivism which lean towards discovery learning, such as Papert's constructionism (Papert, 1980), the role of *scaffolding* – structure within opportunities for discovery, much as a tutor structures a learner's activity (Wood *et al.*, 1976) – is one of the central topics in the field (Quintana *et al.*, 2004; B. Reiser, 2002).

Methods and assumptions

What contributions can the learning sciences make to the study of e-learning? Here, some of the methods and assumptions of the Learning Sciences can be of use. What follows is not a complete characterization of learning sciences, nor are the attributes specified below unique to the learning sciences. However, in combination they help show how Learning Sciences are aligned with the products of e-learning research (theories, tools, activities, and design models).

Emphasis on multidisciplinary empirical understanding

First of all, the learning sciences are generally empiricist, i.e., they rely on systematic collection and use of data. This is not to put down non-empirical methods, such as philosophical enquiry or critical deconstruction. It does, however, support the development and refinement of theories, and in many cases the development and refinement of design models. Through evaluation, it can be used to refine particular designs including tools and activities.

The learning sciences are pluralist when it comes to research methods, theories, and even basic paradigms, which is particularly useful in e-learning research; in the 1990s the learning sciences underwent a heavy debate between situated, sociocultural views of learning and positivist, cognitive understandings of learning. As described above, this has led to some useful blendings of theories such as cognitive apprenticeship (Collins *et al.*, 1991), useful blending of methods of cognitive and cultural analysis (Pea, 1993a; Salomon, 1997; Saxe, 1992), and entirely new methods such as design-based research methods (Brown, 1992; Collins *et al.*, 2004; Design-Based Research Collective, 2003) which 'boils down to trying to understand the world by trying to change it' (Hoadley, 2005a: 46).

Problematizing context

A second characteristic of Learning Sciences is problematizing social context. E-learning often involves online collaboration, which both violates many assumptions we have about learning contexts and permits engineering of new contexts. This theme has been taken up both by CSCL researchers and by learning scientists generally. Design-based research methods have been defined as:

> an emerging paradigm for the study of learning in context through the systematic design and study of instructional strategies and tools … We propose that good design-based research exhibits the following five characteristics: First, the central goals of designing learning environments and developing theories or 'prototheories' of learning are intertwined.

Second, development and research take place through continuous cycles of design, enactment, analysis, and redesign (Cobb, 2001; Collins, 1992). Third, research on designs must
lead to sharable theories that help communicate relevant implications to practitioners and
other educational designers (cf. Brophy, 2002). Fourth, research must account for how
designs function in authentic settings. It must not only document success or failure but also
focus on interactions that refine our understanding of the learning issues involved. Fifth, the
development of such accounts relies on methods that can document and connect processes
of enactment to outcomes of interest.

(Design-Based Research Collective, 2003: 5)

DBRM has, in particular, challenged a number of assumptions that previously
kept different methodologies in the learning sciences distinct. Positivist, experimental methods presume that there are regular laws in the universe and that,
through controlled experimentation, random assignment, and objective measurement, these laws can be uncovered and used to predict the future (Levin and
O'Donnell, 1999). On the other hand, anthropological and ethnographic methodologies assume that social contexts are largely unique and often inaccessible to
outsiders; that no claims about human activity can be made from an objective,
neutral perspective but rather always bear the signature of the observer's history,
background, and point of view; and that prediction is not nearly as important as
description and interpretation (Lincoln and Guba, 1991). This has, within the
social sciences generally, led to 'methods wars' between so-called 'quantitative
versus qualitative' methodologies (although the debate has little to do with
counting versus categorizing). These wars revolve around what is 'scientific'
and, more pragmatically, whether prediction is the primary goal of research or
understanding, what generalization may or may not be possible, and whether any
truth can be called reasonably objective. Design-based research has violated
both of these major traditions, by embracing the idea that contexts are in fact
unique and prediction may be difficult, and by simultaneously trying to make
empirical claims through interventionist manipulation. In general, learning scientists take seriously problems of how contexts differ (i.e., how the culture of
one class may differ from another, or the cultural background of one learner may
differ from another) in attempting to design solutions for learning problems.

The challenges of design and accountability to practice

Another noteworthy feature of the learning sciences is a focus on studying educational interventions *in situ*. Northwestern University's graduate program in
Learning Sciences, the first in the world, describes Learning Sciences as the
confluence of social context, cognition, and design. Historically, Learning
Sciences have begun at a relatively small grain size of individuals' cognition and
their use of isolated tools or curriculum, but have increasingly become concerned with the relationship of different grain sizes (Lemke, 2001) and levels of
analysis (Collins, 1996; Pea, 1993b; Salomon, 1996; Sandoval, 2002). For
instance, a designer of an online learning unit for secondary education might be

deeply concerned with the relatively small grain size of 'What will the user think here, and what psychological, technical, or other constraints must I work within?' But this same designer may need to be equally concerned with different grain sizes, such as 'Will this unit meet different types of learning standards in different states?' or 'What are the social and cultural realities that will shape how this unit is perceived?' or even 'What kinds of systemic change might this unit either demand or support to be used effectively?'

As mentioned before, the learning sciences are relatively agnostic towards design of artefacts (technology, but also educational materials) versus the design of intangibles such as activities, preferring instead to discuss design of 'learning environments', taken to include the entire educational package (Bell, 2004; Hoadley, 2004b; Joseph, 2004). Hence a learning scientist creating a middle school science learning environment might be concerned with aspects of the design such as a novel technology introduced into the classroom, or they might be concerned with a different kind of innovation, such as block scheduling, wherein student class periods are rearranged to allow long blocks of time for science experiments. Indeed, identifying which aspects of any learning environment (whether engineered by the researcher or 'naturally' occurring) constitutes the spirit or meat of the intervention is a significant challenge. This applies directly to e-learning, which is an intervention that may simultaneously affect teaching, technology design, and program design. By studying learning 'in the wild', so to speak, researchers are forced to confront practical realities influencing implementation of learning interventions, as well as aspects of how particular contexts of implementation might differ (Hall, 1996).

This contextualization of research in real settings connects to all four of e-learning research's outcomes discussed above, but especially bridges theories with tools and activities. A simple way to sum it up is that because the learning sciences study learning in real settings, they must rely on the existence of some minimally functional learning environment – something that works in practice as well as in theory – and hence are culpable to what is practical. This type of knowledge has been termed *usable knowledge* (Design-Based Research Collective, 2003; Fishman *et al.*, 2004; Lagemann, 2002).

As a result of the need to create learning environments to study, the learning sciences have paid attention to the role of design both as a component of meaningful research (Edelson, 2002; Hoadley, 2002; Sandoval, 2004) and as a means to produce further innovations through accretion of design models or design knowledge (Baumgartner and Bell, 2002; Bell, 2002; Hewitt and Scardamalia, 1998; Kali, 2006; Norman, 1992; Underwood *et al.*, 2005). Furthermore, as Learning Sciences increasingly connect to traditional design disciplines such as instructional design (historically grounded in the design of curricular materials and media) and human–computer interface design (historically tied to ergonomics and human-factors engineering), the field increasingly attempts to deliberately codify design knowledge for learning settings (Brown and Campione, 1990; Hoadley, 2002; Newman *et al.*, 1989; Resnick *et al.*, 1991; Saxe, 1992; Tabak, 2004).

The focus on knowledge derived from realistic settings occasionally causes conflict between traditional standards for scientific inferencing and the pragmatics of implementing interventions. diSessa has termed this type of work a *local science* (diSessa, 1991), in that attempts are made in research to build locally coherent understandings of phenomena, while recognizing that the generalizability of those findings, and indeed the basic assumptions of the research, may not hold true in all cases. In the instructional design field, the distinction is made between design models and learning theories (R. A. Reiser, 2001) whereas learning scientists may not see these as sharply distinct categories (e.g., Barab *et al.*, 2000). Indeed, for a computer scientist who participates in the learning sciences, the distinction between a design model and a theory may seem somewhat nonsensical, since computer science research often involves empiricism only through design, frequently within an engineering paradigm that emphasizes the explanation of artificial, rather than natural, phenomena (cf. Simon, 1969), and in which theories are embodied by implementations in hardware or software (Computing Research Association, 1999).

To sum up, the learning sciences are often characterized by three types of methods or assumptions: multidisciplinary, empirical understanding (and hence multiple assumptions and methodologies), a commitment to contextualizing research in terms of not just universals but also particulars of setting and practice, and finally accountability to implementation, practicality, and, thus, design.

CONNECTIONS BETWEEN LEARNING SCIENCES AND E-LEARNING

Earlier I listed four desirable outcomes of e-learning research (as contrasted with e-learning practice): theories to support, constrain, and explain phenomena that take place within online learning environments; research on tools for e-learning; research on what types of activities are useful in which applications; and design methods that allow the tailoring of more general knowledge in e-learning to particular situations or applications.

With respect to e-learning theories, the learning sciences draws on many traditions to explain one of the most central phenomena of interest, namely how people learn. While this is by no means the only kind of theory of interest in e-learning (for example, economic theory has much to offer university administrators trying to grapple with e-learning as a new angle on their traditional 'business'), it is central to course designers, technology designers, and e-learning instructors or facilitators. A particular strength of learning sciences is their use of theories that encompass both individual learning and group learning, which is especially germane in e-learning (as contrasted with, for instance, correspondence courses, in which individual learning is much more important). For instance, the theory of cognitive apprenticeship helps suggest both what types of information should be useful to individuals and how this information might be shared from one peer to another through the strategy of 'making thinking visible.' Another strength of theories from the learning sciences is that taking context seriously means that the Learning Sciences community has means to examine how, for instance, an online context differs from face-to-face context, or to help study how shifting cultural norms regarding online behaviour might influence or modulate e-learning; one might ask how e-learning differs in the 1990s compared to the 2000s, or from country to country, or from one cultural group to another.

Tool-oriented research is also important to both e-learning and Learning Sciences researchers. First, the design and implementation orientation of the learning sciences, coupled with the interdisciplinarity and historical inclusion of computer science in the learning sciences, enables the work to address some of the engineering concerns in e-learning. While other domains such as software engineering, information science, library science, and even low-level concerns such as databases and networking have a great deal to offer to e-learning researchers, learning sciences contains a body of research on and a number of fascinating designs for the uses of technology to support learning individually and collectively. Many of these research programs link technology to other concerns. For instance, work might look at how online representations are understood and used by people (Dwyer and Suthers, 2005), what sorts of ontologies, metadata, and information retrieval methods are useful for systems development (Hoppe *et al.*, 2005), or attempt to design multi-device frameworks suitable for collaborative learning activities (Lyons *et al.*, 2006). Another important link between learning sciences and e-learning research on tools is the use of design-oriented research methodologies (such as design-based research) that permit tool refinement as a side effect of social science research.

With respect to the e-learning goal of activity design and research, the learning sciences' neutrality towards both tangible and intangible aspects of learning environments is helpful. The situated learning perspective, or considering learning as inherently contextualized in a social setting, allows the designer to consider the whole 'package', including both activities or practices as well as artefacts and the ways that these combine to form outcomes (Pea, 1993a; Roth and McGinn, 1998; Salomon, 1996). For instance, Brown described the highly effective reciprocal teaching activity structure, and connects this to the artefacts and contexts that supported the activity (Brown and Campione, 1990). Sometimes artefacts are far less important than cultural or situational factors affecting learning activities (Esmonde and Saxe, 2004). Modern work examines connections between theories, tools, and activities as actually enacted in practice. Note that the connection between intended and actual practices or activities is in many cases a fundamental design challenge (Cobb, 2001; Hmelo-Silver *et al.*, 2005; Kirschner *et al.*, 2004; Tabak, 2004).

The final goal of e-learning research, the production of design models and methods, is also increasingly a focus of learning scientists. As described above, the problem of producing phenomena to study them, and the additional pressure to take innovations 'to scale,' – to broadly disseminate them (Fishman *et al.*, 2004) – means that by necessity learning scientists have become designers. This has led to reflection on not only the design outcomes but also the design process itself (Edelson, 2002) and ways of sharing design knowledge (Baumgartner and Bell, 2002; Bell, 2002; Carroll *et al.*, 2003; Kali, 2006). Strikingly, these types of design knowledge can be subject to empirical validation (Underwood *et al.*, 2005) despite the fact that applying design knowledge is notoriously dependent on professional judgement and does not lend itself to regimentation (Argyris and Schön, 1991). In the particular case of design-based research, the researcher produces a rich literature not only on findings but also on how design trajectories unfold over time, providing cases and design narratives that may prove essential to e-learning designers as well (Hoadley, 2002).

CONCLUSION

To sum up, this chapter has examined the products of e-learning research, provided a historical and theoretical background to work in the learning sciences, and made connections between the learning sciences and e-learning research needs. E-learning research aims to provide theories, tools, activities, and design models. The learning sciences are a multidisciplinary, empirical discipline that studies learning both through modern, situated and cognitive learning theories and through learning environment designs (both activities and artefacts or technologies) that are implemented in real contexts. Particular attention is paid to the connection between design and learning and to the context-sensitivity of learning interventions. These features allow the learning sciences to inform e-learning research and development and suggest that Learning Sciences may play a greater role in e-learning research in the future.

NOTES

1   WebQuests, developed initially by Bernie Dodge and Tom March in 1995, are a type of learning activity that uses Web-based resources to permit students to do an enquiry-based learning activity. According to Dodge's original description at http://webquest.sdsu.edu/about_webquests.html, a WebQuest has six features, including introduction, task, information resources, a process or steps for the learners, guidance on synthesis of the information resources, and some sort of conclusion or wrap-up. The model has proven widely popular with teachers due in part to its simplicity and reusability.

2   http://www.tisip.no/E-LEN.

REFERENCES

Argyris, C., and Schön, D. A. (1991) *Theory in Practice: Increasing Professional Effectiveness* (first Classic Paperback edn). San Francisco, CA: Jossey-Bass.

Avgeriou, P., Papasalouros, A., Retalis, S., and Skordalakis, M. (2003) 'Towards a pattern language for learning management systems', *Educational Technology & Society*, 6 (2): 11–24.

Barab, S. A., Squire, K. D., and Dueber, W. (2000) 'A co-evolutionary model for supporting the emergence of authenticity', *Educational Technology Research and Development*, 48 (2): 37–62.

Baumgartner, E., and Bell, P. L. (2002) 'What will we do with Design Principles? Design Principles and principled Design Practice'. Paper presented at the annual meeting of the American Educational Research Association, New Orleans.

Bell, P. L. (2002) 'Developing New Representational Forms for Educational Design Knowledge: Moving beyond Design Principles and Case Studies'. Paper presented at the annual meeting of the American Educational Research Association, New Orleans.

Bell, P. L. (2004) 'On the theoretical breadth of design-based research in education', *Educational Psychologist*, 39 (4): 243–53.

Brown, A. L. (1992) 'Design experiments: theoretical and methodological challenges in creating complex interventions in classroom settings', *Journal of the Learning Sciences*, 2 (2): 141–78.

Brown, A. L., and Campione, J. C. (1990) 'Communities of learning and thinking: a context by any other name', *Contributions to Human Development*, 21: 108–26.

Bruner, J. S. (1968) *Toward a Theory of Instruction*. New York: Norton.

Carroll, J. M., Rosson, M. B., Dunlap, D., and Isenhour, P. (2003) 'Frameworks for sharing knowledge: toward a professional language for teaching practices', in *Proceedings of the XXXVI Hawaii International Conference on System Sciences* (HICSS) Honolulu, HI: IEEE. pp. 1–10.

Cobb, P. (2001) 'Supporting the improvement of learning and teaching in social and institutional context', in S. M. Carver and D. Klahr (eds.), *Cognition and Instruction: Twenty-five Years of Progress*. Mahwah, NJ: Erlbaum. pp. 455–78.

Collins, A. (1996) 'Design issues for learning environments', in S. Vosniadou, E. De Corte, R. Glaser and H. Mandl (eds.), *International Perspectives on the Design of Technology-Supported Learning Environments*. Mahwah, NJ: Erlbaum. pp. 347–61.

Collins, A., Bielaczyc, K., and Joseph, D. (2004) 'Design experiments: theoretical and methodological issues', *Journal of the Learning Sciences*, 13 (1): 15–42.

Collins, A., Brown, J. S., and Holum, A. (1991) 'Cognitive apprenticeship: making thinking visible', *American Educator* (winter): 6–11, 38–46.

Collins, A., Brown, J. S., and Newman, S. E. (1989) 'Cognitive apprenticeship: teaching the crafts of reading, writing, and mathematics', in L. B. Resnick (ed.), *Knowing, Learning, and Instruction: Essays in Honor of Robert Glaser*. Hillsdale, NJ: Erlbaum. pp. 453–94.

Computing Research Association (1999) *Best Practices Memo: Evaluating Computer Scientists and Engineers for Promotion and Tenure*. Wasington, DC: Computing Research Association.

Design-Based Research Collective (2003) 'Design-based research: an emerging paradigm for educational inquiry', *Educational Researcher*, 32 (1): 5–8.

Dewey, J. (1929) *My Pedagogic Creed*. Washington, DC: Progressive Education Association.

diSessa, A. (1991) 'Local sciences: viewing the design of human computer systems as cognitive science', in J. M. Carroll (ed.), *Designing Interaction: Psychology at the Human–Computer Interface*. New York: Cambridge University Press. pp. 162–202.

Driscoll, M. P. (1984) 'Alternative paradigms for research in instructional systems', *Journal of Instructional Development*, 7 (4): 2–5.

Dwyer, N., and Suthers, D. D. (2005) 'A Study of the Foundations of Artifact-mediated Collaboration.' Paper presented at the Computer-Supported Collaborative Learning Conference, Taipei, Taiwan.

Edelson, D. C. (2002) 'Design research: what we learn when we engage in design', *Journal of the Learning Sciences*, 11 (1): 105–21.

Esmonde, I., and Saxe, G. B. (2004) '"Cultural Mathematics" in the Oksapmin Curriculum: Continuities and Discontinuities'. Paper presented at the International Conference of the Learning Sciences, Santa Monica, CA.

Fishman, B., Marx, R. W., Blumenfeld, P. C., Krajcik, J., and Soloway, E. (2004) 'Creating a framework for research on systemic technology innovations', *Journal of the Learning Sciences*, 13 (1): 43–76.

Gardner, H. (1985) *The Mind's New Science: A History of the Cognitive Revolution*. New York: Basic Books.

Hall, R. (1996) 'Representation as shared activity: situated cognition and Dewey's cartography of experience', *Journal of the Learning Sciences*, 5 (3): 209–38.

Hewitt, J., and Scardamalia, M. (1998) 'Design principles for distributed knowledge building processes', *Educational Psychology Review*, 10 (1): 75–96.

Hmelo-Silver, C. E., Derry, S. J., Woods, D., DelMarcelle, M., and Chernobilsky, E. (2005) 'From parallel play to meshed interaction: the evolution of the eSTEP system', in T. Koschmann, D. D. Suthers and T.-w. Chan (eds.), *CSCL 2005: The next ten Years. Proceedings of the International Conference on Computer Supported Collaborative Learning 2005*. Taipei, Taiwan: Erlbaum. pp. 195–204.

Hoadley, C. (2002) 'Creating context: design-based research in creating and understanding CSCL', in G. Stahl (ed.), *Computer Support for Collaborative Learning 2002*. Mahwah, NJ: Erlbaum. pp. 453–62.

Hoadley, C. (2004a) 'Learning and design: why the learning sciences and instructional systems need each other', *Educational Technology*, 44 (3): 6–12.

Hoadley, C. (2004b) 'Methodological alignment in design-based research', *Educational Psychologist*, 39 (4): 203–12.

Hoadley, C. (2005a) 'Design-based research methods and theory building: a case study of research with SpeakEasy', *Educational Technology*, 45 (1): 42–7.

Hoadley, C. (2005b) 'The shape of the elephant: scope and membership of the CSCL community', in T. Koschmann, D. D. Suthers and T.-w. Chan (eds.), *Computer-supported Collaborative Learning (CSCL) 2005*. Taipei, Taiwan: International Society of the Learning Sciences. pp. 205–10.

Hoppe, U., Pinkwart, N., Oelinger, M., Zeini, S., Verdejo, F., Barros, B., et al. (2005) 'Building Bridges within Learning Communities through Ontologies and "Thematic Objects"'. Paper presented at the Computer-Supported Collaborative Learning conference, Taipei, Taiwan.

Hung, D., Looi, C.-K., and Hin, L. T. W. (2005) 'Facilitating inter-collaborations in the learning sciences', *Educational Technology*, 45 (4): 41–4.

Hutchins, E. (1995) *Cognition in the Wild*. Cambridge, MA: MIT Press.

Joseph, D. (2004) 'The practice of design-based research: uncovering the interplay between design, research, and the real-world context', *Educational Psychologist*, 39 (4): 235–42.

Kali, Y. (2006) 'Collaborative knowledge building using a design principles database', *International Journal of Computer Supported Collaborative Learning*, 1 (2): 187–201.

Kirby, J., Hoadley, C., and Carr-Chellman, A. A. (2005) 'Instructional systems design and the learning sciences: a citation analysis', *Educational Technology Research and Development*, 53 (1): 37–48.

Kirschner, P., Strijbos, J.-W., Kreijns, K., and Jelle Beers, P. (2004) 'Designing electronic collaborative learning environments', *Educational Technology Research and Development*, 52 (3): 47–66.

Kolodner, J. L. (1991) 'The *Journal of the Learning Sciences*: effecting changes in education', *Journal of the Learning Sciences*, 1 (1): 1–6.

Lagemann, E. C. (2000) *An Elusive Science: The Troubling History of Education Research*. Chicago, IL: University of Chicago Press.

Lagemann, E. C. (2002) 'Usable knowledge in education: a memorandum for the Spencer Foundation board of directors'. Chicago, IL: Spencer Foundation.

Lave, J., and Wenger, E. (1991) *Situated Learning: Legitimate Peripheral Participation*. New York: Cambridge University Press.

'Learning Sciences and Instructional Systems: Beginning the Dialogue' (2004) *Educational Technology*, 44 (3), special issue.

Lemke, J. L. (2001) 'The long and short of it: comments on multiple timescale studies of human activity', *Journal of the Learning Sciences*, 10 (1): 17–26.

Levin, J. R., and O'Donnell, A. M. (1999) 'What to do about educational research's credibility gaps', *Issues in Education*, 5 (2): 177–229.

Lincoln, Y. S., and Guba, E. G. (1991) *Naturalistic Inquiry*. Newbury Park, CA: Sage.

Lyons, L., Lee, J., Quintana, C., and Soloway, E. (2006) 'MUSHI: A Multi-device Framework for Collaborative Inquiry Learning'. Paper presented at the International Conference of the Learning Sciences, Bloomington, IN.

Newell, A. (1990) *Unified Theories of Cognition*. Cambridge, MA: Harvard University Press.

Newman, D., Griffin, P., and Cole, M. (1989) *The Construction Zone: Working for Cognitive Change in School*. New York: Cambridge University Press.

Norman, D. A. (1992) 'Design principles for cognitive artifacts', *Research in Engineering Design*, 4 (1): 43–50.

Papert, S. (1980) *Mindstorms*. New York: Basic Books.

Pea, R. (1993a) 'Practices of distributed intelligence and designs for education', in G. Salomon (ed.), *Distributed Cognitions: Psychological and Educational Considerations*. New York: Cambridge University Press. pp. 47–87.

Pea, R. (1993b) 'Seeing what we build together: distributed multimedia learning environments for transformative communications', *Journal of the Learning Sciences*, 3 (3): 285–99.

Piaget, J. (1970) 'Piaget's theory', trans. G. L. Gellerier, in P. Mussen (ed.), *Carmichael's Manual of Child Psychology* (3rd edn) I. New York: Wiley. pp. 703–32.

Quintana, C., Reiser, B., Davis, E. A., Krajcik, J., Fretz, E., Duncan, R. G., et al. (2004) 'A scaffolding design framework for software to support science inquiry', *Journal of the Learning Sciences*, 13 (3): 337–86.

Reigeluth, C. M. (1999) 'What is instructional-design theory and how is it changing?', in C. M. Reigeluth (ed.), *Instructional-Design Theories and Models: A New Paradigm of Instructional Theory* (II) Mahwah, NJ: Erlbaum. pp. 5–29.

Reiser, B. (2002) 'Why scaffolding should sometimes make tasks more difficult for learners', in G. Stahl (ed.), *Computer Support for Collaborative Learning (CSCL) 2002*. Mahwah, NJ: Erlbaum. pp. 255–64.

Reiser, R. A. (2001) 'A history of instructional design and technology' II, 'A history of instructional design', *Educational Technology Research and Development*, 49 (2): 57–67.

Resnick, L. B., Levine, J. M., and Teasley, S. D. (eds) (1991) *Perspectives on Socially Shared Cognition*. Washington, DC: American Pyschological Association.

Roth, W.-M., and McGinn, M. K. (1998) 'Inscriptions: toward a theory of representing as social practice', *Review of Educational Research*, 68 (1): 35–59.

Salomon, G. (1996) 'Studying novel learning environments as patterns of change', in S. Vosniadou, E. De Corte, R. Glaser and H. Mandl (eds), *International Perspectives on the Design of Technology-Supported Learning Environments*. Mahwah, NJ: Erlbaum. pp. 363–77.

Salomon, G. (1997) *Distributed Cognitions: Psychological and Educational Considerations*. New York: Cambridge University Press.

Sandoval, W. A. (2002) 'Learning from Designs: Learning Environments as Embodied Hypotheses'. Paper presented at the annual meeting of the American Educational Research Association, New Orleans, April.

Sandoval, W. A. (2004) 'Developing learning theory by refining conjectures embodied in educational designs', *Educational Psychologist*, 39 (4): 213–23.

Sawyer, R. K. (Ed.) (2006) *The Cambridge Handbook of the Learning Sciences*. Cambridge and New York: Cambridge University Press.

Saxe, G. B. (1992) 'Studying children's learning context: problems and prospects', *Journal of the Learning Sciences*, 2 (2): 215–34.

Saxe, G. B. (1999) Cognition, development, and cultural practices', in E. Turiel (ed.), *Development and Cultural Change: Reciprocal Processes* (XXXIII). San Francisco, CA: Jossey-Bass. pp. 19–35.

Simon, H. A. (1969) *The Sciences of the Artificial*. Cambridge, MA: MIT Press.

Skinner, B. F. (1968) *The Technology of Teaching*. Englewood Cliffs, NJ: Prentice-Hall.

Skinner, B. F. (1974) *About Behaviorism* (1st edn). New York: Knopf.

Tabak, I. (2004) 'Reconstructing context: negotiating the tension between exogenous and endogenous educational design', *Educational Psychologist*, 39 (4): 225–33.

Ulich, R. (1954) *Three Thousand Years of Educational Wisdom* (2nd edn). Cambridge, MA: Harvard University Press.

Underwood, J., Hoadley, C., Stohl, H., Hollebrands, K., diGiano, C., and Renninger, K. A. (2005) 'IDEA: identifying design principles in educational applets', *Educational Technology Research and Development*, 53 (2): 99–112.

Vygotsky, L. S. (1974) *Mind in Society: The Development of Higher Psychological Processes,* (trans. M. Cole). Cambridge, MA: Harvard University Press.

Wertsch, J. (1985) *Vygotsky and the Social Formation of Mind*. Cambridge, MA: Harvard University Press.

Wood, D., Bruner, J. S., and Ross, G. (1976) 'The role of tutoring in problem solving', *Journal of Child Psychology and Psychiatry and Allied Disciplines*, 17 (2): 89–100.

PART II

Theory

7

From Distance Education to E-learning

Melody M. Thompson

For many educators, the phrase 'from distance education to e-learning' conjures up the view of an 'evolutionary' progression that began with correspondence study and developed through ever more sophisticated technologies to its current identification with computers, the Internet, and the World Wide Web. For others, particularly those with little knowledge of (and often equally little interest in) the field of distance education, e-learning represents a totally new phenomenon with the potential to transform traditional higher education.

Both views reflect an implicit faith in expanded possibilities. However, the term currently used to denote these expanded possibilities – that is, 'e-learning' – in fact represents a *narrowing* of rhetoric that has already resulted in conceptual confusion and could, over time, have specific negative implications for faculty, students, and researchers. Even assuming that this change in terminology is inevitable at this point, it is important to emphasize elements of this expanding activity that, while not readily apparent in the term 'e-learning' itself, must be understood and included in theorizing about, planning for, and conducting research about the phenomenon.

This chapter will discuss changes that have led to an increasingly circumscribed conceptualization of a broad area of educational practice; examine some implications of this way of thinking based on linguistic theory; offer a rationale for a more holistic approach; and suggest research considerations for the educational practice referred to variously as distance education, online education, online learning, and e-learning. The views discussed here are informed by almost twenty years in the field of distance education.

DISTANCE EDUCATION AND ITS TERMINOLOGY

Anderson and Elloumi (2004) report that in the last 150 years distance education has 'evolved' through four generations, beginning with correspondence study, through those characterized by the mass media (television and radio), synchronous technologies (video- and audio-conferencing), and computer conferencing, to the emerging fifth generation, 'the educational Semantic Web'. They further note that each new generation has been added to the succeeding ones, with the result that currently all five are operating in the overall educational context at the same time.

The changes occurring in the field of distance education have had a profound impact on its recognition and adoption by traditional educational institutions. During the first three generations, distance education was a relatively minor, often marginalized, activity conducted and promoted by a small group of educators dedicated to broadening access to educational programming to unserved or under-served populations of students. These educators used a variety of media and media combinations to offer programmes to students who, because of physical barriers of distance or personal circumstances, were unable to participate in educational programmes at traditional institutions. Within traditional institutions, serving non-traditional students was usually viewed as ancillary to the core institutional mission. The number of students served by distance education programmes was small, and the institutional support and oversight given were proportionally limited and focused on ensuring that such programmes did not detract from the institution's reputation (Thompson and Irele, 2003).

But now, thanks to the power and reach of the World Wide Web, distance education has been 'discovered'. Recast first as 'online learning', then as 'e-learning', it has moved from the margins into the mainstream. No longer is it tolerated only as long as it conforms and defers to the 'real thing'. No longer is it an alternative primarily for non-traditional students – indeed, it is rapidly being incorporated into programmes serving traditional campus-based students under its newest banner, 'blended learning' (Thompson and Irele, 2003). This rapid movement into the mainstream of higher education reflects a new image for distance education: capitalizing on the *E is for Everything* furore, it promises a technology-based transformation of most if not all aspects of society, including education (Katz and Ohlinger, 2000).

FROM THE MARGINS TO THE MAINSTREAM ... AND BACK?

Yet, even as distance education began to achieve long-deferred recognition for the benefits it has provided and continues to provide, this established field of practice and research was almost immediately threatened with remarginalization. This threat has taken the form of an ahistorical attitude reflected in (1) the almost universal rejection of the term 'distance education' in favour of new terms coined to describe a type of education characterized not by 'distance', which was of little interest to all but a few people, but rather by the term 'electronic' (shortened to 'e'), which was of great interest to most people, and (2) the failure of 'e-learning' researchers to build on earlier theories and studies of prior forms of distance delivery. It is unnecessary to review here the story of the world's ever deepening love affair with technology in general (i.e., all things 'e'), or the computer in particular. We all not only know the story, but have contributed to it. What I want to explicate is not that story, but some implications of it – as reflected in these two attitudes – for students, faculty, and institutions.

Those who reject the term 'distance education' have presented a variety of reasons for doing so, among them the ideas that the term is associated with a marginalized activity, particularly correspondence study; that many 'e-learners' are physically present on campuses rather than at a distance; and that 'distance' references physical positionality characterized by institutions and teachers at the centre, a perspective that is inappropriate in a 'learner-centred' context.

Although this change in terminology may be inevitable, I believe that the reasons for change presented above have at best only partial validity, and that substitution of the term 'e-learning', while solving some difficulties, introduces others. For this reason I would like to present an argument, if not for retaining the term 'distance education', at least for (1) recognizing the crucial nature of both elements of the term and (2) respecting and building on the history of distance education by incorporating a focus on both 'distance' and 'education' in the developing theories, practice, and research of e-learning.

Distance is not dead

Mark Twain once noted that rumours of his death were greatly exaggerated; the same is true today of rumours relating to the 'death of distance' (Cairncross, 1997). The term 'distance' in distance education is assumed by many outside the field to refer simply to a physical property: the physical space separating learners from institution, teacher, and each other. Thus when arguing to 'update' terminology, some educators have suggested that new information and communications technologies effectively bridge that space, making it inappropriate to keep distance as the defining characteristic of teaching and learning supported by such technologies.

Saba (2005) points out two problems with this line of thinking. First, while arguing for the inadequacy of one physical property for defining a particular activity, it merely replaces the property of distance with another physical property – 'online', 'electronic' (shortened to 'e'), 'blended', etc. – which is both conceptually confusing and at least equally inadequate as a defining property of the phenomenon. For example, 'online', which originally referred to actual connection to a physical line, provides little conceptual or definitional guidance when connections *may* be maintained by physical 'lines' but just as often are supported by wireless means.

Similarly, the 'e' in e-learning stands for electronic, which appropriately applies to a wide range of technologies, although it is used almost always – but not exclusively – in reference to computer networks. Saba (2005) suggests that none of the terms currently proposed to replace distance education has been demonstrated to be a valid descriptive, explanatory, or organizing construct.

Second, for distance educators, the term 'distance' and their conceptualization of their activity as educators was never limited to a paradigm wherein they worked to bridge a merely physical distance. Rather it reflected a social science perspective that recognized that 'distance' was a factor that strongly influences all interpersonal interaction, including that known as 'education' (Saba, 2005). For distance educators, 'distance' has always referred to both a physical space that needs to be bridged, and, even more important, the psychological distance that characterizes any educational activity (Moore, 1983; Saba and Shearer 1994). As Jane Vella states in *Learning to Listen, Learning to Teach*, 'A significant issue when educating adults is the perceived distance between teacher and students' and finding dialogic ways to close this distance (Vella, 2002: xiv). Saba (2003: 17) concurs when he comments that:

> [Physical] separation can be bridged by communication technology, a fact demonstrated by teachers and students everywhere. But if students and teachers are separated by the total absence of dialog, as occurs in many classrooms across the country and around the world, bringing them together until they stand nose to nose will not offer a solution.

Clearly, the concept of distance can never be irrelevant to either technologically mediated or face-to-face education; to think that it can is to lack a fundamental understanding of a universal educational challenge.

Education versus learning

The second element in the term 'distance education' is equally important and equally out of favour with proponents of up-to-date terminology. In response to a perceived need to shift the focus from the instructor or the institution to the student, new terms have been coined that effectively eliminate one half of the social interaction formerly referred to as education. Whereas education is by definition a multi-faceted activity understood to involve a variety of players and activities – teachers and teaching, students and studying, information, knowledge and, it is hoped, learning – e-learning is a term comprising one letter representing a physical property of technology (e for electronic) and the *hoped-for* outcome (learning) for one participant in the interaction. Although some might argue that the learning refers to an outcome for all participants, the ubiquitous use of the term 'learner-centred' as a quality indicator leaves little doubt as to whose learning is being designated.

In one sense, substituting 'learning' for 'education' falls comfortably within the call to 'democratize' education by empowering students or learners. In another sense, it has the feel of magical thinking about it: name the promise (learning) and it's yours. This goes along well with other ideas we have about technology and its ability to deliver a variety of astonishing results completely divorced from any need to understand how and why it works. While this may work well with our DVD players and iPods, it is more of a problem when we begin to use shorthand thinking for complex social systems such as education. The question is, does shorthand terminology really lead to shorthand thinking?

THE POWER OF LANGUAGE

Linguistic theory and research suggest that language is a social process that both reflects an already established reality and contributes to the construction of an ever-changing reality. In other words, 'it is necessary to examine not only the social determination of language use but also the linguistic determination of society' (Fairclough, 1989). It is this latter idea, the linguistic determination of society – particularly that part of society represented by professional educators – that is of interest here.

Issues of language are central to understanding work communities, including communities of educators. Language, particularly in the form of texts, dynamically creates and maintains a particular profession or work community; it first structures human activity within it to shape initial visions of professional reality and then shapes the subsequent actions of individuals within that community (Bazerman and Paradis, 1990). Such shaping takes place through a variety of textual channels, including institutional policy documents and the newsletters, journals, and conferences of professional organizations.

All of this discourse works together to influence a variety of judgements regarding, among other things, research agendas, prioritization of institutional support, and who makes and who implements decisions related to institutional planning and change. To the extent that particular linguistic conventions make it more or less difficult to conceive of or to communicate about certain ideas, they limit or expand a profession's views of reality: not only of what is, but also of what could be and should be (Bazerman and Paradis, 1990). For this reason it is extremely important to ensure that the way we communicate about what we do not only reflects the reality of practice, but also enables and encourages its robust development in ways that maximize the benefits to all participants.

Re-marginalizing distant students

The 'exclusionary power' of language (Porter, 1986) is such that things that are not named (whether through spoken word, text, or images) are commonly devalued or ignored. Belief in this dynamic is reflected in society's efforts over the last several decades to more equitably represent women and minorities in a variety of textual and visual contexts. Similarly, thought must be given to how we name educational activities and how we communicate about them if we want to maximize their effectiveness and ensure that their value is recognized practically through institutional resource, planning, and research decisions. The differences in terminology discussed above are not mere hair-splitting distinctions. Rather, they have very real and potentially profound implications for excluding from our thinking important aspects of education. Specifically, unless care is taken to forestall this result, there is the potential to remarginalize both true distant students (e.g. those who never attend a physical campus) and all those who teach via 'e-learning'.

Many institutions that in the last decade became interested in Web-based education were motivated by a desire to increase institutional enrolments with students outside their traditional service areas (NCES, 2003). These institutions quickly learned what distance education providers had long known: students at a distance have unique needs related to physical and psychological separation, and the cost of providing appropriate services to bridge that distance is high. At the same time, the higher education community was becoming aware that its 'traditional' resident students were no longer traditional in either their characteristics or their expectations. Faced with both the unforeseen costs of serving distant students and the technological expectations of 'a generation hardwired since birth ... [and] impatient with a lack of technological sophistication in others' (Taylor, 2006: 103), many institutions began to rethink their plans to expand delivery to new populations and decided instead to incorporate the concept of e-learning into the traditional educational environment. 'E-learning' promises no focus on distant students and indeed the newer activity and its successor, 'blended learning,' are in many cases being viewed as a way to revitalize, in some cases even transform, traditional campus-based teaching and learning. This is indeed a benefit that we should not undervalue, particularly in that it not only enhances the educational experience of traditional students but also truly increases access for some students: those who have the flexibility to pursue a portion, but not all, of their studies on a physical campus. At the same time, it is important to note that resources initially planned to support extension of programmes to distant students are in many cases now being used to strengthen campus-based education, giving renewed credence to charges that technology-based education, rather than decreasing the gap between the educational 'haves' and 'have-not,' gives more educational capital to those who already have it (Bates, 1999; Tait, 1999).

The invisible teacher

A major determinant in the ultimate success of online higher education programmes will be a strong faculty commitment to teaching in this new environment. To date, a number of faculty members have voluntarily embraced online technologies and many of these have reported benefits that make the new educational environment a satisfying addition or alternative to traditional face-to-face instruction (Frederickson *et al.*, 1999; NEA, 2000; Hartman and Truman-Davis, 2001; Thompson, 2001).

However, the fact that some faculty members (erroneously labelled 'early adopters' based on a misapplication of Everett Rogers's diffusion of innovations theory) have embraced e-learning is not necessarily evidence of the gradual but ultimately universal adoption of e-learning by all faculty members (deJager, 2005). Many others have signalled resistance to participating in e-learning, and much of the resistance seems to be grounded in concern about the ability of e-learning experiences to provide the personal and professional satisfaction people naturally seek in their vocations. Such concerns make the linguistic invisibility of the teaching function in the term 'e-learning' particularly problematic.

Those who teach in higher education are more than service providers or content experts; they are professionals who seek personal as well as professional satisfaction from their chosen fields. Although we speak easily and frequently of student needs related to networked teaching – learning environments, recognition of the equally legitimate personal needs and motivations of faculty are often lost in today's 'learner-centred' rhetoric. The 2000 American Faculty Poll reported that, for higher education faculty, 'one of the most important factors … in their decision to pursue an academic career was the enjoyment of working with students' (Bower, 2001). Other research has shown that satisfaction with teaching in the online environment is directly related to the extent to which it allows faculty members to attain this and other personal rewards, including 'self-gratification' and 'overall job satisfaction' (Schifter, 2002).

Unfortunately, much of the recent e-learning discourse has in effect relegated teachers to a minor role. Naming their activity 'e-learning' obscures their professional contribution (i.e. teaching or educating), while calls for their 'disaggregation' and 'training' in the skills they need and the tasks they must perform essentially deprofessionalize faculty. As a participant in one research study on faculty satisfaction noted, '[T]his change in the pattern of my working day … has reduced and decentered intellectual tasks to competency and generic skill' (Brabazon, 2001). Jaffee (1998) suggests that this type of faculty dissatisfaction results not from the fact of a new innovation and the change it entails, but rather from a fundamental challenge to one's core professional identity. This challenge is exacerbated by a shift in power relations resulting from a perceived need on the part of institutions to exercise more-than-usual administrative control over this academic endeavour in order to justify and 'protect' institutional investments. As Shedletsky and Aitken (2001: 212) observe, 'Although administrators may have no expertise in computer pedagogy, scholarship, or general computer operation, administrators often make decisions on behalf of faculty,' with the result that faculty success becomes more and more dependent on factors outside of their control. These authors go on to note that this generalized shift in power relations leads to other changes that leave many faculty members feeling that their roles have been deprofessionalized, including:

- Required training workshops in which faculty are made to feel incompetent or ignorant by 'impatient, patronizing, or insolent support staff' (p. 214),
- Assumption of ownership by the institution of faculty members' online courses,
- Lack of recognition for e-learning work within the institutional reward structure.

bell hooks (1994: 15–16), writing about higher education in general, quotes Thich Nhat Hanh's statement that 'the practice of a … teacher or any helping professional should be directed toward his or herself first, because if the helper is unhappy, he or she cannot help many people'. hooks adds that 'it is rare … to hear anyone suggest that teachers have any responsibility to be self-actualized'. Rather than 'the objectification of the teacher' that seems to 'denigrate notions of wholeness', our practice and research should reflect a holistic approach to learning *and* teaching that stresses not only learner self-actualization, but also teacher self-actualization. In conceptualizing, labelling, and communicating about this form of teaching and learning we must keep teachers, as well as students, at the centre of a process that should always be aimed at fostering the personal growth of all participants. Failure to do so threatens to perpetuate the ambivalence many higher education faculty members feel about participating in this new form of education (Thompson, 2002).

FROM DISTANCE EDUCATION TO E-LEARNING: RESEARCH CHALLENGES

Let us accept that e-learning is the current 'term of art' for an activity whose name belies its true complexity: a form of education characterized by a multi-faceted, interactive system of structures, activities, responsibilities, and stakeholders that is networked to minimize physical and psychological distance. Given this robust understanding of the term, what are some important e-learning research challenges?

The ahistorical challenge

As noted earlier, recent and current e-learning research and practice are unfortunately unconnected to many years of distance education theory building and research. Kanuka and Conrad (2003), in response to a National Governors Association statement that 'e-learning has the potential to revolutionize the basic tenets of learning', suggest that such claims

> fail to acknowledge that the 'basic tenets of learning' rest on a long and significant past: twentieth century contributions by researchers and theorists such as Dewey, Piaget, Bloom, Gardner, Maslow, Skinner, Watson, Freud, Pavlov, Bruner, Papert, Erickson, Malaguzzi, and Vygotsky – built upon insights of philosophical giants Aristotle, Socrates, Sartre, and Plato. Claims of revolutionary advances in learning not only slight the contributions of these and other educational researchers and theorists, but also fail to recognize [that] … [w]ithin the field of distance education itself, decades of research have resulted in theory that guides both current practice and research.

(p. 390)

It is not possible in the context of this chapter to make all relevant connections between early distance education theories and research and current practice and research questions. Instead I will identify a few representative early distance educators whose work would seem to provide useful insights into current issues as well as at least partial foundations for further research in these areas.

Three leading distance education theorists, Charles Wedemeyer (1981), Michael G. Moore (1983, 1993), and Börje Holmberg (1983, 1991, 2003), based their theories on the centrality of the learners and their interactions with others. In particular, Moore's theory of 'transactional distance', which is not merely the physical distance but, more important, the *psychological* distance in the relationship between students and teachers, 'is important because it grounds the concept of distance in education in a social science framework ... a significant paradigm shift of the kind described by [Thomas] Kuhn' (Saba, 2003: 5). This theoretical construct was later validated through research conducted by Saba and Shearer (1994).

Many current e-learning researchers are focusing on interaction and collaborative learning as important affordances of e-learning and as key elements in high quality educational experiences. A number of distance education researchers, including Harasim (1987, 1989), Feenberg (1989, 1990), Hiltz (1986, 1994), Wagner (1994), and Gunawardena (1995) have been exploring interaction and collaborative learning in computer-mediated communication (CMC) for almost twenty years. May (1994), Burge (1994), and Gibson (1996; Gibson and Graff, 1992) are among the many researchers who examined distance education from the perspective of the student experience. Murphy (1991) focused on cross-cultural issues in the design of distance education programmes, and Kember and his associates (1991) conducted quantitative research on student progress to develop a theoretical model of student drop-out in distance education. Dillon and Walsh (1992) investigated issues related to the 'neglected resource in distance education': the faculty.

These researchers and many others produced a body of work that, although in some cases led to dead ends, in many others resulted in fruitful lines of further enquiry and improved practice in areas of interest to current e-learning researchers. To continue to neglect the progress made by earlier distance education theorists and researchers is to condemn ourselves to the proverbial reinvention of the wheel, with its accompanying waste of scarce resources. Both solid scholarship and responsible stewardship argue for an exploration of connections between past and current theory building and research.

'Best practices' challenge

One unfortunate result of the lack of knowledge of and connection to previous research and practice is a way of thinking that views e-learning as a totally new phenomenon. Rapid adoption of this largely unproven innovation has raised significant concerns about impact and quality that can only be addressed by research. As Bates (2000: 198) points out:

[Because of] the rapid speed with which new technologies for teaching are infiltrating even the most cautious and conservative of universities, and the lack of experience in the use and management of such technologies, the case for researching and evaluating the applications of these new technologies is obvious.

However, in large part due to the ahistorical attitude discussed above, study of e-learning has too often reflected the relatively superficial examinations that characterize a new field rather than the more robust studies that can be built on the foundational theories and research of a more mature field. In any new area, practice tends to outstrip theory building, research, and policy development (King *et al.*, 2000). In other words, new practices are introduced and publicized well before the research that can validate their effectiveness and the policies that can guide, monitor and control their impact. Lacking a connection to earlier distance education theories and research, the study of the e-learning phenomenon has been overwhelmingly represented by programme evaluations, 'how to' reports, and 'best practice' descriptions. As Moore (2003: x) laments, 'an impatience for moving to action without adequate comprehension of previous experience characterizes not only the research but virtually all American practice in the field'.

In the most positive situation, the best-practices approach can benefit the field by allowing good practices to quickly become established and to serve as models. However, while this 'quest for practical solutions' may reflect 'traditional American pragmatism' in action (Saba 2003: 3), it can also allow less than ideal or poor practices to be adopted without regulation or oversight, to the detriment of students, institutions, and the field as a whole. While a best-practices approach is perhaps inevitable in a new field, it is troubling given the history of theory building and research in distance education (Moore and Thompson, 1997; Saba, 2003; Anderson and Elloumi, 2004).

A cycle of practice to research to improved practice is necessary to move to ever higher levels of understanding in any area of practice. Building on earlier distance education theories and research, as well as testing their validity in the light of new practices made possible by the affordance of the Internet and World Wide Web, will advance our knowledge of e-learning more effectively than will compilations of largely anecdotal best practices.

Philosophical and axiological challenges

Research begins within and reflects particular philosophical stances or world views and the values associated with them. It is widely suggested that even the supposedly value-free approach epitomized by experimental research methods operates within a particular assumptive framework: not only that 'it is possible to describe the physical and social world scientifically so that, for example, multiple observers can agree on what they see' (Shavelson and Towne, 2002: 25), but also that describing the world in ways that forestall multiple perspectives and interpretations leads to 'truer' knowledge and, therefore, is more valuable than other approaches. For those who take qualitative approaches that attempt to understand the meaning as opposed to the 'reality' of a phenomenon, the end is not researcher agreement on what is seen, or correspondence with an objective reality, but rather a deeper understanding of multiple, mutually coexisting realities.

Differences in philosophy and values also are reflected in the presumptive ends or goals of e-learning and the research about it. Is e-learning and e-learning research intended to meet individual, social, and/or global needs? Should it be used to improve education for those who already have access or to extend access to the 'have nots'? Should it be focused on identifying factors correlating with individual success, or on answering questions relating to the development of human resources and capital? Should it study education as a means of addressing the structural inequalities that characterize much of traditional higher education? How should scarce programming and research dollars be invested? Answers to these and other questions are embedded in the philosophical frameworks and values of individual researchers, educational institutions, and funding agencies. In today's diverse global context an assumption of common theoretical frameworks and research agendas is increasingly difficult to maintain. And as Feuer *et al.*, (2002: 7) point out, uniformity of approach is seldom an appropriate goal: 'The challenge of the field of education is to bring diverse communities, both scientific and otherwise, together to integrate theories and empirical finding across domains, cultures, and methods.'

Epistemological challenges

The question of what counts as knowledge has been the subject of heated debate for millennia. Disagreements over the meaning, relative value, and ways of obtaining data, information, knowledge, and wisdom continue to divide researchers along philosophical and disciplinary lines: 'Unfortunately, it is often the case that those who work within one theoretical framework find others unintelligible' (St Pierre, 2002: 25).

Such lack of understanding is of course lamentable given the complexity of educational problems to be informed by research and the potential for untangling them through coordinated approaches from multiple perspectives. However, this distrust of 'the other's' approach to research takes on more powerfully negative connotations when it characterizes the largest single funder of educational research in the US: the US federal government.

Perhaps precisely because of its updated terminology and its seemingly inevitable integration into most segments of society, e-learning has received the attention of funding agencies, including the US government, well beyond that ever afforded to 'distance education'. But acceptance can be accompanied by a high price tag. Commenting on new legislation requiring research proposals to conform to 'scientific principles for education research', Feuer *et al.* (2002: 4) suggest that 'unprecedented federal legislation exalts scientific evidence as the key driver of education policy and practice… .' Thus the question 'What counts as knowledge?' becomes the question 'Who decides?' If the entity holding the funding purse strings proclaims that 'adherence to scientifically-based research will be a critical factor in … funding decisions' (Beghetto, 2003), then that 'five-hundred-pound gorilla' – in this case the federal government – becomes a major adjudicator of what counts as knowledge. Minimizing the potentially negative impact of such a unidimensional approach to knowledge while maximizing the motivation and ability of educational researchers to monitor the quality of research as a community is a major challenge for the field of educational research in general and e-learning research in particular.

Methodological challenges

Matching methods to questions and context appropriately is an ongoing challenge in educational research: 'The question drives the methods, not the other way around' (Feuer *et al.*, 2002: 8). And while the question *should* drive the method – as opposed, for example, to being driven by federal policy makers – the questions themselves are situated in particular times and places, necessitating the factoring of contextual variables into methodological decisions, as well:

> [Educational] research forces us to deal with particular problems, where local knowledge is needed. Therefore, ethnographic research is crucial, as are case studies, survey research, time series, design experiments action research, and other means …
>
> (Berliner, 2002: 19)

In other words, no single research method can provide us with answers to questions about 'the hardest science of all', educational research (Berliner, 2002: 19). Unfortunately, as noted above, at the same time that educational researchers themselves are expanding their repertoire of methodological tools for studying an increasingly complex educational environment, many funders of research – most notably the federal government, but others as well – are narrowing their focus to 'scientific research', which can answer some questions very well but many questions poorly. Although presumably done with the best of intentions in the name of 'accountability', this trend has the potential to greatly hamper e-learning research efforts by excluding many of the methods best suited to answering the important questions associated with this incredibly complex phenomenon, a number of which are suggested below.

E-LEARNING RESEARCH OPPORTUNITIES

Opportunities related to e-learning research are ever-expanding and limited only by the researcher's imagination and, unfortunately, funding constraints. The following focuses on two broad areas of opportunity: under-researched topic areas and interdisciplinary/international research collaborations.

Under-researched areas

Researchers have proposed a number of categories for research related to e-learning. Common categories include the student experience, the faculty experience, and institutional policy and management. A fourth and as yet little mentioned focus area is the ethics of e-learning. A broad examination of the literature reveals a number of gaps in each of these categories where research is needed. Of particular importance will be to examine what has already been learned by distance educators and to integrate that knowledge into new e-learning research in each of these areas.

The student experience

Positive student outcomes represent the ultimate goal of all educational programming, including technology-based higher education. The many aspects of this topic, as well as the complexity and interconnectedness of factors contributing to it, provide numerous research questions in the following areas.

*   *Design and support factors in enhanced student learning.* What design factors are associated with positive student learning outcomes? What is the role of dialogue and community in e-learning? How do the need for and effect of interaction and community differ in relation to different types and levels of content? Different student populations? What support needs are characteristic of e-learners in general? Of particular populations of students?
*   *Comparison of the needs and experiences of adult and traditional-aged students.* What are the distinctive characteristics and commonalities of these different populations? How do their needs differ? What are the differences in dynamics between homogeneous classes and multi-generational classes of students? Does earlier distance education research, conducted primarily on adult students, provide insights into the experience of younger students?
*   *Factors in the retention of e-learners.* What does retention mean in the e-learning environment? Are there differences in retention rates between those in different levels of study or types of programme? What design, delivery, and/or support factors are related to higher levels of student retention? Is community a factor in retention? Do answers to these questions vary by level of study, type of programme, or student characteristics?
*   *The meaning and measurement of student needs and/or satisfaction.* How do institutions define student needs, and how do they balance them in relation to the needs of other higher education stakeholders (faculty, institution, employers, society, etc.)? How should courses be designed to meet the conflicting needs of some students to study independently and others to study in community? What assessment approaches provide actionable data? What performance standards can be developed and shared across higher education to provide the basis for both informed student decision-making and continuous quality improvement?

The faculty experience

The success of online higher education programmes is dependent on a strong faculty commitment to teaching in this new environment. Ensuring such commitment over the long term and for the increasing numbers of faculty members who will be needed to participate will depend on a number of factors that suggest needed research:

- *Changing roles.* What aspects of the faculty role do faculty members themselves believe need to be changed? What aspects of change do faculty members believe result in 'deprofessionalization?' How do perceptions differ between faculty and administrators? At the level of practice, what has been the actual experience of faculty members who are filling new or changed roles? What are the experiences and relative concerns of those in the roles of course author and course facilitator? What differences, if any, in faculty satisfaction or student outcomes result from different arrangements of faculty roles?
- *Faculty resistance.* What are the philosophical, psychological, and/or cultural bases for faculty resistance? What differences exist in faculty and administrative perceptions of the sources of resistance? What are appropriate administrative responses to faculty resistance? What has been the relative success of different approaches?
- *Governance and curricular control.* What institutional policies govern online programme quality? Are such policies developed by administrators or by faculty? Does the faculty role in quality assurance differ between traditional and online programming?

Institutional policy and management

A number of organizational issues and challenges become prominent with the introduction of e-learning into higher education. Research into the implications of this integration, particularly as it relates to institutional policy, is necessary to provide a firm basis for planning, decision making, and effective implementation. Particularly needed are studies focusing on the following topics.

- *Analysis of existing policies and policy gaps.* To what extent do existing policies support the integration of e-learning into the institutional mainstream? What changes and additions to the current policy framework are necessary to support and guide the mainstreaming of e-learning? What is the institutional environment – the beliefs, values, expectations, and norms – that is, the culture – within which policies are developed, implemented, and accepted or resisted?
- *Finance.* What is the range of institutional financial structures for supporting and integrating technology-based programmes into higher education? What changes in existing business structures and levels of financial support will facilitate the integration of online and traditional programming? What sources of funding are extant and projected? Is there a relationship between source of funding and sustainability of programmes? What institutional budget structures and policies are necessary to realize cross-institutional efficiencies?
- *Intra-institutional competition.* What are the governance and fiscal issues related to service areas, student credit hours, and course ownership that must be resolved? How can the various, often conflicting, stakeholder needs and cultures be balanced to ensure the social and fiscal stability of both the overall institution and its constituent campuses?
- *Faculty support and rewards.* What is the appropriate institutional response in cases of documented heavier work load related to e-learning, especially given contextual imperatives for increased institutional productivity and a better 'bottom line'? What incentives can institutions offer that will encourage innovation in pedagogy without creating conflict and equity issues between participating and non-participating faculty members? What changes have been made or should be made in institutional reward structures to encourage participation?
- *Quality assessment, control, and improvement.* How are institutions defining quality in relation to e-learning? Are definitions structurally, process-, or outcomes-based? Do quality definitions go beyond parity with traditional programmes? Are approaches to quality based on generalities or specific performance indicators? Is there congruence between institutional strategic goals and the foci of quality assessment activities? Is quality being viewed from the perspective of maintaining an acceptable *status quo* of educational value or about gradually raising minimum standards?

Ethical issues

Ethical issues can be identified for many of the topical areas presented above, as well as for other areas. Although these issues are intertwined with many of those topics already discussed, they can also serve as triggers for specific ethics-focused research to answer questions about the following issues.

- *Access.* For whom has access increased and for whom has it decreased? Who are the 'winners' and 'losers', and how does this result relate to institutions' legitimate (that is, publicly articulated) missions? Are students being adequately prepared and supported in the convergence of traditional instruction and e-learning?
- *Integrity of institutions.* Do institutional structures and resource allocations reflect commitment to high-quality e-learning programming? How are e-learning programmes marketed relative to traditional programmes? What aspects of the programme are stressed, and with what result? Are programmes presented fairly or are advantages highlighted and disadvantages downplayed? Do institutions give potential students the information they need to make informed choices about the appropriateness of e-learning programmes for their particular situations and educational needs?
- *Integrity of students.* Are problems of identity assurance and plagarism more prevalent in e-learning than in traditional education? What 'best practices' for security have institutions implemented to ensure student identity? Are there forms of assessment less amenable to cheating that have been successfully used in the online environment? What steps can institutions take to promote a culture of integrity that minimizes the threat of misrepresentation or cheating on the part of all of its students?
- *Integrity of researchers.* What are the risks and benefits associated with e-learning research? How do these differ from research on traditional educational communities? How are the concepts of 'public' and 'private' different in traditional and e-learning communities, particularly in terms of dialogue and community interactions? What are the implications of these differences for e-learning research? What changes have institutions made in their human subjects research policies to reflect differences?
- *The coercive, consensual, or supportive nature of change management.* To what extent should faculty be *required* to adopt new ways of teaching, especially when new methods and formats fundamentally change the character of their work? To what extent have institutions 'unbundled' or 'disaggregated' faculty roles, and with what results in terms of both faculty satisfaction and student outcomes? To what degree do faculty members have a choice in/control over such decisions and processes? To what extent do institutions provide adequate support for changes in roles, and how do different levels of support affect faculty satisfaction?

Interdisciplinary research and international collaboration

The disciplinary areas relevant to distance education or e-learning research are many and varied. Anderson and Elloumi (2004: xiii) suggest that 'distance education is a discipline that subsumes the knowledge and practice of pedagogy, of psychology and sociology, of economics and business, of production and technology'. The report of a group of academics sponsored by the Economic and Social Research Council, the Engineering and Physical Sciences Research Council, and the e-Science Research Council in the United Kingdom categorized the relevant disciplines into 'technical domains (e.g. Computer Science, Technology, Artificial Intelligence); design disciplines (e.g. Design, Human-Computer Interaction

(HCI); the learning sciences (e.g. Educational Technology, Psychology, Education) and the disciplines studying communication, communities and discourse (i.e. Social Sciences, Linguistics)' (Taylor *et al.*, 2004).

Yet, while there is widespread recognition that all of the disciplines named above relate to e-learning, to date there have been few efforts to explore the connections between them and to exploit the multi-faceted perspectives that can result from conducting research across disciplines. As Zare (quoted in EU Research Advisory Board, EURAB, 2004, n.p.) notes, 'Knowledge is extracted from a fully integrated world. Knowledge is "dis-integrated" by disciplinary units called Departments in Universities.'

Research within disciplines has provided and will continue to provide answers to many of the questions related to e-learning. Yet the complex, multi-faceted nature of the individual and aggregate actors and systems involved in e-learning, as well as the complexity of problems in areas such as globalization, the environment, health, and defence and security that many hope can be at least partially addressed by education, argue for a breaking down of divisions and a reintegration of knowledge through a multi-disciplinary approach to research.

With the opportunity of interdisciplinary research comes a challenge. Co-ordination and co-operation among researchers from various disciplines will require first that researchers gain an understanding of and respect for norms and approaches to research other than their own. To the extent that such a cross-disciplinary community of researchers can be built and maintained, however, we will come closer to untangling some of the complexities of educational research that can be addressed only through multiple perspectives and approaches.

International collaborations in e-learning research offer some of the same opportunities and challenges, as does interdisciplinary research. Difficulties are inherent in the negotiation of approaches based in different cultural and intellectual perspectives, as well as negotiation among norms and standards of practice. However, as the context within which e-learning is practised becomes more global, the pay-offs for overcoming such difficulties become higher. The synergy possible from co-ordinating approaches to major educational problems and questions and the resource maximization possible from reducing duplication of effort argue for both support of and participation in international collaborative efforts.

In the same way that interdisciplinary research can reintegrate knowledge by bringing to bear different disciplinary perspectives, international research collaborations can result in knowledge that goes beyond particular national or cultural contexts as theories, practices, and research questions are compared, contrasted, and more deeply explored. Several activities of the Worldwide Universities Network (WUN), including collaborative research projects, international research workshops, and collaborative seminars on e-learning research presented via the Access Grid, have established an initial framework for international collaborative research.

CONCLUSION

What is currently being referred to as e-learning is part of a field of practice with a long tradition of theory building and research. Change in terminology is an inevitable aspect of social change; however, we must make sure that in making such changes we neither lose important meaning and knowledge associated with earlier practice nor limit our thinking by unnecessarily circumscribed discourse.

Three things are necessary to support a robust understanding of the activity currently labelled e-learning: conscious awareness of and focus on the 'distance' inherent in the activity; consideration of the multidimensional aspects of 'education', which include but are hardly coterminous with 'learning'; and awareness of and appropriate connection to earlier research and practice that can inform current and future efforts. The potential of e-learning research and practice will be increased to the extent that we maintain a focus on *all* of the essential elements of this activity

REFERENCES

Anderson, T. and Elloumi, F. (2004) 'Introduction', in T. Anderson and F. Elloumi (eds), *Theory and Practice of Online Learning*. Edmonton, Alta: Athabasca University. pp. xiii–xxii.

Bates, A. (1999) *Cultural and Ethical Issues in International Distance Education*. Paper presented at the Engaging Partnerships: Collaboration and Partnership in Distance Education UBC/CREAD conference, Vancouver, Canada, 21–23 September, 1999.

Bates, A. W. T. (2000) *Managing Technological Change: Strategies for College and University Leaders*. San Francisco, CA: Jossey-Bass.

Bazerman, C. and Paradis, J. (1990) *Textual Dynamics of the Professions*. Madison, WI: University of Wisconsin Press.

Beghetto, R. (2003) 'Scientifically based research', *Research Roundup*, 19 (3). Clearinghouse on Educational Policy and Management, University of Oregon. Retrieved 17 January 2005 from: http://eric.uoregon.edu/publications/roundup/spring2003.html.

Berliner, D. (2002) 'Educational research: the hardest science of all', *Educational Researcher*, 31 (8): 18–20.

Bower, B. (2001) 'Distance education: facing the faculty challenge', *Online Journal of Distance Learning Administration*, 4 (2). Available online at: http://www.westga.edu/~distance/ojdla/summer42/bower42.htm.

Brabazon, T. (2001) 'Internet teaching and the administration of knowledge', *First Monday*, 6 (6), available online at: http://firstmonday.dk/issues/issue6_6/brabazoon/index.html.

Buchanan, E. (2004). *Perspectives on Online Mentoring from a Graduate School of Library and Information Science Web-based Programme*. Paper presented at the XXth Annual Conference on Distance Teaching and Learning, Madison, WI.

Burge, E. J. (1994) 'Learning in computer conferenced contexts: the learners' perspective', *Journal of Distance Education*, 9 (1): 19–43.

Cairncross, F. (1997) *The Death of Distance: How the Communications Revolution will Change our Lives*. Boston, MA: Harvard Business School Press.

deJager, P. (2005) *The Danger of the 'Early Adopter' Myth*. Retrieved 4 May 2006 from: http://technobility.com/docs/article032.htm.

Dillon, C. L., and Walsh, S. M. (1992) 'Faculty: the neglected resource in distance education', *American Journal of Distance Education*, 6 (3): 5–21.

European Research Advisory Board (EURAB) (2004) *Interdisciplinarity in Research* (April). Retrieved 3 January 2006 from: http://europa.eu.int/comm/research/eurab/index_en.html.

Fairclough, N. (1989) *Language and Power*. New York: Longman.

Feenberg, A. (1989) 'The written world', in A. Kaye and R. Mason (eds), *Mindweave: Communication, Computers, and Distance Education*. Oxford: Pergamon Press. pp. 22–39.

Feenberg, A. (1990) 'Social factors in computer mediated communication', in L. Harasim (ed.), *Online Education: Perspectives on a New Medium*. New York: Praeger. pp. 67–97.

Feuer, M., Towne, L. and Shavelson, R. (2002) 'Scientific culture and educational research', *Educational Researcher*, 31 (8): 4–14.

Frederickson, E., Pickett, A., Swan, K., Pelz, W. and Shea, P. (1999) 'Factors influencing faculty satisfaction with asynchronous teaching and learning in the SUNY learning network', in *Online Education I, Learning Effectiveness and Faculty Satisfaction*. Needham, MA: Sloan Center for Online Education.

Gibson, C. C. (1996). 'Toward an understanding of academic self-concept in distance education', *American Journal of Distance Education*, 10 (1): 23–36.

Gibson, C. C. and Graff, O. A. (1992) 'Impact of adults' preferred learning styles and perception of barriers on completion of external baccalaureate degree programmes', *Journal of Distance Education/Revue de l'enseignement à distance*, 7 (1): 39–51.

Giguere, P., Formica, S. and Harding, W. (2004) 'Large-scale interaction strategies for Web-based professional development', *American Journal of Distance Education*, 18 (4): 207–24.

Gunawardena, C. (1995) 'Social presence theory and implications for interaction and collaborative learning in computer conferences', *International Journal of Educational Telecommunications*, 1 (2–3): 147–66.

Harasim, L. (1987) 'Teaching and learning online: issues in computer-mediated graduate courses', *Canadian Journal for Educational Communication*, 16 (2): 117–35.

Harasim, L. (1989) 'Online education: a new domain', in R. Mason and A. Kaye (eds), *Mindweave: Computers and Distance Education*. Oxford: Pergamon Press. pp. 50–62.

Hartman, J. and Truman-Davis, B. (2001) 'Factors relating to the satisfaction of faculty teaching online courses at the University of Central Florida', in *Online Education II, Learning Effectiveness, Faculty Satisfaction, and Cost Effectiveness*. Needham, MA: Sloan Center for Online Education. pp. 109–28.

Hiltz, S. R. (1986) 'The "virtual classroom": using computer-mediated communication for university teaching', *Journal of Communication*, 36 (2): 95–104.

Hiltz, S. R. (1994) *The Virtual Classrom: Learning without Limits via Computer Networks*. Norwood, NJ: Ablex.

Holmberg, B. (1983) 'Guided didactic conversation in distance education', in D. Stewart, D. Keegan and B. Holmberg (eds), *Distance Education: International Perspectives*. London: Croom Helm. pp. 114–22.

Holmberg, B. (1991) 'Testable theory based on discourse and empathy', *Open Learning*, 6 (2): 44–6.

Holmberg, B. (2003) 'A theory of distance education based on empathy', in M. G. Moore and W. G. Anderson (eds), *Handbook of Distance Education*. Mahwah, NJ: Erlbaum. pp. 79–86.

hooks, b. (1994) *Teaching to Transgress: Education as the Practice of Freedom*. New York: Routledge.

Jaffee, D. (1998) 'Institutionalized resistance to asynchronous learning networks', *Journal of Asynchronous Learning Networks*, 2 (2). Available online at http://www.aln.org/alnweb/journal/jaln_vol2issue2.htm#jaffee.

Kanuka, H., and Conrad, D. (2003) 'The name of the game: why "distance education" says it all', *Quarterly Review of Distance Education*, 4 (4): 385–93.

Katz, R. and Ohlinger, D. (2000) *The 'E' is for Everything*. San Francisco, CA: Jossey-Bass.

Kember, D., Murphy, D., Siaw, I. and Yuen, K. (1991) 'Towards a causal model of student progress in distance education: Research in Hong Kong', *American Journal of Distance Education*, 5 (2): 3–15.

King, J. W., G. C. Nugent, J. J. Eich, D. L. Mlinek and E. G. Russell (2000) *A Policy Framework for Distance Education: A Case Study and Model*. Available online at http://www.ed.psu.edu/acsde/deos/deosnews.html.

May, S. (1994) 'Women's experience as distance learners: access and technology', *Journal of Distance Education*, 9 (1): 81–98.

Moore, M. G. (1983) 'The individual adult learner', in M. Tight (ed.), *Adult Learning and Education*. London: Croom Helm. pp. 153–68.

Moore, M. G. (1993) 'Theory of transactional distance', in D. Keegan (ed.), *Theoretical Principles of Distance Education*. Abingdon: Routledge. pp. 22–38.

Moore, M. G. and Thompson, M. (1997) *The Effects of Distance Learning* (rev. edn). American Center for the Study of Distance Education, Pennsylvania State University.

Moore, M. G. (2003) Preface to M. G. Moore and W. G. Anderson (eds), *Handbook of Distance Education*. Mahwah, NJ: Erlbaum. pp. ix–xii.

Murphy, K. (1991) 'Patronage and an oral tradition: influences on attributions of distance learners in a traditional society (a qualitative study)', *Distance Education*, 12 (1): 27–53.

National Center for Education Statistics (2003) *Distance Education at Degree-granting Postsecondary Institutions, 2000–2001*. Washington, DC: US Department of Education. Retrieved August 2003 from http://nces.ed.gov/pubsearch/pubsinfo.asp?pubid=2003017.

National Education Association (2000) *A Survey of Traditional and Distance Learning Higher Education Members*. Washington, DC: NEA.

Porter, J. (1986) 'Intertextuality and the discourse community', *Rhetoric Review*, 5 (1): 38–9.

Saba, F. (2003) 'Distance education theory, methodology, and epistemology: a pragmatic paradigm', in M. Moore and W. Anderson (eds), *Handbook of Distance Education*. Mahwah, NJ: Erlbaum. pp. 3–20.

Saba, F. (2005) *Is distance education losing its identity? Or what should our field be called these days?* Paper presented at the XXth Annual Conference on Distance Teaching and Learning, Madison, WI, 3–5 August.

Saba, F. and Shearer, R. L. (1994) 'Verifying key theoretical concepts in a dynamic model of distance education', *American Journal of Distance Education*, 8 (1): 36–59.

St Pierre, E. (2002) '"Science" rejects postmodernism', *Educational Researcher*, 31 (8), 25–7.

Schifter, C. (2002) 'Perception differences about participating in distance education', *Online Journal of Distance Learning Administration*, 5 (1). Available online at: http://www.westga.edu/%7Edistance/ojdla/spring51/schifter51.html.

Shavelson, R. and Towne, L. (2002) *Scientific Research in Education*. Washington, DC: National Academy Press.

Shedletsky, Leonard J. and Aitken, Joan E. (2001) 'The paradoxes of online academic work', *Communication Education*, 50 (3): 206–17.

Tait, A. (1999) 'The convergence of distance and conventional education: some implications for policy', in A. Tait and R. Mills (eds), *The Convergence of Distance and Traditional Education*. New York: Routledge. pp. 141–60.

Taylor, J., Rodden, T., Anderson, A., Sharples, M. Luckin, R., Conole, G. and Siraj-Blatchford, J. (2004) *An E-learning Research Agenda*. Retrieved 3 January 2006 from: http://www.epsrc.ac.uk/.../ReviewsAndConsultations/ Ane-LearningResearchAgenda.htm.

Taylor, M. L. (2006) *Generation NeXt comes to college: 2006 updates and emerging issues*. Retrieved 3 May 2006 from: http://www.taylorprogrammes.org/pages/1/index.htm.

Thompson, M. (2001) 'Faculty satisfaction in Penn State's World Campus', in *Online Education II, Learning Effectiveness, Faculty Satisfaction, and Cost Effectiveness*. Needham, MA: Sloan Center for Online Education. pp. 129–44.

Thompson, M. M. (2002) 'Faculty satisfaction in the online environment', in J. Moore (ed.), *Online Education* IV. Needham, MA: Sloan Center for Online Education. pp. 189–212.

Thompson, M. M. and Irele, M. (2003) 'Evaluating distance education programmes', in M. Moore and W. Anderson (eds), *Handbook of Distance Education*. Mahwah, NJ: Erlbaum. pp. 567–84.

Vella, J. (2002) *Learning to Listen, Learning to Teach: The Power of Dialogue in Educating Adults*. San Francisco, CA: Jossey-Bass.

Wagner, E. D. (1994) 'In support of a functional definition of interaction', *American Journal of Distance Education*, 8 (2): 6–29.

Wedemeyer, C. A. (1981) *Learning at the Back Door: Reflections on Non-traditional Learning in the Lifespan*. Madison, WI: University of Wisconsin Press.

8

E-learning and the Reshaping of Rhetorical Space

Terry Locke

Much have I travell'd in the realms of gold,
   And many goodly states and kingdoms seen;
   Round many western islands have I been
Which bards in fealty to Apollo hold.
Oft of one wide expanse had I been told
   That deep-brow'd Homer ruled as his demesne;
   Yet did I never breathe its pure serene
Till I heard Chapman speak out loud and bold:
Then felt I like some watcher of the skies
   When a new planet swims into his ken;
Or like stout Cortez when with eagle eyes
   He star'd at the Pacific – and all his men
Look'd at each other with a wild surmise–
   Silent, upon a peak in Darien.

With the help of Google or other search engines, it is an easy matter to enter cyberspace and download a facsimile of 'On first looking into Chapman's Homer', the poem the English poet John Keats showed his friend, Charles Cowden Clarke, one morning in October 1816. He had walked through physical space – some two miles – to deliver the poem, which was first published, in slightly edited form, the following December.

Digitally mediated cyberspace was not available to Keats, but *rhetorical space* certainly was. There are ample references to *places* in this poem: 'realms', 'states', 'kingdoms', 'islands'. But in the last eight lines which pivot on the qualifier 'Yet' there is a sense of *space* opening up – pure, undifferentiated extension – like a blank frame into which something wondrous (a 'new planet', a new ocean, a new poetic) is about to enter and change for ever the status/state of pre-existing knowledge. What is clear is that this space, for Keats, is largely textual and that he is a respondent, not just a seer but also a hearer, seeing himself as engaging with time-honoured bards – Homer and especially Chapman himself, whose textual Homer is a very special link in a long intertextual chain (that also includes Alexander Pope). It is a chain which includes, by implication, texts such as Robertson's *History of America* (published in 1777), faultily remembered by Keats, who confused Cortez with Balboa. Furthermore, it is a chain that includes the initial addressee, Clarke himself, as well as the unseen but anticipated audience with whom Keats wanted to share his 'teeming wonderment' at reading Chapman.

The theme of this chapter is Web-based Asynchronous discussion – or the Asynchronous Bulletin Board (ABB) – and its effectiveness as a medium for learning. Starting with the notion of rhetorical space allows one to view this medium as a particular example of a rhetorical space and involves a number of important recognitions. The first of these is that a speaker is always, as Bakhtin noted, a respondent:

> He [sic] is not, after all, the first speaker, the one who disturbs the eternal silence of the universe. And he presupposes not only the existence of the language system he is using, but also the existence of preceding utterances – his own and others' – with which his given utterance enters into one kind of relation or another (builds on them, polemicizes with them, or simply presumes that they are already known to the listener). Any utterance is a link in a very complexly organized chain of other utterances.

> (1986: 69)

As Bakhtin further noted, the notion of being a respondent not only involves a relationship to 'preceding utterances'; it also includes a relationship to those to whom one's utterance (written or spoken) is potentially addressed. We have moved here beyond the literal space of the Greek forum, to think of the rhetorical space as metaphorical – as having a temporal or historical dimension. This first recognition might be thought of as about audience, even though members of this audience may no longer be living. The second recognition, again using a spatial metaphor, recognizes the discursive positions available historically in relation to the topic that is subject to discussion or debate.

If space is rhetorical, then it can also be thought of as epistemic. As Payne points out:

> Space creates frameworks for conception, action, and interaction; its design – whether natural or artificial – limits and directs what we think and do, as well as with whom we do it. Space is not a neutral conduit within which social productions occur; it is itself social produced, and as such it is shot through with the very ideologies of identity and power with which much of our disciplinary work contends.

> (2005: 485)

One can think of James Gee's well known used of the biker bar as illustrative of the way in which a socially produced space operates to constrain discourse – through ways in which particular Discourses (Gee capitalizes here) act to elicit particular 'ways of behaving, interacting, valuing, thinking, believing, speaking … that are accepted as instantiations of particular roles … by specific *groups of people*' (1996: viii). Visitors to an asynchronous bulletin board, then, are not entering a neutral arena. Rather they are entering a space that is value-laden and, for some, potentially intimidating.

DIMENSIONS OF RHETORICAL SPACE

Starting with Keats is a way of suggesting that everything and nothing is new under the sun. In a recent article, Morten Søby quotes Freud – 'Man has, as it were, become a sort of prosthetic God' (Freud, 1962: 38, cited in Søby, 2005: 'Formatting cyberspace', paragraph 6) – and notes that ICT can be thought of in prosthetic terms, as an extension of the body and the senses. As a way of gaining perspective, however, it is sometimes necessary to de-heroize the current moment (as per, we live in 'New Times') and think of all technologies as prosthetic (including Keats' pen and paper). And before we pronounce on multiply-selved cyborgs at play in technologically mediated and constructed virtual worlds as something new, we might recognize that there is a sense in which the human imagination has always been a virtual capability.[1] You could say that, in or through his poem, Keats enters/constructs a virtual world, which effectively enables him to try on a new self.

A corollary is that technology is not just an add-on that enhances human cognition. As Walter Ong (1982) argues, in respect of writing, technology has the power, directly and indirectly, to shape human thought processes (consciousness). A technology, then, is more than just an aid to learning. It shapes the cognitive processes that underpin learning. Furthermore, because the uses of technology are culturally mediated, technologically mediated learning (via asynchronous learning networks) is necessarily shaped discursively by the practices around technology privileged in a particular cultural milieu. We inhabit a text-saturated world, which we negotiate via a repertoire of textual practices that are at once cognitive, social, and *themselves* technologies.

There are two dimensions of Bakhtin's chain metaphor that are relevant to any consideration of a speaker's communicative activity in a rhetorical space, whether it be a Greek forum or the digitally constructed space of an asynchronous bulletin board. These are *reach* (chains vary in length); and *connection* (the links in a chain can connect in differing ways).

Reach

There are two aspects to the dimension of reach: field[2] and company (or membership). In respect of field, we might distinguish two kinds (or axes):

- *Depth of historical field*. This refers to the temporal scope of intertextual and interdiscursive historical reference, both retrospective and anticipative. This is the historical axis of reference.
- *Breadth of contemporary field*. This refers to the range of intertextual and interdiscursive reference that can be thought of as roughly contemporaneous.

In respect of the aspect of company, we can distinguish three kinds:

- *Overt company*: those conversants or participants who regularly engage in utterance exchange, for example, an 'access list'.
- *Covert company*: onlookers who have opportunities to observe the exchanges of the overt company but whose presence will be unsuspected. This includes site administrators for an asynchronous learning network but also extends to 'lurking' members of an ABB discussion who are enrolled in a course but who decide to be non-participants.
- *Implied company*: those conversants or 'addressees' whose 'presence' is implied in a particular utterance.[3] The writer of an article on a course reading list would be an example of this. However, should that writer be invited to participate in the discussion as a guest, he or she would become a member of the overt company.

Connection

The term 'connection' is used here to embrace various aspects of participant activity within a rhetorical space, however 'natural' or technologically mediated.

The first of these relates to duration and continuity. *Duration* refers to the real time taken up by a discussion and is marked by a beginning and end point. In terms of an asynchronous online discussion, duration is typically marked by an imposed beginning date and completion date. *Continuous discussion*, in a face-to-face classroom setting, for example, has a beginning and end point in real time and no breaks. *Continual discussion*, on the other hand, has a beginning and end point in real time and is intermittent. Asynchronous online discussion is an example of continual discussion.

The second and third aspects relate to an individual member's participatory behaviour. The second relates to a participant's participation rate:

- *Absolute participation rate*: the number of utterances a participant makes in a single discussion.
- *Relative participation rate*: the number of utterances a participant makes as a percentage of all utterances in a single discussion.

The third aspect relates to the concept of feedback, a verbal or non-verbal signal that acknowledges an utterance.

- *Feedback spread*: the number of participants in the overt company a particular participant offers unsolicited feedback to, expressed as a percentage of the number of participants in the overt company minus one.
- *Feedback rate*: the total number of feedback instances a participant produces as a percentage of his or her total number of utterances in a discussion. A percentage of more than 100 would indicate that a participant is at times acknowledging the contributions of a number of participants within a single utterance.[4]

A fourth aspect of connection has to do with ways in which the overt company collectively addresses the topic of a discussion.

- *Degree of convergence*: the extent to which the overt company appears to be achieving a consensus on a particular topic, that is, a kind of discursive alignment.
- *Degree of divergence*: the extent to which the overt company appears to be failing to realize a consensus on a particular topic, that is, a kind of discursive non-alignment.
- *Degree of congeniality*: the extent to which the overt company appears comfortable with divergence.

Neither convergence nor divergence is *per se* a desirable outcome of a discussion. However, different discourses of learning vary in respect of their valuing of either of these. Rhetorical spaces differ in terms of their tolerance and/or encouragement of dissent. As Payne puts it, 'hegemony inherent in the production of space functions by degree', so that whether a space is totalitarian or dialogic will depend on what he calls the 'margins of maneuver', the extent to which the discursive structures embedded allow for resistance and agency (2005: 489).

Finally, *structuration* refers to the logic or principles governing the sequence and interrelationship of utterances within a discussion. It is clear that the factors that govern turntaking and cohesion in an online asynchronous discussion differ from those that operate in synchronous, face-to-face discussion. They may be teacher-initiated design features that impact upon sequence. They may relate to the interactive behaviour and predispositions of various members of the overt company. They may relate to aspects of the platform itself. It is possible that at least in part the structuration of such discussion is likely to be characterized by rhizome-type connectivity (Deleuze and Guattari, 1987), described as follows by Semetsky:

> Rhizome as embedded in the perplexity of the situation, going in diverse directions instead of a single path, multiplying its own lines and establishing the plurality of unpredictable connections in the open-ended, what Deleuze called smooth, space of its growth.

> (Semetsky, 2003: 18)

Putting it another way, considerations of the structuration of asynchronous online discussion need to be posited on the coexistence of both hierarchical and non-hierarchical principles of order/disorder.[5]

The preceding section works, Bakhtinian-style, in dialogue with Nicholas Burbules's (2002) notion of the Web as a rhetorical *place*. Burbules prefers 'place' to 'space' because the former is socially meaningful.

> It has an objective, locational dimension: people can look for a place, find it, move within it. But it also has a semantic dimension: it means something important to a person or a group of people, and this latter dimension may or may not be communicable to others.
>
> (2002: 78)

Burbules identifies two broad kinds of strategies whereby spaces become transformed into places: *mapping* (the development of 'schemata that represent the space, identify important points within it, and facilitate movement within the space') and *architecture* (the shaping of space via 'enduring structures') (2002: 78–80). The dimensions of reach and connection, discussed above, can be seen as one way of representing the transition from space to place.

ASYNCHRONOUS DISCUSSION IN THE CONTEXT OF ONLINE LEARNING

In an essay on distance education Natriello produced a range of statistics to underline its burgeoning growth, fuelled (as he argues) by a general growth in demand for education, especially among the young, and by perceived advantages in online learning itself.

- In the 2000–01 academic year, 56% of two- and four-year degree granting institutions of higher education in the US offered collectively 127,400 different distance education courses.
- Distance education courses in the US most often employed the Internet and two video technologies, with 90% of institutions reporting the use of asynchronous course delivery, 43% reporting synchronous Internet courses, 51% reporting use of two-way video and audio and 43% reporting use of one-way video.
- Half of China's 92,000 engineering and technology graduates obtained degrees through distance learning (2005: 1886).

It should be noted that distance learning and online learning are not the same. Many tertiary courses taught in traditional ways in traditional settings are hybridizing and incorporating online features. In respect of the advantages of distance learning, Natriello offered the familiar trio of: the collapse of distance as a deterrent ('space shifting'); 24/7 programme access ('time shifting') and a reduced need for physical structures and elaborate locations ('resource shifting') (2005: 1888). The title of Natriello's essay, 'Modest changes, revolutionary possibilities', was designed to draw attention to what he sees as a dichotomy between current utilization of the potential of the platform (i.e. online learning) and its possibilities.

Power, surveillance and the 'big picture'

A 'big picture' view such as Natriello's is useful for contextualizing a discussion of the usefulness for learning of a particular technology, in this case, an asynchronous bulletin board, whether this be embedded in a totally online, asynchronous learning network[6] or used as an adjunct to a traditional, face-to-face course. Just how 'revolutionary possibilities' might be realized in practice is contingent on a range of factors. The nature of this contingency is reflected in Lankshear and Knobel's statement that:

> The historical and contingent nature of discursive practice becomes readily apparent within cyberspaces. To experience oneself as engaged with others in constructing, refining and monitoring social practices which comprise amalgamations of reading–writing–imaging, values, purposes, theories, roles, identities, etc., is necessarily to envisage one's activity as simply so many representations of what social practice(s) might be, and to be aware of alternative possibilities within and outside cyberspace. It is to realize there is nothing necessary about inhabiting any particular discursive space or spaces: all such spaces are contingent and historical. This insight is central to meta-level awareness of discursive practice and the possibilities for transformative praxis predicated upon it.

(1997: 158)

Payne's (2005) analysis of course management software, with a particular focus on Blackboard, is a reminder of the importance of viewing any educational technology in relation to the wider, socio-contextual picture.

In a press release dated 12 October 2005, a proposal to merge was announced by Blackboard and WebCT, two North American companies which have specialized in the production and marketing of Web-based software for institutions building an online learning environment. The release claimed that this combined enterprise would have a client base of more than 3,700 institutions, and termed this grouping a 'global e-Learning "Community of Practice"'.[7] Elsewhere in the ether, another American company, Web Crossing, was describing itself as 'the world's leading collaboration server platform'.[8] Typically the Web sites of these software production companies feature success stories. The *modus operandi* of an asynchronous bulletin board, featuring as part of an online learning environment, cannot be separated from the (global) marketing ambitions of companies such as Blackboard and Web Crossing.

Drawing on Foucault's concept of the 'panopticon', one can view the 'covert company' present in a rhetorical space as those groups and interests which have managed to obtain a kind of hegemonic sway over the discursive practices permissible in an online learning environment in general and an asynchronous bulletin board in particular (1977: 195). In this sense, power is both diffuse and productive. In his discourse analysis of Blackboard's space, Payne drew on the geographical metaphor of the suburb and noted a tendency towards homogeneity, conformity and acquiescence to an American middle-class ideal (calling to mind the film *Edward Scissorhands*), the embodiment of a 'dominant cultural rhetoric'. 'Blackboard,' he argued, 'serves the interests of the dominant culture by naturalizing and commodifying its space/rhetoric' (2005: 495). Of particular note in his analysis was his attention to issues of surveillance and control and his insistence on the need to scrutinize the '*degree* of agency enabled' (italics Payne's)' by spaces such as Blackboard (2005: 499).

To illustrate power issues at the micro level of asynchronous online discussion, the following examples are drawn from an online learning platform called Class Forum, powered by PLACE, a customized version of the American engine Web Crossing. In considering the overall system or framework within which an online delivery system is embedded, it is useful to distinguish between front-end users, platform administrators (for example, technical support staff in a school or faculty) and engine designers, developers and maintainers. Generally, both technical support staff and system administrators are bound by a code of conduct and are required to enter a formal verbal agreement in respect of their role *vis-à-vis* asynchronous discussions. Both groups can access a particular discussion if there is reason to believe that it is being improperly used or that there is a problem that may be affecting the performance/users. Both are also members of the 'covert company', the presence of which implies a prospect for direct surveillance (in a less Foucauldian sense).

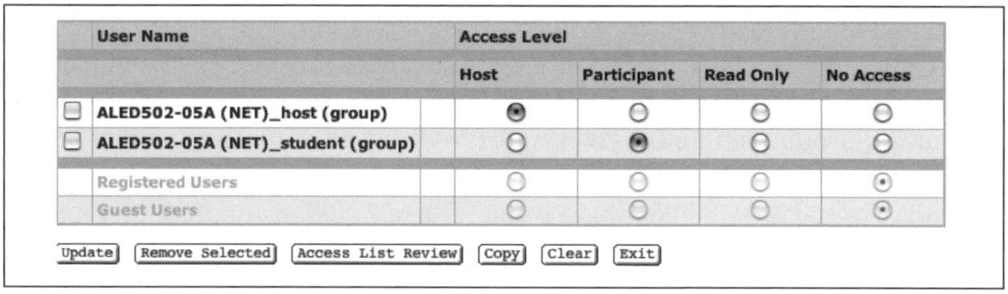

User Name	Access Level			
	Host	Participant	Read Only	No Access
☐ ALED502-05A (NET)_host (group)	⦿	○	○	○
☐ ALED502-05A (NET)_student (group)	○	⦿	○	○
Registered Users	○	○	○	⦿
Guest Users	○	○	○	⦿

[Update] [Remove Selected] [Access List Review] [Copy] [Clear] [Exit]

Figure 8.1   Access level control panel

Issues of access, control, and therefore power differentiation, are necessarily implicated in asynchronous bulletin board design. Figure 8.1 shows the control panel that a course host (either course co-ordinator or lecturer) has available to govern access to a discussion in Class Forum. Table 8.1 sets out the privileges associated with 'Host' and 'Participant'. (The meaning of 'Read only' is self-evident.)

Table 8.1 Comparing host and participant privileges

Host	Participant
Can add folders and discussions	Can *not* add folders and discussions
Can add, delete, edit and move folders and discussions	Can *not* add, delete, edit and move folders and discussions
Can delete or edit student messages	Can *not* delete or edit other users' messages
Can determine access privileges	Can *not* determine access privileges
Can view class lists (photos, various student details)	Can *not* view class lists (photos, various student details)
Can write and submit messages	Can write and submit messages
Can edit messages at any time	Can edit messages within thirty minutes of posting

In practice, a course host (that is, co-ordinator or lecturer) can accord students 'host' status. However, there are ethical implications for such an action. For example, it would give students access to one another's details and the ability to interfere with other students' access. There is also provision for students to be given 'host' privileges in a particular folder within a course. However, the same ethical dilemma arises. In terms of this design, the simplest way of enabling students to initiate a discussion is via a lecturer who can perform the initial 'host' function in the student's name. But there is clearly an imbalance of power here. Finally, it might be noted that there is a 'guest user' provision in the control panel. This allows, for example, a lecturer to provide guest access to a colleague from another university, so that that colleague can participate in a particular discussion. In short, these design features privilege some over others in respect of access and have implications for ways in which the 'overt company' is constructed.

Duration, continuity and rates of participation

Unsurprisingly, the academic literature related to asynchronous online discussion is more likely to focus on operational aspects than issues of power, control and surveillance.

How important is the duration (in real time) of a single, asynchronous online discussion? Does a longer duration affect rates of participation or increase rates of response? On the basis of a cross-case analysis of nine naturalistic case studies of online classes, Dennen suggested that duration was a factor in increasing the number of instances of dialogue between participants. However, she wondered whether the time interval between message and response meant that the original sender would be unlikely to read the delayed response (2005: 136).

In a more elaborate study of duration effects, Im and Lee mapped changing patterns of interaction over time among their student participants, using for analytical purposes five categories of content (topic-related, learning-related, related to discussion management, related to social interaction, and technical management-related) and a model for staged development in an online learning community:

- S_1 Social bond formation ('the first stage of learning community development, where participants introduce themselves and get to know each other'),
- S_2 Information sharing ('where participants feel comfortable in exchanging and sharing knowledge and information'),
- S_3 Advanced stage ('where participants apply advanced metacognitive skills such as awareness, reflection, and evaluation'). (Im and Lee, 2004: 158)

They found that while synchronous discussion was more useful in promoting social interaction, asynchronous discussion was more useful for task-oriented communication. Indeed, the synchronous discussion content failed to lead into 'meaningful learning ... but remained at the level of the social bond formation stage as the course progressed' (2004: 166). While duration appeared to have little impact for synchronous discussion, it was clearly a factor for asynchronous discussion, with stage 2 postings (information exchange) decreasing over time and stage 3 postings (advanced stage) becoming more prevalent by the conclusion of the discussion (2004: 163).

Several researchers have explored the advantages and disadvantages for learning of synchronous (continuous) and asynchronous (continual) discussion. A number of studies comparing asynchronous online discussion with face-to-face discussion in classrooms suggest collectively that 'the critical success factors for asynchronous collaborative learning may be different than in FTF environments' (Hackman and Annabi, 2005: 'Background', paragraph 2). Markel, drawing on a case study involving students in a graduate course on 'Professional Problems of Teachers', argued that in slowing down students' time for reflection, asynchronous discussion fostered a process of deep learning through acts of writing free from 'the tyranny of the ever present "now" of the face-to-face classroom' (2005: 'Summary', paragraph 1) Similarly, Vess, comparing the impact of asynchronous discussion in a fully online course with its impact in a face-to-face course enhanced with asynchronous discussions, found students stating a preference for online debating because they found it easier to participate and allowed research and preparation time prior to posting a message (2005: 360).

Other studies concern themselves with comparing synchronous and asynchronous discussion online. Lim and Tan, based on findings from a case study using a bulletin board as the basis for a focus group discussion, argued that asynchronous discussion allowed more reflection time, more opportunities for discussion management and more time for conflict resolution (2001: 58). Poole (2000), drawing on findings from a case study involving fourteen students enrolled in a two-unit graduate course on 'Social Perspectives of Technology in Education', reported that students 'preferred the more time-independent communication facilitated through the bulletin board' (2000: 175).

A number of research findings suggest that this time-independent aspect of asynchronous online discussion has the potential to mitigate the effects of certain inequalities. On the basis of their research, Sorensen and Baylen argued that the equality of 'speaking' time in computer-mediated discussion environments fostered more equal participation and more idea generation (2004: 118). In their case study of an online course involving both Pakeha (European) New Zealanders and Chinese nationals, Locke and Daly found that a large majority of students indicated that they found it easier to express their views in an online discussion than in a face-to-face, classroom situation. All Chinese students in the course (taught in English) took this position, one commenting: 'In the Class Forum, non-native English speakers can express themselves better than face-to-face learning because online learning give them time to properly put their ideas into English' (2006: 6).

In setting up their study of forty pre-service teacher education students, Im and Lee were mindful of studies suggesting that, in traditional classroom settings, male students appear to dominate discussion (2004: 157). Over a thirteen-week period they gathered and analysed 336 asynchronous discussion postings from thirty-nine students, and 2,820 synchronous postings from twenty-one students (across five separate discussions). In respect of gender, they found female students to be more active than males in online discussions, suggesting that a 'more egalitarian atmosphere' and 'social distance' had lessened male dominance (2004: 166). However, they also found that the difference between genders was less in respect of initiating postings, males preferred to initiate postings than respond to the postings of others (2004: 162).

Dennen attempted to identify factors in course design and facilitation that impacted positively on student participation in terms of quantity, quality, timing, and nature of messages posted (2005: 128). She found:

- A correlation between quantity of participation and quality of participation (p.132).
- More dialogue when instructors were actively involved in discussion (p. 136).
- Certain structures – 'instructor expectations; learner instructions; or prompts, deadlines, and feedback' – affected student willingness to participate (p. 137).
- Students were motivated by being assessed (p. 140).

Dennen's research tends to corroborate earlier research by Swan which found that general factors of clarity of design, interaction with online teachers and active discussion among course participants affected students' satisfaction with asynchronous online learning and whether they felt their learning was effective (2001: 306).

Another issue related to participation is the *relative* participation in discussion of teacher/tutor and student. In a content analysis comparison of learning processes in online and face-do-face discussions, Hackman and Annabi found that student-to-student interactions tended to predominate in asynchronous online discussions whereas instructor–student exchanges tended to dominate in classroom face-to-face discussions (2005: 'Discourse process', paragraphs 2 and 3). Vess's research with tertiary history students found, similarly, that 'Students in the fully asynchronous class … were inclined to continue a discussion thread, while those in face-to-face discussions generally tended to respond only to the instructor's questions and not to each other'. Her research also confirmed Hackman and Annabi's claim that '… student-to-student interactions engendered by asynchronous discussion often demonstrate a great many cognitive indicators of involvement and elaboration' (2005: 362).

On the basis of this study, then, one can conclude that asynchronous discussion in an online setting is better able to facilitate and support learning for a greater range of students than synchronous discussion. However, there are other aspects of rhetorical connection that have a bearing on learning: feedback, convergence and structuration.

Feedback, convergence and structuration

Feedback, convergence and structuration all relate to patterns of interaction operating among the company present, really or virtually, in a rhetorical space. All are in differing ways problematic in the context of an ABB discussion. Immediate feedback is not available to online bulletin-board participants, nor is non-verbal feedback. (Emoticons can be thought of as quasi-non-verbal feedback.) It is clear, however, that feedback patterns in asynchronous online discussion have a bearing on such things as convergence and structuration (Dennen, 2005). Locke and Daly identified feedback as a factor contributing to the success of an online course whose transcripts they analysed. For the students who participated in the course, the feedback spread averaged 80 and the feedback rate averaged 187. The latter figure indicated that all students frequently incorporated multiple feedback instances in single utterances across a range of discussions. These measures, they concluded, equated with a high degree of responsiveness in all participants (2006: 7).

Sorensen and Baylen's (2004) study comparing patterns of communication of the same students from a 'hybrid' class across face-to-face (FTF) and asynchronous online discussion settings is particularly pertinent to the dimension of feedback. They used five categories to code types of communication:

1 *Initiating:* for example, 'stating an opinion or insight to get the conversation started',
2 *Supporting:* for example, 'sharing evidence to support a position',
3 *Challenging:* for example, 'offering different opinions',
4 *Summarizing:* for example, 'when a participant states in a concise way the essence of someone else's remarks',
5 *Monitoring:* for example, 'statements that keep the group on task and focus the discussion on the topic'.

(2004: 119)

The researchers used a further coding system for response levels, which they called the 'Initiate–Response–Reply' (IRR) Framework, where responses were coded as an initial posting (IP), response to a post (RP), reply to a response (RR), or reply to a reply (RR#). Level 4 responses were deemed to be high, and level 1 low, as indicators of interactions among participants (2004: 120).

In respect of online discussion, Sorensen and Baylen found that patterns 1 and 2 (initiating and supporting) dominated. They also found more evidence for initial levels of response patterns. 'Students were most likely to respond to an initial posting (level 2), and much less likely to reply to a response (level 3) and not likely at all to reply to a reply (level 4). Thus the interactions appeared much less like a discussion, in which conversation builds upon previous responses, and more like a question-and-answer scenario' (2004: 124).

The authors drew a number of implications from their research:

- If metacognition is going to occur, students may need to learn and apply new communication patterns (such as challenging, summarizing and monitoring),
- There is a case to be made for designing online tasks that demand that students engage in both synthesizing and challenging,
- Use can be made of models or exemplars of expected online role behaviour, and these expected roles clearly defined and illustrated,
- It is best to choose topics that lend themselves to high-level patterns of communication and interaction,
- Instructors 'need to pay attention to instructional design principles that enhance the learning environment. The use of online discussion should allow learners to focus on key components of what they are learning. They must be able to connect what they know prior to this experience and to make those connections to what they are currently learning.'

(2004: 124–5)

In respect of convergence, Sorensen and Baylen noted, 'While computer-mediated group interactions may be more focused on tasks and less on personal interactions, they also may result in greater processing time and create difficulty in consensus building' (2004: 118). The nature of consensus, the forms it might take and how desirable it is take one into the realm of educational philosophy. In their brief literature review, Sorensen and Baylen further noted a leadership void and lack of structure as potential disadvantages of ABBs and related these to difficulties in 'consensus building' (2004: 118), calling to mind Hammond's (1997) view that much online debate is serendipitous and hard to structure.

While agreeing with Hammond, Hackman and Annabi (2005) have nevertheless developed a rigorous research framework for analysing the 'structuring processes' that underpin both asynchronous online discussion in ALNs and classroom-based face-to-face discussion. In their framework, they distinguish between social process, cognitive process, teaching process and discourse process, with each of these further sub-divided into second-level sub-categories. For instance, they sub-divide social process into affective response, cohesive response and interactive response. The particular value of their work is in their development of third-level specific indicators that enable code-based analyses of ABB transcript data.

Another issue related to convergence and congeniality is communicative competence and style. In this regard, (critical) discourse analysis with an emphasis on pragmatics can identity factors that foster or hinder the kind of collaboration that facilitates online learning. In their analysis of ABB transcripts from a course involving both Chinese and European students, Locke and Daly identified the important role played by such positive politeness strategies as the use of in-group address forms; the intensification of interest in another; and the assertion of common ground. The latter played a key role in the achievement of convergence. They also found some striking differences between Chinese and European students in respect of modes of group address and in the management of such speech acts as expressing disagreement and responding to a challenge. They concluded that politeness practices specific to Chinese culture had contributed to congeniality in the group as a whole (2006: 7–9).

A major issue with the management of asynchronous discussion is the role of online tutor. Involved here are questions of professional identity, desirable pedagogy and – last but not least – work load. In a review article addressing the last of these, Dunlap asserted that 'facilitating discussions is the single most time-consuming and effort-intensive component of an online course' (2005: 21). She addressed this issue by drawing on the literature to bring together a range of instructional strategies designed to help teachers achieve 'presence' without their being constantly online. She divided these strategies into three categories: 'course orientation and management; assessment of learners during online activities; and discussion facilitation and management' (2005: 18).

In a systematic review of sixty-two case-study papers dealing with the role of asynchronous online discussion in higher education, Hammond (2005) highlighted four interrelated issues as impacting on student learning: curriculum design, instructor support, learners' behaviour and attitudes and software. The first two of these are clearly related to feedback, convergence and structuration as discussed here. (The third can be thought of as related to the overt company but impacting on feedback and structuration, while the fourth has a pervasive effect on reach and connection.)

A radical approach to work load, and issues of structuration and convergence (or lack of it) has been proposed by Eleuterio and Bortolozzi, who worked from the premise that systems such as ABBs are 'passive tools designed to merely organize discussions in threaded structures, with no mediating capability to promote interaction, or handle disagreements and conflicts among the group' and are demotivating for students and beyond the mediational capacity of tutors (2004: 13).

The Amanda method allows for 'very little or no interference of a human mediator' (p. 13):

> The AMANDA method consists of launching a set of issues for group debate and then redistributing the corresponding answers and argumentations among the participants to be collectively validated along successive discussion cycles. At each discussion cycle, the method detects disagreements and proposes new interactions among the group, so that the focus of the discussion is intentionally controlled and the debate advances according to specific interaction objectives. New discussion cycles are successively opened until the discussion cannot be advanced any further or until the discussion time expires.
>
> (2004: 14)

Their report of field experiments noted improved student motivation, brought about, the authors explained, because the method shaped the discussion into a 'regular and disciplined activity', with participants 'receiving "personal" discussion forms to work on and being challenged to argue over conflicting positions from their peers' (2004: 20). The writers themselves put the word 'personal' in inverted commas. It is certainly a challenging thought that an algorithmically based system may be superior to a human tutor and that student motivation may be enhanced by replacing or supplementing the teacher in the overt company by a machine.

Irrespective of the Amanda findings, most studies posit a central role for the teacher as both facilitator and designer. In respect of the former, Im and Lee argued on the basis of their research that 'Tutors should take on a variety of roles to successfully promote online discussion, such as guiding students in the online discussion, providing prompt input and feedback, and offering summaries of the discussions' (2004: 167). In his systematic review Hammond, in developing his 'broad consensus on best practices', suggested, among other things, that instructors should 'show teaching presence but encourage critique and divergence; fade as appropriate; have an administrative role ... have a pastoral role ... suggest activities and roles to generate debate; and take responsibility for monitoring the nature and scope of discussion and group processes' (2005: 18).

The role of the tutor (pre-discussion, during discussion and post-discussion) was also the major focus of research carried out by Lim and Cheah, who used questionnaires, focus group interviews and analyses of discussion records with a sample of 700 pre-service teacher education students and four online tutors. They found that tutor involvement varied across the discussions and that students identified a number of areas where tutors could improve. On the basis of this, they identified six important tutor roles:

- Meaningful task-setting,
- Providing guidelines in respect of online discussion 'technicalities' (for example, length and structure of messages),
- Active participation (answering queries, offering feedback, playing devil's advocate).[9]
- Maintaining the focus of discussion,
- Drawing conclusions and offering expert knowledge, especially in the post-discussion stage.
- Suggesting further resources for learning (especially Web-based).

(2003: 43–4)

In another study focusing on online instructor roles, Havard *et al.* claimed that 'The roles of the instructor are critical in the implementation of discussion strategies and design of student tasks for significant learning in online collaborative environments'. Their research examined three productive roles for instructor – class member, initiator, and discussant – and linked these with 'three strategies for dynamic online discussion: flexible peer, structured topic, and collaborative task discussion' (2005: 134).

On the other hand, Poole's case study, mentioned earlier, which required students to take on a leadership role as discussion 'moderator', suggested the possibility of positive benefits for discussion when traditional role differentiation is challenged. She commented: 'It is likely that moderator responsibilities also contributed to students' sense of community, because acting as moderator was a common experience for all class members' (2000: 175). Dennen also identified instructor presence as a key in generating quality student dialogue. But she also noted that instructors can be too dominant (thereby creating a work load rod for their own backs) (2005: 145).

Janks (2005) provided a good example of teacher-initiated instructional design. Typical of a new kind of Web-mediated, inter-institutional arrangement, Janks teaches, from her home study in Johannesburg, a University of South Australia course on 'A Critical Language Awareness (CLA) Approach to Literacy Education' to students enrolled at Mount Saint Vincent University in Nova Scotia, Canada, who could be living anywhere in the world. She wrote: 'I have tried to use my face-to-face experience to design activities that develop and scaffold students' understanding (Bruner, 1985) by using interactive activities and keeping information and definitions to a minimum' (2005: 88). As an example, Janks described a scaffolding sequence of four activities, which take students from a commonplace understanding of the word 'critical' to a more specialized, scientific understanding of it:

- Students simply list the different meanings of the word 'critical' that they can think of (bearing in mind collocations such as 'critical condition').
- Students are referred to the British national corpus Web site (http://sara.natcorp. ox.ac.uk/lookup.html) where a word can be entered and fifty random uses generated. A further entry generates a further random sample of fifty. Students are required to enter the word 'critical' and categorize the different meanings that emerge.
- Students are required to find five examples of the word 'critical' used in the context of educational documents of various kinds pertinent to their own setting.
- Students are directed to readings in critical literacy/CLA in order to discover the meaning of the word 'critical' so contextualized.

A number of points can be made in respect of this example of activity design. First, the sequence is underpinned by a philosophy of teaching and learning. Second, the tasks require students to be actively engaged in learning. Third, the tasks require students to access both prescribed and independently sourced texts, and sources in both print and digital modes. (Students were therefore encouraged to expand the 'implied' company, as defined earlier.) Fourth, the sequence of tasks is dictated by a learning logic. Fifth, the tasks are designed to allow students to develop and bring individualized perspectives to the co-operative task of co-constructing knowledge.

Relevant to structuration in relation to course design is a distinction Hammond makes in suggesting that: 'Cooperative learning involves the completion of a task by breaking it down into subtasks that team members solve independently, whereas collaborative learning involves team members working together to develop a joint solution to a problem' (2005: 13–4; see also Klemm, 2005: 1). The task used by Janks is a good example of collaborative learning. Another approach was reported by Lundin (2003). The issue addressed in the research was the design of asynchronous learning activities to support synchronization in collaborative learning. Using a Net scenario (based on a multimedia-enhanced story to support collaborative role playing for learning), the study tested three types of 'synchronization point': *locked scenes*, *written instructions* and *collaborative production*.

The *locked scenes* were effective in synchronizing all participants but slowed down the group's progress and did therefore make the most active participants lose motivation. The *written instructions* were successful in gathering the active group but failed to engage the less active participants. The *collaborative production* was successful in gathering the active group in collaborative activities and to engage the less active participants individually.

Though the research was based in a workplace, it has relevance for tertiary online learning environments.

LOOKING AHEAD: ISSUES AND RESEARCH AGENDAS

There is no neutrality in naming. Using an acronym like ICT as the generic category for ABBs privileges information and communication functions of technology and overlooks ways in which technologies also have a representational function – extending the human capability to perceive, express, order, construct, render and position. The acronym ICRT (Information, Communication and Representation Technologies) might better express the complex of functions of technology that are being referred to. Naming is an issue for any researcher, because ways in which aspects of a domain are 'worded' affect the formulation of research questions and methodological design.

The terms one uses in addressing the potential of ABBs for learning and teaching inevitably locate one within a particular discursive frame. In his synthesis, Hammond stated that 'Researchers express broad agreement that the argument for using asynchronous online discussion rests in a commitment to interaction between learners and adherence to a social constructivist approach to teaching and learning', focusing on the value of social interaction and learner involvement in active meaning making (2005: 18).

The major point to be made here is that a view of how rhetorical space might be shaped, via the medium of an ABB in educational settings that have bought into the need to provide online learning environments, is going to depend on the philosophy which underpins both platform and programme design. Hammond notes that most of the sixty-two papers he drew on 'had an action research element to them' and were focused on 'improving curriculum design or instructor practice rather than establishing the value of asynchronous online discussion *per se*' (2005: 15). So much is reassuring, but needs to be viewed from the perspective that these studies tend to be single cases and are a drop in the ocean when compared with Natriello's statistics referred to previously. They do not provide an overview of what is generally occurring in online settings using ABBs.

Two paragraphs occur near the conclusion of Natriello's article that further highlight the naming or 'wording' issue:

It is possible to envision scenarios in which teaching is diminished as an element of the education sector with many functions once performed by teachers now shifted to advanced information and communication technologies or at least to lower cost instructors far from the site where education is actually delivered. This, indeed, is the nightmare that causes many educators to avoid distance learning and all that it portends.

It is equally possible to envision scenarios in which teaching is elevated as a profession supported by a range of new technologies based on an enhanced understanding of learning
and the conditions that sustain it. This is the picture of the teacher as a powerful professional able to deliver desired results on a predictable basis whenever well understood
conditions are attained. This is also the vision of the educational enterprise as more varied
and complex with many of the less demanding tasks necessary to support learning shifted to
technologies yet to be invented.

(Natriello, 2005: 1900–1)

A noteworthy naming here is the word 'deliver'. Natriello's two paragraphs, of
course, are meant to evoke contrasting dystopian/utopian extremes. However,
there will be some whose philosophy will lead them to find the concept of education as *delivering* 'desired results on a predictable basis' also nightmarish.
They will argue that 'naming' learning thus is effectively commodifying or
packaging it.[10] Likewise, decisions between wordings such as 'teacher', 'tutor'
and 'instructor' have discursive implications.

In his systematic review Hammond noted a general absence of focus on the
characteristics of particular software programmes (2005: 17). Payne's (2005) critique of Blackboard is an exception to this absence. Such critiques are useful in
rendering visible the discursive underpinnings of particular ALNs and online learning environments in general. As suggested earlier, they provide the necessary act of
social contextualization in terms of which issues related to asynchronous online
discussion can be framed. They also suggest that a move towards increased commodification may be at odds with a commitment to social constructivist pedagogy.

On another level, a focus on the characteristics of particular software programmes is necessary to address issues of functionality and interface design. It
can be argued that ALN system engineers need to find ways to enable users of
ABBs and other ALN technologies access to more multimodal representational
resources. Klemm (2005) has argued against the over-reliance in ALNs on bulletin boards and for greater use of shared-document conferencing. In the latter,
'learners work with applications files such as documents, spreadsheets, and
Power Point presentations. They can check these out and make changes in the
files, provided that they have the requisite application software on their local
PCs' (2005: 1). His argument is that shared-document conferencing is better
suited than bulletin boards to constructivist and co-operative learning.

Desirable focuses for future research are those two aspects of rhetorical reach
termed 'field' and 'company'. If, as is argued here, the rhetorical space of an ABB
is discursively constructed, then (in Foucauldian terms) certain privileged discourses will be operating to regulate what can and cannot be said in respect of the
field. Analyses such as Payne's are important ways of identifying the nature and
degree of the hegemonies operating in a particular online learning environment. It
is interesting to note that Payne's antidote to the social conformity he sees operating in the suburban Levittown of Blackboard is another kind of space, an 'urban
ideal' he finds aptly expressed in a passage from Christy Friend:

In cities, complex networks of production, distribution, transportation, exchange, entertainment, and communication are coordinated across a wide, diverse geographic area. At the same time, individuals retain connections to multiple groups, some of which are small and homogeneous, and others comprised mainly of [sic] strangers. The play of identification and difference is thus continually present, yet continually shifting.

(Friend, 1999: 660, cited in Payne, 2005: 502)

An ABB capable of being viewed in terms of such a metaphor would be characterized by the encouragement of self-reflexivity, diversity, resistance to and critique of naturalized 'common sense', and the valuing of difference.

Questions of what constitutes an ideal rhetorical space can be couched in terms of how one envisages the composition and qualities of the overt, covert and implied company. Questions such as, 'Whose space is it?' 'Who is privileged in this space and who is not?' 'Who is excluded?' 'Who is represented, and how, and for whose ends?' are useful ones for discourse analyses of ABBs and the online learning environments they are embedded in (Payne, 2005: 503). So are questions such as: 'To what extent are participants enabled to enlarge the overt company?' 'How broad is the implied company in a discussion?' 'How is the covert company to an ABB and its online milieu constituted?'

Notions of 'instructor presence' in an ABB, explored by researchers such as Dennen (2005), can usefully be linked to Bakhtin's idea of addressivity discussed earlier. In Bakhtin's terms, a student message writer in an ABB is both respondent to previous utterances and addressor to those in a position to respond to his or her message. A key focus of future research should be to find ways of helping student participants to move beyond a situation where the online teacher is viewed as a dominant member of the overt company to a situation where they see themselves as entering into dialogue with a bigger company: the overt company in total, the implied company, and even the covert company as reflected in the discursive underpinnings of the sociocultural environment that the ABB is contextualized by.

Hammond's systematic review calls for research that focuses on the qualities of participating learners, a critical feature of any overt company. In his consensus of best practices, he includes among these qualities: an appreciation of the benefits of group work; ICT competence and access; lack of face-to-face (FTF) access; willingness to critique authority; text-based communication as a preferred learning style; willingness to interact publicly both constructively and critically; and some fluency and proficiency in the language of the forum (2005: 18–19). Many of the papers analysed are critiqued for their failure to 'critically address the responsibility of learners to participate, the characteristics of the learners to whom online discussion would most or least appeal' (2005: 20). Future research needs to focus on ways of developing proactively the desirable qualities of asynchronous online participants.

The place of assessment and its relationship to participation rates is another issue that warrants future research (Dennen, 2005). A finding from Goodwin *et al.*'s Geelong study is pertinent here:

The tutors and many of the active students argued for more marks to be assigned to the group work to force greater participation by all students. The question remains as to what percentage of marks should be allocated but there is no doubt that unless some marks are awarded, participation will be very low.

(2001: 46)

It is doubtful, however, whether the simple award of marks is going to solve the problem of ensuring an adequate rate of student participation. Indeed, the studies Hammond reported on offered conflicting views, sometimes favouring summative assessment, sometimes suggesting that summative assessment had the potential to increase the number of postings without improving their quality (2005: 16).

There is plenty of scope for research to be done on issues related to structuration. There are no simple answers or general prescriptions in respect of such questions as 'How involved should the online teacher be in discussion?' 'How directive should the teacher be in respect of their stance?' 'How much intervention?' All teachers, regardless of the rhetorical space that is their setting, are confronted with questions in respect of instructional design. Potentially aiding such work are the attempts by researchers such as Sorensen and Baylen (2004) and Hackman and Annabi (2005), both of whom have developed frameworks for analysing the discourse of asynchronous online discussion. What makes Hackman and Annabi's work particularly pertinent is their suggestion – worthy of corroboration by further research – that the discourse patterns of ABBs differ markedly from the teacher-centred discourse of traditional FTF discussion in classroom settings. If this is the case, there will be implications for the work load concerns raised by Dunlap (2005).

Because the Web-based ABB offers the potential for a radical reshaping of rhetorical space, there is plenty of scope for researchers to reflect on the kinds of instructional design principles that best exploit this potential. It is likely that such researchers will continue to base their work in case studies within an action research frame. A comment made by Donald Leu in respect of the impact of technology on literacy applies equally to the effectiveness of ABBs in teaching and learning: 'Our understanding may be informed more often by individuals who use various technologies on a daily basis and less often by traditional forms of research' (2000: 762).

Finally, there are a number of ethical considerations that need to borne in mind in the development of future research agendas, keeping in mind that all teaching is an ethical undertaking and that there is always an ethical dimension to the educational philosophy one subscribes to. In respect of ABBs in particular, there are issues at the macro level related to surveillance, for example the nature and limits of the covert company and the discursive pressures operating in a rhetorical space, that need to be constantly kept in mind. There are also ethical issues on the micro level, related to how members of the overt company manage their interactive behaviour and how course designers and teachers assign, construct and reward specific roles and behaviours. And when courses attract culturally diverse participants, modes of cultural inclusivity, reflected in participant behaviour and environmental design, need to be explored, so that difference is viewed as a resource and not a deficit.

NOTES

1 In *Imagined Communities*, Benedict Anderson argues that 'All communities larger than primordial villages of face-to-face contact (and perhaps even this) are imagined' (1983: 6).

2 My use of the word 'field' here is roughly synonymous with Hallidayan grammar's use of the term 'field of discourse', the general sense of what a text is on about, referring to 'what is happening, to the nature of the social action that is taking place' (Halliday and Hasan, 1985: 12).

3 The term 'utterance' is being used in the Bakhtinian sense of a unit of speech communication (spoken or written) determined by a change of speaking subject (Bakhtin: 1986).

4 I concede that these are crude measures and overlook qualitative differences in types of feedback, depth of feedback and considerations such as delay (how much 'time' has elapsed between the feedback message and the original message) in a thread.

5 In an interesting discussion, Hackman and Annabi suggest that 'the traditional Socratic questioning and feedback functions are to some extent dependent on the linear nature of the FTF dialogue' and that instructors in ABB contexts may need to 'choreograph' discussions differently from those in FTF mode (2005: 'Discussion', paragraphs 7–8). Considerations may also need to be posited on the assumption that besides 'individual' intelligence some kind of 'collective' intelligence is at work in an asynchronous online discussion as it begins to reflect an emerging 'community of practice' (see Lévy, 1997; Wenger *et al.*, 2002).

6 An asynchronous learning network (ALN) is a learning environment which involves a student in both self-study and in significant, asynchronous interaction with teachers and other students via networked computers and other technologies (mobile phones, iPods), without the need for synchronous interaction (see Goodwin *et al.*, 2001).

7 The press release was hotlinked from the Blackboard index page and retrieved on 9 March 2006 from http://www.blackboard.com/company/press/release.aspx?id=767025.

8 Web Crossing's index page (retrieved 9 March 2006) is http://www.webcrossing.com/Home/.

9 Students in this study expected their tutors to visit discussions daily. The authors quote a number of studies highlighting the importance of tutor participation. See also Goodwin *et al.*, (2001); Markel (2001).

10 A critical discourse analysis of this sentence would note, for example, that it suppresses information about *whom* these desired results are to delivered to and *whose* desires these results are serving.

REFERENCES

Anderson, B. (1983) *Imagined Communities*. London: Verso.

Bakhtin, M. (1986) 'The problem with speech genres', in C. Emerson and M. Holquist (eds), *Speech Genres and Other Late Essays: M. M. Bakhtin*, trans. V. McGee. Austin, TX: University of Texas Press. pp. 60–102.

Burbules, N. (2002) 'The Web as a rhetorical place', in I. Snyder (ed.), *Silicon Literacies*. Abingdon: Routledge. pp. 75–84.

Deleuze, G. and Guattari, F. (1987) *A Thousand Plateaus: Capitalism and Schizophrenia*, trans. B. Massumi. Minneapolis, MN: University of Minnesota Press.

Dennen, V. (2005) 'From message posting to learning dialogues: factors affecting learner participation in asynchronous discussion', *Distance Education*, 26 (1): 127–48.

Dunlap, J. (2005) 'Workload reduction in online courses: getting some shuteye', *Performance Improvement*, 44 (5): 18–25.

Eleuterio, M. and Bortolozzi, F. (2004) 'AMANDA: an intelligent system for mediating threaded discussions', *International Journal on e-Learning*, 3(3): 13–20.

Fairclough, N. (1992) *Discourse and Social Change*. Cambridge: Polity Press.

Foucault, M. (1977) *Discipline and Punish*, trans. A. Sheridan. London: Penguin Books.

Freud, S. (1962) *Civilization and its Discontents*, trans. J. Strachey. New York: Norton.

Friend, C. (1999) 'From the contact zone to the city: Iris Marion Young and composition theory', *JAC*, 19: 657–76.

Gee, J. P. (1996) *Social Linguistics and Literacies: Ideology in Discourses* (2nd edn). London: Taylor and Francis.

Goodwin, C., Graham, M. and Scarborough, H. (2001) 'Developing an asynchronous learning network', *Educational Technology and Society*, 4 (4): 39–47.

Hackman, R. and Annabi, H. (2005) 'A content analytic comparison of learning processes in online and face-to-face case study discussions', *Journal of Computer Mediated Communication*, 10 (2), article 7. Retrieved 11 April 2006 from: http://jcmc.indiana.edu/vol10/issue2/hackman.html.

Halliday, M. and Hasan, R. (1985) *Language, Context, and Text: Aspects of Language in a Social-Semiotic Perspective*. Geelong: Deakin University Press.

Hammond, M. (1997) 'Professional learning and the online discussion', *Information Research*, 3 (1). Retrieved 16 November 2005 from: http://informationr.net/ir/3-1/paper34.html.

Hammond, M. (2005) 'A review of recent papers on using online discussion within teaching and learning in higher education', *Journal of Asynchronous Learning Networks*, 9 (3): 9–23.

Havard, B., Du, J. and Olinzock, A. (2005) 'Deep learning: the knowledge, methods, and cognition process in instructor-led online discussion', *Quarterly Review of Distance Education*, 6 (2): 125–35.

Im, Y., and Lee, O. (2004) 'Pedagogical implications of online discussion for preservice teacher training', *Journal of Research on Technology in Education*, 36 (2): 155–70.

Janks, H. (2005) 'Engaging students online: a module in an international M.Ed in Language and Literacy Education', in T. Welch and Y. Reed (eds), *Designing and Delivering Distance Education: Quality Criteria and Case Studies from South Africa*. Braamfontein: NADEOSA (National Association of Distance Education Organisations of South Africa). pp. 87–96.

Klemm, W. (2005) 'Interactive e-learning: why can't we get beyond bulletin boards?', *Educational Technology and Society*, 8 (3): 1–5.

Lankshear, C. and Knobel, M. (1997) 'Literacies, texts and difference in the electronic age', in C. Lankshear, with J. Gee, M. Knobel and C. Searle, *Changing Literacies*. Buckingham: Open University Press. pp. 133–60.

Leu, D. Jr. (2000) 'Chapter 39: Literacy and technology: deictic consequences for literacy education in an information age', in M. Kamil, P. Mosenthal, P. Pearson and R. Barr (eds), *Handbook of Reading Research III*. Mahwah, NJ: Erlbaum. pp. 743–64.

Lévy, P. (1997) *Collective Intelligence: Mankind's Emerging World in Cyberspace*, trans. R. Bononno. New York: Perseus Books.

Lim, C. and Cheah, P. (2003) 'The role of the tutor in asynchronous discussion boards: a case study of a preservice teacher course', *Educational Media International*, 40 (2): 33–47.

Lim, C. and Tan, S. (2001) 'Online discussion boards for focus group interviews: an exploratory study', *Journal of Educational Enquiry*, 2 (1): 50–60.

Locke, T. and Daly, N. (2006) 'Politeness and face in digitally reconfigured e-learning spaces'. Paper presented at the Language, Culture and Technologies conference, May 2006, Kaunas University of Technology.

Lundin, J. (2003) 'Synchronizing asynchronous collaborative learners', in M. Huysman, E. Wenger and V. Wulf (eds), *Communities and Technologies: Proceedings of the First International Conference on Communities and Technologies: C&T 2003*. Dordrecht: Kluwer. pp. 427–43.

Markel, S. (2001) 'Technology and education online discussion forums: it's in the response', *Online Journal of Distance Learning Administration*, 4 (2). Retrieved 22 November 2005 from: http://www.westga.edu/~distance/ojdla/summer42/market42.html.

Natriello, G. (2005) 'Modest changes, revolutionary possibilities: distance learning and the future of education', *Teachers College Record*, 107 (8): 1885–904.

Ong, W. (1982) *Orality and Literacy: The Technologizing of the Word*. London: Methuen.

Payne, D. (2005) 'English Studies in Levittown: rhetorics of space and technology in course-management software', *College English*, 67 (5): 483–507.

Poole, D. (2000) 'Student participation in a discussion-oriented online course: a case study', *Journal of Research on Computing in Education*, 33 (2): 162–77.

Semetsky, I. (2003) 'Deleuze's new image of thought, or Dewey revisited', *Educational Philosophy and Theory*, 35 (1): 17–29.

Søby, M. (2005) 'Identity and learning in cyberspace'. Retrieved 28 September 2005 from: http://mt.sh.se/summerschool2005/identity_and_learning.pdf.

Sorensen, C. and Baylen, D. (2004) 'Patterns of communicative and interactive behaviour online', *Quarterly Review of Distance Education*, 5 (2): 117–26.

Swan, K. (2001) 'Virtual interaction: design factors affecting student satisfaction and perceived learning in asynchronous online courses', *Distance Education*, 22 (2): 306–31.

Vess, D. (2005) 'Asynchronous discussion and communication patterns in online and hybrid history courses', *Communication Education*, 54 (4): 355–64.

Wenger, E., McDermott, R. and Snyder, W. (2002) *A Guide to Managing Knowledge: Cultivating Communities of Practice*. Boston, MA: Harvard Business School Press.

9

Researching the Cognitive Cultures of E-learning

Andrew Whitworth

This chapter discusses how e-learning research can account for the nature and impact of organizations, in both theory and practice. E-learning is not spontaneously generated, but shaped by organized activity. In its turn, it becomes part of the environment, and goes on to shape further organized activities. Because this cycle of e-learning research, development and use is an organized process, it is also a *political* process. The politics of e-learning can be studied at the macro-level of governmental policy (see Coupal, 2004; Estabrook et al., 2007), and such work is valuable, for external pressures like these are very significant. However, when studying innovation, the internal, micro-level practices and negotiations are just as important. Such activity takes place not only in educational organizations, but in other organizations (governments or ICT companies, for instance) that have a stake in e-learning, or otherwise influence its development.

Two intellectual traditions combine in this investigation: the Social Shaping of Technology (SST) thesis (Williams and Edge, 1996); and the sociopolitical study of organizations. As this chapter will explain, the two perspectives depend on each other; technologies and organizations are in a symbiosis, co-evolving through interactions between researchers, developers, users and managers in which organizational processes, structures and latent conflicts are potentially reflected. Technologies are not spontaneously generated; neither are organizations random agglomerations of individuals. There is an element of intentionality to both (Kerr, 2004: 115). Both are designed or shaped to meet specific needs; to fit inside certain environments; and to solve particular problems. Both can develop in ways unintended by their designers. Technologies and organizations are closely related, methodologically, and difficult to separate.

E-learning researchers must therefore be aware of how their participants' – and their own – ability to develop, understand and use these technologies is partly generated by, and concealed within, existing technologies, organizational forms, and the vested interests that exploit and rely on them. Educational organizations are not environments in which all possibilities are, in principle, available for selection, with the most effective or efficient being chosen based only on the results of objective research. Organizations are fragmented, and permeated with a variety of *cognitive cultures* that may be in competition with each other to shape both e-learning technologies and the university itself.

ORGANIZATIONAL ENGINEERING

The study of organization, whether for academic or managerial purposes, is often based around 'implicit images or metaphors that lead us to see, understand and manage organizations in distinctive yet partial ways' (Morgan, 1999: 4). The partiality of metaphors is significant; the study and management of organization are not a unified field. Metaphors – to use a metaphor – are like lights shining on a stage. Without illumination, the stage (the situation being addressed) is invisible, but each light illuminates only part of the whole. Focusing too strongly on one metaphor can lead to a 'rigid and inflexible' approach (Morgan, 1999: 4) to the study of organizational and technological change. (For the role of metaphor in language and life see Lakoff and Johnson, 1980.)

But, *combined*, spotlights provide a full view of the whole – and a richer view than when only 'natural' light is used. Therefore, the following discussion uses several of Morgan's metaphors: the organization as machine; organism; brain; psychic prison; cultural artefact; and instrument of domination. One metaphor is not being proposed as more suitable for e-learning researchers than others. Rather, the intention is to expose the assumptions behind each, and then use it to enrich our view of e-learning research by critically analysing examples with reference to these metaphors and the theories that exploit them.

Morgan's first metaphor is the organization as *machine*: 'invented and developed to aid in performing some kind of goal-oriented activity' (Morgan, 1999: 15). Within the mechanistic organization (Burns and Stalker, 1961), human pursuits are translated into the language of engineering (Mitcham, 1994: 63). People become components in a technical design, put to work to efficiently fulfil organizational objectives; not autonomous individuals with goals, needs and values of their own.

Mechanistic organizations are characterized by: strict division of labour; hierarchical stratification between work force and mangement; decision making by executives based on 'rational' analysis, and insulated from public scrutiny; strictly classified roles and procedures; and formal training processes designed to 'fit' workers into predefined roles. The organization works on problems to which convergent solutions – 'one best' design, product or system (cf. Tyack, 1974) – have been identified through objective research and analysis and solutions to which are assessed against quantifiable criteria; an approach which Fay (1975: 51) terms *policy science*. The classic example of mechanistic organizational theory is the 'scientific management' of Frederick Taylor (1911), though Morgan (1999: 25) points out that he was 'part of a much broader social trend involving the mechanization of life generally'. These trends can be seen in the history of educational technology (see Capel, 1992). When 'effective' education is quantified, the result is an interest in measures such as higher grades, efficiency and technology use (curriculum hours, spending or machine/student ratio) or employability. If policy scientists calculate that increased ICT use will improve these measures, technology will therefore be proposed as *adding value* to the work of educational organizations. It becomes a rational investment, a technological imperative even.

The machine metaphor is outdated, as the following discussion will indicate, but it still makes occasional appearances in contemporary e-learning research. Techniques such as instructional design – 'scientific, value neutral and precise' (Kerr, 2004: 130) – are applied to the new technology. The change from traditional to online learning is discussed as something that will increase 'teacher effectiveness' (Mällinen, 2001). Technical (programming) solutions are sought for educational problems (Clark and Mayer, 2003). Users (academics or students) are reduced to abstractions through modelling (Schewe *et al.*, 2005; Shyu *et al.*, 2004).

It is not that the machine metaphor has no use, nor work based on it no value. But it is a very limited, rather crude way of understanding real-world organizations. As early as the 1940s, the Tavistock Group (see Mumford, 1987) recognized that the metaphor simply cannot account for the full range of responses of human organizational 'components', but emotional, social and political responses to technology are often a strong motivating factor for action. They cannot therefore be ignored. And, unlike machines, organizations are in a complex, interactive relationship with other organizations and the environment as a whole. Different metaphors of organization are therefore required.

DYNAMIC ORGANIZATIONS

In accounting for an organization's relationship with technology, one cannot separate the social system from the technology. Mitcham (1994) states that technologies cannot be studied only as *objects*. Technologies are also:

- *Activities*: design, production, planning, everyday use.
- *Knowledge*: on which production decisions are based.
- *Volition*: underlying motivations for the technology's creation.

Ultimately, 'the definition of technology itself must incorporate the social arrangements within which it emerges and becomes embedded' (Williams and Edge, 1996: 875). This principle – essentially, SST – has implications at each of Mitcham's 'stages', though that word implies a linear process, rather than a complex intermingling and co-evolution of products, activities, knowledge and motivations (here see *activity theory* (Engeström *et al.*, 1999)).

Writers in fields such as soft systems methodology (Checkland, 1999) or collaborative design (Arias *et al.*, 2002) – also referred to as participatory or user-centred design – have suggested how users' perspectives can be embedded in technological solutions not through using models, proxies, representatives or assumptions, but 'the active involvement of users throughout the design process. User involvement is seen as critical both because users are the experts in the work practices supported by these technologies and … will be the ones creating new practices in response to new technologies' (Zaphiris *et al.*, 2004: 164). The aim is to develop systems toward which all stakeholders can feel a sense of ownership.

However, simply acknowledging the influence of human factors is not *sufficient* to move e-learning research and development away from the mechanistic model. Human factors may still be considered variables, the impact of which can be minimized by managerial interventions or Business Process Engineering (in which 'an organization may be broken down into, and is understood in terms of, its core value-adding processes' (Cornford and Pollock, 2002: 176)). Human responses to technology are admitted, but the belief is still that these can be engineered away, if only *best practice* could be found.

'Best practice' in e-learning implementation can include techniques appropriate to the social sphere as well as the technical, but the philosophy remains similar. Models, toolkits or benchmarks are developed to help managers orchestrate the necessary technological and cultural change. Research in this genre includes, but is far from limited to: Bates (2000); Conole and Oliver (2002); Hosie and Schibeci, (2005); Garrison and Anderson (2003, particularly chapter 10). Where e-learning is not implemented as planned (McPherson and Nunes, 2004b), has unintended effects (Harwood, 2005) or is abandoned after a short time (Jervis and Gkolia, 2005), the failures are often ignored or written off. At best they are interrogated for 'lessons learnt' (McPherson and Nunes, 2004b) which can be recycled into new 'best practice' models (Maitlis and Lawrence, 2003). Or failures may be blamed on laggard or 'Luddite' (Glover and Miller, 2001) teachers or students. Responses then range from developing training programmes (Bennett and Bennett, 2003) and/or 'selling' the product to resistant individuals (Gigliotti-Guridi, 2003) to manipulating funding streams and adjusting promotion criteria to penalize those slow to change behaviour.

None of the works cited here is being criticized as inadequate. But, organizationally, they represent merely one approach to e-learning research, and one with a limited area of application. These reductionist, procedural approaches can produce useful general models, but the plans still have to be implemented 'on the ground', within real-world organizations in all their diverse configurations (Kerr, 2004: 120; Mintzberg, 1989; Suchman, 1987). Best practice can struggle to account for *resistance* to change: organizations are resilient (Lakomski, 2001) when subjected to pressure, unlike the ideal machine.

Investigations of resistance and complexity in organizations have been assisted by a different metaphor: not machine, but *organism* (Morgan, 1989: Chapter 3). Organisms depend on an environment for resources, and tend to be better adapted to certain environments than others. If conditions change, and an organism cannot adapt, it will struggle to acquire resources and will possibly die. The *organizational ecology* perspective (see DiMaggio and Powell, 1983; Trist, 1976) suggests that these processes can be observed in organizations. An organization's environment includes natural resources, but also social framing factors such as legislation, funding and available labour. It includes cognitive resources such as skills and research; other organizations; and technology.

But there is reciprocity in this relationship; organisms are not at the mercy of their environment. Even very simple ones can manipulate their environment to help preserve certain conditions. A mutual stability – or *homeostasis* (Marion, 1999: 55–61) – can arise between an organism and its environment. Organizational ecology therefore also accounts for the ways organizations manipulate their environment in order to flourish. Laws are lobbied for, funding streams secured and technologies developed in order that the organization can survive and profit.

Despite these efforts, environmental change still occurs – and e-learning is an example of such a change (Whitworth, 2006). The organism metaphor is more useful at showing how adaptation to change can occur (see Chapter 1 of this volume). Mechanistic research, and the organizational engineering it encourages, is oriented toward finding and implementing single, convergent solutions. This approach works well when environments are stable, but becomes slower and riskier when environments are dynamic and turbulent and a more innovatory approach to developing strategies and products is therefore required (Mintzberg, 1989: Chapter 8).

Bates (2000: 124) writes that a particular rational management technique (cost analysis) 'is not rocket science. Compared with understanding human behaviour or predicting the weather, cost analysis is relatively simple'. But, judged against those tasks, rocket science is relatively simple too. The currents and trajectories in the social sphere are subject to a multitude of influences far less predictable than gravity and wind resistance. We can land rockets – gently – on tiny, swift comets thousands of miles away (as with 2006's 'Stardust' probe), but cannot accurately predict the weather a week hence, let alone the news. Organizations are dynamic and unpredictable (Abrahamsson, 1993: 7–20; Marion, 1999); and, as an organization's environment essentially consists of other organizations, so do the environments in which they have to function.

Dealing with environmental change, including technological change, is therefore a constant process of negotiation, strategizing, planning and acting. Policy science can provide plans and other such resources for action, but its insights must still be applied on the ground, in unpredictable situations where management becomes more a process of negotiation than of planning (Suchman, 1987). E-learning is not a one-off transitional step to be taken by educational organizations, but a profound shift in the environment within which these organizations (and their members) exist and must continue to function. Universities have developed planning procedures and decision-making infrastructures appropriate for the relatively stable environment in which they emerged, but may be less able to produce the rapid responses and flexible production strategies needed in the new era of ICT and the resultant globalization (Bates, 2000: Chapter 10; Trow, 2002).

Though little empirical work has been done to substantiate these claims (Kerr, 2004: 120), it is fair to state that e-learning research cannot take for granted that the educational environment will remain in its current configuration. Innovations catalyse further change. Even the most effective model of 'best practice' will need to adapt to future developments (which it may provoke). Successful innovations may become redundant through no reason other than environmental turbulence (Sørensen and Levold, 1992: 31).

Dynamic systems therefore 'constantly present opportunities for learning' (Russell, 2002: 76). Adaptable technologies and organizations must have the possibility of flexibility and creativity built into their structure. They must, in short, become *learning organizations*, ideally engaging in self-sustaining innovation that continuously adapts the organization to changes in its environment (Senge *et al.*, 1999; and below).

Nevertheless, while these conclusions are now accepted by many organization theorists, the organism metaphor still struggles to account for situations where different parts of the organization fail to pull together around a single agenda. According to Kerr, much work by educational technologists can be 'characterized by an astonishing naïveté as regards the *political* and bureaucratic environments in which they had to try to exist' (Kerr, 2004: 129). We need to consider how some authors have attempted to derive a more political understanding of turbulence, innovation and environmental change as reflected in organizations (Whitworth, 2005).

MULTIPLICITY AND POWER RELATIONS

Viewing organizations as cultures – or, better, an agglomeration of multiple sub-cultures (Turner, 1971) – sheds light not only on the differences *between* organizations, but the divisions *within* them. Organizations are not monolithic and harmonious, but multiplicitous and fragmented. Technologies 'are usually developed in the midst of the lively interplay of group life in organizations in which wants [of different stakeholders] conflict, not all wants can be satisfied simultaneously, and in which key relationships are slowly changing' (Kling, 1987: 121). Within an organization there may be multiple perspectives on how a technological solution should be designed, what problem it is to solve, or whether there is a problem in the first place (Billett, 2002).

Williams and Edge (1996) note that various disciplines such as economics, the history of science and psychology are all useful to SST. But when analysing an organization's culture, subcultures and group interactions, *sociology* has much to offer. The relevant areas are (Kerr, 2004: 114):

- *Sociology of organizations*: 'schools as bureaucracies ... the expectations of actors within the school setting of themselves and of each other (in sociological terms, the roles they play); and the sources of power and control ...'
- *Sociology of groups and classes*: 'the ways that education deals with such groups as those based on gender, class, and race, and how educational technology interacts with those groupings'
- *Sociology of social movements*: the study of change, the role of ideology, which is 'not an explicit, comprehensive and enforced code of beliefs and practices to which all members of a group are held, but rather a set of implicit, often vague, but widely shared set of expectations and assumptions about the social order ...'

Some of the internal partitions within educational organizations are obvious; for example, the relationship between universities' and academics' roles as teachers (knowledge disseminators) and researchers (knowledge producers). Different academic disciplines define knowledge and perceive technology in different ways (Lee, 2004; Russell, 2005). But in addition to these historic differences, e-learning increases the division of labour in education, bringing still more subcultures into play. As work environments (learning and administrative) become more technologically complex, it is harder for single individuals to acquire all skills necessary to care for them. The resultant burden of software production is sometimes shouldered by educators, but may be delegated to developers: whether in-house instructional designers, open source communities or corporate vendors of 'off the shelf' tools. The study of e-learning will therefore benefit from appreciating the workings of not just schools and universities, but software developers (Whitworth and Benson, 2006); nor must it ignore educational pressure groups and campaigners (Kerr, 2004: 129), trade union, policy makers (Coupal, 2004); and others.

Each group's perception of the environment, and how to 'translate' and then 'solve' specific problems, may differ. Diercks-O'Brien and Sharratt (2002: 81) write that: 'Each professional group has different understandings, perceptions and expectations of multimedia, based on their particular professional culture. Consequently, understandings of what multimedia learning can and should do may differ quite dramatically'. (Each group, in short, possesses a different *cognitive culture:* see below, and cf. Lakomski, 2001: 73.) McCurry (2003: 421) says: 'It is not the prescribed or preferred ways of using technology (the so-called "best practices" inventories which are currently being promoted) that should be the centerpiece for discussion, it is the reason (or multiple reasons) we are compelled to pick up technology and implement it to further learning.' Meredith and Newton (2004) list several motivations (or *volition:* see above) behind the introduction of e-learning: a desire to explore new technologies; to increase efficiency; enthusiasm; and an entrepreneurial spirit. They can be admonished for omitting educational motivations (de Castell *et al.*, 2002), but further illustrate how it is hard for research to generalize about motivation. Indeed, the research community itself has a partial perspective on e-learning (Castano, 2003). Researchers have their own needs, values and assumptions. They define their field of interest by focusing on certain groups or environmental factors to the exclusion of others. Whether through time and resource constraints or unstated assumptions, researchers tend to define in advance the questions to be addressed and the methodologies used (cf. Russell, 2002: 67).

Multiplicity does not necessarily block organizational change. In fact, the reverse may be true, as later sections of this chapter will argue. In either case it is rare that decision makers rationally *choose* between all relevant competing opinions. Rather, different world views – some of which may be external to the organization – have more or less power to shape the direction of the organization (and technology) according to factors such as: access to resources; their ability to mobilize support; and their control over the information infrastructure, including research (Berg and Östergren, 1979; and below).

There are pragmatic reasons to include multiple stakeholders in e-learning research. Mitcham criticizes what he calls the 'humanities philosophy of technology' for 'thinking on the cheap' (Mitcham, 1994: 141) – that is, for ignoring the insights of technicians and how they conceive of their work. Technicians have practical knowledge of production processes which users – and planners – may not have. But there are also methodological advantages, in that inclusive research can help draw a more complete picture of the organizational structures that both produce and will be affected by the e-learning solution, instead of relying on a single perspective.

The work of Cervero and Wilson (and associates) is a useful example of a socio-political study of education, though their interest is more in educational programme planning than technology (Cervero and Wilson, 1994; Sandlin and Cervero, 2003; Umble *et al.*, 2001; and Benson, 2002, who does consider e-learning directly). Different interests, interpretations and motivations are negotiated as programmes are planned, and it is in such negotiations that SST and organizational politics combine. *Whose* interests are permitted to, and/or are able to, socially shape technologies? The answer could be read from the resultant (techno-organizational) systems, whether front-end – applications, interfaces – or back office – operating systems, infrastructure, technical support (see Star, 1999). By such 'readings' of the technology, researchers may develop insights into the organization: by 'reading' the organization, one may develop ideas about the sort of technologies it could produce (or socially shape).

Not all significant negotiations directly concern technology *per se*. 'Substantive' negotiations shape the surface details of a system, but are themselves constrained by 'meta-negotiations'. Two types of meta-negotiation are identified:

- 'those that are primarily about power relations, or more specifically, which actors have the most influence over the planning process' and
- 'those that are primarily about frame factors, or more specifically, the fundamental ideational structure and material limits for the programme being planned'

(Umble *et al.*, 2001: 131).

Power can be viewed in several ways within organizations and society (Wrong, 1995); this model exploits Foucault's view of power as ubiquitous, using all available conduits (procedure, law, technology, etc.) to control actions, knowledge and thought in order to maintain existing regimes (Foucault, 1980: 78–108). Power can be wielded to restrict access to decision-making spaces, thus limiting the voices that can contribute to the decision. It can be defined by and distributed through legal or bureaucratic procedures, deviation from which might bring censure, financial penalties and loss of status. The charter of an organization may formally allocate power to certain subgroups (though formal authority and real power are not always the same thing). In a real-world situation, therefore, organizational control over an innovation (such as e-learning) can be asserted by those holding power. Cervero and Wilson (1998) note, for example, how the manager of one professional development programme had the power to exclude certain interests from the planning process. By doing so he effectively discounted the view of 'consultation' as something where those consulted could have actively shaped the programme. Instead, the manager saw consultation as only advisory, and had the power and authority to dismiss not only the contributions of workers but even the possibility of their making any contributions in the first place.

Power relations are one reason why 'user-centred design' does not always produce systems towards which users feel a sense of ownership. In an organization characterized by centralized authority, user-centred design may be viewed as little more than the engineering of 'consent to the technological presence' (Mitcham, 1994: 255) rather than the consensual shaping of change. Bates (2000: 48) declares that all members of an organization should see that it is in 'everyone's interest to participate' in goal setting and design; but many end users may not see the innovation as desirable, nor consultation processes as genuine. Associated e-learning research could provoke resentment, and be rejected or at best ignored.

Those in power have to devote a certain amount of effort and resources to suppressing conflict within an organization, in order that the organization can work towards (their) goals instead of stagnating (Mintzberg, 1989: Chapter 13). Here, further power relations are revealed in the 'framing factors', the second set of meta-negotiations. Power can appear as control over knowledge and research, either directly (restrictions on information, for example) or indirectly, through, say, discounting data not produced through policy scientific methodologies. Power can work through an organization's informal aspects, such as its culture (see Lakomski, 2001), or socialization, induction and recruitment processes (see Turner, 1971). Finally, power can manifest itself as the ability to apportion the risks of a decision (Beck, 1992). Costs and benefits may be described as objective, but Mitcham (1994: 228) notes that they are more often socially determined in accordance with the interests of particular subgroups.

In short, concealed power relations can limit in advance those perspectives that are permitted to influence formal negotiations in any planning process. Concealed conduits of power thereby become part of the organizational substructure. Subcultures are not therefore of equal status.

COGNITIVE BIAS AND COGNITIVE CULTURES

Some have read organizations as little more than dominating instruments wielded by one subculture over another (management over workers, say: Morgan, 1999: Chapter 9). Certain writers on e-learning have been strongly influenced by this metaphor (e.g. Noble, 2002). Yet we should not take the emergence of unequal distributions of organizational power for granted. We must ask why hierarchy is such a dominant organizational form.

Recent work in organizational sociology illuminates ways in which organizational infrastructures, hierarchies, cultures, relationships and communications networks can affect the ways individuals and groups *think* and, thus, constrain the possibilities that they can perceive. Hierarchies exploit universalist tendencies in human information processing to such an extent that Blaug (2007) goes so far as to claim that we cede some of our cognition to organizations: in effect, allowing them to do much of our thinking for us. The link between organizations and technologies suggests that this is also true of technologies. Through such dependence we limit our ability to envision and enact alternatives. Consequently, the ideological 'kernels' of decisions are often implicit (Kerr, 2004: 117) and 'for many people, the ideas that guide their lives may not be held with conscious awareness or full articulation' (Mitcham, 1994: 277).

The world contains too many data for our limited cognitive resources. To understand sensory data, we select from what is available, usually subconsciously: 'subjects are aware of that to which they are attending, but not of the selection process directing their attention' (Evans 1989, 16). For example, until you think about it, it is unlikely you are conscious of the feeling of your backside against a chair. The sensory data are gathered constantly but filtered out. Without consciously registering them, they slip beneath awareness, fading into the background over which we engage in other work.

Filtering is biased, however. We take short cuts when reducing cognitive loads. Blaug (2007) lists four 'cognitive biases': 'simplification', whereby we expect things to conform to patterns and stereotypes (cf. Mitcham, 1994: 1); 'confirmation', whereby we seek evidence that validates prior beliefs (Evans, 1989: 42); 'affirmation', whereby we overestimate what we know and are overconfident in our reasoning, filtering out evidence which challenges our self-assessment (Augoustinos and Walker, 1996: 93); and 'reification', whereby we believe that social constructions have empirical reality, and what is a challengeable belief comes to seem a universal law.

Without filtering we would be overwhelmed by information in even the most stable environment, but the processes are difficult to bring forward into full awareness. Our general ignorance of them is one reason cognition becomes 'automated' and can be manipulated to serve the interests of power (Blaug, 2007). Cognitive schemas – frameworks of assumptions, values, beliefs, procedures, motivations, etc., that are used to produce and disperse knowledge – become embedded into organizational infrastructures. These are then 'pushed' at the organization's members. Enculturation processes, communications networks, technological innovations and other everyday activities continually promote certain objectives, procedures and values in members. This enhances organizational efficiency, for just as we function in the world by reducing sensory input, so organizations can work without stagnation when members are not continually questioning the premises of every activity (Morgan, 1999: 95). Shared *cognitive cultures* give individuals habits and routines (Blaug, 2007), streamlining activity by limiting possibilities; they are reified and thus perceived as real (Sandelands and Stablein, 1987: 13–14).

Yet this sharing of cognitive cultures is, again, a political process. The study of knowledge processing in organizations has exploited the idea of 'distributed cognition' (Salomon, 1993) – the idea that learning is distributed among groups, a concept which has itself benefited from the increased use of communications technologies. But the distribution of cognition is lumpy, not smooth. There is a *separation* of cognitive cultures in hierarchies. Individuals are confined to particular organizational locations. Managers become insulated from subordinates, not just administratively, but cognitively. Different wings of an organization have different cognitive (sub)cultures (Turner, 1971). For example, educators may find it difficult to adopt the viewpoint of administrators, or that of faculty from different disciplines. The multiplicity of organizations makes it likely that cognitive cultures may be conflicting or contradictory.

Nor are all cognitive cultures given equal status. Cultures based around different assumptions from dominant cultures – which can define modes of enquiry into given situations – become characterized as primitive or unsophisticated. This historically informed studies of 'underdeveloped' peoples (see Kerr, 2004: 133); it remains in accusations of 'Luddism' towards those suspicious of e-learning or other (imposed) innovations. Suspicion may arise not through technophobia but through cultural separation from the innovators. Subordinate cultures have sophisticated philosophical and cognitive structures of their own which are adapted to their particular environment; an environment partly defined by, and including, dominant cultures.

Cognitive cultures are among the background or framing factors that influence an organization's ongoing formal and informal negotiations. They influence volition, knowledge management and everyday activity. As a result, cognitive cultures become embedded into an organization's technological infrastructure. They help explain why each organization has a unique technological configuration from which, via historical and sociological research, one can read a history of certain organizational events and subcultures (Star, 1999). And technology, in turn, helps generate culture (Kerr, 2005: 1007). The everyday activities of educational organizations have always 'unfolded within, and because of, a complex collective of technologies' (Luke, 2002: 256). For example, in the design of a lecture theatre, assumptions about pedagogy have been embedded into architecture. These assumptions – often unrevealed and unquestioned – constitute a historically formed background which can constrain action: 'Those who create and first use new technologies take for granted the values and frameworks of previous eras and previous technologies and assume that new generations will have those same values and frameworks' (Barber, 1998). But 'for the second generation of users, this can be corrupting in ways invisible to the pioneers and inventors' (ibid.).

Both researchers and practitioners of e-learning must recognize that assumptions about an innovation's suitability, intended purpose, criteria of success or failure, and even the nature of the original problem, have not been freely formed. Instead, they are the product of the organizational and technological structures within which such thinking occurs. Innovations (whether new curricula, procedures or technologies) are disturbances to a system. Different stakeholders react to these disturbances in different ways, so any 'innovation process is either consistent with or divergent from the main characteristics of the system. In the former case the process is one of dissemination, and in the latter of a political battle' (Berg and Östergren, 1979: 262).

CRITICAL E-LEARNING RESEARCH

Even relatively mainstream organization theory now notes that successful organizations are adaptable: that in the face of environmental change, they *learn* (see Senge *et al.*, 1999). And constructivist theories of learning propose that truly creative and self-sustaining learning requires not the transmission of 'one best' approach to the subject, but a more individualized approach in which learners apply new knowledge to real-world problems in a spirit of self-exploration. The socio-psychological concept of 'cognitive cultures' finds educational expression in *communities of practice* which help members learn their way round problems in the technological/organizational environment (Lave and Wenger, 1991). In principle, e-learning is a field where organizational learning and communities of practice would seem to have particular salience, thanks to issues such as: the rapidity of change; the increased emphasis on electronic communication; and the diverse and empirical nature of educational problems (Carr and Kemmis, 1986).

As we have seen, not all communities of practice (cognitive cultures) are equal. The distribution of cognition throughout an organization is lumpy, not smooth. Yet we must once again remind ourselves that multiplicity does not automatically lead to conflict. In fact, it is from a multiplicity of perspectives that organizational creativity and adaptability emerge. Should a single solution to a problem (such as, say, a theory of education, or a monolithic course management system) be hegemonically imposed, this could lead to difficulties in questioning the underlying assumptions of that decision (McCurry, 2003: 421) if the solution ceased to be relevant in a changing environment. Effective management, therefore, does not involve the repression of multiple perspectives but their orchestration (cf. Senge *et al.*, 1999). Management is involved in 'distributing' shared interpretations of a situation, or 'mediating' between contesting interpretations (Jarzabkowski, 2003). Any organization must foster a certain amount of creativity to survive (Morgan, 1999: 51–2). Innovatory organizations need to engage in a process of 'double-loop learning' (Argyris, 1999) – the interrogation not just of particular decisions but of the premises underlying them.

Yet this is a paradox for managers. Questioning the premises – the cognitive cultures, infrastructures and procedures – on which a decision is based may prove disruptive to an existing organizational form, simply because it may reveal occurrences of automated cognition. Learning can be *emancipatory* for the members of an organization; this is one reason why it is frequently repressed, overtly or implicitly. It is not easy to reveal cognitive cultures and the ways in which they constrain one's options within an organizational setting, yet they '*can* be hauled up into consciousness, properly evaluated and changed' (Blaug, 2007). Yet organizations and technologies both press down on cognition, producing feedback processes which make it easier for organizations to build on existing strengths than seek radically new products (Williams and Edge, 1996: 877). This is why large, mature organizations find innovation difficult (Mintzberg, 1989: Chapters 8–10).

Despite the consequent pressures brought to bear to retard it, 'the kind of learning required to participate and learn fully at work … [requires] individuals … to be richly engaged and shape the practice as well as being shaped themselves' (Billett, 2002: 94; Lave and Wenger, 1991). Notice the use of 'as well as', rather than 'instead of'; the external drivers of technological change cannot be simply ignored. But the work of Fay and Blaug suggests that researchers into, and managers of, technological change must be aware of the need to overcome the cognitive separation which can arise between themselves and practitioners. Only that way can practitioners *actively* (rather than symbolically or passively) shape the process of innovation.

One way of dealing with the partiality of cognitive cultures is holistic research. Berg and Östergren (1979) base their studies of higher education innovation on the 'field theories' of Lewin (1951) in which researchers are exhorted to characterize the situation as a whole, establishing not only the field's composition but what motivates each force within the field. These insights suggest, that, at the very least, critical study into e-learning must include and assess the perspectives of developers, planners and managers as well as users. A range of cognitive cultures competes to shape e-learning, and without investigating these other forces, researchers cannot draw a complete picture of the field (Benson, 2002; Whitworth and Benson, 2006). As well, e-learning research can look at the ways in which group interactions are managed, not simply the surface differences between them. For instance, Kordaki (2003) shows how computer engineers hold assumptions about teaching and learning which are not necessarily shared by the teachers on whose behalf they are working (cf. Whitworth and Benson, 2006). Yet, through establishing a constructivist learning environment in which these perspectives can be revealed and shared, both groups can learn from each other and, ultimately, improve the quality of software.

The crucial insight here is that *all* parts of the organization can engage in self-reflective learning around (and with the help of) e-learning technologies. This should not – must not – be a task undertaken only by academic faculty. In fact, to make the assumption that all resistance to e-learning innovation comes from faculty (e.g. Bennett and Bennett, 2003: 54; Glover and Miller, 2001) is a dangerous generalization. E-learning can at times be characterized as a 'social movement' (Kerr, 2004: 129) in which individual innovators ('lone rangers' – Bates, 2000) sidestep institutional restrictions and engage in autonomous design and development. As often, conflict over e-learning arises through an institution failing to offer support to innovators, or corrupting the innovation to the extent that interested faculty no longer identify with it (see Bates, 2000: 105). Claiming that all problems arise through bad design or lack of training is clearly misplaced.

In addition, casting all e-learning as commodifying, industrial and/or corrupting of educational goals is unfair to those using it to enhance the quality of teaching and/or to deliver syllabuses that challenge cultural paradigms: 'these technologies clearly can support cultural pursuits beyond the world of work and apart from the conduits of commerce, particularly if people *consciously organize them* to serve these ends' (Luke, 2002: 278, emphasis added).

Carr and Kemmis (1986) propose that all educational problems are innately practical, involving 'on the ground', situated action (cf. Suchman, 1987); their solutions therefore require continuous, conscious organization to educational ends. These situations cannot be reduced to abstractions or models. They suggest, therefore, that policy scientific approaches are inappropriate in education. Instead, what is required are (self-)critical enquiry and double-loop learning. Fay describes how *critical* research aims not to

> provide knowledge of quasi-causal laws to a policy scientist who will determine what causal conditions are to be manipulated in order to effect a particular goal, but rather *to enlighten the social actors so that, coming to see themselves and their social situation in a new way, they themselves can decide to alter the conditions* …
>
> (Fay, 1975: 103, original emphasis)

For this to happen, the organization of e-learning research must itself become a subject of enquiry. Through investigating its own underlying premises, the e-learning research community can engage in double-loop learning and achieve the self-awareness that is a prerequisite of conscious action and organization.

Carr and Kemmis suggest that *action research* (AR) – self-motivated research into one's own practice – removes the separation between the cultures of researcher and practitioner, or researcher and subject. AR participants define for themselves the problems that require investigation. Situations are not studied from outside, through models, proxies or objective methods such as surveys (cf. Kerr, 2004: §5.8). These tools may provide valuable information, but only as a part of a wider process of self-reflection. AR is participatory; human-oriented; action-oriented; practical; and emergent (Reason and Bradbury, 2001: 2).

There is a considerable body of e-learning research that involves researchers enquiring into their own practice, particularly in higher education. Several such articles have already been cited (for example, Bennett and Bennett, 2003; Gigliotti-Guridi, 2003, Harwood, 2005; McPherson and Nunes, 2004b). While this work is valuable, researchers must remember the partiality, even parochialism, of singular perspectives; without attention to these limitations, such research can become insular, and thereby repeat the failure to note the reasons lying behind conflict (Gigliotti-Guridi, 2003, is one example of this). E-learning (action) research that involved *diverse* stakeholders would be less likely to be dominated by a single cognitive culture. Combining practice with AR and self-reflection on that practice by both designers and users could enhance all aspects of the work (Mitcham, 1994: 271–2). AR might be more likely to give participants a sense of ownership of innovations that emerge from it, lessening the risk of rejection through incompatibility with their needs (Zuber-Skerritt, 1992). It may increase the effectiveness of the innovations that emerge, reducing the risk of failure due to lack of attention to the constraints imposed by particular organizational environment into which it is introduced, but which the designers had not the cognitive schemata to perceive.

AR is innately educational. It 'explains the need for an ongoing, continuous, cyclical process of "coming to know"...' (Zuber-Skerritt, 1992: 89). To flourish, AR requires a sympathetic environment, but also contributes to that environment – its prevalence would be the sign of a democratic and self-reflective culture. Double-loop learning can help members of an organization learn their way past the limits imposed by parochial cognitive cultures, and AR therefore has an active role to play in the political development of higher education; e-learning is merely one node around which empowerment may coalesce. This applies to practitioners and users alike. Ideally, AR can and should be emancipatory, enabling participants in a system to fulfil the potential they have to not just report on, but creatively change the parameters of a system.

CONCLUSION

The previous paragraph may seem idealistic to some readers and, judged alone, it probably is. AR, with its goals of emancipation and change, is as much the result of singular metaphors as is 'rational' Business Process Engineering. What is important is that insight can be gained through consolidating the results of diverse approaches, avoiding a single, parochial focus on only one. It has been the aim of this chapter to discuss a range of approaches to studying e-learning as the product of organized activity. The various metaphors – organizations as machines, organisms, agglomerations of subcultures, instruments of domination and psychic prisons – are generalizations, but also act as framing factors for real, everyday negotiations within organizations. These formal and informal processes interact with the information storage systems of organizations, their communications networks, the diverse ways and places in which technology is implemented, and external drivers to produce a unique socio-technological configuration within each organization (Mintzberg, 1989). Ultimately, every organization is different, and the research process itself must account for this diversity.

Declaring that e-learning researchers should be interested not only in the technology but in the research processes that produce it is not meant to create a feedback loop akin to a dog chasing its own tail. The learning process is reflexive (cf. Beck, 1992) and cyclical (cf. McPherson and Nunes, 2004a) but does not preclude the emergence of new possibilities. Indeed, it facilitates them. Understanding cognitive cultures and their role in knowledge production, storage and reproduction within organizations can prevent multiplicity acting as a barrier to progress. Instead, the stock of understandings embedded within cognitive cultures can be productively drawn out, combined with the world views of other stakeholders, and embedded into technologies which benefit all interested parties rather than just an exclusive minority. Inherent assumptions which shape this important technology cannot be left concealed, but must be revealed, understood, communicated and (if necessary) challenged and reworked. Objective science and subjective values thereby validate each other in an atmosphere of continuous double-loop learning.

REFERENCES

Abrahamsson, B. (1993) *Why Organizations? How and Why People Organize*. London: Sage.

Argyris, C. (1999) *On Organizational Learning*. Oxford: Blackwell.

Arias, E. G., Eden, H., Fischer, G., Gorman, A. and Scharff, E. (2002) 'Transcending the individual human mind: creating shared understanding through collaborative design', in J. M. Carroll (ed.), *Human–Computer Interaction in the New Millennium*. New York: ACM Press. pp. 347–72.

Augoustinos, M. and Walker, I. (1996) *Social Cognition*. London: Sage.

Barber, B. R. (1998) 'Which Technology and Which Democracy?'. Talk given at *Democracy and Digital Media conference*, MIT, May 8–9. Retrieved online 4 December 2005 at: http://web.mit.edu/m-i-t/articles/barber.html).

Bates, A. W. (2000) *Managing Technological Change: Strategies for College and University Leaders*. San Francisco, CA: Jossey-Bass.

Beck, U. (1992) *Risk Society: Towards a New Modernity*. London: Sage.

Bennett, J. and Bennett, L. (2003) 'A review of factors that influence the diffusion of innovation when structuring a faculty training programme', *Internet and Higher Education* 6 (1): 53–63.

Benson, A. D. (2002) 'Using online learning to meet workforce demand: a case study of stakeholder influence', *Quarterly Review of Distance Education* 3 (4): 443–52.

Berg, B. and Östergren, B. (1979) 'Innovation processes in higher education', *Studies in Higher Education*, 4 (2): 261–8.

Billett, S. (2002) 'Workplaces, communities and pedagogy: an activity theory view', in M. R. Lea and K. Nicoll (eds), *Distributed Learning: Social and Cultural Approaches to Practice*. Abingdon: RoutledgeFalmer. pp. 83–97.

Blaug, R. (2007) 'Cognition in a hierarchy', forthcoming in *Political Psychology*.

Burns, T. and Stalker, G. M. (1961) *The Management of Innovation*. London: Tavistock.

Capel, R. (1992) 'Social histories of computer education: missed opportunities?', in J. Beynon and H. Mackay (eds), *Technological Literacy and the Curriculum*. Abingdon: Falmer. pp. 38–64.

Carr, W. and Kemmis, S. (1986) *Becoming Critical: Knowing through Action Research*, Geelong: Deakin University Press.

Castano, M. S. (2003) 'Researcher's Voice in Web-based Course Management Systems', paper, *American Educational Research Association*, Chicago, 22–24 April.

de Castell, S., Bryson, M. and Jenson, J. (2002) 'Object lessons: towards an educational theory of technology', *First Monday*, 7 (1). Retrieved online at: http://www.firstmonday.org/issues/issue7_1/castell/index.html.

Cervero, R. and Wilson, A. (1994) *Planning Responsibly for Adult Education: A Guide to Negotiating Power and Interests*. San Francisco, CA: Jossey-Bass.

Cervero, R. and Wilson, A. (1998) *Working the Planning Table: the Political Practice of Adult Education*. San Francisco, CA: Jossey-Bass.

Checkland, P. (1999) *Soft Systems Methodology: a Thirty-year Retrospective*. Chichester: Wiley.

Clark, R. C. and Mayer, R. E. (2003) *E-learning and the Science of Instruction*. San Francisco, CA: Wiley.

Conole, G. and Oliver, M. (2002) 'Embedding theory into learning technology practice with toolkits', *Journal of Interactive Media in Education* 8. Retrieved from http://www.jime.open.ac.uk/2002/8/conole-oliver-o2-8-t.html.

Cornford, J. and Pollock, N. (2002) 'The university campus as a "resourceful constraint": process and practice in the construction of the virtual university', in M. R. Lea and K. Nicoll (eds) *Distributed Learning: Social and Cultural Approaches to Practice*. Abingdon: RoutledgeFalmer. pp. 170–81.

Coupal, L. V. (2004) 'Constructivist learning theory and human capital theory: shifting political and educational frameworks for teachers' ICT professional development', *British Journal of Educational Technology*, 35 (5): 587–96.

Diercks-O'Brien, G. and Sharratt, R. (2002) 'Collaborative multimedia development teams in higher education', *Educational Technology and Society*, 5 (1): 81–5.

DiMaggio, D. and Powell, W. (1983) 'The iron cage revisited: institutional isomorphism and collective rationality in organizational fields', *American Sociological Review*, 48: pp. 147–60.

Engeström, Y., Miettinen, R. and Punamäki, R.-L. (eds) (1999) *Perspectives on Activity Theory*. Cambridge: Cambridge University Press.

Evans, J. St. B. T. (1989) *Bias in Human Reasoning: Causes and Consequences*. London: Erlbaum.

Fay, B. (1975) *Social Theory and Political Practice*. London: Allen and Unwin.

Foucault, M. (1980) *Power/Knowledge*. New York: Random House.

Garrison, D. R. and Anderson, T. (2003) *e-Learning in the Twenty-first century: a Handbook for Research and Practice*. Abingdon: RoutledgeFalmer.

Gigliotti-Guridi, C. L. (2003) 'Cheerleader, used car salesman and more: selling Blackboard to faculty', *College and University Media Review*, 9 (2): 11–21.

Glover, D. and Miller, D. (2001) 'Running with technology: the pedagogic impact of the large scale introduction of interactive whiteboards in one secondary school', *Journal of Information Technology for Teacher Education*, 10 (3): 257–76.

Harwood, I. (2005) 'When summative computer-aided assessments go wrong: disaster recovery after a major failure', *British Journal of Educational Technology* 36 (4): 587–98.

Hosie, P. and Schibeci, R. (2005) 'Checklist and context-bound evaluations of online learning in higher education', *British Journal of Educational Technology*, 36 (5): 881–95.

Jarzabkowski, P. (2003) 'Strategic practices: an activity theory perspective on continuity and change', *Journal of Management Studies*, 40 (1): 23–56.

Jervis, A. and Gkolia, C. (2005) '"The machine stops": one school's rejection of integrated learning systems', 10 (4): 305–21.

Kerr, S. T. (2004) 'Toward a sociology of educational technology', in D. Jonassen (ed.), *Handbook of Research on Educational Communications and Technology* (2nd edn). Mahwah, NJ: Erlbaum. pp. 113–42.

Kerr, S. T. (2005) 'Why we all want it to work: towards a culturally based model for technology and educational change', *British Journal of Educational Technology*, 36 (6): 1005–16.

Kordaki, M. (2003) 'Challenging prospective computer engineers to design educational software by engaging them in a constructivist learning environment', *Education and Information Technologies*, 9 (3): 239–53.

Kling, R. (1987) 'Computerization as an ongoing social and political process', in G. Bjerknes, P. Ehn and M. Kyng (eds), *Computers and Democracy*. Aldershot: Avebury. pp. 117–36.

Lakoff, G. and Johnson, M. (1980) *Metaphors we Live by*. Chicago, IL: University of Chicago Press.

Lakomski, G. (2001) 'Organizational change, leadership and learning: culture as cognitive process', *International Journal of Education Management*, 15 (2): 68–77.

Lave, J. and Wenger, E. (1991) *Situated Learning: Legitimate Peripheral Participation*. Cambridge: Cambridge University Press.

Lee, S. (2004) 'Designing and developing for the disciplines', *Journal of Interactive Media in Education*, 11. Retrieved December 4, 2005 online at: www-jime.open.ac.uk/2004/11.

Lewin, K. (1951) *Field Theory in Social Science*. Abingdon: Routledge and Kegan Paul.

Luke, T. (2002) 'Digital discourses, online classes, electronic documents: developing new university technocultures', in K. Robins and F. Webster (eds), *The Virtual University? Knowledge, Markets and Management*. Oxford: Oxford University Press. pp. 249–81.

Maitlis, S. and Lawrence, T. B. (2003) 'Orchestral manoeuvres in the dark: understanding failure in organizational strategizing', *Journal of Management Studies,* 40 (1): 109–40.

Mällinen, S. (2001) 'Teacher effectiveness and online learning', in J. Stephenson (ed.), *Teaching and Learning Online: Pedagogies for New Technologies*. London: Kogan Page. pp. 139–49.

Marion, R. (1999) *The Edge of Organization: Chaos and Complexity Theories of Formal Social Systems*. London: Sage.

McCurry, D. S. (2003) 'Democratic education with technology: towards a theory-foundation of democratic information and communications technology practice in teacher preparation', *Education, Communication and Information* 3 (3), 417–35.

McPherson, M. A. and Nunes, J. M. (2004a) *Developing Innovation in Online Learning: an Action Research Framework*. Abingdon: RoutledgeFalmer.

McPherson, M. A. and Nunes, J. M. (2004b) 'The failure of a virtual social space (VSS) designed to create a learning community: lessons learned', *British Journal of Educational Technology,* 35 (5): 305–21.

Meredith, S. and Newton, B. (2004) 'Models of eLearning: technology promise versus learner needs – case studies', *International Journal of Management Education*, 4 (1): 39–52.

Mintzberg, H. (1989) *Mintzberg on Management*. London: Collier Macmillan.

Mitcham, C. (1994) *Thinking through Technology: The Path between Engineering and Philosophy*. Chicago, IL: University of Chicago Press.

Morgan, G. (1999) *Images of Organization* (2nd edn). London: Sage.

Mumford, E. (1987) 'Sociotechnical systems design: evolving theory and practice', in G. Bjerknes, P. Ehn and M. Kyng (eds), *Computers and Democracy*. Aldershot: Avebury. pp. 59–76.

Noble, D. (2002) 'Rehearsal for the revolution', in K. Robins and F. Webster (eds), *The Virtual University?: Knowledge, Markets and Management*. Oxford: Oxford University Press. pp. 282–300.

Reason, P. and Bradbury, H. (2001) 'Introduction: inquiry and participation in search of a world worthy of human aspiration', in P. Reason and H. Bradbury (eds), *Handbook of Action Research*. London: Sage. pp. 1–14.

Russell, C. (2005) 'Disciplinary patterns in adoption of educational technologies', in *Exploring the Frontiers of e-Learning: Borders, Outposts and Migration. Proceedings of the XII International ALT-C Conference*, Manchester, 6–8 September.

Russell, D. R. (2002) 'Looking beyond the interface: activity theory and distributed learning', in M. R. Lea and K. Nicoll (eds), *Distributed Learning: Social and Cultural Approaches to Practice*. Abingdon: RoutledgeFalmer. pp. 64–82.

Salomon , G. (1993) *Distributed Cognition: Psychological and Educational Considerations*. Cambridge: Cambridge University Press.

Sandelands, L. E. and Stablein, R. E. (1987) 'The concept of organizational mind', in *Research in the Sociology of Organizations*. Greenwich, CT: JAI Press.

Sandlin, J. A. and Cervero, R. M. (2003) 'Contradictions and compromise: the curriculum-in-use as negotiated ideology in two welfare-to-work classes', *International Journal of Lifelong Education*, 22 (3): 249–65.

Schewe, K.-D., Thalheim, B., Binemann-Zdanowicz, A., Kaschek, R., Kuss, T. and Tschiedel, B. (2005). 'A conceptual view of Web-based e-learning systems', *Education and Information Technologies*, 10 (1-2): 83–110.

Senge, P. and associates (1999) *The Dance of Change: Challenges of Sustaining Momentum in Learning Organizations*. London: Nicholas Brearley.

Shyu, H.-Y., Hsieh, S.-H. and Chou, Y.-H. (2004) 'Integrating concept mapping into designing a course management system', *Journal of Educational Multimedia and Hypermedia*, 13 (4): 483–506.

Sorensen, K. and N. Levold (1992) 'Tacit networks, heterogeneous engineers and embodied technology', *Science, Technology, and Human Values*, 17 (1): 13–35.

Star, S. L. (1999) 'The ethnography of infrastructure', *American Behavioral Scientist*, 43 (3): 377–91.

Suchman, L. (1987) *Plans and Situated Action*. Cambridge: Cambridge University Press.

Taylor, F. W. (1911) *Principles of Scientific Management*. New York: Harper & Row.

Trist, E. L. (1976) 'A concept of organizational ecology', *Australian Journal of Management*, 2: pp. 161–75.

Trow, M. (2002) 'Some consequences of the new information and communication technologies for higher education', in K. Robins and F. Webster (eds), *The Virtual University?: Knowledge, Markets and Management*. Oxford: Oxford University Press. pp. 301–17.

Turner, B. (1971) *Exploring the Industrial Subculture*. London: Macmillan.

Tyack, D. B. (1974) *One Best System: A History of American Urban Education*. Cambridge MA: Harvard University Press.

Umble, K. E., Cervero, R. M. and Langone, C. A. (2001) 'Negotiating about power, frames and continuing education: a case study in public health', *Adult Education Quarterly*, 51 (2): 128–45.

Varvel, V., Montague, R.-A. and Estabrook, L. (2007): 'E-learning and policy', in R. Andrews and C. Haythornthwaite (eds), T*he Sage Handbook of E-learning Research*. London: Sage, pp.269–85

Whitworth, A. (2005) 'The politics of virtual learning environments: environmental change, conflict and e-learning', *British Journal of Educational Technology*, 36 (4): 685–92.

Whitworth, A. (2006) 'Dynamic but prosaic: a methodology for studying e-learning environments', *International Journal of Research and Method in Education*, 29 (2): 151–63.

Whitworth, A. and Benson, A. D. (2006): 'Mapping eLearning: visualising the negotiated social shaping of educational technology'. Paper, *ALT-C 2006: The Next Generation: Research Proceedings*, Edinburgh, 5–8 September.

Williams, R. and Edge, D. (1996) 'The social shaping of technology', *Research Policy*, 25 (6): 865–99.

Wrong, D. (1995) *Power: its Forms, Bases, and Uses*. New Brunswick, NJ: Transaction Publishers.

Zaphiris, P., Zacharia, G. and Rajasekaran, M. S. (2004) 'Distributed constructionism through participatory design', in C. Ghaoui (ed.), *E-education Applications: Human Factors and Innovative Approaches*. London: Idea Group. pp. 164–79.

Zuber-Skerritt, O (1992) *Professional Development in Higher Education: a Theoretical Framework for Action Research*. London: Kogan Page.

10

A Theory of Learning for the Mobile Age

Mike Sharples, Josie Taylor and Giasemi Vavoula

A society which is mobile, which is full of channels for the distribution of a change occurring anywhere, must see to it that its members are educated to personal initiative and adaptability. Otherwise, they will be overwhelmed by the changes in which they are caught and whose significance or connections they do not perceive.

Dewey (1916: 88)

When John Dewey wrote *Democracy and Education* the industrialized world was undergoing a huge technological and social disruption. Railways and paved roads had enabled mass travel, wireless communication had bridged the Atlantic, and a mechanized war was being fought across continents. Today, we are experiencing similar social and technological disruption, with the Internet and mobile technologies providing global access to information and mobility of knowledge. Ten years ago a school in Russia teaching English had no access to contemporary language sources; now it has the World Wide Web. Five years ago, a farmer in rural Kenya had no communication with the nearest city, now he carries a mobile phone. We live in a society in which the channels for distribution of change are carried with us as part of daily life.

Every era of technology has, to some extent, formed education in its own image. That is not to argue for the technological determinism of education, but rather that there is a mutually productive convergence between the main technological influences on a culture and the contemporary educational theories and practices. Thus, in the era of mass print literacy, the textbook was the medium of instruction, and a prime goal of the education system was effective transmission of the canons of scholarship. During the computer era of the past fifty years, education has been reconceptualized around the construction of knowledge through information processing, modelling and interaction (Duffy and Cunningham, 1996). Now, as we enter a new world of global digital communication, it is no surprise that there is growing interest in the relations between mobile technology and learning. What we need, however, is an appropriate theory of education for the Mobile Age.

Many theories of learning have been advanced over the 2,500 years between Confucius and the present day, but almost all have been predicated on the assumption that learning occurs in a school classroom, mediated by a trained teacher. A few educational thinkers have developed theory-based accounts of learning outside the classroom, including Argyris (Argyris and Schön, 1996), Freire (Freire, 1996), Illich (Illich, 1971) and Knowles (Knowles & Associates, 1984), but none has put the mobility of learners and learning as the focus of enquiry.

Our aim is to propose a theory of learning for a mobile society. It encompasses both learning supported by mobile devices such as cellular (mobile) phones, portable computers and personal audio players, and also learning in an era characterized by mobility of people and knowledge (Rheingold, 2002) where the technology may be embedded in fixed objects such as 'walk up and use' information terminals. For brevity we shall refer to these together as mobile learning.

CRITERIA FOR A THEORY OF MOBILE LEARNING

A first step in postulating a theory of mobile learning is to distinguish what is special about mobile learning compared to other types of learning activity. The obvious, yet essential, difference is that it starts from the assumption that learners are continually on the move. We learn across space as we take ideas and learning resources gained in one location and apply or develop them in another. We learn across time, by revisiting knowledge that was gained earlier in a different context, and more broadly, through ideas and strategies gained in early years providing a framework for a lifetime of learning. We move from topic to topic, managing a range of personal learning projects, rather than following a single curriculum. We also move in and out of engagement with technology, for example as we enter and leave cell (mobile) phone coverage (Vavoula and Sharples, 2002).

To portray learning as a mobile activity is not to separate it from other forms of educational activity, since some aspects of informal and workplace learning are fundamentally mobile in the ways outlined above. Even learners within a school will move from room to room and shift from topic to topic. Rather, it illuminates existing practices of learning from a new angle. By placing mobility of learning as the object of analysis we may understand better how knowledge and skills can be transferred across contexts such as home and school, how learning can be managed across life transitions, and how new technologies can be designed to support a society in which people on the move increasingly try to cram learning into the gaps of daily life.

Second, a theory of mobile learning must therefore embrace the considerable learning that occurs outside offices, classrooms and lecture halls. A study by Vavoula (2005) of everyday adult learning for the MOBIlearn project, based on personal learning diaries, found that almost half (49 per cent) of the reported learning episodes took place away from home or the learner's own office, i.e. the learner's usual environment. The learning occurred in the workplace outside the office (21 per cent), outdoors (5 per cent), in a friend's house (2 per cent), or at places of leisure (6 per cent). Other locations reported (14 per cent) included places of worship, the doctor's surgery, cafés, hobby stores, and cars. There was no consistent relation between the topic of learning and the location of learning. An example of a connection between location and learning was a person learning the names of different kinds of foreign beer in a pub while conversing with friends. An example of no connection was a person discussing with a colleague over coffee at a bar and discovering references related to their work.

A central concern must be to understand how people artfully engage with their surroundings to create impromptu sites of learning. For example (from Vavoula's diary studies), a person wants to learn how to pre-programme a video recorder and so creates a context for learning out of a recorder, a television and a friend with some knowledge of video technology who offers explanations and clarifications.

Third, to be of value, a theory of learning must be based on contemporary accounts of practices that enable successful learning. The US National Research Council produced a synthesis of research into educational effectiveness across ages and subject areas (National Research Council, 1999). It concluded that effective learning is:

- *Learner-centred*. It builds on the skills and knowledge of students, enabling them to reason from their own experience.
- *Knowledge-centred*. The curriculum is built from sound foundation of validated knowledge, taught efficiently and with inventive use of concepts and methods.
- *Assessment-centred*. Assessment is matched to the ability of the learners, offering diagnosis and formative guidance that builds on success.
- *Community-centred*. Successful learners form a mutually promotive community, sharing knowledge and supporting less able students.

These findings broadly match a social-constructivist approach, which views learning as an active process of building knowledge and skills through practice within a supportive group or community (for an overview, see Kim, 2000). Learning involves not only a process of continual personal development and enrichment, but also the possibility of rapid and radical conceptual change (see Davis, 2001).

Lastly, a theory of mobile learning must take account of the ubiquitous use of personal and shared technology. In the UK, over 75 per cent of the general population and 90 per cent of young adults own mobile phones (Crabtree *et al.*, 2003). These figures mask the huge disparities in access to technology around the world, but they indicate a trend towards ownership of at least one, and for some people two or three, items of mobile technology, including mobile phones, cameras, music players and portable computers. A trend relevant to a theory of learning in the mobile world is that some developing countries, particularly in sub-Saharan Africa, are by-passing fixed network telephony to install mobile phone networks in rural areas. These offer the opportunity for people in rural communities not only to make phone calls, but to gain the advantages of mobile services such as text and multimedia messaging. For example, a project in Kenya is employing text messaging to co-ordinate in-service training of teachers (Traxler, 2005).

We are now seeing a well publicized convergence of mobile technologies, as companies design and market mobile computer-communicators, combining into a single device the functions of phone, camera, media player and multimedia wireless computer. Another equally important convergence is occurring between the new personal and mobile technologies and the new conceptions of learning as a personally managed lifelong activity.

Table 10.1 Convergence of learning and technology

New learning	New technology
Personalized	Personal
Learner-centred	User-centred
Situated	Mobile
Collaborative	Networked
Ubiquitous	Ubiquitous
Lifelong	Durable

Just as learning is being re-conceived as a personalized and learner-centred activity (Leadbetter, 2005), so too are new digital technologies offering personalized services such as music play lists and digital calendars. Just as learning can be seen as a situated and collaborative activity (Brown *et al.*,1989), occurring wherever people, individually or collectively, have problems to solve or knowledge to share, so mobile networked technology can enable people to gain and share information wherever they have a need, rather than in a fixed location such as a classroom.

Computer technology, like learning, is ubiquitous – computers are embedded in everyday devices such as photocopiers and televisions. Computing is also becoming more durable, in that although the hardware may last only for two or three years, personal software packages and storage formats (such as PDF) evolve through successive versions, with a large measure of backward compatibility. Personal technology now offers people the opportunity to preserve and organize digital records of their learning over a lifetime (Banks, 2004).

To summarize, we suggest that a theory of mobile learning must be tested against the following criteria:

- Is it significantly different from current theories of classroom, workplace or lifelong learning?
- Does it account for the mobility of learners?
- Does it cover both formal and informal learning?
- Does it theorize learning as a constructive and social process?
- Does it analyse learning as a personal and situated activity mediated by technology?

From these general criteria we propose a tentative definition of mobile learning as 'the processes of coming to know through conversations across multiple contexts among people and personal interactive technologies'. We shall now attempt to unpack the definition, indicating how conversation and context are essential constructs for understanding mobile learning, and offering implications for the ownership of learning and the integration of mobile learning with conventional education.

The focus of our investigation is not the learner, nor their technology, but the communicative interaction between these to advance knowing. At a first level of analysis we shall make no distinction between people and technology, but explore the dynamic system that comprises people and technology in continual flux. We shall show how this leads to learning as a conversational process of becoming informed about each other's 'informings', to cognition as diffused among interactions and reciprocally constructed conversations, and context not as a fixed shell surrounding the learner, but as a construct that is shaped by continuously negotiated dialogue between people and technology. We shall indicate how this allows us to understand the ecologies of learning in a world of networked mobility. It also leads to intrinsic contradictions, relating to the ontological status of technology in learning and ownership of the means of communication. We suggest that we can begin to resolve these contradictions only by understanding the relationship between traditional and mobile learning, and by creating a society in which learning as a global conversation can be given a central role in our system of education.

LEARNING AS CONVERSATION

Central to our definition is the claim that conversation is the driving process of learning. It is the means by which we negotiate differences, understand each other's experiences and form transiently stable interpretations of the world. Dewey claimed that not only is social life identical with communication, but all communication (and hence all genuine social life) is educative:

> To be a recipient of a communication is to have an enlarged and changed experience. One shares in what another has thought and felt and in so far, meagerly or amply, has his own attitude modified. Nor is the one who communicates left unaffected. ... Except in dealing

with commonplaces and catch phrases one has to assimilate, imaginatively, something of another's experience in order to tell him intelligently of one's own experience. ... It may fairly be said, therefore, that any social arrangement that remains vitally social, or vitally shared, is educative to those who participate in it.

(Dewey, 1916: 5–6)

The problem with Dewey's claim is that it is unclear what he meant by the term 'communication'. On the one hand, a communication is a token that is sent and received ('to be the recipient of a communication'). On the other hand, communication is the sharing of experience ('one shares in what another has thought'). Freire (1996) refers to 'co-intentional learning', where teacher and learner jointly develop understanding through dialogue:

The teacher is no longer merely the one-who-knows, but one who is himself taught in dialogue with the students, who in turn while being taught also teach. They become jointly responsible for a process in which all grow.

(Freire, 1996: 61)

The description we give here of learning as conversation is primarily based on the work of Gordon Pask (Pask, 1976). It derives from cybernetics, the study of communication and control in natural and artificial systems, and its more recent extension to second-order cybernetics, the study of the mechanisms by which a system can understand itself. This 'radical constructivism' (von Glaserfeld, 1984) extends the notion of learning as a constructive process beyond individuals to describe how distributed systems including teams, organizations and societies learn and develop. As an aside, there is a direct link between Freire and Pask, through the attempts by Stafford Beer (a colleague of Pask) and Fernando Flores (best known for his work with Terry Winograd on applying models of conversation to the design of a computer e-mail system: Winograd and Flores, 1987) to create a national cybernetic communications network for Chile during the Allende government in the early 1970s.

Pask broke with the model of communication as the efficient transmission of information that has been a foundation both for communications technology (Shannon and Weaver, 1949) and traditional education. With a prescience that foreshadows recent developments such as the Semantic Web (the development of the World Wide Web into a knowledge-based medium (Berners-Lee et al., 2001)) and smart mobs (groups of interconnected people forming a distributed intelligence: Rheingold, 2002), Pask proposed a new conception of communication. Rather than seeing communication as the exchange of messages through an inert and transparent medium, he reconceived it as the sharing of understanding within a pervasive computational medium (Pask, 1975). Thus media are active and responsive systems within which mind-endowed individuals converse.

The general approach makes no distinction between people and interactive systems such as computers, with the great advantage that the theory can be applied equally to human teachers and learners or to technology-based teaching or learning support systems. The concomitant problem is that on its own the theory does not give sufficient importance to the unique moral and social worth of human learners in their interaction with technology. We shall address this issue later.

Pask's definition of a 'mind' was broad, to encompass any organization expressed in a mutual language (able to accommodate commands, questions and instructions) that gives rise to thought, feeling and behaviour. This includes human minds, but also some computer programmes, and even theatre scripts and political manifestos. Minds, by expressing language and instantiating different systems of belief, provide the impetus for conversation. For example, a political ideology instantiates a system of language and beliefs which, when expressed in a party manifesto, gives rise to debate and discussion. On a smaller scale, two children with different views of a shared phenomenon such as a physics experiment, and capable of expressing their views in a mutual language, engage in conversation to try and come to a shared interpretation.

Thus conversation is not the exchange of knowledge, but the process of becoming informed about each other's 'informings' (what Pask described as the 'coordination of coordinations of coordinations') (Scott, 2001). Higher-level co-ordinations are 'tokens' for lower-level co-ordinations (objects and events) which are themselves tokens for stabilities of sensori-motor activity and 'structural coupling' with the environment. In order to constitute a 'conversation', the learner must be able to formulate a description of himself and his actions, explore and extend that description and carry forward the understanding to a future activity. In order to learn, a person or system must be able to converse with itself and others about what it knows.

Central to these learning conversations is the need to externalize understanding. To be able to engage in a productive conversation, all parties need access to a common external representation of the subject matter (an agreed terminology, and also notes, concept maps or other learning resources) that allows them to identify and discuss topics.

More recently, Pask's Conversation Theory has been applied by Laurillard (2002) and by Sharples (2003a) to examine the processes of learning with technology. Learning requires more than transparent channels of communication and a means of transmitting knowledge; we also need a shared language (among learners, and between learners and computational systems), a means to capture and share phenomena, and a method of expressing and conversing about abstract representations of the phenomena. Learning is a continual conversation with the external world and its artefacts, with oneself, and also with other learners and teachers. The most successful learning comes when the learner is in control of the activity, able to test ideas by performing experiments, to ask questions, collaborate with other people, seek out new knowledge and plan new actions (Ravenscroft, 2000).

Though primarily concerned with the application of educational technology to university-level teaching, the analysis by Laurillard (2002) can be applied more broadly across learning settings and subject areas. Figure 10.1 shows an adapted version of her framework for learning as conversation. Conversations can take place at two levels. At the level of actions, a learner and partner may converse about the performance of some educational activity, such as carrying out a scientific experiment, through discussion establishing a shared understanding of the phenomenon ('What's happening here?' 'What do we do next?'), producing a cycle of setting goals and building and refining practical models to test those goals.

At the level of descriptions, the learner and partner discuss the implications of the actions, to make sense of the activity through a process of proposing and re-describing theories and offering and adjusting explanations ('Why did that happen?' 'What does this mean?'). They may also be informing each other of their viewpoints ('I think it's because...') in order to uncover differences in conception or experience and so move towards a shared understanding. These conversations can be mediated by external representations to assist the learners in negotiating agreements, such as lab notebooks or shared concept maps. In addition to these external conversations, each learner holds a continual internal dialogue, making sense of concrete activity by mental abstraction and by forming theories and testing them through actions in the world.

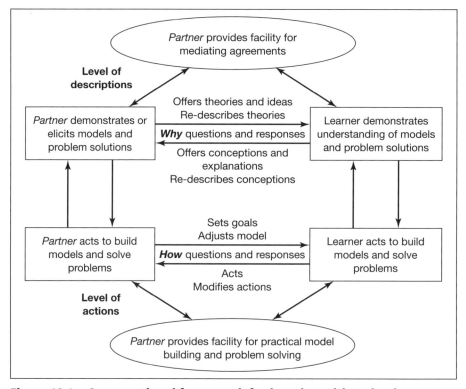

Figure 10.1   Conversational framework for learning with technology
Adapted from Laurillard (2002)

It should be emphasized that the conversational framework is not a normative lesson plan, but a means to describe the process of coming to know through conversation. Laurillard proposes that for learning to succeed, the student must:

- apprehend the structure of the discourse
- interpret the forms of representation
- act on descriptions of the world
- adjust actions to fit the task goals
- adjust descriptions to fit the topic goal
- reflect on the cycle of goal, action, feedback.

Some educational activities, such as science lab classes, are explicitly designed to support this structure of conversation. Most conversations, though, cover only one part of the framework, either because the learner has no conversational partner available, or there are no tools for model building to hand, or learners lack the language and concepts to converse at the level of descriptions. That is where technology can assist. The conversational framework shows a conversation between learner and partner. The partner may be a teacher, or another learner, or it may be computer interactive technology.

Technology may take the place of the teacher, as in drill and feedback. The difficulty here is that the computer can hold a limited dialogue at the level of actions – 'Look here' 'What's this?' 'Do that' – but is not able to reflect on its own activities or its own knowledge. Although some 'intelligent tutoring systems' have been developed which attempt to model the student and to tailor feedback to the perceived student needs, the computer is not engaging in developing a shared understanding. And because it cannot hold a conversation at the level of descriptions, it has no way of exploring students' misconceptions or helping them to reach a shared understanding.

The technology may provide or enrich the environment in which conversations take place. It can provide tools for collecting data and for building and testing models. It can extend the range of activities and the reach of a discussion, into other worlds through games and simulations, and to other parts of this world by mobile phone or e-mail. The technology provides a shared conversational learning space, which can be used not only for single learners but also for learning groups and communities. Technology can also demonstrate ideas or offer advice at the level of descriptions, as with the World Wide Web or online help systems, or through specific tools to negotiate agreements, such as concept maps and visualization tools.

In all these conversations (among learners and teachers, between learners and interactive technology) there is a fundamental need to establish and sustain a language that can enable shared understanding. One means to do this is through 'teachback' (a term coined by Pask) where one person attempts to re-describe what they have learned, to check if it matches the understanding of the other participants in the conversation. This can form part of deliberate learning or can occur naturally, for example when we repeat back a set of instructions over the telephone. It does not mean that every concept must be negotiated and agreed. Such rigour rarely occurs in practice, and pinning down the meaning of terms can often be counterproductive. Not only can debate over the meaning of language stifle discussion, but social solidarity can often be fostered by ignoring precision (Boyd and Pask, 1987).

So far we have described conversations for learning as taking place in the abstract, but every human partner to a conversation (though not necessarily every computational partner) is situated in one physical location. A significant problem with conversations in a mobile world is that not only does the language of communication need to be continually negotiated, but also its context.

CONTEXT AND LEARNING

All activity is performed in context. Cole (1996) makes an important distinction between context as 'that which surrounds us' and context as 'that which weaves together'. This mirrors the distinction made in the technical literature on pervasive computing between context as a 'shell' that surrounds the human user of technology and context as arising out of the constructive interaction of people and technology.

The 'context as shell' model, exemplified by the Shannon and Weaver (1949) informational model of communication, situates the learner within an environment from which the senses continually receive data that are interpreted as meaningful information and employed to construct understanding. Thus a learner in a classroom may receive information from a teacher, a whiteboard and a textbook, all of which must be assimilated and integrated to form a composite understanding of the topic being studied.

Learning not only occurs in a context, it also creates context through continual interaction. The context can be temporarily solidified, by deploying or modifying objects to create a supportive work space, or forming an *ad hoc* social network out of people with shared interests, or arriving at a shared understanding of a problem. But context is never static. The common ground of learning is continually shifting as we move from one location to another, gain new resources, or enter new conversations (Lonsdale *et al.*, 2003)

Traditional classroom learning is founded on an illusion of stability of context, by setting up a fixed location with common resources, a single teacher and an agreed curriculum that allows a semblance of common ground to be maintained from day to day. If all these are removed, as may be the case with learning in the Mobile Age, then creating temporary islands of relatively stable context is a central concern. In this respect, the historic construction of context, the process by which we arrive at current understanding, assumes greater importance.

Current activity can be fully understood only by taking an historical perspective, to understand how it has been shaped and transformed by previous ideas and practices (Engeström, 1996). This is particularly true of mobile learning, where both the immediate history of activity and the wider historical process of coming to know merge to create new understanding. For example, a visitor to an art gallery stands in front of a painting. She has arrived at a current understanding of the painting from the path she has taken through the gallery – taking in the ambience, stopping at other paintings, reading the guidebook – and also from a lifetime of creating and interpreting works of art, starting with childhood drawings. In one sense, context can be seen as an ever-playing movie, with each frame of current context being a progression from earlier ones and the entire movie being a resource for learning. But it is a movie that is continually being constructed by the cast, from moment to moment, as they share artefacts and create mutual understanding through conversation.

THE DIALECTICAL RELATIONSHIP BETWEEN LEARNING AND TECHNOLOGY

We have characterized learning as a process of coming to know through conversation across continually reconstructed contexts. Now, we turn to the role of computer and communications technology in that process. Vavoula (2005) showed that 52 per cent of everyday learning episodes involved one or more pieces of electronic technology: mobile and fixed phones, laptop and desktop computers, televisions and video-recorders. To support mobile learning according to our definition, it is not necessary for the device itself to be portable. Our definition of mobile learning embraced both learning with portable technology, and also learning in an era characterized by mobility of people and knowledge. Vavoula's studies showed that people create settings for learning out of technology or resources that are ready to hand. For example, a person driving out of London in their car with a partner finds out about alternative ways of getting to London by train through on-street advertisement displays. Currently, these two aspects of mobile learning (learning with portable devices and learning while mobile) are somewhat separate but they are starting to converge as handheld and wearable devices interact with their surroundings and static objects respond to people on the move. Thus in the Caerus project (Naismith *et al.*, 2005) visitors to the University of Birmingham botanic gardens were given handheld location (GPS) devices that automatically offered audio commentary on the flowers and shrubs as they walked around the gardens. Conversely, museum visitors can wear 'active badges' that identify them to the fixed exhibits and displays, which provide information displays tailored to their interests (Bristow *et al.*, 2002). In the future, people may be able to create *ad hoc* spaces for individual or shared learning, deploying a combination of mobile and fixed technology, for example in homes, tourist locations or hotel lobbies (Sharples, 2003b).

A paradox arises from this analysis. In order to understand the complexity of learning we need to analyse a distributed system in which people and technology interact to create and share meaning. But putting people on a par with computers and phones fails to take account of the unique learning needs and moral worth of each individual person. We have attempted to address this paradox by describing the activity system of mobile learning, in a way that problematizes the dialectical relationship between people and technology. The analysis draws on cultural-historical activity theory as it applies to learning (Daniels, 2001) through an adapted version of Engeström's expansive activity model (Engeström, 1987).

As with Pask's Conversation Theory, the model (Figure 10.2) describes a system of activity among interacting actors, showing the structural properties of the system. In the model, the subject is the focus of analysis (applied to learning systems, the subject is typically a learner). The object refers to the material or problem at which the activity is directed. This is shaped and transformed into outcomes through physical and symbolic, external and internal mediating instruments, including both tools and signs. The community comprises multiple individuals and/or subgroups who share the same general object and who construct themselves as distinct from other communities. The division of labour refers to both the horizontal division of tasks between the members of the community and to the vertical division of power and status. Finally, the rules refer to the explicit and implicit regulations, norms and conventions that constrain actions and interactions within the activity system.

Following Engeström, we analyse learning as a cultural-historical activity system, mediated by tools that both constrain and support the learners in their goals of transforming their knowledge and skills. However, to explain the role of technology in

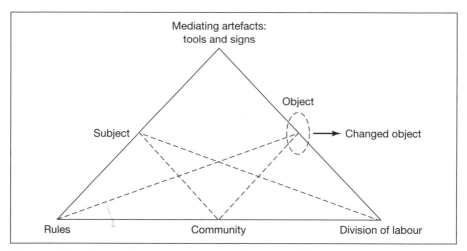

Figure 10.2   Engeström's expansive activity model.
Adapted from Engeström (1987: 78)

learning we separate two perspectives, or layers, of tool-mediated activity. The semi-otic layer describes learning as a semiotic system in which the learner's object-oriented actions (i.e. actions to promote an objective) are mediated by cul-tural tools and signs. The learner internalizes public language, instantiated in writing and conversation, as private thought which then provides the resource for control and development of activity (Vygotsky, 1978). The technological layer shows learn-ing as an engagement with technology, in which tools such as computers and mobile phones function as interactive agents in the process of coming to know, creating a human–technology system to communicate, to mediate agreements between learn-ers (as with spreadsheets, tables and concept maps) and to aid recall and reflection (as with Web logs and online discussion lists).

These layers can be prised apart, to provide either a semiotic framework to promote discussion with educational theorists to analyse the activity and dis-course of mobile learning, or a technological framework for software developers and engineers to propose requirements for the design and evaluation of new mobile learning systems. Or the layers can be superimposed (as in Figure 10.3), to examine the holistic system of learning as interaction between people and technology. Here, the semiotic fuses into the technological to form a broader cat-egory of technology than physical artefacts. Following Dewey (Hickman, 1990), we could describe technology from the merged perspective as any tool that serves the purpose of enquiry, enabling people to address problems in context

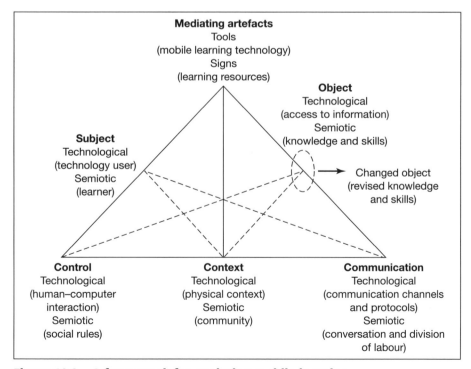

Figure 10.3   A framework for analysing mobile learning

and to clarify and transform them into new understanding. Thus hammers, computers, languages and ideas may all qualify as technologies for enquiry, and there is no clear distinction between the semiotic and the technological.

We need to make clear that, for our framework, we are proposing neither the separation of the semiotic and the technological, nor the fusing of the two. Rather, we want to set up a continual dynamic in which the technological and the semiotic can be moved together and apart, creating an engine that drives forward the analysis of mobile learning.

Learning occurs as a sociocultural system, within which many learners interact to create a collective activity framed by cultural constraints and historical practices. Engeström analyses the collective activity through an expanded framework that shows the interactions between tool-mediated activity and the cultural Rules, Community and Division of Labour. As we have adapted Engeström's framework to show the *dialectical relationship* between technology and semiotics, so we have taken the liberty to rename the cultural factors with terms – Control, Context and Communication – that could be adopted either by learning theorists or by technology designers. The terminology is important. Engeström's terms were drawn from a Marxist lexicon of cultural–historical materialism. We would suggest that these terms may hinder rather than assist dialogue between educational theorists and technology designers, so we have adopted related terms that are in the currency of both professions. Of course, this risks the possibility that the terms will be interpreted differently by both groups and simply lead to misunderstanding and mutual incomprehension, so we shall attempt to clarify their meaning.

Control

The control of learning may rest primarily with one person, usually the teacher, or it may be distributed among the learners. Control may also pass between learners and technology, for example in a dialogue for computer-based instruction. The technological benefit derives from the way in which learning is delivered: whether the learners can access materials when convenient, and whether they can control the pace and style of interaction. These are issues of human–computer interaction design.

However, technology use occurs within a social system of other people and technologies. Social rules and conventions govern what is acceptable (e.g. how to use e-mail, who is allowed to e-mail whom, what kinds of document format should be used). A person's attitudes to technology can be influenced by what others around them think about it, for example whether they are resentful at having to use the technology or are keen and eager to try it out. Individuals and groups can also express informal rules about the ways they like to work and learn.

Context

As we have proposed earlier, the context of learning is an important construct, but the term has many connotations for different theorists. From a technological perspective there has been debate about whether context can be isolated and modelled in a computational system, or whether it is an emergent and integral property of interaction. (See for example Lonsdale *et al.*, 2004, who describe an interactional model of context for mobile learning.) Context also embraces the multiple communities of actors (both people and interactive technology) who interact around shared objectives, mutual knowledge, orientations to study, styles and strategies of learning.

Communication

The dialectical relationship between the technological and semiotic layers is perhaps the easiest to see in relation to communication. If a technological system enables certain forms of communication (such as e-mail or texting), learners begin to adapt their communication and learning activities accordingly. For example people are increasingly 'going online' at home, creating networks of interaction through phone conversation, texting, e-mail and instant messaging that merge leisure and work activities into a seamless flow of conversation. As they become familiar with the technology they invent new ways of interacting – 'smilies', text message short forms, the language of instant messaging – that create new rules and exclusive communities (Grinter and Eldridge, 2001).

This appropriation of technology not only leads to new ways of learning and working, it also sets up a tension with existing technologies and practices. For example, children can subvert the carefully managed interactions of a school classroom by sending text messages hidden from the teacher. On a broader scale, technology companies see markets for new mobile technology to support interactions such as file sharing and instant messaging.

DIALECTICAL RELATIONS AND APPROPRIATION

We propose that there is a dialectical relationship between nodes in the two planes of the mobile learning framework. This enables us to represent something of the process of appropriation that occurs when people are using technology to support their learning. Waycott (2004) provides an account of the internal workings of this process. When faced with a new tool, people examine both the possibilities and the constraints it offers. This leads to a process in which the users adjust the 'fit' of their tools to their activities. Sometimes tools will cause their users to change their own behaviour to accommodate a feature or shortcoming in the tool; sometimes users will shape the tool to suit their specific requirements. Doing either of these things may initiate further changes as the users begin to exploit the technology, hence the dialectical nature of the process.

Thus there is a continual co-evolution of technology and human learning (Bruckman, 2004), with individuals, groups and societies simultaneously developing new modes of interacting with technology (such as text messaging) in parallel with adopting new patterns of learning (such as just-in-time learning and mobile collaborative learning). Each new development in either learning or technology creates pressures that drive the next innovation. This is characteristic of activity systems, which evolve over lengthy periods of time, and are not simply reducible to actions, as Engeström points out:

> Activity is a collective, systemic formation that has a complex mediational structure. An activity system produces actions and is realized by means of actions. However, activity is not reducible to actions. Actions are relatively short-lived and have a temporally clear-cut beginning and end. Activity systems evolve over lengthy periods of socio-historical time, often taking the form of institutions and organizations.[1]

Furthermore, activity systems are in perpetual flux, with movement between the nodes of a given system, and between one activity system and another. This dialectical shaping can emerge at various nodes in the activity framework and provides the process that binds its two levels together.

A CASE STUDY OF MOBILE LEARNING

To illustrate how our theory of mobile learning relates to real activity, we draw upon our experience in a large, multinational, European-funded research project, MOBIlearn (IST–2001–37440). The aim of the project was to define what functions and services a pedagogically sound mobile learning environment would need to be effective, and to implement and evaluate a system delivered on currently available mobile technologies (Da Bormida *et al.*, 2003; Taylor, 2004). The project used several scenarios to investigate learning in mobile environments, and we use one of these, the Museum Scenario, to illustrate the use of the mobile learning framework described above.

The purpose of the following discussion is not to report the evaluation of the trial. Selected elements of the data are used to illustrate the use of the framework, and the value of representing these to enable conversations between the various stakeholders: educators, pedagogy experts, system designers, technical implementers, museum curators and so on. To set the scene, we provide an overview of the trial.

Background to the Museum trial

The first MOBIlearn trial took place in the Uffizi Gallery in Florence in December 2004 (Brugnoli *et al.*, 2005) in two galleries:

- The Leonardo Gallery, containing eleven canvases including 'The adoration of the Kings' and 'Annunciation', by Leonardo da Vinci.
- The Botticelli Gallery, containing nineteen canvases including 'Allegory of spring' and 'The birth of Venus' by Sandro Botticelli.

It is important to bear in mind certain specific characteristics of the Uffizi and of the two galleries used for the trial:

- The Uffizi provides very little information for visitors (just the name of the painting, the date and artist's name).
- The Uffizi is a spacious environment that does not always appear to have a rational layout. Most galleries are larger than 100 m².
- The Uffizi displays a very large number of artworks in each gallery; this is especially true for the Botticelli Gallery.
- The gallery displays a huge number of works which, although well known to the general public, are complex and hard to interpret.

A variety of devices, all incorporating the MOBIlearn system, were available, which included mobile phones, Personal Digital Assistants (PDAs), Pocket PCs and Notebook computers.

Participants were free to walk around the two galleries, inspecting the paintings, using one of these devices to find out more about them, and to communicate with one another. Altogether, twenty-eight participants took part in the trials, in three groups. The groups were a group of 'foreign' (i.e. non-Italian) students, a group of Italian students and members of the Amici degli Uffizi (Friends of the Uffizi), who played the part of art experts.

During the Uffizi trial, both qualitative and quantitative methods of data collection were used (see Brugnoli *et al.*, 2005, for more detail). The following extracts from the initial evaluation report provide an interesting mix of semiotic and technical detail which we will analyse with reference to the mobile learning framework.

Age-related attitudes

Young participants. Participants in this group appeared to be the most satisfied, using the system extensively, and adopting a playful, interactive approach. The general feeling of these participants was that the trial provided an opportunity for dynamic learning. They frequently returned to works they had already seen, exploring first the rooms and then the system. They were interested in 'harnessing … making the most of' the content offered by the system. 'I really like it. I want to find out about everything!'

Adult participants. Older participants were more critical of the system, especially where they had relevant experience and/or considered themselves 'art experts'. Criticisms were not motivated by a lack of satisfaction with the MOBIlearn system but rather by the presumed 'sacredness' of a museum like the Uffizi, which participants saw as a 'special place'. These perceptions became weaker as the trial went on, and a positive appreciation of, and interest in, the system began to emerge. The 'art experts' were also highly critical of the information provided by the system, even when they were completely satisfied with the way it worked. The way that they used the information was, however, different from that of other participants. For example, all participants listened to audio files giving information about the art works. However, the art experts (unlike most other participants) did not use this information to learn about the works but as a starting point for discussion, a way of kicking off a debate on artistic issues.

Experience with systems functions and tasks

Chat. All participants enjoyed using chat for the first time and were satisfied by the service. There was little or no need to deploy chat as a communications tool due to the limitations of the trial environment, an empty museum with a group of no more than eight participants. Despite this, people had fun using the facility and appreciated chat as facilitating enjoyable exchanges. In many instances, participants were enthusiastic about the idea of being able to use chat if they were visiting the gallery in a large group. Participants thought that the ability to share information and to chat would be practical and thus popular. Many, especially younger participants, were keen on the idea of using the service to save, download and print conversations. They would thus have a 'textual photograph' to remind them of their visit to the museum.

Experience with devices

Participants received a variety of devices (either a mobile phone, a PDA, a pocket PC or a notebook) and so had different experiences during the trial. Moreover, the interface of each device was slightly different, meaning that accessibility and usability changed between devices. The pocket PC and notebook interfaces featured better usability than the mobile phone and PDA interfaces. Therefore, participants using these devices had inferior accessibility not only regarding their device, but also in terms of the MOBIlearn system as a whole. People allocated PDAs or notebooks typically sought technical support only to confirm that they were using their instrument or the system correctly. Those with a general familiarity with new technologies who were using the more accessible interfaces typically needed little training or support from technical staff. Below, we describe participant responses to the three different types of device and identify user needs

Mobile phones. Mobile phones were the least popular and least used devices. Most participants had to repeatedly ask for assistance from technical staff. Participants found it difficult to navigate the system and to understand its capabilities. This meant that the vast majority of participants tended to interact very little either with the MOBIlearn system or with the museum exhibits themselves.

PDAs. These devices were quite popular. PDAs were much more than a 'compromise between an audio guide and a mobile phone'. They were perceived as providing attractive multimedia information. The only criticism participants had was that navigating the system proved difficult. Many people asked technical staff for help with navigation. It is worth highlighting that people using the PDA responded enthusiastically to the MOBIlearn system. They thought that MOBIlearn services offered a 'little something extra'. The device, however, was generally considered not particularly useful.

Pocket PCs and Notebooks. These were the most popular devices. Participants given pocket PCs and Notebooks used them more than users with PDAs or phones used their devices. Participants explored the functions of these devices extensively. People using pocket PCs and Notebooks spent longer on their tour and had a more intensive experience than those using other devices. Young people, especially young women, were particularly enthusiastic. They saw the devices as an extension of their personal diary or calendar, a place to write, note down appointments, play games and exchange messages. This tendency to associate the best interfaces with an object as personal as a diary meant that Notebooks and Tablet PCs were well appreciated by participants. People liked using the system and were quick in learning how to use the functions provided. Participants using pocket PCs and notebooks were the most sociable, sharing their device with others and exchanging information and opinions. People with these devices worked well together thanks to the devices' ease of use, larger screen and accessible interface.

(from the initial evaluation report for the Museum trial, quoted with permission)

Dialectical relations: conflict and support in the Museum Scenario

The semiotic learn-space for the Museum Scenario is illustrated in Figure 10.4, where we use a combination of the museum scenario definition and the evaluation data to label the nodes.

The labels reflect the situation of the museum trial – the semiotic subject is a museum visitor, the social rules are those applied to gallery visiting (i.e. a 'sacred space' with no shouting, no running, only whispered conversations, etc.). The semiotic context reflects the community's mix of age and expertise. Communication would take place in the semiotic level as conversation between participants.

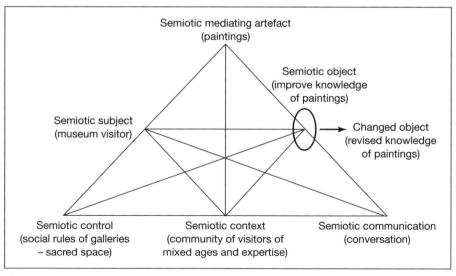

Figure 10.4   Semiotic view of the MOBIlearn museum scenario

The complementary technological space is illustrated in Figure 10.5. Here we see the corresponding equivalents in the technological domain that, in principle, are meant to augment the experience in the semiotic domain. Of course, in cases such as this trial, where new technology is introduced, the technology not only augments the experience but can also become the object of learning for part of it. So there is alternation in the object of learning being to better understand the paintings, to understand the new technology, and to understand how the new technology can help you better understand the paintings.

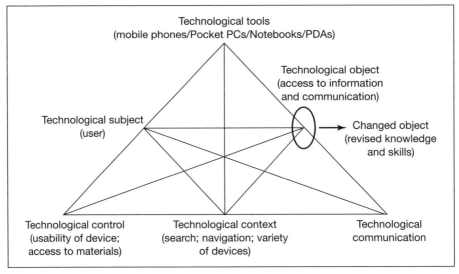

Figure 10.5   Technological view of the MOBIlearn museum scenario

So, as in any representation of activity, the level of detail can vary. We should ideally have a representation for each of the groups visiting, as the issues of control, context and communication are different. Similarly, we need representations of the levels for each of the technological tools. Space prevents us from pursuing this level of detail.

Pocket PCs and Notebooks

The dialectical relationship between control, context and communication, as well as between the semiotic and technological spaces, is evident in the case where Pocket PCs and Notebooks were used. When visitors had devices with good multimedia facilities and high levels of usability, they enjoyed their experience in the museum much more. The young women in the group formed an association between them and other personal 'devices' (e.g. diaries and calendars) for whom presumably such artefacts have high value, and the levels of communication and sharing increased.

It was particularly interesting that many younger participants were keen on the idea of using the Chat service even though it wasn't strictly necessary in the trial situation. Chat creates a conversational space within the 'sacred space' of the museum, to communicate with multiple participants without anyone else being aware.

The 'textual photograph' concept is an example of the dialectic between device and activity. It represents emergent behaviour that could not have been part of a museum experience prior to the introduction of the mobile devices.

In all these cases, the technological aspects of the scenario were supporting and augmenting the semiotic activities, contributing a much richer experience for visitors. This is represented in Table 10.2. The dialectical shaping behaviour emerging in the semiotic level in the control, context and communications nodes as a result of supporting technological underpinning becomes evident. The dialectic is occurring between all three, and from each of those to the corresponding node in the technological space.

Table 10.2 Support in the Museum trial

Support	Technological space	Semiotic space
Tool	Pocket PC/Notebook computer	Paintings
Subject	Experienced technology user	Museum visitor
Control	Usability good	Social rules: sacred space can be respectfully de-sanctified (little noise)
Context	Interesting, well presented content	Young people, especially young women
Communication	Good communication facilities; chat	Exchange of information and opinion; textual photographs
Object	Access to information	Learning about paintings: achieved

Mobile phones and PDAs

In the case of the other technologies (mobile telephones and PDAs) we find that the relative lack of usability in the technological domain inhibits all these developments in the semiotic space (Table 10.3). PDAs tended to be 'under-used due to accessibility and usability problems'. People who were allocated phones and PDAs sought much more technical support, and, in the case of the mobile phones, tended to interact very little with the MOBIlearn system, the museum exhibits or other visitors. In this case, the technological domain is not supporting development of activity in the semiotic domain. Despite the communications infrastructure being excellent, it was simply not used because the participants never arrived at a point where it would have been useful to use it. The technological subject (the user) was in conflict with the semiotic subject (the museum visitor), resulting in an unrewarding experience.

Table 10.3 Contradictions in the Museum scenario

	Technological space	Semiotic space
Tool	Mobile phone/PDA	Paintings
Subject	Experienced technology user	Museum visitor
Control	Usability poor	Social rules: sacred space remains intact and is violated by technology
Context	Difficult interface, poor search	No engagement or sharing
Communication	Good communications facilities; chat	Communication not used
Object	No access to information	Knowledge and skills development: inhibited

One other aspect of the data from the trial was of particular interest. It was clear that participants valued the role of communicating with friends and colleagues in the museum. Younger people who knew less about the paintings were interested in the content provided by the MOBIlearn system, and were keen to preserve their comments and chat about them. The older, better informed 'art experts' were more critical of the content provided at one level, but it was noted by the evaluators that they used it differently. It provided the beginning of a conversation, or argument, about the pictures, which in itself is an indicator of a more mature learner (Lea and Street, 1998).

EDUCATION IN THE MOBILE AGE

Our aim has not been to celebrate experiential learning, nor to promote learning through informal knowledge sharing as intrinsically more valuable than institutional education. Instead, we have attempted to explore the system of learning enabled by mobility of people and technology, through an analytic framework that does not assume that learning arises from individual experience, or that education occurs only in a traditional classroom mediated by a teacher. Our illustration of mobile learning was located in one of the world's great educational institutions, the Uffizi Gallery, and we describe the benefits both of receiving and of discussing information provided by expert art historians. Equally, we could have explored learning on a school field trip, or by medical trainees in a hospital.

Activity theory can be employed to identify tensions and contradictions in activity systems that typically inhibit the subject from achieving the object of the activity. The classic example of a contradiction provided by Engeström, taken from Leont'ev (1981), is within the vocation of a doctor, who is impelled to heal the sick and make everyone well, but who also has to make a living, so must hope that people do not stop being ill. One consequence of our analysis of learning as a technology-mediated process of coming to know through conversations across contexts is that it reveals new contradictions with institutional education. These tensions do not arise from some wish by the authors to challenge formal education; they already exist in society.

A world in which children own powerful multimedia communicators and where they practise new skills of online file sharing and informal text communication does not fit easily with traditional classroom schooling. It challenges the classroom as an environment in which both the structure and content of discourse are regulated externally by the curriculum and the examination system, and where communications are mediated by the teacher. The carefully bounded discourse of formal education contrasts with the rich interactions that children engage in outside school, through mobile calls, texting and computer messaging, and by conversing in online communities. These two worlds are now starting to conflict as children bring mobile phones into the classroom or share homework online:

> [T]he highly significant coupling of young people and mobile technologies has not been well received in educational quarters. Alongside well-publicised health scares has been a steady stream of confusion, conflicting advice and moral panic within the media, government departments and the educational community. Debates over the rights of schools to regulate and control students' use of mobile phones during school hours still rage amidst high-profile court cases and ambiguous government guidance … Concerns over rising levels of youth crime relating to mobile technologies also proliferate, as well as more spurious issues such as cheating in examinations and truancy. Put simply, schools and the wider educational community have been caught up in dealing with the minutiae of student ownership of mobile phones without fully considering the wider implications of such mobile technologies.

> (Selwyn, 2003: 132)

The analysis of learning as a conversational system might imply that a teacher has no ontologically privileged position, but is simply another participant in a continual conversation. We recognize that our theory of mobile learning does not give sufficient importance to what it is that makes a learning activity valuable, to the role of teachers in promoting effective learning, to classrooms as well organized locations for study, and to educational institutions in extending and validating learners' knowledge. Traditional education needs to be explored in relation to the new world of global knowledge and mobile technology. It is not sufficient to assert that authoritative knowledge is always located in the specialist professions and disciplines. Nor can we say that knowledge emerging from the new conversational communities such as Wikipedia (www.wikipedia.org) is more trustworthy because it is the product of many inter-regulating minds, or invalid because it has been created through a self-organizing community rather than by a body of experts.

Instead of seeing mobile communication and online communities as a threat to formal education, we need to explore how learning can be transformed for the Mobile Age, through a dialogue between two worlds of education: one in which knowledge is given authority through the curriculum, the other in which it emerges through negotiation and a process of coming to mutual agreement. Thus Richards (2004) argues that 'the challenge of ICT integration may be a crucial focus for educational reform in terms of productive new modes of learning which reconcile the active learner's construction of knowledge with a reinvigorated sense of teacher agency' (p. 347). Describing learning as a process that extends beyond individuals to distributed systems that learn and develop raises issues about the ontological role of technology as a participant in learning. In distributed learning systems as they have been described here, learning and cognition are diffused. The creation of meaning lies in the act of exchange: the unique interaction that takes place between the elements of the system (humans or technology) within a distributed context. The learning system as a whole evolves in a continuum of advancing knowing through conversations and interactions. Knowledge is embodied in both the elements of the system and their interactions. At the end of a learning episode, what the elements take away is knowledge in the form of the experience of the learning system that was. This cyclic process underlies the continually changing activity systems we represent.

Finally, the view of learning as the process of coming to know through continuous conversations across multiple contexts among people and interactive technologies raises the issue of where the ownership of learning lies. We argue that learning systems need to take shared ownership of learning. The agency is not with a single individual, nor with the technology; it lies in the democratic synergy between the different parts of the system with the aim to advance knowing. Learning needs to be conceptualized in terms of interactions between individuals, humans or non-humans, which take place in order to achieve evolving states of knowing as they are shaped by mutually (and continuously) negotiated goals. Such a concept, of shared ownership of the development of knowledge, raises tensions with copyright and intellectual property, as is being shown in the growing Open Source (www.opensource.org) and Open Knowledge Initiatives (www.okiproject.org).

The implications of this reconception of learning, as conversations across contexts, are profound. It removes the solid ground of education as the transmission or construction of knowledge within the constraints set by a curriculum, and replaces it with a cybernetic process of learning through continual negotiation and exploration. This can be seen as a challenge to formal schooling, to the autonomy of the classroom and to the curriculum as the means to teach the knowledge and skills needed for adulthood. But it could also be an opportunity for technology to bridge the gulf between formal and experiential learning. Thus, Dewey contends:

> As societies become more complex in structure and resources, the need for formal or intentional teaching and learning increases. As formal teaching and training grow in extent, there is the danger of creating an undesirable split between the experience gained in more direct associations and what is acquired in school. This danger was never greater than at the present time, on account of the rapid growth in the last few centuries of knowledge and technical modes of skill.

> (Dewey, 1916: 9–10)

New mobile and context-aware technology can enable young people to learn by exploring their world, in continual communication with and through technology. Instant messaging, for example, enables people to create learning communities that are both contextual, in that the messages relate to locations and immediate needs, yet unbounded, since the messages can be exchanged anywhere in the world. Mobile technology can also enable conversations between learners in real and virtual worlds, such as between visitors to a museum or heritage centre, and visitors to its virtual counterpart. A person standing in front of an exhibit has the benefit of being there, of experiencing the full physical context, whereas the visitor to an online museum can call on the rich informational resources of the World Wide Web. If we can design technology to enable rich conversations between these two learners-in-context, then they gain an educational experience that, in Dewey's phrase, is 'vitally shared'. Education in the Mobile Age does not replace formal education, any more than the World Wide Web replaces the textbook; rather it offers a way to extend the support of learning outside the classroom to the conversations and interactions of everyday life.

NOTE

1   The description given is adapted from www/edu.helsinki.fi/activity/pages/chatanddwr/activitysystem/

REFERENCES

Argyris, C., and Schön, D. (1996) *Organizational Learning II, Theory, Method and Practice.* Reading, MA: Addison-Wesley.

Banks, B. (2004) 'E-portfolios: their Uses and Benefits'. Retrieved 25 June 2005, from: http://ferl.becta.org.uk/content_files/ferl/resources/organisations/fd%20learning/e-portfoliopaper.pdf.

Berners-Lee, T., Hendler, J., and Lassila, O. (2001) 'The semantic web', *Scientific American,* 284 (5), 34–43.

Boyd, G., and Pask, G. (1987) 'Why do instructional designers need conversation theory?', in D. Laurillard (ed.), *Interactive Media: Working Methods and Practical Applications.* Chichester: Ellis Horwood. pp. 91–6.

Bristow, H. W., Baber, C., Cross, J., Woolley, S. and Jones, M. (2002) *Minimal Interaction for Mobile Tourism Computers.* The workshop 'Mobile Tourism Support' at MobileHCI 2002. Retrieved from: http://www.eee.bham.ac.uk/pcg/docs/Mobiletourismv4.1.pdf.

Brown, J. S., Collins, A., and Duguid, P. (1989) 'Situated cognition and the culture of learning' *Educational Researcher* (January–February 1989): 32–42.

Bruckman, A. (2004) 'Co-evolution of technological design and pedagogy in an online learning community', in S. A. Barab, R. Kling and J. H. Gray (eds), *Designing for Virtual Communities in the Service of Learning.* Cambridge: Cambridge University Press.

Brugnoli, C., Bo, G., and Murelli, E., (2005) 'Augmented Itineraries: Mobile Services Differentiating what Museums have to Offer', contribution to the MOBIlearn Deliverable D11.2, 'Evaluation of the MOBIlearn Final System', ed. J. Taylor, and P. McAndrew.

Cole, M. (1996) *Cultural Psychology: A Once and Future Discipline.* Cambridge, MA: Harvard University Press.

Crabtree, J., Nathan, M., and Roberts, S. (2003) 'MobileUK: mobile phones and everyday life', London: Work Foundation.

Da Bormida, G., Bo, G., Lefrere, P. and Taylor, J. (2003) 'An Open Abstract Framework for Modelling Interoperability of Mobile Learning Services', *V*[th] *International Conference on Enterprise Information Systems (ICEIS 2003)* as part of the international workshop on 'Web Services: Modelling, Architecture and Infrastructure'.

Daniels, H. (2001) *Vygotsky and Pedagogy*. Abingdon: Routledge.

Davis, J. (2001) 'Conceptual change', in M. Orey (ed.), *Emerging Perspectives on Learning, Teaching, and Technology*. E-book, retrieved from: http://www.coe.uga.edu/epltt/conceptualchange.htm.

Dewey, J. (1916) *Democracy and Education*. New York: Free Press.

Duffy, T. M., and Cunningham, D. J. (1996) 'Constructivism: implications for the design and delivery of instruction', in D. H. Jonassen (ed.), *Handbook of Research for Educational Communications and Technology*. New York: Simon & Schuster Macmillan. pp. 170–199.

Engeström, Y. (1987) *Learning by Expanding: An Activity-theoretical Approach to Developmental Research*. Helsinki: Orienta-Konsultit.

Engeström, Y. (1996) *Perspectives on Activity Theory*. Cambridge: Cambridge University Press.

Freire, P. (1996) *Pedagogy of the Oppressed*, (20th anniversary edn revised). New York: Continuum.

Grinter, R. E. and Eldridge, M. (2001) 'y do tngrs luv 2 txt msg?', in W. Prinz, M. Jarke, Y. Rogers, K. Schmidt and V. Wulf (eds), *Proceedings of the VII*[th] *European Conference on Computer-supported Cooperative Work ECSCW '01*. Bonn and Dordrecht: Kluwer. pp. 219–38.

Hickman, L. (1990) *John Dewey's Pragmatic Technology*. Bloomington, IN: Indiana University Press.

Illich, I. (1971) *Deschooling Society*. London: Calder and Boyars.

Kim, A. J. (2000) *Community Building on the Web*. Berkeley, CA: Peachpit Press.

Knowles, M. S., & Associates. (1984) *Andragogy in Action: Applying Modern Principles of Adult Education*. San Francisco, CA: Jossey Bass.

Laurillard (2002) *Rethinking University Teaching: A Framework for the Effective Use of Learning Technologies*, (2nd edn). Abingdon: RoutledgeFalmer.

Lea, M. and Street, B. (1998) 'Student writing in higher education: an academic literacies approach', *Studies in Higher Education*, 23 (2): 157–72.

Leadbetter, C. (2005) Learning about Personalisation: how can we put the learner at the heart of the education system? Retrieved 25 June 2005, from: http://www.standards.dfes.gov.uk/innovation-unit/pdf/Learningaboutpersonalisation.pdf?version=1.

Leont'ev, A. N. (1981) 'The problem of activity in psychology', in J. V. Wertsch (ed.), *The Concept of Activity in Soviet Psychology*. Armonk, NY: Sharpe. pp. 37–71

Lonsdale, P., Baber, C. and Sharples, M. (2004) 'A context awareness architecture for facilitating mobile learning', in J. Attewell and C. Savill-Smith (eds), *Learning with Mobile Devices: Research and Development*. London: Learning and Skills Development Agency, pp. 79–85.

Lonsdale, P., Baber, C., Sharples, M., Costicoglou, S., Pouliakis, A. and Mason, J. (2003) *MOBIlearn Context Awareness Subsystem Specification: Literature Review, Proposed Architecture, and Pre-prototype Demonstrator*, MOBILearn Project Report D6.1. University of Birmingham: MOBIlearn IST Project.

Naismith, L., Sharples, M. and Ting, J. (2005) 'Evaluation of CAERUS: a context aware mobile guide', in H. van der Merwe and T. Brown (eds), *Mobile Technology: The Future of Learning in Your Hands. mLearn 2005 Book of Abstracts*, IVth World Conference on mLearning. Cape Town, 25–28 October 2005. Cape Town: mLearn, p. 50.

National Research Council. (1999) *How People Learn: Brain, Mind, Experience, and School*. Washington, DC: National Academy Press.

Pask, G. (1975) 'Minds and media in education and entertainment: some theoretical comments illustrated by the design and operation of a system for exteriorizing and manipulating individual theses', in R. Trappl and G. Pask (eds.), *Progress in Cybernetics and Systems Research* IV. Washington, DC and London: Hemisphere Publishing. pp. 38–50.

Pask, G. (1976) *Conversation Theory: Applications in Education and Epistemology*. Amsterdam and New York: Elsevier.

Ravenscroft, A. (2000) 'Designing argumentation for conceptual development', *Computers and Education*, 34, 241–55.

Rheingold, H. (2002) *Smart Mobs: the next Social Revolution*. Cambridge, MA: Perseus Publishing.

Richards, C. (2004) 'From old to new learning: global imperatives, exemplary Asian dilemmas and ICT as a key to cultural change in education', *Globalisation, Societies and Education*, 2 (3), 337–53.

Scott, B. (2001) 'Gordon Pask's conversation theory: a domain independent constructivist model of human knowing', *Foundations of Science*, 6 (4), 343–60.

Selwyn, N. (2003) 'Schooling the mobile generation: the future for schools in the mobile-networked society', *British Journal of Sociology of Education*, 24 (2): 131–44.

Shannon, C. E., and Weaver, W. (1949) *The Mathematical Theory of Communication*. Urbana, IL: University of Illinois Press.

Sharples, M. (2003a) 'Disruptive devices: mobile technology for conversational learning', *International Journal of Continuing Engineering Education and Lifelong Learning*, 12, (5–6): 504–20.

Sharples, M. (2003b) 'Imagine a future where buildings or public spaces are "learning enabled"'. *e-Learning Europa Info*, 20 January 2003. Retrieved from: http://82.194.71.130/index.php?page=docanddoc_id=593anddoclng=6andmenuzone=1

Taylor, J. (2004) 'A task-centred approach to evaluating a mobile learning environment for pedagogic soundness', in J. Attewell and C. Savill-Smith (eds), *Learning with Mobile Devices* (Learning and Skills Development Agency) pp. 167–71.

Traxler, J. (2005) 'Using mobile technologies to support learning in sub-Saharan Africa', in H. van der Merwe and T. Brown (eds.), *mLearn 2005: Book of Abstracts*. Cape Town: mLearn.

Vavoula, G., (2005) 'A Study of Mobile Learning Practices', internal report, Deliverable 4.4 for the MOBIlearn project (IST–2001–37440)

Vavoula, G. N., and Sharples, M. (2002) 'KLeOS: a personal, mobile, Knowledge and Learning Organisation System', in M. Milrad, U. Hoppe, and Kinshuk (eds), *Proceedings of the IEEE International Workshop on Mobile and Wireless Technologies in Education* (WMTE2002), 29–30 August, Vaxjo, Sweden, pp. 152–6.

von Glaserfeld, E. (1984) 'An introduction to radical constructivism', in P. Watzlawick (ed.), *The Invented Reality*. New York: Norton. pp.17–40.

Vygotsky, L. S. (1978) *Mind in Society: the Development of Higher Psychological Processes*. Cambridge, MA: Harvard University Press.

Waycott, J. (2004) 'The Appropriation of PDAs as Learning and Workplace Tools: an Activity Theory Perspective'. *Unpublished Ph.D. thesis*. Milton Keynes: Open University.

Winograd, T. and Flores, F. (1987) *Understanding Computers and Cognition: A New Foundation for Design*. Norwood, NJ: Ablex.

ACKNOWLEDGEMENTS

This chapter has benefited from discussion among members of the Philosophy of Technology Enhanced Learning Special Interest Group of the Kaleidoscope European Network of Excellence and from detailed written responses from the members of the group to a draft. We are grateful to Chip Bruce for indicating the connection with Dewey's theory of inquiry, and to the MOBIlearn Fifth Framework IST project (IST–2001–37440) for supporting extensive research into the theory and practice of mobile learning.

11

Computer Supported Collaborative Learning

Naomi Miyake

Computer Supported Collaborative Learning (CSCL) is an emerging field of research and practice in learning, aiming at both enhancing the quality of learning and promoting its scientific understanding.

We are living in a society with changes at a speed no one has ever experienced in history. This situation requires learning of high quality, which no existing theory of learning appears to be adequate to guide. The situation calls for a 'community of learners' (Brown and Campione, 1996) where learning does not end at the point of learning but is expected to sustain itself over time, across different situations. The goal of such learning is not the learning of facts, but of flexible, generative knowledge not bound by the concrete situations where it is learned. To fulfil such a goal, new research on learning takes collaboration seriously, and implements and evaluates technological support to materialize effective learning designs. Research in CSCL allows researchers, practitioners, and other stakeholders to design successful practices of fostering the growth of intellectual societies, and to build scientific theories of learning, so that successful practices and robust theory building can feed into each other.

Current CSCL research has seen some consensus in regarding learning as a social process, where each individual participant, or learner, is responsible for creating his or her own knowledge through social interaction with other human beings by interacting with physical objects in everyday situations. Each learner is an 'epistemic agent' (Scardamalia and Bereiter, 1994), working to achieve 'adaptive' or generalizable expertise (Hatano and Inagaki, 1986). One of the most popular types of such learning is collaborative learning. The theoretical foundation of CSCL has to explain why collaborative cognitive processes lead to the acquisition of generative, adaptable pieces of knowledge.

Computers are an inevitable component in CSCL because of the following two reasons. One is that the new type of learning research requires recording and analysing the processes of learning (Granott and Parziale, 2002) with greater detail for a much longer period than conventional, laboratory-based learning studies. The other reason comes from the design requirements for collaborative learning, which call for making thinking visible, sharable, reflectable, and modifiable by the participating learners. Currently, computers and computer-controlled recording and analysing tools are promising with regard to meeting these requirements.

To introduce the depth and breadth of the theories and practices of CSCL in more detail, I divide this chapter into three sections. First, I will describe briefly its historical perspectives. I will then elaborate on some theoretical perspectives on collaboration as the basic form of high-quality learning, with research evidence. In the third section I will also explain how technology, particularly computers and computer networks, can support effective collaborative activities often utilized in classrooms. I will conclude the chapter with some remaining challenges for future studies in CSCL.

HISTORICAL PERSPECTIVES ON CSCL

The beginning

The term 'computer-supported collaborative learning' was first used in the title of an international gathering in 1989, a NATO-sponsored workshop held in Maratea, Italy. (See Stahl *et al.*, 2006, as well as Sawyer, 2006 for more details.) The 1980s were an interesting decade in cognitive studies. Following the call for ecologically valid cognitive studies by Neisser and others (cf. Neisser, 1976) and some views on cultural cognition in real world practices (cf. Cole and Scribner, 1974; Lave and Wenger, 1991) in the 1970s, cognitive studies saw the emergence of the 'situative' perspective (Greeno, 2006). The importance of this perspective quickly spread among researchers, particularly among those who had serious concerns about the reality of cognition which humans experience in everyday life. The influence was immediately taken up and elaborated by researchers who engaged in works bridging cognitive science and learning (Brown *et al.*, 1989).

The 1980s were also an interesting period in studies of computer use in the real world. People began to regard computers as tools to unite people, across time and space; to open up a new type of collaboration for effective work. A research field emerged specifically to focus on how computers could support collaborative work, the first conference on which was held in Austin, Texas, in 1986. One of the research themes that emerged there was related to learning because, researchers came to realize, a new tool or environment always required the users to 'learn' not just its operations but the effective ways of collaboration itself. In the field of human–computer interaction studies in general, the mid-1980s can also be marked as the emerging point of the user-centred system design (Norman and Draper, 1986). In a merger of these trends, the April 1996 issue of *CACM* (*Communications of the American Computational Machinery*, Vol. 39, No. 4) featured 'Learner-centered design' (Norman and Spohrer, 1986). In a column article in this issue, Soloway and Pryor (1986) characterized this movement in three elements: the need (computer software had to be developed beyond ease of use to support for learning), the challenge (computer software was to scaffold learners and learning), and its real promise. They cite Edison's optimistic view in 1922 of television replacing textbooks in a few years, in which he said, 'I believe that the motion picture is destined to revolutionize our educational system and that in a few years it will supplant largely, if not entirely, the use of textbooks' (Edison, 1922).

> Similar quotations on the potential educational impact on TV and computer abound. However, it is safe to say that electronic technologies have 1) not revolutionized education, and in fact have 2) had little – if any – impact on education. However, this time it will be different: this time digital technologies will go beyond telling stories and presenting information to support individuals and groups in undertaking activities.
>
> (Soloway and Pryor, 1986: 18)

Their claim was indeed correct. In fact, the authors who contributed to this special issue have formed the core of CSCL activities since then, and identified the current forms, if not the direct continuation, of almost all the systems introduced here. In other words, we could mark the beginning of CSCL quite confidently at around the middle of the 1980s.

CSCL's development as an established research field

This beginning was followed by a biennial conference series. The first CSCL conference was held at Indiana University in the fall of 1995, followed by the University of Toronto conference in 1997. These were small conferences, with seventy-six and thirty-eight presentations respectively. The presentations were, however, of interdisciplinary mixtures of innovative use of technology, implemented and evaluated in classrooms with real students, who often showed improved learning as a research outcome. The third CSCL at Stanford University in 1999 contained eighty-two presentations, with a doctoral consortium of seven presentations, and gathered many more attendants than previous conferences. In alternating years the international conferences of the learning sciences were held; both of them had grown to gather new participants, including classroom teachers as well as practitioners from informal learning settings. After this the conference sites became more international, CSCL being held at the University of Maastricht in the Netherlands in 2001, the University of Colorado in 2002, the University of Bergen in Norway in 2003, and the National Central University in Taiwan in 2005.

Currently the field has a number of journals, including the *International Journal of Computer-Supported Collaborative Learning*, and the *Journal of the Learning Sciences*. Based on these movements, in 2002 the International Society of the Learning Sciences was incorporated. According to its Web statements, it is a professional society dedicated to the interdisciplinary empirical investigation of learning as it exists in real-world settings and how learning may be facilitated both with and without technology (http://www.isls.org/index.html). The entire community now covers many nations worldwide.

COLLABORATIVE LEARNING: HOW IT WORKS

CSCL emphasizes collaboration as its core method of learning. In this section I will elaborate on the theoretical basis for this perspective: the sociocultural perspective on how people become experts in everyday situations, and the cognitive analyses added to the sociocultural perspectives to reveal mechanisms of how collaboration works to improve both motivation for comprehension and the degrees of understanding. Understanding these theories and mechanisms secures the foundation of how e-learning in the form of CSCL practices should be designed and assessed.

Sociocultural studies on collaborative learning

When we want to renovate learning, one good strategy is to take a close look at already successful learning. Studies on expertise (Chipman and Meyrowitz, 1993), originating from the study of the memory of a grandmaster of chess (Chase and Simon, 1973; de Groot, 1965) and having gone into many different skills like abacus use, piano playing, and sports, offer many definable elements about expertise, particularly how sociocultural those expert processes are. Ericsson *et al.* (1993), for example, having scrutinized a rich set of data taken from interviews with expert players of musical instruments and sport, pointed out the importance of 'deliberate practice' which almost inevitably is supported by the coaches, clubs, families as well as peer groups, to make possible the long and hard process of the 'tuning' phase (Norman, 1982). Literature on 'situated learning' (Lave and Wenger, 1991; Nasir, 2000) has also analysed the cognitive behaviour of novices and experts in everyday situations such as tailoring and playing dominos, and clearly shows that such learning occurs through social interaction.

From these studies, some features of successful learning can be identified as follows:

- Learners are strongly motivated to learn by themselves.
- Such motivation is often supported socially by others, and sometimes culturally.
- There are other people around to mutually teach and/or discuss with.

- Often there is a community such as a mixture of members on different performance levels, not just 'some others' around.
- The establishment of self-esteem in the community directly connects to the results of learning.
- Learning to be a professional requires a long time, possibly around several thousand hours.
- In the long run, learners experience many successes and failures which the learners themselves integrate into some abstracted, conceptual understandings.
- Intentional, deliberate and systematic practices are often effective.
- The intermediate goals are continuously re-examined and new goals are set.
- The community itself re-examines the goal continually and resets it.

If these features are applied efficiently in an instructional design, it will be possible to 'practise' a type of 'learning' at a level different from that achieved in the past. Current CSCL research takes these features seriously to implement them by supporting collaborative activities in both formal (classroom) and informal settings. In such successful cases, factors that have improved learning can be identified through the analysis of the processes, which could serve as a guide to design a further generation of practices. This cyclical method of research has been termed 'design experiments' (Brown, 1992; Collins, 1992) and has established itself as one of the standard research methods of CSCL and the learning sciences. Barab (2006) calls this design-based research, and summarizes its characteristics as follows:

> Design-based research (DBR) is used to study learning in environments that are designed and systematically changed by the researcher. The goal of DBR is to use the close study of a single learning environment, usually as it passes through multiple iterations and as it occurs in naturalistic contexts, to develop new theories, artifacts, and practices that can be generalized to other schools and classrooms.

(p. 153)

To make this iteration happen, it is clear that research requires technological support, from development and the dissemination of the target curriculum to record keeping and data analyses, as well as intensive collaboration not just among the learners but among the research team members as well.

Collaborative enhancement of motivation for comprehension

Sociocultural approaches combined with more process-oriented, cognitively focused studies provide explanations on the mechanisms of collaboration. It has been widely acknowledged that a collaborative situation promotes motivation for learning. Hatano and Inagaki (1991) analysed students' protocols of a well established Japanese collaborative science class to provide some evidence to such intuitive claims.

They used as their research target a widely practised Japanese collaborative curriculum, Hypothesis–Experiment–Instruction (Itakura, 1967), originally devised by Itakura and used in science classes in elementary and junior high schools. The following procedure is usually adopted with this method:

- Students are presented with a question having three or four alternative answers. The question specifies how to confirm which alternative is right (see example below).
- Students are asked to choose one answer by themselves, individually.
- Students' responses, counted by a show of hands, are tabulated on the blackboard.
- Students are encouraged to explain and discuss their choices with one another (in the entire class). The teacher plays the moderating role.
- Students are again asked to choose an alternative. They may change their choices.
- Students are allowed to test their predictions by observing an experiment (usually conducted by the teacher in front of the class) or reading a passage.

An example question might be 'Suppose that you have a clay ball on one end of a spring. You hold the other end of the spring and put half of the clay ball into water. Will the spring (a) become shorter, (b) become longer, or (c) retain its length?'

These questions are developed by groups of teachers who repeatedly test them to obtain a good balance of choices, so that the selection naturally promotes vigorous discussion among the students. In this example, you could expect to observe that 30–40 per cent of the students would choose either (a) or (c), and some 20–30 per cent would choose (b) at the outset of the class discussion.

Students supporting (a) would try to make their points by saying things like 'I feel lighter in water', while supporters of (b) would claim 'A clay ball will sink.' The alternative (c) might be defended by some expressions implying that 'water has the power to make completely immersed things float, but not if they are only half immersed'. Using the observational data collected from one of such classes, Hatano and Inagaki explain why this kind of carefully designed 'collaboration' promotes the students' motivation for furthering their comprehension.

> The students' enduring comprehension activity was pushed forward by their social, or more specifically partisan, motivation, as well as by cognitive or epistemic motivation. In other words their collective attempt is not pure comprehension activity but aims at winning the academic competition as well as comprehension. As soon as they were divided (psychologically, not spatially or socially) into a few groups according to their choices of answer alternatives, the students seemed to be motivated to work for the group they belonged to, that is, to collect more supporters and eventually win the argument by persuading all the others. Most of the utterances were arguments against other parties that ranged from pointing out errors in reasoning to noting overlooked facts that they thought were crucial. Speakers often gave signs of solidarity to supporters who had chosen the same alternative, and the supporters returned signs of agreement. When their prediction proved to be correct, students were quite excited and again exchanged signs of companionship. When it turned out to be wrong, they were greatly disappointed but tried to console each other.

(p. 345).

The mechanism should be clear. At the outset of the class, the students commit themselves to one of the alternatives, and this is purely an individualistic epistemic action. But once they are put in discussion mode, students who have chosen the same alternative have to take a social perspective, on top of their epistemic argumentation, on how to defend and integrate the opinions of those who had chosen the same alternative, while distinguishing and refuting what the others say. This raises the series of sort-and-integrate activities, which are the core patterns of knowledge integration learning (Linn, 2006). One key characteristic of the Hypothesis–Experiment–Instruction is, needless to say, the learner-centred grouping of the students' epistemology. The teacher should take advantage of it by letting the students discuss among themselves, rather than by taking sides with any of the alternatives. This feature can easily be implemented and modified by today's technology.

Collaboration for constructive comprehensive interaction

Collaboration itself has been a topic of research for many years, in many different disciplines. People want to know whether 'two heads are better than one', and if so, how. Social psychological studies have a long history of studying the effects of pairs and small groups, on puzzles and real world tasks (cf. Hastie, 1986). Cognitive scientists have explored the detailed process of joint problem solving and joint comprehension, to come up with some theoretical framework to understand what understanding is and how it develops. Findings from such research should also form one of the bases of collaborative e-learning design.

One type of explanation of the effectiveness of collaboration is the 'theory of convergence' (Roschelle, 1992). According to this theory, in a collaborative learning situation with multiple participants, various expressions are provided by speeches, gestures, drawings, etc., from multiple viewpoints. When the reflective process is promoted against these, convergence among such multiple viewpoints will be sought, that is, activities will be required to summarize the various viewpoints. As a result, Roschelle and his colleagues maintain, an abstraction of the various solutions will occur. When conversations are carried on further, the level of abstraction and the standard of self-evaluation will rise accordingly and meta-cognition of a higher level will be called for. Roschelle demonstrated this effect through a set of protocol analyses using a conversation exchanged by pairs of students learning about force.

This is an appealing theory, widely cited as explaining the fundamental mechanism of why collaboration promotes deeper comprehension. Roschelle's findings suggest that for the successful design of a collaborative learning environment, it is essential to help the participants generate and externalize many 'initial' thoughts, or different viewpoints. This does not explain, however, why the convergence is required when there are multiple expressions from multiple viewpoints.

In order to answer this question, other research has focused on individual courses of understanding during the collaboration, while keeping the basic unit of analysis on the pair (Miyake, 1986; Shirouzu et al., 2002). Their research has focused on how participating individuals maintain the freedom to construct one's own knowledge through constructive interaction. Joint tasks include comprehending how a sewing machine works or what would be the area of three-quarters of two-thirds of a square sheet of paper, or two-thirds of three-quarters. On the sewing machine problem, even knowledgeable pairs could take three to four hours to understand the hidden mechanism of how the internal bobbin works, through which each participant eventually constructed his or her own understanding, clearly different from the partner's comprehension. The detailed protocol analyses of such interaction also demonstrated that when caught in the cul-de-sac, it was often the person who was monitoring the situation, not the person who was taking the initiative for the problem-solving at the moment, who came up with an idea to radically change the situation to 'save' them. These findings could be summarized to imply that, even during a highly collaborative comprehension activity, social sharing of the situation does not impede each participant from pursuing individualistic knowledge construction. Rather, the interactive process supported each to realize different perspectives to check and modify their understandings by making explicit the different perspectives, which are not within their individual repertoire (Miyake, 1986). On the square sheet area problems, paired participants, not individuals, could take alternating perspective shifts, from the local, task-oriented view to a more abstract perspective, and this alternation of the perspectives helped each participant to talk about their solutions in more abstract ways toward the latter part of the interaction (Shirouzu *et al.*, 2002).

This mechanism offers an explanation of why there could be different learning outcomes from paired learners. It is because the abstraction level for each participant depends on the degree of the integration of the shared task-undertaking and the monitoring, during and at the end of the interaction. This also explains why a more knowledgeable participant, or the person who preceded the other in his/her understanding, could still benefit from the interaction. The model implies that for the design of collaborative learning situations it is important to encourage perspective exchanges and to secure ample chances for each individual learner to reflect upon the shared resources. This model is not necessarily the one widely shared among ordinary learners. They do not always grasp the value of interaction according to this model, and may complain, when put in collaborative environments without much preparation, that the more capable participants may not learn much. The model provides explanations why this is not so. To make a collaborative curriculum successful, it is often key that this piece of knowledge is shared among the students, teachers, and the designers as well.

The notion of scaffolding

The notion of scaffolding has also been an important concept in successful CSCL. The construct was first introduced to the field by Bruner and his colleagues (Wood *et al.*, 1976) who experimentally compared how much 'help' or scaffolding that four-, five-, and six-year-olds need in order to achieve a complex block-building task. In essence, the same, pre-trained instructor needed more acting out for the four-year-olds, less behavioural but more verbal suggestions for the five-year-olds, while the six-year-olds needed only verbal suggestions. Scaffolding was achieved through functions like reducing the degrees of freedom available to a learner, accentuating relevant features of the task, and modelling solutions to the task. With this support, very young children attained higher levels of performance than they could have alone. Since then scaffolding has been regarded as an implementation of the more theoretical construct of the 'zone of proximal development' (Vygotsky, 1978). Collins and Brown and their colleagues (Brown *et al.*, 1989; Collins *et al.*, 1991; Collins, 2006) have incorporated the notions of scaffolding and fading into the balanced construct of 'the cognitive apprenticeship'.

Scaffolding implies that, given appropriate assistance, a learner can attain a goal or engage in a practice otherwise out of reach. It can be devised not only by more able adults or peers but also by well designed technological tools and activity structures. By adopting this perspective, classrooms can be considered to be highly complex systems.

With technological support more prevalent as potential scaffolding in regular classrooms, new research issues have emerged around the construct. Reiser (2004), for example, pointed out that there are two mechanisms for scaffolding: structuring, and problematizing. The structuring scaffolding basically serves to simplify tasks for learners, and has been, according to Reiser, the main focus of research so far. Yet Reiser argues that the second mechanism, problematizing, could be as important as the first. Problematizing scaffolding directs learners' attention to issues or tasks the teacher (and any one of the curriculum design team members) wants the learners to focus on, but which might otherwise be ignored. The students are expected to engage in very complex data processing, though highly interesting and attractive from a scientifically oriented perspective. One of the illustrative tasks was to find the reason why a particular type of finch in the Galapagos Islands survived the drought while some others died out. The students were encouraged to tackle extensive data that were collected by scientists. Besides the 'reality' of the data and their analyses, Reiser's research team scaffolded the problematization by guiding the search, helping the students keep records of what they had tried, and by letting them juxtapose their inferred hypotheses.

Some researchers have begun to try to sort out the various types and functions of scaffolding, so that researchers and practitioners can select, or even combine them to best effect. Tabak (2004), for example, examined different types of scaffolding used in complex settings, and identified three distinguishable patterns of scaffolding: differentiated, redundant, and synergistic. She argues that synergy among scaffolding provided from multiple sources like teachers, software, and other agents is critically important in promoting learning in complex learning situations. Sherin *et al.* (2004) devised a new framework for analysing the effects of scaffolding, by contrasting two learning situations, a base and a scaffolded learning environment. The distinction was to help guide the design of scaffolded learning environments and studies of those environments.

While new research topics develop on the issue of scaffolding, some very basic assumptions remain to be studied. As suggested in the theoretical work on collaboration, the practice of collaboration itself appears to require some 'scaffolding' in practice, because it is not always the natural way of doing things in classrooms, where competition is often the norm. Kolodner *et al.* (2003) noticed this quite early on, and have implemented and tested a series of preparatory activities to make the value of collaboration clear to the students. As one of these launcher activities, the teacher may ask the students to undertake a simple construction, like building in ten minutes a book support with index cards, rubber bands, and paper clips. After the time limit, the students 'gallery walk' around the tables to see the products. When they engage in the second round of this construction, it inevitably invites some copying, or 'borrowing' of others' ideas. Teachers can take advantage of such occasions to introduce the notion of 'crediting when borrowing' and 'explicating good ideas so that the others can borrow'. They report that the teachers, who may feel reluctant to spend their precious teaching time on this approach at first, reluctant to keep using it once they realize how much it helps to make the following collaborative classes more productive. This kind of care appears to be particularly important when collaborative activities are implemented in distant e-learning environments.

FORMS OF COLLABORATIVE ACTIVITIES AND HOW TECHNOLOGY SUPPORTS THEM

CSCL research has identified some standard classroom activities to solicit productive collaborations. In this section, I illustrate some such activities, and show how they can be supported by technology.

From ideas exchange to knowledge building

Writing can be a strong support for a wide variety of learning activities. Knowledge Forum (Scardamalia and Bereiter, 1994, 2006) is one of the oldest and the most successful knowledge-building environments relying on collaborative writing. Based on their basic research on what writing is, they distinguished 'knowledge reformation' writing from 'knowledge telling' writing and have created and expanded a networked knowledge-base system to enhance the former into a knowledge-building environment. Students write notes on to a knowledge base over a computer network, by investigating problems in different subject areas over a period of time. They are encouraged by the system to write not just what they find out, but also what they need to know, and comments on other students' notes. As the notes accumulate the system also encourages them to 'rise above' the current discussion so that they can start working on abstract levels of knowledge construction. Students are treated as 'epistemic agents' responsible for building their own knowledge and the intellectual community at the same time.

Articulation of thoughts

Many CSCL tools aim at 'making thinking visible' (Linn and His, 2000), as a way to support collaboration. Those tools make visible the thinking of not just the learners but also the experts so that the learners can compare what they do with what is expected to be done. Among these, Bell *et al.* (1995) developed and tested the SenseMaker, a component of the Knowledge Integration Environment, on which the students were requested to categorize, assign weight to (according to their importance) and visually display the pieces of evidential information that they found during a science investigation. The students were also required to use them while debating their positions, to make them available for open examination. The debate was supported by the display, because the listeners could 'point' to the pieces of evidence for further discussion if needed. By viewing how the students categorized the evidential pieces of information, they found, the teachers could also analyse their current understanding and how it develops.

The tools to support modelling also work by helping students articulate their thoughts. The Collaboratory Notebook (Edelson *et al.*, 1996), Biology Guided Inquiry Learning Environment (BGuILE; Sandoval and Reiser, 2004), WorldWatcher (Edelson *et al.*, 1997), and Model-it (Lehrer and Schauble, 2006) share the approach of introducing professional tools to students to increase their sense of participation. These and other modelling aids are often components of a bigger project, where tool use is embedded in a content-rich curriculum, with project-based pedagogy.

Reciprocal teaching

Palincsar and Brown (1984) devised an interactive support system for reading, for students who were markedly below their required reading levels. They focused on gaining metacognitive, self-guiding questions while reading. The teacher coaches students by asking questions, and then they change roles so that the students have to ask questions themselves to guide the others. This guidance is somewhat ritualistic, but through experiencing this, the students were found to gain the skill to guide themselves.

An intriguing and very promising extension of this approach is the notion of 'Teachable Agents' (Schwartz *et al.*, 1999). Students teach a computer agent by identifying important components and the causal relationships as links, like 'increase' and 'decrease' among them, on which the system creates a relational map. Based on this structured database, the agent can answer questions, and give explanations for her answers by tracing through the links. Teaching the agent reciprocally makes the student's understanding highly visible, making it a resource for further learning.

The jigsaw method

The jigsaw method was first developed by Aronson and his social psychology team for the purpose of 'teaching cooperativeness as a skill' (Aronson and Patnoe, 1997: 14). The method was developed then expanded into a more sophisticated system to turn culturally diverse situations into learning resources. (Some current reports can be found at http://www.jigsaw.org/.)

In an ordinary jigsaw class, students first study a piece of material in an 'expert group', and then form a separate study group, or a 'jigsaw' group, consisting of one member from each of several 'expert' groups. This situation makes each and every student responsible for his or her own learning, and also helps the entire class to understand there is benefit in respecting others. After the groups bring all the explained pieces together, the students are ready to undertake a project that requires them to use all the information. A typical example could be a comprehension test, to demonstrate that they understand the material as a whole. This method has been carefully tested for its effects on a diverse set of topics, including children's acceptance of their classmates as intellectual peers, their self-esteem, and their mastery of classroom materials. According to Aronson and his colleagues, the effects are consistently positive.

The jigsaw method can create a rich environment for intellectual collaboration, and has been used widely in CSCL also (e.g. Brown, 1997). It is highly flexible and modifiable to facilitate many different types of collaboration. Suppose complex and highly structured course work needs to be delivered in a class. Such a goal can be accommodated by a 'matrix' type of jigsaw, wherein college students move in and out of hierarchically structured 'expert' groups and 'jigsaw' groups. Suppose you could prepare the learning materials in an n by m matrix, of perspectives A and B. Assign a student, say S1, to a cell Ai by Bj in the matrix. By doing this, S1 automatically becomes responsible for a particular viewpoint Ai on dimension A, as well as of another viewpoint Bj on dimension B. The course work can then be structured to require him or her to work in one of the expert groups on perspective A at one time, while at other times he or she is required to be an expert on B. Note-sharing software, or a concept-mapping tool could aid the students to express their ideas and integrate them among themselves as well as with others. This kind of technological support works well with the course structure, both of which have been found to promote the students' knowledge integration (Miyake et al., 2001).

The jigsaw can take a much more dynamic form. Suppose a course is to involve collaborative understanding of twenty to thirty kinds of learning material, each representing classic research in three different domains of e-learning research. We expect the students to collaboratively read, explain, exchange, and discuss the materials to integrate them, to the level where each participating student would come out of the course with the ability to verbally explain what the entire field is, with many evidential pieces of knowledge they could cite by identifying relevant research. This could be implemented, at least theoretically, in a dynamically expansive jigsaw.

This dynamic jigsaw models common activities of real-world researchers. Professional researchers take different responsibilities to study a common theme and exchange their interpretations of existing work and new findings from their own community. They most often do this repeatedly, explaining their thoughts to different audiences so that they can examine them from different perspectives for different integration possibilities. This series of activities helps them achieve a coherent comprehension that could evolve dynamically over time. While researchers receive information from others, they are also required to expand their explanations to include the new, and relate these to their own earlier knowledge structure. They then integrate these explanations to form a new explanation, to improve overall understanding.

The dynamic jigsaw class replicates this more systematically. In the first phase, a student becomes expert on one aspect of the learning materials. S/he exchanges his/her understanding with one other student, to create an explanation of two elements of the material. Then the students are ready to exchange their two-part explanations with a neighbouring pair, who are also ready to give their two-part worth. At the end of this phase, each student is expected to know four elements, two of his/her own plus two more explained by another student. They can now exchange four to four, to cover eight research elements, enough to cover a sub-domain. Towards the end of the term, such domain experts share by exchanging explanations of the domains, or some eight elements of information. Some assessment analyses of their performance accumulated over the last six years reveal (1) a fair amount of retention of the learning materials four to six months after the end of the course, (2) an explicit knowledge integration surrounding each student's personal needs, and (3) some conscious learning of learning skills such as asking specific, content-driven questions (Miyake, 2005a, b; Miyake, *et al.,* 2005; Miyake and Shirouzu, 2006).

Metacognitive and reflective activities

Although most of the technological scaffolding supports some metacognitive activities, Collins (2006) gives a succinct summary of what technology can do to this end. According to him:

> [t]here are three forms that reflection can take, all of which are enhanced by technology: (1) reflection on your process, (2) comparison of your performance to that of others, and (3) comparison of your performance to a set of criteria for evaluating performances.

(p. 57)

Because technology makes it possible to record performances, people can look back at how they did a task (1). Tablet PCs and small PDAs for easy recording of the events *in situ* coupled with a networked, large repository for secure storage and stress-free retrieval would lay the ground for better applications, to be valuable in collaborative classrooms as well. Bransford and his colleagues once maintained that one of the most effective ways that people learn is by comparing one another's performance, including their own (Bransford *et al.*, 1989). Thus (2) has a promising future. Also, Collins claims, one of the most effective ways to improve performance is to evaluate how you fared with respect to a set of criteria that determine good performance. When learning physics, students who had explicit criteria to evaluate their performance learned better than those who did not have such an aid (White and Frederiksen, 1998). Collins concludes:

> The essential way people get better at doing things is by thinking about what they are going to do beforehand, by trying to do what they have planned, and by reflecting back on how well what they did came out. If they can articulate criteria for evaluating what they did, this will help them as they plan what to do on the next cycle. The wide availability of computers and other recording technologies makes performances easier to produce and to reflect on.

(p. 58)

Many CSCL systems intend to help students to self-control their own learning, not just during a single course to tackle one learning objective, but to cover a longer period of time, to learn lifelong skills. The Legacy (Schwartz *et al.*, 1999), and the Symphony planning workspace (Quintana *et al.*, 2006) are prominent examples, consisting of a possible scenario of the enquiry activities that the students could take.

SOME CHALLENGES FOR THE FUTURE

CSCL has an expanding research field, with energetic new directions spreading out as the technology advances. This advance needs to be balanced with theoretical and pedagogical evolution on human learning. To conclude, let me pick out just two such future challenges: one is the problem of assessment and communicating the research findings of long-term, gigantic-scale learning projects, with rich and complex data. The other is the seemingly soluble but difficult problems surrounding the CSCL endeavour, which are rooted in our everyday lives.

As CSCL matures as a research field, new challenges are emerging. One of the biggest challenges is to disseminate successful practice to wider recipients, so that the outcome of research in CSCL may achieve real impact in the world. This is often quite difficult, because large-scale projects are packed with a great deal of data, and several findings, each with meaningful implications. Against these odds, Clark and Linn (2003) of WISE/CLP (Web-based Inquiry Science Environment/Computer as Learning Partner, Linn and Hsi, 2000; Linn *et al.*, 2004) offer an interesting presentation. Based on their ten years of research, with one teacher having taught 3,000 students, they succeeded in boiling down their research outcomes into a single, powerful, practical message: streamlining the learning time deteriorates the learning outcome only if you care about deep comprehension.

What they did in terms of their analyses was very simple. They compared multiple-choice test scores and the descriptive answers over four different versions of their thermodynamics curriculum, each taking twelve weeks, ten, eight, and six weeks, covering the same materials categorically. The multiple-choice scores of these courses stayed the same, seemingly unaffected by shortening the learning time. When they scored the explanations given to the multiple-choice answers, however, the performance nicely paralleled the streamlined length of the courses. The power of this report comes, I believe, from their choice of the problem, or the research question they chose to answer. CSCL is a theoretical endeavour, but it is the researchers' responsibility to keep an eye on where we should focus our efforts to have maximum impact. We may at the stage of the CSCL research setting decide to reflect upon what we do, in order to sort out real-world-oriented questions we will collectively try to answer, rather than looking into diverse possibilities that the technology lets us foresee.

By reviewing what changes are possible in our societies with the revolution in technology, Harlverson and Collins (2006) claim that the main core of the conventional teaching–learning system is very robustly against change, because it is institutionalized socially. Thus, they also claim, the new technology or the new technology-supported practices will not dominate or take over the core practice of schooling, but provide learners with ample chances to enjoy alternative forms and goals of learning. Based on these claims, they express their fear that if the new technology remains only as a provider of such alternatives, there could be a divide between people who benefit from it and those who do not. This could increase the inequity in chances of receiving higher levels of education, possibly leading to the inequity of the quality of life learners would end up with in the real world, after graduation.

It might, of course, take a different shape in different contexts (that is, countries) where there could be other contributing factors educational researchers might need to consider. This possible divide could be tied to learning English as a second language, not just as a communicative tool for everyday work, but as a sophisticated, intellectual tool to advance one's own conscious construction of knowledge, usable worldwide. Might technology provide us with some solution in the near future, without deeper understanding of how we use language in learning? Trying to find the answer can open up a set of challenging research topics.

As Soloway and Pryor (1986) suggested, this time things may be different. To make the difference felt by a wider audience, particularly the students who are still struggling with older systems and a somewhat stale pedagogy, there is much work that needs to be done.

REFERENCES

Aronson, E., and Patnoe, S., (1997) *The Jigsaw Classroom: Building Cooperation in the Classroom*. New York: Longman.

Barab, S. (2006) 'Design-based research: a methodological toolkit for the learning scientist', in K. R. Sawyer (ed.), *The Cambridge Handbook of the Learning Sciences*. New York: Cambridge University Press, pp. 153–69.

Bell, P., Davis, E. A. and Linn, M. C. (1995) 'The knowledge integration environment: theory and design', in J. L. Schnase and E. L. Cunnius (eds), *Proceedings of the Computer Supported Collaborative Learning Conference '95*. Hillsdale, NJ: Erlbaum. pp. 14–21.

Bransford, I. D., Franks, J. J., Vye, N. J., and Sherwood, R. D. (1989) 'New approaches to instruction: because wisdom can't be told', in S. Vosniadou and A. Ortony (eds), *Similarity and Analogical Reasoning*. New York: Cambridge University Press. pp. 470–97.

Brown, A. (1992) 'Design experiments: theoretical and methodological challenges in creating complex interventions', *Journal of the Learning Sciences*, 2 (2): 141–78.

Brown, A. (1997) 'Transforming schools into communities of thinking and learning about serious matters', *American Psychologist*, 52 (4): 399–413.

Brown, A., and Campione, J. (1996) 'Psychological theory and the design of innovative learning environments: on procedures, principles, and systems', in L. Schauble and R. Glaser (eds), *Innovations in Learning: New Environments for Education*. Mahwah, NJ: Erlbaum, pp. 89–325.

Brown, I. S., Collins, A., and Duguid, P. (1989) 'Situated cognition and the culture of learning', *Educational Researcher*, 18 (l): 32–41.

Chase, W. G. and Simon, H. A. (1973) 'Perception in chess', *Cognitive Psychology*, 4: 55–81.

Chipman, S. and Meyrowitz, A. L. (1993) *Foundations of Knowledge Acquisition: Cognitive Models of Complex Learning*. Boston, MA: Kluwer.

Clark, D. B. and Linn, M. C. (2003) 'Scaffolding knowledge integration through curricular depth', *Journal of the Learning Sciences*, 12 (4): 451–94.

Cole, M. and Scribner, S. (1974) *Culture and Thought: A Psychological Interlocution*. New York: Wiley.

Collins, A. (1992) 'Toward a design science of education', in E. Scanlon and T. O'Shea (eds), *New Directions in Educational Technology*. Berlin: Springer-Verlag, pp. 15–22.

Collins, A. (2006) 'Cognitive apprenticeship', in K. R. Sawyer (ed.), *The Cambridge Handbook of the Learning Sciences*. New York: Cambridge University Press, pp. 47–60.

Collins, A. Brown, L. S. and Holum, A. (1991) 'Cognitive apprenticeship: Making thinking visible', *American Educator*, 15 (3), 6–11, 38–39.

de Groot, A. (1965, 1946) *Thought and Choice and Chess*. The Hague: Mouton.

Edelson, D. C., Gordin, D. N., Clark, B. A., Brown, M. and Griffin, D. (1997) 'WorldWatcher [computer software]', Evanston, IL: Northwestern University.

Edelson, D. C., Pea, R. D., and Gomez, L. M. (1996) 'The collaboratory notebook', *Communications of the ACM*, 39 (4): 32–3.

Edison, T. A. (1922) cited in H. A. Wise, *Motion Pictures as an Aid in Teaching American History*. New Haven, CT: Yale Unversity Press, p. 1.

Ericsson, K. A., Krampe, R. T. and Tesch-Romer, C. (1993) 'The role of deliberate practice in the acquisition of expert performance', *Psychological Review*, 100 (3): 363–406.

Granott, N. and Parziale, J. (2002) *Microdevelopment: Transition Processes in Development and Learning*. New York: Cambridge University Press.

Greeno, J. G. (2006) 'Learning in activity', in K. R. Sawyer (ed.), *The Cambridge Handbook of the Learning Sciences*. New York: Cambridge University Press, pp. 79–96.

Halverson, R. and Collins, A. (2006) 'Information technologies and the future of schooling in the United States', *Research and Practice in Technology Enhanced Learning*, 1 (2): 145–55.

Hastie, R. (1986). 'Review essay: Experimental evidence on group accuracy', in B. Grofman, and G. Owen, (eds), *Decision Research I, Information Pooling and Group Decision Making: Proceedings of the Second Conference on Political Economy*. Irvine, CA: University of California, pp. 129–57.

Hatano, G., and Inagaki, K. (1986) 'Two courses of expertise', in H. Stevenson, H. Azuma and K. Hakuta (eds), *Child Development and Education in Japan*. New York: Freeman. pp. 263–72.

Hatano, G., and Inagaki, K. (1991) 'Sharing cognition through collective comprehension activity', in L. Resnick, J. Levin and S. D. Teasley (eds), *Perspectives on Socially Shared Cognition*. Washington, DC: American Psychological Association, pp. 331–48.

Itakura, K. (1967) 'Instruction and learning of concept "force" in static based on Kasetsu–Jikken–Jugyou (Hypothesis–Experiment–Instruction): a new method of science teaching', *Bulletin of National Institute for Educational Research*, 52: 1–121 (In Japanese).

Kolodner, J. L., Crismond, D., Fasse, B. B., Graym, J. T., Holbrook, J., Ryan, M. and Puntambekar, S. (2003) 'Problem-based learning meets case-based reasoning in the middle-school science classroom: putting a Learning-by-Design curriculum into practice', *Journal of the Learning Sciences*. 12 (4): 495–548.

Lave, J. and Wenger, E. (1991) *Situated Learning: Legitimate Peripheral Participation*. New York: Cambridge University Press.

Lehrer, R. and Schauble, L. (2006) 'Cultivating model-based reasoning in science education', in K. R. Sawyer (ed.), *The Cambridge Handbook of the Learning Sciences*. New York: Cambridge University Press, pp. 371–87.

Linn, M. (2006) 'The knowledge integration perspective on learning and instruction', in K. R. Sawyer (ed.), *The Cambridge Handbook of the Learning Sciences*. New York: Cambridge University Press, pp. 243–64.

Linn, M. C. and Hsi, S. (2000) *Computer, Teachers, Peers*. Mahwah, NJ: Erlbaum.

Linn, M. C., Davis, E. and Bell, P. (2004) *Internet Environments for Science Education*. Mahwah, NJ: Erlbaum.

Miyake, N. (1986) 'Constructive interaction and the iterative processes of understanding', *Cognitive Science*, 10 (2): 151–77.

Miyake, N. (2005a) 'Multifaceted Outcome of Collaborative Learning: Call for Divergent Evaluation'. Paper presented at the meeting of the XIIIth International Conference on Computers in Education (ICCE 2005), Singapore.

Miyake, N. (2005b) 'How can Asian educational psychologists contribute to the advancement of learning sciences?'. Invited talk at the meeting of the Korean Society of Educational Psychology, 2005 International Conference, Seoul, Korea.

Miyake, N. and Shirouzu, H. (2006) 'A collaborative approach to teaching cognitive science to undergraduates: the learning sciences as a means to study and enhance college student learning', *Psychologia*, 49 (2): 101–13.

Miyake, N., Masukawa, H., and Shirouzu, H. (2001) 'The complex jigsaw as an enhancer of collaborative knowledge building', *Proceedings of European Perspectives on Computer-Supported Collaborative Learning*, pp. 454–61.

Miyake, N., Shirouzu, H., and Chukyo Learning Science Group (2005) 'The Dynamic Jigsaw: Repeated Explanation Support for Collaborative Learning of Cognitive Science'. Paper presented at the meeting of the XXVIIth annual meeting of the Cognitive Science Society, Stresa, Italy.

Nasir, N. (2000) '"Point ain't everything": emergent goals and average and percent understandings in the play of basketball among African-American students', *Anthropology and Education Quarterly*, 31 (3): 283–305.

Neisser, U. (1976) *Cognition and Reality: Principles and Implications of Cognitive Psychology*. New York: Freeman.

Norman, D. A. (1982) *Learning and Memory*, San Francisco, CA: Freeman.

Norman, D. A., and Draper, S. W. (eds) (1986) *User-centered System Design: New Perspectives on Human–Computer Interaction*. Hillsdale, NJ: Erlbaum.

Norman, D. A. and Spohrer, J. C. (eds) (1986) 'Learner-centered education', *Communications of the ACM*, 39 (4): 24–49.

Palincsar, A. S. and Brown, A. L. (1984) 'Reciprocal-teaching of comprehension fostering and monitoring activities', *Cognition and Instruction*, 1 (2): 117–75.

Quintana, C., Shin, N., Norris, C., and Soloway, E. (2006) 'Learner-centered design: reflections on the past and directions for the future', in K. R. Sawyer (ed.), *The Cambridge Handbook of the Learning Sciences*. New York: Cambridge University Press, pp.119–34.

Reiser, B. J. (2004) 'Scaffolding complex learning: the mechanisms of structuring and problematizing student work', *Journal of the Learning Sciences*, 13 (3): 273–304.

Roschelle, J. (1992) 'Learning by collaborating: convergent conceptual change', *Journal of the Learning Sciences*, 2 (3): 235–76.

Sandoval, W. A. and Reiser, B. J. (2004) 'Explanation-driven inquiry: integrating conceptual and epistemic scaffolds for scientific inquiry', *Science Education*, 88 (3), 345–72.

Sawyer, K. R. (2006) 'Introduction: The new science of learning', in K. R. Sawyer (ed.), *The Cambridge Handbook of the Learning Sciences*. New York: Cambridge University Press, pp. 1–16.

Scardamalia, M. and Bereiter, C. (1994) 'Computer support for knowledge-building communities', *Journal of the Learning Sciences*, 3 (3): 265–83.

Scardamalia, M. and Bereiter, C. (2006) 'Knowledge building: theory, pedagogy, and technology', in K. R. Sawyer (ed.), *The Cambridge Handbook of the Learning Sciences*. New York: Cambridge University Press, pp. 97–115.

Schwartz, D., Lin, X., Brophy, S., and Bransford, J. D. (1999) 'Toward the development of flexibly adaptive instructional design', in C. D. Reigeluth (ed.), *Instructional-design Theories and Models: A new Paradigm of Instructional Theory*, X. Mahwah, NJ: Erlbaum. pp. 183–213.

Sherin, B., Reiser, B. and Edelson, D. (2004) 'Scaffolding analysis: extending the scaffolding metaphor to learning artifacts', *Journal of the Learning Sciences*, 13 (3): 387–421.

Shirouzu, H., Miyake, N., and Masukawa, H. (2002) 'Cognitively active externalization for situated reflection', *Cognitive Science*, 26 (4): 469–501.

Soloway, E. and Pryor, A. (1986) 'Log on education: the next generation in human–computer interaction', *Communications of the ACM*, 39 (4): 16–18.

Stahl, G., Koschmann, T. and Suthers, D. D. (2006) 'Computer-Supported Collaborative Learning', in K. R. Sawyer (ed.), *The Cambridge Handbook of the Learning Sciences*. New York: Cambridge University Press, pp. 409–25.

Tabak, I. (2004) 'Synergy: a complement to emerging patterns of distributed scaffolding', *Journal of the Learning Sciences*, 13 (3): 305–35.

Vygotsky, L. S. (1978) *Mind in Society: The Development of Higher Psychological Processes*. Cambridge, MA: Harvard University Press.

White, B. Y. and Fredericksen, J. R. (1998) 'Inquiry, modeling, and metacognition: making science accessible to all students', *Cognition and Instruction*, 16 (1), 3–118.

Wood, D., Bruner, J., and Ross, G. (1976) 'The role of tutoring in problem solving', *Journal of Child Psychology and Psychiatry and Allied Disciplines*, 17 (2): 89–100.

ACKNOWLEDGEMENTS

The writing of this chapter was partly supported by SORST/JSP 2005–2007 and JSPS Grant-in-Aid 15200020 (2004–2006).

PART III

Policy

12

Policy and E-learning

Virgil E. Varvel, Rae-Anne Montague and
Leigh S. Estabrook

When programme administrators seek to implement e-learning they are often challenged by institutional and governmental policies that proscribe such critical areas as how many credits students may earn at a distance or whether students who do not take courses physically offered on campus are eligible for financial aid. These regulations – adopted with the intent of ensuring educational quality – tend to advantage face-to-face, synchronous instruction. As Chaloux (2003: 170) cautions, distance learning may be '"hamstrung" by a myriad of policies and practices that, while effective for a traditional-aged population studying full-time on traditional classrooms are barriers to access' in e-learning environments. Simonson and Bauck note that those policy issues can span academic, fiscal, faculty, legal, student, technical, and philosophical realms (2003: 418).

This chapter addresses these areas at two levels: (1) policies set by the educational institutions that affect the design and delivery of e-learning courses and programmes; and (2) laws and policies of external regulating bodies that circumscribe the ways e-learning is structured and taught. The area of institutional policy is addressed at a relatively general level because our evidence suggests policies vary widely. To our knowledge no researchers have, to date, collected systematic data about institutional practices at the national or global level. The analysis of the legal framework focuses on the US.

INSTITUTIONAL POLICIES AND E-LEARNING

Policies affecting students

Institutions embarking on e-learning initiatives may adapt existing courses and/or programmes or create new ones; but whatever the technologies of learning they develop, they cannot help but be challenged by existing policies: ones that do not recognize the different profile of distance students, and ones designed for face-to-face delivery. First, the students themselves are often different. Not only do they live at a distance from campus (often continents away), but also incoming e-learners bring new expectations, experiences, and needs. They are often older than on-campus students and they may already have – or be unable to use – health insurance, athletic facilities or other such benefits colleges and universities typically offered as a bundle to students. Academic policies may require students with disabilities to be certified disabled by a campus-level person – not an outside physician. The registrar may have a policy of listing on student transcripts that a course was taken via e-learning and thus labelling it in ways that may be interpreted as a statement on relative quality of courses. Campus registration may be secured such that students must register, at least initially, face-to-face through a campus system as a way to confirm identity. Policies limiting financial aid or other kinds of services to part-time students, while not applied only to e-learning students, can disproportionately affect this group, many of whom will be part-timers.

Campuses also struggle to develop policies for evaluating the academic work of their e-learning students. If 'nobody knows you're a dog' when you are on the computer, how do educational institutions know their e-learning students are really the ones doing the work they submit? And what existing policies are fair under the new circumstances of learning? How can distributed exams be conducted, for example? If they take place in real time, is it fair to students in different time zones (e.g. who might be completing the exam in the middle of the night)? Some institutions have policies that require e-learning students to have their exams proctored at a library or other trusted place. Some retain policies that students must come to campus to take certain exams. Cornford and Pollock (2002: 178) argue that institutions should 'change the mode of assessment for the course'. This requires resources, but it may be the only real alternative, especially for 100 per cent online programmes. Shifting to alternative methods of assessment (projects, papers, postings, etc.) implies redesigning courses and shifting faculty (and/or staff) responsibilities, and, as such, has significant implications for policy.

Colleges offer a variety of opportunities to support and enhance students' learning; but these opportunities often fail to accommodate students who never or rarely visit the campus. Since this chapter focuses on policy, it will only list but cannot address the myriad of practices within academic institutions that also place e-learners at a disadvantage. These include providing counselling services only 'in person' or not providing guest lectures in a format that allows students at a distance to hear a recording or even listen live while the lecture is presented. Along with course-level support, students involved in fully online degree programmes 'need academic advising, tutoring, and career counseling, just like students who enroll in on-campus programmes' (Johnstone, 2004: 396). We mention them because the lack of opportunity for e-learners in many institutions suggests a vacuum in policy that assures equity of access and support to e-learners. We also mention them because certain national policies can drive students to look to their colleges and universities to provide social services otherwise unavailable to them. Some students, for example will enrol to obtain health insurance – something they would not need were there universal health care (and thus a condition that differs across countries).

The exception on campuses has been those services for which electronic delivery has become important even for on-campus students. One of the most successful areas of support on many campuses appears to be policies on access to library services. As Searing (2004: 395) describes, online 'students and faculty expect and deserve the same level of library support that their on-campus peers enjoy'. Perhaps one reason library policies have changed so rapidly is that the demands are coming as loudly from individuals on campus as from those taking courses at a distance: students in their dormitory can be as demanding as e-learners. Supporting distance access to library materials necessitates broader, deeper, and faster online migration. In the case described by Searing, this includes new online services for electronic course reserves (http://www.library.uiuc.edu/lsx/reserves.htm), a virtual new bookshelf (http://www.library.uiuc.edu/lsx/acquis.htm), and a collection of electronic books licensed from netLibrary (http://www.netlibrary.com). As students become more familiar with searching for information online, librarians provide new tools and support via toll-free phone access to reference services as well as e-mail and chat reference.

A broad range of collaborative multi-institutional initiatives have been developed to promote growth in other aspects of e-learning, such as course management systems (e.g. Sakai, www.sakaiproject.com) and educational resource repositories (e.g. MERLOT, www.merlot.org). Those course management systems that support both teaching and enrolment management can help a campus address a host of e-learning administrative issues; but many other student needs are outside the domain of these systems. As these evolve, universities face entirely new challenges to policies as they try to make these systems interoperable and available.

Institutional policies governing faculty

One of the most contentious internal policy issues has been related to faculty obligations in teaching e-learning courses. In some institutions faculty are paid on an 'overload' basis, i.e. they are paid an additional sum for teaching an e-learning course that is in addition to their regular course load. In other institutions distance courses are included as part of a faculty member's regular teaching assignment.

But there is little agreement on what a course is and the number of students who should be in an e-learning class. As a result existing policies about faculty 'load' (the amount of work normally expected of a faculty member, including sometimes the average number of students in class, number of advisees and frequency of class meetings) fail to reflect adequately the new reality of e-learning.

Equally at issue are policies surrounding faculty ownership of course materials. Historically faculty members have held copyright on their course materials. When faculty members receive royalties or compensation for publishing books or articles that money has been theirs. Colleges and universities have not generally treated these products as work made for hire. Nor have the academic institutions claimed copyright. They have not insisted on taking a portion of the revenue. But colleges and universities have begun to treat differently those course materials developed for e-learning, often noting that faculty members use significant institutional technological resources and support staff in both design and delivery of e-learning instruction. When course modules are created as self-standing units that can be replicated and taught easily by other instructors, colleges see them as potential sources of revenue and become reluctant to grant the same rights of ownership as they have in the past. These issues of intellectual property sit at the boundary of institutional policy and US law and require deeper analysis. By that we mean that institutions do not have sole authority to determine how course materials are handled; but that copyright law will govern their range of choice.

THE US LEGAL ENVIRONMENT FOR E-LEARNING POLICY

As background to examining the laws relevant to e-learning policy, it seems useful to identify the reasons e-learning is so challenging for law makers. For at least fifty years, legislators and courts have struggled to shape copyright legislation that recognizes the ways new technologies allow easy and inexpensive duplication of materials. Under US copyright law, individuals have certain 'fair use' rights to copyrighted materials. Whether copies fall under fair use is determined by (1) the purpose and character of the use (with fair use favoured for not-for-profit, educational purposes), (2) the nature of the copyrighted work, (3) the amount and substantiality of the portion used in relation to the copyrighted work as a whole, and (4) the effect of the use upon the potential market for or value of the copyrighted work.

The design of e-learning courses often challenges the application of these factors. First, because some colleges and universities have seen e-learning as a possible source of profits, some not-for-profit institutions have formed for-profit companies through which to provide e-learning. Certain copyright exemptions do not apply to for-profit companies, and 'fair use' arguments are reduced. When the Registrar of Copyright, a federal official responsible for overseeing US copyright, held hearings about the application of 'fair use' to e-learning she specifically asked, 'How do you draw the boundary [between not-for-profit and for-profit e-learning]?'[1] Second, the technologies that support e-learning also have supported digitization of a broad range of resources, including books, film, and audio recordings. This digitization makes it as easy to give students access to the entire resource as to just a part of it. Publishers question the impact of e-learning on their profits and thus the 'fair use' of the materials they publish. At issue for some publishers is their entry into the e-learning market; thus, publishers may be in competition with educational institutions for students. The publisher Harcourt, for example, has several divisions involved directly in e-learning. Harcourt School Publishers, according to their Web site, are 'a premier publisher of exemplary school textbooks and related instructional materials, including innovative eLearning components, in a wide range of subject areas'.[2] We can understand the ways policies have been developing by recognizing that the courses and modules created as part of e-learning are increasingly seen as commodities by institutions of higher learning – by-products that can be bought and sold. Publishing, technology, and other industries that support e-learning, lobby to obtain policies that will favour their interests. But the territory is contested: students, faculty, some educational associations, librarians, and organizations concerned with free speech rights, such as the ACLU, push hard for more open access to information, including that developed as part of e-learning. The following discusses current policies in this area. However, because of these pressures, the policies discussed below can be expected to change and evolve at a rapid pace.

INTELLECTUAL PROPERTY POLICY

Ownership

Intellectual property (and more specifically copyright) issues can be found in nearly every list of important policy considerations in higher education today. Intellectual property is defined as those legal ownership rights granted to tangible expressions of ideas. Examples include books, syllabuses, poetry, inventions, music, and art. Laws about intellectual property rights affect such things as the rights of faculty to play music to their students while showing slides from a picture book, but also pertain to faculty members' right to claim ownership of a course they have developed. The American Council on Education (2000) lists intellectual property policies as one of seven critical policy areas for distance education. Simonson and Bauck (2003) and the Council for Higher Education Accreditation & Institute for Higher Education Policy (1999, 2000), among many others also list intellectual property issues among primary concerns for e-learning.

Still, unlike their face-to-face counterparts, many online programmes lack clear policies with regard to ownership of materials created for use in the virtual classroom. In an online course on intellectual property taken primarily by college and university faculty in Illinois, only twenty-seven out of ninety-three participants have been able to find a policy on their campus regarding online courses and intellectual property. Many of them are unable even to find who is responsible for such a policy if it happens to exist. (Data are from seven iterations of a copyright course taught by Virgil Varvel from 2001 to 2006.) This is a recognized problem, one some are trying to alleviate.

For instance, the Center for Intellectual Property and Copyright in the Digital Environment (2005) at the University of Maryland University College has been conducting an as yet unpublished survey of intellectual property policies. A selection of model policies is available on its Web site (http://www.umuc.edu/distance/odell/cip/links_policy.html). The American Association of University Professors Special Committee on Distance Education and Intellectual Property Issues (n.d.) provides faculty with assistance by placing model policy guidelines online as well.

Despite the current push to achieve a common understanding of models of ownership, problems still remain. While students maintain the copyright on most if not all of their creations within an online course, and most employment agreements with general staff make their creations the ownership of the institution, faculty and administrators (and even courts) have differed in their interpretations of who owns faculty work such as online courses.

In the US, most university faculty are considered employees (see provisions determined by *CCNV versus Reid* (490 U.S. 730, 1989) such as providing employment benefits), in which case any work that they perform could fall under the Work Made for Hire (WMFH) provisions of US copyright law (Title 17 U.S. Code), causing initial ownership to reside with the employer or, in this case, the institution. However, work practices in higher education make it difficult for policy makers to interpret WMFH. First, the work must be prepared within an authorized time and space, something especially difficult to delineate in the age of telecommuting and online instructional development, and with the non-structured work day of teaching faculty. If an instructor spends personal time at home on a personal computer working on course development, the time and space apply only to the time frame of employment and the virtual space, but no longer to time at work and physical space. Second, the purpose of employment is a WMFH determinant. In the case of faculty, the exact purpose of employment may be more in line with teaching and research than the actual development of course materials used to teach, although the latter may be a requirement embedded within the former, creating course materials can be embedded within teaching. Finally, under agency law (a guiding principle in interpreting the statutory definition of WMFH according to *CCNV versus Reid*) a fundamental determinant is whether the employer has and executes the right to control the manner and means by which the faculty member prepares the materials. In some cases, the institution clearly makes decisions in this respect, such as the selection of a single course management system. In other cases, such as how an instructor may go about producing educational videos for use online, the institution may have no say beyond curricular needs.

Organizations such as the American Association of University Professors strongly maintain that faculty scholarly work is *not* WMFH. According to their Statement on Copyright (AAUP, as quoted in Springer, 2005), '[I]t has been the prevailing academic practice to treat the faculty member as the copyright owner of works that are created independently and at the faculty member's own initiative for traditional academic purposes.' Yet, as Lape (quoted in Springer, 2005, online) states, 'The most common standard employed by universities for claiming ownership of faculty works is the "use of university resources" or "significant or substantial use of university resources".' One therefore has to ask what rights of the instructor in terms of intellectual property are carried over into a virtual environment to which access is under the control and authority of the employer.

Confounding the issue further, an unwritten 'academic exception' has evolved with respect to university faculty and copyright policy that may or may not traverse the virtual/traditional barrier. From a practical standpoint, such a tradition of permitting faculty to retain ownership of their works even in the presence of policy to the contrary can draw exemplary faculty to an institution. The 'academic exception' predates the Copyright Act of 1976, although the 1976 Act clearly is superordinate to common law predecessors. For example, in *Sherrill versus Grieves* (57 Wash. L.R. 286, S. Ct. D.C. 1929) a US Army instructor was found to own the copyright to the written version of his lectures. More recently, in *Hays versus Sony Corporation of America* (847 F.2d 412, 7th Cir. 1988), the courts ruled that although academic writing is part of a faculty member's employment responsibility, and university resources may be widely used during the production of such works, it is a 'universal assumption and practice' that the work belongs to the faculty in the absence of an explicit agreement otherwise. However, in *Weinstein versus The University of Illinois* (811 F.2d 1091, 7th Cir. 1987), the court stated that the US copyright code is general enough to make all academic works a work made for hire, especially in the case of a university-funded project. Any recognized teaching exception in higher education may be regional as well. In 2005, a Kansas appellate court decided that intellectual property is subject to work made for hire and is furthermore not a mandatory subject of collective bargaining (*Pittsburg State University/Kansas NEA versus Kansas Board of Regents, PSU and PERB*, 101 P.3d 740 (table), 2004 WL 2848767 (Kan. App. 2004)); However, the Supreme Court of Kansas later overturned this decision (http://www.umuc.edu/distance/odell/cip/links_policy.html). If such policies were not subject to collective bargaining, then institutions could change ownership rules without input from the faculty and any union representation.

Important to consider are such cases as *Vanderhurst versus Colorado Mountain College District* (208 F.3d 908, 10th Cir. 2000) and *Williams versus Weisser* (273 Cal. App. 2d 726, 1969) where the manner in which material is presented and produced is widely recognized as a matter of teaching expression entitled to First Amendment protection, and thus in some ways under the control of the instructor. As the court announced in *Tinker versus Des Moines Independent Community*

School District (393 U.S. 503, 506, 1969), 'It can hardly be argued that either students or teachers shed their constitutional rights to freedom of speech or expression at the schoolhouse gate.' In other cases, such as *Miles versus Denver Public Schools* (944 F.2d 773, 775, 10th Cir. 1991), not all speech is considered protected in the classroom, such as that with no pedagogical initiative. For example, while speech fulfilling an educational purpose is often protected, if there is no pedagogical initiative to the speech it is usually not considered protected (see *Hazelwood School District versus Kuhlmeier*, 484 U.S. 260, 273, 1988). In public higher education, the Pickering analysis (see *Pickering versus Board of Education*, 391 U.S. 563, 574, 1968) establishes the necessity of educational institutions to balance protection of faculty speech with the institution's public responsibilities.

E-learning and online education have characteristics that lead academic institutions to push strongly for university ownership rights over products created by their faculty, particularly when courses are reproducible independent of the instructor or course designer. When the academy constructs policy, Shores (1996) and the American Association of University Professors (n.d.) provide several primary issues to address. Rephrased, these issues include: over what aspects of the course and its materials ownership will be exerted; how ownership will be exerted in cases of single and joint ownership, and in terms of revenue dispersal when appropriate; who may use the materials once ownership is established; how and when materials not owned by the institution will be used; how disputes will be resolved; and how and by whom these decisions will be made. Initially, though, the institution must ask whether exerting control over a given property is in its best interests when considering hiring and retaining the best faculty and in supporting a scholarly working environment.

Materials dissemination

Along with ownership of online materials, institutional policies must address handling of all materials placed on campus networks. Institutions can face the problem of using materials of which neither they nor the instructor is the owner. Such problems happen independently of the mode of delivery, but new issues arise online. For example, although the US Copyright Office (1999) maintains that the fair use factors discussed earlier are technologically neutral, the manner in which the four fair use factors are applied within those rules changes in e-learning where different market and distribution factors exist. Furthermore, not only may the four legal factors be applied differently in an online course, but various agreed-upon fair use guidelines that are often referred to in traditional educational settings currently in place for traditional education, were not agreed-upon for use in an online setting and thus do not necessarily apply at all. (For a listing of fair use guidelines, see http://www.ion.uillinois.edu/resources/tutorials/ip/index.asp.)

In 2002, the Technology, Education, and Copyright Harmonization Act (P.L. 107–273) was signed into law. This amendment to the US copyright law allowed for non-profit, educational institutions to extend exemptions normally limited to the traditional classroom. Through the TEACH Act, institutions are authorized to digitize works within reasonable limits provided a list of requirements are met (American Library Association, 2005; Harper, 2005; Kankakee Community College, 2005; North Carolina State University, 2005). The requirements of the TEACH Act are not necessarily easy to meet. In addition to being a non-profit, accredited educational institution, the work must have a pedagogically valid reason to be used in mediated instructional activities. A self-paced tutorial course would not meet the second of these requirements. Next, the institution must have a written copyright policy and a programme to educate faculty and students about copyright, although the exact nature of such a programme is not delineated. Some requirements are ethical as well in that the copy must be legally obtained in the first place. The transmission of the materials must also be limited as technically feasible only to students in the course to avoid illegality. Institutions are thus forced to put security measures on their online courses that until recently could have been prohibitively expensive to smaller colleges.

Even when requirements are met, there are many instances in which the institution may still have to purchase or acquire permission to use the materials. If the materials are marketed or produced primarily for performance or display as part of an instructional activity through digital transmission, then the materials are not eligible for exemption. Also, like traditional classroom use, only selected portions of most works may be displayed. Only non-dramatic literary and musical works may be used in their entirety. When an entire work is needed, then the materials must be distributed to the students somehow, whether mailed as in correspondence education, or delivered online through a library reserve system. In other words, if the students had to go to the library to get the materials in the face-to-face classroom, then they will likely have to acquire the same materials through a library or digital course reserve system in the online course.

Infringement and liability

Of primary concern in policy development is the limitation of any infringement liability that may present itself to the institution or individuals involved. Violating the exclusive rights granted to a copyright holder can render severe criminal and civil penalties. In Australia, for instance, the unmodified maximum penalty for an individual guilty of a criminal copyright offence is AU$60,500, and it rises to AU$302,500 for a corporation ('Dramatic rise in authors publishing in open access journal', 2004). In the US, copyright violation can be a criminal offence. First-time copyright infringement penalties as outlined in 17 U.S.C. § 506(a) and 18 U.S.C. § 2319 can begin with a maximum of five years in prison and AU$250,000 in fines (see 17 U.S.C. § 506(a) & 18 U.S.C. § 2319).

Infringement can take several forms. Direct infringement occurs when any entity directly violates a copyright holder's exclusive rights without falling within an exception or fair use provision. An entity can also be liable for contributory infringement in which others are authorized or required by the entity to infringe upon a copyright. It can be argued that contributory infringement may occur even without direct infringement, since copyright owners are also granted the right to authorize the execution of their copyrights. In vicarious infringement, even in the absence of any actual knowledge of an infringement, if someone had the right and ability to supervise the infringing action of another in which the party holds a financial interest, then copyright infringement may have occurred (see *Famous Music Corp. versus Bay State Harness Horse Racing & Breeding Association* or *KECA Music. versus Dingus McGee's Co.*). In all forms of infringement, 'innocent' or unwitting infringement is still considered infringement.

To limit liability, institutions and individuals must remain mindful of the exceptions that have been set forth as outlined earlier and additional provisions as found throughout copyright law. As the rights of the end users have expanded, there are increasing requirements in return for those rights. There has also been a shift away from mere avoidance of direct infringement towards monitoring materials use across entire systems and mentoring of users of a system in the law in order to avoid liability. For example, 17 U.S.C. § 108(f)(1) requires a notice that the making of copies using equipment such as photocopiers may be subject to copyright law. The TEACH Act requires a copyright education programme be in place for all employees, not just those that use the network. Requirements within 17 U.S.C. § 512 suggest that an institution may need to actively engage in network monitoring in order to qualify for liability exemptions as an ISP. The difficulty in maintaining the legality of materials use prompts many to simply pay a licensing fee for all materials use in order to ensure safe protocol.

Privacy

Techno-critics and futurists often bemoan the increasing loss of privacy resulting from an increasingly technologically dependent society. Educational institutions face particular challenges in assuring their students' privacy. This issue is relevant for on-campus students as well as e-learning ones, but it is perhaps most salient for e-learners because of their dependence on electronic communications. Increasingly most student information – including student records and applications – are being made available on the Web; but how are they protected? The 2005 breach of the Harvard, Stanford, MIT, Carnegie Mellon, Dartmouth, and Duke Business School admissions Web sites that allowed people to see their own – and others' – admission status is but one example of a breach of privacy (CBS News, 2005). In many countries, laws regulate the sharing of information about and by students, especially when they are under certain ages. It therefore becomes both a legal and ethical imperative to protect student information in an online programme.

In the US, the Family Educational Rights and Privacy Act (*FERPA*, 20 U.S.C. § 1232g; 34 CFR Part 99, 1974) and the Child Online Privacy Protection Act (*COPPA*, 17 U.S.C. § 1301–08, 1998) both contain provisions with possible implications to online education and educational research. These issues are not limited to the US. Many countries have privacy regulations for students and/or citizens as a whole. Rules similar to FERPA and COPPA include Australia's National Privacy Principles, various EU data directives, and Canada's Privacy Act and Personal Information Protection and Electronic Documents Act, to name a few. Without addressing the issue of jurisdiction such as where the student, researcher, faculty, or institution is located, implications specific to FERPA and COPPA are discussed next.

In general, FERPA provides students with the right to see their educational record, to seek amendment to that record, to consent or not consent to the disclosure of that record to others (some information may be released without student permission under certain circumstances such as court proceeding requirements), and to file a complaint with the FERPA office in Washington, DC. The term 'educational record' has particular implications to online educators. In effect, any exchange occurring in text in which a student is involved becomes part of that student's educational record if it is assessed in some way. Thus not only is the exchange protected under copyright, as the student would own his/her contribution, the exchange is also protected under FERPA. When research is conducted on such discourse, or when non-institution-affiliated faculty are invited to speak online, the researcher or guest is actually accessing part of the student record and, depending on the features of the course management system, may also have access to a class roster containing personal student information. As such, additional safeguards may need to be met for such activities.

COPPA specifically protects the rights of children under the age of thirteen when they are online. It has applications to online education in situations such as the collection of information in a survey in such a way that it might be shared or used outside the immediate teacher–student educational context. Theoretically, this would even include the use of a survey to gather information about the students in an online course where the automatic reporting of that information provides statistical analysis that all can see (a common feature in many course management systems). COPPA can also cause difficulty when using external for-profit services such as plagiarism detection sites, since even the use of an e-mail address to create an account for the site might be seen as a COPPA violation. In effect, any personally identifying information about those under the age of thirteen should be avoided.

The conduct of online courses often includes text-based discourse between students and faculty members, and among students. Because such discourse includes the identity of the student through his or her e-mail address, it is possible to violate those students' privacy when such information is used as a basis for online research or used by guest lecturers not affiliated with the institution. Unlike a traditional setting, information about the students such as e-mail address and their entire posting history may be readily available without request in many online systems. Varvel (2005) discusses several implications of this situation.

Primarily, policies need to exist and students need to be informed of how any submitted information will be used prior to enrolment in an online course. In some cases, such as when the student is under eighteen years of age, signed consent is required from the student, parent, or legal guardian before information, which may even include part of a graded assignment, can be collected.

Financial aid

One purpose behind distance education in general is to extend access to education beyond the campus reach. However, simply placing a programme online does not in itself extend access. Students must be supported in order to make use of the new educational opportunity. All regional accreditation associations and the Distance Education Training Council reinforced this view in their Statement of Commitment for the Evaluation of Electronically offered Degree and Certificate Programs (Council of Regional Accrediting Commissions, 2001a) and in Best Practices for Electronically offered Degree and Certificate Programs (Council of Regional Accrediting Commissions, 2001b). One aspect of that support that many still struggle with is financial aid.

In 1992, Congress passed what is known as the Fifty Percent rule that excluded colleges that offer more than half their courses by distance education or enrol more than half their students in e-learning programmes from enrolling in federal financial aid programmes. Its purpose was to try to curtail 'diploma mills' with the assumption that programmes that exceed 50 percent in either category cannot provide a good education. In 2005, Congress established an experimental programme in twenty-four such colleges and universities and in 2006 Congress extended federal financial aid to institutions regardless of percent of courses taught online or percentage of students enrolled online. This change will not necessarily improve financial assistance for e-learning students since it now extends the appropriation for federal grants across a larger number of institutions, but it will mean more students will be competing for such assistance.

Looking to the future

Financial aid

Financial aid to students has represented a significant hurdle for e-learning programmes because lack of aid means exclusion of those without the means to pay their own way. The change in federal financial aid may suggest that e-learning is gaining greater acceptance among the public – or it may just mean that for-profit institutions have become more successful lobbyists. Whatever the reason, federal aid to both distance and on-campus students is a source of continuing discussion, as aid per student has declined.

Intellectual property

While financial aid may be a critical issue for some students, much more important to the future of e-learning will be the policies regarding intellectual property. What will e-learning look like if content is too restricted or too expensive to design courses as needed? There is evidence already that instructors may substitute items in course reading packs with less expensive copyright costs than preferred readings that cost more, or online accessible items (at whatever cost) compared to non-accessible items. Although the federal government in the US, the World Trade Organization and other bodies are still developing policies regarding fair use of materials for educational purposes, educators are justifiably concerned about their legal rights to present an array of visual and print materials to their students online.

Global reach

This article has focused on US law, but many of its provisions will impact e-learning globally. To the extent that these US approaches to intellectual property become embedded in such organizations as the World Trade Organization treaties and the World Summit on the Information Society (WSIS), these issues will apply equally to those nations that co-operate and sign treaties with the US. Since e-learning depends on instructors' ability to teach content to their students, and since scientific communication is not restricted by national boundaries, faculty members' right to use the creative works of others is essential to their teaching and to their students' learning.

Advocates of strong copyright protection insist it is necessary to provide an incentive not only to creators of intellectual property but also to colleges and universities that are investing in the infrastructure to assist the development of e-learning materials. Opponents counter that tightly restricted copyright is a disincentive both to creators of creative works and to course development. Some of these arguments revert to classic discussions regarding the merits of capitalist and socialist economies, but to characterize them as such oversimplifies the policy debate. Globally there are also significant cultural differences in the ways people think about intellectual property – even the term 'property' as part of the equation is seen by some as strange. Since e-learning itself naturally and easily transcends national boundaries, future developments in each of these areas of policy will necessarily involve negotiations that cross geographic boundaries.

NOTES

1   Personal question to Leigh S. Estabrook at hearing in Chicago (date unknown).
2   http://www.harcourt.com/about/.

REFERENCES

American Association of University Professors Special Committee on Distance Education and Intellectual Property Issues (n.d.) *Suggestions and Guidelines: Sample Language for Institutional Policies and Contract Language*. Retrieved 5 June 2005 from: http://www.aaup.org/Issues/DistanceEd/ Archives/speccmt/ipguide.htm.

American Council on Education (2000) *Developing a Distance Education Policy for Twenty-first Century Learning*. Washington, DC: Author. Retrieved 28 November 2005 from: http://www.acenet.edu/AM/ Template.cfm?Section=Search&template=/CM/HTMLDisplay.cfm&ContentID=7819.

American Library Association (2005) *Distance Education and the TEACH Act*. Retrieved 30 November 2005 from: http://www.ala.org/Template.cfm?Section=distanceed&Template=/ContentManage-ment/ ContentDisplay.cfm&ContentID=25939.

Arvan, L. (2004) 'The view from campus administration', in C. Haythornthwaite and M. M. Kazmer (eds.), *Learning, Culture and Community in Online Education: Research and Practice*. New York: Peter Lang, pp. 283–90.

CBS News (4 March 2005) *Hacker Hits Top Business Schools*. Retrieved 24 July 2006 from: http://www.cbsnews.com/stories/2005/03/04/tech/printable678049.shtml.

Center for Intellectual Property and Copyright in the Digital Environment (2005) *Copyright Ownership Policies in Distance Education: A Survey*. Adelphi, MD: University of Maryland University College. Retrieved 28 November 2005 from: http://www.umuc.edu/distance/odell/cip/survey_news.html.

Chaloux, B. N. (2003) 'Removing barriers to access: policy initiatives to make distance learning accessi-ble, affordable, and available to all learners', in J. Bourne and J. C. Moore (eds.), *Elements of Quality Online Education: Practice and Direction*. Needham, MA: SCOLE. pp. 159–85.

Cornford, J. & Pollock, N. (2002) 'The university campus as "resourceful constraint": process and prac-tice in the construction of the virtual university', in M. R. Lea and K. Nicoll (eds.), *Distributed Learning: Social and Cultural Approaches to Practice*. New York: RoutledgeFalmer. pp. 170–81.

Council for Higher Education Accreditation & Institute for Higher Education Policy (1999) 'Distance learning in higher education', *CHEA Update, 1* (February). Retrieved 28 November 2005 from: http://www.chea.org/Research/index.asp.

Council for Higher Education Accreditation & Institute for Higher Education Policy (2000) 'Distance learning in higher education', *CHEA Update, 3* (April). Retrieved 28 November 2005 from: http://www.chea.org/Research/index.asp.

Council of Regional Accrediting Commissions (2001a) *Statement of Commitment by the Regional Accrediting Commissions for the Evaluation of Electronically Offered Degree and Certificate Programs*. Retrieved 30 September 2005 from: http://www.wcet.info/resources/accreditation/index.asp.

Council of Regional Accrediting Commissions (2001b) *Best Practices for Electronically Offered Degree and Certificate Programs*. Retrieved 30 September 2005 from: http://www.wcet.info/resources/ accreditation/index.asp.

'Dramatic Rise in Authors Publishing in Open Access Journals' (2005) Retrieved 14 August 2006 from http://www.managinginformation.com/news/content_show_full.php?id=4415.

Harper, G. (2005) The TEACH Act. Retrieved 30 November 2005 from: http://www.utsystem.edu/ogc/ intellectualproperty/teachact.htm.

Johnstone, S. M. (2004) 'A policy perspective on learning theory and practice in distance education', in T. M. Duffy and J. R. Kirkley (eds.) *Learner-Centered Theory and Practice in Distance Education: Cases from Higher Education*. Mahwah NJ: Erlbaum. pp. 395–403.

Kankakee Community College (2005) *TEACH Act Guidelines*. Retrieved 30 November 2005 from: http://www.kcc.edu/faculty/resources/copyright/teachact/guidelines.asp.

North Carolina State University (2005) *The TEACH Toolkit*. Retrieved 30 November 2005 from: http://www.lib.ncsu.edu/scc/legislative/teachkit/.

Searing, S. E. (2004) 'All in the family: library services for LIS online education', *Journal of Library Administration*, 41 (3–4): 391–405.

Shores, C. (1996) 'Ownership of faculty works and university copyright policy', *ARL Newsletter*, 189. Retrieved 30 September 2005 from: http://www.arl.org/newsltr/189/owner.html.

Simonson, M., and Bauck, T. (2003) 'Distance education policy issues: statewide perspectives', in M. G. Moore and W. G. Anderson (eds.), *Handbook of Distance Education*. Mahwah, NJ: Lawrence Erlbaum, pp. 417–24.

Springer, A. (2005) *Intellectual Property Legal Issues for Faculty and Faculty Unions* (18 March). Retrieved 12 December 2005 from: http://www.aaup.org/Legal/info per cent20outlines/05intellprop.htm.

US Copyright Office (1999) *Report on Copyright and Digital Distance Education*. Washington, DC: Author. Retrieved 30 November 2005 from: http://www.copyright.gov/reports/de_rprt.pdf.

Varvel, V. E. (2005) 'Student privacy issues, ethics, and solving the guest lecturer dilemma in online courses', *ELearn Magazine* (26 September). Retrieved 15 October 2005 from: http://elearnmag.org/subpage.cfm?section=articles&article=28-1.

CASES CITED

Community for Creative Nonviolence versus Reid (490 U.S. 730, 1989).

Famous Music Corp. versus Bay State Harness Horse Racing & Breeding Association, 554 F.2d 1213 (1st Cir. 1977).

Hays versus Sony Corporation of America, 847 F.2d 412 (7th Cir. 1988).

Hazelwood School District versus Kuhlmeier, 484 U.S. 260, 273 (1988).

KECA Music versus Dingus McGee's Co., 432 F. Supp. 72 (W.D. Mo. 1977).

Miles versus Denver Public Schools, 944 F.2d 773, 775 (10th Cir. 1991).

Pickering versus Board of Education 391 U.S. 563, 574 (1968).

Pittsburg State University/Kansas NEA versus Kansas Board of Regents, PSU and PERB, 101 P.3d 740 (table), 2004 WL 2848767 (Kan. App. 2004).

Sherrill versus Grieves, 57 Wash. L. R. 286 (S. Ct. D.C. 1929).

Tinker versus Des Moines Independent Community School District (393 U.S. 503, 506, 1969).

Vanderhurst versus Colorado Mountain College District, 208 F.3d 908 (10th Cir. 2000).

Weinstein versus The University of Illinois, 811 F.2d 1091 (7th Cir. 1987).

Williams versus Weisser (273 Cal. App. 2d 726, 1969).

OTHER PERTINENT US CASES NOT CITED

A&M Record versus Napster, 239 F.3d 1004 (9th Cir. 2001).

America Geophysical Union versus Texaco, 60 F.3d. 913 (2d Cir. 1995).

America versus MAPHIA, 948 F. Supp. 923 (N.D. Cal. 1996).

Art Rogers versus Jeff Koons, 960 F.2d 301 (2d Cir. 1992).

Atlantic Recording Corp. versus Does 1-3, 371 F.Supp. 2d 377 (W.D.N.Y. 2005).

Avtec Systems versus Pfeiffer, 805 F. Supp. 1312 (E.D. Va. 1992); 21 F.3d. 568 (4th Cir. 1994).

Basic Books versus Kinko's Graphics Corp., 758 F.Supp. 1522 (S.D.N.Y. 1991).

Boz Scaggs Music versus KND Corp., 491 F. Supp. 908, 913 (D. Conn. 1980).

Campbell versus Acuff-Rose, 510 U.S. 569 (1994).

Columbia Pictures Industries versus Redd House, 749 F.2d 154 (3rd Cir. 1984).

Computer Associates International. versus Altai, 982 F.2d 693 (2d Cir. 1992).

Dastar Corp. versus Twentieth Century Fox Film Corp., 539 U.S. 23 (2003).

Davis versus E. I. Du Pont de Nemours & Co., 240 F. Supp. 612, 621 (S.D.N.Y. 1965).

Dawson versus Hinshaw Music, 905 F.2d 731 (4th Cir. 1990).

Demetriades versus Kaufmann, 690 F. Supp. 284, 292 (S.D.N.Y. 1988).

Donald versus Zack Meyer's T.V Sales & Service, 426 F.2d 1027, 1030 (5th Cir. 1970).

Eldred versus Ashcroft, 537 U.S. 186 (2003).

Ellison versus Robertson, 357 F.3d 1072, 1080 (9th Cir. 2004).

Encyclopedia Britannica Educ. Corp. versus Crooks, 558 F. Supp. 1247 (W.D.N.Y. 1983).

Feist Publications versus Rural Telephone Service Co., 499 U.S. 340 (1991).

Fogerty versus Fantasy, Inc. 510 U.S. 517 (1994).

Folsom versus Marsh, 9 F. Cas. 342 (1841).

Fonivisa versus Cherry Auction, 76 F.3d 259 (9th Cir. 1996).

Futuredentics versus Applied Anagramics, 152 F.3d 925 (9th Cir. 1998).

Gershwin Publishing Corp. versus Columbia Artists Management, 443 F.2d 1159, 1162 (2d Cir. 1971).

Gulf Oil Corp. versus Copp Paving Co., 419 U.S. 186 (1974).

Harper & Row Publishers versus National Enterprises, U.S. (1985).

Hotaling versus Church of Latter Day Saints, 118 F.3d 199 (4th Cir. 1999).

In re: Aimster Copyright Litigation Appeal of, 334 F.3d 643 (7th Cir. 2003).

Intellectual Reserve versus Utah Lighthouse Ministry, 75 F. Supp. 2d 1290 (Dist. Utah 1999).

Kelly versus Ariba Soft Corp., 280 F.3d 934 (9th Cir. 2002).

Marcus versus Rowley, 695 F.2d 1171 (9th Cir. 1932).

Marobie-F versus National Association of Firefighter Equipment Distributors, 983 F. Supp. 1167 (N.D. Ill. 1997).

Marshall versus Miles Laboratories, 647 F. Supp. 1326 (N.D. Ind. 1986).

Mazer versus Stein, 347 U.S. 201 (1954).

Metro-Goldwyn-Mayer Studios versus Grokster, 125 S. Ct. 2764 (545 U.S. 2005).

New York Times Co. versus Tasini, 531 U.S. 483 (2001).

Online Policy Group versus Diebold, 337 F.Supp.2d 1195, 1198 (N.D. Calif. 2004).

Peter Pan Fabrics versus Martin Weinter Corp., 274 F.2d 487 (2d Cir. 1960).

Playboy Enterprises versus Frena, 839 F. Supp. 1552 (M.D. Fla. 1993).

Playboy Enterprises, versus Webbworld, 991 F. Supp. 543 (N.D. Tex. 1997).

Princeton University Press versus Michigan Document Services, 99 F.3d 1381 (6th Cir. 1996).

RCA Records versus All-Fast Systems, 594 F. Supp. 335 (S.D.N.Y. 1984).

Religious Technology Center versus Netcom On-Line Community Service, 907 F. Supp. 1361 (N.D. Cal. 1996).

Rockford Map Publishers versus Directory Serversus Co., 224 U.S.P.Q. 851 (C.D. Ill. 1984).

Roth Greeting Cards versus United Card Co., 429 F.2d 1106 (9th Cir. 1970).

Salinger versus Random House, 650 F. Supp. 413 (S.D.N.Y. 1986).

Sega Enterprises of America versus MAPHIA, 948 F. Supp. 923 (N.D. Cal. 1996).

Shapiro Bernstein & Co. versus H. L. Green Co., 316 F.2d 304, 307 (2d Cir. 1963).

Sid & Marty Krofft Television Prods versus McDonald's Corp., 562 F.2d 1157 (9th Cir. 1977).

Sony Corporation of America versus Universal City Studios (464 U.S. 417, 1984).

Southern Bell Telephone & Telegraph versus Associated Telephone Directory, 756 F.2d 801 (11th Cir. 1985).

Stewart versus Abend, 495 U.S. 207 (1990).

Teleprompter Corp. versus Columbia Broadcasting System, 415 U.S. 194 (1974).

Twentieth Century Music Corp. versus Aiken, 422 U.S. 151 (1975).

UNG Recordings versus MP3, 92 F. Supp. 2d 349 (S.D.N.Y. 2000).

United States versus LaMacchia, 871 F.Supp. 535, 545 (D. Mass. 1994).

Universal City Studios versus Reimerdes, 82 F. Supp. 2d 211 (S.D.N.Y. 2000).
Universal Pictures Co. versus Harold Lloyd Corp., 162 F.2d 354, 366 (9th Cir. 1947).
University of Colorado versus American iCyanamid, 880 F. Supp. 1387 (D. Colo. 1994).
United States versus Elcom 2002 WL 1009662 (N.D. Calif, 2002).

13

An International Comparison of the Relationship between Policy and Practice in E-learning

Gráinne Conole

It could be argued that e-learning is one of the key catalysts for change in current higher education. As an area, e-learning is highly political – numerous rhetorical promises and hype have surrounded each introduction of technological change (radio, television, video and the Internet) and the ways in which these technologies will transform education (Mayes, 1995). This rhetoric sits within a wider policy context and the present chapter aims to explore this and consider the relationship between policy and actual practice.

In particular the chapter will consider how policy directives in different countries affect practice, distilling key similarities and differences. Comprehensive information on e-learning internationally is patchy at best (Kumar *et al.*, 2005) and it would be impossible to provide an all-embracing review of policy directives and their impact on e-learning, therefore this chapter seeks only to give exemplars which demonstrate some of the key rhetoric and aims to link these to both local and worldwide agendas. This chapter draws on a number of major reviews. In particular, Carr-Chellman (2005) provides a more detailed review of international developments in e-learning through an edited collection that describes different policy directives around the introduction of e-learning and a critique of the gap between the rhetoric and reality; Kearns (2002) provides an international overview of the trends in ICT policy in education.

CONTEXT

This section provides an overview of the context of modern higher education and in particular some of the factors that shape this context. Higher education has changed in the past thirty years, in part in response to changing societal needs and drives, and in part from a changing perspective on the purpose of education in a modern context. These changes sit within a wider context of modern society which is in a constant state of change; a globalized, networked society (Giddens, 2000; Castells, 1996) fraught with unintended consequences and manufactured risks (Beck, 1992), risks which arise as a direct result of our impact on the environment – such as the threat of global warming as a consequence of our burning of fossil fuels or our increasing dependence on technology (Virilio, 2000). The Internet provides access to an almost unlimited amount of information; new forms of communicative channels abound, offering opportunities for new ways of working and new forms of distributed collaboration. The information revolution has produced vast amounts of new and often contradictory information that forces people to reflect on experience and make decisions (Dyke, 2001). Dyke *et al.* (2007) argue that within this context 'e-learning needs to be extended beyond behaviourist principles; to nurture initiative, provide students with opportunities for experimentation, dialogue, reflection, "higher level" conceptual thinking and reasoning'. New technologies are resulting in a shift in education from a focus on information to the processes of finding and critiquing, and from the solo learner to learning in social settings.

Thus our environment is that of a networked and information society – offering the potential for global communication through a range of mechanisms (e-mail, chat, video-conferencing, mobiles, etc.). Many current sociological thinkers (such as Giddens, 2000; Beck, 1992; Castells, 1996; Lash and Urry, 1994) suggest that our modern society is also characterized by changing norms and values; with fragmentation of the traditional religious hold across the globe (leading to some parts of society essentially being irreligious while others have become more fundamentalist), changing views on marriage and the family and the breakdown of the class divide. This change in societal norms and values also impacts on the nature of education and its purpose. Traditionally higher education provided a grounding for entry into a particular profession; individuals tended to follow one career pathway. However, the pace of change in society and across subject disciplines means that there is much more of a need now for continuing professional development; furthermore it is increasingly common for individuals to change careers more than once. This impacts both on the type of provision offered by educational institutions and the pedagogical focus – with a shift in emphasis needed from knowledge acquisition to development of the higher-order skills and competences needed to make sense of our complex, constantly changing modern world.

An understanding of this wider context is important because it is so evident throughout the policy rhetoric surrounding e-learning. For example, in his introduction to a comparative review of international policy directives Kearns (2002) states that:

> The conjuncture of the impact of globalisation, information and communication technologies, and the accompanying shifts in the economy, labour market, and the operations of enterprises have led to fundamental changes in the economy and society that have profound implications for the role of education and training. Policy for ICT in education is positioned at the frontier of this transition to an information society.

> (Kearns, 2002: ii)

Similarly, in her introduction Carr-Chellman (2005: 1) states that 'Online education has been heralded as the next democratizing force in education'. She goes on to say (2005: 2) that 'open access' and democracy are often the predominant justification for online education as opposed to economic profit. These quotations echo the factors discussed above and highlight some of the ways in which policy and practice are interwoven.

DRIVERS

Conole, Smith *et al.* (2007) argue that institutions are influenced by a range of drivers, of which e-learning is only one, and that these drivers can act as perturbations or catalysts for change. These drivers are a direct result of the factors influencing the wider societal context and there is an intimate connection between the context, policy directives and actual practice.

Current drivers evident in higher education include targets for widening participation (for example in the UK the aim is to increase participation in higher education to 50 per cent), the desire to ensure accessibility and inclusion, increased emphasis on lifelong learning, requirements for quality assurance and regulation, development of competence-based outcomes and assessment, and the identification of new markets and models for delivery to capitalize on the potential of both globalization and emergent technologies. These drivers are evident in recent policy directives. Examples include the quality assurance imperatives developed in the UK and Australia (see Oliver, 2005; QAA, 2004), the range of accessibility directives (Seale *et al.*, 2006), economic imperatives and the development of the work force (Commission on Technology and Adult Learning, 2000; Duderstadt, 2000), the recognition of the need to provide lifelong learning opportunities (see for example Government of Ireland, 2003; Council of European Union, 2002; DfEE, 1998; OECD, 1996) and the imperatives around widening participation (see Selwyn and Gorard for a critical review of widening participation and e-learning, 2003). There is a visible link between these policy drivers and actual practice, for example the increasing requirement for quality assurance has led to institutions needing to provide evidence of the quality of their educational provision and to establish mechanisms for monitoring and evaluating the creation and delivery of courses. Similarly institutions now need to be more mindful of accessibility issues and ensure provision for learners with a range of disabilities. These drivers mean that institutions need to be cognizant of external factors, are required to be more accountable and to ensure that the courses they offer are meeting the needs of a modern work force.

E-learning is seen by many as one means of supporting these agendas and as an essential element in delivering higher education efficiently and effectively to a diverse, mass audience. This view is in part driven by economic imperatives but is also driven by beliefs in 'open access', democracy and social inclusion. For example, Simpson notes that the current directives in the UK can be traced back to the New Labour government's roots in social democratization (Simpson, 2005: 91). Coupled with these national agendas, with the growth of globalization, institutions have become increasingly interested in exploring the potential to develop international alliances (such as the Universitas 21 and Worldwide Universities Network), as well as different business models for distance learning (Guri-Rosenbilt, 2005).

Carr-Chellman cites a number of overarching themes in relation to considering e-learning. The first is 'open access' and the notion that ICTs have the potential to provide educational opportunities across all aspects of society, leading to a greater massification of education, which in turn will lead to enhanced economic development. The second theme is the shift towards 'individualization, customization and globalization', although she notes that one of the concerns with this shift is that globalization might lead to the eradication of local culture with a global, predominantly Westernized hegemony. Finally she notes the tension between public versus corporate funding to support e-learning developments, with the latter being driven by business imperatives rather than educational goals.

Within the policy rhetoric a number of perceived benefits of e-learning are evident. First, it is seen as offering the potential to provide new forms of provision, new models of delivery and the development of new niche markets. Second, it is cited as having the potential to widen access, provide more personalized learning opportunities and offer new business models for educational provision through the creation of different types of distance-based and blended learning courses. Third, it is offered as a solution to meet the needs of both 'traditional' educational offerings and as a mechanism for continuing professional education, just-in-time training and lifelong learning. However, not everyone valorizes the potential of e-learning; there are a number of perceived disadvantages being voiced. First, there are those that are concerned with the potential dumbing down of education and the production of 'digital mills' as a result of unregulated expansion and inclusion of e-learning (Hansson, 2005; Noble, 1998). Second, there are issues about individual rights and privacy within an online environment, where sophisticated surveillance and monitoring tools are now emerging. Third, many are simply concerned that academic staff lack the necessary skills to take advantage of e-learning and that current institutional structures and processes are inadequate.

This introductory section has set the scene in terms of the wider context within which e-learning policy directives operate and has attempted to give an indication of some of the overarching themes with respect to this context. The next section considers specific policy directives across six very different national contexts, before concluding with some overarching themes and issues for research which emerge from this review.

INTERNATIONAL CASE STUDIES OF THE IMPACT OF POLICY DIRECTIVES ON EDUCATIONAL PRACTICE

Policy directives in the UK

E-learning is a central aspect of UK policy, a fact that is reflected in the range of funding initiatives specifically focusing on the development and use of e-learning. Conole, Smith *et al.* (2007) provide a critique of the relationship between policy and practice in e-learning in the UK. This critique is contextualized in terms of the relationship between e-learning and other current policy directives such as widening participation, accessibility and quality assurance. Conole, Smith *et al.* extend Smith's (2005) earlier work that reviewed e-learning policy in the UK over the past forty years, tracing the development of the area from the Flowers Report (1965), which was the first policy paper that discussed the use of computers in higher education. Conole, Smith *et al.* divide the policy arena into four time frames.

- The first (1965–79) was dominated by centralized mainframe computers, operated by computer experts who acted essentially as gatekeepers to the technology; users were mainly scientists undertaking large-scale number-crunching applications.
- The second phase (1980–89) saw the introduction of desktop computers, the use of computers as office tools and the emergence of software for teaching and learning. What was evident from initiatives in this phase was that they were characterized by two things: the exploration of the potential of technologies through the 'let a thousand flowers bloom' approach and the emergence of a complementary dissemination mechanism through the establishment of a network of subject-based centres providing support and advice on the use of ICT.
- The third phase (1990–99) continued the exploration of the potential of technologies in terms of their use in learning and teaching, aided by significant funding initiatives such as the Teaching and Learning Technology programme (TLTP). The emergence of the Internet had wide-ranging implications across all aspects of institutions and enabled practitioners to explore the potential of Internet technologies for supporting online collaboration and communication. This period demonstrated that e-learning initiatives were moving from being considered as peripheral innovations to affecting all aspects of learning and teaching. There was the start of evidence of a better consolidation at national level with the introduction of more coherent programmes.
- The fourth phase (2000 – present) showed evidence of consolidation of the area with the emergence of more coherent strategic discourse at a national level, better engagement with technologies within institutions and the development of national e-learning strategies (HEFCE, 2004; DfES, 2004).

What is evident from this overview of activities in the UK is that there is a fairly coherent relationship between policy directives (and associated funding) and e-learning practice. This is in part a consequence of the reasonably small size of the UK but is also related to the associated infrastructure available to support these developments – both at the policy level (for example, funding is directed through a number of core funding bodies such as the Higher Education Funding Council for England (HEFCE) and the Joint Information Systems Committee (JISC)), and through the associated professional bodies and support mechanisms available for the sector (such as the Association of Learning Technology, http://www.alt.ac.uk, and the Higher Education Academy and associated subject centres, http://heacademy.ac.uk).

Policy directives in mainland Europe

Social inclusion is at the heart of much of the rhetoric behind European policy directives (Carr-Chellman, 2005). A central issue for Europe is that of language and local culture and how these can be maintained in an increasingly English-language-dominated online environment.

The European e-learning developments are driven by the European Frameworks Programme. Research activities are structured around consecutive four-year programmes, or so-called Framework Programmes. The Sixth Framework Programme (FP6) set the priorities for the period 2002–06, with a stated vision of 'anywhere anytime natural access to IST services for all' (see http://cordis.europa.eu/ist/activities/activities.htm). It focused on four main themes: (1) applying IST research that addressed major societal and economic challenges, (2) communication, computing and software technologies, (3) components and microsystems, and (4) knowledge and interface technologies.

The rhetoric behind this vision is that Information Society promises potentially significant benefits for Europe's economy and society and that to achieve this it is important that Information Society projects are linked to relevant European policies: 'The information society by its very nature cuts across traditional boundaries' (European Commission, 2001). As part of this initiative a detailed audit was carried out mapping projects against key areas of policy: European society, governance, competitiveness, sustainable development, research and innovation and international developments. Following on from these themes, there is a raft of technological and educational programmes such as Socrates, Leonardo da Vinci, Youth, MINERVA and IST (see European Commission and associated links). Across these programmes is the concept of recognition of the importance of lifelong learning, the development of the work force and social inclusion through educational use of ICT and dissemination of good practice. Together these projects have generated significant outputs in terms of innovations in the use of technology. One disadvantage is that the complexity and array of these different initiatives and their objectives are daunting and militate against a cohesive overall picture of ICT developments in Europe.

These ICT directives sit within a wider policy context in Europe. Of particular importance is the EU's action plan – the Lisbon strategy – which focused in particular on innovation as a key agent for economic change, the learning economy and social/environmental renewal. A central tenet is that in an emerging knowledge-based society success depends crucially on realizing human potential and that this will require a fundamental transformation of education. E-learning is clearly evident throughout the surrounding policy rhetoric as a key means of achieving this transformation as is evident from the following (European Commission, n.d.: 2):

> The boundaries of learning are changing all the time. Technological developments such as the Internet, mobile communications and virtual environments, create possibilities to support learning in new ways. In addition, our definitions of learning are changing, as we gain new insights into how people learn and what they need to learn to adapt to changing economic and social conditions.

Policy directives in the US

In contrast to the common vision presented in the rhetoric from Europe, the US adopts a more fragmented approach driven by local agendas, complex partnerships and business imperatives. In many respects the US provides a snapshot of the myriad of different policy directives evident in other countries. Much of the discourse talks of the potential of e-learning in offering greater access, flexibility and cost efficiency; however, there are also concerns that e-learning is pedagogically unproven and that it raises fundamental issues about quality control and mechanisms for federal funding (Kumar *et al.*, 2005). E-learning is seen as providing opportunities for both career development and lifelong learning.

There is no central funding directive or programme for e-learning across the US as there is in the UK or mainland Europe. Harley (2004: 1) states that:

> Within the United States there is a fair amount of *ad hoc* policy at the state and institutional levels. At the national level the traditional 'Big 6' nonprofit associations find themselves challenged to compete with for-profit associations and corporations ...

Byers *et al.* (2002) argue that e-learning policy is not just created by government agencies but is significantly influenced by educational institutions and associated professional associations. They argue that the influence of each of these is subtly different. Educational institutions usually focus at state or regional level in a practical, pragmatic way; professional bodies generally influence through overarching recommendations or policy standards; while government agencies provide opportunities through funding programmes and in particular targeted, specialized programmes.

Nowhere else in the world is e-learning seen as such a commodity as in the US (Byers *et al.*, 2002, Newman, 2000). Byers *et al.* (2002) point to concerns of a shift towards too much of a market-driven perspective, concerned primarily with 'bottom-line profit' rather than the needs of students. Numerous reports have suggested that e-learning is one of the fastest-growing sectors of education, with over 80 per cent of all two- and four-year colleges offering distance learning courses (Byers *et al.*, 2002; Thompson, 2000). Policy documents and rhetoric are peppered with reference to the commercial opportunities and potential of e-learning. The range of types of provision is complex and closely aligned to local needs and institutional strategies; these include non-profit and for-profit degree granters, co-operative universities, partnership consortia and new forms of delivery driven by emerging technologies (Kumar *et al.*, 2005; Harley, 2004; Waight *et al.*, 2002; Newman, 2000; Thompson, 2000). Eaton (2001) argues that distance learning is creating alternative models of education, new roles and new types of providers. She cites three types: credit-bearing institutions, new providers (such as free-standing online institutions, higher education consortia, corporate universities and unaffiliated online providers) and partnerships between institutions and the corporate sector.

At the same time the US is also the source of much of the forward thinking and visionary aspects of e-learning, with active communities of researchers (enabled through organizations such as The Alfred P. Sloan Foundation and the National Science Foundation) and evidence of providing leadership in a number of forward-thinking developments such as the increasing interest in open content (Hewlett Open Content Initiatives, Hewlett Foundation, n.d.), and the development of international technology standards and specifications, through organizations like the W3C consortium (www.w3.org), IEEE (www.ieee.org) and IMS (www.imsglobal.org).

New forms of organizations concentrating on distance learning provision include the Western Governors University, California Virtual Campus and Phoenix University, which aim to capitalize on the commercial potential of e-learning. (See http://www.adec.edu/virtual.html for a more comprehensive list of virtual universities.) Thompson categorizes some of this variety into conventional online courses, networked colleges, aligned systems, independent virtual universities, privatized non-credit courses and online proprietary training schools. He cites a number of examples, such as the Michigan Virtual University (MVU), that do not develop courses but instead offer a brokerage service, and the for-profit National Technological University (NTU), designed to develop non-degree products and market courses globally.

Thompson (2000) identified that states were using multiple strategies to exploit the potential of e-learning, including development of e-learning systems, assurance of quality and identification of associated governance issues (such as privacy and security). He describes a range of initiatives being implemented such as the development of digital libraries, development of tutor e-learning skills, infrastructure and financial incentives and the use of public–private partnerships.

E-learning initiatives are funded through a variety of both for-profit and not-for-profit bodies and only a selection of illustrative examples is provided here. The Sloan Foundation funds the Sloan-C consortium (www.sloan-c.org), which is designed to 'help learning organizations continually improve quality, scale, and breadth of their online programmes'. 'Five pillars' of e-learning (learning and cost effectiveness, faculty and student satisfaction, and access) are used as a means of communicating best practice through research findings, events and projects. In contrast the National Science Foundation (www.nsf.gov) is an independent federal agency that funds about 20 per cent of all federal-supported basic research in colleges and universities. E-learning is evident across a number of the research strands funded by NSF, in particular in relation to their cyber-infrastructure and digital libraries programmes. An interesting example of the latter is a US/UK digital libraries programme funded in conjunction with JISC. Two important examples of initiatives funded by the US Department of Education were the Distance Education Demonstration Program (DEDP) (http://www.ed.gov/programmes/disted/index.html) and the Learning Anywhere Anytime Partnerships (LAAP) (http://www.ed.gov/programs/fipselaap/). Under DEDP fifteen institutions were exempt from restrictions on financial aid in relation to virtual provision. The LAAP grants enabled partnerships to build and deliver distance programmes, exploring themes such as models of provision, identification and measurement of skills and innovative support services, plus the drawing out of evidence of best practice.

Carr-Chellman argues that a prevalent aspect of the political discourse in the US is technological determinism and states that 'In North America, the idea that we simply have to prepare our children for a technological society is nearly an unquestioned premise' (Carr-Chellman, 2005: 128). While there may be an element of truth in this, the reality will invariably be more complex and dependent on a number of other contextual factors, as the discussions throughout this chapter illustrate. Another dominant feature of developments in the US from the policy rhetoric is the economic imperative to commodify, package and sell learning online and to export educational provision abroad. This feature aligns with Hutton's argument that American culture is dominated by capitalism and belief in personal liberty and independence, which contrasts with Europe's roots in social democratization (Hutton, 2002). However, at the other end of the spectrum the issue of access and inclusion is also a central feature of US discourse. Byers *et al.* (2002) cite several examples of US initiatives that focus on access and inclusion, such as President Clinton's 'e-rate' affordable access to the Internet for public schools. More broadly, opinion on the extent of the digital divide is mixed – a World Bank report (OBHE, 2005) suggests that it is rapidly closing, whereas a UN report (United Nations, 2005) suggests that there are still huge disparities in access to and use of information technologies (see Haythornthwaite's chapter in this volume, pp. 97–118). Lenhart and Horrigan (2003) argue for re-visualizing it as a digital spectrum, suggesting that 'Internet access may be intermittent for some users, nearby for others … and a remote possibility for others.'

Policy directives in Australia

Australia, because of its size and dispersed population, has a long history of distance education. Australia shares much in common with both the UK and America; the predominant discourse in the development and use of e-learning is about independence and innovation. In 2002, the Australian government commissioned two important reports – one summarizes ICT policy in Australia (Kearns and Grant, 2002), and the second provides an international comparison (Kearns, 2002).

These reports suggest that there has been a strengthening of partnerships to meet the challenges of ICT in Australia; these include collaborations between the States, Territories and Commonwealth and in the development of a national action plan for ICT in education and the Le@rning Federation. An important example of partnerships in Australia is the emergence of international consortia, some of which are linked with commercial partners. The best known of these is Universitas 21; interestingly such international consortia are also evident elsewhere – the UK has led the development of the Worldwide Universities Network (http://www.wun.ac.uk), for example; others include the Global University Alliance (Aoki, 2004) and CEVU (http://www.cevu.org/).

As in the UK, the quality assurance agenda is an important driver; Oliver (2005) recently undertook a comparison of quality assurance approaches in the UK and Australia. He compared the QAA in the UK with the Australian University Quality Agency (AUQA), which acts under the authority of the Commonwealth government and conducts regular quality audits, providing public reports on the quality assurance arrangements of self-accrediting higher education institutions in Australia.

An initiative that illustrates the cross-institutional approach being adopted in Australia is the CAUDIT programme aiming to disseminate and promote good practice in the use of ICT across universities. Examples of specific strategic interventions include RMIT's top-down/bottom-up approach (McNaught and Kennedy, 2000), as well as the University of South Australia's Teaching and Learning framework and the University of Wollongong's Digital Media Centre, which are both quoted in the review by Kearns and Grant (2002). An example of Australian activities in terms of cross-institutional staff development and evaluation activities is the CUTSD project. Funded by the Australian government Committee for University Teaching and Staff Development (CUTSD) it consisted of a series of staff development projects evaluating the use of ICT and involved forty-one staff supported by eleven mentors.

Kearns and Grant (2002) make a number of observations about ICT developments in Australia. First, that Australia has been particularly active in terms of cross-institutional collaboration and the development of cross-sector partnerships. Second, that there has been an emergence of what they referred to as 'whole-of-government' strategic framework that they argue has led to the mainstreaming of ICT policy in education. However they conclude by stating that 'whilst there has been significant policy development for ICT in education … there is further work to be done if … education and training is to be transformed to enhance the achievements of the knowledge society'.

Policy directives in China

China is experiencing an intense period of change and this is particularly evident in education. China has put in place an ambitious programme for change in education, within which e-learning is seen as playing a central role.

However, such a change must be understood within the context within which it is taking place. China's educational approach is radically different from Western notions of education, being firmly rooted in the traditions of Confucianism. There is a complex relationship between power and cultural tradition within the context of China wanting to be a global world leader. As part of this aspiration there is a need to increase the skills of the work force – education and in particular e-learning are seen as central to this process – as is evident in the policy directives outlined here and in particular the e-learning policy directives outlined by Feiyu and Gilsun (forthcoming).

ICT has been a central part of government rhetoric for a long time, with a focus on providing an ICT infrastructure across the whole country; ICT developments in China are very much driven by top-down directives. This approach is echoed by the following UNESCO Web site (UNESCO) statement 'The Chinese government believes that modernisation of education by applying information technology, a process referred to as educational "informationisation" is essential in order to transform the heavy population burden into valuable human resources.' Huang and Zhaung (forthcoming) and Feiyu and Gilsun (forthcoming) provide an overview of e-learning in China, the implementation of a technological infrastructure for China and the phenomenal growth in the number of students entering education. China is also experiencing the highest broadband subscription increase in the world; one-third of the broadband development in China is now attributed to the education sector. The massive growth in broadband take-up has the potential to increase the sharing of knowledge, resources, interactivity and communication in teaching and teacher training.

Conole and Dyke (forthcoming) explore Chinese policy directives. They cite the fact that the Chinese government is planning to improve compulsory education throughout China through curriculum reform aimed at moving from a model of knowledge transfer and testing to a more student-centred approach that promotes lifelong learning, problem solving, team building and communication. An example of this is the UK–Sino initiative e-China (http://www.echinaprogramme.org/), which consists of collaborative UK/Chinese teams developing innovative e-learning courseware to train teachers (at secondary and tertiary levels).

Policy directives in Africa

Policy in Africa is dominated by the continent's strive towards development, amidst a complex and mixed cultural heritage. Mackintosh (2005) notes that Africa faces challenges of immense proportions and complexity and ICT is seen as offering unprecedented opportunities in terms of access, cost and quality of education. The overarching aim is massification of education, which is seen as the key catalyst for change.

One of the most ambitious projects is the African Virtual University (http://www.avu.org/), which aims to 'build capacity and support economic development by leveraging the power of modern telecommunications technology to provide world-class quality education and training programmes to students and professionals in Africa'. It is funded by the World Bank and now has over fifty-seven Learning Centres in twenty-seven African countries. Africa's vision is to 'lead from behind'. Mackintosh (2005) suggests that within this context 'new technologies provide a vehicle to "leapfrog" legacy communication infrastructure.' Indeed, Africa instigated the first large-scale distance education institution with the formation of the University of South Africa as long ago as the 1940s. A central issue for Africa will be to develop an ICT infrastructure in rural locations, where basic amenities (such as water, electricity and transport infrastructure) are inadequate.

CATEGORIES OF E-LEARNING INTERVENTIONS

This section provides a summary of the nature of these types of intervention, before concluding the chapter by considering in what ways e-learning policy actually impacts on and changes practice. Kearns (2002) notes that countries progress through a number of phases in their implementation of ICT policy. The first is concerned with the roll-out of technologies and associated staff development. The second shifts to mainstreaming, integration and adoption of a more strategic approach. He asserts that the third phase is about moving towards a more radical transformation of the way people learn, arguing that, although no country is yet at this stage, a number are on the threshold.

Conole, Oliver *et al.* (2007) argue that associated with the increased impact of e-learning there have been a range of interventions; some concentrate on the technical or educational aspects, while others focus on policy developments, staff development or changing organizational structures. They have categorized e-learning interventions into three main types (educational, technological and organizational); examples of these are evident across the international case studies described above.

Education interventions primarily focus on the development of innovative approaches to teaching and learning. These developments may be funded through national bodies (such as NSF in the US, JISC in the UK and the European Framework in mainland Europe) or through industrial or institutional funding. Many institutions, for example, have set up funds to enable practitioners to experiment with the use of technologies in their practice and to report back their evaluation findings. Although funding for these kinds of initiatives is often quite modest, their impact on institutional change can be far-reaching.

Initiatives that are essentially about staff development also fall into this category (again either funded externally or within institutions); examples include initiatives that enable the development of support materials or workshops for effective use of technologies or institutional 'show and tell' conferences; or themed learning and teaching semesters to promote dissemination of activities across an institution. The EU has been particularly strong in providing funding for the development of networks, such as the Kaleidoscope network (http://www.noe-kaleidoscope.org/), NETTLE (http://www.nettle.soton.ac.uk:8082/) and the UNFOLD consortium (http://www.unfold-project.net:8085/UNFOLD). One of the most common types of educational intervention is an approach based on providing small grants to enable practitioners to explore the use of learning technologies in their teaching. White (forthcoming) notes many institutions are engaged in this type of small-scale experimentation whereas large-scale systematic interventions are less common.

Technological interventions are those that are primarily driven by either the development or implementation of technologies. Examples include the increased interest across the sector in the past decade in the use of Learner Management Systems, Virtual Learning Environments and Managed Learning Environments. A number of institutions have invested significantly in this area, instigating campus-wide initiatives, particularly in terms of adoption of two of the key international commercial packages, WebCT and Blackboard (which have now merged). Most institutions, however, have adopted a more cautious approach to the introduction of VLEs, usually letting practitioners decide the extent to which they wanted to use VLE in their teaching.

Some institutions have concentrated on particular types of technological use, for example, Loughborough University in the UK has implemented an institution-wide use of Computer Assisted Assessment (CAA), exploring the potential of CAA for summative assessment (Danson, 2003). Recently activities have shifted to the implementation of institution-wide Managed Learning Environments as well as the use of open source approaches. For example, the Open University is integrating an open-source VLE with its existing administrative and e-learning systems with the aim of providing a fully integrated online learning experience for the student.

Kumar (2005) describes MIT's announcement of the OpenCourseWare initiative, which involved MIT making the content of over 700 of its courses available free on the Web. He quotes Vest as saying:

> OpenCourseWare looks counter-intuitive in a market-driven world. It goes against the grain of current material values. But it really is consistent with what I believe is the best about MIT. It is innovative. It expresses our belief in the way education can be advanced – by constantly widening access to information and by inspiring others to participate.

The JISC in the UK funded a major programme focusing on technological interventions, through its Managed Learning Environment programme. The lessons learnt from the projects are summarized by Conole, Oliver *et al.* (2007). The overarching finding was that organizations are complex and multi-faceted; that successful e-learning implementation is dependent on context and that human and organizational issues, rather than technological ones, are usually the main barriers to success.

Organizational interventions tend to be either top-down, directed through the formulation and implementation of strategies (such as e-learning, teaching and learning, or information strategies), or in response to external requirements (such as quality assurance). Often strategic interventions follow a top-down/bottom-up mixed-mode approach to intervention of the type described by McNaught and Kennedy (2000). Salmon (2005) describes an institution-wide implementation which draws on the development and use of an appropriate e-learning strategic framework. Using the metaphor of flight, she suggests that in terms of e-learning 'the introduction of ICT into the world of learning and teaching in universities is now in transition from "flapping" to mass take-off'. She goes on to describe the approach adopted at the University of Leicester that consists of a four-quadrant framework which takes account of integration of both mainstream and peripheral technologies. Quality assurance is an important example of an externally imposed intervention. Oliver (2005) provides a comparison of quality assurance activities in the UK and Australia and contends that there are two main ways by which the quality of a process or activity can be assessed, through benchmarking or by the specification of standards.

IMPACT

This section considers the way in which e-learning developments (as instantiated in practice driven by policy directive) have an impact on higher education, in particular considering the longer-reaching consequences of these factors. A number of ways in which e-learning development has an impact on practice are evident from this review of international policy directives in e-learning and can be categorized as follows:

- Local culture versus global hegemony
- Urban versus rural developments
- Commercial imperatives versus government directives
- Funding models
- Complexity and change management
- Changing roles and organizational structures
- Research versus teaching
- Risk and unintended consequences
- Dissemination and impact
- Evaluation and reflection.

Figure 13.1 shows the relationship between the wider contextual factors which impact on education outlined at the beginning of the chapter, the resultant key drivers and examples of policy and related practice, and the consequential impact factors as described here.

Context

Globalization, dynamic environment, Information and networked society, changing social norms and values

Drivers

Widening participation, e-learning, accessibility, economic developments, workforce development, lifelong learning, quality assurance, commercial imperative, democratization

Policy	Practice
UK: fifteen ICT recommendations (NICHE, 1497), 'let 1000 flowers bloom'	UK: TLTP projects, CTI network, HE Academy JISC ICT programmes
EU: framework programmes; vision – significant impact across all aspects of society	EU: EUMEDIS – developing ICT in the Mediterranean region, IST programme
US: fragmented policy, driven by individual and commercial imperatives	US: education/industry partnerships, learning as commodity, open courseware initiative
Australia: learning for knowledge society	Australia: from roll-out to mainstreaming; partnerships
China: government-directed, open access and massification	China: Sino-UK e-China programme, developing ICT across country, education for all
Africa: leading from behind	Africa: African Virtual University

Impact

Local culture versus global hegemony, urban versus rural, commercial versus government, funding models, complexity and change management, changing roles and structures, conflicting demands, risks and consequences, dissemination and impact, evaluation and reflection

Figure 13.1 Drivers, policy, practice and impact in e-learning

Local culture versus global hegemony

No more is the impact of e-learning more evident than in relation to the tension between individualization/local culture and global hegemony. On the one hand the communicative dimensions of the Internet offer unprecedented opportunities for global reach and access, development of new forms of collaboration and virtual communities. The new communicative possibilities have the potential to preserve and develop local cultures and communities. However, many are increasingly concerned with the insidious domination of the Internet by Western norms and the emergence of English as the *de facto* language of communication. Furthermore, it could be argued that even the structure and layout of the Internet are culturally loaded and biased towards Western ideals. However, to counteract these issues, a number of countries, particularly in Europe, have prioritized the importance of linking ICT and culture, seeing technologies as a mechanism for preserving local culture and making cultural heritage more accessible.

Urban versus rural developments

The case studies in Carr-Chellman's (2005) book repeatedly demonstrate the differences in the application of e-learning in rural and urban settings. These differences are particularly prevalent in fast-developing areas such as China and Africa. The difference between rural and urban populations is evident in a number of respects; rural communities in developing countries tend to have very poor basic infrastructure (down to the level of water, electricity and transport infrastructure) as compared with their urban counterparts. Educational levels can also be dramatically lower in rural communities where basic survival rather than educational advancement may be the priority. This difference highlights the much quoted digital divide (see Haythornthwaite in this volume, pp.97–118), with rural communities being patently unprepared in terms of either technological or educational readiness to embrace the potential of e-learning – an ironic state of affairs, given the rhetoric which surrounds e-learning as being one of the principal drivers for widening access and increasing societal equity.

Commercial imperatives versus government directives

Another emerging feature from the examples cited in this chapter is the tension between e-learning developments that are driven by commercial imperatives and those that emerge from government directives or more socially oriented drivers. Indeed, this tension echoes Carr-Chellman's statement that the rhetoric underlying e-learning is either for-profit or based on open access and democracy.

Commercial drivers clearly focus on associated economic models and the protection of copyright and intellectual property rights. However, the economics of the Internet is by no means clear-cut (as the dot-com bubble in the 1990s demonstrated) particularly given the Internet's roots as a free, interconnected global resource.

Partnerships are one mechanism adopted by a number of countries for implementing change in the use of ICT. Kearns (2002) suggests that these include new forms of public/private partnership, educational cross-sector collaboration, local and regional community partnerships and innovative partnerships in federal systems.

Funding models

The scale of funding and the model of funding adopted have a direct impact on the nature of developments undertaken, and on their long-term sustainability. Funding for e-learning that is based on a short-term model tends to militate against long-term sustainability and limits the degree to which e-learning can become embedded within institutions. As Conole, Smith *et al.* (2007) argue, this short-term approach dictates not only what can be achieved but what can be promised within such time scales and who can undertake the work. Furthermore they argue that internal cohesiveness and collegiality, necessary for successful embedding of e-learning, are not favoured by the short-term approach. Such short-termism militates against the development of longer-term and more reflective research. This type of short-term funding mechanism is common in the UK, Europe and North America – where funding is provided by a range of funding bodies with conflicting agendas and interests. Researchers have to adapt their interests to fit in with the funders' imperatives if they are to be successful in securing funding. A different model may be evident in countries that have more of a centralized, government-directed drive to funding. Such systems may be seen, for example, in the funding models in China and Africa.

Complexity and change management

An inherent characteristic of ICT is the exponential pace of change and its consequential impact on education, the economy and society more broadly. E-learning is complex and multi-faceted; e-learning developments – whether small- or large-scale – have a raft of implicit and explicit consequences across an institution. Many believe that e-learning initiatives need to be undertaken by multidisciplinary teams, drawn from across the institution (educationalists, technologists, subject specialists and support staff). At the heart of the success of such teams are the adoption and management of a collaborative approach; however, successful collaboration is notoriously difficult. The complex nature and importance of collaboration are key features of learning technology work that have long been recognized. E-Learning has been cited by many as a key catalyst of change in higher education – in part because it makes visible good (and bad) existing practices and raises more general questions about the whole learning, teaching and assessment process. But change is complex and needs to be managed. Models of change management abound and a number have been specifically adapted and applied to e-learning developments, with varying degrees of success. However, Kearns (2002: 4) concludes in his review that 'traditional top-down ICT policies are too slow and no longer work in the turbulent context of an information society'.

Changing roles and organizational structures

One of the most evident indicators of the impact of technology is the way in which professional roles are changing (Conole, Oliver *et al.*, 2007, Oliver, 2002, Gosling, 2001). Evidence of such impact includes the emergence of new roles as a consequence of the development and implementation of learning technologies, as well as changes in existing roles.

A review by Conole (2006) demonstrates how even simple tools such as Microsoft Word have had a dramatic impact on practice. The most obvious example of such change is the demise of the secretary, as there is now no longer a need for dictating and typing. The funding opportunities and subsequent developments in e-learning have led to changes in traditional roles with educational institutions – both in support services and in academia.

Job titles and structural units within support services, for example, have been in a constant state of flux in the last few decades as institutions struggle to keep up with the impact of changing technologies and try to introduce appropriate structures and roles to provide support for teaching and research activities within the institution. In many countries, particularly in the West, the 1990s saw the emergence of new support units to provide support to staff on using technologies. However, there was no consistency in terms of either the location or the status of such units – some were located in central information services, others in educational development centres, whilst others still were located in academic departments; institutional 'learning technologists' ranged in status from senior management positions to lower-level support service roles. Furthermore there were differences that reflected the predominant teaching and learning paradigms within each country; for example, the US often had instructional design units whereas in the UK the focus tended to be more on educational development.

Academic roles have also changed. There is greater expectation of evident outcomes and productivity; demonstration of worth through peer-reviewed publications and success in competitive funding for research projects. Lifelong security is no longer guaranteed; there has been an increase in the number of research contract staff and short-term contracts. Managerial-speak has crept into the academy; there is increased emphasis on structures and line management, on overall project management and deliverables. As Conole, Oliver *et al.* (2007) state, 'academics are less likely to view themselves simply as researchers, but are instead required to undertake a multifunctional role with an emphasis on research, teaching and attracting external funding through grants or consultancy'.

E-learning has also had an impact at the organizational level. Conole, Oliver *et al.* (2007) describe a range of approaches that have been adopted to manage the organizational change that arises as a result of the introduction of new technologies. These include those which focus on the impact of learning technologies (Timmis *et al.*, 2003; Beetham *et al.*, 2001); those which focus at the strategic level (Salmon, 2005; McNaught, 2002); or others highlighting support and staff development issues (Oliver and Dempster, 2003; Smith and Oliver, 2000).

Conflicting demands: research versus teaching

Successful implementation of e-learning requires time and investment. Who should undertake this work and for what reward? In many cases to date e-learning developments have been undertaken by academics (or at least by mixed teams which include academics). This clearly creates a tension: academics are expected to undertake both teaching and research. However, in many institutions research output is significantly prized over teaching and learning. Therefore where are the incentives for investing in e-learning when there are few evident benefits?

Risks and unintended consequences

Given the pace of change of technologies there is a raft of risks associated with e-learning developments and resultant unintended consequences. Conole and Dyke (2004) warn that the pace of change 'leaves no space for contemplation and considered judgement, and promotes a more pragmatic, reflexive immediate response to new information'. They go on to argue that technologies have not necessarily been taken up or used in the ways originally intended. For example, they cite the fact that the increase in the volume of information available on the Web has led to new forms of plagiarism, and that e-mail has resulted in increasing commercial exploitation and unwelcome mail. They also argue that new technologies present new forms of surveillance, citing Land and Bayne (2005), who have critiqued the inclusion of monitoring tools within virtual learning environments that mean teachers have the power to monitor student activities more closely than ever before and the fact that these tools means that practitioners can also be surveyed and/or made to comply with institutional norms, which in turn raises issues about the nature of the professional roles/identities and the trust relationship within institutions.

Dissemination and impact

Another aspect which impacts on how successful an e-learning initiative is, or is perceived to be, is the degree to which it is visible and accessible to relevant stakeholders. It is encouraging to note that funders in many countries are more aware now of the importance of ongoing strategically directed dissemination of project outcomes. Many re-purpose research outputs to target the findings for particular audiences. Similarly, extensive use is now made of the medium itself as a dissemination vehicle, through information transmission via specialized mailing lists, online conferences and workshops, plus interactive toolkits providing guidance and support. The demonstration of impact is another important feature to have emerged. Of particular note is the fact that the NSF in the US now has a requirement for all projects that it funds to demonstrate explicitly the tangible benefits of and impact on the sector.

Evaluation and reflection

One of the key lessons that can be drawn from reviewing the relationship between policy, funding and practice as discussed in this chapter is the importance of setting in place formative evaluation mechanisms alongside initiatives so that individuals and the sector as a whole can critically reflect on the initiatives' impact and distil recommendations for future directions. Encouragingly, this message appears to be hitting home as most funding calls now have evaluation as a standard requirement of the workplan and many also put in place overarching external evaluations to draw out cross-programme lessons.

THE ROLE OF RESEARCH

This chapter has described some of key international policy directives concerned with e-learning and the way in which they impact on educational practice. What is evident is that higher education institutions operate in a complex environment, influenced by a range of often conflicting policy directives and external drivers. The situation is further complicated in that the pace of change of technology and its potential impact is phenomenal. E-learning offers the potential to create new and innovative educational provision and improve the student learning experience. However, *how* this can be achieved is not straightforward or obvious. Given this gap in knowledge, more research is needed to understand the context of modern education and analysis of associated policy, as well as research into understanding the ways in which technologies can be used to support education. The findings can then be used to both inform and shape future policy in this area and help to improve practice.

Research in e-learning covers a broad spectrum of issues: organizational, pedagogical and technical. The challenge in terms of policy is how to distil the findings emerging from this research so that they can impact on policy. However, much research in this area is primarily anecdotal and case-based, such that the findings are not scalable or transferable. There is a need for more meta-synthesis of findings to draw out key themes and translate these into practical guidelines to inform practice. The issues raised in this chapter highlight a plethora of research issues and questions, around the core themes that emerge as a result of linking policy and practice. What do the findings from an analysis of, say, a discussion forum in one institution mean in terms of policy directives? How can an understanding of the changing nature of technology developments be translated into tangible guidelines for institutions in terms of the development of their technical infrastructure to support learning? How can what we know about the changing skills base of teachers and learners inform staff development activities and the way in which learners are supported? Other themes to explore include:

- Are current intellectual property policies adequate to cover the implications of e-learning?
- How are governance issues (and in particular issues to do with privacy and individual rights) being addressed?
- How do e-learning policies and developments integrate with other policies (such as those concerned with access and inclusion, widening participation, development of the economy)?
- How are changing academic and student roles being addressed? What provision is being put in place to meet new and emerging literacy skills?
- What new markets and models for higher education might be appropriate to capitalize on the potential of e-learning and an increasingly competitive globalized environment?
- Recurrent trends in e-learning research include: the effectiveness of e-learning, academic and student-related issues, the impact on organizational structures and processes, and a host of associated issues such as quality mechanisms, privacy rights and security issues. How will these trends develop in the future, what new factors are likely to emerge and how can both be taken account of in policy directives?
- How can we ensure that policy makers are aware of and take account of the multitude of research activities in e-learning and how can we ensure the future research developments are of benefit to and feed into policy directives?

CONCLUSION

Conole, Smith *et al.* (2007) argue that it is evident that there has been an increased interest in the role of technology within education and policy directives over the last twenty years that, in turn, has led to funding opportunities that have provided opportunities to experiment with the development and use of e-learning in education. These e-learning focused policy directives and associated funding opportunities have led to better engagement of senior management and policy makers in considering ICT developments at an institutional and national level, although arguably they are still not making appropriate, informed decisions. The funding opportunities and the increased publicity of the importance of e-learning have led to an influx of researchers from different cognitive domains bringing together different theoretical models and ways of interpreting research findings. However, such a development is also problematic in that these researchers, as of yet, have no shared language or understanding and the area lacks good theoretical models to explain findings. It is hoped the present volume will provide the beginnings of such a common language.

Conole, Smith *et al.* (2007) go on to argue that any snapshot of change within an institution will be complex, with factors being co-dependent and interrelated. Policy makers need to have an understanding of the nature of each of these catalysts for change and the relationships between them. Examples in the current climate as discussed in this chapter include the quality assurance agenda, widening participation, lifelong learning, accessibility, skills and employability, the drive for research excellence and the development of enterprise activities. At a national level, strategic directives are driven through policy and more tangibly through targeted funding. E-learning in a number of countries – particularly the UK and mainland Europe – has had significant funding ring-fenced to increase its impact and promote innovation. There is a strong political rhetoric around e-learning but this is in many ways naïve, containing unrealistic expectations about potential. Decision making is often based on ill-informed perspectives of what is achievable and it seems that there needs to be a closer relationship between the nature of education, technology and sector-wide/institutional models or structures.

In reviewing policy and funding arrangements for this chapter, one thing is evident: that practice follows policy directives and the general trend of technological developments, rather than informing them. This suggests that research and development activities in this area are necessarily pragmatic rather than forward-thinking. Furthermore, the complexity of the area and the wealth of policy directives, initiatives and funding programmes make overall clear, coherent thinking difficult.

One of the key lessons to emerge from this review is that policy (and in particular associated funding) fundamentally and radically impacts on practice. As Conole, Smith *et al.* (2007) note:

> Time shows that sadly there has been too much evidence of knee-jerk policy that does not take account of evidence emerging from research. The demise of the UKeU[1] in the UK is the most publicly visible example of this. But many of us wonder about the tone of policy

documents in this area and that although these areas are filled with laudable aims and aspirations about the future use of technology, they leave one with an unease about how realistic this rhetoric is and how will it be achieved, with what level of resourcing.

The present chapter has demonstrated that there is a close relationship between policy and practice that is in turn driven by broader educational and technological factors. Numerous initiatives and funding programmes have focused on the development and use of learning technologies over the last two decades, resulting in significant changes within educational institutions and indeed impacting on society more broadly: increased uptake and use of learning technologies, impact on policy and strategy within institutions, as well as impacting on organizational structures and roles. The increased use of technologies has raised many new questions and issues. One of the most fundamental is that, given the interconnection of policy directions and subsequent impact on practice, what factors need to be taken into account to make appropriately informed policy decisions? This question is central if we are to see a better, more strategic and more targeted use of technologies in the future.

NOTE

1   UKeU: the UK e-University initiative.

REFERENCES

Amiel, T. and Sargent, S. L. (2003) 'Individual Differences in Internet Usage Motives'. Paper presented at the annual conference of the international Communication Association, San Diego, CA.

Aoki, K. (2004), 'Globalization of higher education through e-learning: case studies of virtual universities based on international collaboration of universities across national boundaries', *Journal of Mulitmedia Education Research*, 1: 99–105, available online at http://64.233.183.104/search?q=cache:G02quAViqbMJ:www.nime.ac.jp/journal/10aoki.pdf+international+university+consortia+GUA&hl=en, last accessed 31 August 2005.

Beck, U. (1992) *Risk Society: Towards a new Modernity*. London: Sage.

Beetham, H. (2002). 'The Learning Technology Career Development Scoping Study', available online at http://www.jisc.ac.uk/index.cfm?name=project_career, last accessed 29 July 2003.

Beetham, H., Jones, S. and Gornall, L. (2001) *Career Development of Learning Technology Staff: Scoping Study Final Report*. JISC Commutee for Awareness Liason and Training, available online at http://www.jisc.ac.uk/uploaded_documents/cdss_final_report_v8.doc (accessed 18 December 2006).

Byers, A., Lockee, B. *et al.* (2002) 'Distance education policy: facing the issues of access', *Australian Association for Institutional Research*, 11 (1).

Carr-Chellman, A. A. (ed) (2005) *Global Perspectives on e-Learning: Rhetoric and Reality*. London: Sage.

Castells, E. (1996) *The Information Age: Economy, Society and Culture* I. *The Rise of the Network Society*. Oxford: Blackwell.

CAUDIT, Council for Australian University Directors of Information Technology, available online at http://www.caudit.edu.au/, last accessed 21 September 2006.

Commission on Technology and Adult Learning (2000) A Vision of e-Learning for American's Workforce: Report of the Commission on Technology and Adult Learning, available online at http://www.masie.com/masie/researchreports/ELEARNINGREPORT.pdf (accessed 18 December 2006).

Conole, G. (2006) 'What impact are technologies having and how are they changing practice?', in I. McNay (ed.), *Beyond Mass Higher Education*. Slough: Society for Research into Higher Education; Buckingham: Open University Press. pp 81–95.

Conole, G. and Dyke, M. (2004) 'What are the affordances of information and communication technologies?', *ALT-J*, 12 (2), 113–24.

Conole, G. and Dyke, M. (2007) 'Complexity and interconnection: steering e-learning developments from commodification towards "co-modification"', in H. Spencer-Oatley (ed.), *Learning in China: e-China Perspectives on Policy, Pedagogy and Innovation*, Abingdon: RoutledgeFalmer.

Conole, G., Smith, J. and White, S. (2007) 'A critique of the impact of policy and funding', in G. Conole and M. Oliver (eds), *Contemporary Perspectives in e-learning Research: Themes, Tensions and Impact on Practice*. Abingdon: RoutledgeFalmer.

Conole, G., Oliver, M., Falconer, I., Littlejohn, A. and Harvey, J. (2007) 'The impact of e-learning on organisational roles and structures', in G. Conole and M. Oliver (eds), *Contemporary Perspectives in e-Learning: Research*. Abingdon: RoutledgeFalmer.

Council of European Union (2002) *Council Resolution on Lifelong Learning*, available online at http://europa.eu.int/eur-lex/pri/en/oj/dat/2002/c_163/c_16320020709en00010003.pdf, last accessed 20 September 2006.

CUTSD (n.d.) *Staff Development in Evaluation of Technology-based Teaching Development Projects*, available online at http://www.tlc.murdoch.edu.au/project/cutsd01.html, last accessed 31 August 2005.

Danson, M. (2003) 'Implementing Online Assessment in an Emerging MLE: a Generic Guidance Document with Practical Examples', JISC project report. Loughborough: University of Loughborough.

DfEE (1998) *The Learning Age: a Renaissance for a new Britain*, government Green Paper, available online at http://www.lifelonglearning.co.uk/greenpaper/, last accessed 31 August 2005.

DfES (2004) *Towards a Unified e-Learning Strategy*, DfES paper, available online at http://www.dfes.gov.uk/e-learningstrategy/, last accessed 31 August 2005.

DfES (2005) *DfES e-Learning Strategy: Harnessing Technology – Transforming Learning and Children's Services*, available online at http://www.dfes.gov.uk/publications/e-strategy, last accessed 31 August 2005.

Duderstadt, J. J. (2000) *The Future of Higher Education in the Knowledge-driven, Global Economy of the Twenty-first Century*, available online at http://milproj.ummu.umich.edu/publications/toronto/download/Toronto_103102.pdf#search=%22Duderstadt%20the%20future%20of%20higher%20education%20in%20the%20knowledge-driven%22, last accessed 21 September 2006.

Dyke, M. (2001) *Reflective Learning and Reflexive Modernity as Theory Practice and Research in Post-compulsory Education*. Guildford: Department of Education, University of Surrey.

Dyke, M., Conole, G., Ravenscroft, A. and de Freitas, S. (2007) 'Learning theory and its application to e-learning', in G. Conole and M. Oliver (eds), *Contemporary Perspectives in e-Learning Research: Themes, Tensions and Impact on Practice*. Abingdon: RoutledgeFalmer.

Eaton, J. S. (2001) *Distance Learning: Academic and Political Challenges for Higher Education Accreditation*, CHEA monograph series, available online at http://www.chea.org/Commentary/distance-learning/chea_dis_learning.pdf, last accessed 21 September 2006.

European Commission (2001) *eEurope: an Information Society for all. Making a European Area of Lifelong Learning a reality*, available online at http://ec.europa.eu/education/policies/lll/life/index_en.html, last accessed 22 September 2006.

European Commission (ND) *Information Society and Education: Linking European Policies*, available online at http://europa.eu.int/information_society/activities/policy_link/documents/leaflets/education.pdf, last accessed 21 December 2005.

Feiyu, K. and Gilsun S. (forthcoming) 'e-Learning in China: an overview', in H. Spencer-Oatley (ed.), *Learning in China: eChina Perspectives on Policy, Pedagogy and Innovation*. Abingdon: RoutledgeFalmer.

Flowers Committee (1965) 'Computers for research – a report of a working party for the University Grants Committee', UGC 7/635. London: HMSO.

Giddens, A. (2000) *Runaway World: How Globalization is Reshaping our Lives*. New York: Routledge.

Gosling, D. (2001) 'Educational development unit in the UK – what are they doing five years on?', *International Journal for Academic Development*, 6 (1): 74–90.

Government of Ireland (2003) *The Progress Report on the New Connections Action Plan*. Dublin: Government Publications Office.

Guri-Rosenbilt, S. (2005), '"Distance education" and "e-learning": not the same thing', *Higher Education*, 49, 467–93.

Hansson, H. (2005) *ICT and E-learning:, the Road to Hell or Paradise? The Need for a Strategic Thinking on Sustainable Digital Environment for E-learning*, available online at http://www.wanfangdata.com.cn/qikan/periodical.Articles/kfjyyj/kfjy2005/0503/050314.htm, last accessed 22 September 2006. *Open Educational Research* 11 (3).

Harley, D. (2004) 'Regulation of e-learning: new national and international policy perspectives: proposal to the ford foundation'. Regulation of e-Learning: New National and International Policy Perspectives.

HEFCE (2004) *Consultation on HEFCE e-learning strategy*, available from http://www.hefce.ac.uk, last accessed 21 September 2006.

Hewlett Foundation (n.d.) *Hewlett Open Education Content Initiatives*, available online at http://www.hewlett.org/Programs/Education/OER/openEdResources.htm, last accessed 22 September.

Huang, R. J. X. and Zhang, H. (forthcoming) 'Informatization in higher education', in H. Spencer-Oatley (ed), *Learning in China: e-China Perspectives on Policy, Pedagogy and Innovation*. Abingdon: RoutledgeFalmer.

Hutton, W. (2002) *The World we're in*. London: Abacus.

Kearns, P. (2002) *Towards the Connected Learning Society: An International Overview of Trends in policy for Information and Communication Technology in Education*, available online at http://www.dest.gov.au/NR/rdonlyres/7AC0E17C-C0C6-4BE3-9017-88CA7B983D42/1916/TowardstheConnectedLearningSociety.pdf, last acccessed 22nd September 2006.

Kearns, P. and Grant J. (2002) *The Enabling Pillars: Learning, Technology, Community and Partnership*, report on Australian policies for information and communication technologies in education and training, available online at http://www.dest.gov.au/sectors/higher_education/publications_resources/profiles/enabling_pillars_learning_technology_community_partnership.htm, last accessed 31 August 2005.

Kumar, M. S. V. (2005). 'Discussion piece: from open resources to educational opportunity', *ALT-J*, 13 (3): 241–7.

Kumar, V. J., Matkin, G. W. *et al.* (2005). *Regulation, e-Learning and the Changing Structures of Higher Education: A White Paper to Guide Discussion for the international seminar 'Regulation of E-Learning: New National and International Policy Perspectives'*, http://127.0.0.1:4664/redir?url=C%3A%5CDocuments+and+Settings%5Cgcc64%5CMy+Documents%5CGrainne%5CResearch%5CBooks%5CSage%5Cwhitepaper%5Fkumar%5Fmatkin%5Fgarrett%5F2005nov16%2Edoc&src=8&schema=6&start=0&s=AtZ8AdCfA1voWrdWaW4U24gYyn8, last accessed 31 August 2005.

Land, R. and Bayne S. (2005) 'Screen or monitor? Issues of surveillance and disciplinary power in online learning environments', in R. Land and S. Bayne (eds), *Ideas in Cyberspace*. Abingdon: RoutledgeFalmer.

Lash, S. and Urry, J. (1994) *Economics and Signs and Space*. London: Sage.

Lenhart, A. and Horrigan, J. B. (2003) 'Re-visualing the digital divide as a digital spectrum', *IT and Society*, 1 (5): 23–39.

Mackintosh, W. (2005) 'Can you lead from behind? Critical reflections on the rhetoric of e-learning, open distance learning and ICTs for development in sub-Saharan Africa', in A. A. Carr-Chellman (ed.), *Global Perspectives on e-Learning: Rhetoric and Reality*. London: Sage. pp. 222–40.

Mayes, J. T. (1995) 'Learning technology and groundhog day. Hypermedia at work: practice and theory in higher education', in W. Strang, V. B. Simpson and D. Slater (eds). Canterbury: University of Kent Press.

McNaught, C. and Kennedy, P. (2000) 'Staff development at RMIT: bottom-up work serviced by top-down investment and policy', *ALT-J*, 8 (1): 4–18.

Morgan, K. and Macleod, H. 91992) 'Results from Exploratory Investigations into the Possible Role of Personality Factors in Computer Interface Preference'. Best paper, Second Interdisciplinary Workshop on Mental Models, Robinson College, Cambridge.

Newman, F. (2000) *The Futures Project: Policy for Higher Education in a Competitive World*. Providence, RI: Futures Project.

Noble, D. (1998) *Digital Diploma Mills: The Automation of Higher Education*, available online at http://www.firstmonday.org/issues/issue3_1/noble/, last accessed 22 September 2006.

OBHE (2005) 'World Bank argues that the digitial divide is rapidly closing: as United Nations prepares to launch a costly ICT initiative in the developing world', Observatory on Borderless Higher Education.

OECD (1996) *Lifelong Learning for All*. Paris: OECD

Oliver, M. (2002) 'What do learning technologists do?', *Innovations in Education and Training International*, 39 (4): 245–52.

Oliver, M. and J. Dempster (2003) 'Strategic staff development for embedding e-learning practices in HE', in R. Blackwell and P. Blackmore (eds), *Towards Strategic Staff Development?* Buckingham: Society for Research into Higher Education and Open University Press.

Oliver, R. (2005) 'Quality assurance and e-learning: blue skies and pragmatism', *ALT-J*, 13 (3): 173–87.

QAA (2004) *Code of Practice for the Assurance of Academic Quality and Standards in Higher Education?* Section 2, 'Collaborative provision and flexible and distributed learning (including e-learning)', retrieved 31 August 2005, from http://www.qaa.ac.uk.com/academicinfrastructure/codeOfPractice/ sections2/collabo2004.pdf.

Salmon, G. (2005) 'Flying not flapping: a strategic framework for e-learning and pedagogical innovation in higher education institutions', *ALT-J*, 13 (3): 201–18.

Seale, J. (2006) Editorial and articles in special issue on accessibility, *ALT-J*, 14 (1).

Selwyn, N. and Gorard, S. (2003) 'Reality bytes: examining the rhetoric of widening educational participation via ICT', *British Journal of Educational Technology*, 34, 2: 169–81.

Simpson, O. (2005) 'E-learning, democracy and social exclusion: issues of access and retention in the United Kingdom', in A. A. Carr-Chellman (ed.), *Global Perspectives on e-Learning: Rhetoric and Reality*. London and New Delhi: Sage. pp. 89–100.

Smith, J. and Oliver, M. (2000) 'Academic development: a framework for embedding learning technology', *ALT-J*, 13 (1): 49–65.

Smith, J., (2005) 'From flowers to palms: forty years of policy for online learning', *ALT-J*, 13 (2): 93–108.

Thompson, C. (2000) 'The state of e-learning in the States', issues brief, National Governors Association, available online at http://www.nga.org/cda/files/060601E-LEARNING.pdf, last accessed 22 September 2006.

Timmis, S. (2003) *ELTI Workshop: Institutional Audits to inform the Embedding of Learning Technologies and promote Cross-boundary Working in our Institutions*, ALT-C 2003, workshop, Sheffield, available online at http://www.shef.ac.uk/alt/abstracts/90work/1/ws3-211.htm, last accessed 29 March 2006.

UNESCO (n.d.). UNESCO Web site, available online at http://www.unescobkk.org/index.php?id=1374, last accessed 31 August 2005.

United Nations (2005) *Global e-Government Readiness Report, 2005: from e-Government to e-Inclusion*, available online: http://unpan1.un.org/intradoc/groups/public/documents/un/unpan021888.pdf#search=%22Global%20e-Government%20readiness%20report%2C%202005%3A%20from%20e-Government%20to%20e-inclusion%22, last accessed 22 September 2006.

Virilio, P. (2000) *The Information Bomb*. London and New York: Verso

Waight, C. L., Willging, P. A. and Wentling, T. L. (2002) 'Recurrent Themes in e-Learning: a Meta-analysis of Major e-Learning Reports', available online at http://learning.ncsa.uiuc.edu/papers/AHRD2002_waight-willging-wentling.pdf#search=%22Recurrent%20themes%20in%20e-learning%3A%20a%20meta-analysis%20of%20major%20e-learning%20reports%22, last accessed 22 September 2006.

White, S. (2006) 'Higher Education and Learning Technologies: an Organisational Perspective', Ph.D. thesis. Electronics and Commuter Science. Southampton: University of Southampton.

14

Community-embedded Learning

Michelle M. Kazmer

E-learners are often described as sitting alone at their computer screens, working online with others, and in the best cases engaging interactively with their instructor and other students. Often overlooked is that learners, when they are at their computers and when they are not, are situated in a real world of colleagues, family, and community. This chapter discusses the benefits and experience of e-learning that is embedded in a local context, in particular in work and knowledge communities that complement the online learning. This *community-embedded learning* (CEL) is a rich feature of e-learning, too often ignored in the drive to create more sophisticated online environments.

The chapter starts by defining CEL and explaining its significant characteristics, continuing with a review of existing constructs such as situated learning, active learning, and reality-based learning and how these relate to CEL. This is followed by a discussion of the benefits and drawbacks of CEL. The chapter concludes by discussing emerging trends of research and practice associated with CEL.

While this chapter focuses exclusively on CEL in e-learning, CEL is not associated only with e-learning. CEL and associated concepts discussed later may also apply to on-campus, face-to-face, and other types of traditional and distance learning.

Primary and secondary students in the US traditionally remain in their communities while attending school; boarding schools have not been the primary mode of education at those levels. In the US, however, college is a time for young adults to go away from home and join a new community – the college campus – while (temporarily, at least) cutting ties to their home towns. Thus, in the US, the phenomenon of CEL via e-learning is most interesting to study at the college level and beyond, i.e., professional development, continuing education, and lifelong learning (e.g. Solem *et al.*, 2006).

In any setting, online continuing education for professionals is almost always CEL because such professionals usually have careers and are working to keep their certification and/or improve their services. Online learning in higher education, including postgraduate education, is often CEL because students who take advantage of e-learning are those who cannot or choose not to relocate to a campus. The degree to which students can apply course content directly depends on their involvement in activities related to what they are learning. These related activities are usually in the workplace, but may be in another local setting (volunteer, civic, religious) or another virtual setting (a virtual community).

COMMUNITY-EMBEDDED LEARNING

Community-embedded learning encompasses the knowledge built and applied by online learners who do not leave their home settings while taking e-learning courses (Kazmer, 2005a). CEL is predicated on ties students already have to their communities, with family and friends, memberships in clubs and social groups, and civic and volunteer activities (Kazmer and Haythornthwaite, 2001). Inherent to the definition of community embeddedness is that students are employed in workplaces in their communities, and the jobs they hold are often directly related to the academic degrees they are earning. In addition, the workplace is part of the local community and is shaped by the norms of the community. When students embedded in communities take courses at a distance, they bring what they learn in their courses into a community that they know well and that knows them. Taken together, these conditions define the concept I have named community-embedded learning, or CEL (Kazmer, 2005a).

The idea of embeddedness derives from Granovetter's (1985) concept developed to explain the relationship between (as per the title of his paper) 'economic action and social structure'. Granovetter found the need for an embeddedness construct to avoid what he identifies as two 'theoretical extremes' (p. 487) that had influenced the scholarly analysis of human actions. The first extreme is 'under-socialization', a perspective that assumes individual actors make decisions and behave outside a social context. The other extreme is 'over-socialization' in which individual actors are assumed to 'adhere slavishly to a script written for them by the particular intersection of social categories that they happen to occupy' (p. 487). The embeddedness concept avoids under-socialization by acknowledging that humans are 'closely embedded in networks of interpersonal relations' (p. 504) that provide a social context to their actions. Granovetter argues that embeddedness also avoids over-socialization by acknowledging that decisions are contingent and occur within changing networks of social relations rather than being influenced by an unchanging 'generalized morality' (p. 493). While Granovetter's argument is made within the field of economics, he concludes by saying he 'believe[s] this [i.e., embeddedness] to be so for all behaviour.' Thus the current discussion of community-embedded learning uses embeddedness to combine a review of the empirical research and practice of e-learning to explain an association between e-learning and social structure.

Using the term 'community' can confuse discussions of e-learning because it may be unclear when 'community' refers to a local physical community and when it refers to an online or virtual community of learners (Barab *et al.*, 2002). To reduce confusion about what constitutes 'community' in CEL, different terms are used to distinguish the students' local communities from the shared experience they engage in with their fellow online learners. Community-embedded students form an online learning *social world* in which members communicate with one another and share activities, technology, and space (Strauss, 1978). Students in the e-learning social world create friendships, provide emotional support, work together, study together, and develop future professional networks. Throughout this chapter, this distinction is maintained (Barab, 2003): students are members of a local *community* and of an online learning *social world*.

The framework of CEL is established via the transfers of knowledge that occur between social world members and the local community. Five major types of transfer (Kazmer, 2005a) can be identified in community-embedded learning:

- *Community knowledge to social world*: knowledge and information that the individual learners, from their embedded positions, provide to other individuals with whom they take courses and to the learning world in general.
- *Course knowledge to workplace*: students take delivered course content and their collaboratively built knowledge and apply them to the workplaces in which they are embedded.
- *Social world contacts to home community*: the connection of weak ties, or indirect contacts shared from community to community through the students' social world. This array of weakly tied people is specifically characteristic of community-embedded learners, because their local community ties are constant and ongoing.
- *Course knowledge to home community*: e-learning taken from specific courses, and knowledge shared by the learning social world as a whole, are brought by embedded individuals into home, social, educational, civic, and other non-work activities.
- *Institutional connections*: e-learning CEL provides institutions of higher learning with opportunities to build relationships with communities and other institutions in ways not possible before.

These five types of transfers occur when students interact frequently with one another and with their teachers primarily in the e-learning mode, using many technologies to communicate individually and in groups. Students also communicate with others locally using a combination of face-to-face and mediated communication (Fuller and Soderlund, 2002; Haythornthwaite and Kazmer, 2004). Settings in which interactions between the e-learning social world and the local community are encouraged are also referred to as 'community-centred' learning environments (Bransford *et al.*, 2000; Swan, 2005). In such settings students may be said to occupy a 'hybrid space', defined by Harrison and Dourish (1996: 72) as a space 'which comprises both physical and virtual space, and in action is framed simultaneously by the physical space, the virtual space, and the relationship between the two'. In CEL each student is embedded in a proximate local setting with associated physical limitations and cultural norms while simultaneously engaged in an e-learning setting online (Kazmer, 2005b).

This type of interactive learning draws on the tradition of active learning and constructivism. Swan (2005) traces the development of constructivism through the scholarship of Piaget (cognitive constructivism), Papert (constructionism), Vygotsky, Bruner and Dewey (social constructivism), and Leonte'ev (learning situated in activity structures). In turn, she ties constructivist theory to community-centred learning by concluding that 'constructivist theory views learning as … a social activity. It situates learning in communities and cultures. Thus constructivist approaches emphasize the importance of designing learning environments that are also community centred' (p. 21). Swan goes on to describe two types of community-centred design. The first type focuses on the development of a 'learning community' that allows the 'social construction of knowledge' among students (p. 21). The second type addresses 'the degree to which it [the learning environment] connects to students' larger community and culture' (p. 21). This second type of community learning directly overlaps with the concept of CEL because it focuses on connecting and linking students' learning to their local communities.

COGNATE AREAS ASSOCIATED WITH CEL

Situated learning

According to Lave and Wenger (1991), situated learning is the process of becoming a member of a Community of Practice (CoP) via Legitimate Peripheral Participation (LPP). A community of practice has at least three dimensions: mutual engagement, joint enterprise, and a shared repertoire of actions. People become members of the CoP when they participate in the CoP in an apprenticeship-type process called legitimate peripheral participation. CoP/LPP is related to CEL because learning is both created and applied in a community setting. The difference between CEL and the CoP/LPP framework is that, in CEL, not all the learning comes from within a specific CoP. In CEL, knowledge also comes from the outside via course work (i.e., the social world of e-learning, which is also often a CoP in its own right), and from the application of new knowledge in the local community. In postgraduate or other professional e-learning, the CoP most related to course learning is that of a discipline or profession, not of the local community in which the student resides and works, and not of the e-learning social world.

Lave and Wenger's work is entwined with and only slightly pre-dated by that of Brown *et al.* (1989) and their application of situated cognition to educational learning settings. Very similarly to LPP, Brown *et al.* reason that activity and perception come before – they assert 'must' come before – conceptualization of what is being learned (p. 41). In other words, concepts are developed from 'continuing authentic activity' (p. 30). As such, learning is a process of enculturating (p. 40).

Situated learning and situated cognition have been applied extensively in the business world but also in the field of e-learning. For example, Guldberg and Pilkington (2006) use Lave and Wenger's (1991) model of communities of practice as a theoretical framework to examine 'a networked learning course that offers post-experience professional training to non-traditional university students' (p. 159). In doing so, they present findings consistent with CEL because the students in the e-learning course help each other align the norms and practices of their individual workplaces with the e-learning community. De Laat and Lally (2003) use, in part, the concept of situatedness to analyse tutoring and learning processes in a research learning community of students in a master's programme in e-learning. The students in their study demonstrate CEL because they are 'professionally engaged with teaching responsibilities within their organizations' while at the same time 'engaged in collaborative learning and tutoring processes as they support each other and the group as a whole in a range of structured activities' (p. 15). De Laat and Lally conclude that additional theoretical work is needed to account for all their empirical findings. CEL may provide a key to such additional theory development.

Oliver and Herrington (2003) use situated learning to present a framework for the 'design of online learning settings' (p. 19). Their framework echoes CEL in that it focuses on authenticity, requiring authentic context for knowledge, authentic activities, and authentic assessment mechanisms that all reflect the real-world setting of knowledge application. Malpas (2000: 110) argues that 'knowledge, even in the context of the Internet, is fundamentally tied to place and to our active engagement in place'. On this basis Kazmer (2005b) argues that the co-creation of knowledge by community-embedded learners sharing an e-learning social world must be tied to their virtual place and their physical locales.

Reality-based learning

Reality-based learning applies to the many kinds of learning initiatives that involve real-world application and settings. The category of reality-based learning perspectives here includes various terms developed before the advent of e-learning, such as: action learning (Aronstein and Olsen, 1974); co-operative education (Knowles, 1971); service learning (Jacoby, 1996); community-based learning; problem-based (Rankin, 1999) and problem-centred learning; and experiential (Kolb, 1984) and experience-based learning (McClure *et al.*, 1977). The benefits of community-based learning initiatives in which students in higher education classes apply their learning through work with community members have been realized in content areas such as public health (Hartwig *et al.*, 2004; Citrin, 2001), librarianship (Leonard and Pontau, 1991; Roy, 2001; Yontz and McCook, 2003), and citizenship instruction (Koulish, 1998), but all of those examples reflect on-campus face-to-face learning environments and not e-learning.

Thus community-embedded learning as a type of reality-based learning is not a completely new concept, but its development in the e-learning environment is distinct. Hunter (2002), for example, describes such embedded learning in discussing the National School Network, an online learning community for teachers. She states that there is 'interdependence between NSN [National School Network] as a virtual community and the changing practices in its member institutions and communities' (Hunter, 2002: 103). Other studies and projects have examined the role of online learners in their local communities, exploring instances where a desired outcome is that learners 'use newfound skills within their local context' (Page and Scott, 2001: 548; see also Edwards, 1996; Hollister and Mehrotra, 1999). Many of these studies are about online professional development or other support programmes for schoolteachers (Schlager and Fusco, 2003). Several such studies examine the implementation of agenda-based programmes for teachers, online learning programmes designed so that the teachers will spread the message of the programme to their local colleagues and students. Lakatos *et al.* (2003) describe a programme for teaching Sustainable Development (SD) to teachers in order that they can teach SD to their students and implement SD in their communities. Kreisler *et al.*, (1997–98) evaluate the use of distance education to support community activism by instructing teachers in an anti-smoking campaign aimed at teenagers. Teemant *et al.* (2005) describe 'sociocultural pedagogy' in e-learning, in which e-learning not only teaches the content at hand (professional development in teaching English as a second language for professional teachers) but also models the pedagogical techniques the teachers are to use in teaching ESL. The overall finding of these disparate programmes is that achieving community outcomes when teachers are involved in distance learning is a viable option.

Problem-based learning has been used most heavily in the medical arenas, and has been incorporated with e-learning technologies with the advent of telemedicine and other integrations of learning technology into medical curricula. In many ways, e-learning was a natural setting for all of the reality-based learning techniques because e-learning allows the student to be embedded in a 'real' setting while simultaneously engaged in active and interactive learning. For example, Uden and Beaumont (2006) discuss integrating e-learning into problem-based learning. Kolb's (1984) general discussion of experiential learning has provided the basis for work in e-learning as a way to support experiential learning in professions such as medicine. For example, Stanton and Grant (1999) describe how experiential learning can be integrated with distance learning in medicine. Another study that measures the impact of applied knowledge in public health, and compares online with face-to-face classes, uses the term 'practice contexts' and concludes that in order to achieve the desired results, distance learning has to relate directly to the practice contexts (Umble *et al.*, 2000).

Community informatics

The area of community informatics broadly covers the use of communication technologies to support community activities and meet community objectives (Gurstein, 2000). Community informatics often has a specific education or learning goal, and thus provides a method of approach to CEL that has not previously been formalized. In community informatics-based projects with an educational focus, most designers have assumed a learning network that is a mirror of the local community (Baker and Ward, 2002; Carroll and Rosson, 2001; Kubicek and Wagner, 2002). Students share both a physical location and an interactive learning network, and they do not interact with students in other geographic areas as an explicit part of their learning experience. Such approaches include 'overlaying' the online learning social world on to the local community (Baker and Ward, 2002: 216) and the community network, where a variety of technologies are deployed specifically to support local community activities (Carroll and Rosson, 2001; Kavanaugh *et al.*, 2005; Kubicek and Wagner, 2002). In either of those cases, the participants in the online learning social world also live in the same on-ground community.

Community informatics typically focuses on lifelong learning – rather than degree- or course-based education – that is not only physically but also conceptually based in communities of learners (Kodama, 2001). Community informatics typically focuses on the technology and often on its installation, training, and use. This focus on technology use emerges in particular as community networks can be used to span the 'digital divide' and create e-learning opportunities for individuals who otherwise would not have educational access. Then, community informatics explores how interaction can improve lives, often with an e-learning focus. This includes both informal e-learning through information provision and sharing, and also that offered by an educational institution, in both cases leveraging the technology of the community network (Kodama, 2001). The outcomes of community informatics could thus be improved by considering aspects of CEL in the design of community networks.

BENEFITS AND DRAWBACKS OF CEL

Benefit: collaborative knowledge

One benefit of CEL is that community-embedded students build collaborative course knowledge in addition to learning the basic materials delivered as part of the curriculum, such as by readings and lectures. This benefit is indicated in Motteram's (2006: 19) discussion of blended learning for teachers' continuing professional development, which highlights the importance of 'the interrelationship between knowledge and skills and its impact on what the participants bring to the classroom and then what is added to that and taken away'. In other words, students bring their own knowledge, share it together, combine it with the course materials, and come away with more knowledge than they could have if each individual had worked solely with the course materials. Students in LIS have been found to build collaborative knowledge by sharing knowledge from their work and community settings and using that knowledge collaboratively to contextualize the content delivered in the courses they take together (Kazmer, 2005a). Geography students learning at a distance have been able to extend their experience beyond national boundaries and incorporate materials provided by students who actually live in a variety of global contexts (Solem *et al.*, 2006). For these learners, the geographic diversity enabled by e-learning directly reinforces the content being taught and creates an environment in which students are positioned to contribute and build new knowledge.

Benefit: professional networks

A second benefit of CEL is that the learning-based social worlds created using ICT turn into professional networks that can continue to rely on ICT to provide wider access to dormant relationship ties (Nardi *et al.*, 2002). Dormant relationships occur between people who, at one time, had a close relationship during which they interacted frequently using a variety of media and for many purposes. Such a close relationship might involve, for example, interactions via e-mail, telephone, and face-to-face meetings, and centre around topics as varied as school work, careers, families, and popular culture. When a close relationship occurs in a transient or temporary setting – such as an online learning community – there is usually a shift when the relationship changes because the participants no longer belong to the setting that fostered their close interaction. This shift leads to a dormant relationship in which participants no longer interact regularly. Instead, they feel comfortable contacting one another only as needed, relying on their shared friendship history to provide a basis for sporadic interactions in the future (Kazmer, 2002: 168; Kazmer, 2007).

Benefit and drawback: applied learning outcomes

A third difference in outcomes afforded by CEL arises from the assumption that one way to measure outcomes is through application. In a traditional classroom environment, student learning outcomes are assessed through familiar techniques such as examinations, papers, and group projects. In traditional face-to-face education settings that require practical learning, such as internships, there has typically been a close relationship between the instructor and the internship supervisor. Learning outcomes of practical experience are measured under close supervision of the instructor, who is experienced in academic learning assessment. When we turn to CEL, the focus will be on applied outcomes, not learning outcomes. In other words, this difference is not in the learning outcome itself, but in how it is measured (see Wood *et al.*, 1998). According to Rudestam (2004), online learning in distributed settings (such as those intrinsic to CEL) is most compatible with competence-based outcomes. This reliance on applied learning outcomes can lead to difficulty assessing student performance because the employers cannot or will not take on the task of academic assessment, and because it is difficult to create objective measures of applied learning (Andresen *et al.*, 2000; Kazmer, 2005a). Wood *et al.* (1998) suggest alternative assessment mechanisms, such as portfolios, to counter problems in assessing field-based experiences.

Witmer (1998) addresses the opposite of this point: e-learning, instead of presenting difficulties in assessment, can be of great help and support to on-campus students doing physically remote internships. In other words, if students will be doing off-site internships anyway, distance learning and its associated communication technologies can help give students a shared forum for asking questions and seeking help, keeping them from feeling isolated or abandoned at their internship sites (in particular if something goes wrong with the field experience).

Drawback: community resistance to change

Learners engaged in CEL may encounter resistance to change among the members of their local communities. Individual learners, separated physically from the support of fellow classmates, may find that when they try to implement what they learn within the community they encounter the resistance of community members who are reluctant to change. This is one way the familiarity of the students with their communities can be a drawback rather than a benefit. As Granovetter describes (1985: 498), an embedding environment generates 'standards of expected behavior'. The implication of these standards for CEL is that community members are already familiar with the students and expect their behaviour not to change drastically. Similarly, implementation of classwork concepts can also encounter resistance to change similar to the 'not invented here' phenomenon (Katz and Allen, 1988). As Granovetter explains (1985: 491), while ongoing social relations engender trust, they do not guarantee an absence of malfeasance and thus equally generate distrust. In a CEL setting, community members, even others in the workplace, may thus distrust 'academic' ideas being brought into their environment even while they trust the student/co-worker. This distrust is compounded by e-learning because colleagues, clients, and others may doubt the effectiveness or quality of education obtained 'through the computer'. It remains an open question whether such resistance is more likely met in the case of e-learning CEL, or in the case of a newly graduated professional who enters a new workplace and a new town and meets resistance on the same grounds. Is resistance more likely to be met in the case of CEL because of continuing distrust of online education?

Drawback: workplace as classroom

Community-embedded learners may face difficulties that arise because they are using their workplaces as extensions of the classroom. The students are in work situations that have immediate and long-lasting significance to the students' careers. Students are in their homes and their communities with the colleagues and clients they will continue to see daily, even after they have finished their education. As a result, students might think that there is little room for error as they practise what they learn because they need their co-workers and clientele to continue to trust their performance. This point also emerged from Granovetter's discussion of embeddedness (1985: 490) in which he argues that trustworthy behaviour needs to be maintained over time to secure continuing relationships. Students taking a practicum, internship, or other type of experiential learning are expected to learn as they go and are allowed some leeway for mistakes in the application of their classroom knowledge. The student who is being paid full wages and is expected to be 'doing his or her job' does not enjoy either the same tolerance of error or the explicit instructional support that is provided in experiential learning situations.

Drawback: limited world view

Students who stay in their (overly) familiar environments while they go to school miss the opportunity to experience new physical and geographical places (see also Hearn and Scott, 1998). At the same time, they do not get the chance to be out of their home environments and cast a distanced eye over their circumstances there. While they are gaining from interacting via ICT with other students from a variety of cultural, geographical, and professional settings, they are not gaining perspective from time away from home, or from living in the academic environment or, at the very least, in a new town. This loss of distance and perspective may be a detriment to the overall learning achieved by each student.

Drawback: forced interactivity

A fourth possible issue that emerges when CEL, which requires a highly interactive learning environment, becomes integral to e-learning is that some students choose distance learning specifically because they want to be alone (Wilson and Bagley, 1999: 362). These students are not necessarily loners and introverts but may be people whose learning style causes them to work best without various types of outside distractions, or who do not find that interactivity is a successful mode of learning. Empirical results of work by Simpson and Du (2004) reinforce this point; they found that pedagogy must match learning styles to 'maximize students' success' (p. 133).

For students like those in Simpson and Du's research, required interactivity detracts from a main advantage of distance learning for some students. On the other hand, Hillier *et al.* (2005) completed empirical research indicating that for some topics that involve 'the discomfort of personal experience of psychosocial issues' (p. 279), but where those issues are vital to successful learning outcomes for the topic at hand, students may find an interactive e-learning model better than a face-to-face classroom – but not because they can avoid dealing with problems directly; instead because it can offer a '"safe" environment to explore sensitive issues' (p. 279).

Drawback: tunnel vision in the classroom

The last issue is 'tunnel vision' in the classroom. It is true for students in any set-ting – on-campus or distance, e-learning or face-to-face – that students may focus on what they think they need or want to know rather than on the spectrum of knowledge being offered or encouraged by the instructor. For community-embedded learners, the pressure to stay focused on the specific needs of the local community rather than on the broad variety of concepts being developed in the e-learning environment is constant and driven by the student and the local community simultaneously. Tunnel vision as it occurs among community-embed-ded learners is also highlighted by Wilson and Bagley (1999), who provide the results of a study indicating that students (in their case, community pharmacists) decide what distance learning modules they prefer based on whether or not they address 'commonly encountered problems' (p. 363). Such students focus their attention toward course materials they believe will address their current situations and ignore course materials that seem irrelevant. This ability to focus on what is needed sounds like it could be of great benefit to the learner and to the commu-nity. It should be that students can target the needs of their local community, efficiently gleaning from their education exactly what they need and no more. Alternatively, it may mean that community-embedded learners have tunnel vision in the online classroom and pay attention only to those things that they already think they need to know. At the same time, students may ignore other topics (often conceptual or theoretical topics) and other details they think are unneces-sary to their specific situation. This could be seen as a benefit in that the student is able to focus on what is important. From an educational standpoint, it has more potential as a down side because students receive an incomplete education. Unless the teaching is geared toward making connections clear and plausible to all students, students may only learn what they think they want to learn.

EMERGING TRENDS RELATED TO CEL

How are innovations in e-learning likely to influence further research and prac-tice of CEL? The influence of reality-based learning is likely to increase, with an ongoing focus shift away from learning *per se* and toward the ability of com-munity-embedded learners to provide services – professional and otherwise – related to their areas of study (cf. Wood *et al.*, 1998). In addition to an overall shift in outcomes assessment to applied outcomes assessment which was referred to above ('Applied learning outcomes'), further changes in CEL are likely to emerge from changes in delivery of e-learning content and its articulation with the technology lifestyles of learners.

Blended and hybrid learning

Blended learning and hybrid learning have typically reflected a combination of online (usually Web-based) learning and classroom face-to-face learning (Reasons *et al.*, 2005). Blended learning may incorporate the strengths of e-learning with the strengths of classroom learning to provide a successful learning experience, but only if appropriate pedagogical methods are retained in both environments (Alonso *et al.*, 2005; Ausburn, 2004). Motteram's (2006) explication of blended learning for teacher education at the master's level accounts for the community-embeddedness of the learners: 'For blended learning in general, it is important to take into account the nature of the communities that the participants are involved in on a day-to-day basis' (p. 29), a finding corroborated by Ausburn (2004). As blended learning becomes more common, the impact of community-embeddeness on instruction and assessment will need to be incorporated into e-learning design.

Mobile learning

Mobile learning is designed for students who work in multiple physical locations, whether it is the day-to-day movement of someone who learns at home, at work, at the library, and at the coffee shop or the larger-scale movements of students who relocate residence one or more times while pursuing their learning objectives. This mobility is facilitated by the ability to use a suite of mobile technologies – telephones, computers, and other digital devices – to access learning materials and communication channels.

Stoskopf and Moorash (2005) describe one model of mobile learning deployed for the US Army, called 'EArmyU'. While the military setting may be limited in scope, this model is important for thinking about the future of community-embedded learning because it accommodates a 'highly mobile' population. As people in general – not just in the military – become more mobile and more connected with technology, the nature of the communities in which they are embedded shifts away from a traditional physically local community and becomes more like networked individualism (Boase and Wellman, 2006), in which the personal network comes into the foreground and the spatially proximate community makes up the background. With the local community fading into the background, CEL might change; instead of students embedded in one local community, they may be embedded in several different communities, networks, and social worlds.

Mobile learning also has design implications associated with embedded students, because the mobility of students and technology combined with the realistic limitations of local space and the mutability of technology means students can personalize their e-learning spaces in ways not necessarily predicted by the instructor or designer (Kazmer, 2005b). Schwabe and Goth (2005) highlight design issues associated with this type of embedded e-learning, specifically because the portability of technology and the physical limitations and sociocultural norms of technology use in specific settings necessitate design of systems that are complex and adaptable (cf. also Churchill and Munro, 2001; Kirkley and Kirkley, 2005). Like blended learning, the increased mobility of learners and their technological devices – and the associated influences of local environments on the e-learning process – will need to be accommodated in e-learning design.

NEEDED RESEARCH IN CEL

As e-learning continues to grow, and more learners undertake online course work while remaining embedded in local settings, several areas of research pertaining to CEL are open for exploration. Swan's (2005) discussion of community-centred learning speculates that the dearth of research in CEL may exist because the connections between students' e-learning environments and their local community seem logical and obvious, and because e-learning using the Internet facilitates easy links among students, communities, and cultures. She concludes with a call for research in this area, writing: 'Anecdotal accounts suggest such strategies are very effective in supporting learning, but rigorous research in these areas is clearly indicated' (Swan, 2005: 22).

The first need is for rigorous research to test and modify the CEL conceptual framework presented above by verifying whether the five types of knowledge transfer occur generally in e-learning. Further work is needed to reinforce and supplement the eight potential benefits and drawbacks of CEL. The five types of community/social world transfer, and the eight potential benefits and drawbacks associated with CEL, lead to research questions that will allow scholars to verify and adapt them according to empirical data. For example, there is in particular scant research on how e-learning social worlds become professional networks of dormant ties, useful for furthering community outcomes, individual careers, and the health of professions. Research into this and other benefits of CEL can help clarify the impact of e-learning on individuals, communities, and professions.

As well, further research can help to incorporate more tightly the aspects of e-learning that are intrinsic to CEL with existing research areas of situated learning, reality-based learning, and community informatics. With the increase in hybrid and blended learning, students will be embedded in both classroom and online settings while engaging with the same course material, and attention to CEL may help us understand their experiences. As mobile learning continues to increase, research will be needed to explore how being embedded in ever-changing local settings influences learning.

CONCLUSION

Contrary to perceptions that e-learners spend most of their time at the computer, engaged in a solitary act of acquiring knowledge and skills, most e-learners live and work in community settings. The influences of community settings affect what students learn online, how they co-create knowledge in their shared online learning social worlds, and how they implement their learning. Community-embedded learning, or CEL, provides a framework for understanding the mechanisms of interaction between the local community in which a student is embedded and the online social world of which they are an active part. As well, CEL provides a way to assess the potential benefits and drawbacks of e-learning for the embedded learner, in turn helping learners and educators maximize the benefits and avoid the pitfalls. Continued research into the area of CEL, combined with attention to the increasing use of personal and adaptive technologies by students and the application of mixed and blended learning by educators, can improve the educational experience and outcomes of community-embedded learners.

REFERENCES

Alonso, F., Lopez, G., Manrique, D. and Vines, J. (2005) 'An instructional model for Web-based e-learning education with a blended learning process approach', *British Journal of Educational Technology*, 36: 217–35.

Andresen, L., Boud, D. and Cohen, R. (2000) 'Experience-based learning', in G. Foley (ed.), *Understanding Adult Education and Training* (2nd edn). Sydney: Allen and Unwin. pp. 225–39.

Aronstein, L. W. and Olsen, E. (1974) *Action Learning: Student Community Service Projects*. Washington, DC: Association for Supervision and Curriculum Development.

Ausburn, L. J. (2004) 'Course design elements most valued by adult learners in blended online education environments: an American perspective', *Educational Media International*, 41: 327–37.

Baker, P. M. A. and Ward, A. C. (2002) 'Bridging temporal and spatial "gaps": the role of information and communication technologies in defining communities', *Information, Communication and Society*, 5: 207–24.

Barab, S. (2003) 'An introduction to the special issue: Designing for virtual communities in the service of learning', *Information Society*, 19: 197–201.

Barab, S., Kling, R. and Gray, J. H. (eds) (2004) *Designing for Virtual Communities in the Service of Learning*. New York: Cambridge University Press.

Boase, J. and Wellman, B. (2006) 'Personal relationships: on and off the Internet', in A. L. Vangelisti and D. Perlman (eds), *The Cambridge Handbook of Personal Relationships*. Cambridge: Cambridge University Press. pp. 709–26.

Bransford, J. D., Brown, A. L. and Cocking, R. R. (2000) *How People Learn: Brain, Mind, Experience, and School*. Washington, DC: National Academy Press.

Brown, J. S., Collins, A. and Duguid, P. (1989) 'Situated cognition and the culture of learning', *Educational Researcher*, 18: 32–42.

Carroll, J. M. and Rosson, M. B. (2001) 'Better home shopping or new democracy? Evaluating community network outcomes', in *Proceedings of the SIGCHI Conference on Human Factors in Computing Systems*. pp. 372–9.

Churchill, E. F. and Munro, A. J. (2001) 'Work/place: mobile technologies and arenas of activity', *ACM SIGGROUP Bulletin*, 22 (3): 3–9.

Citrin, T. (2001) 'Enhancing public health research and learning through community–academic partnerships: the Michigan experience', *Public Health Reports*, 116: 74–8.

De Laat, M. and Lally, V. (2003) 'Complexity, theory and praxis: Researching collaborative learning and tutoring processes in a networked learning community', *Instructional Science*, 31: 7–39.

Edwards, T. A. (1996) 'Community learning with an "intelligent" college: a new way to learn', *Journal of European Industrial Training*, 20: 4–14.

Fuller, T. and Soderlund, S. (2002) 'Academic practices of virtual learning by interaction', *Futures*, 34: 745–60.

Granovetter, M. (1985) 'Economic action and social structure: the problem of embeddedness', *American Journal of Sociology*, 91: 481–510.

Guldberg, K. and Pilkington, R. (2006) 'A community of practice approach to the development of non-traditional learners through networked learning', *Journal of Computer Assisted Learning*, 22: 159–71.

Gurstein, M. (2000) *Community Informatics: Enabling Communities with Information and Communications Technologies*. Hershey, PA: Idea Group.

Harrison, S. and Dourish, P. (1996) 'Re-place-ing space: the roles of place and space in collaborative systems', in *Proceedings of the ACM Conference on Computer Supported Cooperative Work*. New York: ACM Press. pp. 67–76.

Hartwig, K. A., Pham, K. and Anderson, E. (2004) 'Practice-based teaching and learning: an example of academic–community collaboration', *Public Health Reports*, 119: 102–9.

Haythornthwaite, C. and Kazmer, M. M. (eds) (2004) *Learning, Culture and Community in Online Education: Research and Practice*. New York: Peter Lang.

Hearn, G. and Scott, D. (1998) 'Students staying home: questioning the wisdom of a digital future for Australian universities', *Futures*, 30: 731–7.

Hillier, D., Mitchell, A. and Millwood, R. (2005) '"Change of heart!": a new e-learning model geared to addressing complex and sensitive public health issues', *Innovations in Education and Teaching International*, 24: 277–87.

Hollister, C. D. and Mehrotra, C. M. N. (1999) 'Utilizing and evaluating ITV workshops for rural community leadership training', *Journal of Technology in Human Services*, 16: 35–45.

Hunter, B. (2002) 'Learning in the virtual community depends upon changes in local communities', in K. A. Renninger and W. Shumar (eds), *Building Virtual Communities: Learning and Change in Cyberspace*. New York: Cambridge University Press. pp. 96–126.

Jacoby, B. (1996) *Service-learning in Higher Education: Concepts and Practices*. San Francisco, CA: Jossey-Bass.

Katz, R. and Allen, T. J. (1988) 'Investigating the Not Invented Here (NIH) syndrome: a look at the performance, tenure, and communication patterns of fifty RandD project groups', in M. L. Tushman and W. L. Moore (eds), *Readings in the Management of Innovation*. Cambridge, MA: Ballinger. pp. 293–309.

Kavanaugh, A., Carroll, J. M., Rosson, M. B., Zin, T. T. and Reese, D. D. (2005) 'Community networks: where offline communities meet online', *Journal of Computer-Mediated Communication*, 10 (4). Available online at: http://jcmc.indiana.edu/vol10/issue4/kavanaugh.html.

Kazmer, M. M. (2002) 'Disengagement from Intrinsically Transient Social Worlds: The Case of a Distance Learning Community'. Unpublished doctoral dissertation, University of Illinois at Urbana-Champaign. *Dissertation Abstracts International*, 63: 3770.

Kazmer, M. M. (2005a) 'Community-embedded learning', *Library Quarterly*, 75: 190–212.

Kazmer, M. M. (2005b) 'Cats in the classroom: online learning in hybrid space', *First Monday*, 10 (9). Available online at: http://www.firstmonday.org/issues/issue10_9/kazmer/index.html.

Kazmer, M. M. (2007) 'Beyond CU L8R: disengaging from intrinsically transient online social worlds', *New Media and Society*, 9: 111–38.

Kazmer, M. M. and Haythornthwaite, C. (2001) 'Juggling multiple social worlds: distance students online and offline', *American Behavioral Scientist*, 45: 510–29.

Kirkley, S. E. and Kirkley, J. R. (2005) 'Creating next generation blended learning environments using mixed reality, video games and simulations', *TechTrends*, 49 (3): 42–53.

Knowles, A. (1971) *Handbook of Cooperative Education*. San Francisco, CA: Jossey-Bass.

Kodama, M. (2001) 'New regional community creation, medical and educational applications through video-based information networks', *Systems Research and Behavioral Science*, 18: 225–40.

Kolb, D. A. (1984) *Experiential Learning: Experience as the Source of Learning and Development*. Englewood Cliffs, NJ: Prentice Hall.

Koulish, R. (1998) 'Citizenship service learning: becoming citizens by assisting immigrants', *Political Science and Politics*, 31: 562–7.

Kreisler, A., Snider, B. A. and Kiernan, N. E. (1997-98) 'Using distance education to educate and empower community coalitions: a case study', *International Quarterly of Community Health Education*, 17: 161–78.

Kubicek, H. and Wagner, R. M. (2002) 'Community networks in a generational perspective: the change of an electronic medium within three decades', *Information, Communication and Society*, 5: 291–319.

Lakatos, G., Csobod, E., Kiss, M., Meszaros, I. and Szabo, J. (2003) 'A distance learning course as a tool to implement SD in Hungary', *International Journal of Sustainability in Higher Education*, 4: 25–32.

Lave, J. and Wenger, E. (1991) *Situated Learning: Legitimate Peripheral Participation*. New York: Cambridge University Press.

Leonard, B. G. and Pontau, D. Z. (1991) 'Sculpting future librarians through structured practicums: the role of academic librarians', *Journal of Academic Librarianship*, 17: 26–30.

Malpas, J. (2000) 'Acting at a distance and knowing from afar: agency and knowledge on the Internet', in K. Goldberg (ed.), *The Robot in the Garden: Telerobotics and Telepistemology in the Age of the Internet*. Cambridge, MA: MIT Press. pp. 108–25.

McClure, L., Cook, S. C. and Thompson, V. (1977) *Experience-based Learning: How to Make the Community your Classroom*. Portland, OR: Northwest Regional Educational Laboratory.

Motteram, G. (2006) '"Blended" education and the transformation of teachers: a long-term case study in postgraduate UK higher education', *British Journal of Educational Technology*, 37: 17–30.

Nardi, B. A., Whittaker, S. and Schwarz, H. (2002) 'NetWORKers and their activity in intensional networks', *Computer Supported Cooperative Work*, 11 (1–2): 205–42.

Oliver, R. and Herrington, J. (2003) 'Exploring technology-mediated learning from a pedagogical perspective', *Journal of Interactive Learning Environments*, 11: 111–26.

Page, M. and Scott, A. (2001) 'Change agency and women's learning: new practices in community informatics', *Information, Communication and Society*, 4: 528–59.

Rankin, J. A. (ed.) (1999) *Handbook on Problem-based Learning*. New York: Forbes.

Reasons, S. G., Valadares, K. and Slavkin, M. (2005) 'Questioning the hybrid model: student outcomes in different course formats', *Journal of Asynchronous Learning Networks*, 9 (1). Available online at: http://www.sloan-c.org/publications/jaln/v9n1/v9n1_reasons_member.asp.

Renninger, K. A. and Shumar, W. (eds) (2002) *Building Virtual Communities: Learning and Change in Cyberspace*. New York: Cambridge University Press.

Roy, L. (2001) 'Diversity in the classroom: incorporating service-learning experiences in the library and information science curriculum', *Journal of Library Administration*, 33: 213–28.

Rudestam, K. E. (2004) 'Distributed education and the role of online learning in training professional psychologists', *Professional Psychology, Research and Practice*, 35: 427–32.

Schlager, M. S. and Fusco, J. (2003) 'Teacher professional development, technology, and communities of practice: are we putting the cart before the horse?', *Information Society*, 19: 203–20.

Schwabe, G. and Goth, C. (2005) 'Mobile learning with a mobile game: design and motivational effects', *Journal of Computer Assisted Learning*, 21: 204–16.

Simpson, C. and Du, Y. (2004) 'Effects of learning styles and class participation on students' enjoyment level in distributed learning environments', *Journal of Education for Library and Information Science*, 45: 123–36.

Solem, M., Chalmers, L., Dibiase, D., Donert, K. and Hardwick, S. (2006) 'Internationalizing professional development in geography through distance education', *Journal of Geography in Higher Education*, 30: 147–60.

Stanton, F. and Grant, J. (1999) 'Approaches to experiential learning, course delivery and validation in medicine', *Medical Education*, 33: 282–97.

Stoskopf, L. D. and Moorash, A. (2005) 'EArmyU: expanding education access and excellence to highly mobile online learners', *Journal of Asynchronous Learning Networks*, 9 (2). Available online at: http://www.sloan-c.org/publications/jaln/v9n2/v9n2_stoskopf_member.asp.

Strauss, A. (1978) 'A social world perspective', *Studies in Symbolic Interaction*, 1: 119–28.

Swan, K. (2005) 'A constructivist model for thinking about learning online', in J. Bourne and J. C. Moore (eds), *Elements of Quality Online Education* VI. *Engaging Communities*. Needham, MA: Sloan-C. pp. 13–30.

Teemant, A., Smith, M. E., Pinnegar, S. and Egan, M. W. (2005) 'Modeling sociocultural pedagogy in distance education', *Teachers College Record*, 107: 1675–98.

Uden, L. and Beaumont, C. (2006) *Technology and Problem-based Learning*. Hershey, PA: Information Science.

Umble, K. E. Cervero, R. M. and Yang, B. (2000) 'Effects of traditional classroom and distance continuing education: a theory-driven evaluation of a vaccine-preventable diseases course', *American Journal of Public Health*, 90: 1218–24.

Wilson, V. and Bagley, L. (1999) 'Learning at a distance: the case of the community pharmacist', *International Journal of Lifelong Education*, 18: 355–69.

Witmer, D. F. (1998) 'Staying connected: a case study of distance learning for student interns', *Journal of Computer-Mediated Communication*, 4 (2). Available online at: http://jcmc.indiana.edu/vol4/issue2/witmer.html.

Wood, W. M., Miller, K. and Test, D. W. (1998) 'Using distance learning to prepare supported employment professionals', *Journal of Rehabilitation*, 64 (3): 48–53.

Yontz, E. and McCook, K. de la P. (2003) 'Service-learning and LIS education', *Journal of Education for Library and Information Science*, 44: 58–68.

15

The Challenges of Gender, Age and Personality in E-learning

Konrad Morgan and Madeleine Morgan

Technological advances in the fields of information and communications technology have allowed the creation of a range of new digital technologies that can act as a vehicle for human expression, communication and behaviour. These new digital technologies pervade all aspects of life and this worldwide technological revolution raises fundamental questions about how these changes impact on the lives of all who use these systems, whether it be for education, communication, entertainment or creative expression.

One of the long-term conceptual challenges that face those involved with digital learning is the goal of documenting, understanding and developing solutions that are sympathetic to the many and varied individual, group and cultural differences that exist within the user populations. In this chapter we will explore the complex interplay of factors associated with an increasingly diverse user population in terms of age, gender and psychology to explore how these differences affect user attitudes and behaviour when using digital learning technologies.

In terms of psychological divergence we will explore factors including:

- Technical aptitude and attitudes
- Personality and intelligence.

In terms of physical divergence we will explore the technology-related impact of the perceptual and mental differences and user attitudes associated with gender, maturation (with younger populations) and ageing (with older populations). Specifically:

- Gender differences in use, attitudes and access to technology and technology-related artefacts or occupations

- The effect of ageing on the comprehension and competence of user populations when using digital technology
- Attitudes and behaviours associated with older user populations.

ETHICAL CONSIDERATIONS WHEN INVESTIGATING DIVERSE POPULATIONS

Historically many issues have developed around the ethical and equitable use of technology, especially in education. These include not only ethical issues related to informed consent of subjects used within the development and evaluation of new digital systems but also the equity issues implicit in the right of access and consideration for individuals in terms of gender, age, disability, ethnic origin, religion and socio-economic status. Before we consider the various differences that have been found to exist within diverse user populations we must first consider the vital importance of the ethical commitment towards individuals within user populations who may be different from the designers of the digital learning system and also from the majority of typical users.

Ethics commitment

It is important that any study of population diversity has an awareness of the equity issues that may arise from identifying differences and that researchers and workers within this area have a clear commitment to understanding the application of ethical principles and 'socially just' practices to digital technologies. Such underlying ethical values are:

- Recognition of the rights and dignity of all individuals
- Equality of opportunity in access and use of technology enhanced systems, education, training and employment
- Enhancing diversity in gender, age, culture, beliefs, attitudes, language and social circumstance in the successful use of technology enhanced systems
- Recognition of the right of all individuals to well maintained, safe and productive digital environments.

AGE AND DIGITAL LEARNING TECHNOLOGY

Of all the factors that affect the reach of digital learning that we will consider in this chapter, none is so poorly understood or supported as the impact of age or maturation (Johnson and Kress, 2003; Kent and Facer, 2004). Indeed, in many texts the process of ageing is presented as an inevitable decline of mental and physical powers, which we now know is an over-simplification, since in many highly complex domains, especially those of a social or psychological nature, true mastery of subjects occurs only much later in the life course. It is only relatively recently that there has been recognition that we need to have a greater understanding of the changes that occur to computer users as they age. In order for the reader to gain some understanding of these issues we will present the literature related to both younger and older users as many of the existing designs within e-learning have ignored the age-related dimension of design and have instead focused on young adult populations.

Ironically these ignored factors of age are also probably the most important for most nations within the developed economies of the world as they face a dramatic increase in the proportion of older people in their populations. If the goal of lifelong learning is to truly live up to its promise then ways must be developed to allow digital technology to address the changes in perception, motor skills, cognitive ability, motivation (life priorities) and attitudes within older and younger populations (Johnson and Kress, 2003). Although considerable investment is being made in designing and developing technology for populations between the ages of fourteen and forty there is surprisingly little investment or interest in the technological support required either by extremely young computer users or the changes that take place in older user populations (Kent and Facer, 2004).

Conceptual and cognitive development in the young

Although many perceive technology to be the domain of the young there is in fact little grounded empirical research that defines the levels of conceptual development that occurs as younger users of technology interact with these systems (de-Beaune, 2004; Meszaros, 2004; Okita, 2004). Most systems aimed at young computer users assume that similar functionality and interface modalities can be used successfully with both adult user populations and extremely young users (Okita, 2004). There is no empirical evidence to support this approach and indeed there is a large body of human developmental literature that suggests that young children do in fact pass through a number of quite distinct major conceptual changes which would influence the ways in which they could understand and interact with computer systems and the user interface metaphors used within modern learning systems. Until detailed research is completed that enables us to fully understand these cognitive developmental stages and their possible impact on conceptual understanding in terms of computer usability in digital learning systems, there will remain questions over the validity and reliability of using digital learning and assessment tools with extremely young computer users (Johnson and Kress, 2003). We are never sure if online education systems are assessing the ability of the student in the subject domain or are instead assessing basic technology competence and understanding. This problem remains one of enormous potential for future researchers within the field of digital learning (Kent and Facer, 2004; Okita, 2004).

Conceptual and cognitive changes in mature and ageing populations

Until recently the literature on the decline in the efficiency of mental and physical processes with increasing age were extremely negative (Marx, 2003), showing dramatic slowing in cognitive processes and complex decision making. More recent research has shown that with appropriate physical and mental exercise there is no reason for an individual to suffer such an extreme decline in their mental or physical performance as they get older (Perry *et al.*, 2003; Wagner and Wagner, 2003). There is relatively little literature available to specifically guide designers of digital learning systems with older learners (Morris and Vankatesh, 2000; Meszaros, 2004). There are certainly known and quantifiable declines in visual and auditory sensitivity, as there are with some very fine motor movements, but none of these changes precludes the older user from interacting successfully with digital technology provided some provision is made for larger type faces, clear fonts and clearly defined interaction spaces (such as large click boxes). Indeed, many of the better user interfaces in modern learning systems have more than adequate user interface configuration features to allow all of these declines in perception and motor performance to be easily accommodated (Wagner and Wagner, 2003).

The areas that are not adequately addressed are how the learning materials and assessments themselves should be adapted to older minds (Morris and Vankatesh, 2000; Johnson and Kress, 2003). There is in fact very little reliable research that has attempted to address how older individuals learn when using digital learning resources and how that learning might differ from the learning processes of younger individuals (Morris and Vankatesh, 2000; Marx, 2003; Meszaros, 2004). Until such research is completed this remains an important and under-researched theme that awaits future study (Perry *et al.*, 2003).

MEN AND WOMEN AND DIGITAL LEARNING

During the past thirty years of investigations into the ratios of males and females using technology there have been consistent reports of males being more positive towards technology and being more likely to adopt the use of new technology on a voluntary basis (Volman and Van-Eck, 2001). This trend has been reported from early school through to adult life and from all over the world (Broos, 2005; Heemskerk *et al.*, 2005). Although some scientists have argued that this pattern is changing (Durndell and Thomson, 1997; Colley and Comber, 2003) surveys continue to show an imbalance between the sexes favouring adoption of technology by males over that by females, and although some reports do show females more likely to use communication-based technology, the majority of students still show a male predominance overall (Colley and Comber, 2003; Heemskerk *et al.*, 2005).

The consequences of this gender bias are significant not only in terms of maximizing the whole potential work force but also because there is some evidence (Morgan, 2005) that males design information- and knowledge-based systems in ways that are different from females; often these differences favour male users in communication and searching methods. The gender imbalance may become of increasing importance as high-technology industries, such as knowledge engineering and e-learning, become the normal methods of conducting such activities throughout the global economy (Trauth, 2006).

A scarcity of females in computing can be detected from the earliest levels in educational systems all over the world (Durndell, and Haag, 2002). It pervades all levels of education and industry (Jackson *et al.*, 2001). This trend could not only pose a threat to the economic growth and stability of the global economy by permitting only half the available population to work in specific careers, but it also reflects a continuing gender inequality in society and educational access (Trauth, 2006).

Gender, along with age, is often considered the primary attribute that differentiates people from each other. In comparison with many of the differences such as intelligence, cognitive style or social grouping, the difference of gender is relatively easy to determine; but like racial origin or social grouping the topic of gender is often sensitive and highly controversial (Morgan, 2004). Explanations for these reported gender differences have been varied, but include genetic and hormonal influences (Brosnan, 2004), brain chemistry (Bransford *et al.*, 1999), cerebral lateralization (Brosnan, 2004) and social roles (Morgan, 1991, 2005). Reviews of the literature of gender and technology show a consistent trend of male domination in the computing industry and education (Volman and van-Eck, 2001). Although there appears to be no single reason for this domination, social roles and stereotypes are now thought to be of major importance in shaping education and vocational choices (Durndell and Thomson, 1997; Morgan and Morgan, 2000).

Parental influence

There is a growing body of evidence that suggests that there are strong parental influences on the attitudes and behaviours that we develop in later life. These influences include not only our views on appropriate gender-based behaviour (Witt, 1997; Snyder *et al.*, 1997; Tidwell, 2002) but also our attitudes towards technology and even our self-rated proficiency in using technology (Morgan, 1991, 2005).

Summary of gender attitudes and technology

As yet there are no universally accepted explanations for the sex differences found in computing. Broos (2005) conducted a large quantitative analysis of previous studies of the gender divide in ICT attitudes and found, in general, females had more negative attitudes towards computers and the Internet than did men. As we have seen there is strong evidence that social and cultural effects play a large role in gender differences. Several researchers have surveyed the sex roles portrayed in the mass media. These researchers have found that males are portrayed as being the predominant users, and being in a dominant role in any mixed-sex portrayals.

One other factor that could explain the lack of females in computing is the male harassment of females who work in traditional male occupations. Sources of such harassment include supervisors, peers, subordinates and clients (Morgan, 2005).

Within e-learning we have a duty to ensure that female perspectives are included within the design process of digital learning environments and course materials. In terms of learning materials it is important that positive female role models are portrayed in course materials as these help break down any prejudice related to women and their use of technology.

PERSONALITY AND DIGITAL LEARNING

Personality plays a role in the use of digital technology in several ways: it influences the manner in which users prefer to interact with other users and with the technology itself, but it has only been within the last thirty years that researchers have begun to explore the possible role that personality could have in digital learning.

Van Muylwijk *et al.* (1983) were among the first to recognize that personality traits would have a major impact on both behaviour and attitudes when using technology. This idea of looking at personality and interaction styles was followed up by both Van der Veer *et al.* (1985) and Singleton (1989). Van der Veer proposed a more general approach where various personality factors would have some effect on attitudes towards and use of the system. In contrast Singleton proposed intelligence as a single factor that he believed would predict the degree of success in using computer systems and in having positive attitudes towards computer systems.

Later investigations into the role of personality included a series of experimental studies by Van Hoe *et al.* (1990), who attempted to look at the role of personality and preferences for menu characteristics, and Weil *et al.* (1990) who tried to find links with computer phobia. Neither Van Hoe nor Weil was successful in the attempt to find links between personality styles and computer use or attitudes. This may have been because they were simply looking at more high-level personality factors or that the tasks they selected were so far removed from day-to-day experience that classical personality theory was overwhelmed by the primitive system characteristics that existed at that time.

By the early 1990s computer systems had advanced enough to allow for Computer Mediated Communication (CMC) that permitted more naturalistic communication styles. It is not therefore surprising that when Adrianson (1991) investigated the role of extroversion in computer-mediated communication he found significant differences connected with the extroversion factor but that these were much weaker than in normal face-to-face communication. We must again recognize that in the early 1990s although CMC provided naturalistic communication it did not support video or audio-conferencing except in rare research settings.

Research has been continuing within this area, investigating the effects of the users' personality on the way they interact and perform in technological environments. The increasing use of the Internet and e-learning has provided a rich arena for investigating personality differences (Hills and Argyle, 2003).

Amiel and Sargent (2003) also looked at the relationship between the personality types described by Eysenck and Eysenck (1969) and Internet use. Their findings demonstrated that distinctive patterns of interaction exist within the personality sub-categories. A further study (DeYoung and Spence, 2004) used factor analysis to establish individuals' attitudes towards information technology and used the results of this investigation to commence development of a technology profile inventory.

The role of social interaction

The role of computers as social devices and the influence that personality has in such interactions was first raised by authors such as Lieskovsky (1988) and Huebner *et al.* (1988), who believed that risk taking, or personality factors associated with risk taking, would be among the largest predictive factors for successful computer use. This theme has been taken up by more recent authors such as Reeves (Reeves and Nass, 1996) who proposes that our reactions to technology and technological artefacts are the same as our reactions to humans. In addition Reeves proposes that our behaviour in virtual space is similar to that in real physical space. We should therefore find identical personality factors in cyber-space as we do in day-to-day life. Kiesler's work (Kiesler *et al.*, 1996) seems to support Reeves's idea. In Kiesler's experiments human subjects tended to keep promises to computers in the same manner that they do to real life human beings. Such work has been felt by many (Loevinger, 1996) to form a potential threat to the stability of the personality of computer users.

Further experimental tests have been undertaken investigating the different group influences when interacting via computers as opposed to interacting with computers (Lee and Nass, 2002). Two tests were carried out, the first investigating how the participants were influenced to conform by other human participants; the second replaced interaction among humans with interaction solely with the computer. The results of the study showed that visual representation of interaction partners (as conducted in the first test) had a greater social influence on the participants and their desire to conform.

Personality factors in educational technology

Much of the potential for successful use of personality factors within digital systems lies within the area of educational information technology. As early as 1966 Hilgard proposed that there would be optimum personality factors for various styles of computer-based training. For example, Arnone *et al.* (1994)

proposed that curiosity would be the major factor in deciding how effective a student would find a computer-based teaching environment. While there appears to be little doubt among researchers that personality factors are of great importance in determining the successful use of information technology in educational settings (Clements, 1995; Hartley, 1998; Calvert, 1999; Harris, 1999; Shavinia and Loarer, 1999) comparatively little work has actually been reported in the general personality literature.

Those studies which have been reported have either looked at abnormal and pathological computer users (Gackenbach, 1998), who are hopefully not representative of a general student body, or have reported finding no differences in personality between predicted groups of users (Davis, 1997a, b). Other studies have concentrated on the most negative areas of information technology use, such as gender imbalance (Harrison, *et al.* 1997), the role of personality in repetitive strain injury (Kiesler and Finholt, 1988) or the personality factors involved in computer-based stress (Kahn and Cooper, 1991; Henry and Stone, 1997).

More recently, researchers have been looking at the relationship between student personality and the students' choice of traditional or online college classes (Mattes *et al.*, 2003). The results of this study found that differences in personality and other human factors (age, computer experience) were evident among the two different student populations that may be of use both for those designing online environments and for the instructors who have to implement the technology.

Previous work by the authors

In contrast to some of the less successful studies described in our review, we have found significant differences in computer attitudes and behaviour associated with major personality factors (Morgan and MacLeod, 1992). Specifically we found possible relationships between a stated preference for command line systems and extreme scores on a high-order control scale, and stated preferences for graphical interfaces and extreme scores on high-order extrovert scales. These promising findings prompted us to undertake further studies where we investigated the computer-based attitudes and behaviour of students using computer-mediated collaborative learning environments.

Current personality measures in e-learning

Throughout the study of the mind various types of personality have been proposed, ranging from the 'humours' proposed by the early Greek philosophers to the personality factors investigated by psychologists in the twentieth century (John, 1990; Eysenck, 1991). Although different personality theorists have used different terms to describe the important (non-cognitive) dimensions of personality, more recent research has isolated five broad dimensions of personality, which are often called the 'Big Five'. One frequently cited organization of these

Big Five is Goldberg's FFI (Five Factor Inventory) (Goldberg, 1992, 1993a, b) where the Big Five are associated with the following types:

- Extraversion
- Agreeableness
- Conscientiousness
- Emotional stability
- Openness.

In contrast to these formal descriptive types the less discriminatory measures derived from Jung's (1971) personality theory are called the Myers–Briggs Type Inventory (MBTI). Within the MBTI the 'Big Five' are associated with the following types:

- Extraversion versus Introversion
- Feeling versus Thinking
- Judging versus Perception
- No match made, since an evaluation is felt to be judgemental
- Intuition versus Sensing.

The Myers–Briggs personality test

The Myers–Briggs Type Indicator is a self-report personality inventory designed to give people information about their Jungian psychological type preferences. The measure was developed by Isabel Briggs Myers and Katherine Cook Briggs in the early 1940s to try and make Jung's theory of human personality understandable and useful in everyday life. Its increasing popularity in educational settings is in part due to its non-judgemental nature.

The Myers–Briggs personality Type Inventory in education

The history of the use of the Myers–Briggs Type Inventory (MBTI) within education is relatively long. As early as the late 1960s Richek (1969) had proposed that the MBTI might be a suitable instrument to determine the best teachers with regard to teaching style and material presentation to students. However, although the history of the MBTI within education is long it took some considerable time for it to gain widespread support. Early evaluations compared the MBTI and other personality measures such as Cattell's 16PF in the role of predicting successful learning styles and grade point averages (Eison and Pollio, 1985) and although researchers such as Lorr (1991) had problems recognizing the usefulness of the MBTI on the whole by the early 1990s there was growing support and recognition for both the validity and reliability of the MBTI in education (Murray, 1990; Brown et al., 1991). Since that time although there have been some studies which raised concerns that the MBTI was being taken out of context from Jungian theory

(Garden, 1991) and that it might not truly reflect unconscious desires (Barbuto, 1997) it has been found to be one of the best predictors for many aspects of education and educational technology (Eison and Pollio, 1985; Jackson et al., 1996).

Some of these studies which involved large samples (n more than 1,000) have not only found the MBTI to be among the best personality descriptors but also that there was no support for the separate gender scoring commonly recommended for the MBTI (Jackson et al., 1996).

Learning styles

As early as the mid-1970s researchers in education were investigating the possible links between Carl Jung's typology of conscious functioning (1971) and general learning styles among students. Early results from studies such as Millott and Cranney (1976) found significant links between the MBTI types INP and learning style differences in reading comprehension. Later work by Lyons (1985) proposed that teaching styles matched the teacher's own learning style and factors identified by the teacher's MBTI scores. Following Lyons's proposal Provost and Anchors (1987) reported the importance for the teacher to match their teaching style to the preferences of the students' learning styles as determined by the MBTI. Indeed, work by Jensen (1987) showed that there was a strong link between the students' MBTI type and their preferred and most effective learning style. However, it took nearly another decade before researchers could define specific MBTI types to students' preferred learning styles. One of the first researchers to investigate this area was Drummond (Drummond and Stoddard, 1992) who proposed that there were strong links and overlaps between the MBTI type of student and their preferred Gregorc Style Delineator (GSD) (Drummond and Stoddard, 1992).

By the mid-1990s researchers had begun to specify the actual learning styles preferred by specific MBTI types such as Harasym's work (Harasym et al., 1996) with the GSD such that MBTI type SJ had a marked preference for GSD learning styles of a concrete sequential nature. In contrast MBTI type NP preferred concrete random GSD learning styles and MBTI type T showed a marked preference for GSD learning style of abstract sequential. Finally MBTI type F preferred GSD learning styles of an abstract random nature. In terms of MBTI types and group interactions the work of Johnson (1997) showed that MBTI type Ts liked learning environments with competition against other students, MBTI type F preferred learning groups which focused on accommodation, MBTI type E preferred group working where individuals collaborated and finally MBTI type I preferred group activities where conflicts were avoided.

Researchers have further investigated the use of the MBTI as an assessment tool for remedial programmes for students who believe that they lack the knowledge of how to study effectively (Fearn, 2005). The objective of this study was to investigate if the students would be able to better understand how they and others learn by means of studying their learning preferences. The hypothesis of the study was that by enabling the students to look more thoroughly at their own personalities they would be able to identify old learning impediments and overcome them. Although the findings of the study were inconclusive, it is an interesting and worthwhile area for further future research.

Such research is of major importance when we take students and force them to use computer-supported collaborative environments. It is therefore vital to gain further understanding of the consequences in terms of student satisfaction performance and effectiveness of putting students with different MBTI types into one common environment.

Among the literature on learning styles we also find some research that looked at MBTI type and student performance (Guangyu, 2004). We must, however, take these kinds of studies with the consideration that they may merely be showing indications of which MBTI types are most suited to the existing single e-learning styles implemented in many educational settings. It may well be that by varying the ways in which teaching is presented to the students we will change dramatically the various MBTI scores reported as being prevalent among successful students. Support for this comes from studies that have shown that student satisfaction levels are directly related to how well the learning situation matches their MBTI type (Tsuzuki and Matsui, 1998). Of those studies which have reported a significant relationship between an MBTI type and academic success, an example would be the work of Rosati (1997), who found that top male students predominantly had the MBTI type ITJ.

MBTI in subject study prediction

Most modern research with the MBTI has not focused on trying to identify the MBTI type of the highest scoring students, since we have already recognized that this may simply be a result of the learning style imposed in that particular educational environment. Instead research has focused on the possible use of the MBTI in predicting which subjects or disciplines would be best suited for students with specific MBTI types. In the late 1980s researchers such as Kean (Kean et al., 1988) and Crockett and Crawford (1989) proposed the central role that the MBTI could play in career and education guidance. Indeed, Crockett and Crawford (1989) determined that MBTI I type students were more comfortable with multivariate career counselling as opposed to more simplistic single factor counselling (fewer items considered) in their future career counselling.

Other studies tried to determine if a student's MBTI type could predict if they would complete a study programme once they had enrolled upon it. Although the work of Schurr et al. (1997) reported that MBTI types among students were poor predictors of degree completion rates in comparison with social and environmental factors, research by Sears et al. (1997) showed that trainee teachers with an MBTI type SFJ were more likely to graduate and complete their teacher training than any other personality profile. Studies have shown that MBTI factors were responsible for a more significant percentage of a student's communication skills and general knowledge variants than any other factor (Schurr *et al.*, 1989).

Researchers have reported finding different MBTI types as being most suitable or predictive of success in the study of various disciplines. For example, Moody (1988) reported that MBTI types IT were most successful in the study of science topics while later research by Boreham and Watts (1998) reported that the single TF dimension was the most successful predictor of the preferred topic of study. More recently, researchers have looked at the MBTI preferences of aviation and aviation business students (Kutz *et al.*, 2005) where the findings show that both groups of students shared three of the four preferences: the aviation management students registering ESTJ and the pilot students registering ESTP. This single letter difference could have meaningful implications for aviation instructors with regard to the development of courses and effective teaching strategies.

Interestingly, research which has looked at the MBTI profiles for student populations who do not choose a certain subject or student group categorization still share the same MBTI basic types. For example, Humes (1992) reported finding that a high percentage of educationally disadvantaged students fell in the MBTI EP types. One could speculate, given that we know how important it is to match an individual student's MBTI type to the e-learning style presented in an educational environment, that current educational environments do little to support the e-learning style preferred by students with an MBTI type EP.

It is known that students' communication when working in groups is strongly predicted by those students' combined MBTI scores (Kagan and Grandgenett, 1987) and this may have a direct link with findings that have shown that students in non-typical learning situations, for example, television presentation of lectures or other distance e-learning settings, do best if they have an MBTI type N profile (Dawson and Guy, 1994). Indeed, it has been known since the late 1980s (Kern and Matta, 1988) that non-standard teaching environments such as distance e-learning settings or Computer-Based Teaching (CBT) give preference to different MBTI types and different learning styles than traditional learning settings. For example, early experiments reported finding that students with MBTI type S performed better on computer-based teaching systems than N types (Kern and Matta, 1988). However, we must realize that these early CBT systems did not involve a distance component and that the findings may well have changed as the nature of computer-based teaching and learning environments has changed.

Modern computer-based teaching systems place an emphasis on collaboration. The overall activity and types of interactions undertaken by a group are known to be also under the influence of MBTI types such that the overall combined MBTI types of the individuals in a group accurately describe and predict that group's behaviour (Stever, 1995). This means that it is possible for an educator to gauge accurately the overall MBTI types of a particular cohort of students before formal educational practices begin. The potential for allowing modification of teaching style or learning environment to match individual MBTI types or even group MBTI types is enormous. For example, when controlled studies are performed where professors deliberately teach in the manner matching their students' MBTI scores, student satisfaction ratings and overall grade performance are significantly enhanced (Provost and Anchors, 1987; Cooper and Miller, 1991; McCutcheon et al., 1991; Fisher et al., 1998). Even though this fact is known widely in the literature relatively few educators make a conscious effort to try and determine their students' MBTI scores or make an effort to teach in a manner that will match the likely MBTI scores of their students. For example, it has been found that most professors at universities teach in an MBTI type I manner while students generally prefer an MBTI type S manner of teaching (Cooper and Miller, 1991).

Analysis of MBTI teaching types has shown that there are significant alterations in the way that teaching styles are delivered, depending on the MBTI types EI and SN (Schmidt, 1989). Such that MBTI dimensions EI are directly linked to student reinforcement rates and the MBTI dimension SN is directly related to teacher implementation of a learning style and teaching pace. With the increase in mature adult students in higher educational settings we should perhaps make more use of MBTI typing of students at enrolment to ensure that educators are given feedback on what the most appropriate teaching styles will be and if there are significant numbers of mature adult students in a student body then educators should be aware of the MBTI type shift that is likely to have taken place from young students who are mostly MBTI type ES to more mature students who are reported to be predominantly MBTI type IS (Lynch and Sellers, 1996).

In our own work (Morgan and Morgan, 2000; Morgan et al., 2004) we have investigated the possible links between MBTI types and the attitudes and behaviour of students using computer-supported collaborative learning environments. We have found statistically significant differences between the major personality factors in terms of the use of the learning environment and attitudes towards the various components of the online collaborative learning system. Based on our findings we strongly support the idea that the MBTI can be a useful tool in configuring such online learning environments to students' personalities and preferred learning styles. Of the MBTI types investigated in our study the dimensions of E/I and S/I appear to be most promising as major predicting factors in learning styles and system component preferences. These can be summarized such that the E/I dimension appears very useful in determining primary learning and interacting style and preference and the S/I dimension appears most useful as a predictive tool for the use or avoidance of certain system components. The remaining dimensions T/F and J/P appear more related to attitudes toward group work and may reflect some previous experience within our subject population.

Although Myers–Briggs and Jung did not include maturity of the individual within their personality types in our subject population there does appear to be a strong trend within the T/F and J/P dimensions correlated with greater age and experience. Within our sample the older and more experienced individuals disliked group work and were more likely to report system-based problems linked with group-based activities. It is uncertain if these findings related to the T/F and J/P scales will be reflected in a more general subject population.

It is to be hoped that future research will investigate methods in which MBTI type tests for E/I and S/I can be directly linked with real-time online changes within the collaborative learning environment to more closely match students' preferred interaction styles and preferred learning tools.

OVERALL CONCLUSIONS AND FUTURE RESEARCH DIRECTIONS

As we have shown in this chapter, research in the effects of population diversity and e-learning is still in its infancy. There are several areas that are specifically of great potential for future researchers. The first is age, where greater understanding is needed in age-related competences that we can expect from young children and the effect these have on the child's understanding of computer-based learning and assessment. In terms of older populations there is little known about the most appropriate learning approaches or assessment procedures. When we consider the issue of gender it is clear that some investment is needed to ensure female perspectives are incorporated in the design of digital learning systems and that the role models provided within courses address and correct any preconceptions about the appropriateness of females using technology. Finally in terms of personality we hope that further research will be performed to clarify the possible applications of the MBTI to enhance the learning system so it more perfectly fits the best learning and communication styles of both students and educators.

REFERENCES

Adrianson, L. and Hjelmquist, E. (1991) 'Group processes in face to face and computer mediated communication', *Behaviour and Information Technology*, 10 (4): 281–96.

Amiel, T. and Sargent, S. L. (2004) 'Individual differences in Internet usage motive', *Computers in Human Behavior*, 20 (6): 711–26.

Arnone, M. P., Grabowski, B. L. and Rynd, C. P. (1994) 'Curiosity as a personality variable influencing learning in a learner controlled lesson with and without advisement', *Educational Technology Research and Development*, 42 (1): 5–20.

Aspinall, A. and Hegarty, J. (2002) 'ICT for adults with learning disabilities: an organisation-wide audit', *British Journal of Educational Technology*, 32 (3): 365–72.

Barbuto, J. E. Jr (1997) 'A critique of the Myers–Briggs Type Indicator and its operationalization of Carl Jung's psychological types', *Psychological Reports*, 80 (2): 611–25.

Boreham, B. W. and Watts, J. D. (1998) 'Personality type in undergraduate education and physics students', *Journal of Psychological Type*, 44: 56 ff.

Bowman, C. A. and Jaeger, P. T. (eds) (2004) *A Guide to High School Success for Students with Disabilities*. Westport, CT: Greenwood Press.

Bransford, J. D., Brown, A. L. and Cocking, R. (eds) (1999) *How People Learn: Brain, Mind, Experience and School*. Washington, DC: National Academy Press.

Broos, A. (2005) 'Gender and Information and Communication Technologies (ICT) anxiety: male self-assurance and female hesitation', *CyberPsychology and Behavior*, 8 (1): 21–31.

Brosnan, M. J. (2004). 'The neuropsychology of human–computer interaction', in K. Morgan, J. M. Spector and C. Brebbia (eds), *Human Perspectives in the Internet Society: Culture, Psychology and Gender*. Boston, MA and Southampton: WIT Press, pp 21–33.

Brown, V. L. and DeCoster, D. A. (1991) 'The Myers–Briggs Type Indicator as a developmental measure: implications for student learners in higher education', *Journal of College Student Development*, 32 (4): 378–9.

Calvert, S. L. (1999) *Children's Journeys through the Information Age*. New York: McGraw-Hill.

Cattell, R. (1936) *A Guide to Mental Testing*. London: University of London Press.

Clements, D. H. (1995) 'Teaching creativity with computers', *Educational Psychology Review*, 7 (2): 141–61.

Colley, A. and Comber, C. (2003) 'Age and gender differences in computer use and attitudes among secondary school students: what has changed?', *Educational Research*, 45 (2): 155–65.

Cooper, S. E. and Miller, J. A. (1991) 'MBTI learning style/teaching style discongruencies', *Educational and Psychological Measurement*, 51 (3): 699–706.

Crockett, J. B. and Crawford, R. L. (1989) 'The relationship between Myers–Briggs Type Indicator (MBTI) Scale scores and advising style preferences of college freshmen', *Journal of College Student Development*, 30 (2): 154–61.

Davis, D. M. (1997a) 'The perpetual novice: an undervalued resource in the age of experts', *Mind, Culture, and Activity*, 4 (1): 42–52.

Davis, D. M. (1997b) 'Review of "The perpetual novice: an undervalued resource in the age of experts": response to reviewer comments', *Mind, Culture, and Activity*, 4 (1): 55–6.

Dawson, Betty G. and Guy, Rebecca F. (1994) 'Personality type and grade performance in a TV assisted course', *Journal of Psychological Type*, 29: 38–42.

de-Beaune, S. A. (2004) 'The invention of technology: prehistory and cognition', *Current Anthropology*, 45 (2): 139–51.

DeYoung, C. G. and Spence, I. (2004) 'Profiling information technology users: en route to dynamic personalization', *Computers in Human Behavior*, 20 (1): 55–65.

Drummond, Robert J. and Stoddard, Ann H. (1992) 'Learning style and personality type', *Perceptual and Motor Skills*, 75 (1): 99–104.

Durndell, A. and Thomson, K. (1997). 'Gender and computing: a decade of change?', *Computers and Education*, 28: 1–9.

Durndell, A. and Haag, Z. (2002). 'Computer self-efficacy, computer anxiety, attitudes towards the Internet and reported experience with the Internet, by gender, in an East European sample', *Computers in Human Behavior*, 18: 521–35.

Eison, J. A. and Pollio, H. R. (1985) 'A multidimensional approach to the definition of college students' learning styles', *Journal of College Student Personnel*, 26 (5): 434–43.

Eysenck, H. J. (1991) 'Dimensions of personality: 16: 5 or 3? Criteria for a taxonomic paradigm', *Personality and Individual Differences*, 12: 773–90.

Eysenck, H. J. and Eysenck, S. B. G. (1969) *Personality Structure and Measurement*. London: Routledge and Kegan Paul.

Fearn, W. L. (2005) 'Higher Learning using type theory to generate individual awareness and development', *Dissertation Abstracts International Section A: Humanities and Social Sciences*, 65 (7–A): 2455.

Fisher, D., Kent, H. and Fraser, B. (1998) 'Relationships between teacher–student: interpersonal behaviour and teacher personality', *School Psychology International*, 19 (2): 99–119.

Gackenbach, Jayne (ed.) (1998) *Psychology and the Internet: Intrapersonal, Interpersonal, and Transpersonal Implications*. San Diego, CA: Academic Press.

Garden, Anna Maria (1991) 'Unresolved issues with the Myers–Briggs Type Indicator', *Journal of Psychological Type*, 22: 3–14.

Goldberg, L. R. (1992) 'The development of markers for the big-five factor structure', *Psychological Assessment*, 4: 26–42.

Goldberg, L. R. (1993a) 'The structure of phenotypic personality traits', *American Psychologist*, 48: 26–34.

Goldberg, L. R. (1993b) 'The structure of personality traits: vertical and horizontal aspects', in D. C. Funder, R. D Parke, C. Tomlinson-Keasey, and K. Widaman, (eds), *Studying Lives through Time: Personality and Development*. Washington, DC: American Psychological Association. pp. 169–88.

Guangyu, Guo (2004) 'A preliminary study of Myers–Briggs Types with academic aptitude and grades', *Psychological Science* (China), 27 (1): 34–8.

Harasym, P. H., Leong, E. J., Juschka, B. B. and Lucier, G. E. (1996) 'Relationship between Myers–Briggs Type Indicator and Gregorc Style Delineator', *Perceptual and Motor Skills*, 82 (3, Pt 2): 1203–10.

Harris, Roger W. (1999) 'Attitudes towards end user computing: a structural equation model', *Behaviour and Information Technology*, 18 (2): 109–25.

Harrison, A. W., Rainer, R. K. Jr and Hochwarter, W. A. (1997) 'Gender differences in computing activities', *Journal of Social Behavior and Personality*, 12 (4): 849–68.

Hartley, J. (1998) *Learning and Studying: A Research Perspective*. New York: Routledge.

Heemskerk, I., Brink, A., Volman, M. and ten-Dam, G. (2005) 'Inclusiveness and ICT in education: a focus on gender, ethnicity and social class', *Journal of Computer Assisted Learning*, 21 (1): 1–16.

Henry, J. W. and Stone, R. W. (1997) 'The development and validation of computer self efficacy and outcome expectancy scales in a nonvolitional context', *Behavior Research Methods, Instruments and Computers*, 29 (4): 519–27.

Hilgard, E. R. (1964) 'Contemporary learning theory', *Indian Psychological Review*, 1 (1): 12–20.

Hills, P. and Argyle, M. (2003) 'Users of the Internet and their relationships with individual differences in personality', *Computers in Human Behavior*, 19 (1): 59–70.

Huebner, M., Krafft, A. and Ortmann, G. (1988) 'Auf dem Rüecken fliegen. Thrills am Computer/Stunt flying: Thrills with a computer', *Psyche. Zeitschrift füer Psychoanalyse und ihre Anwendungen*, 42 (12): 1096–128.

Humes, C. W. (1992) 'Career planning implications for learning disabled high school students using the MBTI and SDSE', *School Counselor*, 39 (5): 362–8.

Jackson, L. A., Ervin, K. S., Gardner, P. D., *et al.* (2001) 'Gender and the Internet: women communicating and men searching', *Sex Roles*, 44: 363–79.

Jackson, S. L., Parker, C. P. and Dipboye, R. L. (1996) 'A comparison of competing models underlying responses to the Myers–Briggs Type Indicator', *Journal of Career Assessment*, 4 (1): 99–115.

Jensen, G. H. (1987) 'Learning styles', in Provost, J. A., Anchors, S. *et al.* (eds) *Applications of the Myers–Briggs Type Indicator in Higher Education*. Palo Alto, CA: Consulting Psychologists Press. pp. 181–206.

John, O. P. (1990) 'The "Big Five" factor taxonomy: dimensions of personality in the natural language and in questionnaires', in L. A. Pervin, (ed.) *Handbook of Personality: Theory and Research*. New York: Guilford.

Johnson, A. K. (1997) 'Conflict handling intentions and the MBTI: a construct validity study', *Journal of Psychological Type*, 43: 29–39.

Johnson, D. and Kress, G. (eds) (2003) 'Redesigning pedagogy and assessment', special issue: *Assessment, Literacies and Society*. London: Taylor and Francis.

Jung, C. (1953–1971) *Collected Works*. London: Routledge.

Kagan, D. M. and Grandgenett, D. J. (1987) 'Personality and interaction analysis', *Research in Education*, 37: 13–24.

Kahn, H. and Cooper, C. L. (1991) 'The potential contribution of information technology to the mental ill health, job dissatisfaction, and alcohol intake of money market dealers: An exploratory study', *International Journal of Human–Computer Interaction*, 3 (4): 321–38.

Kean, R. C., Mehlhoff, C.and Sorensen, R. (1988) 'Using the Myers–Briggs Type Indicator to assess student needs', *Clothing and Textiles Research Journal*, 6 (2): 37–42.

Kent, N. and Facer, K. (2004) 'Different worlds? A comparison of young people's home and school ICT use', *Journal of Computer Assisted Learning*, 20 (6): 440–55.

Kerchner, L. and Kistinger, B. (1985) 'Language processing/word processing: Written expression, computers and learning-disabled students', *Learning Disability Quarterly*, 7 (4): 329–35.

Kern, G. M. and Matta, K. F. (1988) 'The influence of personality on self-paced instruction', *Journal of Computer Based Instruction*, 15 (3): 104–8.

Kiesler, S. and Finholt, T. (1988) 'The mystery of RSI', *American Psychologist*, 43 (12): 1004–15.

Kiesler, S., Sproull, L. and Waters, K. (1996) 'A prisoner's dilemma experiment on co-operation with people and human-like computers', *Journal of Personality and Social Psychology*, 70 (1): 47–65.

Kutz, M. N., Brown, D. M., Carmichael, D. B. and Shandiz, M. (2005) 'Preliminary implications for academic professionals of aviation student Myers–Briggs Type Indicators (MBTI) preferences', *International Journal of Applied Aviation Sciences*, 4 (2): 221–8.

Lee, E. J. and Nass, C.d (2002) 'Experimental tests of normative group influence and representation effects in computer-mediated communication: when interacting via computers differs from interacting with computers', *Human Communication Research*, 28 (3): 349–81.

Lieskovsky, P. (1988) 'Personality and social determinants of attitudes toward computers in university students', *Studia Psychologica*, 30 (2): 115–24.

Loevinger, J. (1996) 'In defense of the individuality of personality theories', *Psychological Inquiry*, 7 (4): 344–6.

Lorr, M. (1991) 'An empirical evaluation of the MBTI typology', *Personality and Individual Differences*, 12 (11): 1141–5.

Lynch, A. Q. and Sellers, P. A. (1996) 'Preferences for different educational environments and psychological type: a comparison of adult learners and traditional age college students', *Journal of Psychological Type*, 39: 18–29.

Lyons, C. A. (1985) 'The relationship between prospective teachers' learning preference/style and teaching preference/style', *Educational and Psychological Research*, 5 (4): 275–97.

Marx, G. (2003) 'Some information age techno-fallacies', special issue: 'Privacy in an Information Society', *Journal of Contingencies and Crisis Management*, 11 (1): 25–31.

Mattes, C., Nanney, R. J. II and Coussons-Read, M. (2003) 'The online university: who are its students and how are they unique?', *Journal of Educational Computing Research*, 28 (2): 89–102.

McCutcheon, J. W., Schmidt, C. P. and Bolden, S. H. (1991) 'Relationships among selected personality variables, academic achievement and student teaching behaviour', *Journal of Research and Development in Education*, 24 (3): 38–44.

Meszaros, P. S. (2004) 'The wired family: living digitally in the Postinformation Age', *American Behavioral Scientist*, 48 (4): 377–90.

Millott, R. and Cranney, A. G. (1976) 'Personality correlates of college reading and study skills', *Journal of Reading Behavior*, 8 (3): 335–6.

Moody, R. (1988) 'Personality preferences and foreign language elearning', *Modern Language Journal*, 72 (4): 389–401.

Morgan, K. (2005) 'Thirty Years of Gender and Technology Research: What have we learnt and how can it be applied?'. Invited keynote presentation IADIS Virtual Multi Conference on Computer Science and Information Systems (MCCSIS, 2005).

Morgan, K. and Morgan, M. (2000) 'Gender issues in technology use', in A. Voiskounsky (ed.), *Cyberworlds: Research into New Technology and Psychology*. Moscow, pp. 267–289.

Morgan, K., Spector, J. M. and Brebbia, C. (eds) (2004) *Human Perspectives in the Internet Society: Culture, Psychology and Gender*. Boston. MA and Southampton: WIT Press.

Morgan, K., Gibbs, S., Macleod, H., and Morris, R. (1991) 'An exploration of some possible gender differ-ences in computer attitudes, interface preference and simple task performance', in G. Lovegrove and B. Segal, (eds), *Women into Computing: Selected papers, 1988–1990*. BCS Workshops in Computing series. Dordrecht: Springer-Verlag. pp. 161–72.

Morris, M. and Vankatesh, V. (2000) 'Age differences in technology adoption decisions: implications for a changing work force', *Personnel Psychology*, 53 (2): 375–403.

Murray, J. B. (1990) 'Review of research on the Myers–Briggs Type Indicator', *Perceptual and Motor Skills*, 70 (3, Pt 2): 1187–202.

Okita, S. Y. (2004) 'Effects of age on associating virtual and embodied toys', *CyberPsychology and Behavior*, 7 (4): 464–71.

Perry, E., Simpson, P., NicDomhnaill, O. and Siegel, D. (2003) 'Is there a technology age gap? Associations among age, skills, and employment outcomes', *International Journal of Selection and Assessment*, 11 (2–3): 141–9.

Provost, J. A. and Anchors, S. (eds) (1987) *Applications of the Myers–Briggs Type Indicator in Higher Education*. Palo Alto, CA: Consulting Psychologists Press.

Reeves, B. and Nass, C. I. (1996) *The Media Equation: How People treat Computers, Television, and new Media like real People and Places*. New York: Cambridge University Press.

Richek, H. G. (1969) 'Jung's typology and psychological adjustment in prospective teachers: a prelimi-nary investigation', *Alberta Journal of Educational Research*, 15 (4): 235–43.

Rosati, P. (1997) 'Psychological types of Canadian engineering students', *Journal of Psychological Type*, 41: 33–7.

Sarnoff, S. (2001) 'Ensuring that course Web sites are ADA compliant', *Journal of Technology in Human Services*, 18 (3–4): 189–201.

Schmidt, C. P. (1989) 'Applied music teaching behaviour as a function of selected personality variables', *Journal of Research in Music Education*, 37 (4): 258–71.

Schurr, K. T., Ruble, V. E., Henriksen, L. W. and Alcorn, B. K. (1989) 'Relationships of National Teacher Examination Communication Skills and General Knowledge scores with high school and college grades, Myers–Briggs Type Indicator characteristics, and self-reported skill ratings and academic problems', *Educational and Psychological Measurement*, 49 (1): 243–52.

Schurr, K. T., Ruble, V., Palomba, C. and Pickerill, B. *et al.* (1997) 'Relationships between the MBTI and selected aspects of Tinto's model for college attrition', *Journal of Psychological Type*, 40: 31–42.

Sears, S. J., Kennedy, J. J. and Kaye, G. L. (1997) 'Myers–Briggs personality profiles of prospective educa-tors', *Journal of Educational Research*, 90 (4): 195–202.

Shavinina, L. V. and Loarer, E. (1999) 'Psychological evaluation of educational multimedia applications', *European Psychologist*, 4 (1): 33–44.

Singleton, W. T. (1989) *The Mind at Work: Psychological Ergonomics*. Cambridge: Cambridge University Press.

Snyder, D., Velasquez, J., Clark, B. and Means-Christensen, A. (1997) 'Parental influence on gender and marital role attitudes: implications for intervention', *Journal of Marital and Family Therapy*, 23 (2): 191–201.

Stever, G. S. (1995) 'Gender by type interaction effects in mass media subcultures', *Journal of Psychological Type*, 32: 3–22.

Szymanski, E. and Parker, R. (eds) (2003) *Work and Disability: Issues and Strategies in Career Development and Job Placement*. Austin, TX: PRO-ED.

Tidwell, J. (2002) 'Gender Development in Children with atypical Parental Socialization: An Example of Lesbian Feminist Mothers'. Ph.D. thesis, Georgia State University.

Trauth, E. (2006) *Encyclopedia of Gender and Information Technology*. London: Ideas Group.

Tsuzuki, Y. and Matsui, T. (1998) '"Subordinates" JP preferences as a moderator of their responses to supervisory structure behaviour: a simulation', *Journal of Psychological Type*, 45: 21–8.

Van der Veer, G. C., Tauber, M. J., Waern, Y. and Van Muylwijk, B. (1985) 'On the interaction between system and user characteristics', *Behaviour and Information Technology*, 4 (4): 289–308.

Van Hoe, R., Poupeye, K., Vandierendonck, A. and de Soete, G. (1990) 'Some effects of menu characteristics and user personality on performance with menu driven interfaces', *Behaviour and Information Technology*, 9 (1): 17–29.

Van Muylwijk, B., Van der Veer, G. and Waern, Y. (1983) 'On the implications of user variability in open systems: an overview of the little we know and of the lot we have to find out', *Behaviour and Information Technology*, 2 (4): 313–26.

Volman, M. and van-Eck, E. (2001) 'Gender differences and information and communication technology in education: two decades of research', *Pädagogische Studien*, 78 (4): 223–38.

Wagner, L. and Wagner, T. (2003) 'The effect of age on the use of health and self-care information: confronting the stereotype', *Gerontologist*, 43 (3): 318–24.

Weil, M. M., Rosen, L. D. and Wugalter, S. E. (1990) 'The etiology of computerphobia', *Computers in Human Behavior*, 6 (4): 361–79.

Witt, S. (1997) 'Parental influence on children's socialization to gender roles', *Adolescence*, 32 (126): 253–9.

PART IV

Language and Literacy

16

Bilingualism and E-learning

Janina Brutt-Griffler

A number of forces in modern society have combined to thrust bilingualism to centre stage on the educational agenda of a growing number of countries: attention to endangered and heritage languages, an emphasis on foreign language education, patterns of international migration, the economic imperatives of globalization, and new research in cognitive science. They have combined to produce a recognizable trend toward introducing language education earlier and more fully into school curricula with the goal of developing advanced levels of proficiency in two or more languages for a growing proportion of the world's population. Without a doubt, bilingualism entails the growth of one's communicative knowledge, the linguistic reservoir that is often acquired and is required to participate in the new electronic world. E-learning therefore is an integral part of bilingual development. Perhaps the most visible manifestation of this relationship is in English language learning, which has seen an explosion of the incorporation of the Internet and digital technologies worldwide.

This chapter grounds its discussion of contemporary issues of bilingualism in the context of e-learning research. It argues that the current research base on the use of technology in second language learning is of an unbalanced nature: the majority of research studies focus on the potential of technology/e-learning and on what is believed to promote language learning (e.g., interaction, authentic input, acculturation, motivation) as opposed to research that reports the measurement of outcomes. The research base in language education and the use of technology also has a limited population of subjects: it shows a greater focus on college-level language learning as opposed to early language learning (cf. Leloup and Ponterio, 2003). According to Liu *et al.* (2002), this is where much bilingual language instruction takes place in countries such as the USA.

Given the fact that foreign language education and bilingual proficiency are becoming a centre piece in school curricula worldwide, e-learning is serving to bridge significant resource gaps in the provision of bilingual education and foreign language learning in many societies. The chapter shows that even without an extant research base the potential of new technologies and e-learning has been embraced by a sizeable number of language educators working with early language learners as well as those who work at the college level. It has gained institutional support in countries such as the USA and the UK as well as in the other nations making up the EU. While underscoring the advantages of e-learning in language education, and bilingualism in particular, the chapter highlights the need for a closer empirical investigation of the points of intersection between bilingualism and e-learning. Such investigation needs to go beyond the exploration of the benefits and potentials of technology. It needs to employ outcome measures with clear reliability and validity, and methodologies that yield results generalizable across studies. Researchers in bilingual studies and e-learning need to move toward *explaining* how technology can be used to support language learning (cf. Liu *et al.*, 2002).

BILINGUALISM

Recent scholarly debate regarding the maintenance of heritage languages (Nettle and Romaine, 2002) and a renewed emphasis on foreign language learning (Brumfit *et al.*, 2005; Kramsch, 2005) has come with a concomitant de-stigmatization of bilinguals. Laurie (1890), a professor at Cambridge University, expressed the traditional view:

> If it were possible for a child to live in two languages at once equally well, so much the worse. His intellectual and spiritual growth would not thereby be doubled, but halved. Unity of mind and character would have great difficulty in asserting itself in such circumstances

(Quoted in Baker, 2003: 135)

This viewpoint, as Baker (2003) notes, was buttressed by early research, such as that of the Welsh researcher, D. J. Saer (1923), whose data, derived from a sample of 1,400 children aged seven to fourteen from rural areas in Wales, showed a ten-point average higher score for monolingual over bilingual children on IQ tests. Baker (2003) points out that this deficit view of bilingualism that understood the learning of a second language to come at the cost of efficiency of cognitive processing, predominated until the 1960s. In that decade, a number of methodological flaws were identified in earlier research. These included the construct of 'intelligence' and how it was measured on IQ tests. It was found, as well, that statistical analysis was not sensitive enough to other variables such as the degree of bilingualism, students' age, social and cultural class and home literacy among the bilingual and monolingual groups. According to Baker (2003), a re-analysis of the study by W. R. Jones (1966) found no statistical difference between monolingual and bilingual groups (p. 138).

The turning point in research on the effects of bilingualism came with the work of Canadian scholars Peal and Lambert (1962). In a study involving 364 children aged ten who were selected from middle-class French schools in Montreal, Canada, it was shown that bilinguals scored significantly higher on fifteen out of eighteen variables on IQ tests. Baker (2003) summarizes its significance: 'The research found evidence that bilingualism need not have detrimental or even neutral consequences. Rather, there is the possibility that bilingualism leads to *cognitive advantages* over monolingualism' (p. 140). Subsequent work offered greater theoretical and empirical specificity on the link between bilingualism and cognition.

Researchers have since compared monolinguals and balanced bilinguals on a variety of measures of divergent thinking, which include fluency, flexibility, elaboration, and originality. The findings have pointed to the superiority of bilinguals on these measures. Bilingual cognitive gains, however, might be constrained by linguistic threshold. Cummins (1977) argues that:

> There may be a threshold level of linguistic competence which a bilingual child must attain both in order to avoid cognitive deficits and allow the potentially beneficial aspects of becoming bilingual to influence his cognitive growth.

(Quoted in Baker, 2003: 146)

Arnberg (1981) suggests that the further the child moves towards balanced bilingualism the higher the cognitive gains they achieve. Studies on bilingualism and metalinguistic awareness suggest that bilinguals score higher on tests of metalinguistic awareness, i.e., the ability to 'reflect upon and manipulate the structural features' of language and treat it as an 'object of thought' (Tunmer and Herriman, 1984: 12). At the same time, Galambos and Hakuta (1988) point out that metalinguistic awareness is tied to the degree of a child's knowledge of the two languages. Carlisle *et al.* (1999) claim that the degree of bilingualism either constrains or enhances metalinguistic performance, thus providing empirical support for the importance of linguistic threshold.

Another area that has drawn researchers' attention is bilingual children's greater analytical orientation toward language processing. Bilingual children seem to develop greater analytical capabilities by working with two systems. Bialystok (1997) found that bilingual children were superior to monolinguals when they were asked to judge syntactic acceptability of sentences and that four- and five-year-old bilingual children develop the concepts of number (cardinality of number) faster than monolinguals. Recent work also suggests cognitive advantages among bilinguals with respect to ageing and memory loss. Using neuro-imaging methodologies, Bialystok (2004) found that while ageing bilinguals are better at retaining their mental capabilities and memory than their monolingual counter-parts, it is reasonable to conclude, as Baker (2003) does in his authoritative assessment of the empirical evidence regarding the cognitive advantages of bilingualism: 'the evidence that currently exists does lead in the direction of bilinguals having some cognitive advantage over monolinguals' (p. 160).

THE CHANGING NATURE OF SOCIETAL BILINGUALISM

The transformed view of the cognitive advantages among bilinguals comes amid significant geopolitical and economic restructuring worldwide that is inaugurating a new phase of societal bilingualism. Until the last few decades, the focus on bilingualism at the societal level in the Western world tended to emphasize nations split between two (or more) large mother tongue groups (for example, French and English in Canada; French, German, Italian and Romansch in Switzerland) or language revitalization of displaced mother tongues (such as Welsh and Irish). Large-scale international migration, however, has redrawn linguistic maps in many parts of the world, with large numbers of bilingual speakers of dozens, and even hundreds, of languages concentrating in the world's urban centres – and increasingly fanning out from there.

Statistics from the largest English-speaking nations are particularly telling in this respect. The 2000 US census returned 17.9 per cent of Americans five years and over as using languages other than English at home, a figure that has been rapidly increasing over the last quarter-century and had already increased to 18.7 per cent, or almost 50 million persons, by the Census Bureau's 2004 American Community Survey (US Census Bureau, 2006). The latter revealed very differential distribution of these non-English mother tongue speakers. For example, in three states, Texas, New Mexico, and California, these comprise one-third of the total – including more than 40 per cent in California. In one-fifth of American states, the non-English mother tongue population comprises more than a fifth of the population, including in all of the nation's five most populous states (California, Texas, New York, Florida, and Illinois) (US Census Bureau, 2006). The 2001 Canadian census found that the mother tongues of 39.9 per cent of the population of Toronto were languages other than English and French, with the corresponding number for Vancouver coming in at 37.6 per cent. The census returned more than 100 different mother tongues in use nation-wide (Canada 2001 census, 2006). While the British census has not so far queried language use, a recent study reports that 30 per cent of London school-children use a language other than English at home, with a total of more than 300 languages represented (Baker and Eversley, 2000). As immigration continues to change the demographics of the world these numbers will continue to grow, with demographers projecting, for example, another 150 million international migrants to the US by 2050.

In the world as a whole, an estimated 175 million people live in nations other than their country of birth (McFalls, 2003: 17). That number increases, currently, by more than 10 million per year, and the number of annual migrants is itself growing (McFalls, 2003:17). The results are more complex than sometimes portrayed. Though the transnational migrations of people are often from a Western perspective seen to be a unidirectional flow of non-Western persons into Western nations, the largest component of that migration is not what we typically hear about – people moving from the global South to the global North. Rather, most of the movement is from one country in the global South to another, often to a regional economic centre. Sometimes the migrants from one country are themselves replaced by migrants from another. For example, South Africa is currently experiencing massive immigration from surrounding countries on a scale comparable to the US or Europe, while the country that provides many of the migrants, Zimbabwe, itself receives many from Mozambique and Malawi. But the pattern is not that simple. South Africa in fact experiences immigration from all over sub-Saharan Africa – a large number, for example, coming from distant Nigeria.

A consideration of international migration alone vastly understates the scale of the process. For if we include all linguistically significant forms of migration, internal migration in multilingual nations, primarily urbanization, accounts for most of the movement. It could be argued that the most powerful force operating in the 'postcolonial' world and driving language use and shift is neither globalization, nation-building, nor ethnic politics, but *urbanization*. The urban population of the global South grew from 304 million in 1950 to 2 billion in 2000 (McFalls, 2003: 30). In fact, we just recently experienced a tipping point – the majority of the world's population now lives in urban areas for the first time (Population Resource Center, 2005). Moreover, the rate of urbanization is actually increasing in many places. In South Africa, for example, the percentage of the population living in urban areas has increased from 50 per cent in 1991 to 58 per cent in 2001 (World Bank World Development Indicators Database) and is projected to increase to 75 per cent by 2020 (Human Rights Watch, 2003). For the continent as a whole, cities grow at an average rate of 4 per cent per year – the highest in the world (Asia is second at 2.6 per cent) (Population Resource Center, 2005). Like their counterparts throughout the world, African cities will attain enormous size – Lagos, Nigeria, is projected to have a population of 23.2 million by 2015 (Population Resource Center, 2005).

The linguistic results are particularly striking. While the number of languages in the world continues to decline, as it has for, perhaps, the last millennium, two other measures of linguistic diversity are increasing: the number of multilingual speakers – or the range of linguistic proficiencies of individual speakers – in many parts of the world and the number of languages represented in most of the large cities of the world. International migrations, together with urbanization in the global South, are bringing together speakers from large numbers of language groups to form perhaps an unprecedented degree of societal bilingualism concentrating up to hundreds of languages represented in the same geographical space.

THE ECONOMIC IMPETUS BEHIND BILINGUALISM

Perhaps the most visible manifestation of the growth of bilingualism has been the spread of English as a second or foreign language, though that language's expansion is not always framed in such terms. As Graddol (2004) puts it, 'Many believe English will become the world language to the exclusion of all others' (p. 1330). It is reasonable to argue that the most significant linguistic effect of globalization has not been either world English or language endangerment, but the increasing prevalence of bilingualism. In this view, the global spread of English is not a step on the way to English Only worldwide but indexes the degree to which we are moving to a world in which *bilingualism and bilinguals are becoming the norm* (cf. Brutt-Griffler, 2002). Graddol (2004) projects, 'English will indeed play a crucial role in shaping the new world linguistic order, but its major impact will be in creating new generations of bilingual and multilingual speakers across the world' (p. 1330). Concomitantly, as Graddol (2004) writes, 'Increasingly, as English spreads across the globe, more people will become bilingual, even multi-lingual, and such skills are highly prized in business' (p. 1329). This is in turn producing renewed motivation for bilingualism in native English speaking nations. There is growing recognition that the ability of nations to produce bilinguals with *advanced* proficiency in at least two languages is becoming a key to global competitiveness. Twenty-first century communicative competence will depend not, as often thought, on possession of advanced proficiency in English, but on *advanced bilingual proficiency* that will be useful in the global market place. Globalization is taking bilingualism from the margins to the mainstream.

The corporate world, cited by some as an engine of English Only worldwide, has in fact embraced bilingualism as a practical economic necessity. The reason is not difficult to discern. As the percentage of the world's commerce that crosses national borders constantly increases (in US dollar figures from $57 billion in 1947 to over $6 trillion in the late 1990s) (Steger, 2003), not just familiarity with, but fluency in, more than one language has increasingly become a prerequisite to effectiveness in more and more segments of global commercial life. A report of the self-described 'pro-business' Washington-based Committee for Economic Development (CED, 2006) stresses that 'full participation in [the] new global economy will require not just competency in reading, mathematics and science, but also proficiency in foreign languages' (p. vii). It argues (p. 6):

> It is becoming increasingly important for US companies of all sizes to succeed in overseas markets. Many small and medium-sized businesses from New England to the Pacific

Northwest are now finding it necessary to do business in the languages and cultural environments of the world's emerging markets. Some small businesses especially need employees with foreign-language skills, as managers must often communicate directly with foreign customers. ... Without foreign-language skills and cultural knowledge, small businesses face greater difficulties exporting to overseas markets.

The necessity extends far up the economic ladder. A survey of global recruiters for executive-level positions in business found that though only 34 per cent of North American respondents considered bilingualism 'critical to succeeding in today's business environment' (as compared to 90 per cent of those questioned in Europe, Asia, and Latin America), a full two-thirds believed it would be so within a decade (identifying Spanish, French, and Chinese as the languages of choice for ambitious North American businesspeople) (Korn/Ferry International, 2005).

The need for advanced bilingual proficiency manifests itself in both expected and less obvious ways. For instance, a US-based call centre trade journal notes that while demand for all employees is experiencing a decline in the US – partly as a result of the outsourcing of such jobs – there is a net shortage of bilinguals in the field, particularly Spanish–English bilinguals (Read, 2004). It is telling that an article in a trade journal for North American chief executives on outsourcing, in recommending potential nations to best fit particular goals, lists the Philippines as 'a base for bilingual Spanish–English language skill' (Fannin, 2004). Bilingualism is among the skills that can be outsourced.

The only remedy is that the educational systems of English-speaking nations must produce highly proficient bilinguals – or lose jobs to nations that do. It is not surprising, therefore, that national self-interest has caused governments across the world to follow the lead of business in concluding that the ability of nations to produce bilinguals with advanced proficiency is a key to global competitiveness. As globalization diversifies language use around the world, English-speaking nations have responded by expressing greater concern for teaching foreign languages to all of their citizens and not only teaching English to immigrant groups.

Nevertheless, the English-speaking nations continue to lag behind. China has launched a major campaign to introduce Chinese–English bilingual education in the schools. The most successful EU nations have achieved bilingualism rates as high as 99 per cent (Luxembourg) and 91 per cent (Netherlands), while the UK comes in at the second lowest (30 per cent) (European Commission, 2005: 3). In the US, only one-third of students in grades 7 to 12 and fewer than one in ten college students take courses in a foreign language (Committee for Economic Development, 2006: 1). As a result, corporate executives in the US self-report an average of 1.5 languages spoken, as against a figure of 3.9 for the Netherlands (Committee for Economic Development, 2006: 7).

EDUCATIONAL CHALLENGES AND GOVERNMENTAL RESPONSE

The implications for education of this linguistic diversity in the era of globalization are profound, as the above-cited statistic of 300 mother tongues present in London schools suggests. In major urban centres in the US, the school-age population is approaching or has reached a preponderance of non-English mother tongue speakers. The proportion of five- to seventeen-year-olds who use a language other than English at home is 48 per cent in New York City, 55 per cent in San Francisco, 66 per cent in Los Angeles and 72 per cent in Miami. Perhaps even more revealing is the picture from a Midwestern city like Minneapolis. Not only does 35 per cent of the school-age population report using languages other than English at home, but the variety of the languages is itself remarkable: about one-third Spanish, another one-third Hmong, with the remaining one-third made up of unspecified African languages (15 per cent), Vietnamese (3.6 per cent), Laotian (2.5 per cent), Arabic (2 per cent), and twenty-six other languages and undifferentiated language groups (Modern Language Association, 2006). The challenges that such linguistic diversity represents are compounded when it is realized that, according to the 2000 US census, more than 4 million children were reported as living in households in which no one over the age of fourteen speaks any English (US Census Bureau, 2006). There are an estimated 5 million K–12 students in the US with limited English proficiency, who, according to Harvard's Catherine Snow, 'arrive with high home-language literacy skills and no English, or with a history of failed and interrupted schooling and no English' (quoted in Guensburg, 2006: 36).

Moreover, as bilingualism increasingly attains the status of requisite to competitiveness in a globalizing world, there is a clear recognition on the part of governments throughout the world of the need to develop advanced competences in *modern foreign languages*. Nor are these limited to the European languages traditionally emphasized in the Western curriculum, as evidenced by the US federal government's allocation of $114 million for encouraging the learning of 'critical' languages like Chinese, Arabic, Hindi, Japanese, Korean, Persian/Farsi, Russian, and Turkish, in which it is deemed crucial to have a supply of highly proficient bilinguals (US Department of State, 2006). The EU's stated goals are even more ambitious, declaring that 'The ability to understand and communicate in other languages is a basic skill for all European citizens' (Commission of the European Communities, 2003: 3). The EU has set a target of every European having 'communicative competence' in 'at least two other languages in addition to his or her mother tongue' (p. 4).

Ministries of Education in such nations as Great Britain, Italy, Korea, and China have begun introducing foreign languages in early education, creating the need for developing effective methods in language pedagogy. This effort to place language education into the curriculum as early in childhood education as possible reflects the notion that 'younger is better' (Ellis, 1994). This line of research provides a justification as to why education specialists might favour the introduction of language teaching at an early stage. Bilingual education specialists provide further support for the potential benefits of early language learning (see, for instance, Bialystok, 2004).

Yet few nations are currently prepared for the challenges that attend to meeting such goals. Even the EU, for example, calls attention to a shortage of 'adequately qualified language teachers' in 'some member states' (Commission of the European Communities, 2003: 10). Among the problems the UK's National Languages Strategy (2002) identifies is a 'shortage of Modern Foreign Language teachers,' particularly those trained in early child development (Department for Education and Skills, 2002: 11).

There is growing awareness, however, that the demographic shifts that are occurring come with a built-in solution. The UK's National Centre for Languages (CiLT) notes, for instance:

> Considerable concern has been expressed in the press about the long-term future of languages in UK schools and universities and about the implications for business. Yet the UK has a major linguistic asset not currently sufficiently recognized in language policy and planning: children from multilingual communities across the UK who are growing up with a knowledge of languages, such as Punjabi, Polish, Somali, or Yoruba, in addition to English. … The linguistic skills and achievements of this group of children are often ignored in discussions of the UK's competence in languages other than English. There is a need to recognize the particular benefits which competence in community languages represents for the children themselves, for their communities and for wider British society, and to identify ways in which their potential can best be realized.
>
> (National Centre for Languages, 2006: 1)

The CiLT reports, 'Mainstream and complementary providers all agree that it is important for students to learn to understand, speak, read and write their community languages well' (National Centre for Languages, 2006: 2).

That goal is not necessarily an easy one to achieve, however:

> It is important to recognize that it takes many years of study for monolingual English-speaking students to acquire high levels of literacy in English, and the same is true for those who speak community languages. Students may gain varying levels of oral fluency at home or in their communities, but learning to read and write the language requires a different sort of attention, particularly when it involves a different script.
>
> (National Centre for Languages, 2006: 2–3)

Even those nations that have long experience in the production of bilinguals may not be prepared for the influxes of non-mother tongue speakers they are currently experiencing. The UK's National Centre for Languages notes:

> A key dilemma for both mainstream and complementary providers is the fact that the range of languages in use in British schools appears to be increasing, but the numbers of students who speak any one language may be small. Moreover, concentrations of students shift from

year to year. Several schools had the experience of recruiting teachers and organizing provision, only to find that numbers of students in that language fell in subsequent years, while the numbers for other languages, not available, rose.

(2006: 3)

As political and market demands increase, what can only be described as a significant resource gap to meet that demand is likely to remain. Though nations like the US and UK have large potential pools of bilinguals in the large numbers of non-English speaking immigrants, these nations lack the bilingual teachers to ensure that students develop literacy in both English and the mother tongues students bring to the classroom. Coming up with adequate solutions to the daunting educational challenges of the provision of bilingual education to these students constitutes one of the principal challenges for language education today, and an area in which e-learning is being increasingly looked to bridge the resource gap many nations are experiencing.

E-LEARNING AND BILINGUAL LANGUAGE DEVELOPMENT

The need to determine specific means for increased and improved instruction in heritage languages and modern foreign languages therefore is of paramount importance internationally. Technology is widely viewed as constituting part of the solution. The UK's Department of Education, for example, suggests, 'Digital technology is already changing how we do business and live our lives. Most schools – and every university and college – now have broadband access' (Department for Education and Skills, 2005: 4). In the spirit of full support for e-learning, it outlined a strategic approach to e-learning to transform teaching and learning and to reach and motivate young learners with special needs. It unequivocally states its intention: 'We need to focus both on e-learning – using ICT to change how we learn, and e-delivery – the mechanisms by which we provide electronic information and services' (p. 8).

Similarly, the Centre for Studies in Advanced Learning Technology suggests that e-learning holds much potential for solving the educational challenges posed by a globalizing world. The Centre defines e-learning as 'the systematic use of networked multimedia computer technologies to empower learners, improve learning, connect learners to people and resources supportive of their needs, and to integrate learning with performance' (2001: 153–4).

The underlying principle in e-learning pedagogy is that technology is a means to an end, not an end in itself. Accordingly, the instructor creates and applies e-learning strategies and resources in teaching and engages students in different e-learning activities. As a delivery system of student-centred, any time–any place learning, e-learning pedagogy, research has shown, increases students' opportunities to interact with content area, promotes communication and collaboration, and adds a worldwide dimension to learning (Waterhouse, 2005).

Scholars rely on the premise that e-learning enhances teaching and learning outcomes. Waterhouse, whose career in technology enhanced teaching and consultancy spans over thirty years, identifies the following strengths of e-learning:

- E-learning facilitates student-centred learning
- E-learing facilitates anytime–anyplace learning
- E-learning facilitates student interaction with course content
- E-learning facilitates and promotes communication and collaboration
- E-learning makes course administration easier
- E-learning helps track students' time on task
- E-learning can reduce the cost of delivering instruction
- E-learning adds a worldwide dimension to courses.

(Waterhouse, 2005: 10)

While stressing the positive outcomes of the e-learning environment, Waterhouse (2005) underscores the importance of applying appropriate *e-learning* pedagogy. She emphasizes that 'e-learning improves learning when instructors focus first on the fundamentals of teaching and learning – that is, on *pedagogical principles* – rather than on e-learning technology' (p. 3, emphasis added). That is, technology is a means to effective learning and teaching and not an end in itself. For Waterhouse, *e-learning pedagogy* involves 'the pedagogical principles and related instructional strategies applicable to an e-learning environment' (p. 4). This will include the instructor's understanding of how to create an *e-learning resource, an activity*, and an *e-learning strategy*. The development of Learning Management Systems (LMS) such as Blackboard or WebCT has allowed instructors to construct a *course site* without requiring advanced programming skills. According to Waterhouse (2005), LMSs play a crucial role in the e-learning environment and e-learning pedagogy. LMSs' functionality extends to four domains (p. 8):

- Distribution of course information
- Student–instructor and student–student communications
- Student interaction with course resources
- Online testing and grading.

Waterhouse's underscoring of *e-learning pedagogy* is particularly important given that scholars have put forth numerous definitions and conceptualizations of what is actually subsumed under *e-learning*. Pedagogical principles would therefore sensibly make the e-learning environment cohere.

From the educational standpoint, the strong advocacy for e-learning comes with calls for teachers to 'innovate' and develop effective and appropriate pedagogies. Garrison and Anderson (2003) point out that educational aspects of e-learning fit well with the communicative potential of new technologies and constructivist and social practice theories of learning.

Research on the effectiveness of e-learning shows positive results in learning outcomes. Kekkonen-Moneta and Moneta (2002) compared learning outcomes among college students in traditional classes and in online courses. It concluded that 'the use of carefully designed interactive eLearning modules fosters higher-order learning' (p. 423). Allen *et al.*'s (2004) meta-analysis comparing the performance of students in distance education and in traditional classes found that distance education students slightly outperformed traditional students on standardized measures (p. 402). This study, however, examined the effectiveness of e-learning in general subject courses. We are yet to determine further the specific impact of e-learning on language learning.

TECHNOLOGY AND LANGUAGE LEARNING

Over the last decades language educators have made significant strides towards the implementation of technology in teaching languages. Within each major phase of the contemporary history of language education, the use of technology found its justification and to a greater or lesser extent some application. In the late 1950s and 1960s, the use of technology in foreign language education was confined to the use of the computer. Language learning informed by the behaviouristic learning theory used the computer as a mechanical tutor which allowed students to 'drill and practise' and they often did so at their own pace. The popularity of communicative language teaching in the 1970s and early 1980s provided a new impetus for the use of technology in the language curriculum. The language teaching profession embraced cognitive theories that viewed learning as a process of discovery, development, and experimentation with language. CALL then was put to the task of creating programmes and simulations that corresponded to the greater cognitive orientation in language learning and teaching. In the late 1980s, language theorists saw the necessity of integrating language skills (listening, speaking, reading, and writing) in language curricula. The *integrated* language instruction broadened communicative language teaching to include both social and cognitive theories of language learning (Warschauer, 1997). During this phase, students were encouraged to use technology and multiple media on an ongoing basis in the classroom, not just once a week in a lab.

The fast-paced development of information and communication technologies (ICT) since the 1990s and language learners' access to it have facilitated different forms of Web-based learning where much communication and interaction takes place in a virtual classroom. By the middle of the 1990s, the Internet introduced new forms of e-learning.

Language educators underscore the following advantages of e-learning in language education:

- Exposure to 'authentic' target language
- Access to wider sources of information and varieties of language
- Opportunities to communicate with the outside world and native speakers
- A learner-centred, task-based approach
- Development of learner autonomy
- Learning in different locations and institutions
- Working at different rates and levels.

(Directorate General of Education and Culture of the European Union, 2006: 19–21)

Research on how technology can enhance the development of specific language skills shows unequal attention to the four language skills. Most of the research studies have focused on the use of technology in writing and reading development; much less research has been carried out to address listening and speaking skills (Liu *et al.*, 2002).

Writing

A sizeable number of studies have addressed the development of specific writing skills such as grammatical accuracy (Gonzalez-Bueno and Perez, 2000), error feedback (Ogata *et al.*, 2000), and the writing process (Thorson, 2000). Much research in the second language writing domain also focuses on the development of written communication skills using synchronous and asynchronous communication tools. CMC studies, for example, highlight the benefits of:

- Equal and increased participation among students when compared to classes that use face-to-face communication (Blake, 2000)
- The use of a wider range of discourse functions (Cubillos, 1998; Sotillo, 2000)
- Greater opportunity for individualized instruction when using technology (Liu *et al.*, 2002).

Reading

Reading has received less research attention when compared to writing. Within this domain, research has focused on the acquisition of lexicon and the use of 'glossing formats', aids that help the reader comprehend unknown phrases and words. There is some evidence to suggest that technology-supported glossing formats help develop reading proficiency (Lomicka, 1998; Nagata, 1999), and multimedia technology significantly enhances vocabulary learning (Grace, 2000).

Speaking

In Liu *et al.*'s (2002) review of research, only six of seventy studies investigated how technology promotes speaking. Liaw's (1997) and Derwing *et al.*'s (2000) studies are worth noting. Liaw (1997) focused on using computer books and investigated the dialogue that took place among the students discussing them.

The study notes that for meaningful discussions to take place students need to have something to talk about. It is argued that computer books could provide the content and stimulus to promote the development of speaking skills. Derwing *et al*. (2000), on the other hand, address the use of speech recognition software and its potential to call attention to learners' production errors. Derwing *et al*., however, caution that the software's feedback on non-native speaker utterance may not always be reliable.

Listening

Relatively few research studies have focused on the development of listening. Leloup and Ponterio (2003) argue that 'The multimedia capabilities of CALL enable learners to engage in a complex listening experience, complete with visual cues from the interlocutor' (p. 2). They point out that the biggest advantage that the research on listening has identified is that 'the multimedia nature of the activities addresses the use of different modalities, thus appealing to a wider variety of learning styles'(p. 2).

E-LEARNING AND BILINGUAL LANGUAGE DEVELOPMENT: THE CASE OF THE UK

The UK has taken the lead in developing a strategy to increase societal bilingualism via the teaching of foreign languages that seeks to make use of the potential power of e-learning. In December 2002, the government issued the National Languages Strategy, *Languages for All: Languages for Life – A Strategy for England*, which sets out the government's plans to transform England's capability in learning languages. One of its key goals is to provide every pupil throughout Key Stage 2 with the opportunity to learn at least one foreign language by the end of the decade. It also outlines plans to 'broaden and enrich the opportunities for language learning at school and beyond' by capitalizing on the notion that 'Languages are a lifelong skill' (Department for Education and Skills, 2002: 1). The clear vision to promote language learning is underscored by the government's recognition that in 'the knowledge society of the twenty-first century, language competence and intercultural understanding are not optional extras, they are an essential part of being a citizen' (p. 5). Its executive summary states that 'For too long we have lagged behind as a nation in our ability to contribute fully as multi-lingual and culturally aware citizens. Likewise in the global economy too few employees have the necessary language skills to be able to engage fully in international business' (p. 5). It states that 'the Government is determined to develop and implement a strategy which will achieve a steep change in language competence and change the country's attitude to teaching and learning foreign languages' (p. 12).

In outlining the *Languages for All* strategy, it states (p. 5) three overarching objectives:

a. To enhance teaching and learning of languages, including 'delivering an entitlement' to study a foreign language for pupils at Key Stage 2. This includes making 'the most of e-learning' and extending it to secondary schools.

b. To develop a system of recognition for students with language skills.

c. To increase the number of people studying languages in higher education and in a work place, including developing Virtual Language Communities across the country, and motivate employers to support language learning.

The government's recognition of the importance of ICT in learning languages – *e-learning* in particular – is worth noting.

Acting upon its strategy, the government has funded nineteen Pathfinder LEAs (partnerships between local education authorities, schools, and other key partners) to design teaching modern foreign languages in primary schools (PMFL), as part of the strategy of introducing them in schools in 2010. The Office for Standards in Education (Ofsted) visited ten of the Pathfinder LEAs in 2004; in July 2005 it issued a study report presenting its findings and samples of best practice. The study notes that the Pathfinder initiative 'has resulted in a significant expansion in modern languages in primary schools'; it notes that, in most schools, 'the modern languages provision was at least satisfactory and often better'; most pupils' listening skills were 'very good'; they showed 'good cultural understanding,' but fewer understood how 'different languages work'. It reports that 'Reading and writing skills were underdeveloped' and that 'Teachers' linguistic competence was at least adequate, although many needed further training to teach at a higher level' (p. 1). It notes that 'few lessons gave pupils opportunities to work independently of the teacher or with information and communication technology (ICT)' (p. 1).

Among the challenges the UK's National Languages Strategy (2002) identifies is a 'shortage of Modern Foreign Language teachers' (p. 11). E-learning represents an important part of the solution to the educational challenges posed by the movement toward societal bilingualism. It can complement the knowledge of the bilingual teacher and enhance the creation of a culturally and linguistically authentic language learning environment. This aspect of e-learning is especially important for students living in remote areas in non-urban contexts and who may lack authentic materials and contact with the target language and culture.

E-LEARNING AND BILINGUAL LANGUAGE DEVELOPMENT: THE CASE OF THE EU

Given its belief that a multilingual citizenry will promote European unity, the EU has launched one of the world's most ambitious language learning programmes, beginning with an emphasis on the necessity of an 'early start' – 'effective kindergarten and primary school level language education' (Commission of the European Communities, 2003: 7) – but including also equal focus on 'a lifetime of language learning' – so it extends beyond schools years. Key areas of strategic development include teacher training (including in early childhood language education) and provision of cross-border educational exchange. The EU's language learning action plan notes (p. 8):

> Socrates/Comenius school language projects, in which a class works together with a class abroad, and which culminate in class exchanges, provide young learners with genuine opportunities to use language skills through contact with learners of the same age. All pupils should have the experience of taking part in such a project and in a related language exchange visit.

In the same manner, under teacher training, emphasis is put on the necessity of teachers having 'adequate experience of using the target language' – to which end it is suggested that teachers 'should have spent an extended period in a country where that language is spoken and have regular opportunities to update their training' (p. 8).

The plan recognizes, however, that, given the prohibitive costs of such programmes, ICT is needed to plug the resource gap. Planners note the impracticality, for instance, of extensive travel and extended stays abroad for language teachers in many contexts, and suggest as an alternative the use of e-learning and distance learning in teacher training. This goal is closely linked to the use of technology to lower the cost of the otherwise prohibitive costs of cross-border educational exchanges. The EU's e-Learning Programme's 'main action' is known as e-Twinning, which electronically links partner schools across national boundaries within the EU. Described as a 'framework for schools to collaborate on the Internet', foreign language education is considered central to the mission of this initiative. e-Twinning is specifically highlighted as 'mak[ing] it possible for all European schools to build pedagogical partnerships with a school elsewhere in Europe, fostering language learning and intercultural dialogue, and promoting awareness of the multilingual and multicultural model of European society'. 'Considerable scope for contact between pupils in other language communities is offered by *e*Learning approaches based on Internet-facilitated school twinnings and on the pedagogical use of ICT for learning (*e*Learning)' (Commission of the European Communities, 2003: 10).

The plan for adult learning, in particular, focuses almost exclusively on building an e-learning-based resource, a Web portal on the Europa server 'giving easy access' to information about language learning resources and giving educational professionals access to materials (Commission of the European Communities, 2003: 16).

E-LEARNING ENVIRONMENT: ITS IMPACT ON THE LANGUAGE LEARNING PROCESS AND LANGUAGE TEACHER AND STUDENT ROLES

The EU Directorate General of Education and Culture commissioned a comprehensive research report entitled *The Impact of Information and Communications Technologies on the Teaching of Foreign Languages and the Role of Teachers of Foreign Languages in Europe*. The group of experts who prepared the report consisted of academics specializing in ICT and foreign language teaching. The steering committee was further supported by a group of practitioners in language education in the seven European countries included in the study. The report examined articles and 'published documentation and forthcoming publications and multimedia' (Directorate General of Education and Culture, 2006: 6) from those EU member states. In addition, it surveyed their Ministries of Education and canvassed the views of 100 experts in the field at the EURO-CALL 2002 conference on the future of new media in foreign language teaching and learning. The report includes over twenty case studies as examples of 'quality innovation' and 'best practice' in the field.

The study found that new media play 'an extremely important role' in foreign language teaching, particularly in the area referred to as 'the new literacies (technical, critical, linguistic and cultural)' knowledge (p. 4). It points out that foreign language teaching is 'different' from 'most other subject areas in the curriculum, namely that it is skill-based as well as knowledge-based, and in this respect it has more in common with Music than, say, History or Geography' (p. 4). This understanding has implications for the selection of technology that is most appropriate to the language learning and teaching domain. In this respect, language teachers working in a media-rich environment need to develop new literacies (scientific, digital, linguistic, cultural) and ICT competences.

It is not surprising, therefore, that the report underscores the importance of teacher training. It points out that the new media do not automatically lead to a new teaching and learning culture; rather, they offer a new platform for change (p. 9). It states, 'Teacher training is shown to be the key to the successful introduction and deployment of the new media' (p. 4). Foreign language teachers need to become aware of their own and their students' changing roles in light of the adoption and use of ICT. The reviewed case studies suggest that 'a shift of paradigm is necessary in teacher/learner roles' (p. 4). The study recommends that language teachers 'focus on the design of situations, sequences and activities conducive to learning languages by encouraging learners to participate in collaborative efforts' (p. 11). The report sums up its findings as follows (p. 4):

> Co-operative, collaborative procedures are called for to harness the wide range of possibilities the new media offer. Teachers are called upon to abandon traditional roles and act more as guides and mentors, exploring the new media themselves as learners and thus acting as role models for their learners.

New media environments allow language learners to communicate rather inexpensively and quickly with other learners or native speakers of the target language worldwide. This gives the learners unprecedented access to authentic target language input. The EU research report indicates that Europe has a 'satisfactory' state of 'network-readiness' and that 'European teachers seem to be overwhelmingly open to technological change'; it states that 'apart from ICT specialists' European teachers are 'the most open to the use of the new media' (p. 5). For instructed foreign language learning, the report provides (p. 8) a set of practical suggestions for the effective implementation of new media:

- Ready access for all learners
- The presence of a full-time technician devoted to servicing and maintaining the functioning of the multimedia laboratory
- The employment of a full-time webmaster
- Adequate training for all new teachers and in-service training for others
- Meaningful use of the multimedia laboratory classes for intensive practice
- Learner-centred approaches to learning
- A total commitment by senior management to the implementation of ICT in language learning classes with vision, support and proactive leadership.

At the same time, the study sounds a cautionary note, stating that the current fascination with technology will give way to 'blended' learning, which will become 'increasingly time and place-independent' (p. 5). It calls for greater attention to be given to a systematic examination of how new media aid language acquisition and learning (p. 5). It also observes the unequal distribution of the use of ICT in foreign language teaching due to a gender and generation divide and suggests that specific training programmes should address it.

THE NEED FOR FURTHER RESEARCH

The need remains to establish a research base on the effectiveness of e-learning in achieving advanced competence in modern foreign languages. There are significant gaps and shortcomings in the existing literature. Among the principal areas of concern are the lack of focus on empirical research, lack of methodological consistency in these studies, and lack of attention to young learners. Liu *et al.* (2002) provide an extensive review of research studies that focus on how technology was used in second and foreign language learning over the period from 1989 to 2000. Out of a total of 246 peer-refereed research studies only seventy were research articles; the vast majority were conceptual discussions or descriptions of projects with respect to (1) the potential of computer technology and its application in specific domains, (2) descriptions of software packages with reference to specific language skills, (3) considerations regarding software design, and (4) considerations regarding computerized language testing.

A second major concern with respect to the body of research on the use of technology in second language learning is that analyses employ an array of methodologies, including some that are entirely experimental and others that rely on qualitative or descriptive statistics (cf. Leloup and Ponterio, 2003). Non-experimental research often results in the use of self-report data, learner discourse, and qualitative studies. The use of such varied methodologies causes problems in categorizing and generalizing across studies (cf. Leloup and Ponterio, 2003) or carrying out meaningful meta-analysis. Furthermore, a sizeable number of research studies in peer-refereed journals fail to use 'well-established measures with clear reliability and validity' (Liu *et al.*, 2002). Low and Beverton (2004) point out that to make research on ICT useful for policy initiatives, it is necessary to examine a range of variables, including the impact of new technologies, the degree of bilingualism in the sample of subjects studied, and to take into account the existing ICT skills of the learners. In some respects, it echoes Chapelle's (2001) observation that 'as possibilities for technology, theory, and pedagogy expand, the need for evaluation has become more urgent' (p. 26). The assessment of the 'value added' of ICT environments is particularly important in light of the numerous national policy initiatives in many countries and universities that are designing their own e-strategy plans.

Finally, the vast majority of studies on the use of technology in second language learning have been carried out with adult populations, subjects that tend to be college-level students. At the same time, the growing number of language learners and bilingual students at the K–12 level necessitates a broadening of the subjects pool in the research base.

Among the central tasks confronting researchers is the need to develop conceptual models for e-learning and literacy development (Andrews, 2004, and see Chapter 1 of this volume) and language pedagogy in particular. We lack a research base that integrates e-learning and bilingualism toward an understanding of specific issues pertaining to the interplay of the individual learning on the one hand and technology on the other hand (e.g., physiological, psychological, cognitive, linguistic, and cultural aspects) in the teaching and learning of modern languages. Researchers must develop synergies between knowledge innovation for language learning and production of educational resources within consistent pedagogical and cultural scenarios. Looking to the longer term, they should aid language educators concerned with innovation and development of specialized materials and curricula for use in foreign languages and bilingual programmes internationally. This new line of research is crucial to developing a greater level of consistency in how e-learning is theorized and how research and implementation of e-learning programmes occur across different institutions and contexts.

REFERENCES

Allen, M., Mabry, E., Mattrey, M., Bourhis, J., Titsworth, S. and Burrell, N. (2004) 'Evaluating the effectiveness of distance learning: a comparison using meta-analysis', *Journal of Communication*, 54 (3): 402–20.

Andrews, R. (2004) 'Reconceptualising Research into the Relationship between ICT and Written Composition', ESRC Research seminar series on Reconceptualising Writing 5–16, Institute of Education, University of London, November.

Arnberg, L. (1981) *Bilingual Education of Young Children in England and Wales*. University of Linkoping, Sweden: Department of Education.

Baker, C. (2003) *Foundations of Bilingual Education and Bilingualism*. Clevedon: Multilingual Matters Press.

Baker, P. and Eversley, J. (eds) (2000) *Multilingual Capital*. London: Battlebridge.

Bialystok, E. (1997) 'Effects of bilingualism and biliteracy on children's emerging concepts of print', *Developmental Psychology*, 33 (3): 429–40.

Bialystok, E. (2004) 'The impact of bilingualism on language and literacy development', in T. K. Bhatia and W. C. Ritchie (eds), *The Handbook of Bilingualism*. Malden, MA: Blackwell. pp. 577–601.

Blake, R. (2000) 'Computer mediated communications: a window on L2 Spanish interlanguage', *Language Learning and Technology*, 4 (1): 120–36.

Brumfit, C., Myles, F., Mitchell, R., Johnston, B. and Ford, P. (2005) 'Language study in higher education and the development of criticality', *International Journal of Applied Linguistics*, 15 (2): 145–69.

Brutt-Griffler, J. (2002) *World English: A Study of its Development*. Clevedon: Multilingual Matters.

Carlisle, J. F. Beeman, M., Davis, L., and Spharim, G. (1999) 'Relationship of metalinguistic capabilities and reading achievement for children who are becoming bilingual', *Applied Psycholinguistics* 20 (4): 459–78.

Centre for Studies in Advanced Learning Technology (2001) *Effective Networked Learning in Higher Education: Notes and Guidelines*. Networked Learning in Higher Education Project JCALT (3), Lancaster University. Online document, retrieved 14 November 2005 from: http://csalt.lancs.ac.uk/jisc.

Chapelle, C. (2001) *Computer Applications in Second Language Acquisition: Foundations for Teaching, Testing and Research*. Cambridge: Cambridge University Press.

Commission of the European Communities (2003) *Promoting Language Learning and Linguistic Diversity: An Action Plan, 2004–2006*. Online document, retrieved 26 March, 2006 from: http://europa.eu.int/comm/education/doc/official/keydoc/actlang/act_lang_en.pdf.

Committee for Economic Development (2006) *Education for Global Leadership: The Importance of International Studies and Foreign Language Education for US Economic and National Security*. Washington, D.C. Online document, retrieved March 26, 2006 from: http://www.ced.org

Cubillos, J. H. (1998) 'Technology: a step forward in the teaching of foreign languages', in J. Harper, M. Lively and M. Williams (eds), *The Coming of Age of the Profession: Issues and Emerging Ideas for the Teaching of Foreign Languages*. Boston, MA: Heinle and Heinle. pp. 37–52.

Cummins, J. (1977) 'Cognitive factors associated with the attainment of intermediate levels of bilingual skills', *Modern Language Journal*, 61: 3–12.

Department for Education and Skills (2002) *Languages for All: Languages for Life: A Strategy for England*. Online document, retrieved 26 March 2006 from: http://www.dfes.gov.uk/languagesstrategy/pdf/DfESLanguagesStrategy.pdf

Department for Education and Skills (2005) *Harnessing Technology: Transforming Learning and Children's Services*. Online document, retrieved 26 March, 2006 from: http://www.dfes.gov.uk/publications/e-strategy.

Derwing, T., Munro, M. and Carbonaro, M. (2000) 'Does popular speech recognition software work with ESL Speech?', *TESOL Quarterly*, 34 (3): 592–602.

Directorate General of Education and Culture of the European Union (2006) *The Impact of New Information Technologies and Internet on the Teaching of Foreign Languages and on the Role of Teachers of a Foreign Language*. Online document retrieved 26 March 2006 from: http://europa.eu.int/comm/education/policies/lang/doc/ict.pdf.

Ellis, R. (1994) *The Study of Second Language Acquisition*. Oxford: Oxford University Press.

European Commission (2005) *Europeans and Languages*. Online document retrieved 3 December 2006 from: http://europa.eu.int/comm/public_opinion/archives/ebs/ebs_237.en.pdf.

Fannin, R. (2004) 'India's outsourcing boom: Sure, the infrastructure is bad. But India's huge labor pool suggests the growth may last', *Chief Executive*, May.

Galambos, S. J. and Hakuta, K. (1988) 'Subject-specific and task-specific characteristics of metalinguistic awareness in bilingual children', *Applied Psycholinguistics*, 9: 141–62.

Garrison, D. R. and Anderson, T. (2003) *E-learning in the Twenty-first Century: A Framework for Research and Practice*. New York: Routledge.

Gonzalez-Bueno, M. and Perez, L. C. (2000) 'Electronic mail in foreign language writing: a study of grammatical and lexical accuracy, and quantity of language', *Foreign Language Annals*, 33 (2): 189–98.

Grace, C. A. (2000) 'Gender differences: vocabulary retention and access to translations for beginning language learners in CALL', *Modern Language Journal*, 84 (2): 214–24.

Graddol, D. (2004) 'The future of language', *Science*, 303 1329–31.

Guensburg, C. (2006) 'Why Johnny (still) can't read', *Edutopia*, February: 35–45.

Human Rights Watch (2003) *Human Rights Watch World Report 2003*. Online document retrieved 24 April 2006 from: http://www.hrw.org/wr2k3/.

Jones, W. R. (1966) *Bilingualism in Welsh Education*. Cardiff: University of Wales Press.

Kekkonen-Moneta, S. and Moneta, G.B. (2002) 'E-Learning in Hong Kong: comparing learning outcomes into online multimedia and lecture versions of an introductory computing course', *British Journal of Educational Technology*, 33 (4): 423–33.

Korn/Ferry International (2005) *Global Survey of Recruiters reveals Demand for Multi-Language Capabilities among Senior Executives will Increase*. Online document, retrieved 28 November 2005 from: http://www.kornferry.com/Library/Process.asp?P=PR_Detail&CID=879&LID=1.

Kramsch, C. (2005) 'Post-9/11: foreign languages between knowledge and power', *Applied Linguistics*, 26: 545–67.

Laurie, S. S. (1890) *Lectures on Language and Linguistic Method in School*. Cambridge: Cambridge University Press.

Leloup, J. and Ponterio, R. (2003) Second Language Acquisition and Technology: A Review of the Research. ERIC Digest. Online document, retrieved from: http://www.cal.org/resources/digest/0311leloup.html.

Liaw, M. (1997) 'An analysis of ESL children's verbal interaction during computer book reading', *Computers in the Schools*, 13(3–4): 55–73.

Liu, M., Moore, Z., Graham, L. and Lee, S. (2002) 'A look at the research on computer-based technology use in second language learning: a review of the literature from 1990–2000', *Journal of Research on Technology in Education*, 34 (3): 250–73.

Lomicka, L. (1998) 'To gloss or not to gloss: an investigation of reading comprehension online', *Language Learning and Technology*, 1 (2): 41–50.

Long, M. (1990) 'Maturational constraints on language development', *Studies in Second Language Acquisition*, 12: 251–85.

Low, G. and Beverton, S. (2004) 'A systematic review of the impact of ICT on literacy learning in English of learners between 5 and 16, for whom English is a second or additional language', in *Research Evidence in Education Library*. London: EPPI-Centre, Social Science Research Unit, Institute of Education.

McFalls, J. (2003) 'Population: a lively introduction', *Population Bulletin*, 58 (4): 3–39.

Modern Language Association (2006) *MLA Language Map*. Online document retrieved 24 April 2006 from: http://www.mla.org/census_main.

Nagata, N. (1999) 'The effectiveness of computer-assisted interactive glosses', *Foreign Language Annals*, 32 (4): 469–79.

National Centre for Languages (2006) *Language Trends 2005: Community Language Learning in England, Wales and Scotland*. Online document retrieved 26 March 2006 from: http://www.cilt.org.uk/key/trends2005/trends2005_community.pdf.

Nettle, D. and Romaine, S. (2002) *Vanishing Voices: The Extinction of the World's Languages*. Oxford: Oxford University Press.

Office for Standards in Education (2005) *Implementing Languages Entitlement in Primary Schools: An Evaluation of Progress in Ten Pathfinder LEAs*. Online document, retrieved from: http://www.ofsted.gov.uk.

Ogata, H., Feng, C., Had, Y. and Yano, Y. (2000). 'Online markup based language learning environment', *Computers and Education*, 34 (1): 51–66.

Peal, E. and Lambert, W. E. (1962) 'The relationship of bilingualism to intelligence', *Psychological Monographs*, 76 (27): 1–23.

Population Resource Center (2005) Executive summary: *World Population Trends*. Online document retrieved 26 March, 2006 from: http://www.prcdc.org/summaries/worldpopupdate02/worldpopupdate02.html

Read, B. B. (2004) 'Wanted: quality agents!' *Call Center Magazine*. Online document retrieved 28 November 2005 from: http://www.callcentermagazine.com/showArticle.jhtml?articleID=18201851.

Saer, D. J. (1923) 'The effects of bilingualism on intelligence', *British Journal of Psychology*, 14: 25–38.

Sotillo, S. (2000) 'Discourse functions and syntactic complexity in synchronous and asynchronous communication', *Language Learning and Technology*, 4 (1): 82–119.

Statistics Canada (2001) *2001 Census of Canada*. Online document retrieved 23 April 2006 from: http://www12.statcan.ca/english/census01.

Steger, M. (2003) *Globalization: A Very Short Introduction*. New York: Oxford University Press.

Thorson, H. (2000) 'Using the computer to compare foreign and native language writing processes: a statistical and case study approach', *Modern Language Journal*, 84 (2): 155–70.

Tunmer, W. E. and Herriman, M. L. (1984) 'The development of metalinguistic awareness: a conceptual overview', in W. E. Tunmer, C. Pratt and M. L. Herriman (eds), *Metalinguistic Awareness in Children*. Berlin: Springer-Verlag. pp. 12–35.

US Census Bureau (2006) *Language Spoken at Home: 2004 Community Survey*. Online document retrieved 24 April 2006 from: http://factfinder.census.gov/servlet/STTable?_bm=y&-geo_id=01000US&- qr_name=ACS_2004_EST_G00_S1601&ds_name=ACS_2004_EST_G00_.

US Department of State (2006) *President introduces Foreign Language Initiative: New and Enhanced Programmes to help Americans study Critical-need Languages*. Online document retrieved 26 March 2006 from: http://usinfo.state.gov/gi/Archive/2006/Jan/06-344515.html.

Warschauer, M. (1997) 'Computer-mediated collaborative learning: theory and practice', *The Modern Language Journal*, 81: 470–81.

Waterhouse, S. (2005) *The Power of e-Learning: The Essential Guide for Teaching in the Digital Age*. New York: Pearson Education.

World Bank *World Development Indicators* Database (2006). Online document retrieved 24 April 2006 from: http://web.worldbank.org.

17

Second Language Learning and Online Communication

Carol A. Chapelle

The potentials of e-learning are likely to be explored for many years to come in view of some of its obvious logistical benefits for learners and apparent financial incentives for institutions. Exploration of teaching practice requires a parallel research programme to investigate the nature and effects of dialogue and communities of enquiry in e-learning in higher education. The commonsense approach to this issue is to compare outcomes of e-learning with those of classroom learning, but this approach has proven to be too simplistic for understanding the characteristics and potentials of e-learning. As Garrison and Anderson (2003) put it, 'Why would we expect to find significant differences if we do exactly the same thing [in the two modes of learning]…?' (p. 6). They conceptualize the changes prompted by e-learning as more radical than what can be captured through assessment of outcomes and comparisons with outcomes from classroom learning. At the core of the issue, in their view, is that education is about ideas, not facts, and that e-learning provides more than access to information: it affords opportunities for communication and interaction. But how does one assess how well learners are formulating ideas through communicative interaction in e-learning activities?

Garrison and Anderson argue that the quality of student assessment rests in the use of a variety of measuring devices, and that some of these need to assess the quantity and quality of learners' participation and contribution in online discussion. This perspective is consistent with the views of those who study second language learning through technology. The second language research additionally emphasizes the specific linguistic character of learners' interactions, which in some studies have been evaluated in view of ideals for the type of communicative language use believed to foster language development. This chapter reviews the questions second language researchers have formulated and methods they have used to investigate online learning. The many exploratory studies of second language e-learning reveal an array of analytic methods for analysis of learners' language and therefore suggest implications for research on learning through online communication.

The research methods illustrated through the study of second language learning through technology reflect what applied linguists do – they study how people make meaning though their linguistic choices. Research on this issue is concerned with describing specific words and phrases that are chosen to create larger units of language referred to as genres (Halliday and Hasan, 1989; Swales, 1990). Genre research in applied linguistics has extended into the study of language in e-discourse (Herring, 1996; Erickson, 1999). In second language studies, researchers typically study linguistic choices that are constrained not only by the context of language use, but also by the linguistic ability of the language user. The goal of research is to understand how language develops through learners' engagement with particular learning conditions. The study of language development through communication is of interest to any researcher studying learning through electronic communication because the language of online interactions reveal learners' growing understanding of ideas and concepts through the increased sophistication in the language they choose to communicate about complex ideas. Learning a subject means learning the language of the subject. Learners' language also reveals increased confidence and expertise through the choices they make for framing and hedging their contributions (e.g. through questions and statements). In a sense, all students are second language students as they attempt to learn the ideas of a subject along with the language that they can use to express these ideas. As a consequence, the methods of applied linguists should be of interest to a range of researchers who study learning through electronic communication.

SECOND LANGUAGE RESEARCH QUESTIONS AND FINDINGS

Most people hold the view that the best way to learn a second language is to go to the country where it is spoken and talk to people. If one cannot go where the language is spoken, can the vital conversations take place online? Following this line of thought, one might even ask whether or not students can learn a second language better through online communication than they do in traditional classrooms? In second language research, like in other areas, a simple answer to this question has proven to be elusive in part because of the variety of approaches that are used for e-learning in second languages, including courses taught completely at a distance, various blended configurations, and short modules of e-communication within a primarily traditional classroom course. Researchers in applied linguistics who are concerned with technology have argued for years that such comparisons fail to yield results that provide insights and recommendations about the use of technology for second language teaching. Instead, researchers have reframed the question and generated new ones about technology and language learning in general and online communication more specifically. The questions that have focused research on second language learning through online communication can be divided into three types – descriptive, evaluative, and critical. Table 17.1 defines these three perspectives with examples of research questions and analytic approaches to data analysis that fall into each type. Examples of studies are included in the right column.

Table 17.1 Summary of research on second language learning through online communication

Analytic perspective	Research questions	Analytic approach to data analysis	Examples of second language studies
Description	What is the nature of interaction in e-learning?	Discourse analysis of functions; applied conversation analysis	Chun (1994), Negretti (1999)
	How do learners engage in language play in a MOO?	Discourse/content analysis	Warner (2004)
Evaluation	Can negotiation of meaning or other language-related episodes occur in online communication?	Discourse analysis of negotiation sequences	Blake (2000), de la Fuente (2003), Garcia and Arbelaiz (2003), Kitade (1999), Lee (2001), Lamy and Goodfellow (1999), Pelletierri (2000)
	How are topics nominated and sustained?	Discourse/content analysis of final exchanges	Stockwell (2003), Schwienhorst (2004)
	How good is written CMC as rehearsal for oral communication?	Discourse analysis and word counts	Weininger and Shield (2003)
	Is there evidence for emergent grammatical competence in online communication?	Longitudinal microanalysis of discourse (referred to as microgenetic)	Belz (2004), Salaberry (2000)
	Can pragmatic competence be developed through online communication?	Microanalysis of discourse (referred to as microgenetic)	Belz and Kinginger (2003), Kinginger (2000)
	Is intercultural competence enhanced through online communication?	Post-task interviews with participants; discourse/content analysis of appraisals	O'Dowd (2000), Belz (2003)
Critical analysis	How do the learners' meaning and use of online communication tools construct their learning experience?	Content analysis and other observations	Thorne (2003)

Description

Descriptive research attempts to characterize the nature of the interactions that learners engage in through online learning. In studies of instructional technology, descriptive research has played an important role (Knupfer and McLellen, 1996) in understanding the new forms of interaction afforded by the medium. Data analysis, which is accomplished through discourse analysis or conversation analysis, is used to reveal the linguistic characteristics of learners' production, the nature of the interaction, or, more recently, the way that play is accomplished.

The nature of interaction

The methodologies used for description of interaction fall within the broad set of analytic perspectives called discourse analysis which examine how writers and speakers use language to express particular meanings in view of the context in which communication takes place. In the study of e-learning, the context is interesting because it is constructed virtually when participants' language intersects in asynchronous and synchronous modes. The best known example of discourse analysis from the classroom is Sinclair and Coulthard's (1975) study of classroom talk, which identified the functional sequences of Initiation, Response, and Follow-up (IRF). From a discourse analytic perspective, one can study the language of online collaborative learning to discover the extent to which the patterns of discourse (IRF) structures found in classrooms are evident. Today researchers studying second language classrooms would argue that the ideal is for learners to engage in other types of discourse functions, and therefore the discourse analytic research on e-learning has tended to seek evidence for the use of a variety of discourse functions. In other words, does e-learning help to construct a context for communication where learners can expand the functions of language they produce from 'response' to other functions such as 'initiate'?

Analysis of functions

The first significant descriptive study of language learning through online communication was conducted by Chun (1994), who identified in learners' language a number of interactional speech acts displaying a number of functions – for example, asking questions and requesting clarifications. She investigated the functions used by first-year German learners in computer-mediated communication in a university classroom in the US. This and other studies have concluded that online communication is valuable for language practice on the basis of the amount of communication that learners participated in enthusiastically. The implicit comparison is with learners' oral language in the classroom, although, except for Warschauer (1995/1996), comparisons were made intuitively. The overwhelming majority of the descriptions of interactive written classroom discourse conclude with the positive finding that the written interactive medium promotes relatively large amounts of participation and that learners practice a variety of communicative language use (Beauvois, 1992; Kelm, 1992; Kern, 1995; Warschauer, 1995/1996; Ortega, 1997; González-Bueno, 1998). For example, learners perform functions such as greeting, questioning, providing information, joking, and managing other students. This is important because second language researchers would agree that learners benefit from engaging in meaningful conversation and that in order to develop their language fully they need to use language for a variety of functions in communication in view of the essential role of meaning-focused linguistic production for second language learning.

Conversation analysis

Conversation analysis is a specific micro-ethnographic approach sometimes placed within the broad umbrella of discourse analysis. Conversation analysis attempts to capture how language users' utterances accomplish communicative intent and social action through conversation. In practice, it is sometimes difficult to distinguish between the range of practices that are included under discourse analysis and the more specific method of conversation analysis. However, in one study of English as a Second Language (ESL) learners in a text chat, Negretti (1999) identifies her method of analysis of data from written online chat communication as conversation analysis with the following rationale:

> Given the present state of [second language acquisition] research in Internet-based environments and computer-mediated communication, a heuristic–inductive approach such as conversation analysis (CA) is the most useful and fruitful because such a hypothesis-generating method is a good way to begin the study of new interaction/acquisition situations.
>
> (Negretti, 1999: 76)

Rather than beginning with functional categories such as asking questions and expressing agreement, Negretti's description discovered the conversational routines that the learners used for openings, closing, topic shifts, and cohesion, for example. In other words, the conversation analysis used in this study served as a means of describing language practices. Detailed examination of the play-by-play deployment of social interaction in a virtual environment described in a conversation analytic style is also provided by Roed (2003), who emphasizes the importance of psychological factors associated with willingness to communicate (MacIntyre *et al.*, 2001) such as low anxiety and strong confidence. Both of these studies suggest how communication and social acts such as openings, closings, and creating cohesion are accomplished in the new forum for second language communication offered by synchronous text-based electronic communication. What is important for second language studies is the fact that learners need to develop a somewhat different set of linguistic resources from those required for writing on paper or communicating face-to-face.

Play

A more specific focus was directed to data gathered over the course of a one-semester project to understand the use of a MOO (a type of text-based virtual reality system) as a supplement for a communicative language class (Warner, 2004). The questions were exploratory, but they focused on playful use of language in the MOO. What types of play do students use? When and how does play appear? Warner examined four sessions for an intermediate communicative German course and two sessions from an intermediate conversation course. She also interviewed the instructors, and asked the students to comment on their language use as they examined the transcripts of the MOO sessions.

The analysis highlighted instances of three categories of play identified from prior theory and research in second language acquisition: (1) play with the linguistic form, such as rhyming, making parallel structures, and repeating, (2) play with content or concepts, such as inventing new things or combinations through language, and (3) play with the frame, such as what can be done when the speaker takes on a different role or adopts a positioning that has already been taken up in previous utterances. Having found such instances in the data, Warner concluded there is a need to expand the scope of what is considered interesting and important in such transcripts beyond referential communication used to accomplish a clear goal. Warner (2004) argued that:

> greater attention must be paid to playful elements in language use that are not limited to the linguistic form. Students in the German classes were not simply playing with the language, but playing within the language. In such instances, it is not primarily meaning that is being negotiated, but also the relations between speakers, their interlocutors, the medium, and the context. What's more, they are negotiating their relation to a foreign language, which to them feels in some ways inauthentic and, as one student noted, like 'just a game'.

Anyone who has conducted synchronous communication in the classroom recognizes that such play is not limited to second language users!

These descriptive studies all characterize some aspect of the online communication with the implicit intent of evaluating the quality of the learning tasks or at least understanding them better. However, the focus is on providing a careful description of the language that occurs when learners at a particular level engage in specific types of tasks online. The evaluation studies, which are described next, are explicitly intended to examine the value of specific aspects of performance of interest to the researcher.

Evaluation

Evaluation research seeks direct evidence of language learning resulting from online activities. Rather than beginning with open questions about how dialogic interaction is constructed, it begins with assumptions about how learning might take place and what evidence would indicate that positive learning episodes are occurring. Evaluation is a challenge for those wishing to study online second language learning for at least these three reasons (Chapelle, 2003):

- Online learning is typically used as one of many forms of language practice for learners in a larger programme of instruction and out-of-class activities, so the idea that learners would learn the language exclusively from the online activities the teacher constructs is at odds with the reality of many e-learning situations.
- Learners, not teachers, frequently select the linguistic points to be the focus of attention in communication tasks, and therefore pre-planned assessment of acquisition of particular linguistic points is not feasible.
- Evaluation that genuinely informs software developers, teachers, and learners about how to learn better through technology requires delicate analysis of the process of learning. Research revealing that one class did better than another does not reveal what aspects of the e-learning were responsible for success or failure of the group, and therefore additional data are needed to document teaching and learning strategies, for example.

In view of these challenges for evaluation of second language e-learning, researchers seek evidence for learning by focusing on key aspects identified in second language acquisition theory and research.

Negotiation of meaning

Several studies of learners' use of online communication for second language tasks have evaluated the quality of interactions by relying on interactionist second language acquisition theory (e.g. Gass, 1997; Pica, 1994) which hypothesizes benefits when communication breakdowns occur and learners have to negotiate meaning (Long and Robinson, 1998). Example 1 below comes from such a study in which the researcher recorded the conversation of two learners communicating over voice chat on the Internet (Sauro, 2001). The key episode begins in the third turn, or contribution to the conversation, where Sumiko, the ESL learner, signals lack of comprehension of Andy's message. Sumiko's 'Pardon?' prompts Andy to modify what he said with a simplification, which she appears to understand. The process of misunderstanding and stopping to obtain a message that can be understood is hypothesized to be beneficial for second language learning, and therefore such sequences are the object of interest to the researcher.

Example 1: Negotiation of meaning (from Sauro, 2001)

Sumiko. All right. So about our friend Harry.

Andy. Yeah, I'm a little concerned about him. I don't know, I'm a little concerned about him. I think he should take some leadership courses so he can gain some confidence. It looks like he's got a choice. He's interested in either Stanford or MIT.

Sumiko. Pardon?

Andy. It looks like Harry is interested in Stanford and MIT.

Sumiko. Yeah.

Andy. I don't know exactly how much you know about Harry, but I do know some things about Harry. And, ah, I think he's got a great personality, but, ah, he's got himself some challenges to deal with. He's having a difficult time trying to pick a university to, to study at. And, ah, I do know some things about him. Maybe if we work together on this problem, we go ahead and solve the issues, maybe we can give a recommendation to Harry.

Blake (2000) drew on the same theoretical perspective in the analysis of text chat data. Fifty intermediate learners of Spanish were assigned several different types of communication tasks that were designed within the guidelines of research investigating face-to-face tasks for second language learning (Pica *et al.*, 1993). Blake assigned jigsaw tasks (requiring learners to piece together a solution with information they did not share) and decision-making tasks (requiring learners to make a decision based on shared information). The jigsaw task requires negotiating who has what information and using the information to reach a goal. In Blake's study, results were consistent with expectations: negotiation of meaning was observed. Similar findings were also obtained from a study in which tasks were designed the same way but each pair of learners consisted of one heritage speaker of Spanish (a learner whose home language was Spanish while growing up) and one learner of Spanish (Blake and Zyzik, 2003). Thus the finding that the jigsaw task helped to create a context in which negotiation of meaning took place has been found repeatedly across different languages, topics, and participants.

Other research provides less clear support for online communication as a forum for fostering negotiation of meaning. Lee examined the communication strategies evident in language produced during online conversations among forty learners of Spanish who were either majoring or minoring in Spanish at a university in the US. Students were organized into groups of three or four, with a mix of language proficiencies. They were given extra credit for participating in open-ended discussions that were initiated by a topic provided by the researcher, such as Halloween or Thanksgiving. Lee reports that:

> The impact of responding to negative feedback or incomprehensible messages proved to be meaningful for learners because it allowed them to try out different vocabulary and language structures in order to modify input and output. The modified interactions, therefore, facilitated mutual understanding. In terms of linguistic accuracy, [however,] learners tended to ignore each other's mistakes and moved on with the discussions. This shows that students focused on the meaning of the communication rather than on the form itself'.

(Lee, 2001: 242)

In a setting where getting the meaning across is the only goal, this finding would be good news, but in conversations intended to help the development of linguistics accuracy and complexity of learners' language knowledge, good negotiation of meaning encompasses attention to linguistic form in order to move beyond communication breakdowns.

Whereas the studies discussed above quantified the instances of negotiation of meaning evident in the data from chat tasks, two more recent studies have compared the amount and effects of negotiation of meaning in chat with that appearing in a comparable task carried out through face-to-face interaction. García and Arbelaiz (2003) compared the negotiation of meaning in face-to-face communication versus written online communication in second language tasks for university learners of Spanish. They found that more communication breakdowns occurred in face-to-face communication in part due to difficulty in perceiving the oral language. The written mode of communication facilitated comprehension, precluding the need for the use of repair strategies. De la Fuente (2003:74) found 'that both face-to-face and CM [computer-mediated], text-based interaction, where learners need to negotiate the meaning of target words, seem to be equally effective in promoting written receptive and productive acquisition and retention of second language vocabulary'.

Other studies drawing on a similar theoretical orientation are concerned with a variety of exchanges that indicate that learners are paying attention to the language in a way that directs their attention to gaps in their knowledge of the second language. Such language-related episodes (Swain, 1998) are hypothesized to be useful for language development. Kitade (2000), for example, analysed transcripts from the chat sessions of Japanese learners, finding instances where the learners had noticed and corrected their errors, either because they had recognized the errors themselves or because other chatters had pointed out the errors to them. In addition to this type of 'productive repair' she also found negotiation of meaning, concluding that the use of Internet chat with 'task-based second language interaction facilitates comprehensible and meaning-making interaction, awareness raising, as well as collaborative learning' (p. 162). She attributes these positive attributes of the communication to the fact that learners do not have to compete under time pressure for turns in the conversation. Instead, they can compose and post their messages at their own speed. Lamy and Goodfellow's (1999) construct of 'reflective conversation' – online discussion among learners about language and language learning – seems to get at the same idea of putting the language under the learners' direct attention. They contrast this with social conversation, which requires little negotiation of meaning or stretching of competence. Overall, this research suggests that online communication can include both the focus on meaning that occurs in social conversation and the focus on form that can push learners' linguistic competence.

Nominating and sustaining topics

Several studies by Stockwell and colleagues have attempted to identify factors that may affect the sustainability of e-mail communications between native and non-native speakers. The idea is that in order to be valuable as language practice for non-native speakers, online communication needs to occur for an extended period of time and that learners need to be actively involved by initiating topics.

Stockwell (2003) focused on characteristics of the final message in an exchange between native and non-native speakers. The e-mail exchanges took place among forty-eight students at an Australian university and thirty-four students at a Japanese university. The Australian students were advanced learners of Japanese and the students in Japan were studying cross-cultural communication. The teachers in the two courses set the topics (e.g. dining out, dating and socializing) but told the students that they could move beyond those set topics. Students were asked to write four to five e-mails in Japanese per week over a five-week period. All the e-mails were stored and the topic threads were analysed to identify messages that marked the end of the thread. In 70 per cent of the cases, the topic thread ended in a manner that the researchers characterized as natural, meaning that 'no reply or request for further information was invited in the final message of a topic thread' (Stockwell, 2003: 40). The majority of the remaining 30 per cent of the topics ended with a message that contained multiple topics in one e-mail ($n = 163$). Other reasons for ending the exchange were: sudden cessation due to assigned topics ($n = 93$), lack of explicitness ($n = 84$), syntactic error ($n = 34$), asking about a question already answered ($n = 16$), pragmatic error ($n = 8$), topic closed by one speaker ($n = 4$), unknown ($n = 90$). These results are intended to point toward directions for helping learners to maintain conversations.

Schwienhorst (2004) examined the extent to which topic initiation was shared between native speakers and non-native speakers in synchronous communication in order to obtain evidence about how topic initiation and maintenance are similar to or different from these discourse patterns in classroom conversation. The comparisons were made based on findings from previous research on oral face-to-face tasks and the chat scripts recorded during collaborative tasks performed by native speakers of German and learners of German. Findings indicated equal sharing of topic initiation moves, which showed that learners were maintaining a position equal to the native speakers in the e-communication. This is one of the ways that the electronic communication is an equalizer among participants who typically have uneven power in a typical face-to-face conversation – an unevenness that works against the learner. A medium that empowers learners to contribute, and indeed share in the control of the conversation, appears very promising for language learning.

Quality of language as rehearsal

Weininger and Shield (2003) evaluated the extent to which the discourse constructed through a written mode can be considered valuable to second language learners as rehearsal for oral communication. Their assumption was that similarities in language use in MOOs, Internet spaces for synchronous written communication, and in spoken registers, as reflected in the use of pronouns, greeting forms, and conversational particles (e.g. 'humm'), would indicate that MOO was good as rehearsal for oral communication. Based on quantitative analysis of data from transcripts of chat in a MOO by second language learners, and native speakers, a large corpus of written language, and a large corpus of spoken language, the authors concluded that the similarities between MOO and oral language were sufficient to pursue the use of MOO as rehearsal. For example, the ratio of first and second-person pronouns to third-person pronouns is higher in oral language (1.97) than it is in written language (0.46) because in conversation it is more typical to talk in terms of *you* and *I*, whereas in written language one is more likely to read about *he* and *they*, for example. In the MOO chat scripts of both native and non-native speakers the ratio is also high, in fact even higher than that of the oral language (4.28 for non-native speakers and 4.57 for native speakers). The criteria for 'similarity' are obviously open to interpretation, but the point is that learners' participation in the MOO environment provides them with some practice that may be beneficial for development of their spoken language.

Emergent grammatical competence

Interesting data on language development in electronic communication have come from a project investigating learners of French and German at Penn State University. Drawing on the German data, Belz's (2004) study described a learner's use of a grammatical construction, the da-compound, over the course of a semester of German study. Da-compounds, which are used to create cohesion within and across sentences, are considered to reflect an advanced level of proficiency in German, and therefore the development of this linguistic device is worthy of examination across time. Belz examined a 100,000-word corpus of online collaborative correspondence through a microgenetic analysis, which 'traces the history of development of particular phenomena (e.g. the appropriate use of a particular grammatical structure) through close examination of its ecology of use in a given task' (Belz, 2004). The students spent at least two hours in online collaboration over an eight-week period. The findings demonstrate the qualitative process of microgenesis of a construction. The idiomatic uses of this feature are the first to appear, followed by those with anaphoric reference, and finally occurrences with cataphoric reference appear over time through the online collaboration. The perspective taken is that this emergence of grammatical competence in use is something that is seen over the course of communication among competent interlocutors, which, practically speaking, could only occur through the type of extended dialogue engaged in by the learners in this study.

The da-compound presents a different learning challenge from the linguistic construction analysed by Salaberry (2000). Based on his comparison of development of the morphosyntactic construction of present-tense verb inflections in oral face-to-face versus written chat interactions, Salaberry concluded that the written conversation is more effective because the distinctions among verb forms are more salient in written exchanges than they are in oral communication. This finding is consistent with Pellettieri's (2000) finding that learners negotiated *form* in addition to negotiating meaning in text chat tasks similar to those used in Blake's (2000) study. Presumably these Spanish learners were able to focus on the details and the correctness of the morphosyntax that they had studied when they were not operating under the pressure of face-to-face communication and the elusiveness of oral language. In other words, the written interactive communication unique to online learning appeared to offer an advantage for learning particular aspects of language.

Development of pragmatic competence

'Pragmatic competence' refers to the knowledge that allows speakers to make contextually appropriate linguistic choices. Pragmatic competence presents a different challenge to language learners from that of development of grammatical knowledge because the 'rules' are different. Typical classroom discourse is not conducive to development of pragmatic competence because of the lack of variety in the social contexts present in the classroom (Kasper, 2001).

Whereas grammatical competence can be learned and practised through communicative classroom activities, pragmatic competence is better developed when learners can observe appropriate linguistic choices made by a variety of interlocutors. Belz and Kinginger (2003) and Kinginger (2000) reported on the analysis of data from a study of the German–English and French–English collaborative teams who communicated with each other over a two-week period during the overlapping segment of their language classes. The students in Germany were preparing to be English teachers, and the students in the US were fourteen undergraduates in fourth-semester German classes. The students were required to engage in telecollaborative activity, first, exchanging introductions and personal information through e-mail, second, discussing through synchronous and asynchronous communication class readings and films, and third, constructing Web sites showing comparisons of their interpretations.

The data that were collected demonstrate the development of pragmatic competence in the choice of the formal versus the informal variety of the word 'you' in French and German. As shown in Example 2, the English speaker uses the formal form of you, *vous*, to say 'But sometimes I would like to write in English for you.' The French speaker, who is also a student of the same status as the English speaker, responds, 'I'm twenty-one years old, so therefore you should say *tu* [familiar 'you'] to me.'

Example 2

English speaker. Mais, quelquefois, je voudrai ecriver en anglais pour vous …

French speaker. J'ai vingt-et-un ans aussi, donc *tu* dois me dire '*tu*'.

(Kinginger, 2000: 36)

The researchers point out that this pragmatic use has certainly been taught in the classroom, but, without the real need to use the appropriate forms to keep from offending the interlocutor, this pragmatic choice is not mastered in the classroom. In contrast, 'The long-distance relationships formed by students offer contexts for language socialization, with support for conscious awareness of, and assisted performance in, the appropriate uses of the second-person pronoun (*tu* versus *vous*)' (Kinginger, 2000: 23). The data from the weeks of collaborative work of the Americans with the Germans and with the French demonstrate many instances of help such as the one shown in Example 2, and demonstrate that most learners improved dramatically in this area.

Intercultural competence

Intercultural competence is one of the goals of second language teaching. It seems to be something for which online distance collaborations would be ideal. Examples of two studies investigating the value of such communication used different methodologies for evaluating the extent to which learners benefited from such collaborations.

Post-task interviews

O'Dowd (2000) used post-task interviews to assess students' views about their development of intercultural knowledge. The projects and online discussion between a Spanish class in northern Michigan in the US and the University of León in Spain focused explicitly on the stereotypical ideas and attitudes that the students held toward each other. The report of interview data highlights areas where students recognized that their knowledge and attitudes had changed as a result of the communication. For example, one participant reported, 'I learned that it is not good to generalize, because even though many Americans don't even know where Spain is, there are definitely some who know that we exist …' (pp. 56–7). This type of result is representative of other studies that have used online communication in order to increase intercultural competence.

Discourse/content analysis of appraisals

Belz (2003) examined the extent to which she could find evidence of learners' development of intercultural competence in the dialogue of learners participating in collaborative cross-cultural exchanges. The analysis focuses on the linguistic realization of appraisal in the learners' language. From a systemic functional perspective, appraisals are evident in the attitudes expressed through the interpersonal functions of language that are evident in expressions such as 'I suppose that …' versus 'I know that …' These are related to intercultural competence (IC), Belz (2003) argues, because:

> IC is centrally concerned with suspending disbelief about the other and belief about the self. In other words, IC entails modifying or re-evaluating one's evaluations of other societies, cultures, and individuals (through confrontation with them) as well as re-analyzing one's evaluations of the self and one's own culture and society. The subsystem of ATTITUDE, therefore, provides a concrete and transparent linguistic procedure for revealing how speakers do this in the empirical details of their talk at the microinteractional level.

Despite that fact that one might wish to construe and investigate culture in a more complex way (Atkinson, 2000), the potential of online learning for helping students to expand beyond their own material and cultural reality is clearly something to pursue for second language learning.

Critical perspectives

Postmodern critical perspectives are expanding the research questions and findings concerning e-learning in the classroom and beyond (Warschauer, 1998). This research is grounded on the assumption that:

> Internet communication tools cannot be fully apprehended from a positivist vantage point as generically 'there' in the world. Cultural artifacts such as global communication technologies are produced by and productive of socio-historically located subjects. Such artifacts take their functional form and significance from the human activities they mediate and the meanings that communities create through them.

> (Thorne, 2003)

Through the use of case study analysis of the content of learners' communications, Thorne was able to identify ways in which the learners' prior knowledge of content as well as their preferences and habits of technologically-mediated communication affected the nature of communication between them and their potential interlocutors, who were native speakers of French living in France.

Another example of the research drawing upon critical perspectives was Lam's (2000) study of an ESL learner in the US who was able to connect with a transnational cohort through the use of his English and technology skills. The critical perspective captures the transformative process afforded by this learner's appropriation of the technology to construct a new, confident English-speaking identity for himself, which is as important as the linguistic knowledge displayed by learners in tasks constructed by others.

Critical perspectives and use of critical discourse analysis for the study of e-discourse for second language learning are likely to appear more and more in the coming years, but at the moment few studies have adopted these methods.

Summary

The results from the research reported should be considered in view of the small-scale studies upon which they are based, but the following positive conclusions seem warranted:

- Learners can gain some second language practice in online communication that may be valuable for performance in other contexts.
- Negotiation of meaning, and negotiation of form, have been observed in online communication, but may not compare favourably with face-to-face conversation quantitatively.
- Learners have been observed developing syntactic, pragmatic, and intercultural competence through online communication.
- The function of online communication is not limited to a tool that teachers can use to construct collaborative tasks for learners; it is potentially a transformative tool that each learner, depending on his or her own knowledge and agency, can use to construct an identity as a user of the second language beyond the classroom.

RESEARCH IMPLICATIONS REGARDING LEARNING THROUGH ONLINE COMMUNICATION

A review of the research on second language learning through online communication demonstrates a complex of issues. Second language learning is itself perhaps the most challenging subject in higher education because of the multiple dimensions that are incorporated into the construct of communicative language ability, which is arguably the goal for many language learners. The introduction of e-learning into second language studies offers a provocative opportunity to re-examine the goals of second language learning and the ways in which learning is evaluated. Studies of e-learning begin to meet this challenge, but in doing so they also point to the need to build a solid research foundation in this area. I have identified four major areas that require attention to strengthen the research in this area, and I believe that the implications are relevant to learning through online communication in general.

The language of learning

Researchers need to have a more sophisticated understanding of how to study the language of learning. The large majority of studies on online communication are based on a simplistic view that allows the researcher to count or describe communication turns that learners take in an online conversation. The studies that combine content with discourse analysis come closer to examining more relevant aspects of learning. The real issue, however, is how learners deploy their linguistic knowledge to make choices that help them construct and display new sophisticated meanings about important ideas in the subjects they study. Therefore, analysis needs to focus on the development of the sophistication of linguistic deployment over time. The research of Belz (2003, 2004) and Belz and Kinginger (2003) provides examples of an approach that might fruitfully be applied to this issue, and therefore is worth looking at more closely. These three studies demonstrate how research can investigate the complexity of development of three central aspects of language ability – syntactic competence, pragmatic competence, and intercultural competence.

In these and other discourse analytic studies, analysis rests on identifying how linguistic choices made to encode ideas and relationships demonstrate knowledge and learning. In the study examining intercultural competence, Belz focused on the language of appraisals as they were variously encoded by learners to indicate their dialogic positioning relative to the ideas presented in the text, in particular showing the openness to ideas other than those put forward in the text. Examples of such expressions given by White (2003: 260) are *perhaps, it has been argued that, naturally, admittedly,* and *I think.* Belz identified these indicators of appraisal as relevant to intercultural competence, and one might argue that such openness and modulation of certainty is indicative of the type of sophisticated understanding of ideas that Garrison and Anderson (2003) refer to when they suggest that education is about ideas. If education is about ideas, then research on the quality of education requires methods that assess the quality of evolving ideas, values, and understandings. The linguistic analysis of e-comunication seems critical for the assessment of what matters in education.

However, in language education as well as in other areas, we are often concerned with a more concrete plane of accomplishment, which one might describe as an increase in the ability to use language to express professional or scientific knowledge. Some would argue that learners are in no position to express openness to alternative ideas if they are unable to use the language of the discipline to engage in discussion about those ideas. In this regard, researchers need a means of examining the degree of sophistication that learners display in their emerging discipline-specific language use. Researchers working on examining learners' development across a mode continuum, or variations in language use situations, draw on systemic-functional linguistic theory (Halliday, 1994; Martin, 1992) to describe the movement across the continuum from here-and-now oral language to the more precise and distant language of academic writing. An example of such research is Gibbons's (2003) study of learners' conversation with their teacher about a science experiment, as shown in Example 3. Two points on a mode continuum are evident as the student describes his observation of the experiment in his everyday spoken language ('it sticks together'), and the teacher's mediation consists of rephrasing the learner's language into the more scientific written mode ('the magnets attract').

Example 3: Interaction helping the learner through the mode continuum

Student. It sticks together.

Teacher. They [are] attracted to each other.

Student. You can feel … that they're not pushing … If we use the other side we can't feel pushing.

Teacher. When they were facing one way you felt the magnets attract and stick together. When you turned one of the magnets around you felt it repelling or pushing away.

(Gibbons, 2003: 258)

The dialogic learning evident in this exchange is described by Gibbons linguistically through the constructs of mode continuum (variations in language style) and mediation (interactions coming between the learner and the language). Together these constructs seem to offer a means of examining interactions of potential value for learning through conversation. Clearly, some such perspective that extends beyond correctness of linguistic form and quantitative comparisons across registers is needed to examine language learning or learning through language. A means of studying the language of schooling (Schleppegrell, 2004) is needed.

The pragmatic and cultural goals that most language learners have today, as well as the goals learners have for advancing knowledge in other subject areas, require a means of examining language and interactions in a way that reveals how assistance is given and taken to increase the quality of learners' meaning making through language (Lantolf, 2000; Ohta, 2000). Accordingly, Gutiérrez (2003) argues that sociocultural theory is valuable for the study of online collaborative tasks, and Wells (1999) points out that a systemic functional linguistics is the ideal match for sociocultural theory for the study of learning through language. The combination of these two analytic perspectives provides valuable tools for the study of second language development through e-discourse, and in fact for the study of learning through language as well.

Assessment of learning

Perhaps it should go without saying that the evaluation of online learning through conversation requires some means of assessing learning, but as I have suggested above, methods for assessing e-learning in second language studies present a thorny issue. The issue in second language learning may be exacerbated by the complexity of what is to be learned, but the basic problem probably crosscuts the subjects of higher education, as well as the general communication goals of higher education. The problem rests in the difficulty of identifying and measuring the specific areas in which learners may have benefited from online communication, because such learning may intersect and combine with learning from other modes, learners often control what is learned, and the most valuable indicators of learning may appear during the process of learning. Even when pre- and post-testing is conducted (e.g. Fotos, 2004), the online communication is embedded in complex ways with the instruction, making the links between learning through online communication and test scores difficult to interpret.

Second language research on online learning has tackled these problems in two ways: (1) by setting research objectives as descriptive or critical rather than evaluative or (2) by identifying some aspect of the observable learning process that can be argued to be valuable for learning. In the first instance, the assessment issue is bypassed, as the research objective does not require the researcher to demonstrate learning has taken place. Instead, results are intended to provide different type of insights to technology use for second language learning. The second approach is worth examination from the perspective of language assessment. Depending on the aspect of the learning process targeted by the researcher, the process data have been argued to indicate language development. For example, researchers seeking evidence of negotiation of meaning in online discussion can argue on the basis of theory and prior research in second language acquisition that such sequences demonstrate the *potential* for language acquisition, but they would not argue that such sequences indicate language development. In contrast, those researchers who focus on the emergence of particular grammatical or pragmatic aspects of language for an individual argue that the appearance of particular forms and uses in the data can be considered as evidence of language development. However, whether or not such an argument is accepted, of course, depends on the person to whom the argument is made! Thus, whatever methods are used for evaluation and assessment, they need to be discussed in view of the broader academic community in which they might be called upon to play a role.

Grounding in educational research methods

Discourse analytic methods might be better accepted and developed if they were contextualized with broader approaches toward educational research. Garrison and Anderson (2003) discuss content analysis of e-learning transcripts as quantitative studies. Their review concludes that 'the main shortcoming of the quantitative content analysis studies in our sample was the failure of researchers to adhere to the principles that make quantitative research valid' (p. 148). Similarly, when viewed by an audience that assumes the correctness and defensibility of quantitative, comparative evaluation methods, the research I have summarized in this chapter appears altogether inadequate.

The methodologies employed are consistent with some of the research conducted on second language acquisition (Ellis, 1999), which some would argue is
intended to inform theoretical perspectives about how second languages are
acquired, as illustrated by the arrow in Figure 17.1. The curved dotted line in
Figure 17.1 indicates that such methods have been borrowed for research on
online communication, which one would hope would have some connection
with curriculum and teaching practices. However, if such second language
acquisition-influenced methods are to be useful for more practice-oriented
knowledge, additional reflection and development of these methodologies are
clearly needed. Evaluation methods in education draw upon complex qualitative
methods; it seems that the second language methods need to be incorporated
into such larger frameworks that make sense and have credibility to relevant
audiences in the educational context.

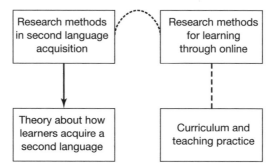

**Figure 17.1 The tentative status of research methods for studying online
second language learning**

Advanced-level study

If ten and twenty years from now we are to have a research basis for making decisions and recommendations about e-learning through online communication,
much more advanced-level study needs to be devoted to the central issues in this
area. The need is evident if one considers the number of Ph.D. dissertations
devoted to issues such as interaction analysis in the teacher-fronted classroom or
internal consistency reliability formulas for dichotomously scored items relative
to the number that have attempted to isolate and study the way in which learning
is construed through learners' language in online communication. The field of
applied linguistics takes issues of discourse analysis within learning tasks and outside the classroom as an area of inquiry offering constructs such as negotiation of
meaning as well as critical reflection on their use (e.g. Nakahama *et al.*, 2001), but

this activity needs to expand to include how these research methods play out in online communication. In other words, the activity of applied linguistics research needs to expand to the new and important issues created by the use of technology in communication and higher education. The complexity of these issues suggests that advanced-level study needs to be designed in a way that allows students wishing to work on these issues to study a combination of technology, linguistic analysis, assessment, and educational research.

CONCLUSION

Despite the exploratory nature of the research on second language learning through online communication, the issues addressed in these studies may offer some useful suggestions for research on learning through online communication in other areas. The data in such contexts are so clearly in need of linguistic analysis that it is difficult to look at them without seeking help from linguists. As the linguist Michael Halliday (1993) put it, 'learning is a semiotic process: learning is learning to mean .... The prototypical resource for making meaning is language' (p. 113). The language of learning is recorded regularly with great efficiency in higher education today – more efficiently than anyone can process it. The technology affords researchers an ideal position to examine how, when, and why students learn to mean through online communication.

REFERENCES

Atkinson, D. (2000) 'TESOL and culture', *TESOL Quarterly*, 34 (1): 625–54.

Beauvois, M. H. (1992) 'Computer-assisted classroom discussion in the foreign language classroom: conversation in slow motion', *Foreign Language Annals*, 25 (5): 455–64.

Belz, J. (2004) 'Learner corpus analysis and the development of foreign language proficiency', *System*, 32 (4): 577–91.

Belz, J. A. (2003) 'Linguistic perspectives on the development of intercultural competence in telecollaboration', *Language Learning and Technology*, 7 (2): 68–117.

Belz, J. A. and Kinginger, C. (2003) 'Discourse options and the development of pragmatic competence by classroom learners of German: the case of address forms', *Language Learning*, 53 (4): 591–648.

Blake, R. (2000) 'Computer-mediated communication: a window on second language Spanish interlanguage', *Language Learning and Technology*, 4 (1): 120–36.

Blake, R. and Zyzik, E. C. (2003) 'Who's helping whom? Learner/heritage-speakers' networked discussions in Spanish', *Applied Linguistics*, 24 (4): 519–44.

Chapelle, C. A. (2003) *English Language Learning and Technology: Lectures in Applied Linguistics in the Age of Information and Communication*. Amsterdam: John Benjamins.

Chun, D. M. (1994) 'Using computer networking to facilitate the acquisition of interactive competence', *System*, 22 (1): 17–31.

De la Fuente, M. J. (2003) 'Is SLA interactionist theory relevant to CALL? A study of the effects of computer-mediated interaction in second language vocabulary acquisition', *Computer Assisted Language Learning*, 16 (1): 47–81.

Ellis, R. (1999) *Learning a Second Language through Interaction*. Amsterdam: John Benjamins.

Erickson, T. (1999) 'Rhyme and punishment: the creation and enforcement of conventions in an on-line participatory limerick genre'. *Proceedings of the XXXIInd Hawaii International Conference on System Sciences*. Los Alamitos, CA: IEEE Computer Society Press.

Fotos, S. (2004) 'Writing as talking: e-mail exchange for promoting proficiency and motivation in the foreign language classroom', in S. Fotos and C. Browne (eds), *New Perspectives on CALL for Second Language Classrooms*. Mahwah, NJ: Erlbaum. pp. 109–29.

García, M. F. and Arbelaiz, A. M. (2003) 'Learners' interactions: a comparison of oral and computer-assisted written conversations', *ReCALL*, 15 (1): 113–36.

Garrison, D. R. and Anderson, T. (2003) *E-learning in the Twenty-first Century: A Framework for Research and Practice*. Abingdon: RoutledgeFalmer.

Gass, S. (1997) *Input, Interaction, and the Second Language Learner*. Mahwah, NJ: Erlbaum.

Gibbons, P. (2003) 'Mediating language learning: teacher interactions with ESL students in a content-based classroom', *TESOL Quarterly*, 37 (2): 247–73.

González-Bueno, M. (1998) 'The effects of electronic mail on Spanish second language discourse', *Language Learning and Technology*, 1 (2): 55–70.

Gutiérrez, G. A. G. (2003) 'Beyond interaction: the study of collaborative activity in computer-mediated tasks', *ReCALL*, 15 (1): 94–112.

Halliday, M. A. K. (1993) 'Towards a language-based theory of learning', *Linguistics and Education*, 5: 93–116.

Halliday, M. A. K. (1994) *An Introduction to Functional Grammar* (2nd edn). London: Edward Arnold.

Halliday, M. A. K. and Hasan, R. (1989) *Language, Context, and Text: Aspects of Language in a Social-Semiotic Perspective*. Oxford: Oxford University Press.

Herring, S. C. (ed.) (1996) *Computer-Mediated Communication: Linguistic, Social, and Cross-cultural Perspectives*. Amsterdam: John Benjamins.

Kasper, G. (2001) 'Four perspectives on second language pragmatic development', *Applied Linguistics*, 22 (4): 502–30.

Kelm, O. R. (1992) 'The use of synchronous computer networks in second language instruction: a preliminary report', *Foreign Language Annals*, 25 (5): 441–54.

Kern, R. G. (1995) 'Restructuring classroom interaction with networked computers: effects on quantity and characteristics of language production', *Modern Language Journal*, 79: 457–76.

Kinginger, C. (2000) 'Learning the pragmatics of solidarity in the networked foreign language classroom', in J. K. Hall and L. S. Verplaetse (eds), *Second and Foreign Language Learning through Classroom Interaction*. Mahwah, NJ: Erlbaum. pp. 23–46.

Kitade, K. (2000) 'Second language learners' discourse and SLA theories in CMC: collaborative interaction in Internet chat', *Computer Assisted Language Learning*, 13 (2): 143–66.

Knupfer, N. N. and McLellan, H. (1996) 'Descriptive research methodologies', in D. H. Jonassen (ed.), *Handbook of Research for Educational Communications and Technology*. New York: Simon & Schuster Macmillan. pp. 1196–212

Kötter, M. (2003) 'Negotiation of meaning and codeswitching in online tandem', *Language Learning and Technology*, 7 (2): 145–72.

Kramsch, C. and Thorne, S. (2002) 'Foreign language learning as global communicative practice', in D. Cameron and D. Block (eds), *Globalization and Language Teaching*. New York: Routledge. pp. 83–100.

Lam, W. S. E. (2000) 'Second language literacy and the design of the self: a case study of a teenager writing on the Internet', *TESOL Quarterly*, 34 (3): 457–82.

Lamy, M.-N. and Goodfellow, R. (1999) '"Reflective conversation" in the virtual language classroom', *Language Learning and Technology*, 2 (2): 43–61.

Lantolf, J. (ed.) (2000) *Sociocultural Theory and Second Language Learning*. Oxford: Oxford University Press.

Lee, L. (2001) 'Online interaction: negotiation of meaning and strategies used among learners of Spanish', *ReCALL*, 13 (2): 232–44.

Long, M. H. and Robinson, P. (1998) 'Focus on form: theory, research and practice', in C. Doughty and J. Williams (eds), *Focus on Form in Classroom Second Language Acquisition*. Cambridge: Cambridge University Press. pp. 15–41.

MacIntyre, P. D., Baker, S. C., Clément, R. and Conrod, S. (2001) 'Willingness to communicate, social support, and language-learning orientations of immersion students', *Studies in Second Language Acquisition*, 23 (3): 369–88.

Martin, J. R. (1992) *English Text: System and Structure*. Amsterdam: John Benjamins.

Nakahama, Y., Tyler, A. and van Lier, L. (2001) 'Negotiation of meaning in conversational and information gap activities: a comparative discourse analysis', *TESOL Quarterly*, 35 (3): 377–405.

Negretti, R. (1999) 'Web-based activities and SLA: a conversation analysis research approach', *Language Learning and Technology*, 3 (1): 75–87.

O'Dowd, R. (2000) 'Intercultural learning via videoconferencing: a pilot exchange project', *ReCALL*, 12 (1): 49–61.

Ohta, A (2000) 'Rethinking interaction in SLA: developmentally appropriate assistance in the zone of proximal development and the acquisition of second language grammar', in J. Lantolf (ed.). *Sociocultural Theory and Second Language Learning*. Oxford: Oxford University Press. pp. 51–78.

Ortega, L. (1997) 'Processes and outcomes in networked classroom interaction: defining the research agenda for second language computer-assisted classroom discussion', *Language Learning and Technology*, 1 (1): 82–93.

Panova, I. and Lyster, R. (2002) 'Patterns of corrective feedback and uptake in an adult ESL classroom', *TESOL Quarterly*, 36 (4): 573–95.

Pellettieri, J. (2000) 'Negotiation in cyberspace: the role of *chatting* in the development of grammatical competence in the virtual foreign language classroom', in M. Warschauer and R. Kern (eds), *Network-Based Language Teaching: Concepts and Practice*. Cambridge: Cambridge University Press. pp. 59–86.

Pica, T. (1994) 'Research on negotiation: what does it reveal about second-language learning conditions, processes, and outcomes?', *Language Learning*, 44 (3): 493–527.

Pica, T., Kanagy, R. and Falodun, J. (1993) 'Choosing and using communication tasks for second language instruction', in G. Crookes and S. Gass (eds), *Tasks and Language Learning: Integrating Theory and Practice*. Clevedon: Multilingual Matters Press, pp. 9–34.

Roed, J. (2003) 'Language learner behaviour in a virtual environment', *Computer Assisted Language Learning*, 16 (2-3): 155–72.

Salaberry, M. R. (2000). 'L2 morphosyntactic development in text-based computer-mediated communication', *Computer Assisted Language Learning*, 13 (1): 5–27.

Sauro, S. (2001) 'The Success of Task Type in facilitating Oral Language Production in Online Computer Mediated Collaborative Projects'. Unpublished M.A. thesis, Ames, IA: Department of English, Iowa State University.

Schleppegrell, M. J. (2004) *The Language of Schooling: A Functional Linguistics Perspective*. Mahwah, NJ: Erlbaum.

Schwienhorst, K. (2004) 'Native speaker/non-native speaker discourse in the MOO: topic negotiation and initiation in a synchronous text-based environment', *Computer Assisted Language Learning*, 17 (1): 35–50.

Sinclair, J. and Coulthard, M. (1975) *Towards an Analysis of Discourse*. Oxford: Oxford University Press.

Stockwell, G. (2003) 'Effects of topic threads on sustainability of e-mail interactions between native speakers and non-native speakers', *ReCALL*, 15 (1): 37–50.

Swain, M. (1998) 'Focus on form through conscious reflection', in C. Doughty and J. Williams (eds), *Focus on Form*. Cambridge: Cambridge University Press. pp. 64–81.

Swales, J. (1990) *Genre Analysis*. Cambridge: Cambridge University Press.

Thorne, S. (2003) 'Artifacts and cultures-of-use in intercultural communication', *Language Learning and Technology*, 7 (2): 38–67.

Warner, C. N. (2004) 'It's just a game, right? Types of play in foreign language CMC', *Language Learning and Technology*, 8 (2): 69–87.

Warschauer, M. (1995/1996) 'Comparing face-to-face and electronic discussion in the second language classroom', *CALICO Journal*, 13 (2–3): 7–25.

Warschauer, M. (1998) 'Researching technology in TESOL: determinist, instrumental, and critical approaches', *TESOL Quarterly*, 32 (4): 757–61.

Weininger, M. J. and Shield, L. (2003) 'Promoting oral production in a written channel: an investigation of learners' language in MOO', *Computer Assisted Language Learning*, 16 (4): 329–49.

Wells, G. (1999) *Dialogic Inquiry: Toward a Sociocultural Practice and Theory of Education*. Cambridge: Cambridge University Press.

White, P. R. R. (2003) 'Beyond modality and hedging: a dialogic view of the language of intersubjective stance', *Text*, 23 (2): 259–84.

18

Literacy, Learning and Technology Studies

Ilana Snyder

WHAT'S IN A NAME?

What's in a name? That which we call a rose
By any other name would smell as sweet.

(Romeo and Juliet, II)

Juliet's famous lines about the importance of words and names are salutary for e-learning research in higher education. Juliet compares Romeo to a rose and reasons that if a rose were given another name it would still be a rose, just as if Romeo renounced his family name he would still be Romeo. Juliet loves the person who is called Montague; she does not love the name Montague. For Juliet, a name is an artificial and meaningless convention, not as important as what it represents.

A far cry from Renaissance Verona, but also illustrative of the tension between a name and what it might mean, is the distinction in contemporary Israel between the two words used to denote the barrier dividing Jewish settlers from Arabs in the West Bank. Many Israelis refer to it as a fence while most Palestinians would describe it as a wall. Although the image that consistently appears on television is of a high concrete construction, when you drive through the West Bank you see that the barrier is both a fence and a wall. In the main, it is a barbed wire construction with only intermittent high, solid sections that resemble the sound barriers on freeways. In the volatile context of Israeli–Palestinian politics, both the names and what they represent are of considerable importance. It is either a wall or a fence depending on your ideological position.

In the field of technology-mediated learning, the issue of names is less charged but, nonetheless, significant. As evidenced by the studies distilled in this handbook, researchers use a number of terms, sometimes distinctively and sometimes interchangeably, to identify the central constructs that inform their work. The editors of this volume have selected e-learning as the organizing principle to signify the body of research that investigates, explores and theorizes teaching and learning mediated by the use of new information and communication technologies in the higher education sector. What we mean by the term 'e-learning', as well as what we mean by other key terms, is important, as it shapes the way the field is conceived, described, examined, understood and critiqued. The explanations have implications for a goal probably implicit in most of the chapters in this volume: to improve teaching and learning when digital technologies are used in higher education.

THE MEANING OF E-LEARNING

In *Keywords*, Raymond Williams (1976) points out that when some people see a word they think the first thing to do is to define it. Dictionaries are produced and an authoritative meaning is provided. For certain words this kind of definition may be effective, but for words that involve ideas and values 'it is not only an impossible but an irrelevant procedure' (Williams, 1976: 17).

The *New Shorter Oxford English Dictionary on Historical Principles* (Trumble and Stevenson, 2002) does not have an entry for e-learning but it does define the prefix 'e' and, of course, 'learning':

e- *prefix*

[from *e-* (in ELECTRONIC *adjective*) after EMAIL *noun*]

Denoting the use of electronic data transfer in cyberspace for information exchange and financial transactions, esp. through the Internet.

e-book *noun* an electronic version of a printed book that can be read on a personal computer or handheld device designed specifically for this purpose. **e-commerce** *noun* commercial transactions conducted electronically on the Internet. **e-zine** *noun* a magazine only published in electronic form on a computer network.

(*Oxford*: 781)

The definition associates the prefix with the use of the Internet, involving electronic form and some kind of electronic exchange. I have always been reticent in using the prefix in the context of learning because of the strong association between 'e', the Internet and commercial activities.

The *Oxford* defines learning as:

1   **a** The action of LEARN *verb.* **b** Education; schooling.

2   Knowledge acquired by systematic study; the possession of such knowledge.

3   A thing learned or taught; a lesson, an instruction; information; a doctrine; a maxim; a branch of learning; an acquired skill.

(Trumble and Stevenson, 2002: 1562)

The definition emphasizes that learning is an active state that involves systematically acquiring knowledge or skills. It presents learning as possible and unproblematic. A definition of e-learning is achieved by combining the meaning for 'e' with that for 'learning'. The result is something like 'learning conducted electronically via the Internet' or 'learning electronically'. But this definition, similar to those in other dictionaries, such as the Macquarie (Yallop *et al.*, 2005), does not convey the idea that learning and gaining knowledge represent complex social and cultural practices.

While Williams argues that historical dictionaries go beyond limited meanings, even the *New Shorter Oxford Dictionary on Historical Principles* does not get us very far in understanding what learning electronically means. As Williams explains, there are difficulties in any kind of definition because the meaning of a word such as 'learning' is embedded in relationships and in processes of social and historical change. In his view, no word ever finally stands on its own; it is always an element in the social process of language.

These understandings of words and their meanings inform the question central to this chapter: to what extent is the mainly Preschool to Grade 12 (end of secondary education) (P-12) research that has investigated critical literacy and learning when digital technologies are used relevant to e-learning in higher education? Following Williams, I have identified and explain below four keywords that are central to the research reports, debates and discussions in the P-12 literature: literacy, learning, technology and critical. Although common in everyday usage, these words are understood in different ways by different people. Further, they are highly contested and value-laden, which means that any explanations are unlikely to be accepted by all readers. However, despite these difficulties, the concepts are integral to an understanding of the research that has concentrated on young people's in- and out-of-school literacy practices since computers were first introduced into schools *en masse* in the early 1980s. Of the four, literacy is the least familiar in the context of higher education, which makes the discussion of its meaning, as well as those of the others, an important preface to the overview of the P-12 literature that follows. Of course, the complex issues surrounding e-learning in higher education cannot be understood simply by considering the words that might be used to discuss them. But at the same time, the issues cannot really be thought through unless we are conscious of keywords as elements of the issues. The discussion of these words represents an inquiry into a vocabulary, a shared body of words and meanings concerned with educational practices and institutions in the twenty-first century (cf. Williams, 1976).

WHY LITERACY, LEARNING, TECHNOLOGY AND CRITICAL?

Although I have argued that these four concepts are central to the research reports, debates and discussions in the P-12 literature, another researcher might have come up with a different cluster of words or, at least, different forms of the words. However, this possibility does no more than affirm Williams's observation that each of us has different values and that we use language differently – especially when strong feelings or important ideas are in question, as they are in the context of Israeli–Palestinian politics and as they also are in relation to e-learning in higher education. I have chosen the terms literacy and learning rather than e-literacy and e-learning to avoid evoking the world of business by adding the prefix 'e', and also because in the P-12 literature the have been used more commonly. As our explanations of literacy and learning need to take account of the expanding use of digital technologies in the production of information and knowledge, I have also chosen technology; others might have chosen computers. I've included the word 'critical', not to signal denigration or crisis, but to emphasize that in the age of the Internet the imperative for critical engagement is stronger than ever. Finding ways to promote critical approaches that enable students in higher education to recognize the constructedness of new media texts is an important goal. I hope that the terms I have selected will be encountered critically as they have meanings that are to be tested, confirmed, asserted, qualified, perhaps changed.

Literacy

Moving beyond narrowly conceived explanations of literacy, rendered simply as encoding and decoding language, more recent explanations take account of social phenomena and often refer to it as a social practice (Street, 1984). These versions also critique inadequate views of literacy that fail to look further than teaching and learning and the classroom: literacy studies investigate reading and writing in diverse areas including everyday life and the workplace (Barton, 2001). Literacy is not fixed but is always changing; it covers a range of cultures and historical periods, as well as multilingual contexts. Literacy is also concerned with the use of digital technologies, including the Internet. Literacy studies recognize that successive advances in technology extend the boundaries of what was previously possible and that each technological advance has seen a corresponding change in how literacy is practised and its social role understood (Lankshear and Snyder, 2000; Lankshear and Knobel, 2003).

Technological literacy (also known as silicon, digital, techno-literacy, information literacy and e-literacy, etc.) refers to the capacity to access networked computer resources and use them (Snyder, 2001, 2002). It is the ability to use and understand information in multiple formats from a wide range of sources when it is presented via computers. The Internet broadens the literacy experience from the world of print by incorporating video, hyperlinks to archived information, sound clips, discussion areas, supporting databases and related software. Acquiring technological literacy involves becoming proficient with a set of important skills. The most essential of these is the ability to make informed judgements about the information that is found online, for, unlike conventional media, much of the Internet is unfiltered by editors. Despite the speed of change in the digital world, core literacies still include Internet searching, hypertextual navigation, content evaluation and knowledge assembly (Gilster, 1997).

Learning

From a sociocultural perspective, learning is a complex activity. It is about becoming proficient participants in social practices. The situated social practice model (e.g. Rogoff, 1984, 1990; Lave and Wenger, 1991), derived from the pioneering work of Vygotsky (1962), is particularly useful. This model emphasizes situated learning within authentic contexts through processes like cultural apprenticeship, guided participation and participatory appropriation (Rogoff, 1995), involving people with different degrees of experience, engaging with each other, and moving through cycles of teaching, learning and practice. Within authentic settings of culturally valued activity, participants learn from each other, are guided by social and cultural values as well as by social partners, and improve their expertise by such means as explaining to and guiding others, and from sheer practice (Lankshear and Snyder, 2000).

Becoming proficient participants in a social practice typically involves a mix of acquisition and learning. As Gee explains (1996: 138), '*acquisition* is a process of acquiring something (usually, subconsciously) by exposure to models, a process of trial and error, and practice within social groups, without formal teaching', while '*learning* is a process that involves conscious knowledge gained through teaching (though not necessarily from someone officially designated a teacher) or through certain life-experiences that trigger conscious reflection'.

Learning is essential if cultural apprenticeship is to be appropriately balanced by cultural criticism and active participation. From a sociocultural perspective, learning focuses not on children or schools, but on human lives seen as trajectories through numerous social practices across a range of social institutions.

In universities, it is teachers who take responsibility for what and how students learn by creating the conditions in which understanding is possible. It is the students who take advantage of opportunities for coming to know (Laurillard, 1993). A vision of learning with growing acceptance is of young people pursuing their own objectives towards knowledge, inspired but not necessarily directed by their teachers. According to this view, when students take responsibility for their own learning they can regard the classroom as offering a set of resources that are largely under their control.

Despite the popularity of this belief that teachers will become less important as students become more independent, engaging in self-directed learning, university teachers now have a heightened role: to deepen and refine students' capacity for response to cultural change, so that the changes can be constantly criticized and their implications understood, and to ensure that 'the technical changes that have made our culture more dependent on literate forms are matched by a proportionate increase in training in literacy in its full sense' (Williams, 1983: 310). Although written before the arrival of Web, Williams's admonition continues to resonate. Teachers are needed more than ever because critical technological literacy practices are cognitively and socially demanding.

Another way of thinking about learning (and literacy) in the twenty-first century is to conceive of the process as knowledge assembly: the ability to collect and evaluate information, defined as data that have been organized and communicated (Gilster, 1997). Effective information gathering can be represented as a balancing act. Used skilfully, networked information possesses unique advantages. It is searchable. It can be customized to reflect users' needs. Moreover, its hypertextual nature connects with a wide range of information sources, allowing users to consider different points of view and to make informed decisions about their validity. The process of using these tools and critically evaluating the results is knowledge assembly.

Technology

It is still common for educators to think of technology in terms of tools, implements and applications. In the age of the Internet, these would include: Web sites, multimedia, video games, CD-ROMs, DVDs and virtual reality. Although it is not wrong to think of technology in this way, it is limiting; it impedes the understanding of technology's social and cultural dimensions. Like literacy, technology is a form of social practice. It represents not just the need to acquire certain skills: technology is 'an expression of the ideologies, the cultural norms, and the value systems of a society' (Bruce, 1999: 225). This means that talk about technology and its effects is inadequate if it remains in the realm of the technical.

Producing a list of the technical things teachers in higher education should know appears easy. A list might include learning how to: explore, evaluate and use a range of computer applications; operate a multimedia system; use certain software such as word processing, databases and spreadsheets. Just as important, however, are the underlying pedagogical values 'that might inform decisions about whether this option is appropriate for particular students in a given context, how it should be used, and how one might judge its success' (Bruce, 1999: 226). A set of questions needs to be asked. On what basis should teachers judge software? What kind of instruction is required to support the software? What do teachers want the software tools to help produce? A list of the technical requirements alone fails to connect with the fundamental issues of teaching and learning. Finding answers to these questions is a central part of everyday teaching: thinking primarily about learning is paramount, but thinking critically about the technologies that support it is also important (Lankshear and Snyder, 2000).

Although activity theory (Engeström *et al.*, 1999) does not specifically address issues of literacy, one of the four concepts discussed in this chapter, it has been increasingly applied to contexts where the use of technology plays a major part in the learning experience. As a heuristic, activity theory enables thinking about both language and technologies as mediating or cultural tools in human learning (Vygotsky, 1962). It is concerned with context that involves a weaving together of learners with both tools and people into a 'web or network of sociocultural interactions and meanings that are integral to the learning' (Russell, 2002: 68).

Pacey's (1983) concept of technology-practice is also useful. As Bruce (1999) has more recently argued, to think of technology in terms of tools, implements, techniques and know-how alone is to limit our conception of technology to just one of its three component dimensions: the technical. If we look beyond the tool itself to see 'the web of human activities surrounding the machine' (Pacey, 1983: 3) we see that technology is a form of social practice and not, as is so often assumed, culturally neutral.

Looking at a machine such as a computer, the opposite may seem to be true. However, once the complex of human activities surrounding the computer's use is considered, it soon becomes apparent that technology is part of life itself and not something that can be kept in a separate compartment. In other words, technology-practice has technical, organizational and cultural dimensions. Moreover, technology is an essential aspect of humanity, since technology is found in all cultures, irrespective of geographic locale or historical period.

Critical

Although 'critical' can be a difficult word because its predominant sense is of either disapproval or impending crisis, in literacy studies it is often used in association with literacy to highlight the complex relationships among language, power, social groups and social practices (Knobel and Healey, 1998). Like literacy, being critical represents a practice or a process. Concerned with the development of social awareness and active, responsible citizenship, a critical approach to literacy argues that the meanings of words and texts cannot be separated from the cultural and social practices in which they are constructed. It recognizes the non-neutrality of texts and is concerned with the politics of meaning: how dominant meanings are maintained, challenged and changed.

Just as a critical approach to literacy has been recommended, so too there is a need to adopt a socially critical stance toward information and communication technologies, taking careful account of their educational applications and implications. A critical stance means understanding the place of digital technologies within contemporary history and culture and in relation to ourselves and everyday social practice. It means adopting a certain kind of orientation and attitude towards digital technologies and developing appropriate understandings and skills that involve more than simply 'learning how to drive them'. Teachers need 'to become appropriately informed and skilled with regard to new technologies, that … means becoming critical consumers or users' (Bigum and Green, 1995: 13).

As the use of the Internet expands, attention increasingly turns to the promotion of critical technological literacy practices. Critical technological literacy is about recognizing and valuing the breadth of information available and learning how to evaluate, analyse and synthesize that information. It is also concerned with the construction of new meanings and knowledge with technology and with the capacity to communicate in a variety of media for different audiences and purposes. Moreover, it focuses on understanding the ethical, cultural, environmental and societal implications of the use of digital technologies (Faigley, 1999).

Using this vocabulary of inquiry, the next section outlines some important questions that have guided the P-12 research and presents, somewhat schematically, several influential theoretical frameworks. Although there are significant differences between the school and the tertiary sectors, such as the funding models, the organizational structures, the resources, the age of the students, the pedagogical approaches and, of course, the language used to designate key constructs, to name just a few, there are research questions and theoretical perspectives useful for all sectors.

QUESTIONS AND THEORIES PERTINENT TO INVESTIGATING DIGITAL TECHNOLOGIES IN HIGHER EDUCATION

The questions and theories presented here are designed to contribute to thinking about critical literacy, learning and technology in the context of higher education. Four keywords have already been discussed. It is useful at this point to define a few more that are used in this chapter. In the main, the term computers signifies the hardware and software central to the research (before widespread connectivity via the Internet). New media and digital technologies are used more or less interchangeably to denote the diverse technologies such as networked computers, video games, the Internet, mobile phones and DVDs that assume the centrality of the screen. Cultural form, derived from Williams'

(1975) study of television technology and cultural form, is explained as a general way used by the culture to represent human experience in the world. In the context of the Internet, a cultural form might be a hypertextual essay, a chat facility, a Web log or a multi-user game.

Questions

The challenge for both teachers and researchers is to make possible the intelligent and informed use of digital technologies so that students can participate productively and ethically in their lives beyond tertiary study in a world increasingly dominated by the use of digital technologies. On the one hand, university teachers are looking for models that offer strategies that take account of digital technologies to teach students what they need to know in the Age of the Internet. On the other hand, researchers are seeking ways to explain the conceptual, visual, textual, artistic, technical and identity processes involved when digital technologies are used that might inform teaching and learning practices. Although much of the research reported here has not focused directly on higher education, it is possible to extrapolate from studies concerned more broadly with young people's engagement with new media and the implications for teaching and learning. The findings of these studies may sometimes challenge, sometimes complement and sometimes support the traditional print-based literacy practices that still dominate many university classrooms.

In their systematic investigations of the contexts in which young people use new media, researchers have asked how teachers might take account of the changes to literacy practices likely to develop in the future and needed to support communication across linguistic, cultural and geopolitical borders. Researchers have also asked what the social practices that develop around young people's growing engagement with new media may mean for critical education. Of particular contemporary importance is researchers' interest in how teachers might handle the tension between calls for more innovative teaching and responsiveness to students' lives, on the one hand, and governments demanding greater control and accountability at the same time as they reduce funding, on the other. This tension is real in Australia, New Zealand, the UK and the US.

Theoretical approaches

Social accounts of literacy as represented in the New Literacy Studies (NLS) offer a potent framework for investigating the use of digital technologies in higher education for teaching and learning. Indeed, the earlier discussion of the keywords was informed by an NLS approach. Researchers who have taken the social turn recognize that reading and writing are always situated within specific social contexts, and that it is these contexts that give meaning to the practices of reading and writing. The New Literacy Studies, conceived as a body of independent yet linked work produced over the past twenty years, across a number of disciplines, including anthropology, history, psychology and sociolinguistics, exemplifies the social approach to literacy research (Scribner and Cole, 1981; Heath, 1983; Street, 1984; Gee, 1996; Barton and Hamilton, 1998).

Rather than defining literacy as a set of static skills, taught in schools and associated with books and writing, NLS research examines literacy practices and events looking at the role of literacy in people's everyday lives (Street, 1995, 2001; Barton and Hamilton, 1998). The NLS rejects the dominant view of literacy as a neutral technical skill, conceptualizing it instead as 'an ideological practice, implicated in power relations and embedded in specific cultural meanings and practices' (Street, 1995: 1). The ways in which language is used in the context of Middle Eastern politics embodies this understanding.

Not only has there been a social turn in literacy studies: there has also been what Kress (2003) calls a visual turn, that is changing the ways communication and meaning-making are understood. Researchers working in this area argue that communication and learning are becoming more and more multimodal (Kress and Van Leeuwen, 1996, 2001; Jewitt and Kress, 2003). In an electronically mediated world, literacy practices include multiple forms of representation: to be literate means recognizing how different modalities are combined in complex ways to create meaning. These other modes incorporate diagrams, pictures, video, gesture, speech and sound, and researchers in the area have produced systematic accounts of the ways in which multimodal texts communicate meaning.

Also pertinent to understanding the textual practices and formations associated with the use of new media is Bolter and Grusin's (1999) theory of remediation, as it offers a compelling explanation of the complex ways in which old and new media interact. They argue that new media achieve their cultural significance by paying homage to, rivalling and refashioning, earlier media such as perspective painting, photography, film and television. Bolter and Grusin call this process remediation and note that earlier media have also remediated one another: photography remediated painting, film remediated stage production and photography, and television remediated film, vaudeville and radio.

Castells (1996: 371) makes a similar point when he explains how different media borrow codes from each other so that 'interactive educational programmes look like video games; newscasts are constructed as audiovisual shows; trial cases are broadcast as soap operas; pop music is composed for MTV'. According to Bolter and Gruisin, the new literacy practices associated with the use of new media do not simply represent a break with the past: old and new practices interact in far more complex ways, producing hybrid rather than wholly new practices.

The ideas presented here have been selected to provide a theoretical context for the thematic analysis of the research that explores the use of digital technologies in a range of educational contexts that follows. Importantly, these theoretical perspectives all encourage critical engagement with culture, language and education. Finding innovative ways of developing *critical* pedagogies remains a central concern for all teachers across all educational sectors. However, even though the New Literacy Studies offer a particularly generative framework for thinking about the issues involved, no one theory is adequate to engage the richness, complexity, variety and novelty inherent in the literacy and learning practices associated with the use of new media (Snyder, 2002).

AN OVERVIEW OF THE LITERACY, LEARNING AND TECHNOLOGY RESEARCH

While the review below begins with a brief account of the first two decades of the literacy, learning and technology research (the 1980s and 1990s), the emphasis is on the second millennium, chosen as the marker of a new epoch and burgeoning research activity in this field of study. Readers will recognize efforts by researchers and practitioners to identify what is central to the project of improving teaching and learning when digital technologies are used. Notable too is the scope of methodologies the researchers bring to their studies. In their move away from cognitive models to concentrate on cultural and social aspects of language practices, many of the studies share common ground with the theoretical approaches and ethnographically oriented methodologies of the New Literacy Studies.

Early research, 1980–2000

The first decade of research was dominated by studies that set out to determine whether the use of computers improved writing and in the main drew upon accounts of literacy conceived predominantly in psychological terms. By the mid-1980s understandings of literacy as a social practice became more widely accepted. With this increased sensitivity to the social setting in that the computers were used, some researchers shifted the focus from the isolated writer to the writer in context (e.g. Eldred, 1991); some began to explore the possibilities of the computer as a site for the social construction of knowledge (e.g. Herrmann, 1987). A number of studies began to adopt multiple perspectives (e.g. Hawisher and Selfe, 1991), while others examined computer-mediated literacies through a particular ideological lens (e.g. Goodson and Mangan, 1996). More generally, there was a growing recognition that computers in classrooms appeared unlikely to negate the influence of 'the differential socialisation of students by social class' and its effects on their success or failure in education' (Herrmann, 1987: 86).

Social understandings of literacy provoked different kinds of questions and research orientations. The *Digital Rhetorics* study (Lankshear *et al.*, 1997; Lankshear and Snyder, 2000) exemplified research informed by the understanding of literacy as social practice. This relatively large-scale qualitative study argued that education must enable young people to become proficient in the operational, cultural and critical dimensions of techno-literacy (Durrant and Green, 2000). However, a central finding was that teachers were so overwhelmed with operational concerns related to the use of digital technologies that they had no time for developing the critical dimension of literacy.

As in the *Digital Rhetorics* study, critical perspectives were gaining attention in this period. Researchers have criticized the short-sighted policy efforts of self-interested governments, corporations and school councils and boards that have rushed to embrace technology, spending huge amounts without first asking some difficult questions about use, support and learning (e.g. Cuban, 1986, 2001). Others have pointed to the non-neutrality of computer technologies (Bowers, 1988) and how over time they tend to become naturalized, thus escaping critical examination (Burbules and Callister, 2000). Yet others have represented computers as instruments of social control and dependence (e.g. Apple, 1987).

Increasingly, the Internet has become a site for research (e.g. Jones, 1999). Informed by the understanding of literacy as a set of social practices, investigations have focused on new literacy practices (e.g. Snyder, 1997), issues of identity (e.g. Turkle, 1995), class and access (e.g. Castner, 1997), the maleness of the Web (e.g. Takayoshi *et al.*, 1999). The findings have emphasized the need to teach students how to critically assess the reliability or value of the information they find on the Web by understanding not only its textual but also its non-textual features such as images, links and interactivity (LeCourt, 1998; Burbules and Callister, 2000).

The early research demonstrates the transition from psychological to more socially constructed conceptions of literacy, as well as the growing interest in critical evaluation as it relates to race, class, gender and information. The social turn focused attention on the importance of history as well as on other contextual influences that play a role in the constitution of classrooms, teaching, learning and achievement. The early research also began to argue for more complex understandings of the relationship between technology and society. Such understandings drew attention to the varied effects of technology in classrooms, suggesting wariness of research investigating the *impact* of technology *on* learning. A more generative direction focused on how to use technology productively in teaching and learning. Rather than regarding technology as a neutral tool for teaching and learning purposes, researchers saw the possibilities for modelling critical engagement with it so that students might recognize that in educational settings technology represents the varied intentions of business, government and education players.

Recent research, 2000–2006

Four general directions informed by critical understandings of literacy, learning and technology that researchers seem to be following are presented here: changing texts and practices; technological literacy practices in formal and informal education; new cultural forms; technology-mediated innovation and change. As these categories often overlap, it is sometimes difficult to make clear distinctions between them.

Although the trend has been there since the early days, more researchers are acknowledging the need to pay attention to the social, cultural and political changes associated with the use of digital technologies. Finding ways to exploit the opportunities for learning offered by digital technologies in productive ways, but at the same time helping students to become capable and critical users, is increasingly seen as a major challenge. Often implicit in reports of research is the understanding that the relationship with technology is never one-way and instrumental: it is always two-way and relational. These understandings, of course, are not universal. Further, as in most research areas, indeed, as this handbook exemplifies, there are available overviews of the research literature (e.g. Snyder, 2000; Andrews, 2004).

Changing texts and practices

Changes to texts, language practices and social formations are associated with students' use of mobile phones, text messaging, the Internet, instant messaging, online games, blogs, search engines, Web sites, e-mail, digital video, music and imaging, and more. Working with the texts produced by these new ways of communicating requires a complex set of literacies: not only verbal literacy, but also visual and audiovisual literacies. Among other things, it requires an understanding of layout and design, not often recognized as necessary with print texts. Finding the language to talk about these practices and discerning how meanings are made with them is a research concern.

Abbott (2002) has examined the ways in that students, including those with special needs, make elegant use of the visual in their Web pages, forming representations of themselves, their practices and their aspirations. Also interested in Web design, O'Hear and Sefton-Green (2004) have investigated online culture and Web authoring by young people. In addition to a consideration of the technical, institutional, aesthetic and generic determinants influencing the nature of Web-based productions, they pay attention to the fusion of visual, textual and structural elements, especially those relating to non-linear navigation features.

Implicit in much of this research are notions of critical literacy, broadly defined, but often mobilized in different ways in online spaces. Such research has a long heritage but continues to argue that digital technologies require different ways of reading. Cranny-Francis (2004) maintains that young people need to know not only how to approach sites as readers looking for information and/or entertainment but also as text producers who need to understand the kinds of meanings different sites generate. Walton (2004) argues that what goes on behind the screen is just as important for users as what is visible on the screen. With a focus on the database, design and interactivity, she draws on evolving conventions in the field of Web design to account for the characteristics of new media. Walton also considers search engine logic and the ways in which it shapes online knowledge and experience. Much of this amounts to a version of critical literacy where the apparent seamlessness of new media environments is understood as the composited and constructed worlds that they are (e.g. Manovich, 2001).

In a similar way, Burbules (1997, 2002) has looked at hyperlinks and the ways they can become invisible and neutral. He considers their dual character as both semantic connectives and navigation elements, suggesting new metaphors for thinking about learning with, through and about digital technologies. These new metaphors posit learning as a kind of mobility that has special importance for reconceptualizing education in an Information Age. As teachers and students consider how some semiotic modes are privileged and others excluded, and how different modes can also be combined in different ways for different purposes, possibilities of thoughtful and critical engagement with a range of new and hybrid text types become available.

Technological literacy practices in formal and informal education

The pervasive take-up and presence of digital technologies, at least in the developed world, mean that students' experience of literacy is shaped by multiple engagements with digital technologies and global digital cultures. As a result, their use of technologies in a range of contexts has implications for equity and identity formation as well as for a range of other important issues. Research can provide important understandings for tertiary educators about the experiences and expectations students bring to formal studies (e.g. Hull and Schultz, 2002; Lankshear and Knobel, 2003). However, as Burbules and Callister (2000) emphasize, access to new media cannot be seen merely as having a way to use a computer with an Internet connection. Access also includes issues of who can afford a computer with an online connection, who knows how to operate the technologies and who knows how to judge what is good and what is not. Users who cannot operate effectively across the full range of opportunities that new media represent cannot be said to have true access.

In a number of large-scale studies, Livingstone and her colleagues provide insight into the complex relationship between the media, the family and the home (Livingstone, 2002). The UK project investigated how far gaining access to media goods determines or frames subsequent use, tracing the slippage between access and use. The study found the contexts of leisure, home and family increasingly aligned but also in tension, particularly in terms of the individualization of leisure, the loss of public leisure, together with the privatization of everyday life, even within the home, and the democratization of cross-generational relationships within the family.

Two large-scale surveys in the US provide detailed portraits of young people's media lives. The PEW Project has found that more than half of American teenagers have created content for the Internet and that most think that getting free music files is easy to do (Lenhart and Madden, 2005). The teens have produced a blog or Web page, posted original artwork, photography, stories or videos online or remixed online content into their own new creations. A survey study of 'Generation M' (Rideout *et al.*, 2005) asked questions that ranged from broad societal issues to health concerns to issues of cognitive development. It found that young people live media-saturated lives and have access to an unprecedented amount of media in their homes. Those with easy access tend to spend more time using those media but age, gender and race influence the amount of time they spend. Those with the poorest grades spend most time with video games. And television and listening to music remain more important in their media lives than the Internet. Although they continue to read, they now spend less time with books. The findings of such surveys remind the higher education sector that students bring sophisticated skills to classrooms that might be better used for critical literacy learning.

On a smaller scale, Snyder *et al.* (2002) compared home and school digital literacy practices in the context of disadvantage. A year-long study investigated the ways in which four families used digital technologies to engage with formal and informal literacy learning in home and school settings. The findings drew together issues of access, equity and cultural capital and explored what it is about digital literacy practices at home and at school in disadvantaged communities that make a difference in school success. Clearly, there are further questions about the complex relations between the use of digital technologies and existing patterns of social and economic disadvantage that need to be asked. These are questions not just about physical access to the most sophisticated technology, but also about the quality and nature of such access as influenced by the cultural resources that individuals and families can bring to bear on their relationship with technology.

New cultural forms

Researchers have taken account of young people's everyday technological literacy practices in P-12 classrooms. Although these practices are largely ignored in school curricula, research is demonstrating the value popular texts offer for consolidating and extending students' understanding of technological literacy (Alvermann *et al.*, 1999). Researchers have examined different cultural forms such as Japanese anime (Chandler-Olcott and Mahar, 2003), online role playing (Thomas, 2005), online auction and news commentary Web sites (Lankshear and Knobel, 2003), culture jamming (Lankshear and Knobel, 2003), horror movies and digital film production (Burn, 2000), blogging (Gurak *et al.*, 2004), Internet chat rooms, instant messaging, and peer-to-peer music and video file sharing (Merchant, 2001; Godwin-Jones, 2005).

In a study of the use of new media, Snyder and Bulfin (2005) are examining the cultural forms with which young people engage in three domains: school, home and community. A central aim is to learn more about the complex connections between literacy practices and cultural form, but, most important, the study will consider the implications of young people's digital lives for formal teaching and learning. Building a case for the use of popular culture texts and activities in secondary classrooms, Carrington (2005: 480) argues that these texts are both 'familiar and authentic' and build links between young people's in school and out of school worlds. When teachers recognize that young people bring expertise and skills to the learning context, they can encourage the students to remix, play around and engage critically with these textual practices. These studies suggest that creative ways of learning can be employed using digital technologies that facilitate greater student motivation, greater responsibility for aspects of their own learning, enhanced technology capabilities, and the experience of achievement and success.

Another perspective on the significance of young people's out of school literacy activities is provided by researchers investigating video and computer games in relation to literacy learning (see McFarlane's chapter in this volume). After examining the theory of learning underpinning good video games, Gee (2003) concludes that it most closely resembles the best kinds of science instruction in schools. Gee does not argue that what people learn when playing video games is always good; rather, what they are doing when they are playing good video games often involves good learning (cf. Prensky, 2005). Gee's research suggests that there are a number of lessons teachers might learn from game designers about situated learning, reducing the consequences of failure and the power of affinity groups – relevant not just to the school sector, but also to higher education.

Technology-mediated innovation and change

When researchers write about the possibilities of creative changes to pedagogical and institutional practices when digital technologies are used, they often ask several questions. What are the optimum conditions under which innovation can thrive? Is conflict between institutional goals and pedagogical objectives inevitable? They raise these questions within the context of a culture of institutionalized education that champions innovation at the same time as it honours the value of preserving the traditional. This is further complicated by those who have a vested interest in commodifying education and who often promote technological innovation as an appealing selling point (Snyder, 1999).

One prerequisite for effective innovation and change is a strong knowledge and understanding of the history of technological literacy. Bruce (2002) takes an historical perspective, asking how literacies, technologies and social circumstances co-evolve and what changes in literacy practices mean for young people today. He argues that literacy becomes inextricable from community, from the ways that communities and society change and from the material means by which knowledge is negotiated, synthesized and used.

Interested in the nexus between schools and the their local communities, Bigum (2002) critiques the widely held assumption that the more schools spend on technology the better the outcomes. A similar view was once held in business and industry. However, analyses have demonstrated that there is little or no association between spending on technology and increased productivity and profitability. Bigum's research on knowledge-producing schools argues for the development of a relationship-based design sensibility for schools that shifts the focus from how to integrate digital technologies into the curriculum towards a consideration of schools as social organizations that have relationships with local communities, government and other schools. Again, the corollary for higher education is evident.

Highlighting how theory and practice can work together effectively, Pahl and Rowsell (2005) see learning as a shared enterprise between teachers and students rather than as an individual cognitive activity, concerned with the acquisition of a set of skills that can be transferred with ease from context to context. They argue that systematic engagement with everyday texts, discourses and practices is at the heart of teaching and learning. They also argue that, by acknowledging students' identities in their literacy practices, teachers can support and sustain their engagement with education. Although their focus is on P-12, it is not too great a leap to see the implications for higher education.

CHALLENGES FACING E-LEARNING IN HIGHER EDUCATION

This examination of P-12 literacy, learning and technology studies reveals some facts about the communication landscape, also pertinent to higher education. The landscape is changing, as it has always done, but more rapidly and more fundamentally. Contemporary texts are being shaped by the new uses they have been put to. They cross communication domains and are remediated to make new or hybrid texts. These changes mean that the literacies required for the future will no doubt be different and thus have significant implications for all sectors of education.

There is growing recognition that digital technologies cannot be dismissed as new tools, employed to do what earlier technologies did, only faster and more efficiently. Researchers and teachers acknowledge the social and cultural significance of digital technologies, warning against overlooking their material bases and the expanding global economic dependence on them. However, opportunities to use digital technologies in educational contexts that exploit their affordances are happening unevenly, within and between nation states, in both the developed and the developing world.

The studies reported in this chapter explore the complexity of technology-mediated education in local settings. The findings demonstrate that the changes in literacy practices can be understood when they are examined within their social, political, economic, cultural and historical contexts. When digital technologies are available in education settings, teachers have an important role to play. As students in higher education are engaging with these technologies, in contexts beyond the academy, and in the various trajectories of their lives, university teachers need to ensure that they learn how to assume a critical and informed approach while still accessible to formal education.

Some questions to guide future research

The challenge for researchers is to devise projects that will inform effective teaching and learning practices in higher education mediated by the use of digital technologies. It would be useful to undertake a longitudinal approach to the study of students immersed in computer culture at university, at home and at work. Attention also needs to be directed towards the intersection of multiple languages and the multiple modalities of the new technologies. There are many universities where multiple languages are present both inside and outside classrooms. Research could investigate the place of multilingualism and multiculturalism in technology-mediated university settings.

There is a need for further research investigating the complex relationships between the verbal and the visual in communication and representation in higher education contexts. There is also a need for further research investigating the complex relationships between literacy, technology and disadvantage. Prompted by concerns about equity, Livingstone and Bober (2005) recommend that research needs to keep up with technological and market developments in relation to access to track shifting and diversifying contexts of use, including the institutional and social influences on young people's Internet use, and to critically examine causes and consequences of exclusion.

Above all else, making critical technological literacy education better is the aim. If this is true, then the challenge for researchers and teachers is how to restructure university classrooms in response to social and technological changes, but at the same time to cater for the needs of students from diverse cultures, races and backgrounds. This chapter concludes by encouraging a critical pedagogy of literacy, technology and learning. Through the study of texts, both print and electronic, an informed critical pedagogy would aim to provide learners with a sense of their place in the world and with the capacity to develop strategies for making it a better place.

REFERENCES

Abbott, C. (2002) 'Writing the visual: the use of graphic symbols in onscreen texts', in I. Snyder (ed.), *Silicon Literacies: Communication, Innovation and Education in the Electronic Era*. Abingdon: Routledge. pp. 31–46.

Alvermann, D. E., Moon, J. S. and Hagood, M. C. (1999) *Popular Culture in the Classroom: Teaching and Researching Critical Media Literacy*. Newark, DE, and Chicago, IL: International Reading Association National Reading Conference.

Andrews, R. (ed.) (2004) *The Impact of ICT on Literacy Education*. Abingdon and New York: RoutledgeFalmer.

Apple, M. (1987) *The New Technology: Part of the Solution or Part of the Problem?* Canberra: Curriculum Development Centre.

Barton, D. (2001) 'Directions for literacy research: analyzing language and social practices in a textually mediated world', *Language and Education,* 15 (2–3): 92–104.

Barton, D. and Hamilton, M. (1998) *Local Literacies: Reading and Writing in One Community*. Abingdon: Routledge.

Bigum, C. (2002) 'Design sensibilities, schools, and the new computing and communications technologies', in I. Snyder (ed.), *Silicon Literacies: Communication, Innovation and Education in the Electronic Era*. Abingdon: Routledge. pp. 130–40.

Bigum, C. and Green, B. (1995) *Managing Machines? Educational Administration and Information Technology*. Geelong, Vic.: Deakin University Press.

Bolter, J. D. and Grusin, R. (1999) *Remediation: Understanding New Media*. Cambridge, MA: MIT Press.

Bowers, C. A. (1988) *The Cultural Dimensions of Educational Computing: Understanding the Non-neutrality of Technology*. New York: Teachers College Press.

Bruce, B. C. (1999) 'Response: speaking the unspeakable about twenty-first century technologies', in G. E Hawisher and C. L. Selfe (eds), *Passions, Pedagogies and Twenty-first Century Technologies*. Logan, UT: Utah State University Press; Urbana, IL: National Council of Teachers of English. pp. 221–8.

Bruce, B. C. (2002) 'Diversity and critical social engagement: how changing technologies enable new modes of literacy in changing circumstances', in D. E. Alvermann (ed.), *Adolescents and Literacies in a Digital World*. New York: Peter Lang. pp. 1–18.

Burbules, N. C. (1997) 'Rhetorics of the Web: hyperreading and critical literacy', in I. Snyder (ed.), *Page to Screen: Taking Literacy into the Electronic Era*. Sydney: Allen and Unwin. pp. 102–22.

Burbules, N. C. (2002) 'The Web as a rhetorical place', in I. Snyder (ed.), *Silicon Literacies: Communication, Innovation and Education in the Electronic Era*. Abingdon: Routledge. pp. 75–84.

Burbules, N. C. and Callister, T. A., Jr (2000) *Watch IT: The Risks and Promises of Information Technologies for Education*. Boulder, CO: Westview Press.

Burn, A. (2000) 'Repackaging the slasher movie: digital unwriting of film in the classroom', *English in Australia*, 127–8: 24–34.

Carrington, V. (2005) 'The uncanny, digital texts and literacy', *Language and Education*, 19 (6): 467–82.

Castells, M. (1996) *The Rise of the Network Society*. Oxford: Blackwell.

Castner, J. (1997) 'The clash of social categories: egalitarianism in networked writing classrooms', *Computers and Composition*, 14 (2): 257–68.

Chandler-Olcott, K. and Mahar, D. (2003) 'Adolescents' anime-inspired "fanfictions": an exploration of multiliteracies', *Journal of Adolescent and Adult Literacy*, 46 (7): 556–66.

Cranny-Frances, A. (2004) 'Spinning the Web: an analysis of a Web site', in I. Snyder and C. Beavis (eds), *Doing Literacy Online: Teaching, Learning and Playing in an Electronic World*. Creskill, NJ: Hampton Press. pp. 145–62.

Cuban, L. (1986) *Teachers and Machines: The Classroom Use of Technology since 1920*. New York: Teachers College Press.

Cuban, L. (2001) *Oversold and Underused: Computers in the Classroom*. Cambridge, MA: Harvard University Press.

Durrant, C. and Green, B. (2000) 'Literacy and the new technologies in school education: meeting the l(IT)eracy challenge?', *Australian Journal of Language and Literacy*, 23 (2): 89–108.

Eldred, J. M. (1991) 'Pedagogy in the computer-networked classroom', *Computers and Composition*, 8 (2): 47–61.

Engeström, Y., Miettinen, R. and Punamaki, R. (eds) (1999) *Perspectives on Activity Theory*. Cambridge: Cambridge University Press.

Faigley, L. (1999) 'Beyond imagination: the Internet and global digital literacy', in G. E Hawisher and C. L. Selfe (eds), Passions, Pedagogies and Twenty-first Century Technologies. Logan, UT: Utah State University Press; Urbana, IL: National Council of Teachers of English. pp. 129–39.

Gee, J. P. (1996) *Social Linguistics and Literacies: Ideology in Discourses* (2nd edn). London: Taylor and Francis.

Gee, J. P. (2003) *What Video Games have to Teach Us about Learning and Literacy*. New York: Palgrave Macmillan.

Gilster, P. (1997) *Digital Literacy*. New York: Wiley.

Godwin-Jones, B. (2005) 'Messaging, gaming, peer-to-peer sharing: language learning strategies and tools for the millennial generation', *Language, Learning and Technology*, 9 (1): 17–22.

Goodson, I. F. and Mangan, J. M. (1996) 'Computer literacy as ideology', *British Journal of Sociology of Education*, 17: 65–79.

Gurak, L., Antonijevic, S., Johnson, L., Ratliff, C. and Reyman, J. (eds) (2004) 'Into the blogosphere: rhetoric, community, and culture of weblogs', University of Minnesota. Retrieved 4 April 2005 online at: http://blog.lib.umn.edu/blogosphere/.

Hawisher, G. E. and Selfe, C. L. (eds) (1991) *Evolving Perspectives on Computers and Composition Studies: Questions for the 1990s*. Urbana, IL: National Council of Teachers of English.

Heath, S. B. (1983) *Ways with Words: Language, Life and Work in Communities and Classrooms*. Cambridge: Cambridge University Press.

Herrmann, A. (1987) 'Ethnographic study of a high school writing class using computers: marginal, technically proficient and productive learners', in L. Gerrard (ed.), *Writing at the Century's End: Essays on Computer-assisted Instruction*. New York: Random House.

Hull, G. A. and Schultz, K. (eds) (2002) *School's Out: Bridging Out-of-school Literacies with Classroom Practice*. New York: Teachers College Press.

Jewitt, C. and Kress, G. (eds) (2003) *Multimodal Literacy*. London: Peter Lang.

Jones, S. (ed) (1999) *Doing Internet Research: Critical Issues and Methods for Examining the Net*. Thousand Oaks, CA: Sage.

Knobel, M. and Healy, A. (1998) 'Critical literacies: an introduction', in M. Knobel and A. Healy (eds), *Critical Literacies in the Primary Classroom*. Newtown, NSW: Primary English Teaching Association. pp. 1–12.

Kress, G. (2003) *Literacy in the New Media Age*. Abingdon: Routledge.

Kress, G. and Van Leeuwen, T. (1996) *Reading Images: The Grammar of Visual Design*. Abingdon: Routledge.

Kress, G. and Van Leeuwen, T. (2001) *Multimodal Discourse: The Modes and Media of Contemporary Communication*. London: Edward Arnold.

Lankshear, C., Bigum, C., Green, B., Honan, E., Durrant, C., Morgan, W., Murray, J., Snyder, I. and Wild, M. (1997) *Digital Rhetorics: Literacies and Technologies in Education – Current Practices and Future Directions*. Canberra: Department of Employment, Education, Training and Youth Affairs.

Lankshear, C. and Knobel, M. (2003) *New Literacies: Changing Knowledge and Classroom Learning*. Buckingham and Philadelphia, PA: Open University Press.

Lankshear, C. and Snyder, I. with Green, B. (2000) *Teachers and Techno-literacy: Managing Literacy, Technology and Learning in Schools*. Sydney: Allen and Unwin.

Laurillard, D. (1993) *Rethinking University Teaching: A Framework for the Effective Use of Educational Technology*. Abingdon: Routledge.

Lave, J. and Wenger, E. (1991) *Situated Learning: Legitimate Peripheral Participation*. Cambridge: Cambridge University Press.

LeCourt, D. (1998) 'Critical pedagogy in the computer classroom: politicizing the writing space', *Computers and Composition*, 15 (3): 275–95.

Lenhart, A. and Madden, M. (2005) 'Teen content, creators and consumers. PEW Internet and American Life Project: Family, friends and community'. Retrieved online 22 December 2005 at: http://www.pewinternet.org/PPF/r/166/report_display.asp.

Livingstone, S. (2002) *Young People and New Media: Childhood and the Changing Media Environment*. London: Sage.

Livingstone, S. and Bober, M. (2005) 'UK children go online: final report of key project findings', London: London School of Economics and Political Science. Retrieved 2 June 2005 online at: http://www.children-go-online.net.

Manovich, L. (2001) *The Language of New Media*. Cambridge, MA: MIT Press.

Merchant, G. (2001) 'Teenagers in cyberspace: language use and language change in Internet chatrooms', *Journal of Research in Reading*, 24: 293–306.

O'Hear, S. and Sefton-Green, J. (2004) 'Style, genre and technology: the strange case of youth culture online', in I. Snyder and C. Beavis (eds), *Doing Literacy Online: Teaching, Learning and Playing in an Electronic World*. Creskill, NJ: Hampton Press. pp. 121–43.

Pacey, A. (1983) *The Culture of Technology* (1st edn). Oxford: Blackwell.

Pahl, K. and Rowsell, J. (2005) *Literacy and Education: Understanding the New Literacy Studies in the Classroom*. London: Paul Chapman Publishing.

Prensky, M. (2005) *Don't Bother Me, Mom – I'm Learning: How Computer and Video Games are Preparing your Kids for Twenty-first Century Success and How you can Help*. New York: Paragon House.

Rideout, V., Roberts, D. F. and Foehr, U. G. (2005) 'Generation M: Media in the lives of 8–18 year-olds'. Retrieved online 22 December 2005 at: http://www.kff.org/entmedia/entmedia030905pkg.cfm.

Rogoff, B. (1984) 'Introduction: Thinking and learning in social context', in B. Rogoff and J. Lave (eds), *Everyday Cognition: Cognitive Development in a Social Context*. Cambridge, MA: Harvard University Press. pp. 1–8.

Rogoff, B. (1990) *Apprenticeship in Thinking: Cognitive Development in a Social Context*. New York: Oxford University Press.

Rogoff, B. (1995) 'Observing sociocultural activity on three planes: participatory appropriation, guided participation, apprenticeship', in J. Wertsch, P. del Rio and A. Alvarez (eds), *Sociocultural Studies of Mind*. New York: Cambridge University Press. pp. 139–64.

Russell, D. (2002) 'Looking beyond the interface: activity theory and distributed learning', in M. Lea and K. Nicoll (eds), *Distributed Learning*. Abingdon: Routledge. pp. 64–82.

Scribner, S. and Cole, M. (1981) *The Psychology of Literacy*. Cambridge, MA: Harvard University Press.

Snyder, I. (ed.) (1997) *Page to Screen: Taking Literacy into the Electronic Era*. Melbourne: Allen & Unwin.

Snyder, I. (1999) 'Packaging literacy, new technologies and "enhanced" learning', *Australian Journal of Education*, 43 (3): 287–301.

Snyder, I. (2000) 'Literacy and technology studies: past, present, future', *Australian Educational Researcher*, 27 (1): 97–119.

Snyder, I. (2001) 'A new communication order: researching literacy practices in the network society', *Language and Education*, 15 (2–3): 117–31.

Snyder, I. (ed.) (2002) *Silicon Literacies: Communication, Innovation and Education in the Electronic Era*. Abingdon: Routledge.

Snyder, I. and Bulfin, S. (2005) 'Being digital in home, school and community'. Retrieved online 3 June 2005 at: http://community.education.monash.edu.au/projects/beingdigital/.

Snyder, I., Angus, L. and Sutherland-Smith, W. (2002) 'Building equitable literate futures: home and school computer-mediated literacy practices and disadvantage', *Cambridge Journal of Education*, 32 (3): 367–83.

Street, B. (1984) *Literacy in Theory and Practice*. Cambridge: Cambridge University Press.

Street, B. (1995) *Social Literacies: Critical Approaches to Literacy Development, Ethnography and Education*. Harlow: Longman.

Street, B. (ed.) (2001) *Literacy and Development: Ethnographic Perspectives*. Abingdon: Routledge.

Takayoshi, P., Huot, E. and Huot, M. (1999) 'No boys allowed: the World Wide Web as a clubhouse for girls', *Computers and Composition*, 16 (1): 89–106.

Thomas, A. (2005) 'Children online: learning in a virtual community of practice', *e-Learning*, 2 (1): 27–38.

Trumble, W. R. and Stevenson, A. (2002) (eds) *New Shorter Oxford English Dictionary on Historical Principles* (5th edn). New York: Oxford University Press.

Turkle, S. (1995) *Life on the Screen: Identity in the Age of the Internet*. New York: Simon & Schuster.

Vygotsky, L. (1962) *Thought and Language*, trans. E. Hanfmann and G. Vakar. Cambridge, MA: MIT Press.

Walton, M. (2004) 'Behind the screen: the language of Web design', in I. Snyder and C. Beavis (eds), *Doing Literacy Online: Teaching, Learning and Playing in an Electronic World*. Cresskill, NJ: Hampton Press. pp. 91–119.

Williams, R. (1975) *Television: Technology and Cultural Form* (1990, 2nd edn). Abingdon: Routledge.

Williams, R. (1976) *Keywords: A Vocabulary of Culture and Society*. London: Fontana.

Williams, R. (1983) [1958] *Culture and Society, 1780–1950*. New York: Columbia University Press.

Yallop, C., Bernard, J. R. L., Blair, D., Butler, S., Delbridge, A., Peters, P. and Witton, N. (2005) (eds) *Macquarie Dictionary*, 4th edn. Sydney: Macquarie Library.

19

Problems in Researching E-learning: The Case of Computer-Assisted Language Learning

Zhao Yuan

It is rather difficult to draw a clear definition of e-learning. E-learning is a general term covering many different approaches such as distance learning, classroom-based online learning and self-access learning that have in common the use of information and communication technology as media in learning activities. Concepts of e-learning are complex. E-learning involves learners, teachers, materials, contexts and distribution of the technology available. More often different terms are used to describe similar approaches, which can make it difficult to understand what is involved in an e-learning programme. This chapter looks at e-learning activities with a special perspective on Computer-Assisted Language Learning (CALL). Whereas e-learning has been associated with all kinds of learning activities involving information communication technology, CALL represents a side of e-learning where computer technology is used in the context of language learning.

Computer-assisted language learning is 'the search for and study of applications of the computer in language teaching and learning' (Levy, 1997: 1). This subject is interdisciplinary in nature. In Levy's words, 'It [CALL] has evolved out of early efforts to find ways of using a wide variety of subject areas, with the weight of knowledge and breadth of application in language learning ultimately resulting in a more specialized field of study' (ibid.). The approaches of CALL application are varied, which mainly include the laboratory-based instructed learning (situated on campus), distance learning under tutors' instruction and online self-study. A CALL programme can be used in different approaches. For example, the Language Centre at the University of Newcastle upon Tyne (UK) piloted an English learning programme, College English, in 2004. There were two ways of using it in the pilot study: as an online self-study programme for students on campus and as a distance learning programme with a tutor's online support for a group of students in Thailand (Gilmour, 2004). At the same time, the English Teaching Centre at the University of Sheffield also used College English in the laboratory-based courses with a tutor around to support learning activities.

The discussion of the effectiveness of computer-based applications in education, and in particular in language education, has been going on throughout the 1980s and the 1990s and into the twenty-first century. On the one hand, a number of studies (Blake, 2000; Chapelle, 2003; Richards, 2005) have suggested that computer technology has enhanced an interactive learning environment. On the other hand, researchers (Clark, 1983, 1991; Liddell, 1994) argue that there is no hard educational evidence in terms of learning benefits to be gained from employing any specific medium to deliver instruction. The reasons for the lack of good published research on CALL effectiveness are set out by Burston: 'most suffer from fatal design flaws, too many uncontrolled variables, inadequate statistical analysis, not infrequently no quantitative data at all' (1996: 30).

Although the situation of CALL is still problematic and not as ideal as assumed, the general direction in which CALL researchers should be moving is clear and generally agreed. After an extensive review of CALL applications, Warschauer and Kern summarize their findings and give the following recommendations: 'The design of networked multimedia applications for language learning should be based on principles of second language acquisition and constructivist learning, as well as on a cognitive approach to the use of hypertext and multimedia' (2000: 159).

Similarly, Chapelle suggests seven hypotheses based on Second Language Acquisition (SLA) that are relevant for developing multimedia CALL. She comments on their implications for multimedia task design:

> The hypotheses outlined above are supported by theory and research on SLA tasks in experimental settings in which L2 learners interact with other learners or proficient target language users. They are not guaranteed to apply directly to design of CALL activities; but they may provide a valuable starting point to look for principles to apply to CALL.
>
> (1998: 26)

These recommendations suggest the trends in recent CALL research: to establish a theoretical basis for CALL and to look for sound application approaches aligned with language learning theories. However, it is also the case that, set against the background of a rapid developing technology, there are theoretical and practical problems that face CALL researchers. Therefore, this chapter is going to identify the problems in researching e-learning in terms of conceptualization of CALL, CALL practice and research methods with a specific perspective on language acquisition. The purpose is to identify the gaps in CALL theories, to improve our understanding of CALL practice, to find better ways of applying computer technology in learning contexts and thus to shed some light on problems in e-learning research and how to solve them.

PROBLEMS IN CONCEPTUALIZING E-LEARNING: THE CASE OF CALL

Although the name is a fairly new one, the study of CALL is undoubtedly one of the rapid-developing research areas in language acquisition. This is, to a large degree, a reflection of the development of computer technology and its expanding application in language learning contexts. However, the effectiveness of CALL applications has also been questioned. Scepticism mostly concerns how to make appropriate use of the computer technology in language learning and how to integrate CALL materials into different learning contexts such as the instructed class, self-access centres and distance learning in its various forms. The scepticism is largely due to the gap between CALL theories and reality, or more specifically, 'a lack of guidelines or standards for the present generation of CALL materials … CALL authors have no reliable conceptual framework, or yardstick by which to measure their work' (Last, 1989: 35; Levy, 1997: 4; Smith, 1988: 5).

In order to make up the gap between CALL theories and practice, researchers and CALL teachers have been seeking for a solution to conceptualize CALL. Theoretical sources that have been proposed and used are diverse and interdisciplinary. The fields which have influence on CALL theoretical development include psychology, communication theories, human–computer interaction, linguistics, second language acquisition and sociocultural study (Chapelle, 1997; Levy, 1997; MacWhinney, 1995; Salaberry, 1996), of which the theories developed from second language acquisition have special implication for our understanding of CALL application and activities. Aligned with the cross-disciplinary research on theoretical frameworks of CALL, the research topics are also diverse, including instruction methods, learning patterns (such as styles, strategies, attitude and motivation), e-communities, CALL material design and cross-cultural communication (Cononelos and Oliva, 1993; Kern, 1996; Muyskens, 1997; Salaberry, 2001; Sanaoui and Lapkin, 1992; Warschauer, 1996a). However, the attempt to set up a sound theoretical framework for CALL practice has encountered difficulties. Special attention needs to be paid to the following problems arising in the conceptualization of CALL.

Theories from other disciplines should be used with caution

Given that CALL is a relatively new and interdisciplinary research field, it is no surprise that the CALL researchers have borrowed established theories from a number of other fields and disciplines. This cross-disciplinary research has a number of acknowledged advantages to the development of CALL. For example, it helps to further the understanding of CALL activities and to set up a theoretical framework for the CALL practice. However, there is always the danger that the theories drawn from other disciplines cannot show clear links and can give only partial explanations for CALL. As Chapelle points out:

> The uncritical statement that another area may be relevant for the study of CALL threatens to make the search for research paradigms a wild goose chase. What is needed to appropriately draw from other disciplines is a clear notion of exactly what they have to offer to the development, use, and evaluation of CALL.

> (1999: 108)

As mentioned earlier in this chapter, theories from other disciplines have had a valuable influence on CALL, but many of these theories are relatively new in themselves, such as educational technology theory (for instance, study on speech technology, multimedia and video-conferencing), information theory (for instance, study of the ability to find, organize and make use of information; electronic information theory also encompasses how to read and write in a new medium), and sociocultural theory (for instance, study of using ethnographic methods to investigate the sociocultural and classroom contexts in which second language acquisition occurs) (Warschauer and Kern, 2000; Watson-Gegeo, 1988); their influence on CALL is not determined. Even the theories from well established disciplines like linguistics and psychology overlap; for example, both disciplines shed light on the characteristics of the individual learner, learner needs and learning strategies. Besides, the modern development of the study of cognitive psychology has been influenced by the developments in linguistics, particularly the work of Chomsky (Anderson, 1985: 8). Bearing in mind the complexity of interrelated theories, CALL researchers have to be cautious and selective when using theories from other disciplines to explain CALL activities.

Theories from other disciplines should be applied to CALL research appropriately

Even if relevant theories from other fields and disciplines are chosen to help our understanding and interpretation of CALL, there is still a problem of adaptation – how to apply those theories to CALL research appropriately. As Nunan comments in the case of language teaching:

> It [language teaching] has suffered from the misapplication and misinterpretation of theory and research from other disciplines. ... This has led to a number of undesirable outcomes. Instead of a cautious programme of research and development, the profession has been characterized by a series of fads and fashions.

(1988: 174)

As for CALL, the application of the theories from other disciplines such as psychology, communication theory, sociology and second language acquisition need to be in line with CALL practice. For example, cognitive psychology has been considered valuable to CALL practice (Sampson, 1986) because its theories provide a number of hypotheses to explain, design and evaluate CALL activities. Cook (1985) discusses the information processing approach as a model of language teaching appropriate for CALL, and Legenhausen and Wolff (1989) adopt qualitative methods from cognitive psychology to evaluate text reconstruction programmes. However, more study is needed to investigate the research questions that the theories suggest in a CALL environment (Chapelle, 1999). Another example of appropriate application of other disciplines to CALL research is that of sociocultural theories. The value of a sociocultural perspective for CALL has been suggested and discussed by a number of CALL researchers (Salaberry, 1999; Warschauer, 1997). For instance, Warschauer and Kern (2000) suggest that by using multimedia components in networked activities such as audio-conferencing and video-conferencing, learners have the opportunity for authentic exchanges in which to practise conversational strategies that lead to improved sociolinguistic and pragmatic competence. Ludvigsen and Mørch take a sociocultural perspective to study the collaborative learning in the technology-based environments. They conclude:

> Learning occurs in and through social interaction ... The knowledge we have about how learning occurs at the individual and collective levels needs to define the premises for design of educational technology for collaborative learning ... Such a generic functionality (customizable, specific technology) represents a step forward toward the second generation of collaborative learning environments, technology-based environments that are allowed to evolve in the wild, by teachers and students, in their classroom.

(2005: 39–43)

But the abundance of theories from other disciplines can benefit CALL research only if they are applied to CALL environments in appropriate ways. As Chapelle argues: 'Research paradigms for CALL can benefit from further exploration of second language classroom discourse perspectives, but only to the extent that they help to frame CALL research questions and suggest methods for addressing these questions' (1999: 108).

In order to develop an appropriate way to apply theories from other disciplines to CALL research agenda, it is necessary to undertake empirical study driven by research questions that are initiated from reality and from the practice of teachers and students. The evidence gathered from the empirical study of CALL would give researchers a deep insight into CALL activities and help them to detect the problems of a research programme, which in turn would help in conceptualizing CALL activities. The importance of empirical study can be explicated in researching CALL from the SLA perspective.

Theories from SLA with implications for CALL research should be tested empirically

The SLA literature contains work representing a variety of objectives and approaches for investigating the process of second language acquisition and development. In particular, the theories of SLA have reliable research methodologies available to properly frame hypotheses and evaluate the result of CALL practice. The implications of SLA theories for CALL have been addressed in CALL literatures by a number of researchers (Holland, 1995a; Krashen, 1982; Long, 1996; Pica *et al.*, 1996; Swain and Lapkin, 1995). The theories of SLA that have been used in CALL study include interaction hypotheses, communicative language theory, instructional design, theories of teaching and learning. However, the abundance of SLA theories has brought problems to the conceptualization of CALL. As Burston points out:

> The failure to provide a firm research base for CALL certainly has not come about for any lack of Second Language Acquisition (SLA) theory to follow. On the contrary, the problem with respect to language learning theory stems from the superabundance of theories to choose from and, concomitantly, no well-defined, generally accepted theoretical basis for SLA.

> (1996: 31)

Burston further explains the reason for this problem:

> The heart of the problem is the monumental chasm which exists between those in linguistics (psycho-socio-applied, as the case may be) concerned with theory construction, on the one hand, and those involved on the chalk face of language teaching in the classroom (at whatever educational level).

> (1996: 31)

One of the effective ways to bridge the gap is 'a perspective on CALL which provides appropriate empirical research methods for investigating the critical questions about how CALL can be used to improve instructed SLA' (Chapelle, 1997: 21).

Research topics need to be expanded

A glance at the CALL literature in the recent decades suggests that there are, in general, five main research focuses: on theories, on learning activities, on learning tasks, on technology and on research methods.

With the booming application of computer technologies in language teaching, the research topics need to keep aligned with CALL practice. There are three concerns in generating CALL research topics. First, the interdisciplinary research on CALL theories makes the research topics diversified, but only those which are in line with the current CALL applications can provide useful guidance to the practice. Therefore, when selecting the research topics, the researcher needs to consider the significance of research topics to the development of CALL practice. Second, there is a lack of research on the comprehensive frameworks that can overview CALL practice. Most of the studies have examined the use of only one element of technology or one aspect of CALL application such as reading, writing, learning styles or learners' motivation (Baugh and Baugh, 1997; Emery and Ingraham, 1991; Hokanson, 2001; Mydlarski, 1998; Thomson, 2003). The last concern is that there is a need for more study on research methods. How to observe students' learning activities on computers? How to collect data of distance learning activities, and how to collect and evaluate data on new types of learning via e-mail and mobile technologies?

PROBLEMS IN PRACTISING E-LEARNING

Difficulties in theoretical exploration are just part of the problem in researching e-learning. The application of computer technologies into practice could also be problematic. The problems have been identified in administration, attitudes towards e-learning by learners and teachers, and integration of computer technology into existing practice particularly in the context of CALL.

Administration problems

E-learning practitioners and researchers need to consider the influence from policy makers and administration because the investment in and installation of computers need support from the administration of schools, departments or institutions. In most cases, the administration's decision to install and integrate computers into the existing organizations is because of the interest in promoting efficiency with the new technologies. However, without careful planning, the integration of the technology will also lead to unanticipated systemic effects, such as change in the way the organization defines itself and its objectives (Slatin, 1998; Sproull and Kiesler, 1991; Zuboff, 1988). Moreover, administrators need to be aware that simply installing computers cannot guarantee an improvement in efficiency; constant technical training for staff, technical support and updating facilities are also essential components of the successful use of computer technology.

Users' attitudes towards e-learning

From an attitudinal standpoint, both learners and tutors are aware of the benefits of computer technology in learning, such as the large volume and wide range of information available online, its open accessibility, its fast processing speed and its interactive nature. However, it is also often reported by tutors and learners that they have found not much difference in the impact on learning made by computer technology compared with traditional instruction methods (Dunkel, 1991; Salaberry, 1996). A number of reasons have been cited for limited practical impact of computer-based instruction: the current limitations of the technology itself (Holland, 1995b; Warschauer, 1996b) and the effective (or ineffective) methods of instruction by computers.

As for the technology, one of the challenges is the stability and advancement of systems (both hardware and software). Online learning requires a stable and fast Internet speed and facilities such as headphones, microphones and Web cameras if software supports visual communication. Some systems allow students to send their voice recordings to each other, but the transfer of voice files requires a large storage space and fast Internet speed. For instance, in the case of voice-based synchronous speech instruction in language education, there are five technological challenges. First, a system must recognize the speech of a variety of individuals. Second, a system must require little pre-training, as a tutor may find it difficult to give lengthy training to every learner in a class. Third, a system must accept continuous speech. Continuous speech refers to the transcription of a large natural vocabulary without pauses between words. Fourth, a system must be reasonably accurate to convert a high proportion of the words spoken to their text equivalent. And last, a system must be sensitive to the speaker's voice, not the background noise.

As for the methods of instruction, it is worth emphasizing that it is not the media but the pedagogy that matters. It is necessary for a tutor to consider the ways to make full use of the advantages of computer technologies. If a computer is used only as a substitute for a tape recorder or just simply requires a learner to fill in blanks, to select the correct answer in multiple-choice questions, or to answer questions after reading or listening to a paragraph, the advantages of computer technologies cannot be fully utilized. A learner benefits from multimedia that combine different visual and aural information such as texts, speeches, drawings, photographs, music, animations and videos. As Gros and Adrian remark:

> For centuries, university teaching focused on the pedagogical model based on the transmission of information. This perspective is currently being modified in favor of a model focused on student learning ... Numerous proposals have been made in recent years ... They all aim to use technology to promote and mediate learning ...

> (2005: 17)

Finally, the lack of integration of e-learning programmes into the existing teaching curriculum is another reason for the lack of impact. For instance, despite the development of CALL practice since the 1990s by enthusiastic and dedicated CALL advocates, CALL programmes mostly remain as supplements to the main curricula. In Burston's words:

> CALL based activities have for the most part remained ancillary. The total number of applications in use is limited, and their pedagogic quality too frequently leaves something to be desired. The range and content of existing CALL applications is similarly problematic.

> (1996: 32)

The problem of e-learning practice in different learning contexts

The commonly recognized e-learning contexts, as stated above, are self-access, instructed and distance learning (Abrioux, 1989; Bax, 2003; Levy, 1997; Littlemore, 2001). In these learning contexts, the ways to apply e-learning programmes, the design of syllabuses, the instruction methods and learning activities are varied. E-learning practice in each of these contexts has its limitations.

Self-access mode

In the self-access learning context, students are supposed to work on computers without the presence of teachers. The main advantage of the self-access approach is that it gives students flexibility in managing their learning activities. They can choose the materials, time and places to study (Atkinson, 1996). However, there are common misunderstandings about self-access programmes.

First, the self-access programme is assumed to be self-instructed. It is true that some students who have good skills in self-management and self-instruction will achieve their learning purposes, but many will not. There is still a need for teachers who can answer questions, provide technical support and give feedback and suggestions (Little, 1991).

Second, 'self-access' is assumed to be a concept equivalent to 'autonomy'. When students study without teachers, they are assumed to be autonomous learners. The concept of autonomy, however, is not that simple.

> According to the theory of adult education, the autonomous learner is capable of managing, monitoring and evaluating his or her own learning; and this capacity for self-regulation enables the learner to transcend the barriers that pedagogy often erects between learning and living.

> (Barnes, 1976: 30)

In reality, the presence of autonomy in learning is not guaranteed, because no single student is a fully autonomous learner. A student who displays autonomy in one area may not be autonomous in another (Little, 1991).

Last but not least, self-access study is assumed to be less interactive because students study on their own. Self-access study is an independent and to some extent an individualized form of study, but it is unlikely to compensate for the necessity of interaction. In self-access study, interaction happens more often between students and computers.

A self-access programme emphasizes the interaction between students and computers. Students have more control over their learning progress. They can interrupt the normal interaction by asking for help or requesting a repetition or requesting a subtitle, or skipping to the next practice. As Chapelle states:

> The computer programme created the opportunities for modified interaction by offering modified input to the learner upon demand. The data documented that the learner actually engaged in modified interactions and received the modified input, thereby constructing potentially beneficial interaction.

(2001: 59)

There are three critical issues affecting the quality of student–computer interaction. First, technology advancement. A stable condition of technology available is a necessary condition for a productive learning activity. Moreover, state-of-the-art technology has expanded interactive activities. For example, there is a new research tendency to create a Visual Language Tutor (VLT), a piece of language learning software that contains an agent (an animated 3D figure) that you can talk to, and that talks back to you (Beskow, 2003; Granström, 2004). Second is detailed feedback: a computer can give sufficient help, tips and feedback when a student requests it. Third is a variety of choices of learning tasks which can individualize a practice according to a student's needs.

However, such technology is unlikely to obviate the need for teachers in a self-access programme. It is necessary and important for teachers to run the programme and give support to students because the system needs to be maintained; programmes need to be updated regularly; and students need help when they require it. Although the interaction between students and teachers in the self-access approach is not direct and timely, for example, by e-mail, it is throughout a study process. First of all, training given by teachers on how to make the most use of computer technology is necessary before students start a computer-aided language programme. Second, teachers are available to solve both the technical and the language problems students meet. Third, the programme is designed, maintained and upgraded by teachers in order to meet students' needs. Lastly, feedback from teachers on students' practice and progress is necessary, particularly when computers fail to give the specific explanation that students require.

Instructed mode

In this context, computer activities are integrated into the lesson as a whole. A number of authors have stressed the importance of carefully integrating computer-assisted work into the curriculum (Farrington, 1986; Garrett, 1991; Hardisty and Windeatt, 1989). Teachers play an important role in successful integration by choosing course material, designing and implementing pedagogy. This point was emphasized by Jones in his paper on CALL entitled 'It's not so much the programme, more what you do with it: the importance of methodology in CALL' (Jones, 1986).

It is also not easy for the teacher to achieve successful integration. For example, as a course designer, how can a teacher choose material that suits all students? How can a teacher keep the balance of students' progress in practice? As a technical supporter, how can a teacher keep up with fast-developing technology? As a knowledge resource, how can a teacher meet every student's needs? What kind of feedback will a teacher give to students?

Distance learning

Distance learning refers mainly to a mode of delivery. It is 'independent learning at a distance through the means of self-study texts and non-contiguous communication' (Sampson, 2003: 103). Despite the acknowledged strength of distance learning as to the convenience, flexibility and adaptability of this mode of education to suit individual students' needs (Holmberg, 1989: 24), at least three significant weaknesses of distance learning have been identified by researchers: its inability to offer face-to-face interaction between students and teachers; the isolation and demotivation of students (Kirkup and Jones, 1996; Strambi and Bouvet, 2003); and its lack of flexibility in content and learning methods.

In the context of distance learning, learners are not able to receive face-to-face instruction from the teacher. With no direct interaction with the teacher, the learner may misunderstand the message from the teacher and feel uncertain as to how to carry out and evaluate the task (Hara and Kling, 1999). Moreover, the learner may also feel disconnected and isolated due to the lack of face-to-face interaction with the teacher and other learners (Egbert and Thomas, 2001; Rovai, 2002, Sampson, 2003). It is also not easy to build sufficient flexibility into the materials to adapt to a variety of learners' styles, interests and skill levels, therefore sustaining learners' motivation (Holmberg, 1986; Strambi and Bouvet, 2003). In order to sustain a high level of motivation of the learner, it requires a great deal of timely support and guidance from the teacher and of an interactive online community where the learner can communicate synchronously with the teacher and other students. But this can make the teacher's task time-consuming and demands advanced hardware and software.

PROBLEMS IN RESEARCH METHODS

The choice of research methods can be constrained by accessibility to the sample

One of the difficulties in carrying out research in e-learning is gaining access to programmes and students. For example, in the case of CALL, it is not easy to locate appropriate computer-assisted language-teaching programmes. An important influence on the use made of ICT in subjects and classes is the amount and range of ICT resources available to students and teachers. Where there are limited numbers of computers available, this limits the use of CALL programmes (Lam, 2000; Strudler *et al.*, 1995; Warschauer, 2002). More often, many language centres in universities and other educational institutions just install CALL programmes on the computers in the language laboratory. There is limited integration with regular class teaching because such integration depends on teachers' interest, time, effort and technical capability. Egbert reports that two participants responded that they had rigid curricula which left them with no time or support to integrate CALL: 'We also have a curriculum to follow and, since we use block scheduling at our school, we already struggle to find enough time to complete the required agenda each year. There never seems to be enough time to incorporate CALL activities' (2002).

The difficulty is emphasized by a small sample of students. For example, a small study on CALL application in teaching English listening and speaking skills was conducted in UK universities in 2003 (Zhao, 2007). When the persons in charge of applying the CALL programmes in the respective language centres were contacted, the response was disappointing. Some universities had given up CALL programmes after an experimental period. Some of the students were full-time language students, preparing for the IELTS (International English Language Testing System) tests in order to study in UK universities; others were university students who took part-time language courses to improve their English. But the students attended the language courses only on a short-term basis. By the end of each term, they simply finished the course and left. Even if there were ongoing CALL programmes in the language centres, the teachers had to consider not overloading the students by participating in my survey. Besides, when a CALL programme was a supplement to the major curriculum in the language centre, it was up to the students as to whether they were willing to do extra practice in their spare time. Students' motivation was usually affected by the availability of the facilities and their course schedules (Zhao, 2004).

Conventional research methods borrowed from other disciplines should be adapted to e-learning contexts

Computer technology has created a new dynamic field for research. In order to investigate the various topics of e-learning – including the features of learning activities; the appropriate teaching methods; the ways of designing and delivering e-learning materials; peripheral features of e-learning in relation to other disciplines such as sociology, culture, psychology and second language acquisition – well established research methods such as questionnaire, interview and observation have all been used in this relatively new research field. However, the methods chosen must be appropriate to the setting and the technology under study (Egbert *et al.*, 1999).

Questionnaire

The questionnaire is a popular research technique for carrying out a survey. It is not only efficient in both time and cost, but also standardizes the questions and simplifies the data analysis. The possibility of respondent anonymity may lead to more candid and honest responses. However, there are three common problems of applying questionnaires in an e-learning context.

First, learning via computers is a new way of learning. When using a computer as a tool to practise English, students hardly pay a second thought to the rationale behind the approach. Therefore, students are easily misled if they do not realize the purposes of questions in a questionnaire. For example, a questionnaire survey was conducted to investigate the impact of computer technology on students' use of learning strategies to practise listening skills (Zhao, 2006). Figure 19.1 is an excerpt from the questionnaire which shows that if the respondents do not understand the rationale(s) behind CALL programme design, they are likely to misinterpret the question(s). Question (g) is about whether a computer would give feedback to students' practice.

Question	Agree (No. of students)	Disagree (No. of students)	Reasons for the disagreement
(g) I can get hints or answers to the exercise questions from the CALL programme	12	4	☐ Some are a little bit difficult to answer ☐ It is very slow ☐ The computer programme is just limited in a few areas

Figure 19.1   Questionnaire excerpt

Several students misinterpreted the question. One answer concerned technical or design problems: 'It is very slow.' Another was about the poor variety of the content: 'The computer programme is just limited in a few areas.' This sort of misinterpretation is explained by Low:

> [In a questionnaire survey] respondents presume that a given question has been designed with them in mind and, in the absence of negotiation, further assume that their initial interpretation is what is wanted. As a result, they may fail to notice where the designer is using words differently from them.

> (1999: 505)

Therefore, it is helpful if the relevant rationale(s) can be explained to respondents before they answer the questionnaire. The second concern in using a questionnaire is that it is also difficult to explore issues in depth. A questionnaire is helpful to investigate the distribution of e-learning application, but is not able to provide detailed information. Moreover, the respondents' literacy problems affect, to some extent, how they understand and answer the questions. As Dörnyei points out, 'Statistics of people who have difficulty reading and the number of those who are uncomfortable with writing is even bigger. It is therefore understandable that for respondents with literacy problems, filling in a questionnaire can appear an intimidating or overwhelming task' (2003: 11). In particular, there are many new terms about e-learning, such as asynchronous learning, discussion boards, Electronic Performance Support System (EPSS) and so on. If respondents are not familiar with the terms, their answers to the questions might be affected.

Interviews

Another conventional method used to research e-learning is the interview. There are particular problems associated with interviews in the e-learning context. For instance, students' language knowledge affects interview results. If students do not have advanced knowledge of the English language, in particular of spoken English, it is difficult to carry out an interview. Moreover, as I found out in my own research (Zhao, 2004), students normally attended more than one language programme. The duration of programmes also varied, some lasting one year, others three or six months. Some programmes used commercial courseware with multimedia while others were developed by teachers. Some programmes were integrated into normal pedagogy with teachers' instruction while others were self-access, installed into universities' networks. Such complexity is likely to result in inaccurate data, as interviewees may answer questions based on the different programmes they use and the different courses they attend. Therefore, it is necessary to make it clear what kinds of programmes they attend.

Observation

Observation has become a mainstay method in second language acquisition research (Allwright, 1988; Allwright and Bailey, 1991; Chaudron, 1988; Johnson, 1995; van Lier, 1988). It is 'one of the most reliable tools for determining how students are progressing in class and can be purposefully employed to gather information about a wide variety of learners' abilities, skills, and competencies' (Egbert, 1999: 260). Observation has also been applied to e-learning research to investigate students' behaviours in class (Chun, 1998) and the impact of computers on learning and teaching (Markley, 1998). But it can be difficult to apply observation in studying e-learning activities, because, as with other learning activities, much of the information in e-learning activities cannot be observed, as it is cerebral and non-behaviouristic; it can be especially difficult when attempting to observe students' learning strategies while they are using computers. Moreover, if e-learning activities happen online, it is difficult to carry out observation without the presence of the students.

It is necessary to search out and practise new research methods of e-learning

The computer itself allows the generation of data for many kinds of analysis. For example, information that has been gathered from synchronous communications like Internet relay chat and Web chat; asynchronous communications like e-mail are widely used to study learning activities in various e-learning contexts (Holliday, 1999; Turbee, 1999).

These methods are alternatives to the conventional methods, but there are problems in access and integrity. For example, there are several challenges to using e-mail to collect data. First, it is not easy to access respondents' e-mails due to privacy and confidentiality. If one of the sample population refuses to provide e-mails, the balance of data will be affected. Another disadvantage of e-mails is that students who have had little experience on the computer may find sending and receiving e-mails frustrating (Kelm, 1998). Another concern is ethical issues. Thampton (2000) notes:

> The online environment may not be reflected in existing codes of ethical practice for research on human subjects. Factors such as the disinhibiting effect of the seemingly anonymous (or pseudonymous) environment, an increased danger of researchers objectifying their 'invisible' research subjects, and the difficulty of obtaining informed consent from members of online groups whose composition changes constantly are representative concerns.

Online chat such as Web chat, Internet relay chat, MOO (Multiple User domains Object Oriented), WOO (Web-enhanced MOO) and GMUK (Graphical Multiple User Konversations) are also considered by e-learning researchers because they are flexible in terms of time and place. However, all these modes of online chat require large memory (data storage space), a fast Central Processing Unit (CPU) and a fast modem. This is a particular problem in the regions or countries that are not advanced in technology. The stability of technology and speed of the Internet may affect the quality of data. For instance, Turbee points out the effect of technology on the quality of online chat: 'Screen refreshes, slow graphics downloads, or other delays may make the reading of the conversation difficult and disjointed' (1999: 348). Besides, the words used in online chat tend to be simple and abbreviated, which may cause misunderstanding and unspecific information. It is also time-consuming to type long sentences.

Video recording is also an interesting means for collecting data about students' behaviour with technology. There are acknowledged advantages to video-recording in study e-learning. First, it can provide information about the speaker's posture, gestures and clothing that can inform the researcher of the social and cultural background of the speaker (Dufon, 2002). Second, visual information can help the researcher to disambiguate verbal messages (Iino, 1999). Furthermore, video- (also audio-) recording can provide denser linguistic information than does note taking (Dufon, 2002). However, there are also challenges to using video-recording in researching e-learning. First, a video can capture only what is observable. Second, the cost of video- and audio-recording equipment can be expensive. Last but not least, there is the possibility that some data may be lost because part of the activity falls outside the range of the lens (Fetterman, 1998; Watson-Gegeo *et al*, 1981).

CONCLUSIONS AND IMPLICATIONS

The further the study of e-learning develops, the more questions emerge regarding the theoretical framework of research, the practice of applying e-learning programmes in different learning contexts, appropriate research methods, and the process of carrying out research.

In order to establish the theoretical framework for e-learning research, researchers have been seeking solutions from other disciplines such as psychology, educational technology and sociocultural studies. The theories from other subjects help us understand e-learning and improve its practice in various learning environments. However, attention should be given to developing cross-disciplinary theories which have to be relevant and helpful to the development of e-learning theories. Another challenge for e-learning theoretical exploration is to apply cross-disciplinary theories appropriately into e-learning practice. Researchers need to identify the theory or theories on which they are drawing (and if there is more than one, how they relate to each other); or, if they are eschewing theory altogether and choosing a problem identification and problem-solving approach that is more pragmatic, explain why they are not referring to theory. This latter approach is more like research and development, and does not necessarily need an epistemological basis from which to gauge progress. Appropriate applications need first to identify the problems of e-learning practice and then to suggest solutions. Empirical study is necessary and helpful to find the problems in e-learning and to discover the gaps between theory and practice.

E-learning practice has also encountered challenges from administration, teachers and students, as the use of computer technology in learning is comparatively new. It takes time to prove its efficacy and to find appropriate ways of integrating it into existing administrative systems, teaching methods and learning contexts. In general, there are three e-learning contexts: a self-access context, an instructed context and a distance learning context. In each context, there is a different way of both organizing learning and delivering course material. But problems also occur in how to enhance interactive learning activities in different learning contexts.

Problems also occur in the process of carrying out research. It is not easy to gain access to a suitable e-learning programme. Secondly, there is no perfect research method for studying e-learning. The conventional methods such as questionnaire, interview and observation are confounded by specific features of an e-learning environment, such as complex learning programmes and interaction between students and computers. The research methods relevant to the use of technology, such as e-mail and online chat, offer researchers flexibility of time and place, but they do require stable technology, and there can also be problems of access and integrity, together with the ethical issues which can affect the validity of the data. One of the solutions is to apply multi-level research methods. The data collected can provide various perspectives on CALL practice.

In conclusion, the solutions to the problems identified in researching e-learning in terms of theories, practice and research methods will almost certainly require changes in technology, in attitudes, in approach, and in practice among teachers and students. This change will not be an easy process. However, if we are committed to finding research solutions based on real problems, future practice will be that much better informed.

REFERENCES

Abrioux, D. (1989) 'Computer-assisted language learning and distance education', *Journal of Distance Education*, 4 (1): 20–35.

Allwright, D. (1988) *Observation in the Language Classroom*. Harlow: Longman.

Allwright, D. and Bailey, K. M. (1991) *Focus on the Language Classroom: An Introduction to Classroom Research for Language Teachers*. Cambridge: Cambridge University Press.

Anderson, J. R. (1985) *Cognitive Psychology and its Implications*. New York: Freeman.

Atkinson, E. (1996) 'Open/Flexible Learning and the Open Learning Initiative', proceedings of the II International Conference on Open Learning, Old Australia, 45–8.

Barnes, D. (1976) *From Communication to Curriculum*. London: Penguin.

Baugh, G. and Baugh, W. (1997) 'Global classroom – e-mail learning communities', *Learning and Leading with Technology*, 25 (3): 38–41.

Bax, S. (2003) 'CALL – past, present and future', *System*, 31: 13–28.

Beauvois, M. (1997) 'Write to speak: the effects of electronic communication on the oral achievement of fourth semester French students', in J. Muyskens (ed.), *New Ways of Learning and Teaching: Focus on Technology and Foreign Language Education*. Boston, MA: Heinle and Heinle. pp. 93–115.

Beskow, J. (2003) 'Talking Heads – Communication, Articulation and Animation'. Paper presented at Fonetik '96, Swedish Phonetics Conference, Nässlingen.

Blake, R. (2000) 'Computer mediated communication: a window on L2 Spanish interlanguage', *Language Learning and Technology*, 4 (1): 120–36.

Block, D. (1990) 'Seeking new bases for SLA research: looking to cognitive science', *System*, 18 (2): 167–76.

Burston, J. (1996) 'CALL at the crossroads: myths, realities, promises and challenges', *Australian Review of Applied Linguistics*, 19 (2): 27–36.

Chapelle, C. A. (1997) 'CALL in the year 2000: still in search of research paradigms?' *Language Learning and Technology*, 1 (1): 19–43.

Chapelle, C. A. (1998) 'Multimedia CALL: lessons to be learned from research on instruction', *Language Learning and Technology*, 2 (1): 22–34.

Chapelle, C. A. (1999) 'Research questions for a CALL research agenda: a reply to Rafael Salaberry', *Language Learning and Technology*, 3 (1): 108–13.

Chapelle, C. A. (2001) *Computer Application in Second Language Acquisition*. Cambridge: Cambridge University Press.

Chapelle, C. A. (2003) *English Language Learning and Technology*. Dordrecht: John Benjamins.

Chaudron, C. (1988) *Second Language Classrooms: Research on Teaching and Learning*. Cambridge: Cambridge University Press.

Chun, D. (1998) 'Using computer-assisted class discussion to facilitate the acquisition of interactive competence', in J. Swaffar, S. Romano, P. Markley and K. Arens (eds), *Language Learning Online: Theory and Practice in the ESL and L2 Computer Classroom*. Austin, TX: Labyrinth.

Clark, R. (1983) 'Reconsidering research on learning from the media', *Review of Educational Research*, 53 (4): 445–59.

Clark, R. (1991) 'When researchers swim upstream: reflections on an unpopular argument about learning from media', *Educational Technology*, February: 34–40.

Cononelos, T. and Oliva, M. (1993) 'Using computer networks to enhance foreign language/culture education', *Foreign Language Annals*, 26 (4): 527–33.

Cook, V. J. (1985) 'Bridging the gap between computers and language teaching', *ELT Document*, 122, 13–24.

Dörnyei, Z. (2003) *Questionnaires in Second Language Research: Construction, Administration, and Processing*. Mahwah, NJ: Erlbaum.

Dufon, M. (2002) 'Video recording in ethnographic SLA research: some issues of validity in data collection', *Language Learning and Technology*, 6 (1): 40–59.

Dunkel, P. (ed.) (1991) *Computer-Assisted Language Learning and Testing: Research Issues and Practice*. Philadelphia, PA: Penn State University Press.

Egbert, J. (1999) 'Classroom practice: practical assessments in the CALL classroom', in J. Egbert and E. Hanson-Smith (eds), *CALL Environments: Research, Practice and Critical Issues*. Alexandria, VA: TESOL.

Egbert, J. and Hanson-Smith, E. (eds) (1999) *CALL Environments: Research, Practice and Critical Issues*. Alexandria, VA: TESOL.

Egbert, J. and Thomas, M. (2001) 'The new frontier: a case study in applying instructional design for distance teacher education', *Journal of Technology and Teacher Education*, 9 (3): 391–405.

Egbert, J., Chao, C. and Hanson-Smith, E. (1999) 'Computer-enhanced language learning environments: an overview', in J. Egbert, and E. Hanson-Smith (eds), *CALL Environments: Research, Practice and Critical Issues*. Alexandria, VA: TESOL.

Egbert, J., Paulus, T. and Nakamichi, Y. (2002) 'The impact of CALL instruction on classroom computer use: a foundation for rethinking technology in teacher education', *Language Learning and Technology*, 6 (3): 108–26.

Emery, C. and Ingraham, B. (1991) 'France interactive: a hypermedia approach to language teaching', *Educational and Training Technology*, 28 (4): 321–33.

Farrington, B. (1986) '"Triangular mode" working: the Littré Project in the field', in J. Higgins (ed.), *Computer-Assisted Language Learning*, special issues of *System*, 14 (2): 199–204.

Fetterman, D. M. (1998) *Ethnography: Step by Step* (2nd edn). Thousand Oaks, CA: Sage.

Garrett, N. (1991) 'CARLA comes to CALL', *Computer-Assisted Language Learning*, 4 (1): 41–5.

Gilmour, B. (2004) 'College English Pilot: Report and Recommendations'. Unpublished report, Newcastle University.

Granström, B. (2004) 'Towards a Virtual Language Tutor', invited paper at *Proc InSTIL/ICALL2004 – NLP and Speech Technologies in Advanced Language Learning Systems*, 1–8.

Gros, B. and Adrian, M. (2005) 'The use of virtual forums to promote collaborative learning in higher education', *Educational Technology*, 45 (5): 17–20.

Hara, N. and Kling, R. (1999) 'Students' frustrations with a Web-based distance education course', *First Monday*, 4 (12). Retrieved on 1 May 2003 from: http://firstmonday.org/issues/issue4_12/hara/index.html.

Hardisty, D. and Windeatt, S. (1989) *CALL*. Oxford: Oxford University Press.

Hokanson, B. (2001) 'Silk and silicon: technology paradigms and education', *Educational Technology*, 41 (3): 42–6.

Holland, M. (1995a) 'Lessons learned in designing intelligent CALL: managing communication across disciplines', *Computer-Assisted Language Learning*, 7 (3): 227–56.

Holland, M. (1995b) 'The case for intelligent CALL', in M. Holland, J. D. Kaplan and M. R. Sams (eds), *Intelligent Language Tutors: Theory Shaping Technology*. Mahwah, NJ: Erlbaum.

Holliday, L. (1999) 'Theory and research: input, interaction, and CALL', in J. Egbert and E. Hanson-Smith (eds), *CALL Environments: Research, Practice and Critical Issues*. Alexandria, VA: TESOL.

Holmberg, B. (1986) *Growth and Structure of Distance Education*. London: Croom Helm.

Holmberg, B. (1989) *Theory and Practice of Distance Education*. New York: Routledge.

Iino, M. (1999) 'Issues of video recording in language studies', *Obirin Studies in Language and Literature*, 39: 65–85.

Jaeglin, C. (1998) 'Learners' and instructors' attitudes towards computer-assisted class discussion', in J. Swaffar *et al.* (eds), *Language Learning Online*. Austin, TX: Labyrinth.

Johnson, K. E. (1995) *Understanding Communication in Second Language Classrooms*. Cambridge: Cambridge University Press.

Jones, C. (1986) 'It's not so much the programme, more what you do with it: the importance of methodology in CALL', *System*, 14 (2): 171–8.

Kelm, O. (1998) 'The use of electronic mail in foreign language classes', in J. Swaffar *et al.* (eds), *Language Learning Online*. Austin, TX: Labyrinth

Kern, R. (1996) 'Computer-mediated communication: using e-mail exchanges to explore personal histories in two cultures', in M. Warschauer (ed.), *Telecollaboration in Foreign Language Learning: Proceedings of the Hawaii Symposium*. Honolulu: Second Language Teaching and Curriculum Center, University of Hawai'i, pp. 105–9.

Kirkup, G. and Jones, A. (1996) 'New technologies for open learning: the superhighway to the learning society?', in P. Raggatt, R. Edwards and N. Small (eds), *Adult Learners, Education and Training* II, *The Learning Society: Challenges and Trends*. Abingdon: Routledge. pp. 272–91.

Krashen, S. (1982) *Principles and Practice in Second Language Acquisition*. Oxford: Pergamon Press.

Lam, Y. (2000) 'Technophilia v. technophobia: a preliminary look at why second language teachers do or do not use technology in their classrooms', *Canadian Modern Language Review*, 56: 389–420.

Last, R. W. (1989) *Artificial Intelligence Techniques in Language Learning*. Chichester: Horwood.

Legenhausen, L. and Wolff, D. (1989) 'Evaluating software: the Düsseldorf CALL project', *CALL Digest*, 5 (1): 7–9.

Levy, M. (1997) *Computer-Assisted Language Learning: Context and Conceptualization*. Oxford: Oxford University Press.

Liddell, P. (1994) 'Learners and second language acquisition: a union blessed by CALL?', *Computer-Assisted Language Learning*, 7 (2): 163–73.

Little, D. (1991) *Learner Autonomy* I: *Definition, Issues and Problems*. Dublin: Authentik.

Littlemore, J. (2001) 'Learner autonomy and the challenge of tandem language learning via the Internet', in A. Grambers and G. Davies (eds), *ICT and Language Learning: A European Perspective*. Lisse: Swets and Zeitlinger.

Long, M. H. (1996) 'The role of linguistic environment in second language acquisition', in W. C. Ritchie and T. K. Bhatia (eds), *Handbook of Second Language Acquisition*. San Diego, CA: Academic Press. pp. 413–68.

Low, G. (1999) 'What respondents do with questionnaires: accounting for incongruity and fluidity', *Applied Linguistics*, 20 (4): 503–33.

Ludvigsen, S. R. and Mørch, A. I. (2005) 'Situating collaborative learning: educational technology in the wild', *Educational Technology*, 45 (5): 39–43.

MacWhinney, B. (1995) 'Evaluating foreign language tutoring systems', in V. M. Holland, J. D. Kaplan and M. R. Sams (eds), *Intelligent Language Tutors: Theory Shaping Technology*. Mahwah, NJ: Erlbaum. pp. 317–26.

Markley, P. (1998) 'Empowering students: the diverse roles of Asians and women in ELS computer class-rooms' in J. Swaffar *et al.* (eds), *Language Learning Online*. Austin, TX: Labyrinth.

Muyskens, J. A. (1997) *New Ways of Learning and Teaching: Focus on Technology and Foreign Language Education*. Boston: Heinle and Heinle.

Mydlarski, D. (1998) 'Shall we dance? Applying the cooperative model to CALL', *Canadian Modern Language Review*, 55 (1): 124–38.

Ng, K. and Olivier, W. (1987) 'Computer-assisted language learning: an investigation on some design and implementation issues', *System*, 9 (2): 85–98.

Nunan, D. (1988) *The Learner-Centred Curriculum*. Cambridge: Cambridge University Press.

Pica, T., Lincoln-Porter, F., Paninos, D. and Linnell, J. (1996), 'Language learners' interaction: how does it address the input, output, and feedback needs of L2 learners?', *TESOL Quarterly*, 30 (1): 59–84.

Richards, C. (2005) 'The design of effective ICT-supported learning activities: exemplary models, changing requirements, and new possibilities', *Language Learning and Technology*, 9 (1): 60–79.

Rovai, A. (2002) 'Building a sense of community at a distance', *International Review of Research in Open and Distance Learning*, 3 (1): 1–16.

Salaberry, R. (1996) 'The theoretical foundation for the development of pedagogical tasks in computer mediated communication', *CALICO Journal*, 14 (1): 5–34.

Salaberry, R. (1999) 'CALL in the year 2000: still developing the research agenda', *Language Learning and Technology*, 3 (1): 104–7.

Salaberry, R. (2001) 'The use of technology for second language learning and teaching: a retrospective', *Modern Language Journal*, 85 (1): 41–56.

Sampson, G. (1986) 'Transition networks for computer-assisted language learning', in G. Leech and C. N. Candlin (eds), *Computers in English Language Teaching and Research*. Harlow: Longman.

Sampson, N. (2003) 'Meeting the needs of distance learners', *Language Learning and Technology*, 7 (3): 103–18.

Sanaoui, R. and Lapkin, S. (1992) 'A case study of an FSL senior secondary course integrating computer networking', *Canadian Modern Language Review*, 43 (3): 524–52.

Slatin, J. (1998) 'The computer writing and research lab: a brief institutional history', in J. Swaffar *et al.* (eds), *Language Learning Online*. Austin TX: Labyrinth.

Smith, W. F. (ed.) (1988) *Modern Media in Foreign Language Education: Theory and Implementation*. Lincolnwood, IL: National Textbook Company.

Sproull, L. and Kiesler, S. (1991) *Connections: New Ways of Working in the Networked Organization*. Cambridge, MA: MIT Press.

Strambi, A. and Bouvet, E. (2003) 'Flexibility and interaction at a distance: a mixed-mode environment for language learning', *Language Learning and Technology*, 7 (3): 81–102.

Strudler, N., Quinn, L., McKinney, M. and Jones, W. (1995) 'From coursework to the real world: first-year teachers and technology', in D. A. Willis, B. Robin and J. Willis (eds), *Technology and Teacher Education Annual*. Charlottesville, VA: AACE. pp. 774–7.

Swaffar, J., Romano, S., Markley, P. and Arens, K. (eds) (1998) *Language Learning Online: Theory and Practice in the ESL and L2 Computer Classroom*. Austin TX: Labyrinth.

Swain, M. and Lapkin, S. (1995) 'Problems in output and the cognitive processes they generate: a step towards second language learning', *Applied Linguistics*, 16: 371–91.

Thompson, M. (2005) 'e-Learning research in the US: challenges and opportunities'. Pre-seminar draft, WUN e-Learning Seminar Series: Research methodological issues in e-learning research. Retrieved on 19 February 2006 from: http://www.wun.ac.uk/e-learning/seminars/seminar_two/papers/Melody.pdf.

Thomson, C. K. (2003) 'The World Wide Web as a teaching and learning resource: observation of learners' performance in the resource-based learning of Japanese as a foreign language', *Australian Review of Applied Linguistics*, 17: 74–90.

Turbee, L. (1999) 'Classroom practice: MOO, WOO, and More – language learning in virtual environments', in Egbert, J. and E. Hanson-Smith (eds), *CALL Environments: Research, Practice and Critical Issues*. Alexandria, VA: TESOL.

van Lier, L. (1988). *The Classroom and the Learner*. Harlow: Longman.

Warschauer, M. (1995) *E-mail for English Teaching*. Alexandria, VA: TESOL.

Warschauer, M. (1996a) 'Motivational aspects of using computers for writing and communication', in M. Warschauer (ed.), *Telecollaboration in Foreign Language Learning: Proceedings of the Hawaii symposium*. Honolulu: Second Language Teaching and Curriculum Center, University of Hawaii. pp. 29–46.

Warschauer, M. (1996b) 'Computer-assisted language learning: an introduction', in S. Fotos (ed.), *Multimedia Language Teaching*. Tokyo: Logos International.

Warschauer, M. (1997) 'Computer-mediated collaborative learning: theory and practice', *Modern Language Journal*, 81: 470–81.

Warschauer, M. (2002) 'A developmental perspective on technology in language education', *TESOL Quarterly*, 36 (3): 453–75.

Warschauer, M. and Kern, R. (eds) (2000) *Network-based Language Teaching: Concepts and Practice*. Cambridge: Cambridge University Press.

Watson-Gegeo, K. (1988) 'Ethnography in ESL: defining the essentials', *TESOL Quarterly*, 22: 575–92.

Watson-Gegeo, K., Maldonado-Guzman, A. and Gleason, J. (1981) 'Establishing Research Goals: The Ethnographer–Practitioner Dialectic'. Proceedings of selected research paper presentations, Theory and Research Division, Association for Educational Communications and Technology. pp. 670–714.

Zhao, Y. (2004) 'Problems in Researching Dialogue in E-learning in Higher Education'. Paper presented in Economic and Social Research Council/Worldwide Universities Network research seminar series 'Researching Dialogue and Communities of Enquiry in E-learning in Higher Education', University of York, December.

Zhao, Y. (2007) 'The Impact of Computer Technology on Teaching and Learning English (Listening and Speaking) as a Second Language in UK Higher Education', Thesis submitted for the award of Ph.D. (March 2007). York: The University of York, Department of Educational Studies

Zuboff, S. (1988) *In the Age of the Smart Machine: The Future of Work and Power*. New York: Basic Books.

PART V

Design Issues

20

New Conceptions for Community Design

Bronwyn Stuckey and Sasha Barab

What makes for a successful online community is often poorly understood. At this time (1996), the tendency of those involved in building graphical virtual worlds is to create visually compelling worlds that look good, but do a poor job of fostering social interaction. Many of these systems have more in common with lonely museums than with the vibrant communities they set out to create.

(Kollock, 1996: 58)

Over the last decade we have seen more and more educators strive to craft community in various online learning contexts (Barab *et al.*, 2001; Jones *et al.*, 2001; Riel and Polin, 2004; Shumar and Renninger, 2002). A fundamental premise of these efforts is that a community-based design will benefit groups of individuals coming together to develop relationships and construct notions of meaningful practice. However, we are still in our infancy in terms of understanding the dynamics that characterize and drive these Internet-mediated communities of practice (CoP), especially where a sponsoring body intentionally develops them to support a particular learning agenda. Although it is ten years since Kollock made the above opening quote, it still serves as a salient warning to those of us charged with designing Web-supported communities of practice. Many attempts to build online community may have failed because of the very design efforts meant to facilitate them. These efforts unduly focused on the implementation of fine-grained design and highly structured Web architectures while neglecting the social infrastructure that is at the heart of any community (Preece, 2000; Rheingold, 1994; Senge, 1999). Experience clearly shows that 'good design' in socially oriented environments is neither a prelude to community nor enough in itself to stimulate and support community. If designers, managers, and facilitators are to succeed in capitalizing on what online community affords, they need to adopt new conceptions of what it means to design for community. These new conceptions will require them to build more than a tolerance for the 'messiness' inherent in social systems, they must learn to leverage it.

This chapter presents, from the authors' varied experiences, a set of critical considerations to move the reader toward an evidence-based conception of community design. Specifically drawing from practical cases, and supported by relevant literature, this chapter describes five ever-present design tensions and proposes ways these tensions can be recognized and harnessed for effective Web-supported community design.

COMMUNITY

'Community' is a complex term and one that belies one particular definition or meaning. The concept of 'community' has a long and rich tradition, and is likely to evoke distinctly different images for each of us. Long before the pundits dreamed of taking the community online, sociologists struggled to find agreement when defining and describing community (Hillery, 1955; Poplin, 1979). Hillery was so struck by the plethora of sociological definitions that he drew together ninety-four of them in an effort to isolate shared definitional concepts. His analysis, still widely cited today, was to find that only one concept was truly common to all. It was acknowledged that community dealt with *people*. Today, agreement on a single definition of community is no more attainable than it was for Hillery in 1955. While drawn from a wide range of domains, theories and disciplines, community online has been popularized over the last decade as:

- *Online communities* (Kim, 2000; Preece, 2002; Williams and Cothrel, 2000).
- *Online social networks* (Borgatti and Molina, 2005; Kimball and Rheingold, 2000; Wellman and Gulia, 1999).
- *Online, virtual or distributed learning communities* (Bruckman, 2002; Kowch and Schwier; 1997: Palloff and Pratt, 1999; Wilson and Ryder, 1998).
- *Communities of interest* (Department of Defense, 2004; Fischer, 2001).
- *Communities of enquiry* (Garrison *et al.*, 2000; Garrison *et al.*, 2004; Farmer, 2004).
- *Knowledge-based communities* (Scardamalia and Bereiter, 1993).
- *Professional learning communities* (DuFour and Eaker, 1998; Hord, 1997; McLaughlin and Talbert, 2006).
- *Communities of practice* (Davenport and Hall, 2002; Lave and Wenger, 1991; Lesser and Storck, 2001; Wenger *et al.*, 2002; Williams and Cothrel, 2000).

In some cases what distinguishes these communities seems merely a matter of semantics. For instance, *professional learning communities* and *communities of practice* both focus on improving professional work practices. In other cases there are fine yet fundamental differences in their contexts and goals. Where *learning communities* are often cited in the literature as part of curriculum and academic course contexts, *professional learning communities* are more likely to be found in the context of in-service professional development. Where a *community of interest* may bring together people who develop an affinity through a shared interest or to solve a particular problem, a *community of practice* draws people who, beyond interest, actually work in a particular practice. Many of the community types serve as vehicles for professional learning through their capacity to share and build knowledge. While no single definition of community suffices, a review of the literature listed above shows that four predominant threads first recognized by Hillery in 1955 still hold true. Communities are comprised of *people*, with *common ties*, engaging in ongoing *social interaction* in a *place* (geographical or virtual) (Hamman, 2000; Poplin, 1979; Hillery, 1955; Stuckey, 2004). This simple view of community may, as Bruckman (cited in Preece and Maloney-Krichmar, 2005) suggests, allow us to move forward, accepting that community as a concept is always going to have 'fuzzy borders'.

There has been a call from several commentators to suggests that it is time to empirically operationalize online communities (Havelock, 2004). Research across diverse fields with and interest in knowledge management suggests that as designers we need to structure our design efforts around three conceptual premises. The *first premise* relates to the knowledge we seek to build when we set out to design for community, recognizing it not as a thing but an active process (Snowden, 2002; Stacey, 2001). Holding to this premise will cause designers to consider ways to facilitate the *flows* between expert and novice, tacit and explicit rather than simply focusing on the content 'to be delivered' (Nonaka and Takeuchi, 1995).

The *second premise* is that communities can never be the result of a design, only a response to it (Wenger, 1998). While it would be eagerly sought after if we could build a road map to community, it seems impossible when community itself is idiosyncratic and organic by nature. A strong body of literature does indicate that community development involves a truly emergent process and cannot simply be prescribed (Baym, 1998; Havelock, 2004; Renninger and Shumar, 2004; Wenger *et al.*, 2002). Literature in the field of knowledge management similarly indicates that communities are complex self-organizing social systems (Brown and Duguid, 1999; Kelly, 1994; Krebs, 1998; Lave and Wenger, 1991; Lemke, 1993; Wiley and Edwards, 2002). This research would suggest community is continually evolving according to the relationships between members and the maturing practices of the community and it is the social activity of the members, not external design efforts, that build those relationships and the sense and value of community (Brook and Oliver, 2003; Havelock, 2004).

If we accept that community development does seem effective when occurring as a natural process, the question arises as to how community managers and facilitators can emulate or foster that natural process? There is evidence that designers can establish enabling online environments that invite, promote or facilitate interactivity and provide fertile opportunities for members to interact and develop the close ties often seen in community (Haythornthwaite, 2002; Wellman, *et al.*, 1996). It was not by accident that a number of the leading theorists in this field explain the process of community design in terms of gardening metaphors; describing how organizations, managers and co-ordinators may act to *cultivate* or *grow* community (Brown and Duguid, 2000; Schlager *et al.*, 2002, Wenger *et al.*, 2002).

The *third conceptual premise* is that community design is never final: it requires a commitment to ongoing and sustained design, and management focus should be on community as a negotiation process as well as a discrete entity (Fernback, 1999). Barab *et al.*, (2004: 496) found in their investigations of a community-based teacher preparation programme that coming to terms with the evolving dynamics of community may be the ultimate challenge for those of us who seek to design for them. They advise us that:

> [T]o speak of communities in a theoretically grounded manner is to acknowledge that communities emerge through interactions rather than design, and gain their richness, complexity, and opportunities for learning through their multigenerational structures and member pathways for movement through the community.

It seems that to design an opportunity from which community might grow requires sustained attention and care just as the gardener continues to tend flower beds long after planting. We cannot front-end-load the community with a 'good' design process and return at given intervals to evaluate our product. Community design requires a commitment to ongoing and sustained processes. For those of us trying to intentionally cultivate community as an environment for learning we must learn to iteratively design opportunities for interaction and openness in online spaces.

In this chapter we have chosen to focus on design for enabling a Web-supported community of practice. The lessons learned for community of practice design we posit will hold true for other communities with a professional learning agenda.

COMMUNITY OF PRACTICE

While there are many rationales for community's recent allure, in academia and instructional design, much of the current interest in community was spurred by work in situated learning by Lave and Wenger (1991). Primarily resulting from their anthropological work examining the interrelations of communities and learning, they advanced the term 'communities of practice'. Wenger (1998) further advanced the concept when he carried out an ethnographic study of community of corporate claims processors. Their community of practice was characterized by three main components: *mutual engagement*, a *joint enterprise* and a *shared repertoire* which when co-present created a context for the negotiation of meaning. In this context, members working in a shared enterprise engaged in discourse about their shared repertoire of practices in efforts to improve them. Engagement in the community discourse surfaced the tacit knowledge of skilled practitioners and allowed that knowledge to be shared, reflected upon and challenged. Through these exchanges, members constructed an identity with regard to the community and the field.

It might be important here to pause and consider what we mean by *practice and identity*, as they are concepts critical to understanding the value of communities of practice. The first step is to differentiate the domain of knowledge from the practices of the field. Snyder (1997) assists us to take on this concept when he relates practice to Schön's (1987) *knowledge-in-action*. Practice in this context is equally about learning and doing. The importance of this difference becomes clear in John Seely Brown's (2000) discussion of the differences between learning the science of physics and becoming a physicist. On one hand a person is engaging with the domain of knowledge, the content of a field. On the other hand she is entering into the practices of the field to do the work of a scientist. Of becoming a physicist Brown advises, 'Acquiring this expertise requires learning the explicit knowledge of a field, the practices of its community, and the interplay between the two. And learning all this requires immersion in a community of practice, enculturation in its ways of seeing, interpreting, and acting' (p. 9).

The anthropologist Jean Lave (1993) argued that 'developing an identity as a member of a community and becoming knowledgeably skillful are part of the same process, with the former motivating, shaping, and giving meaning to the latter, which it subsumes' (p. 65). In this way, being a core member of a community and being knowledgeably skilful with respect to the practices and knowledge of the community are inextricably intertwined (Barab and Duffy, 2000).

This social and situated view of learning is consistent with the paradigmatic shift that has occurred in the learning sciences, from theories emphasizing individual thinkers and their isolated minds to theories that more fully acknowledge the role of the physical and social context in determining what is known (e.g. Barab *et al.*, 1999; Brown, *et al.*, 1989; Greeno, 1997; Kirshner and Whitson, 1997). From a social theory of learning perspective, the community constitutes both the context and the content of learning. It provides implicit and explicit structures some of which are human and social and others reified in material objects, tools and resources. A community-based approach holds great promise for learning, as it does not simply support content acquisition but is focused on transforming practices, and even identities, and does so by putting the power of this transformation in the actions of its members.

WEB-SUPPORTED COMMUNITIES OF PRACTICE

Extending the concept of communities of practice explicitly into the online environment Barab *et al.* (2003: 55) envisioned a Web-supported community of practice as 'a persistent, sustained social and technical network of individuals who share and develop an overlapping knowledge base, set of beliefs, values, history and experiences focused on a common practice and/or mutual enterprise'. The term 'community of practice' ideally refers to a group of individuals that have: (1) a common practice and/or shared enterprise; (2) opportunities for interaction and participation; (3) mutual interdependence; (4) overlapping histories, practices and understandings among members; (5) mechanisms for reproduction, and, ideally, (6) respect for diverse perspectives and minority views.

It is important to note that while talking about communities that leverage technology, there is clear evidence that communities intentionally designed to support learning will rarely be successful if the interaction takes place exclusively online (Cothrel and Williams, 1999; Schwen and Hara, 2004). Many unsuccessful attempts at intentional design of community begin naively with the most extreme set of conditions by working with a wholly distributed group of individuals, not yet known to each other but expected to build relationships, identities, collaboration and trust while interacting exclusively online. In a multi-case study of twelve successful Internet-mediated communities of practice, representing widespread domains and distributed memberships, Stuckey (2006a) found that in some way all communities held face-to-face engagement as a factor in an ongoing pattern of engagement. For some, the face-to-face engagement was a community-hosted annual meeting or series of workshops. In other cases community gatherings were grafted on to external meetings and events likely to be attended by members. For others, the community sprang from a face-to-face activity and, having an established face-to-face base, moved to expand and continue by taking some activity online. For some, the need for face-to-face was met more informally by keeping abreast of each other's travel plans, capitalizing on times where even pairs of members might meet (Preece and Maloney-Krichmar, 2005; Stuckey, 2006a). It is a core assumption underlying this current work that face-to-face, whether formal or informal in design, should be viewed as one of the modes of communication required to support a *Web-supported* community of practice (Barab, Kling *et al.*, 2004).

FIVE TENSIONS OF COMMUNITY DESIGN

Engeström (1987, 1999), in looking at multiple activity systems, argued that tensions fuelled system-level change and innovation. When we refer to system tensions, we are referring to conflicting, and often overlapping, needs that drive a system and that need to be balanced – not eliminated. Further, and consistent with the work of Wenger (1998) and Barab *et al.* (2002), our goal is to treat tensions not as contradictions but as *dualities*, with the challenge being to illuminate and better support their interplay. For Engeström (1987) and Wenger (1998), tensions are necessary, conflicting, and frequently overlapping, functions that energize a system and that need to be weighed and leveraged. We have come to believe that understanding and exploiting these tensions is integral to the process when intentionally and successfully designing *for* a community of practice. Through design-based and case study research in community of practice design and development we have identified five key tensions that are endemic to online community design. What follows is a presentation of each of these five tensions, drawing on multiple examples adapted from various works related to design for community. We begin by describing each tension, suggesting why it exists and highlighting some of the core design challenges. From there, we offer a specific case narrative to concretize the tension while at the same time disentangling the context in such a way as to make it useful to others' design efforts. Finally for each tension we unpack the theory, concepts and relevant research related to our findings.

Tensions arise in the design of Web-supported communities between:

- Content transmission and engaged participation.
- Open-ended participation and bounded participation.
- Pre-defined structure and emergent structure.
- Concern with usability and concern with sociability.
- Instructional design process and value-sensitive design process.

These tensions operate not as opposites but as dualities. They do not represent clear choices to be made and adhered to from an initial design; they represent issues to be mindful of throughout the life of the community. Addressing these tensions causes us to reflect on our assumptions about the social nature of learning and the influence of context on design. These five tensions are provided as the culmination of design-based research and case study work carried out by the authors individually and collectively over seven years.

Much of the research in communities of practice has sprung from a naturalist paradigm drawing from domains such as anthropology, learning sciences and sociology while drawing together such diverse fields as Human-Computer Interaction (HCI), Computer Supported Collaborative Work (CSCW) and Knowledge Management (KM). Much of the research has employed qualitative, most particularly ethnographic and design-based research methods. Case study has proven an effective research strategy when attempting to understand such complex social systems as communities. Cases and stories of successful community development offer powerful insights into the dynamic nature of community and a holistic view honouring the complex set of elements at play within each social context (Denning, 2000; Denning *et al.*, 2002; Snowden, 1999; Snowden, 2005).

In this chapter the relevance of each tension is stated through presentation of a case overview for a successful Web-supported community of practice. The case examples are all drawn from school and teacher education with a diversity of supporting evidence drawn from case studies in other domains such as military, knowledge management and online facilitation. The complexity in each tension and the resultant design decisions are highlighted through the literature and additional case insights. The full history and detail of the case studies and design-based research under-pinning this chapter can be found in the body of recent work published by each of the authors.

Content transmission and engaged participation

Participation in the community includes, but is not limited to, acquiring important resources (tools, instruments, documents and templates). When learning as part of a community, the emphasis is on social interaction and on carrying out the core practices of a community in the context of community-defined goals. Many online communities struggle with getting the right balance of making available practical resources and tools while engaging members in rich dialogue around their practice. When the community focuses heavily on building a body of quality resources, the 'grab and run' action of many new members becomes counter-productive to dialogue (Stuckey, 2006b). At the same time, engaging in collaborative discussions around practice without offering practical tools to the mix may not satisfy the needs of the bulk of novice practitioners. This tension has also been described in terms of the seeming mismatch of community goals of providing a service and fostering ownership (Stuckey, 2006a) and may be bound up in the community's need to tend to the active core membership as well as those on the periphery.

In light of perceived potentialities for online community in teacher professional development, Barab et al., undertook with the support of the National Science Foundation to develop a Web-supported community. The community would draw together in-service and pre-service mathematics and science teachers to share, improve, and create enquiry-based pedagogical practices (see Barab, Kling et al., 2004: Chapters 1, 3, 5, 11). Consistent with the community-of-practice pedagogical commitment, the Inquiry Learning Forum (ILF) (http://ilf.crlt.indiana.edu/) was designed around a 'visiting the classroom' metaphor offering teachers multimedia representations of authentic classroom practice. Through captured and streamed video, teachers could virtually visit actual classrooms where they observed and then discussed the challenges of enquiry-based learning. The rationale for this design was that teachers with a broad range of experience and expertise would come together in a virtual space to observe, discuss and reflect upon pedagogical theory and practice anchored in actual teaching vignettes. A tension in the project arose between teachers wanting to use the Forum as a repository to download lesson plans and a design predicated on teachers engaging in rich discussion with other members about enquiry learning as a practice. The design has not been without problems, with some teachers asking the designers' 'university experts' to just tell them what they were supposed to know about how to support rich enquiry (Barab *et al.*, 2003).

The designers had resisted building a repository of lesson plans and teaching tools seeking to engage teachers through the class visits and dialogue with peers. Over time that design evolved to better meet the immediate and longer-term needs of teachers by supporting them to (1) participate in discussions with other teachers, scientists, and educators; (2) gather and share enquiry-based lesson plans and resources; (3) examine videos of teachers' classrooms; and (4) develop personalized professional development plans. Resources became linked such that when a teacher engaged in learning about a particular topic (e.g. scaffolding, collaborative learning, classroom management or enquiry more generally) they were connected into a network of human and technical resources. The challenge had been to situate resources such that teachers collecting them were likely to also participate in activities that would help them gain a richer appreciation for the topic of interest.

The tension between resource offering and dialogue is borne out in Wenger's notions of *participation* and *reification* as a key duality in negotiating meaning. Where participation is about acting, interacting and living in the world, reification is about the development (process and product) of artefacts and objects that embody aspects of the practice. Reification involves making aspects of the practice tangible, what Wenger calls giving 'thingness' to the often implicit qualities of the practice (Wenger, 1998). And it appears that this tension between content and participation needs to be balanced variously according to the community membership and its current stage of development. When looking beyond academic communities, successful management of this tension can be seen in a number of other Web-supported communities like West Point's Company Command (Dixon *et al.*, 2005) or the Australian Flexible Learning Community (Brook and Oliver, 2002) . The managers of these communities found that the quality of their resource offering became a great hook for new members (and sponsors) and set an expectation of value for further engagement in the community (Stuckey, 2006b). Community managers described a pattern of use where the resources served as 'stranger attractors' to prospective members, whose first visits to the community were to resolve a specific challenge or locate specific instruments, information, solutions or advice. Many new members reported their first activities in the community were to download resources and seek information from experts. If members' experience in their first forays into the community was successful, they recognized quality in those resources, and if they got a high return for their time investment, they were often motivated to look around and see what else the community had on offer.

The process of moving from resource-based use to dialogue and collaboration-based use seems to take significant time and ongoing exposure to the norms and culture of the community. It is important to note that, in mature communities, the resources will be the products of community collaboration rather than just an aggregation of individual member or centrally developed contributions. A key to effectively positioning resources in communities of practice is to contextualize them with surrounding tools such that they serve as a 'gateway' to richer community participation. Resources alone will not sustain community nor will they alone serve to transform practice.

Open-ended participation and bounded participation

With the advent of the Internet, and following the success of commercial ventures like e-bay, Amazon and AOL there was initially a somewhat naive optimism that: (1) developing something like online community was as easy as purchasing a server and a good graphic designer; (2) Internet technologies would necessarily create 'anytime, anywhere' learning; and (3) totally open-ended spaces and activities would be sufficient for establishing an online community (Kling and Courtright, 2003). Beyond the obvious boundary decisions of creating an open or passworded community space, the truth is that openness is important but boundaries do also appear to be very important to communities of practice. They are both considerations at many levels of community design and development, as they impact the membership, goals, engagement and foci of the community.

The *Australian Flexible Learning Community* (archived at http://pre2005. flexible-learning.net.au/community/default.htm) had its roots in an Australian national educational framework designed 'to create and share knowledge about flexible learning and to support its take-up in vocational education and training' (ANTA, 2005). The Australian Flexible Learning Community (AFLC) was an instrument of the Australian Flexible Learning Framework, a four-year national strategy in operation between 2000 and 2004. The purpose of the community was to provide professional development in the area of flexible learning in the vocational education sector. At the start of 2004 the community had in excess of 2,000 members, building a sense of community as they shared teaching resources, collaborated on workplace learning projects and interacted about tools, practices and pedagogy with each other, over the community's largely asynchronous, Web-based environment (Brook and Oliver, 2003)

This community focused on topics integral to the job of a Registered Training Organization (RTO). Topics and agendas included grants and projects, professional development, support programmes, technical support and tool testing over time. The community's rigorous attention to its focus of preparing 'creative, capable people' was integral to its success. To maintain that focus, the community membership was open and the discourse of much of the community was public, but membership was required to join any of the events or discussions and contribute to the community. Further work in tending to the boundaries of the community could be seen in the activities of the community manager or convener. Some of this work served to maintain boundaries and some to puncture them in order to foster open-ness and ownership. The convener worked to maintain the boundaries around the community foci, norms and practices while working to support and scaffold member contribution and ownership. Initially the convener and later core commu-nity members also worked to broker what Star (1989) called *boundary objects*, objects crossing between communities (Davenport and Hall, 2001; Pawlowski *et al.*, 2000), and externally promoting the work of the community in order to main-tain a relationship to the larger community and the domain.

Bounded activities have proven to be an integral part of the creation of the rhythm in a community (Barab *et al.*, 2003; Stuckey, 2006b; Wenger *et al.*, 2002). For instance, in the AFLC a newsletter would announce a series of events for the month ahead. In these activities was an Expert Spruik, an invited thought leader who would lead a discussion on a cutting-edge topic open for the first two weeks of the month. Also, in that month would be a fun poll or competition, related to a flexible learning theme or for fun to a topical issue or technology. These time-bounded regular events and activities, including the newsletter itself, served to draw members back into the community, as the spike on page hits would attest. Often a time-based activity, like a book club discussion or a guest speaker visit, intensified the visible activity and served to revive a flagging com-munity. Members were often drawn to an event, even volunteering for leadership roles, if they knew what depth and length of engagement were required and could come prepared for an intense burst of activity.

Boundaries strictly defined the purpose, domain and topics of the AFLC. Activities bounded by the level of commitment or engagement proved very valu-able for community building. Members in the AFLC could engage in low-commitment activities like polls and games or extensive project team activi-ties. The diversity and levels of engagement allowed members to stay in touch with community themes and activities without always having to carve out large chunks of time from busy schedules. Members do wax and wane in their attention to the community, sometimes collaborating at the centre and at other times read-ing and watching from the periphery, and it is only fitting that design for community activity should allow for this. None would suggest that all community activity should be time-based or bounded, but being able to offer the community members 'light and shade' and to align their own rhythm for engagement with the community rhythm was important to the long-term stability of the community.

In a successful community of practice, boundaries (whether extended, perme-able or distinct) in terms of groups and in terms of particular activities have a part to play in enhancing the membership, engagement commitment and norms of the community. Decisions about community boundaries can be seen as com-munities focus on the development of such aspects as subgroups, time-based activities, delimited foci and topics, and community norms. Pragmatically we can say that while the technology can support ubiquitous usage, individuals do not actually have such open schedules and while the idea of any place, any time learning is attractive in theory, most busy practitioners appreciate some level of boundedness (Barab *et al.*, 2003). How to then support boundary crossing is a key research question that requires further investigation.

Pre-defined structure and emergent structure

The structure of successful communities appears to cross the full gamut of possibilities between being clearly and strictly defined and totally emergent. Webheads in Action, a community of TESOL teachers, is arguably one of the most organically structured and, from the perspective of its members, most successful communities of practice online today (http://www.homestead.com/prosites-vstevens/files/efi/papers/eltoc2001/webheads00.htm). Webheads in Action began life in 1997 in an online 3D multi-user environment, The Palace, and was called English for Webheads. The meetings were where classes of students learning English and teachers would get together. The meetings were informal and unstructured and moved in and out of technologies to suit the mood and interest of the group assembled. By the year 2000 the group had begun to attract more teachers who wanted to experiment with online technologies and language teaching, a trend that continues to the present time. Webheads in Action, the teacher community, was formed in 2002 and is now a vibrant and active community of practice.

The community has met every Sunday online since the summer of 2000, some 400 meetings in total. What to the uninitiated is a disorganized process can actually be thought of as a process that one community member described as 'intuitive chaos navigation' (Nyrop, 2002). The synchronous gatherings last for some three or four hours, and are like an open house for a group of very close friends gathering in a neighbourhood meeting place, and as such are open and rowdy, with the hospitality and housework shared among all the community members present. A typical meeting might start in Tapped In (described later in this chapter), where the community has an office, or Yahoogroups instant messenger or the Learning Times room the community is sponsored with. Somehow people manage to come and go, finding each other across all these technologies during the time. There is no set agenda and yet they never end up without one, having decided it most often on the fly. There are no formal roles or titles and yet someone usually steps up to record the meetings, take notes and do follow-up that might be required. In 2005 the community hosted a highly successful online conference which saw keynote speakers and a distributed team of volunteer members positioned about the globe present to an audience of 300+ people using podcasts, VOIP, MUVEs and other synchronous technology.

There was no discrete process of design in Webheads, rather some very basic community tenets and a very real need to collaborate and learn together. Key here may be the group's ability to tend to the periphery as well as the core of the group. Members serve the community with genuine offers of support, coaching, partnership and peer review, and they have established a high level of interdependence and reciprocity.

In stark contrast to the unstructured design of the Webheads community, but equally impressive in its success, the MirandaNet Fellowship community (http://www.mirandanet.ac.uk) is built solidly on a tried and tested structure and clear member progression. The MirandaNet Fellowship (Cuthell, 2002; Preston, 2005) has been operating for twelve years, supporting educators working together in collaborative action research projects to build capacity in the profession for using information and communication technologies. It has a formal structure that sees members enter and become Fellows as they plan their personal research project and graduate to being Scholars when they publish their findings. Scholars are the members at the centre of the community that work in the consultancy aspects of the community and mentor the Fellows in their action research efforts.

What Webheads and MirandaNet demonstrate is that community developers need to know their prospective membership and the practices they seek to improve, and to have a clear vision of what community can look like in that context. These communities are about the same size and both involve teachers working to improve their respective teaching practices and yet they could not be more different in the structure and development. It is no accident that both of these communities were founded by a well respected, passionate and visionary leader. In both cases the founder was close to the work practices of the prospective membership and could envision ways of being together that would develop and inspire members (Stuckey, 2006a). The community takes time to honour member achievements and to celebrate the community's work and success. Both communities hold open flexible time in the schedule for social activity and celebration – indeed, being highly social and professional is a hallmark of both groups.

Not every community will relish the chaos navigation of Webheads or thrive moving through the professional rites of passage of MirandaNet, but all communities need to view design as an ongoing process built upon closeness to and effective feedback from the members. Design actually begins with those first 'what if' conversations with stakeholders. It begins in listening to their needs and keeping close to the practices they care about. Like the investment in design ethnography that instigated the design of one socially responsive Web-supported community space, Quest Atlantis (Barab *et al.*, 2005), community designers need to invest in finding out what communities, relationships and modes of communication already exist, how people currently share knowledge and what technological affordances they could see themselves leveraging online (Agre, 1998). Many community designers make the mistake, like a child's oversize pair of shoes, of thinking the community will grow into the architecture they have designed. This is rarely the case and as Wenger (E. Wenger, personal communication, 15 May 2003) suggests a community design heuristic should aim to 'design a little and practice a lot'. What this means is that we should design enough to enable social interaction and the first steps in collaboration and put energies into building the social capital, all the while on the alert for new design opportunities in architecture and infrastructure that the community itself may call for. For designers this means having enough technology and infrastructure in place to look like there is value, while being flexible and extensible so that the community can build ownership.

Concern with usability → Concern with sociability

When a community is mediated online the infrastructure requires inclusion of some form of technological architecture. Research has shown that, to the detriment of social development, the technological architecture can assume a precedence for many intentionally developed online groups (Barab *et al.*, 2002; Baym, 1998; Klecka *et al.*, 2002; Stuckey *et al.*, 2001). Shirky (1995: 91) put the technological and sociological aspects of community into perspective when he reduced the online architecture to simple physics: 'the basics of electronic space can be broken into two parts: group dynamics and simple physics. The simple physics is the movement in electronic space and is governed by software and tools. The group dynamics is social interaction governed by human behaviour.' Kling *et al.* (2001) and Kling and Courtright (2003) used the term Socio-technical Interaction Network (STIN) to capture the interactions that the technology was designed to facilitate, with technology simply being a node of the larger network. According to Kling *et al.* (2001), an STIN includes people (including organizations), data, equipment, documents and messages, legal arrangements and enforcement mechanisms, and resource flows. From an interaction network perspective, any characterization of the technology (e.g. an online community) must capture the networks of interactions among people that both define and are defined by the technology.

The literature is dotted with evidence that a design that focuses overly on the technological aspects, attempting to build the community out from the tools rather than harnessing technology to community needs, is doomed to failure (Klecka *et al.*, 2002; Preece, 2000; Saint-Onge, 2003; Stuckey, Hedberg *et al.*, 2001). This does not suggest that the technology has no influence on the activities and style of community discourse that may develop in a space. Preece (2000) reminds us that just as home architecture can influence how we live, online architecture can influence how communities behave. She suggests that community design must attend to both usability and sociability. Usability involves interface design, navigation support, archiving, scalability, software and users and may focus on the experience of the individual user. Sociability is about building social capital (Bourdieu, 1972; Putnam, 2000; Resnick, 2001) in the community and entails aspects of purpose, interaction, presence, codes of practice, etiquette and facilitation and focuses on the collective value of the social group.

Even a more technologically rich context like Tapped In (http://www.tappedin.org) has had to prioritize the 'socio' aspect in order to have success (Schlager and Fusco, 2004). Tapped In began in the US in 1997 under National Science Foundation (NSF) grant funding. The community has throughout its life utilized synchronous communication tools which in the early days the community ran over a purpose-built MOO (Schlager *et al.*, 1999), and an infrastructure that enables members to create a personal space, profile, network while exploring community collaborations and leadership. The vision was that of a shared 'virtual place' (Schlager and Schank, 1997) with an infrastructure designed as a conference centre within which professional dialogue would take place. It is variously described in the literature as a community, a Teacher Professional Development Institute (Craig *et al.*, 2003) and a 'crossroads' (Riel and Polin, 2004). None of these descriptors adequately describes the professional, respectful and supportive atmosphere that the community projects, and the amount of time that the team has targeted to social support over continuing technological developments.

The project has worked to better understand local social networks, and prioritize technological developments that support and expand these existing relationships. Rather than focusing simply on human–computer interactions, interdependence is prioritized as members, operating with appropriate internal scaffolding and support, take on various roles and projects within the community context. It is supporting member interaction and not downloadable acquisitions that is the focus of this community. Multiple volunteer roles within the community, and the ability to move in and out of these roles, allow members to establish credibility and identity. At its core, the project prioritizes human relations, building technology around and in the service of these social interactions, with an emphasis on prioritizing communication and collaboration.

The ILF (discussed above) and Tapped In communities designed and developed their environments in-house, using fairly large financial investments and time from a group of designers. However, many of the other community spaces discussed here have thrived on substantially less technological developments. The point to take away from the diversity of tool sets and designs is that community does not need to be constrained by modest budgets and short deadlines to start up. And this availability of tools is about to make the possibilities for community even simpler while moving control away from the centre. Web 2.0 (O'Reilly, 2005) social software will allow individuals to build and find community themselves. The emphasis on community design, from our perspective, should be less on sophisticated technological developments that allow individuals to interact with the technology (human–computer interactions) and more on how to use the technology to support individuals in connecting with other members (human–human as mediated by computer interactions).

Most recent community of practice and knowledge management literature recognizes that effective knowledge sharing as more than a 'catch and release' programme, again moving away from the concept of knowledge as a thing. It builds on a socially situated view of knowledge as central to any truly effective knowledge-sharing practices (Pollard, n.d; Wenger *et al.*, 2002). The principles of effective knowledge sharing practices are embodied in a series of shifts that acknowledge the social nature of learning and capitalize on the growth of intuitive and readily appropriated social software. These shifts are illustrated in Table 20.1.

Table 20.1 Shifts evident in current knowledge-sharing practices

From	To
Collecting assets	Connecting people
Technical focus	Social focus
Central content management	Personal content management
Top-down strategies	Bottom-up viral evolutions
Compliance	Enabling
Web 1.0 tools	Web 2.0 tools

Today, one does not need to know the answer to every problem but to know where to find a solution. Today, when the problem is complex and the volumes of information are overwhelming, that 'where' is more likely to be found in social contexts than in terabytes of data.

> Expertise location is a big issue in companies today. The goal is not only to provide access to information, but to provide access to people that have the information … I don't want raw data, I don't want information, I want the judgements of people I can trust.

> (Boone, 2001: 22)

Even within the Web 1.0 tools and architectures, sociability and collegiality have proven vital in establishing effective professional learning communities. An embodiment of collegiality can be seen in *Webheads in Action* (Stevens, 2005), MirandaNet social events, or the Tapped In community (Schlager *et al.*, 2002). Sociability has been a high priority in Tapped In as designers, from the first conceptions, held sociability, facilitation and networking as a cultural goal. This is evidenced by the first greetings from a volunteer on duty to the generous offers of support and guidance by regular members.

While collegiality is attainable over online technology there are also strong caveats in the literature to a picture of ready and productive collegiality. Managers and facilitators of online community-based professional development courses report that teachers often proved either reticent to communicate or unwilling to critique each other's work (Riel and Polin, 2004). Some, like Schlager and Fusco (2004), believe the culture of collegiality must be acquired locally first if more than early adopters are to benefit from collegially based online activity. Others have reported that teacher engagement in such online environments has been a struggle to cultivate and sustain (Barab *et al.*, 2001). Many long-lived Internet-mediated communities and networks report various patterns of engagement waxing and waning over time. The long-term sustainability of such activities depends on the critical mass of interaction (Preece, 2001), effective facilitation and moderation (Ferry and Kiggins, 1999; Salmon, 2000) and a clear purpose and value perceived by participants (Wenger *et al.*, 2002).

Instructional design process ←→ Value-sensitive design process

Instructional design in information systems can be described as a content-independent process used to interpret learning theory and develop instructional systems (Reigeluth, 1999; Wilson, 1997). The best-known, the traditional ID process (Main, 1993: 38–9), describes a series of steps in a design cycle. The cyclic process in this model is known by the acronym of ADDIE for the steps Analysis, Define, Design, Implement and Evaluate. There are many other instructional design models that have also advocated different processes for design (Cognition Technology Group at Vanderbilt (CTGV), 1993; Reigeluth, 1999; Young, 1993). Regardless of the steps that one project decides as relevant for their particular project, we advocate that one also must consider the ethical (value-sensitive) principles underlying the design – especially when designing something like community.

Value-sensitive design is a construct that builds on the democratic principles of participatory design but goes further to bring ethics, agency and values into the equation.

> Value-Sensitive Design is primarily concerned with values that center on human well being, human dignity, justice, welfare, and human rights. Specific values include trust, accountability, and freedom from bias, access, autonomy, privacy, and consent. Value-Sensitive Design connects the people who design systems and interfaces with the people who think about and understand the values of the stakeholders who are affected by the systems.

> (Friedman, 1999).

Design for community often requires designers to marry or at least integrate these two visions for learning design. Whereas instructional design focuses on delivery and a more discrete staged process, value-sensitive design focuses on the development of the more intangible aspects of relationships, trust and agency for all stakeholders. Where instructional design might focus on building knowledge, value-sensitive design focuses on ethics, culture and on building safe, enabling and empowering environments.

MirandaNet is a community of educators (teachers, academics, consultants and bureaucrats) working together to carry out high-quality, school-based action research. People apply to join the community and, if accepted, enter as members. When a member takes on a personal action research programme they are promoted to Scholar status. They work on that research project under the guidance of the senior community member known as a Fellow. Upon the completion and acceptance of their research project, and publication on the community Web site, they themselves become Fellows. Fellows are the inner circle of the community and the people drawn upon to work in consultancy, mentoring and leadership roles within the community.

An ongoing stream of research, assessment and demonstration projects since 1994 has provided a rich learning environment in this community. The Fellowship's work is largely funded through these tendered and sponsored action research projects, and industry partnerships. The community activity is clearly situated in authentic contexts for the integration of information communication technologies. This situativity and the community's adherence to quality research make MirandaNet's research capability of compelling interest to teacher researchers, academics and technology vendors alike. In MirandaNet it is professionalism and high teacher morale that are a constant, and its sister community World e-Citizens carries high ideals and moral purpose for world citizenry. Values are evident in almost every aspect of design for this community. The goals of building capacity and raising the professional status of teachers are embodied in the roles, activities and support members receive within the community. The way the community now supports trust, autonomy and accountability was a vision in the value-based design.

A community based on value-sensitive design involves an infrastructure and process where communities do more than take root; they build ownership and establish a safe harbour for learning. Such environments will support the community in collaborative activities promoting formation of identity, relationships and networks. The community infrastructure supports developing, modelling and sustaining community norms. This is about establishing an ethos that pervades all aspects of community life and, in a mature community, is apparent to members from their first entry into the community space. Accessible and active community facilitators have a big role to play in establishing this ethos (Babinski *et al.*, 2001; Brook and Oliver, 2003; Chapman *et al.*, 2005; Marx *et al.*, 1998). Facilitators, who may be community managers but are often different from community leaders (Wenger *et al.*, 2002), serve as the first point of human contact in community. The ways in which they work to model the tone and etiquette of the community cannot be overestimated. Effective facilitators spend a great deal of time in one-to-one relationships in these many-to-many environments, working with members to support psychological safety.

Several other communities of those we have encountered embody value-sensitive design. Webheads, MirandaNet and CompanyCommand have variously designed for values development. In Webheads it is the culture of collaboration and unconditional support that pervades the community activity. CompanyCommand builds on the ethos of the wider military community of integrity and selfless service. Another example is the Quest Atlantis project, a socially responsive play space for elementary children. In this work, the social agenda at first was more subtle, but as the work progressed it became an explicit part of the marketing such that it now plays a core part of the project identity (see http://questatlantis.org) (Barab *et al.*, 2004). In fact, they have organized member identity around participation related to the project life commitments such that for each member their performance in relation to these commitments becomes a core part of how their identity is perceived on their project home page (Barab, Arici *et al.*, 2005).

While not all projects need to explicitly display their identity so centrally, the message we wish to convey is that designing community is a value-sensitive process. While not all would agree that at its core community design has roots in a Marxist, socialist ideology. However, we have argued that community design involves valuing all members and a commitment to ensuring a member-negotiated (not simply a designer-determined) identity. Even if the community agenda might be socially transgressive there remains an element of member empowerment, simply because the designer has chosen to enlist a design type that necessarily encourages local voice. However, value-sensitive design goes one step further, encouraging the designer to integrate ethics, agency and values into the design equation. It serves to create a culture. This means looking beyond how to support content learning, but also to thinking about the nature of that content, as well as how the learning environment facilitates the development of trust, accountability, freedom from bias, autonomy and differential access.

CONCLUSION

The power of the Internet coupled with the learning potential inherent in a community-of-practice model for supporting learning has led to a number of design efforts to develop so-called online communities. Some of these have proven very successful, others partly successful, and still others have failed. While different people have different views of what constitutes community and what counts as success, no one who has tried to develop a Web-supported community in the service of learning could deny the challenges in doing so. Communities are self-organizing structures, continually evolving in ways that cannot be prescribed through some particular design. They grow, evolve and change dynamically, transcending any particular member and outliving any particular task. To truly acknowledge the complexity of communities or practice in a theoretically grounded manner is to acknowledge that they emerge through interactions rather than design, and gain their richness, complexity and opportunities for learning through their multi-generational structures and member pathways not predetermined channels. A central design and research challenge is to understand the dynamics that characterize, drive and maintain community functioning.

In this chapter, we have highlighted five design tensions that, in our experience, lie at the heart of why 'Good Design Isn't Enough' when designing to support something like community. Further, these tensions are not simply overcome and, we have argued, overcoming these tensions or simply working towards one side of the tension should not be the target. Instead, tensions, as discussed in this chapter, need to be continually checked and reflected upon, providing benchmarked reminders that can serve as checks from which to evaluate one's design decisions. If the designer goes too far to one of the poles of these designs, unless this has been clearly warranted by member needs, they run the risk of obfuscating the power of Web-supported communities. The trick is to remain in dynamic interaction, providing features and interactions that sway back and forth between the two sides of the five tensions. Tensions give life to systems and without the interplay among these poles the community, and the learning of individual members, will most likely stagnate. For example, if all a community was about was participation and it had no content, then it would provide less value to its members (Wenger, 1998); similarly, if the designers simply focused on supporting content transmission there would be little sense of community and all that that entails. As another example, while we have argued for bounded participation, if it were too bounded we would be slipping back into traditional course structures and would lose the potential power of a community model for situative learning.

Clearly, designing for the emergence of a Web-supported community is not an easy task. In this chapter we have discussed those particular tensions that we identified in our own work, and have presented them in a manner that we hope will prove valuable to readers as they reflect on their own work. We have described community design as part of the challenge, but have emphasized sociability challenges and how communities are emergent and not simply designed. As such, the lines between design and implementation become blurred, with much of the identity of any particular community taking shape in the unfolding member participation and not the initial design specifications. A great deal of the work is carried out by facilitators in the back-room activity, away from the public gaze of the membership, and involves welcoming, encouraging, building trust, making introductions and linking people, information and activities. In successful Web-supported communities the facilitator is a vehicle for community feedback as their interactions allow them to constantly gauge the temperament of the community.

We have also emphasized that when something like community is being designed it is practically impossible, and – we would argue – undesirable, to remain ethically neutral. Communities have agendas and the potential to accomplish transformative work. If one spends time really trying to understand the systems within (or through) which the technology will transact, one will necessarily become attuned to problematic issues – they exist in all walks of life. For example, spending time in classrooms helped us simultaneously to appreciate the many constraints under which teachers operate while becoming disheartened at the ways in which the current obsession with standardized test scores and breadth over depth has led to impoverished pedagogical practices. It is our hope that this chapter will aid our colleagues in actualizing those agendas that they, and the members of the community with whom they are designing, view as significant. More generally, we have emphasized that the *building* of a community involves a community, and cannot be simply prescribed even by a well-intentioned designer.

REFERENCES

Agre, P. (1998) 'Designing genres for new media: social, economic, and political contexts', in S. Jones (ed.), *Cybersociety 2.0: Revisiting Computer-mediated Communication and Community*. Thousand Oaks, CA: Sage. pp. 69–99.

ANTA (2005) *Australian Flexible Learning Framework for the National Vocational Education and Training System 2005–2007 Business Plan 2005* (retrieved 30 August 2006 from http://pre2005.flexiblelearning.net.au/aboutus/resources/aflframeworkbusinessplan2005.pdf).

Babinski, L. M., Jones, B. D. and DeWert, M. H. (2001) 'The roles of facilitators and peers in an online support community for first-year teachers', *Journal of Educational and Psychological Consultation*, 12 (2): 151–69.

Barab, S. A. and Duffy, T. (2000) 'From practice fields to communities of practice', in D. Jonassen and S. M. Land (eds), *Theoretical Foundations of Learning Environments*. Mahwah, NJ: Erlbaum. pp. 25–56.

Barab, S. A., Arici, A., Jackson, C. (2005) 'Eat your vegetables and do your homework: a design-based investigation of enjoyment and meaning in learning', *Educational Technology*, 65 (1): 15–21.

Barab, S. A., Barnett, M. G. and Squire, K. (2002) 'Building a community of teachers: navigating the essential tensions in practice', *Journal of the Learning Sciences*, 11 (4): 489–542.

Barab, S. A., Cherkes-Julkowski, M., Swenson, R., Garrett. S., Shaw, R. E. and Young, M. (1999) 'Principles of self-organization: ecologizing the learner–facilitator system', *Journal of the Learning Sciences*, 8 (3–4): 349–90.

Barab, S. A., Kling, R. and Gray, J. (eds) (2004) *Designing for Virtual Communities in the Service of Learning*. Cambridge: Cambridge University Press.

Barab, S. A., MaKinster, J. and Scheckler, R. (2003) 'Designing system dualities: characterizing a Web-supported teacher professional development community', *Information Society*, 19 (3): 237–56.

Barab, S., MaKinster, J. G., Moore, J., Cunningham, D. and the ILF Design Team (2001) 'Designing and building an online community: the struggle to support sociability in the Inquiry Learning Forum', *Educational Technology Research and Development*, 49 (4): 71–96.

Barab, S. A., Thomas, M. Dodge, Carteaux, R., and Tuzun, H. (2005) 'Making learning fun: Quest Atlantis, a game without guns', *Educational Technology Research and Development*, 53 (1): 86–108.

Barab, S. A., Thomas, M., Dodge, Squire, K. and Newell, M. (2004) 'Critical design ethnography: designing for change', *Anthropology and Education Quarterly*, 35 (2): 254–68.

Baym, N. K. (1998) 'The emergence of online community', in S. Jones (ed.), *Cybersociety 2.0: Revisiting Computer-mediated Communication and Community*. Thousand Oaks, CA: Sage. pp. 35–68.

Berge, Z. L. (1995) 'Facilitating computer conferencing: recommendations from the field', *Educational Technology*, 35 (1): 22–30.

Boone, M. E. (2001) *Managing Inter@ctivity*. New York: McGraw-Hill.

Borgatti, S. and Molina, S. (2005) 'Toward ethical guidelines for network research in organizations', *Social Networks*, 27 (2): 107–18.

Bourdieu, P. (1972) *Outline of a Theory of Practice*. Cambridge: Cambridge University Press.

Brook, C. and Oliver, R. (2002) *Supporting the Development of Learning Communities in Online Settings*. Conference proceedings, EdMedia Conference, Denver, CO. Retrieved 5 December 2005 from: http://elrond.scam.ecu.edu.au/oliver/2002/edmedia2.pdf.

Brook, C. and Oliver, R. (2003) 'Online learning communities: investigating a design framework', *Australian Journal of Educational Technology*, 19 (2): 139–60.

Brown, J. S. (2000) *Learning, Working and Playing in the Digital Age*. 1999 Conference on Higher Education of the American Association for Higher Education. Retrieved 5 December 2003 from: http://serendip.brynmawr.edu/sci_edu/seelybrown/.

Brown, J. S., and Duguid P. (1999) 'Organizing knowledge', *Reflections: the SoL Journal on Knowledge, Learning and Change*, 1(2): 28–44.

Brown, J. S., and Duguid, P. (2000) *The Social Life of Information*. Boston, MA: Harvard Business School Press.

Brown, J. S., Collins, A. and Duguid, P. (1989) 'Situated cognition and the culture of learning', *Educational Researcher*, 18: 32–42.

Bruckman, A. (2002) 'The future of e-learning communities', *Communications of the ACM*, 45 (4): 60–3.

Bruckman, A. and Jensen, C. (2002) 'The mystery of the death of MediaMOO: seven years of evolution of an online community', in K. A. Renninger and W. Shumar (eds), *Building Virtual Communities*. Cambridge: Cambridge University Press. pp. 21–33.

Chapman, C., Ramondt L. and Smiley, G. (2005) 'Strong community, deep learning: exploring the link', *Innovations in Educational and Teaching International*, 42 (3): 217–30.

Cognition Technology Group at Vanderbilt (CTGV) (1993) 'Designing learning environments that support thinking', in J. Lowyck. D. H. Jonassen and T. M. Duffy (eds), *Designing Environments for Constructive Learning*. New York: Springer.

Cothrel, J. and Williams, R. L. (1999) 'On-line communities: helping them form and grow', *Journal of Knowledge Management*, 3 (1): 54–60.

Craig, J. M. B., Lee, B. Y. and Turner, J. A. (2003) *Tapped-in and Tapped-in 2*. Personal Web site, J. B. Craig, University of Michigan. Retrieved 8 December 2005 from: http://www-personal.umich.edu/~canna/docs/TIFinalReport.doc.

Cuthell, J. (2002) *MirandaNet: A Learning Community – A Community of Learners*. Ilkeston: Actis.

Darling-Hammond, L. (2000) 'Futures of teaching in American education', *Journal of Educational Change*, 1 (4): 353–73.

Davenport, E. and Hall, H. (2001) 'New knowledge and micro-level online organization: "communities of practice" as a development framework', in R. Sprague (ed.), *Proceedings of the XXXIVth Annual Hawaii International Conference on System Sciences*. Los Alamitos, HI: IEEE.

Davenport, E. and Hall, H. (2002) 'Organizational knowledge and communities of practice', *Annual Review of Information Science and Technology*, 36: 171–227.

Denning, S. (2000) *The Springboard: How Storytelling Ignites Action in Knowledge-Era Organizations*. Boston, MA: Butterworth Heinemann.

Denning, S., Pommier, M. and L. Shneier (2002). *Are There Laws of Knowledge Management?* United Nations Online Network in Public Administration and Finance (UNPAN). Retrieved 31 August 2006 from: http://unpan1.un.org/intradoc/groups/public/documents/APCITY/UNPAN007798.pdf#search=%22Are%20there%20laws%20of%20knowledge%20management%22.

Department of Defense (2004) *Data Sharing in a Net-centric Department of Defense*. Directive No. 8320.2, 2 December 2004, ASD(NII)/DoD CIO (retrieved 30 August 2006 from http://www.fas.org/irp/doddir/dod/d8320_2.pdf).

Dixon, N., Allen, N., Burgess, T., Kilner, P. and Schweitzer, S., 2005. *CompanyCommand: Unleashing the Power of the Army Profession*. West Point, NY: Center for the Advancement of Leader Development and Organizational Learning.

Engeström, Y. (1987). *Learning by Expanding*. Helsinki: Orienta-konsultit.

Engeström, Y. (1999) 'Activity theory and individual and social transformation', in Y. Engeström, R. Miettinen and R. Punamaki (eds), *Perspectives on Activity Theory*. Cambridge: Cambridge University Press. pp. 19–38.

DuFour, R. and Eaker, R. (1998) *Professional Learning Communities at Work: Best Practices for Enhancing Student Achievement*. Bloomington, IN: National Educational Service.

Farmer, J. (2004) *Communication Dynamics: Discussion Boards, Weblogs and the Development of Communities of Inquiry in Online Learning Environments*. Proceedings of the Australian Society for Computers in Learning in Tertiary Education conference. Retrieved 30 July 2006 from: http://www.ascilite.org.au/conferences/perth04/procs/pdf/farmer.pdf.

Fernback, J. (1999) 'There is a there there: notes toward a definition of cybercommunity', in S. Jones (ed.), *Doing Internet Research: Critical Issues and Methods for Examining the Net*. Thousand Oaks, CA: Sage. pp. 203–20.

Ferry, B. and Kiggins, J. (1999) *Making Use of a Knowledge Building Community to Develop Professional Socialisation*. Melbourne: UltiBASE, Faculty of Education, Language and Community Services, Royal Melbourne Institute of Technology (RMIT). Retrieved 20 August 2003 from: http://ultibase.rmit.edu.au/Articles/aug99/ferry1.pdf.

Fischer, G. (2001) 'Communities of Interest: Learning through the Interaction of Multiple Knowledge Systems', in Proceedings of the XXIVth IRIS conference, Bergen, Norway, August. pp. 1–14.

Friedman, B. (1999) *Value-Sensitive Design: A Research Agenda for Information Technology* (Contract No. SBR-9729633). Arlington, VA: National Science Foundation.

Garrison D. R., Anderson, T. and Archer, W. (2000) 'Critical thinking in a text-based environment: Computer Conferencing in Higher Education', *Internet and Higher Education*, 11 (2): 1–14.

Garrison, D. R., Cleveland-Innes, M. and Fung, T. (2004) 'Student role adjustment in online communities of inquiry: model and instrument validation', *Journal of Asynchronous Learning Networks*, 8 (2): 61–74.

Goodfellow, R. (2003) *Virtual Learning Communities: Communities of Practice and other Frameworks for Conceptualising, Developing and Evaluating NCSL's Initiatives in Linking Staff and School Communities*. Buckingham: Open University Press.

Gonzalez, D. (2002) *Index of 'Webheads in Action' Web Pages and Related Sites*. Personal Web site, Teresa Almeida d'Eça. Retrieved 13 August 2006 from: http://64.71.48.37/teresadeca/webheads/wia-index.htm.

Greeno, J. G. (1997) 'Response: On claims that answer the wrong questions', *Educational Researcher*, 26: 5–17.

Hamman, R. B. (2000) *Computer Networks Linking Network Communities: A Study of the Effects of Computer Network Use upon Pre-existing Communities*. Cybersoc and Cybersociology: online community research and management. Retrieved 30 August 2006 from: http://www.socio.demon.co.uk/mphil/short.html.

Havelock, B. (2004) 'Online community and professional learning in education: research-based keys to sustainability', *Association of Computing in Education*, 12 (1): 56–84.

Haythornthwaite, C. (2002) 'Building social networks via computer networks: creating and sustaining distributed learning communities', in K. A. Renninger and W. Shumar (eds), *Building Virtual Communities: Learning and Change in Cyberspace*. Cambridge: Cambridge University Press. pp. 159–209.

Hillery, G. (1955) 'Definitions of community: areas of agreement', *Rural Sociology*, 20: 111–23.

Hord, S. (1997) *Professional Learning Communities: Communities of Continuous Inquiry and Improvement*. Southwest Educational Development Laboratory. Retrieved 4 November 2005 from: www.sedl.org/pubs/change34/welcome.html.

Jones, S., Lang, G., Terrell, I., Thompson, K. and Ramondt, L. (2001) *Establishing Online Communities for School Leaders: An Interim Report* (*The NCSL pilot, Talking Heads – January to December 2000*). Paper presented at the British Educational Research Association conference.

Kelly, K. (1994) *Out of Control*. New York: Addison-Wesley.

Kim, A. J. (2000) *Community Building on the Web: Secret Strategies for Successful Online Communities*. Harlow: Addison-Wesley.

Kimball, L. and Rheingold, H. (2000) *How Online Social Networks benefit Organizations*. Mill Valley, CA: Howard Rheingold Associates. Retrieved 3 June 2006 from: http://www.rheingold.com/Associates/onlinenetworks.html.

Kirshner, D. and Whitson, J. A. (eds) (1997) *Situated Cognition: Social, Semiotic, and Psychological Perspectives*. Mahwah, NJ: Erlbaum.

Klecka, C. L., Clift, R. T. and Thomas, A. R. S. (2002) 'Proceed with caution: introducing electronic conferencing in teacher education', *Critical Issues in Teacher Education*, 9 (28–36): 1–18.

Kling, R. and Courtright, C. (2003) 'Group behavior and learning in electronic forums: a sociotechnical approach', *The Information Society*, 19 (3): 221–36.

Kling, R., McKim, G. W., Fortuna, J., King, A. (2000) *Scientific Collaboratories as Socio-technical Interaction Networks: A Theoretical Approach*. Trier, Germany: Digital Bibliography and Library Project. Retrieved 13 November 2005 from: http://arxiv.org/pdf/cs.CY/0005007.

Kollock, P. (1996) 'Design principles for online communities', *PC Update*, 15: 58–60. Retrieved 7 July 2003 from: http://www.sscnet.ucla.edu/soc/faculty/kollock/papers/design.htm.

Kollock, P. and Smith, M. (1996). 'Managing the virtual commons: cooperation and conflict in computer communities', in S. Herring (ed.), *Computer-Mediated Communication: Linguistic, Social, and Cross-cultural Perspectives*. Amsterdam: John Benjamins. pp. 109–28.

Kowch, E. G. and Schwier, R. A. (1997) *Characteristics of Technology-based Virtual Learning Communities*. Occasional Papers in Educational Technology, University of Saskatchewan. Retrieved 20 December 2005 from: http://www.usask.ca/education/coursework/802papers/communities/community.PDF.

Krebs, V. (1998) *Knowledge Networks: Mapping and Measuring Knowledge Creation, Re-use and Flow*. LeaderValues. Retrieved 20 December 2005 from: http://www.leader-values.com/Content/detail.asp?ContentDetailID=914.

Lave, J. (1993) 'Introduction', in J. Lave and S. Chaiklin (eds), *Understanding Practice: Perspectives on Activity and Context*. New York: Cambridge University Press. pp. 3–34.

Lave, J. and Wenger, E. (1991) *Situated Learning: Legitimate Peripheral Participation*. New York: Cambridge University Press.

Lemke, J. L. (1993) 'Discourse, dynamics, and social change', *Cultural Dynamics*, 6 (1): 243–75.

Lesser, E. L. and Storck, J. (2001) 'Communities of practice and organizational performance', *IBM Systems Journal*, 40 (4): 831–41.

Main, R. G. (1993) 'Integrating motivation into the design process', *Educational Technology*, December: 37–41.

MaKinster, J. G., Barab, S. A., Harwood, W. and Andersen, H. O. (2006) 'The effect of social context on the reflective practice of pre-service science teachers: incorporating a Web-supported community of teachers', *Journal of Technology and Teacher Education* 14 (3): 543–79.

Marx, R. W., Blumenfeld, P. C., Krajcik, J. S. and Soloway, E. (1998) 'New technologies for teacher professional development', *Teaching and Teacher Education*, 14 (1): 33–52.

McAndrew, P., Clow, D., Taylor, J. and Aczel, J. (2004) 'The evolutionary design of a Knowledge Network to support knowledge management and sharing for lifelong learning', *British Journal of Educational Technology*, 35 (6): 739–46.

McLaughlin, M. W. and Talbert, J. E. (2006) *Building School-based Teacher Learning Communities: Strategies to Improve Student Achievement*. New York: Teachers College Press.

Nonaka, I. and Takeuchi, H. (1995) *The Knowledge-Creating Company*. London: Oxford University Press.

Nyrop, S. (2002) *Intuitive Chaos Navigation and the Webheads Community*. Virtual online communities in educational practice and research. Retrieved 11 December 2005 from: http://home19.inet.tele.dk/susnyrop/chaos.html.

O'Reilly, T. (2005) *What is Web 2.0? Design patterns and business models for the next generation of software*. O'Reilly Media. Retrieved 30 August 2006 from: http://oreillynet.com/lpt/a/6228.

Palloff, R. and Pratt, K. (1999) *Building Learning Communities in Cyberspace: Effective Strategies for the Online Classroom*. San Francisco, CA: Jossey-Bass.

Pawlowski, S., Robey, D. and Raven, A. (2000). 'Supporting shared information systems: boundary objects, communities, and brokering', in *Proceedings of the XXIst International Conference on Information Systems*, Brisbane, Australia. pp. 329–38.

Pollard, D. (n.d.) *Preparing for Conversations with Dave Pollard. Weblogs and other Social Software for Knowledge Work*. STAR Series the Association of Knowledgework. Retrieved 30 August 2006 from: http://www.kwork.org/Stars/pollard.html.

Poplin, D. E. (1979) *Communities: A Survey of Theories and Methods of Research* (2nd edn). New York: Macmillan.

Powazek, D. M. (2002) *Design for Community*. Indianapolis, IN: New Riders.

Preece, J. (2000) *Online Communities: Designing Usability, Supporting Sociability*. Chichester: Wiley.

Preece, J. (2001) 'Sociability and usability in online communities: determining and measuring success', *Behaviour and Information Technology*, 20 (5): 347–56.

Preece, J. (2002) Special issue: 'Supporting community and building social capital', *Communications of the ACM*, 45 (4): 37–9.

Preece, J. and Maloney-Krichmar, D. (2005) 'Online communities: design, theory, and practice', *Journal of Computer-Mediated Communication*, 10 (4): article 1. Available online at: http://jcmc. indiana.edu/vol10/issue4/preece.html.

Preston, C. (2005) 'The MirandaNet Fellowship: A Community of Practice Developing Self-regulated Learning Environments'. Paper presented at the TACONET conference on Self-regulated Learning in Technology Enhanced Learning Environments, Portuguese Catholic University, Lisbon, Portugal.

Putnam, R. (2000) *Bowling Alone: The Collapse and Revival of American Community*. New York: Simon & Schuster.

Reigeluth, C. (ed.). (1999) *Instructional-Design Theories and Models: A New Paradigm of Instructional Theory* II, *Instructional Design Theories and Models*. Mahwah, NJ: Erlbaum.

Renninger, K. A. and Shumar, W. (2004) 'The centrality of culture and community to participant learning at and with The Math Forum', in S. A. Barab, R. Kling and J. H. Gray (eds), *Designing for Virtual Communities in the Service of Learning*. New York: Cambridge University Press. pp. 181–209.

Resnick, P. (2001) 'Beyond bowling together: socio-technical capital', in J. Carroll (ed.), *HCI in the New Millennium*. Reading, MA: Addison-Wesley, pp. 247–72

Rheingold, H. (1994) *The Virtual Community: Homesteading on the Electronic Frontier*. Reading, MA: Addison-Wesley.

Riel, M. and Polin, L. (2004) 'Learning communities: common ground and critical differences in designing technical support', in S. A. Barab, R. Kling and J. Gray (eds), *Designing for Virtual Communities in the Service of Learning*. New York: Cambridge University Press. pp. 16–50.

Saint-Onge, H. (2003) Guest speaker presentation given by teleconference: Foundations of Communities of Practice Workshop, CPsquare, 3 May 2003.

Salmon, J. (2000) *E-moderating: The Key to Teaching and Learning Online*. London: Kogan Page.

Scardamalia, M. and Bereiter, C. (1993) 'Technologies for knowledge-building discourse', *Communications of the ACM*, 36 (5): 37–41.

Schlager, M. and Fusco, J. (2004) 'Teacher professional development, technology, and communities of practice: are we putting the cart before the horse?', in S. A. Barab, R. Kling and J. H. Gray (eds), *Designing Virtual Communities in the Service of Learning*. New York: Cambridge University Press. pp. 120–53

Schlager, M. and Schank, P. (1997) 'Tapped in: a new online community concept for the next generation of Internet technology', in R. Hall, N. Miyake and N. Enyedy (eds), *Proceedings of the Second International Conference on Computer Support for Collaborative Learning*, Hillsdale, NJ: Erlbaum. pp. 231–40.

Schlager, M., Fusco, J. and Schank, P. (2002) 'Evolution of an online education community of practice', in K. A. Renninger and W. Shumar (eds), *Building Virtual Communities: Learning and Change in Cyberspace*. New York: Cambridge University Press. pp. 129–58.

Schön, D.A. (1987) 'Educating the reflective practitioner', in *Proceedings of the American Educational Research Association*. Kingston, Ontario: Russell. pp 1–15.

Schwen, T. M. and Hara, N. (2004) 'Community of practice: a metaphor for online design?', in S. A. Barab, B. Kling, J. H. and Gray, (eds), *Designing for Virtual Communities in the Service of Learning*. Cambridge: Cambridge University Press. pp. 154–80.

Senge, P. M. (1999) 'Leading learning organizations', in Ken Shelton (ed.), *A New Paradigm of Leadership*. Provo, UT: Executive Excellence Publishing. Chapter 19.

Shirky, C. (1995) *Voices from the Net*. Emeryville, CA: Ziff-Davis Press.

Shumar, W. and Renninger, K. A. (2002) 'On community building', in K. A. Renninger and W. Shumar (eds), *Building Virtual Communities: Learning and Change in Cyberspace*. New York: Cambridge University Press. pp. 1–17

Snowden, D. (1999) 'The paradox of story: simplicity and complexity in strategy', *Scenario and Strategy Planning*, 1 (5): 16–20.

Snowden, D. (2002) *Complex Acts of Knowing: Paradox and Descriptive Self-awareness*. Resources of the Association of Knowledgework. Retrieved August 30, 2006 from: http://www.kwork. org/Resources/snowden.pdf.

Snowden, D. (2005) 'From atomism to networks in social systems', in *The Learning* Organization, 12 (6): 552–62.

Snyder, W. (1997) *Communities of Practice: Combining Organizational Learning and Strategy Insights to Create a Bridge to the Twenty-first Century*, Community Intelligence Labs. Retrieved 15 April 2005 from: http://www.co-i-l.com.

Stacey, R. D. (2001) *Complex Responsive Processes in Organizations: Learning and Knowledge Creation*. New York: Routledge.

Star, S. L. (1989) 'The structure of ill-structured solutions: boundary objects and heterogeneous distributed problem solving', in L. Gasser, and M. Huhns, (eds), *Distributed Artificial Intelligence* II. London: Pitman. pp. 37–54.

Stevens, V. (2002) *Webheads Chat Logs from September 8, 2002*. Personal Web site, Vance Stevens. Retrieved 30 August 2006 from: http://www.homestead.com/prosites-vstevens/files/efi/chat2002/wfw020908.htm.

Stevens, V. (2005) 'Webheads: Intuitive Chaos Management in Online Collaborative Interaction'. Paper presented at Knowtips Conference. Retrieved 20 April 2005 from: http://www.homestead.com/prosites-vstevens/files/efi/papers/horizonlive/2005feb25whjam.htm.

Stuckey, B. (2004) 'Making the "Most of the good advice": meta-analysis of guidelines for establishing and Internet-mediated community of practice', in Piet Kommers, Pedro Isaias and Miguel Baptista Nunes (eds), *Proceedings of IADIS International Conference Web Based Communications*. Lisbon (retrieved 30 August 2006 from http://www.iadis.net/dl/Search_list_open.asp?code=749.

Stuckey, B. (2006a) 'Intentionally Cultivating Internet-mediated Communities of Practice in Educational Contexts'. Paper presented at the annual meeting of the American Educational Research Association, San Francisco, CA.

Stuckey, B. (2006b) 'Cultivating Internet-mediated Communities of Practice'. Unpublished Ph.D. dissertation, University of Wollongong, Sydney.

Stuckey, B. and Smith, J. (2004) 'Building sustainable communities of practice', in P. M. Hildreth and C. Kimble (eds), *Knowledge Networks: Innovation through Communities of Practice*. Hershey, PA: Idea Group. pp. 150–64

Stuckey, B., Hedberg, J. G. and Lockyer, L. (2001) 'Growing an Online Community of Practice: Community Development to Support In-service Teachers in their Adoption of Innovation'. Paper presented at the IX Improving Student Learning using Technology Symposium, Edinburgh, Scotland.

Stuckey, B., Lockyer, L. and Hedberg, J. (2001) 'The Case for Community: Online and Ongoing Professional Support for Communities of Practice'. Paper presented at the Education Odyssey 2001: Continuing the Journey through Adaptation and Innovation, XVth Biennial Forum of the Open and Distance Learning Association of Australia, Sydney.

Wellman, B. and Gulia, M. (1997) 'Net-surfers don't ride alone: virtual communities as communities', in M. A. Smith and P. Kollock (eds), *Communities in Cyberspace*. Abingdon: Routledge. pp. 167–94.

Wellman, B and Gulia, M. (1999) 'Net-surfers don't ride alone: virtual communities as communities', in Barry Wellman (ed), *Networks in the Global Village: Life in Contemporary Communities*. Boulder, CO: Westview Press. pp. 331–67.

Wellman, B., Salaff, J., Dimitrova, D., Garton, L., Gulia, M. and Haythornthwaite, C. (1996). 'Computer networks as social networks: collaborative work, telework, and virtual community', *Annual Review of Sociology*, 22: 213–38.

Wenger, E. (1998) *Communities of Practice: Learning, Meaning, and Identity*. Cambridge: Cambridge University Press.

Wenger, E., McDermott, R. and Snyder, W. M. (2002) *Cultivating Communities of Practice*. Boston, MA: Harvard Business School Press.

Wiley, D.A. and Edwards, E. K. (2002) 'Online self-organizing social systems: the decentralized future of online learning', *Quarterly Review of Distance Education*, 3 (1): 33–46.

Williams, R. L. and Cothrel, J. (2000) 'Four smart ways to run online communities', *Sloan Management Review*, 41 (4): 81–91.

Wilson, B. G. (1997) 'Thoughts on theory in eduacation technology', *Educational Technolgy*, 37 (1): 22–7.

Wilson, B. and Ryder, M. (1998) 'Distributed learning communities: an alternative to designed instructional systems', *Educational Technology Research*. Retrieved 5 May 2005 from: http://www.e-innovation.org/stratinc/files/library/32.doc.

Young, M. F. (1993). 'Instructional design for situated learning', *Educational Technology Research and Development*, 41 (1): 43–58.

21

Researching the Impact of Online Professional Development for Teachers

Wynne Harlen and Susan J. Doubler

A key question to be asked of any professional development course for teachers, whether provided on-campus or online, is 'Does it lead to intended changes in teachers' understanding, skill and classroom practice?' This chapter is about the attempts to answer this question through research in relation to online courses. The first section comprises a narrative review of relevant research on the development, process and impact of online professional development for teachers. The second section considers the challenges to be faced in providing teachers' professional development online. This is followed by a brief account of attempting to meet these challenges in a modular online programme for elementary and middle school teachers aimed at developing their understanding of science and of teaching science through inquiry. The account includes a summary of research designed to enable a comparison to be made between the processes and outcomes of the course content when studied online and in an on-campus version specially set up for the research. The final section brings together points arising from this and other research in considering the pros and cons of online delivery of teachers' professional development.

REVIEW OF RELEVANT RESEARCH

There is a considerable body of research on professional development of teachers spread across different modes, from informal mentoring to formal award-bearing courses and from face-to-face to wholly online interaction. For example, Dede *et al.* (2005) identified nearly 400 empirical studies of online teacher professional development courses. Here we are concerned with studies of teacher professional development that is delivered either wholly or mainly online. This focus reduces the number of studies considerably, but not their diversity. The application of online learning for the professional development of teachers is relatively new compared with its use in other areas of higher education. The development of such courses began in some countries in the late 1990s and it took some time for related research to be undertaken and published. Many early studies were concerned with development of courses rather than the outcomes in terms of change in teachers.

The focus of this chapter is on studies describing the use of the Internet in the development of teachers' classroom practice, as distinct from the development of the use of the Internet in classroom teaching (Vrasidas and Glass, 2005). However, the latter courses are important to consider because they help to illuminate matters relating to course design, the rationale for using online learning in this context, the perceptions of students of learning online and the development of evaluation instruments for online programmes. Thus there are three main headings under which some relevant research studies are outlined here:

- Studies concerned with online course design, development and evaluation and online pedagogy
- Studies of the process of learning online, including teachers' participation and perceptions of online learning
- Studies of outcomes of online professional development in teachers, subdivided into:
  - *Content knowledge,* (e.g. understanding of science or mathematics)
  - *Pedagogic content knowledge,* about how to teach the subject matter, including the use of technology, useful illustrations, analogies and examples (Shulman, 1987)
    Pedagogic knowledge – understanding and reflecting on learning, particularly a social constructivist view of learning.

When discussing professional development for teachers there can be some ambiguity in terminology, since teachers are the learners. In the following, therefore, we refer to 'teachers' meaning those undertaking professional development. 'Students' is reserved for school students taught by the teachers. Those providing tuition or facilitation in the courses are described as instructors or facilitators, following authors' terminology. Those providing other higher education courses are described as university teachers or lecturers.

Online course design, development, evaluation and pedagogy

Dougiamas (1999a) discusses the application of educational theories of reading and writing in supporting online learning in the context of course development. Reading and writing are central to learning from the Internet, particularly when a constructivist view of learning is embraced. This view recognizes that effective learning involves more than just passive absorption of material. Reading and writing play important parts in the active engagement of students with materials, teachers and other students, essential to construct meaningful understandings (Tobin, 1993; Gergen, 1995). Together reading and writing can form a number of types of written discourse through which meaning can be created and shared. Dougiamas (1999a) describes a system he developed to enable teachers to create online courses for any subject. Called Moodle (Dougiamas, 1999b), it provides a framework for teachers to use taking the form of a concept map or 'tree'. Each item on the map is linked to an activity relating to a single concept. Teachers use the framework to develop the courses and in doing so deepen their understanding of the content. For students, reading and using one of these concept maps is an active process in which their navigation of the content encourages comprehension skills such as inference, patterns, summarization and elaboration (Dougiamas, 1999a). Kim and Hannafin (2004) consider the challenges in designing online courses that provide learners with opportunities for scientific enquiry. They suggest design principles that enable students to engage in open-ended enquiries of relevance to their everyday lives.

McLoughlin (2002) claims that an important means of ensuring the effectiveness of instruction in distance and face-to-face settings is through provision of learner support. She offers a conceptualization of the term 'scaffolding' in distance learning and provides examples of how learners can be supported in the processes of constructivist enquiry in a range of learning settings. McLoughlin (2003) summarizes current thinking on quality in online learning and presents a framework for rich online experiences based on learners' needs and learner-centred constructivist principles. Starting from the American Psychological Association's fourteen learner-centred psychological principles (APA, 1993), McLoughlin proposes that online tools should provide learners with 'opportunities to construct knowledge, actively share and seek information, generate a diverse array of ideas, appreciate multiple perspectives, take ownership in the learning process, engage in social interaction and dialogue, develop multiple modes of representation and become more self-aware' (McLoughlin, 2003: 6).

George *et al.* (2004) describe the development of an evaluation instrument for use by course developers for their own courses and for higher education lecturers in evaluating courses developed by others. The instrument, embodying criteria of quality gathered from the literature, enables the self-evaluation and peer evaluation of online courses. It consists of a list of criteria relating to all aspects of the content and pedagogy under four main headings: instructional design, interface design, the use of multimedia to engage learning, and the technical aspects of interactive educational multimedia. For example, under 'instructional design' are criteria such as 'The overall purpose of the course is clearly stated,' 'Objectives or learning outcomes are clearly stated for each section or module' and under 'the use of multimedia' there is 'Video clips include synchronised captions for audio tracks.' A course is judged against each criterion on a five-point scale. Case studies of the use of the instrument and its associated Web site lead the authors to conclude that it guides university lecturers in the development of an online learning environment and also provides a mechanism that enables them to share their experiences and practices with colleagues.

Akkerman *et al.* (2004) used 'pioneer' teachers from five European countries to propose ways to help teachers develop competences they need to use ICT in education. These teachers participated in a two-year project in which they discussed, online and face-to-face, the two questions: 'What competences are important for teachers to employ ICT in their work at school?' 'What are possible ways for teachers to develop these competences?' (Akkerman *et al.*, 2004: 252). The results were grouped into three areas of competence: teaching and learning processes, collaboration and school development. The authors concluded that teachers 'need to be competent in pedagogical matters in general, but also competent in constructivist pedagogy, and moreover competent in a suitable integration of ICT into that pedagogy' (Akkerman *et al.*, 2004: 257). In terms of how to develop the competences, the teachers' preference was for a combination of online courses, face-to-face workshops and in-school learning.

In an action research in professional development of higher education lecturers aimed at improving teaching online, Maor (2004) addressed both the pedagogy and the technology skills of the lecturers. From observation of ten academic members of staff, the researcher categorized them according to their pedagogical approach (implementation of a socio-constructivist approach) and their competence in technology. The intervention was a series of monthly professional development meetings where problems identified by the group were discussed. The results showed that the lecturers' weaknesses in either pedagogy or technology were reduced by seeing the opportunities that developing teaching provided for technology, and vice versa.

Factors inhibiting or facilitating development of online courses in higher education were studied by Haag *et al.* (2004) and Kearsley *et al.* (2004). Data were gathered by Haag *et al.* from faculty, department chairs and administrators in a case study of an online master's programme held at three universities. The findings showed that the development of online courses was inhibited by absence of recognition or financial reward for the extra work involved for faculty when more students enrolled to take advantage of the online facility. These problems were exacerbated by teaching not counting for tenure or for other benefits as a scholarly activity. There were also issues relating to intellectual property rights to be addressed.

These obstacles were confirmed by Kearsley *et al.* (2004), who collected the views of engineering faculty offering a three-year online master's degree comprising ten online courses and a one-week summer residential session in the first and second years. However, they also found that faculty appreciated the rewards, which included the freedom from being on-campus, the experience of trying new approaches, the appreciation of the learners and the mutual learning from the online interaction of faculty and learners. Teaching had become more enjoyable and they saw themselves as enablers rather than tutors, and teaching and learning as collaborative activities. Ways in which they addressed the problems they encountered included offering more choice in assignments to reduce duplication, using a combination of individual and group projects and arranging for students to help and inform each other. Advice to other faculty contemplating developing online courses related to becoming computer-proficient and not dependent on others for technical support, experiencing an online course and observing how other successful faculty create courses. In common with the findings of Haag *et al.* (2004) was the advice to obtain tenure first, as there would probably be no rewards for online developments.

The influence of cultural background, and particularly the prevailing view of teaching and learning, when courses developed in one country are implemented in another, were investigated by Burgess *et al.* (2004). They studied a course developed in Australia and exported to Malaysia. The research questions concerned the attitudes of Malaysian teachers towards new educational technologies and whether the new technologies were used to promote student-centred and independent learning. The learning materials provided technology-based options in addition to more familiar learning resources. They included online lectures, an online discussion board and chat room and a variety of Internet resources. Burgess *et al.* (2004) found that Malaysian lecturers encountered considerable resistance from students to the use of the new technology in the courses. The ambivalent attitude of the students was supported by parents, who expected to see lecturers delivering material to be learned and considered that they were not getting value for money if students were expected to find information for themselves or to help each other learn. However, the lecturers commented that the students were well able to adapt to using new learning tools and that the negativity towards the technology was a result of their exposure to limited learning styles rather than a reflection of the culture.

The processes of learning online

Higher education learners' perceptions of online learning have been widely studied in a range of academic subjects. Walker (2001) collected learners' expectations before studying online and perceptions after the event and compared them with their instructors' views of the same processes and events. Walker found some discrepancy among these three views. This was greatest in respect of the instructor considering that learners were learning at their own pace when learners did not perceive that this was happening. Similarly, the instructor thought that the learners' activities were carefully planned, while learners perceived otherwise. It was also interesting that the learners appeared to have understood more about what was expected of them than the instructor thought they had understood.

Tobin (1998) describes a science course for elementary and middle school teachers in which participants met face-to-face during summer semesters but where the computer was the predominant means of learning at other times. Tobin's study of the learning environment of this course drew on the online experience of twenty teachers and his own experience as a 'participant–observer instructor'. His study was primarily concerned with participants' perceptions of the online learning environment. He identified fifteen dimensions 'considered salient to the learning environment preferred and experienced by the participants in the study' (Tobin, 1998: 150) and encapsulating the essential components of effective learning environments found in the general research on learning environments (for example by Fraser, 1998). Tobin grouped the fifteen dimensions under three broad headings:

- *Emancipatory activities*: convenience (access at convenient times); efficiency (not having to attend on campus saved time); autonomy (choice of when and how to access the material)
- *Co-participatory activities*: flexibility; reflection; quality (of learning); interaction (with others, asynchronously); feedback (from other participants and the instructor); collaboration (with other participants in a variety of activities)
- *Qualia*, a term coined by Tobin to mean: enjoyment (associated with success and master of technology); confidence; success; frustration (with the technology); tedium (associated with posting and responding on a regular basis).

This framework has been adopted by other researchers (Chang, 1999; Chang and Fisher, n.d.; Goh and Tobin, 1999) in developing instruments for assessing the quality of online learning environments as perceived by learners. Chang (1999) and Chang and Fisher (n.d.) describe the development of the Web-based Learning Environment Instrument (WEBLEI), informed by Tobin's (1998) framework. There are four sections to the instrument providing scales relating to Access, Interaction, Response and Results. Learners respond to each of the thirty-seven items by indicating if it is something that they do or feel on a five-point scale from 'never' to 'always'. The results of administering the instrument to 377 learners in a trial are reported, leading the authors to conclude that it can be a useful way of evaluating learners' reactions to online study.

THE IMPACT OF ONLINE PROFESSIONAL DEVELOPMENT ON TEACHERS' KNOWLEDGE AND PRACTICE

Content knowledge

The distinction between content knowledge and pedagogic content knowledge is difficult to make in the context of professional development for teachers. The goals of professional development are necessarily to help the teaching of a subject, which depends on subject knowledge. So when content knowledge is a focus there is generally also some development of pedagogical content knowledge. The study of *Try Science* described later in this chapter was the only one found in a search for research evidence where there was an attempt to measure change in content knowledge as an outcome of teachers' online professional development. Knowledge of the use of technology in education is a borderline case but, since the technology content knowledge is invariably conveyed in the context of teaching a particular subject, studies with this focus are discussed under the heading of pedagogical content knowledge.

Studies of content learning by school or higher education students through various forms of distance learning were summarized by Spooner *et al.* (1999). Of six studies where achievement outcomes were compared for traditional and technology-based distance courses (Kuramato, 1984; Weingand, 1984; McCleary and Egan, 1989; Ritchie and Newby, 1989; Souder, 1993; Thomson and Smith, 1996), in only one was there any difference and this was in two of three measures reported. In other studies (Lombardi *et al.*, 1991; Jones, 1992; Stahmer *et al.*, 1992; Naber and LeBlanc, 1994; Jaeger, 1995), where no comparison was made but where students' perceptions and achievement of goals in distance courses were reported, the distance learning was received positively and considered effective. Twigg (2001) suggested that the reason for the common finding of 'no significant difference' was because 'the vast majority of online courses are organized in much the same manner as their campus counterparts' (Twigg, 2001: 3). This still applies to many online courses, although the developments of guidelines for course design and criteria for course evaluation, such as those mentioned earlier, mean that online courses are increasingly offering more than additional flexibility in relation to access.

Pedagogical content knowledge

Some programmes for teacher professional development use case studies of classroom teachers in action, on video or CD-ROM, to address the questions that teachers raise about the teaching of specific subject or the use of technology. Others use experienced practising teachers to discuss with less experienced or trainee teachers for the same purpose. Greene and Magliaro (2004) reported a project that combined these two approaches. In their study, twenty-seven pre-service teachers with little teaching experience took part in a project in which they viewed CD-ROM-based case studies of teaching by teachers in their own classrooms, spanning elementary to high school classes. Viewing the CDs in class was followed by an online chat session and week-long threaded discussions. This cycle was repeated each month for four cycles. The chats, led by a practising teacher and a university teacher, were designed to follow up particular points raised by the CDs. The threaded discussions were open forums. Data were collected by interview with the teachers, university teachers and the pre-service teachers, observations, field notes, class documents and surveys. Transcripts from chats and threaded discussions were also printed and analysed. The authors claimed that the findings confirmed the value of the case studies in enabling the pre-service teachers to link theory to practice.

However, Savenye *et al.* (2004) showed that case studies alone were not effective in developing teachers' confidence and ability to create the kinds of learning opportunities for students seen in the case studies. Their study describes the development and formative evaluation of a database of case studies of 'best practice' in using technology in teaching. Each case includes an interview with the teacher, a video of the technology-based lesson, the lesson plan and materials developed by the teacher, a reflection by the teacher and a commentary by an educational technology expert. A questionnaire completed by teachers after using a video case for ninety minutes showed that the teachers were positive in their attitude to the cases but were less positive about their own level of confidence in teaching with technology. The evaluation indicated that the teachers wanted more guidance in designing lessons. When asked to produce lesson plans of their own the teachers described lessons produced for other purposes with little reference to the use of technology.

Kupferberg and Ben-Peretz (2004) report on a study of exchanges in an online forum designed to bring together novice and experienced teachers. The participants, all teachers of English as a foreign language, were able to meet and discuss face-to-face both theoretical and practical aspects of interpersonal problem discourse. The online forum was an additional channel of communication that they could use. Each of the twenty eight participants (sixteen novice teachers in their first year and twelve more experienced teachers) initiated an online discussion through a problem-message, leading to 310 messages. The study found that both experienced and novice participants engaged effectively with the problems introduced. The authors noted that delayed online responses 'lacked the urgency characteristic of face-to-face interactions' (Kupferberg and Ben-Peretz, 2004: 115). The novice teachers offered *ad hoc* solutions whereas the experienced teachers provided more systematic reasoned solutions.

In a study by Ge and McAdoo (2004), peer learning was the approach used to provide ongoing technological and pedagogical support for teachers in the integration of ICT into their teaching. To facilitate this, various online tools were provided within the context of establishing a peer learning community. These tools included Web logs, discussion boards, chat rooms, e-mail and the sharing of resources such as documents and templates. The results at an early stage of implementing this model indicated that 'the weblog system provided a tool to make their thinking visible and accessible, not only to themselves but also to other community members, who could provide constructive comments or suggestions to them' (Ge and McAdoo, 2004: 279).

Pedagogic knowledge

The programmes found in this review that were aimed at improving teachers' understanding of pedagogy were designed to achieve this through teachers' reflection on learning – both their own and that of school students. Reflection has already been mentioned in some studies and features in the study of *Try Science* described later in this chapter. Cheng *et al.* (2004) used examples of student work uploaded by participating teachers as a focus for this reflection. This programme, Science Around the World (SAW), sought to provide professional development for teachers of science in countries beyond the originating one. As well as reflecting on their own work in the context of work provided by other teachers, there were online seminars and a forum for discussing ways of improving student achievement. The discussion forum was structured with tasks and questions to provoke critical analysis and reflection. The reactions and experience of teachers in Hong Kong and the US are reported. Uptake of the programme was found to be influenced by several factors relating to the country or district, such as fluency in English and the availability of and familiarity with the technology used. There also has to be trust developed among participants so that they feel able to comment on each other's student work openly. When the necessary learning environment is created then analysing student work and discussion about classroom teaching are very relevant to their work. The teachers also believed that participation helped them to develop communication skills and develop critical thinking skills.

In the online environment, reflection is closely related to writing. In the study reported by Greene and Magliaro (2004), described earlier, the 'chats' about the video case studies of teaching were led by a practising teacher and a university lecturer. Having to write their thoughts and reactions so that others had access to them not only contributed to understanding of the social nature of learning but caused participants to think carefully about what they wanted to communicate.

> Closely tied with these advantages of written communication was the role reflective opportunities played. All three participant groups mentioned the value of reflection. The pre-service teachers stated it helped them synthesize and understand all the information they were learning. The teachers and university teachers stated it allowed them to reflect on their own practice while sharing it with others.

> (Greene and Magliaro, 2004: 57)

Quantitative analyses showed that the pre-service teachers' comments became increasingly more reflective during the semester. The authors concluded that the technology provided opportunities for social learning and reflective thought which enhanced the pre-service teachers' ability to connect theory with practice.

Questioning plays a key role in pedagogy in any context and the type of questions asked determine the nature of interactions to a large extent. Blanchette (2001) studied the syntactic structure, cognitive functions, pedagogical features and communicative characteristics of questions asked by participants in an asynchronous learning environment. Compared with face-to-face interaction, learners online asked more rhetorical questions, using them to think aloud, persuade and indirectly challenge other participants. It was found that, in the online context, questions phrased to elicit a yes-or-no answer did not in fact lead to short responses, nor did they discourage interaction if their content was at a higher level of cognitive functioning. Questioning strategies that may have been effective in the face-to-face classroom may not achieve the expected outcomes in an online environment. At the same time, because asynchronous interaction does not suffer from time constraints as does face-to-face teaching, it is possible to ask more of the higher cognitive level questions that require a longer processing time.

Comment

Although this review falls short of being comprehensive, the emergence of themes from different studies suggests that it has identified at least some of the main points from research relating to change in ways of teaching and learning. A move to online learning is not just to a different way of engaging in the same traditional ways of learning, to which most students are accustomed. Neither is online teaching merely a new way of 'delivering' traditional teaching. More fundamental changes are involved. Indeed, it is clear that lecturers who have attempted to continue the kind of interaction with students familiar in face-to-face teaching after putting their courses online are soon faced with an impossible task. They need to make changes to reduce the learners' dependence on lecturer response and increase learning through interaction among learners. They have also found it necessary to modify assessment procedures.

In relation to the professional development of teachers the research shows that there are both similarities and differences in the characteristics of effective courses. Both online and face-to-face courses that aim to make change in teachers need to:

- Use content that is seen by participants as relevant to their working environment
- Give examples of new pedagogy in action
- Provide support in what is necessary to make change
- Provide sufficient time for change to take place in teachers' understanding and commitment before new practices can take place in the classroom
- Recognize the influence of established expectations regarding learning and teaching
- Establish an ethos of trust among participants so that they freely share their ideas and examples of their work.

Some of the differences between online and face-to-face professional development highlighted by the research are that, online:

- The requirement to communicate in writing can help learning
- The freedom to study when and where convenient, within limits, is appreciated by practising teachers particularly
- Asynchronous communication gives time for reflection and leads to more thoughtful responses
- Questioning by both facilitator and participants operates rather differently than in face-to-face interaction
- The public nature of the communication through the Internet accentuates the need for encouragement and support for all types of response.

As the research shows, it is almost a requirement of the online environment that learners take greater responsibility for engaging with course material than when a teacher is physically present. This means that learners must be provided with learning goals, information and the skills necessary for taking responsibility for constructing their own understanding. Implementing a social constructivist approach to learning would seem to be a greater challenge online, yet this is the aspiration of many online programmes. It is also consistent with current thinking about learning whether by students in school or teachers in pre-service or in-service courses. We now turn to the challenges that this view of learning presents in the development of teachers' professional development.

THE CHALLENGES OF ONLINE PROFESSIONAL DEVELOPMENT

Quality teaching is known to have a strikingly large effect on student learning (Good and Brophy, 1994; Ferguson and Ladd, 1996; Hattie, 2003). In reflecting on curricular and policy change, Atkin and Black (2003) state, 'We have come to believe that it is the teachers themselves and their vision, thoughtfulness, beliefs, and abilities that overshadow virtually everything else' (Atkin and Black, 2003: 55). They argue that to improve our schools we need to understand the work of our best teachers.

In this section, we consider the significant challenges encountered in helping teachers to develop these best practices and how online learning environments can contribute in the context of learning about teaching science through enquiry. The question we ask is: What are the potential benefits and the challenges afforded by this new environment for teacher learning?

Online learning has changed our vision of who can be served when, in what ways and with what quality. Professional learning, once bound to specific sites and times, can now serve teachers regardless of time or place. While wider accessibility is apparent, the question of quality is not. Too often, the environment is viewed as a delivery rather than a teaching forum, and the use of sound pedagogy overlooked. When attention is given to developing quality programmes based on theories of learning and teaching, this quality can be replicated again and again in future offerings. While face-to-face learning relies primarily on the instructor's teaching skills, pedagogical approaches can be built into the structure of online experiences. When this is done, more teachers have access to consistently high-quality professional learning (Doubler and Paget 2005). Increased access to quality professional development, in turn, holds the promise of more equitable teaching across all schools.

Hammerness *et al.* (2005: 386) provide a framework for thinking about the knowledge and professional skills of effective teachers. Their framework includes: a vision of practice; a set of understandings about subject matter, teaching and learning; dispositions; practices that allow teachers to act on their intentions and beliefs; and tools that support their efforts. Here we explore the key needs and the potential contribution on the online environment for meeting each of these factors.

A vision of practice

Teachers come to their teaching with a vision of how schools work. This vision is coloured by their own K-12 learning (Lortie, 1975). Their prior experiences and imprinted images of how classrooms work are tenacious. In their professional learning, teachers may need to unlearn established ideas as well as learn new ones. The online environment provides a context in which established beliefs about teaching can be suspended and rethought (Duffy and Kirkley, 2004). Online, video cases make it possible for teachers to 'visit' the classrooms of other teachers. Together they can see and discuss effective practices for helping children learn. These images and their discussion help to change established images of how school works.

Understanding content, learning and pedagogy

In their professional learning, teachers may develop awareness and verbal understanding of subject matter and practice, but may not be able to put this understanding into practice in the classroom (Kennedy, 1999). Helping teachers to transfer learning to the classroom requires more than the presentation of content and theory, it involves teachers in trying out and developing the processes associated with the understanding. Online courses can be designed so that more of the professional learning takes place in a classroom where teachers try out ideas, reflect on their success and then use the online environment to report and discuss their experiences with their online colleagues.

Dispositions

A key challenge that teachers face in their learning is to develop dispositions associated with the disciplines they teach or with teaching itself. Indeed, how can teachers model dispositions, such as tolerance of ambiguity or respect for evidence, if they have not developed these themselves? In the online environment, access can be provided to experts, such as scientists, writers, mathematicians or master teachers. Teachers can see the expert in action and reflect on how he or she approaches problems, helping teachers to understand the nature of the discipline.

Flexible practices

The act of teaching is extremely complex, often requiring quick, on-the-spot decisions to meet learners' needs and to address events unfolding in the classroom. Established routines allow teachers to work efficiently, but teachers also need to be flexible, to think from multiple perspectives, to innovate, and to continue to modify their teaching based on the circumstances at hand (Hatano and Inagaki, 1986; Schwartz *et al.*, 2005). The online environment provides a time-effective way for teachers to come together and share professional dilemmas and reactions. Through online discussions they can apply their learning to the reality of their school, become familiar with perspectives of other teachers, and a wider range of practical applications for their learning.

Tools

Teachers need tools, such as curriculum materials, in conjunction with their learning to support change in classroom practice. However, a distinction exists between providing such tools and mastering them (Grossman *et al.*, 1999). Tools may be incorporated without significant change in practice unless their underlying values are understood and maintained. Online environments can provide just-in-time professional learning modelling the effective use of tools so that their integrity is maintained.

Professional learning is more likely to be effective when the message and focus are consistent and sustained (Tatoo, 1996; Wideen *et al.*, 1998). Time is a significant factor. Supovitz and Turner (2000) found eighty hours of coherent professional learning were needed to impact teaching. Harlen (2004) reports that changes in understanding and practice happen gradually, with some aspects of teaching requiring more time to develop than others. Online programmes can provide the necessary time flexibility to enable teachers' professional learning to move beyond awareness to nuanced understanding and commitment.

MEETING THE CHALLENGES IN A SCIENCE EDUCATION PROGRAMME

These challenges were foremost in the minds of the developers of an online modular programme in science education for elementary and middle school teachers. The programme (which can lead to a master's degree) was developed by TERC (an educational research and development non-profit organization) and Lesley University. The programme is fully online and supports the learning of science and science teaching with particular attention to the role of enquiry, learning communities and peer-to-peer mentoring. Enquiry was understood in the way defined in the National Science Education Standards (NRC, 1996: 23).

The programme consists of an introductory three-credit thirteen-week course and five six-credit modular courses. Since the courses are developed for online use and not transferred from existing materials, a high level of coherence exists within and across the programme. The science portion of each module uses pedagogical approaches explicitly studied in the teaching portion, and the teaching portion of each module revisits the science experienced in the science portion. Tools, such as a model of enquiry, are used across all science and teaching courses. In the programme, the online environment intertwines science and teaching to reinforce learning the discipline and learning to teach the discipline.

In their course work, teachers engage in a mix of asynchronous on- and offline activity. Each six-credit module is co-facilitated by a scientist and science educator, with the scientist guiding teachers in the acquisition of science content, skills and habits of mind, and the science educator coaching teachers as they learn about and try research-based teaching strategies in their classrooms. Video clips (available online) of other practitioners working with students are analysed and discussed to help create vivid images of how effective teachers support learning. Video of scientists engaged in thinking about common, everyday phenomena are analysed and discussed to make visible the strategies scientists use in their problem solving. In the programme's asynchronous environment the learner decides when to think alone and when to communicate ideas and pose questions to his or her course colleagues.

Evaluation

A longitudinal evaluation study followed a cohort of twenty-two course participants over three years as they completed all courses and modules that comprised the online master's programme. Quantitative data from embedded course assessments (thought experiments) were collected and analysed in order to assess change over time in programme participants' understanding of science concepts. These 'thought experiments' were embedded twice in each of the six course modules, toward the beginning (time 1) and the end (time 2) of the module. The assignment was described to course participants as a mental exercise where they think through a suggested experiment but do not actually conduct it. Two external science experts coded the 'thought experiments' for biology, ecology, Earth science and engineering.

Overall, participants' performance on the embedded thought experiments provided evidence that one of the programme's goals, to further students' understanding of science concepts, was being met. In all but one of the five modules examined, participants' scores increased significantly from the beginning to the end of the course, effectively demonstrating an increased understanding of the particular science content presented in that module.

Comparison of learning online and on-campus

Research was conducted on the introductory module of the programme *Try Science*, which can be studied as a stand-alone professional development course or part of the degree course, in order to evaluate the effectiveness of this part of the programme and to provide an account of the participants' and facilitators' experiences. The criteria of effectiveness to be applied were that teachers would be involved in the intended active enquiry learning processes and would develop their understanding of the science concepts involved, their understanding of enquiry and of enquiry teaching and would gain confidence in teaching science.

There was particular interest in investigating the questions of whether the outcomes of the online *Try Science* course would be similar or different from the outcomes of a course of the same content presented face-to-face, and whether certain learning outcomes of the course are more readily achieved through online or face-to-face learning. To answer these questions, an on-campus course, with eighteen participants, was run as a temporary addition to the Lesley University professional development programme. Data were collected from this on-campus course and from two cycles of the online course, with fifteen and thirteen participants respectively.

It was recognized that there were many inevitable differences in structure and interaction among facilitator, participants and materials that were inherent to the formats of the two courses. Face-to-face learning is essentially synchronous, with participants being able to respond to one another immediately while online learning in *Try Science* is asynchronous. The face-to-face course allows some flexibility, to move more quickly or more slowly to meet the participants' needs, while the online course was laid out from start to finish in weekly packages. In addition, the two components of the online course – for developing scientific knowledge and developing pedagogy – were facilitated by two different people, while, in keeping with the usual University procedures, for the on-campus course one course leader was enlisted to run it. Other uncontrolled differences between the two courses were related to the experience and backgrounds of the participants. These factors, discussed by Harlen and Doubler (2004), need to be borne in mind in drawing conclusions from comparison between the two course formats.

The data collection from the on-campus course was similar, except that direct observation and video-recording were used to collect class experiences in place of the analysis of messages posted by participants in the online course. Despite the uncontrolled differences between the two forms of the course, the data from the on-campus course added an important dimension to the interpretation of the online course outcomes.

A full account of the methods of analysis and the interpretation of findings is given in Harlen and Altobello (2003). Results concerning learning achieved, time spent and confidence indicated that:

- For participants in both courses, there were increases in their understanding of the science content of the course (as measured by a pre–post thought experiment) but this change was significantly greater for the online participants

- Online participants spent on average seven and a half hours per week on the courses, compared with five and a half hours per week spent by the on-campus participants
- Facilitators of the online course spent on average over nine hours per week, 16 per cent more per week than the on-campus instructor
- The confidence that participants in all courses expressed in their capacity to teach science through enquiry increased, but the difference was significantly greater for online than for on-campus participants.

There were many similarities between the responses of the participants in the online and on-campus courses, which could generally be ascribed to the content of the activities. The main differences in experience between the online and on-campus participants were that the former were involved more frequently than the latter in reflecting on their learning and on the process of enquiry. Online participants also experienced, appreciated and commented upon their collaborative learning; they did not feel that they were working alone.

DISCUSSION: POINTS FROM RESEARCH

Professional development of teachers is widely acknowledged to be crucial to improvement in education. Attempting to produce change in classrooms through the provision alone of new materials for students and/or teachers has not resulted in students' access to intended learning experiences. This is particularly so in the case of major change in pedagogy, such as is required for teaching through enquiry, where producing real change in classrooms often requires change in teachers' beliefs about the subject, about enquiry and about how students learn. Many professional development programmes attempt to model, through their procedures and pedagogy, the teaching actions that they wish teachers to adopt. However, provision of such courses on a large scale is clearly problematic. The Internet offers an attractive medium for reaching more teachers without the limitations of geographical location.

The example of the *Try Science* course illustrates the problems faced when a professional development programme attempts to address complex matters of changing teachers' pedagogy. *Try Science* had the dual aim of increasing teachers' understanding in science and raising the level of their ability to teach science through enquiry. As the findings show, it was more successful in developing teachers' understanding of the science studied than in bringing about change in classroom practice. Whilst we can speculate about various reasons for this, the most likely, given what is known about producing change in teachers' practice, is that such change could hardly be expected, even on the most optimistic view, after a single (three-credit hours) module. The work of Rudduck and Kelly (1976), Doubler (1991) and Fullan (1993), for example, indicates that change in teachers' practice has to be built up through various stages. Thus to develop practice in enquiry teaching requires more sustained study by teachers of enquiry learning and teaching than provided within the limits of *Try Science*. What is needed includes opportunities to build up knowledge of students' own ideas and of how to access them, developing understanding of learning with understanding, knowing how to share goals with students and how to enable students to assess their own work. These are all aspects of pedagogy that are included in later modules of the whole science education professional development programme.

Points about the time needed for change in teachers' practice apply, of course, to professional development in general, whether studied online or on-campus. A key question is whether one mode of delivery supports or detracts from the process of change more than the other. Bearing in mind both what is needed to bring about change and the desirable features of a learning environment for teachers, identified by Tobin (1998), it seems that the online learning environment provides these advantages:

- Communication through the written word, requiring greater precision in choosing words and clarifying an idea or observation in order to convey it effectively.
- Asynchronous communication, providing time for reflection and giving opportunity to pursue a point in several exchanges without preventing other threads of discussion.
- Space for asking and answering higher cognitive level questions that require time to process.
- Flexibility, within the limits of the weekly programme, in respect of when to study, when to conduct investigations or pursue other information gathering and for how long to continue to explore and follow up further questions.
- The opportunity to read and re-read others' experiences and to give and receive comments on differences in experiences and/or interpretations.
- Exposure to learning experiences of high quality, giving access to the thinking of a team of experts beyond the immediate facilitators of the course.

At the same time, there were some disadvantages:

- Dependence on written communication could disadvantage some teachers, particularly those not confident in expressing themselves on paper and those whose first language is not English. Research by Burgess *et al.* (2004) also indicated that lack of experience of different ways of learning can inhibit the learning of participants from different countries.
- The written word has a permanence far greater than the spoken word in a face-to-face discourse; thus expressing tentative ideas requires trust in others not to ridicule or misjudge them.
- Written instructions can also be ambiguous and cause frustration if incorrectly interpreted.
- The weekly programme imposed a uniform pace on learning and favoured a certain learning style.
- Not receiving individual feedback from the facilitator can be disconcerting, leading to uncertainty as to whether views are being ignored, not received or not thought worth pursuing.
- Cultural difference may lead to expectations that the facilitator should have a more central role in delivering material (Smith, 2001; Ziguras, 2001).

In developing further professional development courses, steps need to be taken to minimize the disadvantages and to exploit the advantages. Further research can help in understanding how to do this.

Opportunities for further research

There is room for research to extend our understanding of how to promote transfer to the classroom of ideas encountered on a course, particularly when the aim is, as in so many studies reviewed earlier, to promote implementation of a social constructivist view of learning. This requires study of how to promote dialogue, critical review and personal reflection in the context of teachers' professional development. Discourse analysis of the online dialogue would help to illuminate how learning takes place and to inform understanding of adult as compared with student learning. An interesting aspect of this is how the power and status of learning changes when moving between offline and online.

In addition to matters relating to course content, the development of a course or programme also requires attention to the facilitator's role. Aspects that require investigation include how to avoid the discussion among participants wandering into unproductive channels, how to build consensus among participants and yet ensure that inaccurate conclusions are challenged. There is still a great deal to learn about the role of the online facilitator in relation to developing personal understanding of complex matters such as are involved in enquiry-based teaching. Also important is the extent to which, and in what circumstances, such understanding leads to change in professional practice.

Finally, there is the matter of course structure. While many online courses have no on-campus element and participants do not meet each other or the facilitators face to face, many other courses mix online and face-to-face elements on the assumption that the latter have a necessary role. When asked, teachers often express a preference for this mixture (for example, as reported by Akkerman *et al.*, 2004). It is a matter of some importance to investigate what, if anything, is added in terms of learning opportunities and the effect of different combinations of online and face-to-face experience.

REFERENCES

Akkerman, S. F., Lam, I. and Admiraal, W. F. (2004) 'They understand what it takes: a pioneer's view on teachers' professional development', in C. Vrasidas and G. V. Glass (eds), *Online Professional Development for Teachers*. Greenwich, CT: Information Age Publishing. pp. 249–64.

American Psychological Association (1993) *Learner-centre Psychological Principles: Guidelines for School Reform and Restructuring*. Washington, DC: American Psychological Association and the mid-continental Regional Educational Laboratory.

Atkin, J. and Black, P. (2003) *Inside Science Education Reform: A History of Curricular and Policy Change*. New York: Teachers College Press.

Blanchette, J. (2001) 'Questions in the online learning environment', *Journal of Distance Education* 16 (2). Retrieved from: http://cade.icaap.org/vol16.2/blanchette.html.

Burgess, M. Currie, J. and Maor, D. (2004) 'Technology enhancements across cultures in higher education', in C. Vrasidas and G. V. Glass (eds), *Online Professional Development for Teachers*. Greenwich, CT: Information Age Publishing. pp. 159–76.

Chang, V (1999) 'Evaluating the effectiveness of online learning using a new Web-based learning instrument'. *Proceedings of the Western Australian Institute for Educational Research Forum*. Retrieved from: http://education.curtin.edu.au/waier/forums/1999/chang.html.

Chang, V. and Fisher, D. (n.d.) 'The Validation and Application of a New learning Environment Instrument to Evaluate Online Learning in Higher Education'. Retrieved from: http://www.aare.edu.au/01pap/cha01098.htm.

Cheng, M.-H., Stoel, C. F. and Anderson, E. (2004) 'Online professional development of teachers through the Schools Around the World (SWA) program', in C. Vrasidas and G. V. Glass (eds), *Online Professional Development for Teachers*. Greenwich, CT: Information Age Publishing. pp. 177–96.

Collins, A., Seely, J. and Holum, A. (1991) 'Cognitive apprenticeship: making thinking visible', *American Educator: the professional journal of the American Federation of Teachers*, 15 (3): 6–11, 38–46.

Dede, C., Breit, L., Ketelhut, D. J., McClosky, E. and Whitehouse, P. (2005) 'Overview of current findings from empirical research on online teacher professional development', in C. Dede (ed.), *Harvard University Usable Knowledge Conference Report: Evolving a Research Agenda for Online Teacher Professional Development*. Cambridge, MA: Harvard University.

Doubler, S. J. (1991) 'Change in Elementary School Teachers' Practice in Science in the United States'. Unpublished Ph.D. thesis, University of Liverpool.

Doubler, S. and Paget, K. (2005) 'Science learning and teaching: a case of online professional learning', in C. Dede (ed.) *Harvard University Usable Knowledge Conference Report: Evolving a Research Agenda for Online Teacher Professional Development*. Cambridge, MA: Harvard University.

Dougiamas, M. (1999a) *Reading and Writing for Internet Teaching*. Retrieved from: http://dougiamas.com/writing/readwrite.html.

Dougiamas, M. (1999b) 'Developing tools to foster online educational dialogue', in K. Martin, N. Stanley and N. Davison (eds), *Teaching in the Disciplines/Learning in Context*. Proceedings of the VIIIth Annual Teaching Learning Forum, University of Western Australia, February. Perth: University of Western Australia. pp. 119–23. Retrieved from: http://cleo.murdoch.edu.au/asu/pubs/tlf/tlf99/dj/dougiamas.html.

Duffy, T. and Kirkley, J. (2004) 'Introduction: Theory and practice in distance education', in T. Duffy and J. Kirkley (eds), *Learner-centered Theory and Practice in Distance Education: Cases from Higher Education*. Mahwah, NJ: Erlbaum. pp. 3–13.

Ferguson, R. and Ladd, H. (1996) 'How and why money matters: an analysis of Alabama schools', in H. F. Ladd (ed.), *Holding Schools Accountable: Performance-based Reform in Education*. Washington, DC: Brookings Institution. pp. 265–98.

Fraser, B. J. (1998) 'Science learning environments: assessment, effects and determinants', in B. J. Fraser and K. G. Tobin (eds), *International Handbook of Science Education*. Dordrecht: Kluwer.

Fullan, M., (1993) *Change Forces: Probing the Depths of Educational Reform*. Abingdon: Falmer Press.

Ge, X. and McAdoo, S. (2004) 'Sustaining teachers' efforts in technology integration', in C. Vrasidas and G. V. Glass (eds), *Online Professional Development for Teachers*. Greenwich, CT: Information Age Publishing. pp. 265–81.

George, R., Wood, D. and Wache, D. (2004) 'Shifting the teaching paradigm', in C. Vrasidas and G. V. Glass (eds), *Online Professional Development for Teachers*. Greenwich, CT: Information Age Publishing. pp. 283–300.

Gergen, K. J. (1995) 'Social construction and the educational process', in L. P. Steffe and J. Gale (eds), *Constructivism in Education*. Hillsdale, NJ: Erlbaum. pp. 17–39.

Goh, S. W. and Tobin K. (1999) 'Student and teacher perspectives in a computer-mediated learning environment in teacher education', *Learning Environment Research: An International Journal*, 2: 169–90.

Good, T. and Brophy, J. (1994) *Looking in Classrooms*. New York: HarperCollins.

Greene, H. C. and Magliaro, S. G. (2004) 'A computer-mediated community of learners in teacher education', in C. Vrasidas and G. V. Glass (eds), *Online Professional Development for Teachers*. Greenwich, CT: Information Age Publishing. pp. 51–67.

Grossman, P., Smagorinsky, P., and Valencia, S. (1999) 'Appropriating tools for teaching English: a theoretical framework for research on learning to teach', *American Journal of Education*, 108 (1): 1–29.

Haag, S. G., Folkestad, L. S. and Dietrich, S. W. (2004) 'Faculty incentives and development for online learning', in C. Vrasidas and G. V. Glass (eds), *Online Professional Development for Teachers.* Greenwich, CT: Information Age Publishing. pp. 69–85.

Hammerness, K., Darling-Hammond, L., Bransford, J., Berliner, D., Cochran-Smith, M. McDonald, M. and Zeichner, K. (2005) 'How teachers learn and develop', in L. Darling-Hammond and J. Bransford (eds), *Preparing Teachers for a Changing World: What Teachers should Learn and be Able to Do*. San Francisco, CA: Jossey-Bass. pp. 358–89.

Harlen, W. (2004) *Evaluating Inquiry-based Science Developments: A Paper commissioned by the National Research Council in Preparation for a Meeting on the Status of Evaluation of Inquiry-based Science Education*. Washington, DC: National Research Council.

Harlen, W. and Altobello, C. (2003) *An Investigation of Try Science Studied On-line and Face-to-face*. Cambridge, MA: TERC.

Harlen, W. and Doubler, S. (2004) 'Can teachers learn through enquiry online? Studying professional development in science delivered online and on-campus', *International Journal of Science Education*, 26 (10): 1247–67.

Hatano, G. and Inagaki, K. (1986) 'Two courses of expertise', in H. Stevenson, H. Azuma and K. Hakuta (eds), *Child Development and Education in Japan*. New York: Freeman. pp. 262–72.

Hattie, J. (2003) 'Teachers make a Difference: What is the Research Evidence?' Paper presented at the Australian Council for Educational Research annual conference on Building Teacher Quality.

Jaeger, M. (1995) 'Science teacher education at a distance', *American Journal of Distance Education*, 9 (2): 61–75.

Jones, T. (1992) *Students' Evaluation Questionnaire for the Fall Semester of 1991: a Summary and Report*. ERIC Report No. ED 345716.

Kearsley. G. and MEPP faculty (2004) 'The MEPP faculty experience', in C. Vrasidas and G. V. Glass (eds), *Online Professional Development for Teachers.* Greenwich, CT: Information Age Publishing. pp. 121–39.

Kennedy, M. (1999) 'Form and substance in mathematics and science professional development', *NISE Brief*, 3 (2), Madison, WI: National Center for Improving Science Education.

Kim, M. and Hannafin, M. (2004) 'Designing online learning environments to support scientific inquiry', *Quarterly Review of Distance Education*, 5 (1): 1–10.

Kupferberg, I. and Ben-Peretz, M. (2004) 'Emerging and experienced professional selves in cyber discourse', in C. Vrasidas and G. V. Glass (eds), *Online Professional Development for Teachers.* Greenwich, CT: Information Age Publishing. pp. 105–20.

Kuramato, A. (1984) 'Teleconferencing for nurses: evaluating its effectiveness', in L Parker and C. Olgren (eds), *Teleconferencing and Electronic Communications* III. Madison, WI: University of Wisconsin-Extension, Center for Interactive Programs.

Lombardi, T., Bauer, D., Peters, C. and O'Keefe, S. (1991) *Satellite Distance Courses: A Collaborative Effort for meeting Demands for Special Education Teachers*. ERIC Document ED 332 481.

Lortie, D. C. (1975) *Schoolteacher: A Sociological Study*. Chicago, IL: University of Chicago Press.

Maor, D. (2004) 'Opportunities with e-learning: changing teachers' pedagogies', in C. Vrasidas and G. V. Glass (eds), *Online Professional Development for Teachers.* Greenwich, CT: Information Age Publishing. pp. 213–29.

McCleary, I. D. and Egan, M. W. (1989) 'Program design and evaluation: two-way interactive television', *American Journal of Distance Education*, 3 (1): 50–60.

McLoughlin, C. (2002) 'Learner support in distance and networked learning environments: ten dimensions for successful design', *Distance Education*, 23 (2): 149–63.

McLoughlin, C. (2003) *How does the quality debate relate to the nature of the student experience online?* Retrieved from: http://www.ecu.edu.au/conferences/tlf/2003/pub/pdf/19_McLoughlin_Catherine.pdf.

Naber, D. and LeBlanc, G. (1994) 'Providing a human biology laboratory for distant learners', *American Journal of Distance Education*, 8 (2): 58–70.

National Research Council (1996) *National Science Education Standards*. Washington, DC: National Academy Press.

Ritchie, H. and Newby, T. J. (1989) Classroom lecture/discussion vs live televized instruction: a comparison of effects on student performance, attitude and interaction', *American Journal of Distance Education*, 3 (3): 36–45.

Rudduck, J. and Kelly, P. (1976) *The Dissemination of Curriculum Development: Current Trends*. Slough: National Foundation for Educational Research.

Savenye, W., Brush, T., Middleton, J., Igoe, A. and Kurz, T. (2004) 'Developing online teacher video cases for learning technology integration', in C. Vrasidas and G. V. Glass (eds), *Online Professional Development for Teachers*. Greenwich, CT: Information Age Publishing. pp. 317–30.

Schwartz D., Bransford, J. and Sears, D. (2005) 'Efficiency and innovation in transfer', in J. Mestre (ed.), *Transfer of Learning: Research and Perspectives*. Greenwich, CT: Information Age Publishing. pp.1–51.

Shulman, L. S. (1987) 'Knowledge and teaching: foundations of the new reform', *Harvard Educational Review*, 7 (1): 1–22.

Smith, S. N. (2001) 'Approaches to study of three Chinese national groups', *British Journal of Educational Psychology*, 71 (4): 419–41.

Souder, W. E. (1993) 'The effectiveness of traditional vs satellite delivery in three Management of Technology master's degree programs', *American Journal of Distance Education*, 7 (1): 37–53.

Spooner, F., Luann, J., Algozzine, B., and Spooner, M. (1999) 'Student ratings of instruction in distance learning and on-campus classes', *Journal of Educational Research*, 92 (3): 132–40.

Stahmer, G., Smaldino, S., Hardman, R. and Muffaletto, R. (1992) 'A Survey of Students currently enrolled in Interactive Instructional Television Courses in Community Colleges in Iowa'. Paper presented at the meeting of the Association for Educational Communications and Technology, Washington, DC, February.

Supovitz, J. A. and Turner, H. M (2000) 'The effects of professional development on science teaching practices and classroom culture', *Journal of Research in Science Teaching*, 37: 963–80.

Tatoo, M. T. (1996) 'Examining values and beliefs about teaching diverse students: understanding the challenges for teacher education', *Educational Evaluation and Policy Analysis*, 18 (2): 155–80.

Thomson, J. D. and Smith, C. L. (1996) 'Students' perceptions of the affective experiences encountered in distance learning courses', *American Journal of Distance Education*, 10 (3): 37–48.

Tobin, K. (1993) 'Constructivist perspectives on teacher learning', in K. Tobin (ed.), *The Practice of Constructivism in Science Education*. Hillsdale, NJ: Erlbaum. pp. 215–26.

Tobin, K. G. (1998) 'Qualitative perceptions of learning environments on the World Wide Web', *Learning Environments Research*, 1: 139–62.

Twigg, C. A. (2001) *Innovations in Online Learning: Moving beyond No Significant Difference*. Troy, NY: Center for Academic Transformation, Rensselaer Polytechnic Institute.

Vrasidas, C. and Glass, G. V. (eds) (2005) *Preparing Teachers to Teach with Technology*. Greenwich, CT: Information Age Publishing.

Walker, S. L. (2001) 'Online Learning Environments Research'. Retrieved from: http://education.ollusca.edu/tcc2001/online_learning_environments_research_PAPER.htm.

Weingand, D. E. (1984) 'Telecommunications and the traditional classroom: a study of the delivery of education', in L. Parker and C. Olgren (eds), *Teleconferencing and Electronic Communications* III. Madison, WI: Center for Interactive Programs, University of Wisconsin – Extension.

Wideen, M., Mayer-Smith, J. and Moon, B. (1998) 'A critical analysis of the research on learning to teach: making the case for an ecological perspective on inquiry', *Review of Educational Research*, 68 (2), 130–78.

Ziguras, C. (2001) 'Educational technology in transnational higher education in South East Asia: the cultural politics of flexible learning', *Educational Technology and Society*, 4 (4): 8–18.

22

Exploring E-learning Community in a Global Postgraduate Programme

Ellen Roberts and Jane Lund

Higher education institutions are increasingly interested in the potential of e-technologies to enable teaching and learning, for both strategic and pedagogic reasons. One of the issues that have attracted attention as a result is that of the 'e-learning community'. How can a learning community be enabled and fostered when teaching and learning take place through e-technology? What helps and hinders? What issues should form the research agenda? And, more fundamentally, how can we assess the importance of the issue, and what are the measures of success?

This chapter is a contribution to exploring these issues. It sets a theoretical context through a review of concepts relevant to the understanding of e-learning communities; discusses challenges in researching the notion; and relates this theoretical context to an illustrative example drawn from our own experience of e-delivery within a postgraduate programme: the University of York's online master's in Public Policy and Management programme (referred to hereafter as the York programme).

There are some important caveats in presenting this discussion. First, the chapter reflects early indicators. The programme that is the subject of the chapter was launched in the autumn of 2003. At the time of writing, our experiences are based on a period of two years. This is a limited period of enquiry. Secondly, and linked to this, the shape of our understanding is still emerging. Although a number of the theoretical frameworks have proved extremely relevant in making sense of what we see and hear, our understanding is continuing to evolve.

Thirdly and most important, what is presented here are indicators *for* research rather than findings *from* research. The process of developing and launching the programme can certainly be described as a 'high intensity project' (Yourdon, 2001) in which there has to date been only limited space for systematic evaluation. One of the purposes of this chapter is to frame the next stages of an evaluation plan. In this sense, the chapter is very much exploratory, in that it seeks to frame the issues that should be addressed for the future.

COMMUNITIES IN E-LEARNING

Online distance learning programmes owe much to the precedents set by the more traditional paper-based distance learning programmes and yet differ enough from them to excite a plethora of enquiry from within the academies that deliver courses in this way. The potential for action research is obvious and it is in the spirit of this form of enquiry that this chapter is situated, seeking to contextualize the York programme within a wider framework of discourse and, in particular, within the current debates around what constitutes and defines an online learning community.

This chapter begins by discussing some of the thinking behind social learning theory, and then looks at why defining 'community' is problematic and equally why it is important to do so. It will then focus on Garrison and Anderson's (2003) notion of 'social presence' in the light of some of the research that has been done to date. The section ends with a question about how practitioners can design for or design in structures or processes that will encourage the development of a community.

Many of those who work in the field of teaching and learning appear to agree that a strong sense of community among participants increases retention, enhances knowledge construction, and increases student motivation and satisfaction levels. Although a full discussion of this is beyond the scope of this chapter, it seems important to briefly touch on the social constructivist theory of learning that underpins much of the discourse about 'adult learning communities' (Anderson *et al.,* 2001; Bauman, 1997; Brown 2001; Campos, 2004; Garrison and Anderson, 2003; Hiltz *et al.*, 2000; Weller, 2002)

Social constructivism (Vygotsky, 1978) posits that, in order for learning to occur, information must be processed by the learner in a social context, interaction with others allowing the individual to make sense of new information via discourse in such a way as to transform it into meaning, and that this meaning is defined (or 'constructed') via the learner's existing knowledge, beliefs or values.

Lave and Wenger (1991) took this notion and developed it into the theory of 'situated learning' ('situated' in their model meaning located within a social engagement of some kind). They coined the phrase 'community of practice' to describe a group of people whose intentions to learn are engaged, and who use tools and resources within a relational context to create meaning.

Such thinking has underpinned much of the pedagogy in adult education for some time, although it must be said at this point that arguments have been raised about the lack of acknowledgement within social constructivist circles of the possibility that knowledge may be constructed without a relational context, and also that that there may be 'communities of practice' that are weak or may 'exhibit power relationships that seriously inhibit entry and participation' (Smith, 2003).

We acknowledge the suggestion that communities are not necessarily egalitarian but suggest that, in adopting the principles of the theory, the role of educators is to allow for both and attempt to address the latter where it occurs in our own communities.

The principles of social constructivism, situated learning and communities of practice have informed the development of the York programme, and continue to inform how the programme is directed and taught. But defining 'community' is difficult, and the next section looks at why this is and why we must attempt to do so for ourselves, possibly even each time we attempt to develop an online learning community.

PROBLEMATIZING 'COMMUNITY'

What defines an online learning community? Is it the case that 'almost any group of people who interact might be called a community' (Hammon, 1998) or is there a need to create a definition? A choice is important if we as practitioners are to decide how to establish and develop a learning community and work out how to measure its efficacy.

Whilst it is a truism that continued philosophical and empirical enquiry is needed to define the nature of a learning community, not least given the plethora of definitions, indicators and classification systems that exist, it is incumbent on anyone embarking on the quest for such a community as part of an educational experience to identify their own definition – or how can we know when we have achieved it that what we have achieved has educational value (as opposed to the purely 'social' value of other virtual communities)?

The definition debate is intellectually engaging and challenging. As the *Oxford Dictionary of Sociology* says, 'the ambiguities of the term community make any wholly coherent sociological definition … impossible to achieve'. A study by Hillery (1955), quoted in Hammon (1997) identified ninety-four definitions of the term and extrapolated sixteen different definitional concepts. From these sixteen, however, he identified four main themes that repeatedly emerged, summarized by Hamman (1997): '(1) a group of people (2) who share social interaction (3) and some common ties between themselves and other members of the group (4) and who share an area for at least some of the time'. (This last point in the context of e-learning is interesting – would cyberspace qualify as 'an area'?)

Hamman also cites a more recent empirical study (Poplin, 1979) that identifies no fewer than 125 sociological definitions, but notes that 'the above definitional aspects were still present in the majority despite some changes in the usage of the term over the years'.

This definition, however, whilst useful and concise, doesn't go far enough to describe a 'learning community', and postgraduate learning communities in particular, designed to enable 'higher level' learning, by which we mean learning as a process of knowing, thinking, connecting, acting and caring (Fink, 2001) and where 'ideas are conceived, responded to, reframed' (Scardamalia and Bereiter, 1994).

'Communities of enquiry'

Whilst accepting the four indicators illustrated by Hammon, we need to probe further to find a definition that is useful in terms of its application in adult education. One such definition is Garrison and Anderson's (2003) interpretation of the term 'community of enquiry', borrowed from the philosopher Charles S. Pierce (1839–1914). Pierce coined the term to describe interaction between scientists whilst Garrison and Anderson use it to describe a learning community that incorporates the theoretical framework of social constructivism, describing what is required to create, develop and sustain such a community online; one that supports and enhances higher learning.

According to Garrison and Anderson (2003), early adopters of e-learning recognized a potential for collaborative learning that paper-based distance learning did not afford, and devoted considerable time and effort trying to replicate the face-to-face experience of the traditional university. Garrison and Anderson cite the use of CMCs as the technology that allowed educators to see that distance learning could be qualitatively different from face-to-face learning in a positive way, a way that involved rethinking the definition of discursive space. 'With the ubiquity of communications technologies and their multiple forms (e.g. text, visual, voice) we are in the early stages of a true paradigm shift. The application with perhaps the greatest influence on education and society is e-learning' (Garrison and Anderson, 2003: 5).

Garrison and Anderson challenge for instance the oft-cited notion that the lack of face-to-face contact between individuals and the consequent absence of visual and audible clues and cues is a barrier to creating 'social presence' in an online environment, something that is crucial if students are to engage with each other. This is supported by Campos (2004), who suggests that the lack of familiar face-to-face cues can actually lead to greater group cohesion.

According to Garrison and Anderson, the successful use of asynchronous text-based communication media that can facilitate higher learning requires:

- *Social presence* – non-subject-based communication, expressions of personal experience, expressions of acknowledgement of other participants, etc.
- *Cognitive presence* – evidence of academic engagement with the texts, 'thinking out loud', evidence of reflection, critical thinking and further construction of meaning

- *Teaching presence* – design (of the programme), facilitation (of the asynchronous discussions) and direct instruction.

Garrison and Anderson (2003) go on to suggest that, rather than seeing asynchronous text-based communication as a means of compensating for the supposed limitations of remote learning, it may in fact have inherent pedagogical advantages, arising from the opportunities for reflection, the emphasis on written communication and permanence of the written record. The potential for synergy between postgraduate professional development, a constructivist approach and asynchronous communication has also been noted elsewhere.

The idea of 'social presence' is worth expanding on here because one of the arguments espoused in favour of blended learning in preference to distance e-based learning is that it produces a stronger sense of 'community' and thus more motivated students (Rovai and Jordon, 2004); this is assumed to be due to students feeling less isolated. However, the same authors go on to describe research that suggests that isolation isn't the main cause of weakening of 'community ties' but 'lack of prompt or clear feedback from the tutor' (Hara and Kling, 2001). Others would no doubt be able to offer their own rationale for the higher drop-out rate among distance-learning students and this is one of the areas that badly needs more research (although of course talking to those that do drop out is notoriously difficult).

Other research on computer-mediated communication since the 1970s by, for example, Short *et al.* (1976), who introduced the term 'social presence', and Kiesler *et al.* (1984, 1992), Walther (1996), Caldwell and Taha (1993) and Culnan and Markus (1987) addresses issues of 'reduced cues' environments and media-richness and the implications for social interaction and cohesion. A full review of this material is beyond the scope of the present chapter and, although none of it addresses educational contexts *per se*, it is worth highlighting two of them as particularly helpful in illuminating Garrison and Anderson's work.

It seems fair to say that many in our own communities of practice would argue that the lack of face-to-face interaction militates against the development of community because, apart from anything else, the relative anonymity of the medium encourages the kind of 'deindividuation' that produces a loss of personal and social responsibility, which could lead to antisocial behaviour (Le Bon, 1995, quoted in Watt *et al.*, 2002). The apparent threat presented by deindividuation has implications for Garrison and Anderson's suggestion that 'social presence' is critical to successful learning online. If students (and staff?) are at risk of not creating a social presence simply because of the medium, what is to be done?

However, there is evidence (Watt *et al.*, 2002) that suggests that the opposite of 'deindividuation' may be the case in an online environment, and that what transpires is 'depersonalization' rather than deindividuation, which is where 'the reduction in social clues and relative anonymity provided by most Internet communications are more likely to reinforce socially normative behaviour rather than undermine it' (Watt *et al.*, 2002). Watt *et al.* state that 'while deindividuation implies a loss of self, depersonalization implies an increased tendency to define the self in terms of the group'. Watt *et al.* have developed a theory, Social Identity Model of Depersonalization Effects (SIDE), to explain that the 'privileging of group-level information over individuating information in text-based CMC allows a situationally relevant group more influence than in many face-to-face situations where group-level information is submerged by the wealth of interpersonal cues available'.

Walther (1996) also suggests that depersonalization in certain contexts can be beneficial: 'As socioemotional concerns such as conflict or relationship management take time and effort away from task resolution, any mechanism that reduces the need or proclivity to expend effort in these directions should enhance the efficiency of a group's efforts' (Walther, 1996: 6).

So the lack of interpersonal communication can be seen as a benefit. But Walther then goes on to challenge the acceptance of what he calls the 'cues filtered out' theories by suggesting that the research studies upon which these theories are based are flawed because they took place over short periods of time and that in fact, given long enough, sociable CMC can and does develop (Walther, 1996). He concludes by suggesting that CMC benefits from both impersonal and, given time, interpersonal communication, something that is unique to the medium. This apparent paradox is something he calls 'hyperpersonal communication'.

Can community be 'designed' in?

But can all this careful attention to pedagogical design generate a 'learning community'? Wenger (1998) argues that communities are emergent and thus cannot be designed, that they are self-organized and come about because of the desires of the people within them, determined by local conditions. However, Haythornthwaite (2000, 2002, 2005) argues that designers have a key role in laying the groundwork on which communities can be built. An e-learning community, created and engineered to support strangers coming together to learn for the first time, is a different entity from a traditional community. It needs to be bootstrapped. 'While it is possible that just by bringing students together into the programme they may achieve a sense of community, we believe that without attention to community characteristics we would be providing an impoverished environment' (Haythornthwaite, 2000).

It is also recognized that communication online takes more effort. Kling and Courtright (2003) note: 'in online communication, the participants have to work hard [through writing] to communicate something about themselves' and Grabowski and Roberts (1998, quoted in Kling and Courtright, 2003) go further and suggest that 'developing trust in VOs [virtual organizations] requires constant, continual communication among members to build relationships that provide the foundation for trust'.

It is our view that the mechanism and support for this communication must be designed into the programme from the outset, by which we mean that students need to be led and supported in a series of communication exercises with initial tasks being designed to develop confidence and familiarity with the medium used which then build into subject-specific exercises and discussions. Bootstrapping in the case of the programme at York consists of required participation in these exercises, with monitoring of participation and early intervention with students who appear to be failing.

Wenger (1998) concedes that 'minimalist design' in pursuit of community is allowable but we would argue that in an online distance-learning context it is demonstrably possible to design for collaboration and communication between participants and that this is part of the way to put in place the conditions for a community to build upon. We accept, however, that this works best when members of the community have a personal investment in making it happen. An emphasis on the central role of the tutor and the other people who support the learning on the programme is paramount (and we shall revisit this later) not least because, as Kling and Courtright (2003) put it: 'in the end, community development is likely to be a complex accomplishment that is difficult to initiate without purposive interventions from some kind of leaders or stewards. It will rarely happen online alone through self-organizing.'

'COMMUNITY' IN PRACTICE: EXPERIENCE DERIVED FROM THE YORK PROGRAMME

We will now go on to look at the York programme in more detail, relating it as far as we can to some of the theories we raised in the first half of the chapter, indicating too our attempts at 'designing in' a community and what we have learned to date about that.

The York programme (the online masters in Public Policy and Management) is designed to provide professional development through the linking of theory and practice: students study a range of theoretical and case-based material, analyse and debate their understanding of this material and relate it to their professional experience. The outcomes for students should be at several levels. They should become more aware of the context in which they work and able to place their own experience within that context. They should develop understanding of analytical frameworks and tools that can assist their professional work, and develop a range of specific skills. They also place their experience in a wider context, and become better able to critique it, through sharing those experiences with other students.

The programme has been designed from the outset to be internationally relevant. Most modules have been developed by authors from across an international collaboration of which York was a founder member; the Worldwide Universities

Network (WUN). This international context has meant that the programme is designed to engage an international mix of students. Learning from the process of comparison between experiences in different contexts is an important driver for the programme as a whole – one that is especially important in the study of the social and political processes that are at the heart of the programme.

The programme is delivered entirely online. The main components of the programme are: online material organized in modules; links to other material both within the modules and through the university library; and asynchronous discussions in tutorial groups of approximately ten students, via computer-mediated conferencing. The role of the programme's tutors is to support the learning process by facilitating the asynchronous discussions and by providing individual support via e-mail and less frequently by telephone. Although some tutors have been involved in reviewing and refining the module material in the light of their experience of supporting the modules, the tutors' role is otherwise separate from that of the module authors. Thus on this programme the functions of designing the material and teaching it have been split.

Modules are organized around a series of weekly themes, each of which includes a set of resources and a tutorial group discussion. The discussion topics are each completed over a two-week period, the second week overlapping with the first week of the next topic. Students are required to take part in the discussions unless exceptional reasons require absence. In addition to the asynchronous discussions they can also communicate with each other, the tutor and the central programme team via e-mail, and have access to a synchronous chat tool. Telephone conferences are organized at the end of each module and tutors offer a telephone call to each student during each module. There is also an asynchronous 'café', for optional socializing.

Principles of community in the design of the programme

The notion of a 'learning community' has been significant in designing and delivering the programme, for a number of reasons. Pedagogically, 'community' seems important because collaboration and peer-to-peer learning are closely bound up with the aims and rationale of the programme. The linking of theory and practice seems likely to occur best and most fully when practitioners are able to reflect on, and debate, a range of practices, as they will thus be better able to identify common principles, test hypotheses and draw conclusions that are richer and better informed than when based solely on their individual experience. Thus the notion of 'community' is closely tied in this programme to a social constructivist design. Indeed, an explicit aim from the outset has been to use the 'advantages' of the online medium (Garrison and Anderson, 2003) to support these constructivist principles.

In summary, the programme is based on the assumption that the learning experience will be richer if it is informed by a range of experiences and insights shared among fellow practitioners. This stance also reflects the extent to which managers of public services – the main constituency for this programme – share a common frame of reference: despite local differences, public sector organizations across much of the world have been shaped by a similar set of fiscal, ideological and organizational pressures. This set of pressures, referred to by academic commentators as New Public Management (Pollitt and Bouckaert, 2004), provides a shared starting point.

Researching the student experience

Our main concern in the early stages of the programme was to gather as much feedback about the student experience as possible. An overarching concern in this process was to identify what factors act as barriers or enablers to e-learning. This concern reflected an early preoccupation with identifying differences between the experience of e-learning and that of face-to-face learning. As our understanding of and confidence about e-learning has grown, our focus has moved away from the identification of enablers and barriers towards seeking to understand the notion of community in more depth. Despite this shift, the initial focus on barriers and enablers has yielded findings, discussed below, that appear very relevant to understanding the notion of online community.

The main sources of feedback in exploring the student experience on the programme have been: end of module questionnaires (completed online and anonymously); discussions held with students in groups and individually in the course of ongoing academic and pastoral contacts; an evaluation event held at York in July 2004, attended by half of cohort 1, together with a panel of internal and external e-learning experts and the programme team; a second evaluation event held at York in July 2005, attended by a cross-section of students from cohorts 1, 2 and 3.

The student population from whom the feedback has been gathered is approximately eighty in number. This number includes four cohorts, spanning joiners in September 2003 (cohort 1), to joiners in May 2005 (cohort 4). This student population spans twenty-five countries.

Students' perceptions

The following sections summarize key points from students' feedback to date about their experience on the programme. The discussion has been structured around the topics that emerged from the feedback itself. Connections are made to the theoretical context outlined above as appropriate, with Garrison and Anderson's typology of 'presence' proving especially useful as a frame of reference. Thus the organizing framework has been the content of the feedback itself rather than a specific theoretical starting point. This seems important in order for key points to be allowed to emerge on their own terms.

As noted above, much of the evaluation effort in the period identified above was concerned with identifying barriers and enablers to e-learning. This question was asked specifically of students at the two evaluation events identified above.

It is of course a wide question, which further research could help to unpack. There are a number of possible 'sub-questions'. For example, what helps students feel motivated and pleased to be studying on the programme, and what hinders this? What helps to create depth of understanding and what impedes it? The factors relevant to these two questions may of course be quite different. Since the process of creating 'depth' of understanding can be an uncomfortable and puzzling one, it is quite likely that at times it will not sit easily with straightforward enjoyment or satisfaction. While noting these issues, it is nevertheless worth identifying pointers to date in what students have identified as 'barriers' or 'enablers'.

From the feedback to date, a cluster of issues appears to be important. The clusters are around 'pedagogy' and 'systems'. Some of the issues raised bear directly on the notion of 'community' while in others there is a less direct relationship.

Pedagogy

Three pedagogic themes emerge strongly: programme content, student interaction and the role of the tutor.

Programme content

The issue of the 'quality' of the material presented to students is clearly a key one. Students look for depth and breadth in the materials presented to them. A sense of 'institutional security' seems important: the sense students have of the expertise and experience underpinning the programme. The first comments offered by students at the evaluation event with cohort 1, when asked to consider barriers and enablers, were about this topic.

It is easy to take for granted the core importance of 'content' in the effort to focus on the 'process' of e-learning. Students' comments suggest, though, that their perception of quality in relation to the content is a kind of precondition for their active engagement in what they are asked to do.

Student interaction

It is this topic that relates most closely to the theoretical ground discussed earlier, and it is also a topic about which students have provided substantial feedback. The core of their interaction is the weekly process of asynchronous discussion (referred to hereafter as 'the discussions'), guided by tutors and around themes set within the module. Feedback about the discussions indicates their importance from the students' perspective: 'The discussions are the programme,' 'The breadth of the student experience and location enriches the experience' (cohort 1, evaluation event). The opportunity to be part of an international cohort is also mentioned frequently: 'I enjoy the contrast that an international cohort brings' (cohort 2, module evaluation feedback).

These comments would seem to support the social constructivist notion that it is through interaction that learning occurs. Other students have also commented, though, that they find the discussions problematic, for reasons to do either with learning style or logistics. Some students express a preference for being able to study independently: 'I prefer to be left alone' (cohort 1, evaluation event), 'I don't find much value in the discussion groups for my own personal learning. The value to me is that they keep me on track with my timetable for learning' (cohort 1, module evaluation feedback). Logistically, it can be difficult to keep pace with them: 'There is often so much else happening that it is not possible to do them full justice' (cohort 2, module evaluation feedback). The views expressed indicate a tension within the programme between *independence* (students who like to study privately and may have opted for distance learning for that very reason) and *interdependence* (the collaborative principles on which the programme is built). Although only a minority of students express a strong preference for a wholly independent approach, this is an ongoing tension that has to be managed.

There are also differing views among students about what creates 'value' in a discussion. Here we see issues to do with 'cognitive presence' ('the extent to which learners are able to construct and confirm meaning through sustained discourse in a critical community of enquiry' (Garrison *et al.*, 2001: 11). Some students express a clear preference for a 'conversational' style, in which contributions build on each other through frequent, interlinked and often short postings. Others express concern about the extent to which a 'conversational' style might lead to fragmented or superficial discourse (cohort 3, group discussion topic). Students who express this view prefer to present pieces of sustained thought. On the other hand students who prefer the conversational style may see the longer contributions as burdensome ('mini-theses', as described by one student with a preference for a conversational approach). This is an issue that would benefit greatly from further research.

There is a range of views too about social interaction, most readily identifiable in students' views about the 'café'. For some, this is important glue that provides a sense of connection. '[The café] is very important. It is especially important to foreign students, as it gives you a sense of camaraderie that is grossly lacking in e-learning environments. ... I like the feeling that I am at the UK', 'I think it is helpful. It can provide a diversion that allows us to learn more about each other. So on the whole, it's a good idea' (cohort 1, module evaluation feedback). Students from within cohort 1 also commented positively on a sense of support and belonging in general: 'We seem to have formed a sort of mutual support, especially with those of us who have been here [on the programme] since the origin of the species.'

Comments from students about their positive social experiences online are repeated frequently enough to suggest that social interaction is important to them and that they appear to be experiencing some form of group adherence (community?). The use of the word 'camaraderie' is interesting, as it is used by Brown

(2001) in her three-stage model of online community formation, with the development of a sense of camaraderie among participants being the third and final stage.

Students' feedback shows that they have been struck by the amount of interaction that is possible within an e-based programme. A student from cohort 3 who had previously studied face-to-face as a full-time student and part-time on a paper-based distance course, commented as follows in a publication designed for fellow employees in her organization:

> Having studied previously as a full-time university student, and also part-time, I can honestly say that the sense of camaraderie and support from fellow students and tutors via the online Master's is second to none. Don't let the 'remote' aspect put you off. I know my online colleagues better than those I sat with in lectures, and have more contact with my tutors.

Again, the use of the word 'camaraderie' is interesting.

But, as already noted above, it is also clear that not all students are equally interested in contact with fellow students, because of either personal preference or lack of time: 'On a personal basis, I am more interested in studying than socializing, but I also appreciate the value and pleasure of group interaction. I visited [the café] once, but have had no time to go back there' (cohort 1, module evaluation feedback).

Much more work clearly needs to be done to explore in depth the nature of the interactions overall that are occurring within the programme, and the ties and relationships that are being formed. Social network theory (Haythornthwaite, 2002) appears to offer considerable potential as a tool for mapping these relationships, and examining further the different roles being played by students within their tutorial groups. Social network theory also appears highly relevant to the following issue: the role of tutors in shaping the online community.

The role of the tutor

Students' feedback contains some consistent messages about the role of the tutor. Students recognize, first, the importance of the tutor in shaping their experience of the programme: 'If the tutor fails, the discussion fails' (cohort 1, evaluation event). 'Tutor presence' (Garrison and Anderson, 2003) appears to be crucial, and needs to be expressed through both group *and* individual contacts. The motivational effects of individual contacts (addressing students by name and acknowledging individuals within group discussions, plus individual contact via e-mail) was a consistent message at both evaluation events. In summary, the feedback shows that students look for three elements from their tutor: support and reassurance, academic guidance and academic challenge. If any of these elements is missing, they perceive that the tutor and the discussion have been less effective.

It is also worth noting that students who are least enthusiastic about the value of the discussions *per se* nevertheless value the opportunities that they give for tutor feedback: 'Although I personally do not like the discussion groups I find the tutor feedback very useful and as stated above they keep me focused on my timetable' (cohort 1, module evaluation feedback).

Systems

The other main topic identified in relation to factors that help and hinder relates to 'systems'. These are issues to do with structures, roles and procedures. These findings are another area in which there are clear implications for the notion of 'community'.

Support systems are a key issue within this heading. In describing positive aspects of their experience on the programme, the word 'support' is one of those used most frequently. By 'support' students mean the mix of academic, operational and administrative connections that they have with the institution. This includes their module tutors but also encompasses the central course team. Garrison and Anderson's conceptual framework for understanding communities of enquiry consists of three interlinked types of presence: social presence, cognitive presence and teaching presence. Our feedback to date indicates that a fourth dimension should perhaps be added to their framework: institutional presence. This finding connects with Haythornthwaite's emphasis (2002, 2005) on the role of programme designers in laying the foundations on which communities can be developed.

What students appear to value is the interconnectedness of academic, operational and administrative support. This also seems to tie in with the sense that 'belonging' to the institution is important. Students value the symbols of their belonging: the university branding on the Web site, a university newsletter, and so on.

Procedures also appear to play a crucial part in enabling collaboration and the development of a 'community'. Again, we see here an important role for the institution in shaping the life of the programme. The programme team's experience is that procedural issues can have a very significant impact on how students come together, relate to each other and collaborate. Thus they are important for the notion of community.

An example of an important procedural issue is the requirement that students participate in the discussions. This requirement has the effect of bringing students into the discussions in a regular and repeated way. It is hard to know what the effect would be of removing this requirement. Some participants (those who favour purely private study) would be inclined to disappear. This would most likely lead to a downwards spiral of participation, with those who did take part finding less and less activity and value.

A further example is the instigation of a 'rapporteur' role. At the suggestion of the students (cohort 1) each student takes a turn at summarizing the weekly group discussion. Although not universally favoured, this role seems to fulfil a number of functions: the rapporteur benefits from the process of synthesis, the

rest of the group benefits from the summary and the act of taking turns reinforces group citizenship. Thus a small change in 'procedures' can shape group
dynamics and 'cognitive presence' (Garrison and Anderson, 2003).

WHAT DO THESE PERCEPTIONS SUGGEST ABOUT THE ROLE OF 'COMMUNITY' IN HELPING OR HINDERING E-LEARNING?

The pointers discussed above concerning barriers and enablers to e-learning
have implications for the notion of 'community'.

- A sense of belonging is important to many students, but not to all. There is a tension within any
  distance-based programme that seeks to be collaborative between independence (respecting
  the desire of some students to study privately and separately) and the interdependence necessary for learning through collaboration.
- The set 'discussions' are perceived as a key part of the programme and of its value. There are
  interesting indicators here about how 'value' can best be created, and in particular an issue
  about the balance between a conversational and more scholarly style. More work needs to be
  done on this to unpick the implications for *cognitive presence*.
- Students tend to have clear preferences about whether they interact socially, and these preferences throw some light on the notion of *social presence*. For some, connecting in this way is
  important. For others, personal preference or lack of time limits the connections they seek to build.
- Tutors have a crucial role in the value that students perceive within their collaborative work.
  Balance between group and individualized communications appears to be key, and this appears
  to be important for understanding the notion of *tutor presence*.
- Systems (support and procedures) also appear to have a considerable influence on how students
  engage with the programme and each other. *Institutional presence* – a fourth dimension to add
  to Garrison and Anderson's three dimensions of presence – appears to be an important enabler.

THE RESEARCH AGENDA: POINTERS AND NEXT STEPS

This chapter has presented some initial, evolving and exploratory pointers about
what helps and hinders e-based learning, and the part played in this by the
notion of 'community'. Against this background, what should the priorities for
research be in relation to this programme and perhaps more broadly?

Certainly, our experience to date, and the students' feedback, suggest that the
following areas are priorities:

- How collaborative work and dialogue build value. How can asynchronous discussion best support 'sustained critical discourse and higher-order knowledge acquisition and application?'
  (Garrison and Anderson, 2003: 55). What is the role in this of different types of task (debates,
  role-play, case studies, open-ended discussion and so on)? How can depth and breadth of discussion both be maximized? How can theory and practice be linked most effectively through
  this medium? How can independence and interdependence best be held in balance? And how
  should achievement in this be measured?

- How do patterns of contact within the student group, and between students and tutors, affect attachment to the process of study and the nature of the learning?
- How specific types of tutor behaviour impact on group dynamics and on the achievement of higher-order knowledge acquisition and application.
- Whether these issues are affected by the extent to which groups are internationally mixed.
- The role of the institution in shaping a sense of belonging. And should the institution be seen as apart from the learning community, enabling it, or as part of the community?

CONCLUSION

This chapter has reviewed the theoretical context related to the notion of an 'e-learning community', and has identified early findings and indications from the experience of delivering one programme. It has suggested some possible priorities for the future research agenda. The process of reviewing what has been learnt to date from this particular programme has itself has been valuable, and indicates that further work to follow up the points identified to date will be of direct relevance in helping us to 'walk the asynchronous talk'. In particular, we look forward to comparing and contrasting our findings with other distance-based programmes, and to exploring further the notion of 'institutional presence', as discussed above.

REFERENCES

Anderson, T., Rourke, L., Garrison, D. R., Archer, W. (2001) 'Assessing teaching presence in a computer conferencing context', *Journal of Asynchronous Learning Networks* 5 (2).

Bauman, M. (1997) *Online Learning Communities*, http://www-personal.umd.umich.edu/~marcyb/tcc-l.html, retrieved 9 November, 2004.

Brown, R. (2001) 'The process of community building in distance education', *Journal of Asynchronous Learning Networks*, 5 (2).

Caldwell, B. S. and Taha, L. H. (1993) 'Starving at the banquet: social isolation in electronic communication media', *Interpersonal Computing and Technology*, 1 (1), http://hegel.lib.ncsu.edu/stacks/serials/ipct/ipct-v1n01-caldwell-starving, retrieved 29 April 2006.

Campos, M. (2004) 'A constructivist method for the analysis of networked cognitive communication and the assessment of collaborative learning and knowledge-building', *Journal of Asynchronous Learning Networks*, 8 (2).

Culnan, M. J. and Markus, M. L. (1987), 'Information technologies', in F. M. Jablin, L. L. Putnam, K. H. Roberts and L. W. Porter (eds), *Handbook of Organizational Communication: An Interdisciplinary Perspective*. Newbury Park, CA: Sage.

Fink, D. L. (2001) 'Higher-level learning: the first step toward more significant learning', in D. Lieberman and C. Wohlburg (eds), *To Improve the Academy: Resources for Faculty, Instructional and Organizational Development*. Bolton, MA: Anker Publishing.

Garrison, D. R. and Anderson, T. (2003) *E-learning in the Twenty-first Century: a Framework for Research and Practice*. Abingdon: RoutledgeFalmer.

Garrison, D. R., Anderson, T. and Archer, W. (2001) 'Critical thinking, cognitive presence and computer conferencing in distance education', *American Journal of Distance Education*, 15 (1): 7–23.

Glaser, B. G. and Strauss, A. L. (1967) *The Discovery of Grounded Theory: Strategies for Qualitative Research*. Chicago, IL: Aldine.

Hammon, R. (1997) *Introduction to Virtual Community Research*, Cybersoc, http://www.cybersoc.com, retrieved 28 October 2004.

Hammon, R. (1998) *The Online/Offline Dichotomy: Debunking some Myths about AOL Users and the Effects of their Being Online upon Offline Friendships and Offline Community*, Cybersoc, http://www.cybersoc.com, retrieved 28 October 2004.

Hara, N. and Kling, R. (2001) 'Students' distress with a Web-based distance education course', *Information, Communication and Society*, 3 (4): 557–79.

Haythornthwaite, C. (2000) 'Strong, weak and latent ties and the impact of new media', *The Information Society*, 18 (5): 385–401.

Haythornthwaite, C. (2002) 'Building social networks via computer networks: creating and sustaining distributed learning communities', in K. A. Renninger and W. Shumar (eds), *Building Virtual Communities: Learning and Change in Cyberspace*. Cambridge: Cambridge University Press, pp. 159–90. http://alexia.lis.uiuc.edu/~haythorn/hay_bvc.html, retrieved 14 April 2006.

Haythornthwaite, C. (2005) 'Social networks and Internet connectivity effects', *Information, Communication and Society*, 8 (2): 125–47.

Haythornthwaite, C., Kazmer, M. M., Robins, J. and Shoemaker, S. (2000) 'Community development among distance learners: temporal and technological dimensions', *Journal of Computer-Mediated Communication*, 6 (1).

Hine, C. (2000) *Virtual Ethnography*. Thousand Oaks, CA: Sage.

Hiltz, S. R., Coppoloa, N., Rotter, N. and Turoff, M. (2000) 'Measuring the importance of collaborative learning for the effectiveness of ALN: a multi-measure, multi-method approach', *Learning Networks Effectiveness Research*, http://www.alnresearch.org/Data_Files/articles/full_text/le-hiltz.htm, retrieved 19 November, 2005.

Kiesler, S. and Sproull, L. (1992) 'Group decision making and communication technology', *Organizational Behaviour and Human Decision Processes*, 52: 96–123.

Kiesler, S., Siegel, J. and McGuire, T. (1984) 'Social psychological aspects of computer-mediated communication', *American Psychologist*, 39 (10): 1123–34.

Kling, R. and Courtright, C. (2003) 'Group Behaviour and Learning in Electronic Forums: A Socio-technical Approach', in S. A. Barab, R. Kling, and J. H. Gray, (eds), *Designing for Virtual Communities in the Service of Learning*. Cambridge: Cambridge University Press pp. 91–119

Lave, J. and Wenger, E. (1991) *Situated Learning: Legitimate Peripheral Participation*. Cambridge: Cambridge University Press.

Martin, P. Y. and Turner, B. A. (1986) 'Grounded theory and organizational research', *Journal of Applied Behavioral Science*, 22 (2): 141–57.

Myers, M. (2004) *Qualitative Research in Information Systems*, Association for Information Systems, http://www.qual.auckland.ac.nz/, retrieved 19 November 2005.

Pollitt, C. and Bouckaert, G. (2004) *Public Management Reform: a Comparative Analysis*. Oxford: Oxford University Press.

Poplin, D. E. (1979) *Communities: a Survey of Theories and Methods of Research* (2nd edn). New York: Macmillan.

Rovai, A. P. and Jordan, H. M. (2004) *Blended Learning and Sense of Community: A Comparative Analysis with Traditional and Fully Online Graduate Courses*, http://www.irrodl.org/content/v5.2/rovai-jordan.html, retrieved 18 November 2005.

Scardamalia, M. and Bereiter, C. (1994) 'Computer support for knowledge-building communities', *Journal of the Learning Sciences*, 3 (3): 265–83.

Short, J. A., Williams, E. and Christie, B. (1976) *The Social Psychology of Telecommunications*. New York: Wiley.

Smith, M. K. (2003) *Communities of Practice*, www.infed.org/biblio/communities_of_practice.htm, retrieved 19 November 2005.

Taylor, P. and Maor, D. (2000) 'Assessing the efficacy of online teaching with the Constructivist On-Line Learning Environment Survey', in A. Herrmann and M. M. Kulski (eds), *Flexible Futures in Tertiary Teaching*. Proceedings of the IXth Annual Teaching Learning Forum, 2–4 February. Perth: Curtin University of Technology, http://lsn.curtin.edu.au/tlf/tlf2000/taylor.html, retrieved 19 November 2005.

Vygotsky, L. S. (1978) *Mind in Society: The Development of Higher Mental Processes*. Cambridge, MA: Harvard University Press.

Walther, J. B. (1996) 'Computer-mediated communication: impersonal, interpersonal and hyperpersonal interaction', *Communication Research*, 23 (1): 3–43.

Watt, S. E, Lea, M. and Spears, R. (2002) 'How social is Internet communication? A reappraisal of band-width and anonymity effects', in S. Woolgar (ed.), *Virtual Society? Technology, Cyberbole, Reality*. Oxford: Oxford University Press.

Weller, M. (2002) *Delivering Learning on the Net*. London: Kogan Page.

Wenger, E. (1998) *Communities of Practice: Learning, Meaning and Identity*. New York: Cambridge University Press.

Yourdon, E (2001) *Managing High-Intensity Internet Projects*. London: Prentice-Hall.

23

The Place of Digital Video in the Curriculum

Andrew Burn

The moving image has a long history in education. Following the widespread distribution of video-tape player-recorders in the 1980s, the moving image became a source of information in many fields of knowledge. In classrooms, film and television became carriers of curriculum content across all subject areas in the latter half of the twentieth century, in the form of documentary television in the humanities and sciences, filmic adaptations of literature and drama in English, and specialist educational programming as part of public service broadcasting.

The most significant consequence of the digital era, with the increasing availability of digital editing software, has been to open up the possibility of making moving-image texts in the classroom. The production of moving-image texts by young people in schools begins with the history of children's engagement with the cultural forms of film and television. In simple terms, children (like the rest of the general population) have been seen principally as consumers of film, television and video. Because, in their leisure lives, they are positioned as audiences, they continue, along with their teachers, to be positioned as audiences in schools. The general distribution of video-editing software appears to have offered the possibility of a shift from consumption to production.

While there is obvious appeal in the use of an attractive popular medium to convey and consolidate varieties of subject knowledge, media educators have consistently pointed out a risk. Perhaps best represented as a loose international consensus in a 2001 report for UNESCO (Buckingham, 2001), proponents of media education have argued that these widespread extensions of the child as audience in the curriculum, now complemented by the child as producer, are

liable to render the medium itself invisible or transparent, no more liable to critical scrutiny than the traditional textbook which they purport to replace. The
media education community insists that young people's engagement with the
media should be an explicit focus of work in schools, developing critical understandings of media texts, institutions and audiences.

Media education has always been at the forefront of work in the production of
the moving image with children. This tradition, in effect, challenges the notion
of children confined to the role of audiences, positioning them by contrast as
producers. The rationales for this move are several: those summarized by
Buckingham *et al.* (1995: 12) include the arguments that making media texts
might help children to 'deconstruct' their messages, offer opportunities for
expressive, creative work and provide 'pre-vocational' experience of working in
the media industries.

Before the arrival of affordable digital editing software in schools, production
of moving-image texts was always a tiny, marginal activity in formal education,
depending on the energies of enthusiasts for media education, and their ability
to find funding for analogue video-editing suites, which were expensive and
unlikely to be used by other curriculum subjects. While television and video
were widely used across the curriculum to deliver subject content, then, production was confined to a very small minority of schools.

As schools began to acquire digital editing equipment and software from the
mid-1990s this picture began to change in two ways. Media educators were the
first to pick up on the benefits of the new technologies, buying systems such as
the Apple-based Adobe Premiere editing package, typically for courses in media
studies with students at the higher end of the secondary age range, and in further
education. However, as such systems required high-specification computers, and
the software was still expensive, other curriculum subjects remained largely
uninvolved. The wider curriculum, and the ICT in education community, really
began to consider the wider learning benefits of digital video (DV) only with the
arrival of the first free entry-level software, Apple's *i-movie*, now followed by
Microsoft's response, *Moviemaker 2*. In the case of the former, the software
itself played a major role in intervention projects discussed in this chapter, Reid
et al. (2003) and Schuck and Kearney (2004). For the first time, the editing of
DV was available free, on ordinary computers, in an accessible form.

The research literature cited in this article reflects and in some cases antici-
pates these developments. Much of the literature, especially the earlier studies,
displays the interest of media educators in children as potential producers of
media texts, not simply as audiences of film and television. Subsequent studies
reflect a widening interest in the use of DV in other curriculum contexts, repeating, in some ways, earlier debates about the uses of television and film. A broad
question, then, for a review of this field, is how has this long-standing debate
developed? What case is made in the research literature for the use of DV

production as a learning medium across the curriculum? What case is made for children as critical producers in media education? And how do these two rationales relate to each other?

The expansion of moving image work consequent upon the advent of digital editing technologies has seen a corresponding expansion of research studies in this field, though it is a relatively small body of work. I undertook, with a colleague, a systematic review of research literature four years ago, investigating the relation between digital technologies and moving image literacies (Burn and Leach, 2003). This review found only twelve studies internationally which met its selection criteria. Since then, a number of other studies have emerged, which will be referenced in this chapter.

Most of these are small-scale case studies, often describing the work of a single teacher or classroom. Most of the work originates in the UK, though Australia and the US are also represented. There are only three larger-scale studies: Reid *et al.* (2002), which evaluates a pilot DV project in fifty UK schools; de Block *et al.* (2005), which reports the findings of a seven-country European project in the use of DV by migrant children; and Schuck and Kearney (2004), which looks at the use of Apple's i-movie DV editing software across five schools in Australia.

Understandably, a good deal of the literature is produced by proponents of moving image work in schools, such as the British Film Institute in the UK, or a range of practitioners engaged in forms of action research. Some of the authors cited here, for instance, received small-scale funding from the Department for Education and Skills in the UK to develop and reflect on their practice under the supervision of a higher education mentor. Other studies were conducted in collaboration with industrial partners, in particular Apple, who supported both the Australian *Students in the Director's Seat* project (Schuck and Kearney, 2004) and the pilot DV project run by the British Educational Communications and Technology Agency (Reid *et al.*, 2002). For these reasons, it is sometimes difficult to separate out research findings from advocacy, and there is, arguably, a lack of critical distance in many of the studies. Apart from this general remark at the outset, however, this criticism will not be developed in relation to individual studies. Rather, I will accept that research in a new field of this kind is inevitably accompanied by the enthusiasm of early adopters, and point up the need for larger, longer external studies in the future.

Three broad rationales can be identified for moving image production in education across the research literature. By far the largest of these in terms of research is the rationale derived from media education. The second largest rationale is the argument for video production as an expressive form, in the context of arts education. The third largest group represents an argument for the use of video to enhance or mediate learning in other curriculum areas. Accordingly, these will form the headings of this chapter.

MEDIA EDUCATION

Internationally, there is a good degree of consensus about what media education constitutes (Buckingham, 2001), in so far as it revolves around a conceptual framework which young people can be expected to grasp. This framework covers concepts of media institutions, texts, and audiences. For the purposes of this chapter, it also assumes that the learning of this conceptual framework will be attained by both analysis and production of media texts.

As Buckingham points out (2003), media education should lead to the outcome known in many countries as media literacy. This idea is differently understood in different contexts and countries. In the UK, the media regulator OFCOM's defini-tion of media literacy includes access to, understanding of, and creation of media texts. However, statutory curricula in different countries may be much less bal-anced in actually requiring that children learn to make media texts as an entitlement. In the UK National Curriculum, for instance, attention to the moving image is limited to the reading section, so that children in England and Wales are required to 'read' the moving image, but not to 'write' it – so that the statutory requirement is at odds with the media regulator's definition. By contrast, in the Canadian province of Ontario the English secondary curriculum is constructed as four strands, the fourth of which is Media Studies. While this requires that stu-dents both 'learn to understand and interpret media works', it also specifies that they should 'learn about the media through the process of creating their own media works, using a range of technologies to do so'. However, this requirement applies very generally to all media: examples given are book jackets, songs and sample Web pages. The moving image is not, then, prescribed specifically.

In the US, while there is no clear pattern of curricular provision for media education, there is a tradition of such work, often co-ordinated by voluntary organisations such as the Center for Media Literacy. One of most influential articulations of the related notions of media education and media literacy, by Kathleen Tyner (1998), proposes an expansion of traditional literacy into visual media and new technologies, and associates such literacies with access to forms of social power.

A question about this more general notion of media literacy, raised by some studies cited in this chapter, is to what extent it might need to be complemented by more specific competences with particular media. Some studies propose an idea of moving image literacy. However, it is important to realize that there is not simply one model of moving image literacy at work here. Perhaps the dominant model in this field derives from the traditional understanding of filmic conven-tions outlined in its most familiar form by the standard film studies textbook, Bordwell and Thompson's *Film Art* (2004). Even where it is not explicitly refer-enced, the research of practitioners in DV often seems to be using a default model best described in terms of this framework, which incorporates the dramatic aspects of film (*mise-en-scène*) and the twin processes of filming and editing.

Another model in the UK has been the cine-literacy framework proposed by the British Film Institute (FEWG, 1999), which emphasizes the importance of film texts. A third is the multimodal model proposed by Burn and Parker (2003), who argue that the moving image is not one signifying system, but an ensemble of many, and that any model of literacy needs to be responsive to this ensemble.

A strong common feature of much of the research is the relation of DV as a signifying system to the social and cultural interests of the young producers of moving image texts. Perhaps the earliest study (Sefton-Green, 1995) shows how secondary school students making trailers for the film *The Outsiders* feel empowered by their new ability to manipulate the material of filmic texts, to move from the cultural role of audience to that of producer. This theme is echoed in many subsequent studies: Burn and Reed (1999), Sweetlove (2001), Burn *et al.* (2001), Burn and Durran (2006). Judgements about this empowerment are in most cases based on interview or observation data, in which young people report feelings of control, of being the director or editor, and of the excitement of being on the other side of the production process.

A problem for this kind of research is how to account for the motivation of *individual* students. The media production work reported by all the studies is characteristically group work, and there is a danger of collapsing the individual motivations of young film makers into claims about the motivations of the group as a whole. This is balanced to some extent by detailed attention either to aspects of the video work contributed by subsets of the group, or by the use of interview data or written work by students to differentiate between participants. Sweetlove (2001) shows, in the context of a media project within an English language curriculum, that peer tutoring, in pairs made up of a more experienced user of the software and a novice, produces more effective learning of the digital editing process than teacher demonstration or worksheet, but distinguishes finely between different degrees of success with different individuals. This demonstrates the importance of sensitive approaches to individual learning to refine the application of broader pedagogic structures. Kelsall, in Burn *et al.* (2001), shows how UK A level Media Studies students making music videos negotiate differing cultural interests and emphases in their choices of image, sound, rhythm and pace, using recordings of student talk during the editing to reflect different aesthetic preferences. Burn (2000) shows how a group of four boys in a Media Studies class splits into two pairs, in response to different motivations. These pairs are then able to follow their own interests, the pair being a more natural editing unit for computer-based work than the foursome.

Several studies report that a powerful motivating force is self-representation: the use of DV as an expressive form to represent aspects of young people's developing identities, social roles, and aspirations. This is a feature of Sefton-Green's study, in which the teenage heroes of *The Outsiders* provide attractive territory for the exploration of selfhood by the teenage video makers. Reid *et al.* (2002) place considerable emphasis on the value of DV as a medium for the exploration of identity, citing several examples. One example, from a Media Studies class-room, showed how two girls used their documentary film to engage with their relationships with their parents in the aftermath of their fathers' redundancy as workers in South Wales. In another case, Burn and Parker (2003) analysed a skateboarding video made by three sixteen-year-olds, concluding that it allowed aspirational representations of the makers' peer culture, while also addressing a Media Studies examination system in which they wished to perform well.

Another aspect of identity that is explored as a powerful motivating force in a number of studies is the beliefs and convictions of young people. For Goodman (2003), this is a central purpose of the video-making of the teenagers at his centre in New York; indeed, the central use of the documentary genre here pre-supposes that the articulation of social and political beliefs, particularly about the place and rights of young people in modern urban societies, will be a key function of the work with video. Burn and Parker (2001b) analyse an advertise-ment for Fair Trade chocolate made by sixteen-year-old students who struggle to represent the abstract notion of fair trade and the distant phenomenon of African cocoa farming, resorting to symbolic images (tropical plants) and on-screen text to convey these messages. They find themselves torn between these distant cul-tural references and their own more immediate interests in their peer culture, represented by their teenage protagonist and their hip-hop soundtrack.

Another common feature is the exploration of what students learn about the formal systems of signification in the moving image through, in particular, the process of digital editing. For instance, Sweetlove and Tuohey (in Burn *et al.*, 2001) show how twelve-year-old students learn to indicate aspects of place and time through the order of shots and the use of transitions as they edit their own film of a class play.

As remarked above, these systems of signification are differently conceived in different studies. In some studies, a general deployment of well understood notions of camerawork and editing points towards the conventions of filming and editing laid out in standard textbooks of film theory such as Bordwell and Thompson (2004). In other cases, however, these conventions are explicitly ref-erenced. Coxon (2002), for instance, describes how his A level Film Studies students used Adobe Premiere to edit a series of rushes for the UK television adaptation of *Middlemarch*, provided by the *bfi*, in accordance with classic prin-ciples of continuity editing. Reid *et al.* (2002) give examples of specialist Media Studies work with a similar conceptual focus:

> Elsewhere, work was clearly associated with forms of moving image literacy conceptualised in terms of traditional film grammar and the meta-language associated with it. For example, it was reported in one of the school visits that a Scottish Advanced Higher media studies stu-dent had an '… understanding … that the film would highlight and reinforce the various techniques such as 180 degree rule, eyeline match, etc., and also to experience the whole film-making process – from the initial idea through to planning, scripting, shooting, story-boarding, filming and editing'. (2002: 24–5)

However, there is some uncertainty about what kind of 'film language' students are using or learning in many of the studies whose context is Media Studies. This may be because work produced for public examinations in the UK tends to be confined to 'short form' genres, such as television advertisements, film trailers, title sequences and music videos. These forms make frequent appearances: the making of film trailers appears in Sefton-Green (1995), Burn and Reed (1999), Burn (2000), Durran (in Burn *et al.*, 2001); making advertisements appears in Burn and Parker (2001b); and music video appears in Kelsall (in Burn *et al.*, 2001), and Archer (forthcoming). These short forms are not ideal for the teaching and learning of the continuity system of editing as Bordwell and Thompson describe it. The continuity system evolved as a narrative strategy based around the unfolding of events in logical relations between units of space and time. By contrast, trailers, advertisements and music videos are condensed, impressionistic, and not typically subject to straightforward narrative sequence. Arguably, they might be best theorized in terms of classical montage theory (Eisenstein, 1968), which considers how the juxtaposition of moving images and sounds produces new meanings; or more recent formulations of montage theory in the context of new media (Manovich, 2002). Burn and Reed (1999) consider this kind of condensed form in their account of a film trailer made by four girls, who select and edit together key moments from the film, theorized by the authors in terms of Barthes's cardinal points in narrative (Barthes, 1978).

In some studies, questions are raised about the limits of conventional models of 'film language'. Burn and Durran (2006) give an example of a boy who writes about aspects of dramatic movement in Luhrmann's *Romeo + Juliet* which are difficult to account for in terms of Bordwell and Thompson's schema, for instance. They propose instead a multimodal approach, elaborated more fully by Burn and Parker (2003), drawing in particular on Kress and van Leeuwen (2001). In this study of a skateboarding video made by three teenage boys, they propose the idea of the *kineikonic* mode (from the Greek words for move and image), as an overarching idea of how the contributory modes of the moving image are assembled in any given text. While on the one hand these modes include the forms of spatial and temporal design usually associated with the moving image, they also include performative, dramatic, improvised actions and gestures of the subjects of the film, conceived here in terms of Goffman's notion of dramatized selfhood (1959). This theory is applied and further refined in a number of subsequent studies in the context of other curriculum areas considered below.

The model of multimodality used in these studies has a number of clear advantages. It enables the researchers to be quite precise about which semiotic modes and media are used by children and for what purpose. It gives a more complete picture of the use of these modes than earlier models of moving image literacy, where the focus was more on the visual, and on the specific signifying properties of the filming and editing processes. However, these studies, in developing their own analytical framework, are often unclear about how explicitly the children themselves understand what they are doing, or indeed the extent to which this might be necessary. Further research and debate is needed, therefore, on the question of whether a multimodal semiotics is best used as an analytical tool for researchers to explain what children are doing; or whether such a tool, at some level, can be made available to children themselves, and, if so, what the benefits would be.

Most of the studies, from Sefton-Green (1995) onward, suggest that the principal difference made by digital editing software is the ability to revise work endlessly and instantly. This was simply not possible with analogue video, as those practitioners who have moved from analogue to digital point out (Burn and Durran, 1998). This feature of digital editing derives from what Manovich (1998) calls the principle of *variability*: because digital media consist of databases of media objects provisionally configured by algorithms, the configurations are infinitely variable, which the user experiences as the plasticity and provisionality of DV which many of the studies comment on.

Reid *et al.* (2003) identify three affordances of the digital medium, derived from Moseley *et al.* (1999): feedback, dynamic representation and iterative opportunities for editing. The first is noted both in this study, and in other studies: Kelsall and Durran (in Burn *et al.*, 2001) both note the importance of the instant viewing of their work by students, both in terms of motivation and in terms of reflection on the developing edit. Dynamic representation is presented by Reid *et al.,* as the possibilities for screening the finished work on television screens, projectors, intranets and the World Wide Web. These varied platforms for exhibition are certainly at least partly characteristic of the digital medium specifically; though as Reid *et al.* point out, the degree to which they might be described as 'dynamic' varied considerably. Finally, iterative editing refers to the ability to endlessly rework the edited piece, a feature of DV mentioned in many of the studies. Burn and Reed (1999) break this feature down into more specific functions. They point out that the raw material for the edit can be stored in 'bins' in the software in a way that would not have been possible with analogue video, allowing much more ambitious and experimental successive edits. Rather than making a new text each time, each successive edit was a revised version of a previous one – genuinely an 'edit' rather than a complete rethink. The girls using the software also spent some time adjusting the pace of the piece by trimming clips on the timeline of the software, which, again, is a function not possible in analogue video, where the length of shot initially decided on would then be fixed.

The emphasis in nearly all the studies is, as we have seen, on the notion of moving image production: as a technology, as a cultural and critical practice, as a dimension of moving image literacy. One study, however, displaces the emphasis onto the analysis of media texts through the use of digital editing software. Burn and Durran (2006) describe how thirteen-year-old Media Studies students use the free software Microsoft Moviemaker to analyse aspects of a film. This software, like some others, has a 'clip detection' function which splits up incoming media into shots. The teacher had pre-loaded the whole film into the software, so that it showed up as hundreds of individual shots in the 'bin'. Students were then able to sort, analyse, edit together and export shots into PowerPoint to make visual 'essays' about the 'grammar', style and meaning of the film.

In general, then, in the specific context of media education, DV is seen as having a number of significant benefits. In many of these studies, it has provided access to moving image production for the first time. It has extended such work down the secondary age range. It has allowed a more profound learning experience through iterative editing in which students can experiment, and connect the experience of composing moving image sequences with their developing conceptual understanding of the moving image as a semiotic system, however this may be represented by their teachers or by the researchers. In addition, it provides a powerful connection to the moving image cultures in which learners develop their first understandings of the medium, and on which they draw as resources for their own creative work.

DIGITAL VIDEO IN ARTS EDUCATION

This category overlaps with the previous one. This is largely because some of the projects described in these studies, while they are clearly constituted as arts projects in relation either to arts subjects in the formal curriculum or in the informal education sector, are conceived of, by researchers or practitioners or both, as forms of media education.

Like many studies in the other categories, studies of DV-based arts projects frequently emphasize the value of the medium for the exploration of the social identity of young people, enabling forms of self-representation in which young film makers can explore their social roles in the world, play with fantasy identities, and test out aspects of selfhood such as race and sexuality. De Block *et al.* (2005) report on a large EC-funded three-year project in which migrant children in different European countries use DV artwork to represent the experience of migration, working with video artists and educators in after-school clubs. The study shows that the children's identity as migrants can be represented either directly, for instance as a form of narrative, or indirectly, by displacing images of migration and origin in favour of identity claims based in global media cultures. (For an extended discussion of how participants used rap music see de Block and Rydin, 2006.) Though this is an arts project, its rationale and the interpretive framework of the research are those of media education, so that the expressive form is seen as becoming available to the children through a combination of the formal signifying properties of the moving image and the cultural resources on which the children choose to draw, especially those from popular media such as music video, television drama and cartoons.

Overton (2004), an art and drama teacher in a special school for children with physical disabilities, describes his own practice in an action research project funded by the UK's department of education (DfES), and supervised by the

British Film Institute and the Institute of Education, University of London. He shows how children use DV to represent aspects of their disability, transforming these into positive images through dance and sci-fi narratives. Again, the motivation for the work proceeds from the students' sense of self, and the contradictory needs both to face their disabilities and escape them. While this was conceived by the teacher as a drama project, in which DV would compensate for the difficulty for the children in the physical aspects of drama, it resembled a media education project in many ways. In particular, like the projects already referred to, it taught specific moving image conventions, such as shot types and technical roles, which were explicitly reinforced by the teacher, through the use of wordwalls, labels attached to equipment, and group discussion. The teacher also recognized the students' popular cultural experience, such as their interest in video games, making a reference to *Tombraider 4* a central reference for the content and style of the piece.

Potter (2005) describes an arts project in which he works with a primary school class at the end of their last term in the school, using DV cameras and editing software (Pinnacle Studio) to make short films of their memories of the school. He explores how two boys in the class construct playful images of themselves, elaborating on and exaggerating aspects of the social roles they play in the school. This project is conceived in general terms as a digital arts project, and, unlike some of the media education projects described in other studies, avoids emphasis on the formal conventions of the moving image. It finds, however, that a sophisticated grasp of television conventions, from a range of shot types to generic features of chat shows and youth television, are deployed by the two boys.

Burn (2003) describes a project in which six bilingual teenage girls make short films of their performances of their own poems about language and identity. Here, aspects of identity are closely related to how the girls have constructed the moving image text: for instance, a sequence of shots in which a girl faces alternately in different directions represents her bilingualism in English and Bengali. This project also raises questions about the limitations of the conventions of media education: while these are clearly moving image texts, they are not identifiable popular cultural forms. This project takes place in a hybrid context. The poetry exercise originated in the study of a poem for an exam set text in English; the films were supervised by an English and media teacher with an expertise in DV. The emphasis, as in several of the arts projects referred to here, is both on the conventions of the moving image and on expressive forms which are traditionally highly valued, in this case poetry.

An aspect of identity which occurs in several studies is that of cultural taste. Video made by young people often represents specific pleasures in forms of popular music, in televisual and filmic styles and genres, and in dress codes and forms of (sub)cultural performance. Potter shows how the two boys whose video he analyses incorporate music by the Red Hot Chilli Peppers and other bands to indicate their sophisticated tastes in music (2005). De Block *et al.* give several examples of children using music as a cultural marker, either of their own ethnic or national origins, as in a Turkish boy's performance in song and on a traditional instrument; or through global musical forms, such as hip-hop (2005). Doyle shows how two thirteen-year-old girls making a trailer for an imaginary horror film play with conventions of the genre which appeal to teenage fascinations with death (2005), producing images in which they use their friends as 'the two girls who are dead', and construct shots that directly imitate films such as Kubrick's *The Shining*.

A strong emphasis in research into digital moving image production in arts projects is, unsurprisingly, creativity. This theme engages with policy expectations about artistic production as a creative process (cf. NACCCE, 1999). There is some tension between this conception and the more conventional media education rationales in which making the moving image serves the more general aim to develop critical awareness and a conceptual grasp of the nature of media texts. However, media educators also see moving image production as creative in ways that exceed these more limited purposes: Buckingham (2003) devotes a chapter to notions of creativity in media education, for instance. Similarly, the four teacher-researchers whose work is collected in Burn *et al.* (2001) construct a conceptual model of digital editing in which creativity is one of three components, the others being social roles and skills, and literacies.

In Potter (2005) creativity is conceived, following Loveless (2003) and Csikzentmihalyi (1991), as 'interaction between people within specific domains and contexts which give rise to the production of work but also construct the value of that work'. Thus the primary school children described in his research interact through the use of digital editing tools in ways which also relate to the social context of their life in primary school, represented and valued in their film.

Reid *et al.* (2002), in their evaluation of the use of DV across the curriculum in fifty schools in England, make a number of references to the use of DV in the arts. In particular, the wider evaluation contains three detailed case studies, one of which describes the work of an Art teacher who conducts a number of animation projects with different classes of different ages. The children work in a range of media to make drawn and plasticine animations. The media education emphasis on critical understanding and concept development is here replaced by an emphasis on expressive work, on the craft of the artist in different media, and on creativity conceived as originality. In contrast to the reference to popular media encouraged in media education, originality is here seen by the teacher as *opposed* to popular television. However, the normal practices of art education do move in the direction of media education in recognizing the moving image as a structured system of signification: the children storyboard their narratives, and learn basic conventions of shot construction.

As for the value of the digital medium in this project, the feedback and dynamic display functions proposed in the wider study are the most obvious. The teacher gathers the class around the edited film at various stages of its completion to see the progress so far, and comment on how it might develop. And the finished films of the groups are projected in assemblies and parents' evenings (though, again, this exhibition is difficult to distinguish from pre-digital forms of film or video exhibition).

The discussion of creativity in Reid *et al.*, following Sharples (1999), suggests that creativity in the use of digital editing software and digital camcorders is found most clearly in projects where teachers are clear about the constraints of the activity. These constraints are associated in some cases with the conventions of moving image 'language', so that the teachers who give explicit instruction in techniques of shot construction and continuity editing provide greater opportunities for successfully expressive work than those who allow greater 'freedom' for children to experiment. Security with the 'rules' of this language allowed children to produce witty, subversive, ironic pieces with some degree of confidence. What this study was unable to test, however, was whether repeated opportunities to experiment with production would have allowed children to discover and evolve a comparable grasp of techniques and conventions. In this respect, this study is limited in the same way as all the literature in this field, which consists entirely of snapshots and short-term case studies. A clear gap in the research is longitudinal studies that might explore recursive learning with digital editing software (see Chapter 1 of this volume).

Burn and Parker (2001a) describe a media arts project conducted by a consortium of a specialist media arts school and a cinema, providing an artist-in-residence project for a group of local primary schools. The children made animated films using a computer animation software, *The Complete Animator*, with teachers from the secondary school, the Film Education officer from the cinema, and an animator-in-residence. In this study, creativity was conceived as specific forms of work with successive layers of authoring software in the primary school animation project they explore. They consider how the children appropriate basic shapes in a vector-drawing package, Acorn *Draw!*, and invest these with cultural meanings, by, for instance, designing a Red Riding Hood character beginning with a circle which suggested the feminine shapes derived from experiences of teenage pop divas like Britney Spears or a woodcutter modelled on Arnold Schwarzenegger which begins with a more 'masculine' square. These images, subsequently imported by the students into the animation software, are seen as derivative (from popular cultural experience) but also creative, in that they are adapted to represent particular preoccupations and interests of the young authors. Creativity and the moving image here are seen as transformative both of semiotic–cultural resources and of self. However, this project is conceived, both by the practitioners and the researchers, as a form of media education, so that a strong emphasis is placed on shot construction, narrative structure and the conventions of editing. The point of interest, perhaps, is the synthesis of these explicit meaning-making processes which the project was concerned to teach, and the popular cultural references which the children found unaided – indeed, often unnoticed.

As in the studies of media education projects, there is a strong tendency that emphasizes the importance of the moving image's formal properties as a system of signification. Again, this is sometimes conceived in terms of the traditional conventions of the continuity system, so that shot types and edit sequences are explicit features of the teaching, as we have seen, in some of the projects in Reid *et al.* (2002), in Overton (2004), in Burn and Parker (2001a), in Doyle (2004), and in de Block *et al.* (2005). However, the researchers do not always interpret the outcomes of the projects in the same terms. As in the media education literature, one approach which produces a more complex analysis is rooted in theories of multimodal semiotics (Kress and van Leeuwen, 2001). Potter (2005) interprets the film made by the two primary school boys in his study in this way, considering how their film integrates different semiotic modes, such as their own dramatic performances, the music they have selected, culturally salient objects from their world like toys and costumes, and different forms and styles of spoken language. Doyle (2004) analyses how the girls in her study combine the semiotics of filming and editing with the signifying properties of objects, buildings, costumes, make-up, and, again, dramatic action and speech. Burn and Parker (2003) analyse how music, speech and moving image combine in a children's computer animation of an African folk tale, identifying different combinations of the modes, such as anticipation (where the music suggests an event ahead of the image track), complementarity and contradiction, for instance for ironic effect.

Very few of the studies make many claims for the differences made by digital cameras. An exception is de Block *et al.* (2005), who describe how digital cameras helped to speed up the process of learning, providing instant feedback through flip-out LCD screens, which could be viewed by a group of children. Along with 'on-location editing', made possible by laptops with Apple's i-movie, the whole production process was able to keep up with the pace of learning needed by the children, rather than slowing it down and fragmenting it into different phases.

Three other studies address the nature of the digital medium. Reid *et al.* (2002) show that, in some of the schools in their study, computers as editing tools make possible many different social models of editing, from small groups of four to individuals working on their own project, which was much less likely in the days of analogue video edit suites, though of course possible. Sefton-Green and Parker (2000), exploring how primary school children use three different computer animation softwares, observe how the children used the computer as a kind of co-worker, in a 'choric' process which they compare to children's drama. Finally, Burn and Parker (2001a) report how the primary school children making a class animation shared a common bank of digital images on the school's computer network to which they had all contributed and from which they all borrowed to make their designated sequence.

DIGITAL VIDEO ACROSS THE CURRICULUM

Beyond the media education and arts education perspectives, there is a smaller and more recent body of work concerned with DV as a learning technology. Some of these are small studies (e.g., Ross *et al.*, 2003; Swain *et al.*, 2003; Tschirner, 2001), in which DV is presented as a relatively transparent medium through which curriculum content can be mediated, or which can aid the development of concepts specific to a curriculum area such as science or history. In addition, a small number of studies explore the value of DV for students with special needs. Overton's study (2004), which has already been cited above, describes how DV can allow access to physical expressive forms such as Drama and Dance for students with a range of physical disabilities. Dimitriadi and Hodson (2005) find that DV offers valuable forms of multisensory learning, and helps to develop collaborative skills, second-language fluency and reflection among bilingual children with special educational needs in six inner-London primary schools.

Two of the larger studies of DV in the classroom address the wider curricular context. One of these, Reid *et al.* (2002), has already been discussed above, as it also includes discussions of data representing DV in specialist media classrooms and in the arts. However, this project extended to uses of DV in all curriculum areas, though some, such as maths and religious education, took place in only one school (Figure 23.1). The other study, Schuck and Kearney (2004), investigates the use of DV in five Australian schools, in classrooms which ranged from Kindergarten to Year 12, and in subjects which included ICT, RE, History, Maths, Science, ICT and a LOTE (Languages Other Than English).

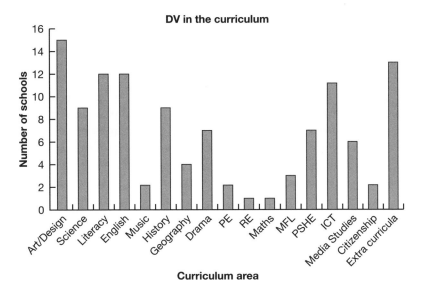

Figure 23.1   Digital video in the curriculum
Source Reid *et al.* (2002)

The findings from these studies echo certain themes of the media education literature. In particular, both studies emphasize the motivating effect of DV, and they take possible explanations further than other studies. Reid *et al.* offer possible explanations for the increased motivation that was widely reported by teachers. First, the use of DV depends on, and engages with, children's experience of television and film, which are widely distributed, in contrast with other ICTs, leading to a democratizing element in DV work. Second, the study identified students' ownership of the work, especially noticed among disaffected students, and in projects where students took the initiative, sometimes where teachers were uncertain of the new medium. Third, the study speculated that the novelty of the medium may have raised motivation among some students.

Motivation is also reported as a key consequence of the use of DV by Schuck and Kearney. Again, it is associated with increased ownership of work, and with a higher than usual degree of autonomy for students. However, this study also suggested that the nature of the medium itself may be partly responsible for increased motivation. Although this idea is not fully explored, it does echo suggestions in other studies, such as Durran's (in Burn *et al.*, 2001), which emphasizes the intense pleasure of the editing process, or Burn and Reed (1999), who describe how the editing activity held a group of girls for many hours after school. While these observations are not theorized, they do point towards later uses of the 'flow' theory of the psychologist Mihaly Csikszentmihalyi (1991) in explaining the immersive experience of using digital media in general (cf. Loveless, 2003).

Both studies also emphasize the importance of attention to the language of the moving image. Reid *et al.* (2002) show how certain of the case studies in their study produce high-quality films through explicit teaching of the conventions and language of the moving image, in some cases consisting of quite formal employment of the rules of continuity editing. This study finds, across the fifty schools in the project, that effective work must, in some way, pay attention to the language of the moving image, in fact, and that there can be no 'transparent' use of DV to convey ideas, information or other content of different curriculum subjects.

Schuck and Kearney emphasize the importance of media literacy, and their examples demonstrate that this includes critical awareness of the medium (a project on advertising), developing understanding of textual structures (a project on narrative in Hollywood films), and learning detailed editing conventions at both practical and metalinguistic levels.

However, both studies make important distinctions between different emphases in the use of DV. Reid *et al.*'s finding that the best work was in many cases related to the most explicit attention to the language of the moving image, and its consequent argument that there can be no transparent use of the medium, also rests on a judgement that those schools which simply used DV as a way of recording subject content were missing out on its expressive potential, and on students' extensive knowledge of moving image culture. In the case of Schuck and Kearney, although they cite examples of attention to the medium, they also find that outcomes relating to autonomy and motivation were more evident than those relating to metacognition or development of conceptual understanding. This finding is less easy to interpret than Reid *et al.*'s clear, though somewhat polemical, argument about the importance of the medium. On the one hand, it could suggest that attention to media literacy as a conceptual framework is less important to teachers of a variety of curriculum subjects than the motivational power of DV simply to enhance students' interest in their subject. On the other hand, Schuck and Kearney develop an argument for 'authenticity' which, while independent of some aspects of media literacy, also captures features of learning with DV which are absolutely complementary to media literacy. The specific points they make are that authentic learning involves engaging with real-world problems and situations (through video journalism, for instance); filming real events or processes rather than learning through simulations; and making films for real audiences, who provide real feedback. This echoes a similar point by Burn and Parker (2001a), who point out that showing children's animations in a real cinema breaks out of the culture of simulation in which many school experiences are locked.

Finally, these two studies make additional points which are important, and which are not developed elsewhere in the literature. Schuck and Kearney find that a critical factor in the successful adoption of DV as a learning tool is the school environment, listing a number of features from supportive head teachers to essential technical support staff. Reid *et al.* make two related points which reach beyond the projects described in their study, to ask how student films might be evaluated, and how learning progression in the moving image might be structured. These points recognize the fact that, outside formal assessment criteria in Media Studies exams, no clear sense has yet emerged of how teachers and students can tell how successful their films are, or of how learning in one course can lead to more advanced learning the next time. These problems are partly consequent upon a situation in which the use of DV typically happens only once or twice in a child's school career, though forms of progression are now being mapped by schools with a particular interest in media forms and technologies, such as the specialist media arts colleges in the UK (Kirwan *et al.*, 2003; Burn and Durran, forthcoming).

One more research focus may be mentioned: the question about how moving image literacy relates to print literacy. This does reflect the curriculum priorities of English and literacy curricula, though in fact all the studies cited here in relation to this focus are clearly within the media education paradigm, and are exploring the extensive shared territory between English and media education. A key hypothesis here is that, by understanding and making moving image texts of their own, children will come to understand and deploy features of print texts better. Parker (1999, 2002) reports on a project in which a class of primary school children improve aspects of their narrative writing such as visual description after having worked on their own computer animation of a Roald Dahl story. Similarly, Henson (2005) finds that a group of under-achieving Year 9 boys score better than predicted in national English tests after working on an animation project. There is some question about the correlation between small qualitative case study accounts of production work and raw scores here; and also a difficulty in distinguishing between the motivating effects of media production work and specific cognitive gains. Also, though these are both accounts of work using digital media production technologies, the difference made by the digital medium is not really isolated. Nevertheless, these studies suggest that digital moving image production does connect with aspects of print literacy, and that exactly how this happens is a question well worth exploring in future research.

CONCLUSION

The research literature summarized here presents a picture that, though unclear and murky in places, nevertheless contains strong indications about the value of digital moving image production and learning. It also clarifies questions that need further research.

The picture is, unsurprisingly, of a new technology in its infancy. Many of the studies represent early forays into digital editing, and are limited by the one-off nature of the project, or by its novelty. Nevertheless, one important theme of the research tells an old story. The use of media technologies, forms and genres as learning tools prompts the question about whether these forms can be used transparently to contain, record and re-present curriculum content with no explicit reference to the system of signification and the cultures from which it derives – what Buckingham (2003) calls learning through the media rather than learning about the media. Like Buckingham, many of the authors represented in this chapter (including the present author) believe that to do so not only misses important learning opportunities but fundamentally misunderstands the medium. The moving image cannot produce 'transparent' meanings: it will always structure meaning through framing, shot type, and the editing of image and sound, as Reid *et al.* argue (2002).

A general point about the moving image, in this respect, is that, although all digital media in a sense have analogue predecessors, digital *editing* softwares are particularly strongly connected with analogue editing of video and celluloid film editing, for three reasons. Firstly, in many ways digital editing is doing essentially the same job as its analogue forebear, that is, producing film and television. Secondly, like earlier editing technologies, digital editing is only half the picture: it depends on its relationship with the process of filming, which is in several respects unchanged by the digital medium, still depending primarily on the composition of shots through a lens and viewfinder. Thirdly, digital editing proceeds in certain very clear ways from a history of a century of film production and half a century of television, and employs the signifying systems, cultural frameworks and social production processes which have evolved through these histories.

Arguably, what is happening here can be related to Lev Manovich's parallel histories of representational technologies and the computer (1998). He proposes that the former begins with Daguerre's daguerreotype and the latter with Babbage's analytical engine, both in the 1830s. The two histories, the first concerned with visual recordings and constructions of the world, the second with calculation and information, proceeded separately until very recently, when the convergence of computers with the representational technologies of photography and the moving image bring them together. Manovich describes this as the fusion of two layers: the computer layer and the cultural layer. The implications for education, perhaps, are that those whose principal concern is the use of ICTs in education, perhaps in the context of e-learning, need to understand the cultural history and uses of the moving image, while media specialists need to understand what it means for their familiar televisual and cinematic texts to become computable.

The difference made by the digital medium has been a focus of attention, as we have seen, in some of these studies, in particular the specific affordances isolated by studies such as de Block *et al.* (2005) and Reid *et al.* (2002). These suggest that DV combines traditional conventions of moving image composition with generic and transferable processes of ICT authoring of the kind described by Sefton-Green (2004). While these begin to suggest what the learning benefits are of DV editing, they also indicate how important it is to see the use of DV as a form of continuity in practices of communication and representation. Rather than seeing DV as a brand new technology, it might be better to see it as a stage of development in a moving image culture that has a history of over a century.

Finally, it is clear that this research field is marked by a preponderance of studies rooted in theories of media education. A consequence of this is a particular view of learning, emphasizing theories of new literacies, such as multimodality, the importance of popular cultural texts and contexts, and the conceptual framework of media education. There is much less evidence of learning theories which are typical more generally of research in e-learning, such as constructivist approaches, though there is, in this field, some accommodation between Vygotskyan learning theory and media education perspectives, which explore forms of progression from children's informal experiences of the media outside school to more formal conceptual learning about the media in school (Buckingham, 2003; Burn and Durran, 2006). Again, the nature of learning in relation to this medium needs further research, and further consideration of how different interpretive traditions might complement each other.

Perhaps the arrival of free editing software on every computer will usher in a new dawn of video-making in schools, taking its place alongside other forms of digital authoring: music composition, Web authoring, game design. Alternatively, it could be argued that, like other artistic or expressive media, filmic forms will struggle for a place in an overcrowded curriculum, as painting, music and photography have before them. Whatever the case, there will be a need for larger studies to produce more authoritative conclusions than the existing small case studies, valuable though their collective suggestions are; and longitudinal studies to develop models of recursive learning in this medium.

REFERENCES

Archer, S. (forthcoming) 'Media education, music video and glocalisation', in A. Burn and C. Durrant (eds), *Media Teaching*. Melbourne: Australian Association for the Teaching of English and Wakefield Press.

Barthes, R. (1978) 'Introduction to the structural analysis of narrative', in *Image–Music–Text*, trans. S. Heath. New York: Hill and Wang.

Bordwell, D. and Thompson, K. (2004) *Film Art: an Introduction* (7th edn). New York: McGraw-Hill.

Buckingham, D. (2001) 'Media Education: a Global Strategy for Development'. Policy paper prepared for UNESCO, sector of communication and information, retrieved online at: http://portal.unesco.org/ci/en/file_download.php/b58899efc30429f265088ac106599f95Policy+paper+by+Pr+David+Buckingham.rtf.

Buckingham, D. (2003) *Media Education: Literacy, Learning and Contemporary Culture*. Cambridge: Polity Press.

Buckingham, D., Grahame, J. and Sefton-Green, J. (1995) *Making Media: Practical Production in Media Education*. London: English and Media Centre.

Burn, A. (2000) 'Repackaging the slasher movie: digital unwriting of film in the classroom', *English in Australia*, 127–8: 24–34.

Burn, A. (2003) 'Two tongues occupy my mouth: poetry, performance and the moving image', *English in Education*, 37 (3): 41–50.

Burn, A., and Durran, J. (1998) 'Going non-linear', in *Trac*, 2 (winter).

Burn, A. and Durran, J. (2006) 'Digital anatomies: analysis as production in media education', in D. Buckingham, and R. Willett, (eds), *Digital Generations*. Mahwah, NJ: Erlbaum.

Burn, A. and Leach, J. (2003) 'A systematic review of the impact of ICT on moving image literacy in English' (EPPI Centre Review), in *Research Evidence in Education Library*. London: EPPI-Centre, Social Science Research Unit, Institute of Education, retrieved from: http://eppi.ioe.ac.uk/EPPIWeb/home.aspx?page=/reel/review_groups/english/review_five.htm.

Burn, A. and Leach, J. (2004) 'ICT and the moving image', in R. Andrews (ed.), *The Impact of ICT on Literacy Education*. Abingdon: RoutledgeFalmer.

Burn, A. and Parker, D. (2001a) 'Making your mark: digital inscription, animation, and a new visual semiotic', *Education, Communication and Information* 1: 155–79.

Burn, A. and Parker, D. (2001b) 'Reading films, selling chocolate: some proposals for a grammar of the moving image', *English and Media Magazine*, autumn.

Burn, A. and Parker, D. (2003) 'Tiger's big plan: multimodality and the moving image', in G. Kress, and C. Jewitt (eds), *Multimodal Literacy*. New York: Peter Lang.

Burn, A. and Reed, K. (1999) 'Digi-teens: media literacies and digital technologies in the secondary classroom', *English in Education*, 33: 5–20.

Burn, A., Brindley, S., Durran, J., Kelsall, C., Sweetlove, J., Tuohy, C. (2001) '"The rush of images": a research report into digital editing and the moving image', *English in Education*, 35: 34–47.

Coxon, D. (2002) 'Editing *Middlemarch*', DfES Best Practice Research Scholarship report, retrieved from: www.bfi.org.uk/education/research/ teachlearn/pdf/06_coxon_daren.pdf.

Csikszentmihalyi, M. (1991) *Flow: The Psychology of Optimal Experience*. New York: Harper Perennial.

de Block, L. and Rydin, I. (2006) 'Digital rapping in media productions: intercultural communication through youth culture', in D. Buckingham, and R. Willett (eds), *Digital Generations*. Mahwah NJ: Erlbaum.

de Block, L., Buckingham, D. and Banaji, S. (2005) 'Children in Communication about Migration (CHICAM)'. Final report of EC-funded project, retrieved from: www.childrenyouthandmediacentre.co.uk; project Web site: www.chicam.net.

Dimitriadi, Y. and Hodson, P. (2005) 'Digital Video and Bilingual Children with Special Educational Needs: Supporting Literacy', BECTA research paper, http://www.becta.org.uk/page_documents/research/bursaries05/bilingual_children.doc.

Doyle, E. (2004) 'Multimodal Media meets ICT: a Key Stage 3 Digital Video-editing Case Study'. Unpublished M.A. dissertation, Institute of Education, University of London.

Eisenstein, S. M. (1968) *The Film Sense*, trans. J. Layda. London: Faber and Faber.

FEWG (1999) *Making Movies Matter*. London: bfi.

Goffman, E. (1959) *The Presentation of Self in Everyday Life*. New York: Anchor Books.

Goodman, S. (2003) *Teaching Youth Media: A Critical Guide to Literacy, Video Production, and Social Change*. New York: Teachers College Press.

Henson, D. (2005) 'Media Literacy and Boys' Achievement'. Unpublished MA dissertation, Institute of Education, University of London.

Kirwan, T., Learmonth, J., and Sayer, M. (2003) *Mapping Media Literacy*. London: bfi.

Kress, G. and van Leuween, T. (1996) *Reading Images: The Grammar of Visual Design*. Abingdon: Routledge.

Kress, G. and van Leuween, T. (2001) *Multimodal Discourses*. London: Arnold.

Loveless, A. (2003) *Creativity: a Literature Review*, NESTA Futurelab, retrieved from: www.nestafuture-lab.org.

Manovich, L (1998) *The Language of New Media*. Cambridge MA: MIT Press.

Manovich, L. (2002) 'Spatial computerisation and film language', in M. Rieser, and A. Zapp, (eds), *New Screen Media*. London: bfi.

Moseley, D., Higgins, S., Bramald, R., Hardman, F., Miller, J., Mroz, M., Tse, H., Newton, D., Thompson, I., Williamson, J., Halligan, J., Bramald, S., Newton, L., Tymms, P., Henderson, B. and Stout, J. (1999) *Ways forward with ICT: Effective Pedagogy using Information and Communications Technology for Literacy and Numeracy in Primary Schools*. Newcastle upon Tyne: University of Newcastle upon Tyne.

NACCCE (1999) *All our Futures: Creativity, Culture and Education*. Sudbury: National Advisory Committee on Creative and Cultural Education: DfEE and DCMS.

Overton, R. (2004) 'Using Digital Video with Disabled Children'. DfES Best Practice Research Scholarships, retrieved from: http://www.teachernet.gov.uk/professionaldevelopment/resourcesan-dresearch/bprs/search/index.cfm?report=1508.

Parker, D. (1999) 'You've read the book, now make the film: moving image media, print literacy and narrative', *English in Education*, 33: 24–35.

Parker, D. (2002) 'Show us a story: an overview of recent research and resource development work at the British Film Institute', *English in Education*, 36: 38–45.

Potter, J. (2005) '"This brings back a lot of memories": a case study in the analysis of digital video production by young learners', *Education, Communication and Information*, 5 (1): 5–23.

Reid, M., Parker, D. and Burn, A. (2002) Evaluation Report of the BECTa Digital Video Pilot Project. BECTa, retrieved from: http://www.becta.org.uk/research/reports/digitalvideo/index.html.

Ross, D., Yerrick, R. and Molebash, P. (2003) 'Lights, camera, science?', *Learning and Leading with Technology*, 31 (3): 18–21.

Schuck, S. and Kearney, M. (2004) 'Students in the Director's Seat: Teaching and Learning across the School Curriculum with Student-generated Video'. Research report, University of Technology, Sydney, retrieved from: http://www.ed-dev.uts.edu.au/teachered/research/dvproject/pdfs/ReportWeb.pdf.

Sefton-Green, J. (1995) 'New models for old? English goes multimedia', in D. Buckingham and J. Sefton-Green (eds), *Making Media: Practical Production in Media Education*. London: English and Media Centre.

Sefton-Green, J. (2004) 'Timelines, timeframes and special effects: software and creative media production', *ECI*, 4 (3).

Sefton-Green, J. and Parker, D. (2000) *Edit-Play*. London: bfi.

Sharples, M. (1999) *How we Write: Writing as Creative Design*. Abingdon: Routledge.

Swain, C., Sharpe, R. and Dawson, K. (2003) 'Using digital video to study history', *Social Education*, 67 (3): 154–7.

Sweetlove, J. (2001) 'Sharing the screen: action research into different methods of learning how to use iMovie 2'. Unpublished paper, British Film Institute/BPRS project.

Tschirner, E. (2001) 'Language acquisition in the classroom: the role of digital video', *Computer Assisted Language Learning*, 14 (3–4), 305–19.

Tyner, K. (1998) *Literacy in a Digital World: Teaching and Learning in the Age of Information*. Mahwah NJ: Erlbaum.

Index